THE ORCHESTRA

Origins and

Transformations

THE
ORCHESTRA

Origins and
Transformations

JOAN PEYSER

EDITOR

CHARLES SCRIBNER'S SONS

NEW YORK

Copyright © 1986 Charles Scribner's Sons

Library of Congress Cataloging in Publication Data

The Orchestra—origins and transformations.

Includes bibliographies and index.
1. Orchestra.   I. Peyser, Joan.
ML1200.075   1986   785'.06'6   86-6618
ISBN 0-684-18068-5

Published simultaneously in Canada
by Collier Macmillan Canada, Inc.
Copyright under the Berne Convention.

1 3 5 7 9 11 13 15 17 19 Q/C 20 18 16 14 12 10 8 6 4 2

PRINTED IN THE UNITED STATES OF AMERICA

The paper in this book meets the guidelines for permanence
and durability of the Committee on Production Guidelines for
Book Longevity of the Council on Library Resources.

Editorial Staff

Contents

Contributors

Michael Beckerman
Washington University, Saint Louis
THE NEW CONCEPTION OF "THE WORK OF ART"

Peter Anthony Bloom
Smith College
THE PUBLIC FOR ORCHESTRAL MUSIC IN THE NINETEENTH CENTURY

Michael Broyles
University of Maryland, Baltimore
ENSEMBLE MUSIC MOVES OUT OF THE PRIVATE HOUSE: HAYDN TO
BEETHOVEN

Lance W. Brunner
University of Kentucky
THE ORCHESTRA AND RECORDED SOUND

J. Peter Burkholder
University of Wisconsin, Madison
THE TWENTIETH CENTURY AND THE ORCHESTRA AS MUSEUM

Gregory G. Butler
University of British Columbia
INSTRUMENTS AND THEIR USE: EARLY TIMES TO THE RISE OF THE
ORCHESTRA

Jon W. Finson
University of North Carolina, Chapel Hill
MUSICOLOGY AND THE RISE OF THE INDEPENDENT ORCHESTRA

Jane F. Fulcher
Indiana University
MUSIC IN RELATION TO THE OTHER ARTS: THE CRITICAL DEBATE

Nancy Groce
TECHNICAL DEVELOPMENT OF MUSICAL INSTRUMENTS: STRINGS

Rufus Hallmark
Aaron Copland School of Music, Queens College, C.U.N.Y.
THE STAR CONDUCTOR AND MUSICAL VIRTUOSITY

Alan Houtchens
University of California, Santa Barbara
ROMANTIC COMPOSERS RESPOND TO CHALLENGE AND DEMAND

Barbara Lambert
TECHNICAL DEVELOPMENT OF MUSICAL INSTRUMENTS: BRASS

Tod Machover
Massachusetts Institute of Technology
THE EXTENDED ORCHESTRA

Katherine T. Rohrer
Columbia University
THE ORCHESTRA IN OPERA AND BALLET

Edward Rothstein
The New Republic
THE NEW AMATEUR PLAYER AND LISTENER

Bryan R. Simms
University of Southern California, Los Angeles
TWENTIETH-CENTURY COMPOSERS RETURN TO THE SMALL ENSEMBLE

Elaine R. Sisman
Columbia University
THE MAIN FORMS OF ORCHESTRAL MUSIC

George B. Stauffer
Hunter College, C.U.N.Y.
THE MODERN ORCHESTRA: A CREATION OF THE LATE EIGHTEENTH CENTURY

Denis Stevens
Accademia Monteverdiana
WHY CONDUCTORS? THEIR ROLE AND THE IDEA OF FIDELITY

R. Larry Todd
Duke University
ORCHESTRAL TEXTURE AND THE ART OF ORCHESTRATION

Nancy Toff
TECHNICAL DEVELOPMENT OF MUSICAL INSTRUMENTS: WOODWINDS

Robert L. Weaver
University of Louisville
THE CONSOLIDATION OF THE MAIN ELEMENTS OF THE ORCHESTRA: 1470–1768

William Weber
California State University, Long Beach
THE RISE OF THE CLASSICAL REPERTOIRE IN NINETEENTH-CENTURY ORCHESTRAL CONCERTS

Introduction

For at least two reasons, the present time appears to be the right time to bring forth the book you now hold in your hands. One is the state of the orchestra itself. A gleaming, efficient ensemble that has achieved all it is likely ever to achieve in precision, virtuosity, and responsiveness, it brings more music to more thousands of listeners with each passing year. Another reason is the state of modern scholarship. Not only would it have been impossible to produce *The Orchestra: Origins and Transformations* without the benefit of modern musicology; the very conception of the book depends on ideas generated by cultural history, a relatively recent discipline. Our predecessors' works not only lack the musicological detail in evidence here; they also manifest little awareness of the social and historical forces that played a role in the orchestra's life.

To say that this book is unique in its coverage, its variety, and its currency is not to denigrate those which came before. Rather is it to emphasize that the moment for a knowledgeable summing up, for some kind of correct reckoning, has only now arrived. When Johann Mattheson, the most important music theoretician of the early eighteenth century, was writing, the instruments had not yet coalesced into the modern orchestra. Even long after they had, as recently as 1940, Adam Carse

encountered problems in his effort to collect historical detail. In his introduction to *The Orchestra in the Eighteenth Century* Carse wrote,

> The searching historian must read page after page about the singing of the
> vocalists and the playing of the violinist or the flutist, and then be truly
> grateful if he is thrown a word about the orchestra.... What little can be
> gleaned about the 18th century orchestras and their playing has been
> scraped together and forms the basis and authority for what is written in
> these pages.

The reason that the present book should prove more useful, then,
than those that went before is not that our authors are brighter than the
others or more endowed with God-given insight. It is because it has only
been in recent times that the depth and caliber of historical research have
permitted the perspective that is critical to a genuine understanding of
the orchestra's genesis and development.

The musical repertory of today's orchestra generally begins with
Mozart and Haydn and ends with Mahler and early Stravinsky. In order
to provide a rich background for our chronicling of events, we begin our
story not in the classic era but in 1470, the date of the first surviving
account of a large body of string instruments. Robert Weaver charts what
happened between then and the last third of the eighteenth century
when, according to George Stauffer, Mozart and Haydn breathed new life
into an idiom then ridden with dry formulas. At this point our other
authors pick up the many threads of the story and go on to bring their
knowledge and imagination to the aesthetic, political, and economic factors that make up the historical tapestry in which the orchestra serves as
the focal point. Tod Machover, a composer who specializes in computer
music technology, contributes the last essay. Despite his remarkable
accomplishments in this field, Machover concedes that "the modernist
mode of purely electronic sounds is quickly passing." The most he fore-
sees is "the incorporation of some electronic instruments into the vast
resources of the orchestra." Such an innovation, it seems to this editor,
would probably be coloristic at most and unlikely to change the orchestra in a substantive way. It would seem in no way to be comparable to
the invention of the horn valve at the beginning of the nineteenth century, a device that transformed trumpets and horns into the chromatic
instruments that enabled Wagner to compose the wandering inner parts
for them that he did.

Although our overall approach is chronological, it does not follow
that the ideas presented here can be neatly compartmentalized into old

and new, conservative and advanced. Take, for example, the notion of meaning in music, the question of whether music is always tied—consciously or not—to a literal idea, or if it is entirely independent, with its own idiosyncratic rules and owes nothing to any other art. Michael Beckerman argues eloquently that all music, even after its emancipation from a dependence on the voice, has kept its deep associations to words. Jane Fulcher, on the other hand, considers music to be an autonomous art that "maintains its distance from linguistic features." In taking opposing viewpoints, our authors present a microcosm of the music world itself. In "The Star Conductor and Musical Virtuosity," Rufus Hallmark attributes to Toscanini the following remark about Beethoven's *Eroica*: "Some say it is Napoleon, some Hitler, some Mussolini. For me it is simply *Allegro con brio*." Yet Toscanini's view of Beethoven's instrumental music as abstract is not shared by André Watts. In 1985, at New York's Metropolitan Museum of Art, the pianist coached several students in an open master class. Leaning over the shoulder of a young German working on the *Appassionata*, Watts pointed to some measures in the score and asked him what they meant. "Modulation," was the reply. "Modulation? No!" Watts countered. "That passage means surprise."

The Orchestra: Origins and Transformations is above all a reference work, and a glance at its table of contents will suggest its wide scope. In our tracing the history of the orchestra from its modest beginnings in the Renaissance to the awesome vehicle that it is today, a genuine effort has been made to find a middle ground between pedestrian listings and lofty philosophizing. Sometimes, in attempting to preserve the individuality of our writers, we may have veered toward one side or the other. But the middle ground is almost always visible, and the reader should come upon fact after fact that not only enlightens but delights. He will learn that at the beginning of the eighteenth century, concert programs were made up of eight to ten short pieces—not the three or four long ones of the present time—and that the only long ones were oratorios or sacred pieces presented in segments with other compositions intervening; that Haydn admitted to introducing that surprising drum stroke in the Andante of his G Major Symphony not for any structural reason or elevated aesthetic purpose but simply to compete for attention with Ignaz Pleyel, his own pupil and rival, in a contest generated by the London critics and followed assiduously by the public; that Mendelssohn, while working on the *Reformation Symphony*, may well have been the first composer to orchestrate measure by measure, "like an immense mosaic," rather than in the then traditional way of filling in all the instrumental parts after completing the outer lines; that it was his deafness that forced

Beethoven to become a composer only, rather than both a composer and a performer. That particular specialization unfortunately became the model for composers who could hear.

We are reminded that during most of their lives, Mozart and Haydn heard their works performed almost as soon as they had composed them and that something unprecedented happened in the 1830s and 1840s: by traditional expectations their music should have dropped out of the repertory about that time. But the fact is that it did not. The intriguing point here is that it was more than a century ago—not recently, as many writers on music believe—that the modern canon of musical masterpieces began to take hold.

Along with the decrease in performance of new works, even older music than that of the classic period eventually made itself heard. Until only a generation ago music written before the eighteenth century was the exclusive domain of scholars; yet today, because of modern musicology, many conductors and chamber music ensembles specialize in so-called early music. Much of this material is presented not only in concert but preserved on recordings. Deutsche Grammophon's Archiv label, founded thirty years ago as a semischolarly one, now produces some of the company's best-selling discs.

Early music is not, of course, the only music of the past in which record companies work at cross-purposes with the living composer. The massive distribution of masterpieces in multiple performances forces today's composer to compete for the listener's time with Mozart, Schubert, Beethoven, Brahms, and Wagner—and that is a heavy burden for him to bear. Lance Brunner's illuminating essay is based on the premise that recording is the most important phenomenon in Western music since the invention of music notation in the ninth century. Less apocalyptic but reasonably substantive factors influencing creativity in music—criticism, performance fees, copyright, and so on—all figure in this portrait which brings the orchestra up to the present day. The irony is that it is now, when its capabilities are at their height, that the fundamental validity of the orchestra as a tool that bends and shapes according to composers' demands is increasingly under challenge. That challenge stems not from inherent limitations in the medium but from the state of the art of music itself.

For our most respected composers have not turned their backs on the orchestra. On the contrary, such gifted artists as Milton Babbitt, Elliott Carter, David Diamond, Jacob Druckman, Morton Gould, Leon Kirchner, Roger Sessions, and Charles Wuorinen have recently devoted much of their energies to composing orchestral works. But if one acknowledges even a modicum of truth to the Hegelian concept that a change in quantity means a change in quality, then one cannot ignore the following facts: that in a much more crowded world there are probably fewer composers than there were in the eighteenth century, and that while Elliott Carter aspires to the composition of one work a year, Alessandro Scarlatti—and he was not alone—completed more than four thousand in his sixty-five-year lifetime.

This said, the orchestra, like the museum, should endure for a considerable time, mounting masterpieces from the past. As the museum occasionally presents an exhibit devoted to the works of a living painter, so will the orchestra program the pieces of a living composer. The danger, then, is not that the orchestra will decay before our eyes. It is rather that the kind of music for which it has served as a perfect vehicle may soon cease to be composed.

Following the age-old sequence of theory following practice, this book comes at the right time not only for the reasons articulated at the beginning of this introduction, but because seventy-five years have passed since the death of Mahler and more than seventy since the composition of *Firebird, Petrouchka,* and *The Rite of Spring.* In an age when packaged electronic entertainment attracts a large part of the total audience, that part demanding novelty in everything it does, the orchestra can still serve those who long for something from an older world. Given the proper circumstances—adequate funding and skillful direction—it should continue to please, to excite the imagination, to move the spirit, and to shape the minds of listeners for centuries to come.

Joan Peyser
June 1986

Editor's note: I would like to acknowledge my indebtedness to Jacques Barzun, literary consultant to Charles Scribner's Sons, whose idea it was to create such a book, and to Kirk Reynolds, Michael McGinley, and Paul Wittke for the considerable contributions each of them made.

THE ORCHESTRA

Origins and

Transformations

The Consolidation of the Main Elements of the Orchestra: 1470–1768

Robert L. Weaver

The elements that compose what is currently called the "orchestra" coalesced about the middle of the eighteenth century into a complex yet remarkably stable tradition. That tradition, now over two centuries old, shows today a vigor that promises a life lasting into the foreseeable future. Although in Western musical history the orchestral tradition took shape later than others, such as those surrounding the liturgical choir, opera company, or oratorio society, it has assumed a dominance that justifies a major reference work devoted to the orchestra alone. In fact, it raises the question of why such a work has been so long delayed.

The word *orchestra* descends from the Greek term for the semicircular space where the chorus stood, in front of the main acting area of a theater. In Roman times it was a reserved section for wealthy patrons and senators, and in the Middle Ages, at least at the time of Isidore of Seville, the stage. Johann Mattheson used the term in the title of his treatise *Das neu-eröffnete Orchestre* (1713) but defined it in an interesting combination of terms as the space in front of the stage where the "Herren Symphonisten" sat (Becker, "Orchester," in *Musik*). The first recorded use of *orchestra* to mean a group of instruments and not a place is found in Abbé François Raguenet's unflattering comment in his *Parallèle des Italiens et des Français* (1702) on the softness of the "orchestre de notre Opéra" (Strunk, 126, obscures the passage by using "band" as the translation of *orchestre*). This meaning took root first in France and then spread through Europe along with the rising cultural influence of France in the mid-eighteenth century. In Jean Jacques Rousseau's *Dictionnaire de musique* (1768), the meaning became attached finally and authoritatively to the players. The date of Rousseau's publication has therefore been chosen as the termination for the present essay.

The initial date of 1470 has been chosen because the earliest account of a large number of string instruments, which are the essential and aboriginal portion of the orchestra, occurred in that year. At a public festival in Breslau in honor of the marriage of the king of Hungary, Matthias Corvinus, there was heard the sound of many trumpets, and (whether simultaneously or afterward is not clear) "of all kinds of string instruments" (Spies, 3). Early in the next century, *concerto* appeared in Italy as a term denoting a group of instruments but not the size of the group. *Band* in France and England in the sixteenth century was normally used for the same meaning. For example, the king's musicians in London were entitled the Royal Band, and Les Vingt-quatre Violons du Roi, the Twenty-four Violins of the King (Louis XIII of France), organized in the early seventeenth century, were called the Grande Bande.

In the baroque era it was the practice to use *violin* (*violon* in French) or *arm-viol* (*viola da braccio* in Italian) to denote several or all of the members of the violin family, that is, violins, violas, violoncellos, plus others such as the tenor violin and bass (*violone*), which have become more or less obsolete. At the same time another family of bowed string instruments was described by the term *leg viols* (*viole da gamba*) because they were played by resting the instruments on the knee. During a time when there were so many string instruments, bowed and plucked (lute, theorbo, chitarrone, and so on), *string instruments* as a term was ambiguous; to use the word *violins*, meaning to include all members of that family, was more specific. Thus the Twenty-four Violins of the King included violins of all sizes. In the present essay the same meaning for *violins* will be maintained whenever historical context makes *string instruments* a too-inclusive term.

The elements of the orchestral tradition that gradually crystallized during the period 1470–1768 are these: (1) the instrumental members of the orchestra, their numbers, and their technological evolution under the formative demands of the orchestra; (2) forms that compose the repertoire of the orchestra, the musical logic by which these forms are embodied, and the musical language or rhetoric by which the forms and the logic are transmuted into human expression; (3) the function of the instruments in the transformation of abstract ideas into orchestral son-ority through the art of orchestration; and (4) geographical stability, which is intimately related to patronage and all forms of public support and to the concert and concert series.

MEMBERS OF THE ORCHESTRA

The primary element in the definition of *orchestra* is the number of instruments. The term is often used with no other meaning than a large group of instruments. Thus, Becker begins his article on the orchestra with a survey of instrumental groups in classical antiquity, Asia, and Africa, and the *Harvard Dictionary of Music* in various articles uses *orchestra* as the designation of a Balinese thirty-piece *gamelan gong kebyar* and a *kuencheu*, or Chinese opera "orchestra," and speaks of the "orchestral" character of African music. To use it in this manner, while useful, never-theless stretches the meaning unmercifully. Here the term is restricted to a musical organization that existed only in Western culture (except where it has been imported by other cultures) and only from about the middle of the eighteenth century to the present.

The size of the orchestra, moreover, is a crude criterion and is not a continuously evolving element through the history of music. All peoples in all times and places have known that in small spaces small numbers are appropriate, and in large, many. The "orchestra" mentioned in 2 Chronicles 5:12–13, consisting of cymbals, psalteries, harps, and 120 trumpets, would hardly be acceptable as an orchestra merely because of the number of instruments.

Not every instrument, no matter how common or popular it may have been, has gained a permanent place in the modern orchestra—the saxophone, organ, banjo, bagpipes, cromorne, and many others. The accepted instruments in the orchestra have arrived at standard construc-tions and ranges, but related instruments have been excluded. Thus, there is no tenor violin, although the instrument was common in the seventeenth century, between the violoncello and viola. Cornets, euphoniums, sousaphones, flügelhorns, and bugles are very seldom called for in orchestral scores. Some instruments present in seventeenth- and eighteenth-century orchestras have been abandoned—specifically, all sizes of lutes and harpsichords. The kinds of instruments, therefore, make the first distinction between the orchestra and other large groups of instruments. Among the instruments of the orchestra, the violin family is essential, a fact that can be demonstrated by current terminology and by a historical account of the growth of the orchestra.

Considering terminology first, the distinction between a solo ensemble and an orchestra is that in the former there is one instrument for each musical part. If the ensemble is composed only of string instruments, the difference is merely the number of instruments for each part. During the baroque era many compositions called "sonatas" were scored for two violins, thorough bass, or basso continuo but were performed as "concertos"—that is, works for orchestra with or without solo instruments. Indeed, the distinction between "orchestra" and "ensemble" for the seventeenth century and the first decades of the eighteenth was a matter of performance practice rather than a specification by the composer in published scores. When other instruments are added, it is the multiplication of violins and their relatives that distinguishes orchestral from solo-ensemble music. Thus, an ensemble such as a septet, composed of one each of violin, viola, violoncello, bass viol, flute, oboe, and bassoon, is converted into an orchestra by doubling the violins, violas, violoncellos, and contrabasses, even if the winds remain one on a part. Significantly, both historically and in common practice, as the whole orchestra increased in size, the numbers of each member the violin family increased, but the kinds remained unchanged. By contrast both the numbers and the kinds of woodwinds, reeds, brasses, and percussion increased.

The strings, whose presence and numbers form the basic component of the orchestra, were also historically the first element of the orchestra to become a coherent, standardized group of instruments. The advantages of the violin family over other families of instruments were for the most part obvious. The plucked strings, such as the lute, harp, and harpsichord, were unable to sustain a tone without renewed attacks. Keyed wind instruments of the Renaissance and early baroque were limited in range and not as easily adjustable in pitch as violins. Renaissance wind instruments were made in one piece and therefore were untunable. The use of more than one Renaissance wind instrument on a part, in general, revealed differences in the construction of each single instrument to no advantage of the unisons. Covered reeds like cromornes were invariable in volume. High brasses were too limited in pitch and too fierce and penetrating in tone. The only low brass instruments capable of playing chromatic tones at this time were trombones, but they lacked the agility of the string instruments.

The only real competitor of the violin family was the viol family. The superiority of the former as orchestral instruments consisted in their not being fretted. A fret was a bar or strip of leather or gut tied across the fingerboard that stopped the string at a fixed point to produce a particular note when the player pressed the string against the fingerboard to the left of the fret. Violin strings are stopped by the player's finger and can produce infinitely adjustable pitches at the will of the player. Differences in structure make the violin's sonority stronger than that of the viol. Because of its soft tone and frets, the viol is perfectly suited to serve as an instrument for amateurs in private musical society. The violin is preeminently the instrument of the professional musician and is capable of carrying in large halls or theaters, especially if there are several instruments playing together. But the fixed pitch of the viol precludes its being played in large numbers on a single part, since unisons cannot be tuned by ear and are inevitably unsatisfactory. Finally, the frets of the viol until the late seventeenth century were tuned in mean-tone temperament. Consequently the viol could not play in the key of C-sharp Minor, for example, and sound in tune. But the new common-practice harmony, which was beginning to be used by the time that theatrical music was demanding large instrumental groups, required that all keys be equally in tune in all instruments of the group. Again, violinists could adjust the tuning of any key by ear even before the system of equal temperament was established.

One instrument of the gamba family did make the transition and find a place in the orchestra: the doublebass viol, which still preserves the typical sloping shoulders, flat back, C-holes, and tuning system in fourths (violins use fifths) of the gamba family.

By the beginning of the seventeenth century, complaints were heard about large groups of instruments containing wind instruments. Agostino Agazzari objected to "the insufficient union [of the wind instruments] with the stringed instruments" (Strunk, 425). Giovanni Battista Doni disparaged mixtures of strings and winds as "Spanish porridge." Monteverdi complained that wind instruments in opera forced singers to use a loud and strained voice, of which he, of course, disapproved.

Under the impact of such criticism, the violins were separated from the wind instruments during the late sixteenth and early seventeenth centuries as violin bands began to be organized for use in theaters and ballrooms. At first they performed as double or triple consorts in a fashion that preserved Renaissance equality of the parts, but soon an unequal balance came to be sought by using more violins than violas or basses and by reinforcing the bass with the instruments of the basso continuo (keyboard, plucked string instruments, and bassoons or extra basses) to reinforce the melodic line and the bass. The distinction was fundamental to the change in musical style and order that produced the orchestra.

THE RISE OF THE STRING ORCHESTRA

During the sixteenth century, it became the general practice of courts, city governments, and wealthy noblemen and bourgeois to maintain more or less continuously an instrumental band to play in various combinations (but not all at once) at public functions, ceremonies, and private entertainments, especially balls. Six French musicians paid by Francis I, king of France, in 1529 were described as "viollons, haulxbois et sacquebuteurs" and were capable of performing three unmixed consorts (that is, solo ensembles) and whatever mixture might be called for on an ad hoc basis (Boyden, 24f.). A letter written in 1546 by an agent of the duke of Piacenza recommended a group of six musicians for employment in the duke's household. The six men played unmixed consorts of trumpets, trombones, pipes, cornetts, shawms, recorders, flutes, and violins, and whatever mixed consorts were desired, and sang very well (Pelicelli, 42f.). In 1550 the English royal musicians, composed of a band of eighty, could play violins, violas, flutes, trumpets, trombones, shawms, and timpani.

These consorts and lists of court musicians convey no hint of the formation of the orchestra. A different kind of instrumental group is suggested by the fact that Charles IX, who ruled as king of France between 1560 and 1574, ordered thirty-eight violins—twelve large and twelve small violins, six violas, and eight basses—from Andrea Amati, the famous violin maker of Cremona. So large a collection disposed in an unequal balance of numbers of instruments suggests (yet without proof) that the string orchestra was taking shape. Charles's mother, Catherine de Médicis, imported a band of Italian violinists led by Baldassare da Belgiojoso, or Balthasar de Beaujoyeulx in French, for the accompaniment of a company of dancers.

Circé, ou Le ballet comique de la reine, lavishly produced as a celebration given by Henry III on the occasion of the marriage of the duke of Joyeuse to his queen's sister in 1581, is the most famous and best documented performance by Beaujoyeulx's band. The music was composed by Lambert de Beaulieu and Jacques Salmon and was published in 1582 to perpetuate the memory of the brilliant production. Two sets of instrumental dances called for ten violins of all sizes in five equal parts; that is, the violins formed a double consort. According to a contemporary description, the two consorts stood (as was common at the time) on opposite sides of the hall.

The association between violins and dance music was formed almost at the birth of the violin itself, or even of its ancestor, the rebec, and was widespread in Europe. The rudiments of bowing, in particular the association of the down-bow with the first beat of a measure, probably originated in Italy as a characteristic of the playing of dances. Supportive of this speculation is the fact that the earliest band of violins in Paris was composed of imported Italian violinists, who brought with them Italian instruments and styles of playing. Since the one bit of evidence that exists concerning the instrumentation used by the Italian band (the *Circé* records) shows a double consort rather than an orchestra, the speculation may reasonably be expanded: the Italians developed the instrument and the elements of playing technique, but the French first conceived of the orchestral sonority.

While the violins of the Grande Bande played the dances, other instruments were used to represent programmatically the characters of dramatic scenes. In 1619 for Pierre Guedron's *Grand ballet du roy sur l'adventure de Tancrède en la forest enchantée*, the dances were accompanied by violins, the voices by viols and lutes, Pan and three satyrs by cornetts, other satyrs who played for the entrance of four elderly silenuses by oboes, still others who played for the entrance of woodland nymphs by flutes, and shepherds by bagpipes and shawms. But there is no indication that these viols, lutes, and wind instruments were at any point members of an "orchestra."

The organization in 1626 by Louis XIII of the famous string orchestra of the French court, the Grande Bande or Les Vingt-quatre Violons du Roi, is a landmark in the history of the orchestra. Marin Mersenne, in his *Harmonie universelle* (book 4, 177), praising the orchestra as the most perfect of instruments on which to play dance music and as the ultimate in ravishing beauty and power, provided a more secure record of a new, truly orchestral sonority. Mersenne added the information that the orchestra was composed of six violins (*dessus*), six violoncellos (*basses*), four violas playing the second-violin range (*hautes-contre*), four violas playing the alto range (*tailles*), and four violas playing the tenor range (*quintes*). All three of the last-named instruments were tuned in unison but played in different ranges. The strengthening of the highest and lowest instruments and the relative subjugation of the internal parts were steps toward the organization of the orchestra.

Jean-Baptiste Lully, discontented with the quality of the performances by the Grande Bande, persuaded Louis XIV to allow him to orga-

nize a new orchestra, Les Petits Violons, some time before its first performance in 1656. The instruments numbered approximately sixteen and
included oboes and bassoons, but the exact distribution is not known.
The orchestra accompanied the *ballets de cour*, danced by the court and
the king himself, and later it was augmented to twenty-one instruments
to serve as the opera orchestra of the Académie Royale de Musique. It
was famous for its discipline and for the restraint with which ornamentation was used. But because in his opera scores Lully expanded the role
of the winds, we will return to this orchestra later.

If it was ballet that spawned the string orchestra in France, it was
opera and oratorio in Italy. It is an exaggeration, however, to use the
word *orchestras* in relation to the early operas in Florence and Rome at
the beginning of the seventeenth century, since these operas were performed in private chambers or theaters and required only ensembles, as
in the case of Jacopo Peri's *Euridice* of 1600. Claudio Monteverdi's *Orfeo*,
performed in Mantua in 1607, was accompanied by an instrumental
group of forty-four, as is made clear by the published score. Under scrutiny this "orchestra" turns out to have been basically two consorts with
equal voicing: a string consort in five voices with two instruments per
part and a seven-part wind consort of five trombones and two cornetts.
Other instruments were added for programmatic color in particular
scenes in the manner of the sixteenth-century *intermedio*. The anticipa-
tion of the characteristics of the orchestra is limited, first, to the heavier
setting of the bass part, which was played by various keyboards, three
chitarroni, and two double basses, in addition to the bass instruments of
each consort, and, second, to the importance of the consort of the violin
family, which did not have such a dominant position in the sixteenth-
century *intermedio*. Monteverdi's *Combattimento di Tancredi e Clorinda*,
composed in Venice in 1624 and first performed in the private house of
the patrician Girolamo Mocenigo, was a later instance of the consort
rather than the orchestra, since the accompaniment required a five-part
string consort and basso continuo. The introduction to the publication
of the score suggests the doubling of all parts equally, according to the
size of the auditorium.

In Roman opera of the first two decades of the seventeenth century,
the preference for string ensembles became well established. Moreover,
the consort principle was abandoned in favor of a typically baroque texture of two (occasionally three) violins and a well-reinforced bass.
Whether the instrumental groups in any one case comprised an ensemble
or an orchestra depended upon the character of the performance, being
in a small chamber or in a large theater. Thus, when the published score

of Giacinto Cornacchioli's *Diana schernita* (1629) called for two violins, a violoncello, and basso continuo, one may suppose that it was an ensemble of one instrument to a part, since it was performed in a private house. But Stefano Landi's *Sant' Alessio,* the inaugural opera in 1632 of Rome's Teatro Palazzo Barberini, which was reputed to have a capacity of more than three thousand, would have required considerable doubling of its three violin parts, supported by unspecified quantities of harps, lutes, harpsichords, theorbos, and contrabass viols, to be equal to the size of the auditorium. Both opera and its orchestra flourished only sporadically in Rome until the last quarter of the century because of the inconsistent attitudes of the papacy toward opera.

Despite the financial instability of Venetian opera houses, theatrical orchestras achieved some continuity of employment after the opening of the Teatro San Cassiano in 1637. The standard Venetian operatic orchestra included a harpsichord, one chitarrone, one or two trumpets, and about ten violins of various sizes. The scores of Venetian operas occasionally mentioned other instruments, such as flutes, viols, and recorders, which were used for particular scenes but not as part of the orchestra. Viola parts were often improvised.

Churches, as well as theaters and courts, supported groups of instrumentalists. From the fifteenth century onward, trombones were the most prominent instruments maintained by court chapels, churches, and cathedrals, but by the end of the sixteenth, such *cappelle* might include a variety of instruments. In Venice during the time of the Gabrielis, San Marco maintained a *cappella* consisting of five trombones, one cornett, and five violins for use in liturgical services. Sixteenth- and seventeenth-century Italian liturgical music specifically calling for trombones was conservative, being closely associated with polychoral traditions that, as the baroque era matured, became one of the most important types of music belonging to the old style (*stile antico*) as opposed to the then modern style (*stile moderno*).

Oratorio, in contrast to the service music of the church, joined opera as one of the two most innovative forms of the baroque and, like opera, provided great impetus to the creation of the string orchestra. Since oratorio flourished earlier and more vigorously in Rome than in any other city, the rise of the string orchestra can be most easily traced in that city. One of the most important patrons of oratorio in seventeenth-century Rome was Cardinal Benedetto Pamphili, who wrote the librettos of several oratorios set by composers such as Alessandro Scarlatti, Bernardo Pasquini, Alessandro Melani, and Giovanni Lorenzo Lulier. The performances took place at various locations: Santa Maria in Vallicella, the

Seminario Romano, Pamphili's Palazzo nel Corso, and elsewhere. Alessandro Melani's *Abele,* performed at Santa Maria in Vallicella in 1678, required a string orchestra composed of six first and six second violins, four violas, a violoncello, and a bass viol, to judge by the number of copies of the parts. While the bass was comparatively weak, the balance was orchestral (Marx, 143).

The orchestra grew through the next decades. In 1685 for a performance of Alessandro Scarlatti's *S. Maria Maddalena* (the alternate title of *Il trionfo della gratia*) at the Seminario Romano, the violins were fifteen in number, with six violas, five violoncellos, three contrabasses, two lutes, and a harpsichord—a standard baroque string orchestra. Significantly, two years later, for a sumptuous performance of *S. Maria Maddalena de' Pazzi,* by Giovanni Lorenzo Lulier, in the palazzo of Cardinal Francesco Maria de' Medici, brass instruments (one trumpet and two trombones) were added. The largest orchestra recorded among those patronized by Cardinal Pamphili was used in 1689 for *S. Beatrice d'Este,* by the same composer. This substantial orchestra consisted of forty violins, ten violas, seventeen violoncellos, seven contrabasses, two trumpets, one trombone, one lute, and one organ (played by Pasquini), for a total of seventy-nine instruments. In 1695 for *Ismaele soccorso dall' angelo* by Carlo Cesarini, a three-member *concertino* consisting of Corelli and Matteo Fornari, playing violins, and Lulier, playing viola, was paid more than the other instrumentalists. This addition of a group of soloists in a performance coincided in time with the appearance of publications in Italy calling for a contrast between the *concertino,* or ensemble, and the *concerto,* or full orchestra.

THE ADDITION OF COLLA PARTE WINDS

No matter how great the dominance of the string orchestra in opera and oratorio, the use of other instruments, at least occasionally, never ceased throughout the seventeenth century. The limited use of wind instruments with strings is indicated by the guarded approval bestowed upon them even by their critics. Agazzari, while disapproving of mixtures of strings and winds, admitted that a bass trombone softly and well played might be substituted for the bass viols, and Doni, who disliked conglomerations of all kinds of instruments, defended the use of recorders and muted cornetts.

The fundamental problem with wind instruments was tuning. Renaissance instruments with fingerholes were made in one piece, were untunable, and were constructed in mean-tone temperament. When they were used in solo ensembles in matched or mixed sets that had been made with compatible tuning, the problem was satisfactorily solved. But the multiplication of instruments on a single part did not always produce acceptable results. The problem became crucial only when music moved from the private chamber to the auditorium suitable for opera and oratorio. The larger space demanded a larger number of instruments on each part.

Renaissance practices, however, perpetuated the use of wind instruments in ballet, opera, and oratorio, wherever the use of certain wind instruments represented particular scenes, according to programmatic associations in the manner of the Renaissance *intermedio*. A *festa teatrale* sometimes recalled the many-colored Renaissance consorts, as in Jacopo Melani's *Ercole in Tebe* performed in Florence in 1661, in which the "orchestra" contained four cornetts and one trombone for an incantation scene, and in Marc' Antonio Cesti's *Pomo d'oro* performed in Vienna in 1668, which called for various consorts of trumpets, trombones, cornetts, flutes, one bassoon, and one regal, to represent infernal, battle, and bucolic scenes, but not in union with the strings in an orchestral manner.

The introduction of woodwind instruments into the now-established string orchestra took place in Paris during the late seventeenth century in a regular and more or less permanent fasion. At the same time in Paris occurred the alterations of the transverse flute and of the bassoon that made them more adaptable for orchestral use and the conversion of the chawm into the oboe, the first treble reed instrument truly adaptable to the demands of the orchestra. The flute's tone was softened by a conical bore, its tuning made more adjustable by joints, and its range extended by keys. The last two changes were applied also to the bassoon, which was adjusted to eliminate the disadvantages of intonation, mentioned by Praetorius, that made it necessary to have two different instruments, one to play flats and the other, sharps. The modern oboe was invented probably around the middle of the seventeenth century by a member of the Hotteterre family, players employed by the French court. With rare exceptions the oboe was used as a ripieno instrument doubling the violins and making the sonority uniform with the basso continuo formed by bass viols, violoncellos, and bassoons. From the beginning, the oboe seems to have been called into existence as an orchestral instrument. These inventions and alterations demonstrate the demands of the orchestra (operatic, oratorio, or independent) on instrumental manufacture, a subject to be taken up in greater detail in a subsequent chapter.

The Petits Violons, cited above, included two oboes and one bassoon, which presumably played colla parte with the violins and the basses, respectively. Becker lists two oboes in the Vingt-quatre Violons in 1610, a doubtful proposition. Lully's operatic scores required trumpets for fanfares and sudden "noises," flutes for pastoral ballets, oboes for rustic and sea scenes, and bassoons. Except for the oboes and bassoons, the winds were used in sectional contrasts and for programmatic illustration of the text. The orchestra of the Opéra (Académie Royale de Musique) in 1713, close to the "classical orchestra," was composed of twelve violin parts, a smaller number of internal parts (two *quintes*, two *tailles*, and three *hautes-contres*), and a strong bass (eight instruments without differentiation between violoncellos and basses). To these were added a wind choir of two each of flutes, oboes, clarinets (possibly shawms), bassoons, and, presumably, at least one harpsichord. Missing still were the brass instruments and kettledrums.

The growth in favor of the outer parts is apparent in the list of instruments in the same orchestra in 1751: eight first and eight second violins, two each of the middle voices, and eight violoncellos and basses. Note here the strengthening of the bass. The clarinets were missing, but a trumpet and timpani had been added to reinforce the tutti passages. In the same year at a Concert Spirituel the same balance was heard but with further compression of the inner strings, the violas having been reduced to two in a four-part (not five-part) string orchestra. Another important addition was a pair of horns.

Italy was not far behind in enriching opera orchestras with wind instruments after the beginning of the eighteenth century. The Teatro San Carlo of Naples, proud of its large opera orchestra, boasted one of the largest in Europe: it fluctuated between forty-five and seventy players. In 1737 it consisted of twenty-four violins, six violas, three violoncellos, three basses, two harpsichords, two oboes, three bassoons, and two trumpets. Note that flutes and horns were missing.

Thus far, only the accumulation of instruments and their relative numbers have been considered. How the instruments were integrated is a separate consideration. Since a true integration is fundamental to the concept of the orchestra and is moreover inextricably linked to harmonic form, which reached maturity in the late seventeenth century, it will be necessary to examine the evolution of harmonic form before the integration itself can be explained. However, there remains to be considered one more particular member of the orchestra—the conductor.

In the mid-eighteenth century, there were several possibilities for conducting: in the Paris Opéra, it was the practice to make an audible beat with a long pole, no doubt a continuation from the *ballets de cour*, in which a large assembly of instrumentalists, singers, and dancers had to be coordinated. Rousseau, complaining about this noise in his article on beating time, denounced not only the Opéra for its noisy beat but all performances in France for the lack of a dependable measure. Foot-stamping by the first violinist was evidently not an uncommon method of keeping an ensemble or orchestra together.

The short baton or even a roll of paper wielded by the *maestro di cappella* was equally well established in France at the same time, and the first descriptions of the movements still used today, at least in conducting classes, were written down in French manuals of instruction: M. de Saint-Lambert's *Les principes du clavecin* (1702) and Michel Pignolet de Mon-téclair's *Nouvelle méthode pour apprendre la musique* (1700). Rousseau recorded the definition of *bâton de mesure* as a short baton or roll of paper and discussed under the entry *Battre le mesure* the differences between the Italian style of beating time and the French, which he described thus: "The French beat only the first time value of the measure and mark the others by different motions of the hand to the right and left" (Rousseau, 52).

In the opera house as well as elsewhere, practice permitted two con-ductors simultaneously, one leading from the harpsichord and the other from the chair of the first violin, whose motions would have been not very different from those of the modern violinist leading an ensemble while playing. The harpsichordist, however, seemed to have taken pre-cedence usually, and it should be recalled that one of the first descrip-tions of the standard gestures for the various meters appeared in a man-ual for the harpsichord, indication enough of the position of the harpsichordist in the direction of the group. The origin of these gestures is to be found in the Renaissance method of beating time values (*tactus*), primarily in church music. The *tactus*, which Bukofzer calls "an even flow of beats," was indicated by up-and-down hand motions without any expression of accentuation. The transition to the French manner, which indicated accentuation by marking the downbeat with the downward motion and subordinating other beats by motions to the right and left (a system still not adopted by the Germans and Italians in 1768, accord-ing to Rousseau), took place during the seventeenth century as dance meters invaded all types of music. It is not surprising that the change should occur in France first, in view of the importance of ballet there. The use of the hand, with or without a baton, by an appointed person who is not performing on an instrument remained throughout the sev-enteenth and eighteenth centuries associated with choral music or with combinations of instruments and voices, as can be seen by innumerable depictions of performances in churches from the period. Its persistence is attested by accounts of Haydn's direction of the masses and oratorios, from which it is evident that he was conducting in the modern manner and that part of his function was to convey to the performers the sentiments contained in the music.

FORM, RHETORIC, AND ORCHESTRATION

A conspicuous element of the orchestral tradition is the repertoire. The relation between players and what is played is so close that twice since the sixteenth century the term for the most frequently performed type of composition became interchangeable with the term for the musical organization itself: *concerto* and *symphony*. At various times during the Renaissance and baroque eras, *concerto* was applicable to a number of musical concepts: to any type of music combining voices and instruments; to a group of instruments; to a musical event (that is, a concert); and to a form that was a staple of the repertoire of the organization. Similarly, in the eighteenth and nineteenth centuries, *symphony*, which earlier had been often used as a synonym of *concerto,* stood for a musical form, for the group of instruments performing it, or for a concert by the group. Plainly, an understanding of the histories of the two terms is essential to the comprehension of the orchestra's repertoire, since the concerto and the symphony are to this day the two primary musical genres that make up the fare of the orchestra, with the suite, overture, descriptive pieces (tone poems, symphonic poems), and concert arias and cantatas trailing behind these.

Concerto.   Throughout this and the following sections, italics have been used to try to distinguish between old *sonate, concerti,* and so on and modern and/or generic uses of terms (Roman). In some cases, Italian forms have replaced English for clarity or consistency. The earliest meaning of *concerto* in common Italian usage was "a solo ensemble." In the 1546 letter of the duke of Piacenza's agent cited earlier, *concerto* held no distinction between instruments and voices. "A mixture of voices and instruments" continued to be the most common meaning into the first half of the seventeenth century. Thus, many seventeenth-century published works entitled *concerti* contained a mixture of vocal and instrumental types and forms, but none were what in the eighteenth to twentieth centuries would have been called a *concerto.* Early-seventeenth-century examples are the *concerti ecclesiastici* by various composers, including Ludovico Viadana, Claudio Monteverdi, and Adriano Banchieri. The meaning of "a combination of voices and instruments" lingered on into the eighteenth century in J. S. Bach's use of *concerto* as a generic term for his church cantatas.

All three terms—*concerto, sinfonia,* and *sonata*—associated with instrumental music are vague and often are used as synonyms. (Sartori gives numerous titles and prefaces that interchange all three terms.) But *sonata* denoted consistently an instrumental composition with one instrument on a part, excepting the basso continuo. The definition held for any mixture of instruments, including the violin, as in the sonatas of Giovanni Gabrieli. But if a sonata was written for two violins and basso continuo, these being the instruments for which the taste of the era allowed multiplication, it could have been played by either solo ensemble or string orchestra. In Bologna the addition of brass instruments, particularly trumpets in the last half of the seventeenth century, identified a *sonata* as an orchestral composition. This conclusion is reached by Enrico, who analyzes the number of copies of the instrumental parts of Giuseppe Torelli's *Sonata D.X.16* for strings and brass instruments, and by Newman, on the basis of the parts for Cazzati's Opus 35 and later works of the same genre. The word *sinfonia* most often indicated a composition for orchestra with the connotation of an introduction or sequel to a vocal composition. At other times it referred to an introductory movement of a dance suite or to a whole dance suite itself.

In the last decades of the seventeenth century and the first half of the eighteenth, distinctions began to be made. *Concerto* took on the specific meaning of an exclusively instrumental group as a whole (that is, an orchestra), identified in scores as the *ripieno* or *tutti*. The exclusion of voices seems to have been the intention of Marco Uccellini's *Sinfonici concerti,* published in Venice in 1667. Torelli's *Concerto da camera a due violini e basso,* Opus 2, (1686) is the first title in which voices were not expected to be part of the designated performing group. Thereafter *concerto* became the standard designation for an orchestra until it was displaced by *orchestra* sometime in the middle of the eighteenth century. Johann Joachim Quantz uses *orchester* as standard terminology in his *Versuch einer Anweisung die Flöte traversière zu spielen (On Playing the Flute,* 1752), and in Italy, while *orchestra* is not to be found in the *Vocabulario della Crusca* of Venice, 1741, the records of payments for the Cocomero theater in Florence in 1754, for example, begin to list the expenses of the instrumentalists under this new term, which had apparently worked its way from France to Italy. By the last quarter of the century, *orchestra* had become the standard designation in librettos. In the meantime, *concerto* changed its primary meaning from an instrumental group to a type of composition played by the orchestra.

Another form of the word, *concertato,* denoted the addition of parts for solo instruments, first, to voices and, finally, to instrumental groups, or the *concerto* proper. The evolutionary sequence of the meanings is reflected in the orthography: (1) *concerto* meant solo ensemble in the sixteenth century. (2) As the violin consort was converted into the string orchestra, *concerto* came, by the mid-seventeenth century, to mean a large group of instruments, especially a string orchestra. (3) In the late seventeenth century the group of soloists detached itself from the *concerto* and was designated the *concertino.* If the second and third stages were reversed, the denomination for the orchestra would have had to be *concertone.*

The line was not distinct between *concertato* and *accompagnato.* A description of masques presented in Florence in 1567 listed music "in six voices concerted [*concertata*] with two viols, two trombones, two traverse flutes, and two lutes, which made a concerto and a most sweet harmony." In the first of these masques, the description said also that the voices were "accompanied [*accompagnate*] and concerted [*concertate*] by two trombones, two cromornes, [and] two cornetts." *Accompagnate* here may refer to the lutes and trombones playing harmonies on a *basso seguente,* and *concertate* to the other instruments playing independent parts in polychoral relation to the voices. Numerous titles accorded with this meaning of *concertato,* such as Martino Pesenti's *Il quarto libro de madrigali . . . alcuni concertati con violini* (1638). While most instances of the use of *concertato* involved vocal music, where the term could have been used to indicate a polyphony of voices and instruments indiscriminately, as in Giovanni Ghizzolo's *Mass, psalms . . . concerted for five or nine voices* (1619) and Valerio Bona's *Eight orders of litanies . . . concerted for two choirs* (1619), the term always applied to instruments in titles that listed the instruments. The reverse did not occur (that is, sonatas for instruments "concerted with two sopranos"). This usage may indeed be the origin of the final association of *concerto* with instruments, to the exclusion of voices.

In any case, the practice of identifying solo instruments as an ensemble within the larger group occurred as the result of two approaches to the transformation of ensemble music into orchestral music. The first and simplest was to identify optional *ripieno* sections, or ritornels, at important cadences. As early as 1602, Gabriele Fattorini in the second edition of his *Sacri concerti a due voci* (first published in 1600) added *ripieni* in four parts. Georg Muffat's famous description of the practice he heard in

Rome in the 1680s whereby Corelli converted his trio sonatas into concertos was the continuation of the first approach (Strunk, 89–92).

The second approach was to add solos to the concerto. In the 1619 *Compositioni armoniche nella quali si contengono motetti, sinfonie, sonate, canzoni & caprici,* by Francesco Usper, there was a *synfonia* with episodes for two solo violins *in concertino,* the first instance of a distinct group of solo instruments so designated. There were several instances in which Alessandro Stradella employed a *concertino:* in some of the *sinfonie* of a serenata of 1675 and in another *sinfonia* in a manuscript entitled *Sinfonia for violins and basses for concertino and grand concerto,* a composition that was called a *sonata* in a second manuscript in Turin. The title of Giovanni Lorenzo Gregori's publication clarified the meaning: *Grand concerti [concerti grossi] for several instruments: two violins concerted with the full orchestra [ripieni]; alto viola, archlute, or violoncello, with a bass for organ* (1698). This title was also the first in which the term *concerti grossi* appeared in a publication.

Torelli's *Concerti musicali,* Opus 6 (1698), was a landmark on several counts. It indicated the music for the *concerto* and the *concertino* by using T. (for *tutti*) and S. (for *soli*). The *ritornelli* were expanded, and the so-called ritornello form was established in which the *tutti* and *soli* regularly alternated. Further, the collection contained the first fully developed solo violin concertos in which the solo instrument had its own distinct material. Corelli's Opus 6 *concerti,* some of which must date from the 1680s, used a *concertino* of two violins and basso continuo. The *concertino* violins were, however, expected to play with the *concerto;* hence, they had the character of a *sonata* in which the cadential sections were reinforced by the addition of the *ripieno* strings. Vivaldi's violin concertos, the best known of which is *L'estro armonico,* Opus 3, and *Il cimento dell'Armonia e dell'Invenzione,* Opus 8 (1725), brought the solo *concerto* and the *concerto grosso* to a classic definition. Others who made major contributions to the form include the great composers of the baroque: Alessandro Scarlatti, Tommaso Albinoni, Georg Philipp Telemann, J. S. Bach, and George Frederick Handel.

By whatever etymological process, *concerto* became the standard designation for two types of musical compositions in the 1680s and 1690s. One was the orchestral dance suite termed *concerto da camera,* or chamber concerto. The other was a more generalized three-, four-, or five-movement form labeled *concerto da chiesa,* or church concerto. The first declined and almost disappeared early in the eighteenth century. The second dropped the label and survived as the standard term for a composition for solo or solo ensemble and orchestra.

Harmonic Form and Dance.   The harmonic form of the *concerto da chiesa,* from the point of view of the harmonic relationships among the movements and the internal organization of a single movement, was a fusion of the polysectional *canzona* of the late sixteenth and early seventeenth centuries with the dance, without regard for the instrumentation (if specified). That is to say, the steps that led to the late-eighteenth-century form of the *concerto* can be found in a variety of instrumental types—from keyboard *canzone* to *sonate, sinfonie,* and *concerti* for ensembles.

The dance and the *canzona* can be conceived of as opposites in a polarity between regularity (dance) and irregularity *(canzona).* The abstracted qualities of dance music are, first, metrical regularity (including not only regularity of the accentuation of each measure but in the combining of measures into two-, three-, or four-measure patterns of phrases and into sections containing four, six, eight, twelve, sixteen, or more measures). Second, dance music typically organizes and identifies these metrical patterns by cadences and half-cadences. Most Renaissance dances are in three sections. However, occasionally dances in two sections occurred that were constructed in a clear, simple binary form. An example is the "Princess's Dance" for lute (from Parrish and Ohl). Its form may be diagramed as follows:

Phrase I: A Minor to C Major (4 mm.)
Phrase II: C Major to C Major (4 mm.) {phrases I and II repeated}
Phrase III: C Major to A Minor (4 mm.)
Phrase IV: repetition of III (4 mm.) {phrases III and IV repeated}

This binary harmonic structure was singled out from Renaissance dance forms as the almost universal harmonic pattern for instrumental music (substituting, of course, in major keys the dominant in the place of the mediant) by baroque composers, who imposed it upon types of compositions not originally dance music. The harmony and meter were combined with a basic homophony, and the resulting emphasis upon periodic melody that emerged by the end of the baroque stood in strong contrast to the vocal polyphony of the Renaissance and early baroque.

Dance music provided, in addition to the internal structure, the first models of instrumental music organized as a series of separate movements, each harmonically organized and self-sufficient. The history of the Italian band of violins imported into France by Catherine de Médicis implies that already the Italian violin bands were renowned and that their principal function was the performance of dance music. As one might expect, then, early in the seventeenth century, publications of dance music for violins (as the first choice among possible instruments) began to appear in quantity. Designated *concerti*, *sonate*, and *sinfonie*, not to mention other more imaginative titles, these dances were subject to the same ambiguity between solo-ensemble and orchestral music discussed above. But to cite a few, Salomone Rossi's four books of works *per sonar due viole da braccio* {or *violini*} . . . *& un chittarrone* (1607, 1608, 1623, 1642) established the three-voiced baroque texture in the imitative *sonate* but did not clearly order the specified dances into suites. Two suites were composed in the sequence, *sinfonia*, *gagliarda*, and *corrente*, a double of the gagliard, in Giovanni Battista Buonamente's *Il quinto libro de varie sonate, sinfonie, gagliarde, corrente & ariette* (1629). The qualification *da*, *di*, or *per camera* initially had only the functional meaning of being suitable for private, secular entertainment, but since dance music was most obviously and exclusively secular, *da camera* gradually came to mean a suite of dances, perhaps mixed with *sinfonie* or characteristic pieces.

An early use of *da camera* in a title was Giovanni Valentini's *Musiche di camera . . . parte concertate con voci sole, & parte con voci, & instrumenti* (1621), which contained a mixture of madrigals and dances. Giacomo Arrigoni's *Concerti di camera* (1635) joined the chamber with the *concerto*, probably meaning here a "string orchestra," at least as the first choice for the performing group. The last among Biagio Marini's twenty-five works, *Diversi generi di sonate, da chiesa e da camera, a due, tre, et a quattro* (1655), by numbering the individual dances, implied that suites or *balletti* were to be assembled by the performers, but the dances were still grouped in four of a kind: *balletti*, *zarabande*, or *correnti*. Maurizio Cazzati began his *Trattenimenti per camera* (1660) with a three-movement suite consisting of a three-part aria, a *ballo dell'aria*, and *sua corente* {sic}. The collection continued with seven two-movement suites made up of a *ballo* and a *corrente*. The suite matured in Giovanni Bonaventura Viviani's *Sonate a violino solo* from the *Capricci armonici da chiesa e da camera* (1678), which included a suite composed of an *introduttione*, *allemanda*, *corrente*, *gagliarda*, *sarrabanda*, and *giga*, and in Giovanni Battista Bassani's *Balletti, correnti, gighe, e sarabande a violino e violone, overo spinetta, con il secondo violino a beneplacito* (1677); the second edition, of 1680, was entitled *Suonate da camera*, wherein the dances comprising the suites were in the order of the title. Other composers who contributed to the great variety of suites in Italy were Giovanni Battista Vitali, Domenico Gabrieli, and Nicola Matteis. A high level of development was reached in Arcangelo Corelli's *Sonate da camera*, Opus 2 (1685), and *Sonate a tre*, Opus 4 (1694), which contained twelve suites each, primarily in four movements.

The ambiguity between ensemble and orchestra began to clear with the twelve suites in Giuseppe Torelli's *Concerto da camera* (1686), which were composed of a variety of combinations of six dances, each suite being headed by an *allemanda*. Comments to the reader in later publications of Torelli's compositions in 1692 and especially in 1709 indicated that for Torelli *concerto* meant orchestra, and while *sonata* after the 1680s could still be ambiguous, *concerto* became less so.

The Italian suite of dances remained characteristically free of fixed orders of dances. Fine examples are to be seen in Antonio Veracini's suites in his two collections of *sonate da camera* (1692 and 1696). Corelli's *Concerti grossi con due violini e violoncello di concertino obligati, e due altri violini, viola, e basso di concerto grosso ad arbitrio che si potranno radoppiare*, Opus 6 (1714), perhaps influenced by German examples made known to him by Georg Muffat, who was in Rome in the 1680s, was one example of fixed order. The concertos were divided into two types: *da chiesa* (eight) and *da camera* (four). The latter four were made up of a prelude and four or five dances in the order allemande, gigue, courente, saraband, gavotte, and minuet.

Another type of orchestral suite was the overture. Its origin was in the practice of playing excerpts from a successful *ballet de cour* or opera, especially those by Lully. This type was cultivated by Johann Kusser in his operatic suites and *Composition de musique* (1682); Georg Muffat in *Florilegium* (1695–1696); J. C. F. Fischer in *Le journal du printemps* (1695); Johann Fux in *Concentus musico-instrumentalis* (1701); J. S. Bach in his four *Overtures*; and others in Germany and Austria.

From Canzona to Concerto da chiesa. At the beginning of the seventeenth century, the canzona's characteristics were first, a greater vivacity of affective expression; second, irregularity or a liberal mixture of regularity and irregularity; and, third, an internal sectional structure composed of contrasts in melodic material, rhythmic patterns, meters, tempi, harmonic behavior, and, in some polychoral canzonas, instrumentation.

The expressiveness of the canzona arose in the Renaissance from the link with vocal part-music, the French chanson in historical fact and the Italian madrigal in essence. In the sixteenth-century expressive style known as *musica reservata*, the musical setting of each line of the text in a madrigal or a motet usually began with a succinct series of notes and rhythmic values that expressed the character and sometimes the literal meaning of the text. This series of notes, the ancestor of the baroque *motto* and the eighteenth- and nineteenth-century motive, was then heard in succession in each of the voices of the composition. The resulting repetitions varied by the changing location in different voices (called a point of imitation) provided the origin of the motivic development of later centuries. The fact that the motive in sixteenth-century music expressed the text through its contours, rhythms, and implied harmonies accounts for the close link in the baroque mind between musical composition and rhetoric, even to the point of applying the terminology of rhetoric to the art of musical composition. The association between motive or motto and text was followed naturally by a more general relationship between rhetoric and the use of the motive in all types of music, including instrumental, with the motive assuming the role of a word or a phrase. By such means, baroque composers gave a general or even programmatic expressive character to instrumental music.

The classification and definition of the proper expression of particular affects preoccupied many theorists in the baroque era. (Rosenthal, 308–311, provides an annotated list of baroque writers on the subject.) Their achievement was sufficiently cogent and consistent that modern musicology has invented two terms for two aspects of the same idea: the doctrines of affects and of figures, the former governing the relationship between affect and motive and the latter governing the rhetorical organization of the motives or figures. The thought in Athanasius Kircher's *Musurgia universalis* (1650), Johann Mattheson's *Das neu-eröffnete Orchestre* (1713) and *Der vollkommene Capellmeister* (1739), Johann Heinichen's *Der General-Bass in der Composition* (1728), and other works established attitudes that have pervaded Western music to the present time. The nineteenth-century concepts of the idée fixe, the leitmotiv, and the germ motive all ultimately derived from the baroque treatment of the motive as an expressive musical symbol.

Expressive intent is not an adequate replacement for the text in instrumental music. A new metrical and harmonic order compatible with the flexibility of the *canzona* was necessary. While metrical rhythm invaded the *canzona*, as it did all other genres of music, the larger groupings of measures retained a freedom not characteristic of the dance. Variability in all elements was the hallmark of the *canzona*. The *concerto da chiesa* (or, by the eighteenth century, simply the *concerto*), then, was the product of the evolution of the polysectional *canzona*, which, as it grew and changed into the *concerto*, absorbed characteristics of the dance without ever yielding up its own properties. The flexibility, variability, and irregularity of the *canzona* were the resources for the *concerto's* expressiveness, without which the concerto could not have competed with opera, cantata, and oratorio for the attention of the audience. And yet without the constraint created by the harmonic-metrical structure of dance the freedom of the *canzona* could not have become more than ele-

gance. While the elaboration of an harmonic arch in the internal structure of each section of the *canzona* was an intrusion of dance form, the
separation into movements of what had been sections of the *canzona* was
a direct mimicry of the dance suite, which from the beginning was composed of separate formal units. Nevertheless, the *sonata* and the *concerto
da chiesa* received an important heritage from the *canzona*, consisting of:
(1) a vague aesthetic and intellectual elevation and a greater intensity of
expression than identified dance forms; (2) a greater irregularity or variability of harmonic motion; (3) a greater dependence upon the motive
and its manipulation (coordinated with harmonic structure) for achieving an expressive end; (4) the reinforcement of cadences by the repetition or the transposition of phrases, periods, or sections; (5) the convention whereby the andante movement will change key (dance movement
will return to the tonic key); and (6) flexibility and variety of instrumentation originating in the contrast of ensemble (*concertino*) and orchestra
(*concerto*).

A reasonable parallel may be drawn now between the orchestra's repertoire and several of its evolving elements. The development of the
monochrome string orchestra as the core of the orchestra in the baroque
era was comparable to the development of a harmonically independent
structure that governed a predominantly monothematic procedure. The
evolution of both the orchestra and the repertoire was one of expansion.
In the case of the orchestral instruments, the resources of instrumental
color increased reinforcements or contrasts to the string orchestra. In the
case of the motivic-harmonic structure, the degree and types of contrast
grew to the point that baroque unity was replaced by classical-romantic
dramatic contrast, which was achieved most remarkably in sonata form,
rondo, and their various combinations in the latter half of the eighteenth
century. The distinctive feature of the realization of these forms in
orchestral music was not merely the presence of the total variety of the
instruments in the orchestra but also the manner of the use of the instruments and their coordination with the motivic-harmonic procedures
described above.

Orchestration. To summarize, three varieties of orchestration have
been described. The first was based upon equality of parts and has been
designated *consort* instrumentation. It was subservient to the voice part
and indeed, all instrumentation within this style could be conceived of
as the replacing of human voices with instruments of appropriate register. The practice called for the mixture of instruments at pleasure but
always in a system of equal and continuous voice parts. Each part is an
integer. Thus, if only one part survived from a motet for five voices, the

duration, the subject matter, the characteristic expression, and the sectional contrasts could all be perceived in the one part.

The second variety entailed the multiplication of violins and their
relatives and the addition of wind instruments to the basic three- or
four-part string orchestra colla parte. The additional instruments were
employed as a matter of performance practice under the control of the
maestro di cappella, whose decision was determined primarily by the size
of the hall. The practice arose as music expanded into the opera house
and concert hall to satisfy the demands of a large audience. This colla
parte accumulation of instruments has been traced through the baroque
era, and the history of the subject can be concluded with a quotation
from Quantz's *Versuch* (1752) in which he made suggestions about the
proper numbers of instruments for orchestras:

> With four violins, use one viola, one violoncello, and one double bass of
> medium size. With six violins, the same complement and one bassoon. Eight
> violins require two violas, violoncellos, an additional double bass...two
> oboes, two flutes, and two bassoons. With ten violins, the same complement,
> but with an additional violoncello. With twelve violins, use three violas, four
> violoncellos, two double basses, three bassoons, four oboes, four flutes, and
> in a pit another keyboard and one theorbo. Hunting horns may be necessary
> in both small and large ensembles, depending upon the nature of the piece
> and the inclination of the composer.   (p. 214)

Since the addition of the winds was conceived as a matter of size only,
Quantz was assuming that, excepting the horns, which are separately
listed and explicitly delegated to the composer, the winds double the
string parts. After all, there is no problem of balance, even in the smallest
group, if the winds play independent parts as equal members of an
ensemble. It is only when they play the same parts with the strings that
the blend and balance are affected. The procedure differed from the first
variety of orchestration only in the general objective of reinforcing the
highest two parts and, secondarily, the bass. Otherwise, the integral, continuous character of the instrumental parts was interrupted only by a
polychoral texture or by the presence of solo ensemble parts within a
composition for orchestra.

In the third variety, which historically evolved concurrently with the
second, the musical continuity of a given voice part was broken up by
the discontinuity of the instrumental setting created initially by the use
of a polychoral texture or of a solo ensemble within the orchestra. Thus,
a single surviving soprano or first-violin part in a polychoral composi-

tion or the surviving viola di ripieno part of a concerto will not necessarily provide clues about all of the subjects and harmonies of the entire
piece. The various varieties of concertos from the last two decades of the
seventeenth century contribute the major examples of this manner.

The fourth variety expanded the simple colla parte doubling in such
a way that not only the continuity in one instrumental part but also the
register of the voice part was altered. In the Renaissance an instrument
played a given part in its standard register. The limited ranges of the
wind instruments did not permit transpositions. There were transposing
instruments, the sopranino recorder, the pochette, and the contrabass
instruments being the principal ones, and their late appearance in the
sixteenth century was probably a harbinger of baroque sonority, since
their use emphasized the outer parts at the expense of the inner. But
throughout the baroque era, flutes, oboes, and trumpets continued to
double the violins in the register of the written violin parts (hence the
standard published scores of *sinfonie* in three or four parts for strings,
which, according to historical records of performances, were played by
orchestras that included wind instruments). Only in the middle of the
eighteenth century did doubling become a complex, sophisticated skill
employed by the composer and not the performers. And one of the
effects of the fourth manner was precisely to free the instruments, and
particularly the wind instruments, from the necessity of uttering musical
ideas (voice parts, melodies, phrases, or motives) so that they could be
employed by the composer to give color to chords, accented tones, or
other fragments, using whatever register of the instrument was effective
without otherwise regarding the musical logic or continuity presented by
the individual instrumental part itself. Thus one can observe over the
centuries, from the Renaissance to the present, a gradual diminution in
the portions of a musical part that may be properly or conventionally
assigned to a particular instrument: (1) at first, an instrument played an
entire part. (2) Then, it played a particular melody within a part containing several distinct melodies played by other instruments (perhaps one
part of a polychoral composition or the second theme of a sonata form).
(3) Next, one instrument was used for one phrase of a melody, other parts
of which were given to other instruments—typical of orchestration by
the classical composers. (4) The reduction continued to the level of a
motive within a phrase—typical of Beethoven; to a single note—typical
of composers since Berlioz; and finally to a changing instrumental color-
ation for a single chord or note—especially typical of modern
techniques.

The proper term for the assignment of instruments to the musical parts in these four ways is *orchestration*. *Instrumentation* is more general and is more appropriately applied to the selection of instruments to perform, for example, a Renaissance motet. Instrumentation may be practiced by the performer or specified by the composer, but orchestration is an act of composition or arranging in which the orchestra is treated as if it were a single instrument of vast possibilities. Since this fourth manner of orchestrating takes place in the *sinfonia* most conspicuously, the development of the *sinfonia* (apart from its meaning of *suite*) must be taken up.

THE SYMPHONY

During the seventeenth century, it has been observed, *sinfonia, sonata,* and *concerto* were more or less interchangeable terms. But with the clarification of the meanings of *sonata* and *concerto* in the last decade of the century, the *sinfonia* also became a more specific term, and the beginnings of a "symphonic" style emerged as orchestration evolved as an art and a discipline and as the form developed distinctive procedures. Of orchestration and form, the former seems to have appeared first and to have been closely tied with the evolution of the specific form. At least, the concept of orchestration is more readily perceived in *sinfonie* than in *concerti*. Alessandro Scarlatti's overture for *La Griselda* (1721) was innovative in the treatment of the wind instruments. Unlike the *sonate* and *concerti* already examined, the wind instruments (two trumpets and two oboes) function in three different relationships with the strings: (1) as harmonic support by playing each chord in the register at which the violins play the active, leading parts (mm. 1–7); (2) as solos in turn supported by strings in the same register (mm. 8–9, 12–13); and (3) as undoubled parts equal to the strings (mm. 11–12, oboes), all in discontinuous musical parts. In the second section, an *adagio*, the trumpets fall silent while the oboes perform as standard obbligato parts. But the third section, which is the most independent of the sections, returns to the orchestration of the first section. The detachment of the metrical accents supplied by the winds is an initial step toward a free application of instrumental color.

What is noteworthy in Scarlatti's overture is that there is no doubling of the instruments, which indicates that in Scarlatti's thinking the use of colla parte instruments was still a notion having to do with the size of the orchestra, as Quantz later proposed. The final distillation of these four techniques, a process taking place primarily in Austria and Germany in the years 1730–1750, is found in the symphony for orchestra, Opus 5, no. 2, scored for two flutes, two oboes, two bassoons, two horns, and strings, by Johann Stamitz. Of the four techniques, doubling was raised by Stamitz to the level of proper orchestration. A copious catalogue of ways to enhance orchestral color by doubling could be composed on the basis of this work alone: winds with winds; winds with strings; at the octave above, in unison, or at the octave below; two octaves apart; in ratios of durations ranging from whole notes to eighths (mm. 75–76, where winds in whole notes double the downbeats of the more active arpeggios of the violins), to one-to-one values (frequent examples throughout).

Another example of the symphonic approach to doubling can be seen in Niccolò Jommelli's overture to *L'Olimpiade* (1761). (References are to the facsimile edition by Howard Mayer Brown, New York, 1978.) On the first measure of page 37, an F-Major harmony is formed by two each of violins, oboes, and flutes. The tones of the chord read from bottom to top in this order: c′ (middle C) in second flute; c″ (an octave above) in first flute; f″ in second oboe; a″ in first oboe, all sustaining a whole note; a trill on a′–g′ is played by the second violins, and f″–e″ by the firsts. The flutes play the fifth of the chord in octaves without any doubling. The oboes double the tones of the violins but an octave above. On page 71, new ways of combining horns and oboes are seen. The oboes are silent in the first two bars, then in their register double the horns in the third measure, and finally play contrapuntal motives to the horns in the last measure of a four-measure phrase. Jommelli is thinking in orchestral sonorities in a distinctive way, by comparison with Scarlatti or any of the earlier composers cited here.

Returning to the Stamitz symphony, the form, too, had undergone transformation. Stamitz' symphony, when compared with a Vivaldi concerto, is seen to have altered the internal structure of the movements, particularly the first. While this symphony preserved the principles of the baroque concerto (the coordination of motive or subject and harmony), the events that make up the forms had changed. The harmonic form now adumbrates two tonal areas before the harmonic arch is explored. These areas are the tonic and the dominant (or mediant), which are now identified further by contrasts in melodic material. As in a Vivaldi concerto, the material is coordinated with, and controlled by, the harmonic rhythm and type of motion—that is, periodic harmonic patterns, which define harmonic areas and evoke tunes; cadencing, which establishes points of arrival that justify repetition at pitch and in transposition; sequencing, which produces motion and calls forth brief motives in rapid repetitions, often in the nature of conversational exchanges among the instruments; and pedal points, which restrain harmonic motion and provoke repetitions of motives usually having the character of scales and arpeggios.

A concept of great importance can also be observed in its infancy in this symphony: the use of instrumental color to reinforce the expressive character of a musical idea or theme. Here the more stentorian opening reiterations of the tonic note and the tonic triad by all instruments (except the flutes) are contrasted with the more lyric woodwind motive stated piano over the dominant pedal in measures 20–24 while the strings and horns strengthen the metrical accents.

The expressive differences among the sonorities of instruments have been observed and used since instruments were invented. Moreover, these expressive characters have won for the instruments associations with social ceremonies (weddings, parades, dances), events (battles, contests, coronations), or activities (sheep grazing, sailing). It is enough to remark at this point upon the use of instruments to represent dramatic, theatrical subjects during the Renaissance and baroque eras.

The choice of instruments to accompany scenes in the sixteenth-century *intermedio* was determined by the subject. Some of the associations between subjects and instruments have remained consistent from that time to the present: strings are associated with love and the gods representing love; reeds, with shepherds, nymphs, satyrs, Pan, rustics, sailors, and common folk in general; horns, with hunting and royal sports and ceremonies; trombones, with spiritual matters, good or evil, and mystical manifestations; trumpets, drums, and pipes, with warfare. Instances of such use of instruments in baroque opera were frequent enough to maintain the continuity of the practice. The infernal and pastoral scenes in Lully's operas, in Cesti's *Pomo d'oro*, in Monteverdi's *Orfeo*, and in Handel's operas, oratorios, and especially in *Acis and Galatea*, all pointed the way to similar uses in Gluck's *Alceste* (the trombones accompanying the voice of the oracle) and *Orfeo*, and in Mozart's *Don Giovanni* (the appearance of the statue in the finale). These traditional programmatic identifications for instruments are comparable in the baroque era to the classification of harmony, melody, and rhythm according to affect. Whether consciously or with that unquestioning acceptance of any "language," the instruments were used as one means of creating contrasts in expressive character between one subject and another, even in nonprogrammatic orchestral works and as a basic technique in programmatic ones.

The external form of the symphony assumed conventional order in the 1730s and 1740s, with either three movements, like the Italian sinfonia, or four. In either case, the first was an allegro with more or less theatrical character and fanfarelike subject matter. The middle movements were a slow, lyric movement and/or a dance in trio form, usually a minuet, and the last movement a lively binary or sometimes a gigue. Composers of symphonies included: in Italy, Giovanni Battista Sammartini (twenty-four symphonies, the earliest in 1734); in Mannheim, Johann Stamitz (seventy-four symphonies) and Ignaz Holzbauer (sixty-nine symphonies); in Vienna, Georg Christoph Wagenseil (thirty symphonies) and Georg Monn; in Paris, where a veritable fever of symphonies broke out, Louis-Gabriel Guillemain (*Six simphonies dans le goût italien,* in 1740) and François-Joseph Gossec (five sets of six symphonies, published between 1744 and 1762); and in London, William Boyce (eight symphonies and twelve overtures) and J. C. Bach. The taste for symphonies spread with amazing rapidity over all of Europe.

THE PATRONS AND THE PUBLIC

During the baroque era the patronage and the audience for music were profoundly altered by the sociopolitical transformations that were laying the foundations for the industrial and political revolutions of the late eighteenth century. The growth of the middle classes and of the cities, two interrelated phenomena, began a new, vigorous phase. The arbiters of taste and principal employers were still the aristocracy. But their own ranks were being diluted by the elevation of the bourgeoisie to the aristocracy, a remuneration and reward that monarchs freely, even gleefully, bestowed on successful entrepreneurs. The pressure of the middle class, whether promoted or not, forced changes of behavior even in the life of the courts, for as the middle class intruded in numbers, the characteristic chamber or private music-making gave way to public concerts in large halls or theaters. Concurrently, cities grew in population: for example, Paris grew from just over one hundred thousand to more than half a million between the fifteenth and eighteenth centuries. These forces changed the madrigal into chamber opera, chamber opera into opera seria and comic opera (eventually converting comic to romantic opera), and the consort into the orchestra. The conversion of the private performances of opera in private theaters into performances before a paying audience, even if the control of the theater remained in the hands of noblemen, made it a financial necessity to respond to the tastes and demands of an ever-widening public. The change accounts for the many protestations by opera librettists that they were obliged to satisfy the low taste of the audience. The effect of these sociopolitical changes upon opera, as the first of the major forms to become popular, is apparent and has been often noted.

Orchestral music also underwent changes that can be ascribed to the broadening of the audience for which it was written. These changes included: (1) the acoustical adjustment of instrumental music to the concert hall by the choice of the violin family as the instruments to be multiplied to create the orchestra, and the subsequent addition of the newly redesigned and constructed winds and timpani; (2) the related acoustical emphasis upon the outer parts of the harmony (the equality of instrumental parts possible in private chambers being no longer effective in large halls); (3) tendencies toward simplification of form and style, especially after around 1740; (4) the rising popularity of both the virtuoso performer and the public celebrity; (5) the advent of the public subscription concert and concert series; and (6) the creation of a society in which it became possible for the composer and performer to exist comfortably by obtaining income from a variety of activities and associations, such as publication, including subscriptions for publications (in which the publisher listed the names of the contributors), teaching, concert-giving for paid and for benefit performances, touring, and individual commissions from a variety of patrons. While the position of musician in the service of a particular nobleman by no means vanished in the baroque era— musicians still defined their own rank by that of their patron it became feasible in the large cities for composers, singers, and instrumentalists to exist independently of the special patronage of a court.

Opera more radically than any other genre altered the economic base upon which the community of instrumental musicians depended, most obviously by providing a new and relatively steady employment outside the service of a court. The popularity of opera, combined with its expense, forced the court to seek other means for the financing of opera than direct outlays of its own funds. The means throughout Europe, but especially in Italy, was the formation of academies with the specific charge of promoting public music. Some of the most famous academies were the Accademia Filarmonica in Verona; the academy of the same name in Bologna; the Sorgenti, the Infuocati, and the Immobili in Florence; and the Académie Royale de Musique, organized by Lully, in Paris. The dominance of the academies was represented in the use of *accademia* or *académie* to mean a concert of music well into the latter part of the eighteenth century. (Brenet provides examples from provincial journals of the seventeenth century. Rousseau in his *Dictionnaire*, under "Académie de Musique," says that the term was used formerly in France and still in

Italy to mean a concert.) The principal effect of the system was to broaden the financial support of music to include, in an organized fashion, the more affluent portions of society (by their membership dues and direct contributions) and the general public (by their purchase of tickets and box rentals), thus setting the pattern for communal support that is still in effect.

The vitality of academic music reinforced the tendency of wealthy nobles and bourgeois to emulate the members of a reigning family. It became fashionable to hire or patronize a small group of musicians. In Rome in the late seventeenth century, the Chigi, Pamphili, Ottoboni, and Colonna families each maintained a small group of composers and players who performed in *conversazioni* in the family palace before a surprisingly broad audience. To these must be added the brilliant salons of Queen Christina of Sweden, whose informal gatherings became after her death the Accademia degli Arcadi, and later the salons of Maria Casimiri of Poland. In Rome the patronage of music by the papal aristocracy reached a genuinely inclusive public through performances of oratorios in churches, especially Santa Maria in Vallicella, San Marcello, San Luigi dei Francesi, and Santa Maria Maggiore. The combination of the small private *cappelle*, the *cappelle* of the churches and especially of the Sistine Chapel, and finally the public theaters, Tor di Nona and Capranica, diffused the economic support of musicians in the city, with the result that the orchestras employed for performances of orchestral music (with or without voices) became remarkably stable. Orchestras hired by the Borghese and Pamphili families and by San Luigi dei Francesi maintained a consistent membership with a continuing leadership. During the period from 1669 to the 1680s the leadership revolved among Alessandro Melani, Bernardo Pasquini, Arcangelo Corelli, and Alessandro Scarlatti. A substantial list of regular members of orchestras can be drawn up from the payment records of the cited patrons and churches. The Roman orchestra existed in all but name, and it was made economically feasible by the free mixture of individual patronage and employment by *cappelle* and theaters, a situation not altogether foreign to modern instrumentalists.

The balance of these resources varied, of course, from city to city and country to country. In Venice, the theaters, some operated by academies, some by private owners, overshadowed the academies, the churches, and especially the salons of private patrons. Here, other elements not present in Rome were to be found: foundling hospitals and orphanages that specialized in providing their students with musical training, including orchestral performances in public concerts. For example, Vivaldi was engaged as a teacher, performer, and *maestro de' concerti* at the Seminario Musicale dell'Ospedale della Pietà between 1703 and 1740.

In Florence, the Medici and Hapsburg-Lorraine governments held a tight reign upon all public entertainments. Under the latter, a bureau was set up to oversee all theaters from 1738 on. A government so inclined to bureaucracy naturally found academies a convenience. Almost without exception, the theaters were owned and operated by the academies, which received the patronage and financial support of the rulers, but were expected to pay dues and to contribute such additional funds as were necessary to pay for public performances beyond what income was produced by the sale of tickets and the rental of boxes. Major Florentine musical and dramaturgical academies were the Immobili, the Sorgenti, and the Infuocati. The first was an academy of nobles that flourished in the mid-seventeenth century and again after 1718 in the Pergola theater. The second was located in the Cocomero and subsequently in other theaters during the seventeenth century. The Infuocati were the eigh-teenth-century successors of the Sorgenti and continued as the operators of the Cocomero. Both were rarities among Italian academies: their mem-bers were commoners, and their long, more or less successful operation of the Cocomero theater (today the Niccolini) is testimony to the impor-tance of the *cittadinanza* as a part of the eighteenth-century system of musical patronage. So strong was the academic tradition in Florence that even religious fraternities such as the Compagnia dell'Arcangelo Raffaelo, at least in its seventeenth- and eighteenth-century activities, and the Filippine Congregazione dell'Oratorio in San Firenze were organized to perform oratorios as if they were secular academies with dues-paying lay and clerical members and special benefactors among the wealthier members. But both opera and oratorio provided occupation for instrumentalists.

When concerts, in the modern sense, became fashionable after 1765, a special group of academicians was formed, *accademici armonici*, com-posed of nobility and ordinary citizens, to underwrite the cost and pro-vide an audience. The programs consisted of a mixture of orchestral and vocal music, and the performers were members of the theatrical orches-tras, gifted amateurs, or guest artists. While some of the Florentine musi-cians were given titles as *musici da camera* to the grand duke of Tuscany, it is clear that the positions were indeed an honor but a source of income less important than formerly would have been the case.

In the German states a comparable movement was the *collegium musi-cum*, which differed from the Italian academic system by being primarily organizations for students. The earliest was founded in Zurich in 1613.

Hamburg followed in 1660 when Matthias Weckmann and Christoph Bernhard established a society for the performance of new music, but it was disbanded after Weckmann's death in 1674. Later Telemann, after having directed a collegium in Leipzig, continued his sponsorship of public concerts in Frankfurt and in Hamburg, where the municipal government contributed to the support of the collegium. In Hamburg in 1743 a *grosses concert* by a sixteen-piece orchestra under the direction of J. F. Doles initiated a series of concerts with admission by ticket sales. The best-known collegium was founded by Telemann in Leipzig in 1704; its directors included Johann Kuhnau and J. S. Bach. However, the true successors of these collegia are the singing unions that have remained a characteristic and popular feature of German musical society to this day.

To London belongs the distinction of having been the city of the first recorded concerts with paid admissions (apart from opera). Perhaps the fact owes much to the Commonwealth's transferring both power and responsibility to the middle class and, between 1649 and 1660, removing the court as a patron of the arts. The peculiarly English habit of holding musical performances in taverns was well documented in Samuel Pepys's diary. The *Memoires of Musik* (1728), by Roger North, recorded a public concert arranged by Ben Wallington, a composer and singer, in the Mitre Inn in 1664. The first continuing series of concerts was founded in a significant revolt by an English musician against the importation of French music that attended the restoration of Charles II, who had grown up in Paris, in 1660. John Banister was the leader of the king's band under Charles II until he criticized the violinists whom Charles had imported and was fired. He then set up a studio as a teacher of violin in London and began regular concerts in his own house with admission by ticket sales. He was soon followed by imitators. Thomas Britton, a music-loving coal dealer, held Thursday concerts from 1678 to 1714 in an attic over his shop. Famous performers at his concerts included Handel. J. W. Franck and Robert King organized vocal and instrumental concerts from 1690 until 1693, building a concert hall in Charles Street to house their series. The Belgian flutist Jean Baptiste (John) Loeillet began concerts in his house in 1710, moving soon to the Queen's Theatre (the first by that name, erected in 1705 in the Haymarket).

Other theaters in London mixed instrumental concerts with opera and spoken drama among their attractions offered to the public. Sadler founded his Music House in 1683, a public "pleasure garden" where dance music was especially cultivated on a popular level. In Goodman's Fields Theatre at Whitechapel a curious reversal of relationship between drama and music took place as the result of legal restrictions on the theaters. Forbidden to perform prose dramas, Henry Gifford, the proprietor, presented orchestral concerts, filling the intervals between the compositions with short dramas. The high point of public concerts in London, however, came in the second half of the eighteenth century.

In seventeenth-century Paris, the private salons produced an extraordinarily rich musical life. Many patrons supported their own virtuosos (perhaps only one musician), who presented weekly concerts in their patrons' salons. Uniquely Parisian were the concerts performed by music teachers themselves on their own premises as a means of attracting students and patronage. One account claims that the first Concert Spirituel ever heard in Paris was the performance arranged some time before 1650 by Pierre de Chambonceau, sieur de La Barre, organist of the Royal Chapel, in his own residence. From the performers cited, the programs must have been a mixture of instrumental and vocal music, probably limited to ensembles. Another notable series of concerts was held each month during the late seventeenth and early eighteenth centuries by a mixture of amateur and professional musicians in the house of a certain very wealthy Crozat (later these concerts were given in the Louvre twice a week). The costs of these elaborate concerts of international performers was borne by a society whose members, honoring the country of origin of the idea, were called *academici [sic] paganti*. Judging by the names cited in various accounts, the patrons and the audiences of these concerts were highly varied, and one needed only to be identified as a lover of music to be invited. The Académie de Musique even brought music to the common Parisian by presenting annually on the eve of Saint Louis's feast day, 24 August, a concert in the courtyard of the Tuileries. Remarkably, there appeared in these concerts a tendency, much noted and often lamented in the present era, toward a standard, constantly repeated repertoire dear in the appreciation of the general public: suites drawn from music of Lully's operas remained a staple of these concerts for almost one hundred years.

Until the beginning of the eighteenth century, there seems to have been no attempt outside of the opera house or the court to concentrate all of this musical enthusiasm into suitable channels for the public support of a stable orchestra. Finally, in the Concert Spirituel established by the professional flutist and composer Anne Danican-Philidor in 1725, the foundation of true public concerts of large-scale music was achieved. The patent granted by Louis XIV to Lully and his descendants forbade any performance of music using French on a stage, and at this time vocal music was virtually synonymous with music itself. The regulations gave the Académie effective control over any presentation of music before a large audience, one of the reasons that private patronage and concerts continued to dominate Parisian musical life so long. Philidor was obliged to stay within the restraint on the use of French and to give his concerts only on those days on which the Opéra, operated by the Académie, was closed. This restriction limited him to about thirty-five days, all of them religious holidays—hence, the necessity of performing only religious music. The performances took place in the Salle des Suisse in the Tuileries, wherein a special wooden platform was constructed for the *symphonistes* and the singers. So large was the room that it required a large number of instruments, thus evoking critical disapproval. Around the middle of the eighteenth century, the orchestra of the Concert Spirituel was relatively stable at about forty instrumentalists.

One other patron of concerts must be mentioned in connection with Paris: A. J. J. Le Riche de La Pouplinière, whose concerts eclipsed all others toward the middle of the eighteenth century. Among the accomplishments of these concerts was the performance of orchestral works by Rameau; by Johann Stamitz, who came to Paris at La Pouplinière's invitation in 1754; and by François Joseph Gossec. According to the testimony of the latter, La Pouplinière's orchestra included two horns, two clarinets, and a harp.

In all of these urban associations seeds existed out of which the symphony orchestra would soon grow. On the one hand, the orchestra would become independent of the court orchestra, with its inevitable ceremonial functions and its double duty with other vocal forms. On the other, it would, in the cities at least, declare its independence from the opera house or the oratorio society. But the orchestra also had to detach itself from the embrace of the academy, with its inescapable introduction of amateur performers and its predilection for vocal music. These events belong to subsequent articles. The stage is set.

BIBLIOGRAPHY

Anthony Baines, *European and American Musical Instruments* (1966). Arnoldo Bonaventura, *Saggio storico sul teatro musicale italiano* (1913). Ercole Bottrigari, *Il desiderio, overo De' concerti di varii strumenti musicali* (1599), Kathi Meyer, ed. (1924). David D. Boyden, *The History of Violin Playing from Its Origins to 1761* (1965). Michel Brenet, *Les concerts en France sous l'ancien regime* (1900; repr. 1970). Nathan Broder, "The Beginnings of the Orchestra," in *Journal of the American Musicological Society*, 13 (1960). Manfred F. Bukofzer, *Music in the Baroque Era* (1947). Adam Carse, *The Orchestra in the Eighteenth Century* (1940; repr. 1950); and *The History of Orchestration* (1925; repr. 1964). C. L. Cudworth, " 'Baptist's

Vein': French Orchestral Music and Its Influence from 1640 to 1750," in *Proceedings of the Royal Musical Association*, 83 (1956–1957).

Archibald T. Davison and Willi Apel, *Historical Anthology of Music: Baroque, Rococo, and Pre-classical Music* (1962). Fabrizio Della Seta, "I Borghese (1691–1731)," in *Note d'archivio*, 1 (1983). Giovanni Battista Doni, *De' trattati di musica*, vol. 2, *Musica scenica* (1763). Eugene Enrico, *The Orchestra at San Petronio in the Baroque Era* (1976). Jürgen Eppelsheim, *Das Orchester in den Werken Jean-Baptiste Lullys* (1961). Karl Geiringer, *Haydn: A Creative Life in Music* (1946; repr. 1982). Federico Ghisi, *Feste musicali della Firenze Medicea* (1939). Hugo Goldschmidt, "Das Orchester der italienischen Oper im 17. J.," in *Sammelbände der Internationalen Musikgesellschaft*, 2 (1900). John Walter Hill, "Oratory Music in Florence," in *Acta musicologica*, 51 (1979).

Hans Joachim Marx, "Die 'Giustificazioni della Casa Pamphily' als musikgeschichtliche Quelle," in *Studi musicali*, 12 (1983). Johann Mattheson, *Das neueröffnete Orchestre* (1713) and *Der vollkommene Capellmeister* (1739), Ernest C. Harriss, trans. (1969). Marin Mersenne, *Harmonie universelle* (1636), Roger E. Chapman, trans. (1957). *Musik in Geschichte und Gegenwart*, Friedrich Blume, ed. (1949–). Reginald Nettel, *The Orchestra in England* (rev. ed. 1956). *New Grove Dictionary of Music and Musicians*, Stanley Sadie, ed. (1980). William S. Newman, *The Sonata in the Baroque Era* (1972).

Carl Parrish and John F. Ohl, eds., *History of Music Before 1750* (1951). N. Pelicelli, "Musicisti in Parma nei secoli XV–XVI," in *Note d'archivio*, 9 (1932). Marc Pincherle, *Corelli* (1933). Michael Praetorius, *Syntagma musicum*, vol. 2, *De organographia* (1618), Harold Blumenfeld, trans. (1980). Johann Joachim Quantz, *Versuch einer Anweisung die Flute traversière zu spielen* (1752), translated as *On Playing the Flute*, Edward R. Reilly, trans. (1966). Jean Jacques Rousseau, *Dictionnaire de musique* (1768).

Claudio Sartori, *Bibliographia della musica strumentale italiana stampata in Italia fino al 1700* (1952; repr. 1968). Arnold Schering, *Geschichte des Instrumentalkonzerts bis auf die Gegenwart* (1927; repr. 1965). *Schirmer History of Music*, Léonie Rosenthal, ed. (1982). H. A. Scott, "London's Earliest Public Concerts," in *Musical Quarterly*, 22 (1936). Hermann Spies, *Beiträge zur Musikgeschichte Salzburgs im Spätmittelalter und zu Anfang der Renaissancezeit* (1941). Denis Stevens, ed., *The Letters of Claudio Monteverdi* (1980). Oliver Strunk, ed., *Source Readings in Music History* (1950). Michael Talbot, "Musical Academies in Eighteenth-Century Venice," in *Note d'archivio*, 2 (1984). Flavio Testi, *La musica italiana nel seicento* (1972). Robert Lamar Weaver, "Sixteenth-Century Instrumentation," in *Musical Quarterly*, 47 (1961); and "The Orchestra in Early Italian Opera," in *Journal of the American Musicological Society*, 17 (1964). Percy M. Young, *The Concert Tradition* (1965).

The Modern Orchestra: A Creation of the Late Eighteenth Century

George B. Stauffer

Given the evolution of the orchestra, a process beginning in the broadest sense in ancient times and continuing down to the present day, we might hesitate to single out one short period and declare that this is when the modern orchestra was born. Yet we see that toward the end of the eighteenth century, musical and sociological forces converged to spark the creation of a new ensemble, the classical orchestra, which prospered and gained international stature, spreading from Italy, Austria, and Germany to the other countries of Europe.

The classical orchestra represents the first fully formed ancestor of the modern orchestra. Indeed, it is the first type of ensemble that we can call an orchestra without hesitation or qualification. It deserves the epithet *classical*, for it has endured. Its assemblage of strings and paired winds and brass remains at the heart of the orchestra today. Its repertoire is still studied, performed, and esteemed. For these reasons, the late eighteenth century must be viewed as a turning point in the long development of our present-day symphonic ensemble.

What stood behind the appearance of the classical orchestra in the late eighteenth century? Three factors were critical to its birth and growth. The first is the standardization and refinement of the orchestral ensemble. After some 150 years of mutation filled existence, the heterogeneous baroque ensemble, with its ability to stress individual lines and colors, gave way to a more homogeneous group of eight parts: four strings (violin I and II; viola; and *basso,* consisting of cello and double bass) and four winds (most commonly oboe I and II and horn I and II). This small band was ideal for performing works in the new *galant* style, and it proved to be a sturdy nucleus around which the orchestra could form in subsequent years.

The second factor was sociological: the rise of the concert and of music printing. By the late eighteenth century, church and court music performances, the mainstays of the baroque, were giving way to public concerts. Concerned aristocrats, then a captivated public, and finally well-organized philharmonic societies replaced the church and court as the principal financial sponsors of ensemble music. This system of general patronage was taking shape during Mozart's time and was firmly in place by the end of Beethoven's. Public patronage, together with the construction of municipally funded concert halls and the founding of multinational publishing houses, made possible the remarkable expansion and technical improvement of the orchestra in the nineteenth century.

The third factor was the creation of classical style. To Giovanni Sammartini, Johann Stamitz, the sons of Bach, and other preclassical composers must go the honor of writing the first "symphonies." But it is questionable whether or not the new orchestral style would have gained permanence, were it not for Franz Joseph Haydn and Wolfgang Amadeus Mozart, who demonstrated its expressive possibilities. With their symphonies and concertos, Haydn and Mozart breathed new life into an idiom that by 1760 was already formulaic and platitudinous. As founders of the classical style, Haydn and Mozart transformed the symphonic concert into theater—theater whose drama has held the public's attention down to the present day.

THE STANDARDIZATION AND REFINEMENT OF THE ORCHESTRA

The change from the baroque ensemble to the early classical orchestra was not a sudden breakthrough but a gradual, logical transformation that occurred in the second quarter of the eighteenth century. During this time Italian opera, with its homophonic textures and singable melodies, emerged as the new musical ideal, and its orchestra became the ensemble of the future. The coming era was heralded symbolically in 1713, when Johann Mattheson chose the term *Orchestre,* instead of the more traditional *General-Bass,* to head a series of volumes on musical instruction

(*Das neu-eröffnete Orchestre,* 1713; *Das beschützte Orchestre,* 1717; and *Das forschende Orchestre,* 1721). In a preface to the first volume, Mattheson acknowledged that the term *Orchestre* was not well known. He explained it as a *galant* expression for the area in front of the stage occupied by instrumentalists and their director; by implication, it denoted the instrumental ensemble that performed in that location.

In his series of books, Mattheson criticized old methods of instruction in favor of new and praised the stylistic possibilities of *galant* homophony. He championed Reinhard Keiser, a North German composer of Italianate opera, as a model of the modern German musician. Mattheson proselytized for a new aesthetic, to which the opera orchestra pointed the way. In Milan, Naples, Dresden, Hamburg, and other urban centers, large professional opera orchestras were already presenting repertoire in the homophonic style, and court orchestras and *collegia musica* were performing the final fruits of the baroque. The next fifty years witnessed the migration of the progressive idiom espoused by Mattheson from the opera to the nonoperatic concert.

The new homophonic style required adjustments in the baroque ensemble. One of the first was the gradual elimination of the more esoteric, specialized instruments. The recorder, the *oboe da caccia,* the *viola da gamba,* the *viola d'amore,* and similar instruments were ideal for highlighting the contrapuntal lines of baroque music in *concertante* fashion, but in the classical style their distinctive, independent sounds became a liability. Moreover, the technical shortcomings of many baroque instruments—limitations of range (in the recorder, for example), of volume (in the *viola da gamba* and *viola d'amore*), and tuning (in the *oboe da caccia*)—also contributed to their exclusion from the classical ensemble.

The shift to homophonic texture had a similarly mortal effect on the *basso continuo.* In the baroque, the *continuo* was the animus of the instrumental ensemble, supplying the motor force that gave the music its rhythmic impetus. It was the center of the ensemble, figuratively and literally, a fact borne out by contemporary illustrations, which normally show the *continuo* in the middle of the performing forces with the other instruments gathered around it. With the advent of classical style, the role of the *continuo* declined as the musical focus shifted from the bass line to the soprano.

This may be observed by comparing a baroque score, such as a portion of Bach's *Brandenburg* Concerto no. 1 (Ex. 1), with a classical score, such as the opening of Haydn's Symphony no. 45 in F-sharp Minor, the *Farewell* Symphony (Ex. 2). In the Bach concerto, the bass has an active, obbligato function, serving as a motivic, as well as harmonic, force. In the

Haydn, the bass plays a more subsidiary part. It provides harmonic support, but it is of little melodic or rhythmic consequence. In the classical orchestra, the violins moved to the foreground, having won the leading part (as can be seen in the Haydn score, where the principal theme of the movement is outlined in the first violins). The *continuo* forces moved to the background and were gradually assimilated into the string or wind sections (in the case of the cello, double bass, and bassoon) or disappeared altogether (in the case of the harpsichord and organ).

The harmonic duties of the *continuo* were assumed mostly by the horns and, in the early stages of the classical orchestra, by the oboes as well. The horns proved to be an ideal vehicle for providing chordal support in the new expressive style. They were certainly more appropriate

Example 2. Haydn: Symphony no. 45 in F-sharp Minor (*Farewell*), movement 1, mm. 1–4

than the organ or harpsichord, whose dynamic possibilities extended no further than terraced *piano* and *forte*. The horns, usually presented as a pair, blended well with the strings. They could play sustained harmonies, and they were capable of realizing a full range of dynamic expression, from whispering *pianissimo* to piercing *fortissimo*. The technical demands on classical horn players were generally less than those placed on their baroque counterparts, as a glance at the Bach and Haydn scores shows. At times, though, virtuoso performers must have been available, to judge from the obbligato writing in several Haydn symphonies (nos. 31 and 72, for example) and in Mozart's horn concertos.

The oboes, too, were normally paired. The third oboe of the baroque *ripieno*, usually an alto instrument, was dropped, leaving two soprano instruments (again apparent in the Bach and Haydn scores). In the early classical ensemble, the oboe was frequently employed for chordal support except in the trios of minuets, where it was often given a solo role. As the classical period unfolded and the violas and other instruments began to assume richer harmonic functions, the oboes were liberated to perform greater melodic tasks.

The string section stood at the heart of the classical orchestra. As an instrumental group, the strings had risen steadily to prominence during the baroque, beginning with the French Vingt-quatre Violons du Roi, continuing through the concerto ensembles of Arcangelo Corelli, Giuseppe Torelli, and Antonio Vivaldi, and ending with the *galant* orchestra of Giovanni Pergolesi and Johann Adolph Hasse. Each of these made a significant contribution. The Vingt-quatre Violons demonstrated the technical capabilities of a disciplined group of strings with several players assigned to each part (distributed 6-4-4-4-6, as far as we can tell); the Italian concertos of Corelli, Torelli, and Vivaldi established the string ensemble as the heart of the concerto orchestra; and the orchestra of Pergolesi and Hasse, with its strong emphasis on string sound, illustrated the suitability of string instruments for interpreting the "singing allegro" style.

Classical composers held string instruments in high esteem for an obvious reason: no other instrument could imitate the expressive nuances of the human voice so closely or sound quite as "natural." Whereas the number of winds in the early classical orchestra was often reduced to as few as four, the number of string instruments was increased in order to produce a thicker, lusher sound. In Milan, the opera orchestra included fourteen first and fourteen second violins by 1770; in Naples the number was eighteen and eighteen. Such figures approach modern proportions. So many violins on a part would have been detrimental for baroque counterpoint, but it was ideal for classical homophony. The Milan and Naples figures also show that the violins, like the horns and the oboes, were being used as paired instruments: violin I and violin II were becoming equal partners. In the music they were frequently assigned homophonic duets. In the early classical orchestra, the strings were divided into four parts in the Italian manner: violin I, violin II, viola, and *basso*. Later this texture was enriched by splitting the violas in the French fashion (in mature Mozart, for instance) and by giving the cello and double bass separate parts (as in late Haydn and Mozart).

These diverse trends point to the codification of an eight-part ensemble, with three pairs of melody instruments (violin I and II, oboe I and II, and horn I and II), a bass part (*basso*), and a distinctly subsidiary middle voice (viola). Playing the *basso* with the cello and double bass were other instruments often unmentioned in the scores: the bassoon and, until it became superfluous, the harpsichord.

This "orchestra," though modest in size and composition when compared to the more variegated opera ensemble, was admirably suited to the needs of early classical composers. It was homogeneous, flexible, and, above all, melodious and sensitive. It was the perfect vehicle for realizing the sudden changes in dynamic level and the graduated crescendos and diminuendos that went with the *Empfindsamkeit* and *Sturm und Drang* of the blossoming classical idiom. (*Empfindsamkeit*, or "sensitivity," and *Sturm und Drang*, or "storm and stress," are terms generally used for two eighteenth-century German cultural movements. The first called for intimate, subjective, "sensitive" expression. The second, coined from Friedrich Maximilian von Klinger's Gothic play *Sturm und Drang* of 1776, called for extreme, sometimes irrational emotionalism.)

By 1761, the year Haydn entered the employ of the Esterhazy family, the eight-part ensemble was firmly established as an international standard, much as the trio had been during the baroque. It was used by progressive composers in Italy, Austria, Germany, and England. It was adopted by Haydn in his symphonies of the 1760s and embraced by the young Mozart in his earliest London and Salzburg works. Indicative of the standardization of the eight-part ensemble is the appearance on the international market of entire series of symphonies (frequently termed "overtures") in eight parts. One such publication was Robert Bremner's *The Periodical Overture in Eight Parts*, issued in the 1760s from London. Bremner presented a new symphony each month—works by Jommelli, Stamitz, and others—in the form of eight engraved instrumental parts: violin I, violin II, viola, *basso* (two copies, both figured), oboe I, oboe II, horn I, and horn II. Bremner's project never attained the stature of the later symphony publications of Artaria, Hummel, and others. But it stands as important evidence that the formalization of the classical orchestra, in its earliest guise, was complete.

This small, versatile ensemble was not without limitations. The most critical can be traced to the construction of the horns and oboes. The horns were essentially the natural, valveless instruments of the baroque, whose diminished, muffled artificial tones (achieved by thrusting the fist into the bell) contrasted greatly with the full, bright "naturals." The number of tonalities usable on these instruments was limited, thus explaining why the vast majority of classical symphonies were written in C, F, G, D, and the other few keys practical for the horns.

The oboes, for their part, were relatively simple affairs, with two or three mechanical levers. The chief problem here was not so much limitation of key as of tuning: the instruments were easily affected by changes in temperature and frequently went off pitch. This difficulty was shared by the bassoons. On his visit to Mannheim in 1772, the English music historian Charles Burney commented that the tuning malady plagued even the superbly skilled players of the Elector Karl Theodor's ensemble:

> I found, however, an imperfection in this band, common to all others, that I have ever yet heard, but which I was in hopes would be removed by men so attentive and so able; the defect, I mean, is the want of truth in the wind instruments. I know it is natural to those instruments to be out of tune, but some of that art and diligence which these great performers have manifested in vanquishing difficulties of other kinds, would surely be well employed in correcting this leaven, which so much sours and corrupts all harmony. This was too plainly the case tonight, with the bassoons and hautbois, which were rather too sharp, at the beginning, and continued growing sharper to the end of the opera.

The shortcomings of the horns, oboes, bassoons, and other brass and wind instruments later added to the classical orchestra were not to be remedied until the first half of the nineteenth century. Only then did instrument makers, responding to the challenges posed by Beethoven, Berlioz, and others, come up with sturdier, stabler instruments capable of staying in tune and achieving comfortably a wide range of keys.

The pairing concept observed in the horns and oboes was extended to other melody instruments as they joined the classical ensemble. Flutes were used sporadically at first, probably because they were commonly played by the same musicians who played the oboes. Thus, a composer was often faced with the choice of using flutes or oboes, but not both at the same time. Oboes were generally deemed more necessary, possibly because they provided fuller, richer harmonic support. But as flutes were introduced into the classical orchestra on a permanent basis (from the 1770s), they were paired. As the bassoons gained independence from the bass line a bit later, they, too, were formally paired and occasionally given melodic duets. Clarinets were a new, specialized instrument, rarely available outside Paris or Mannheim until the 1780s. When employed, they were also used in pairs.

Among the brass instruments, the trumpets were reduced from three to two (the third trumpet of the baroque *ripieno* was eliminated, as was the third baroque oboe), so that the standard classical score called for a pair of trumpets when the instrument was available. Finally, the horns remained two in number until Beethoven's *Eroica* Symphony (which required three), despite a healthy group of experiments by Haydn, Mozart, and others calling for four instruments (or even as many as five, in J. B. Vanhal's Symphony in D Minor). Timpani were normally used with trumpets, and sometimes with horns as well.

Certainly the model of the opera orchestra was a critical factor in the desire to add instruments to the basic eight-part ensemble. As we have noted, opera stood at the forefront of the new musical aesthetic, pointing the way for the formation of a well-blended, string-dominated ensemble. But at the same time, opera, with its magnetic combination of grandeur, spectacle, and exoticism, and its rich assemblage of strings, winds, brass, and percussion, served as an impetus for expanding the classical orchestra into a larger, more colorful band.

The size and makeup of the leading opera orchestras in the classical era could not help but impress composers of the day. If we look at a sampling of ensembles from the 1770s and 1780s, we see that the urban opera orchestras stand out as an almost distinct tradition, one separated from that of the more modest-sized court groups (see Table 1).

The statistics in Table 1 tell us a number of things. First, the court orchestras show an average of twenty-two string instruments and twelve winds, for a total of thirty-four players. These figures, of course, are determined by the particular groups chosen in the present table. Nevertheless, they are not untypical of courts with more than the most modest financial means (as shown by Carse). The opera orchestras in Milan, Naples, and Paris, by contrast, average over forty strings and sixteen winds, for a sum of fifty-six players. Such large ensembles are approached only by the Court Orchestra in Mannheim and the Concert Spirituel in Paris, two unusual groups to which we will turn shortly. One can understand why Leopold Mozart would report so excitedly from Milan in 1770 about the size of the orchestra for the premiere of his son's *Mitridate, re di Ponto* at the Teatro Regio Ducal, or why Burney would so dutifully visit the opera during his stays in Paris, Naples, and Milan in order to verify reports of the orchestras' magnificence. It was not only the dimensions of the string sections in the opera orchestras that impressed, but also the availability of clarinets (in Paris and Milan, at least) and other wind and brass instruments in large numbers.

We also note that by today's standards, the ratio of cellos and double basses to violins and violas is small in both the court and opera ensembles. This may be explained in part by the fact that the cellos and double basses usually played the same *basso* part, which was typically reinforced by the bassoon. It was not until these three instruments went their own ways with independent lines that the cellos and double basses came into closer balance with the violins and violas. We see, too, that the winds stood in much higher proportion to the strings in the classical orchestra than in the modern. The wind-to-string ratio seems to have been roughly 1 to 2 in both the opera and orchestral ensembles; today it is approximately 1 to 3. Thus, Quantz' admonition in *Versuch einer Anweisung die Flute traversière zu spielen* (*On Playing the Flute*; 1752) that the wind instruments must be doubled when the orchestra has more than twenty-one strings, and Mozart's oft-quoted report that the winds were doubled for a performance with sixty-eight strings of one of his symphonies (K. 338?) in Vienna in 1781, ought not be viewed as aberrations. Their testimony is supported by the surviving figures and suggests that we are accustomed to too heavy a string sound when we perform the classical repertory today.

Returning to the opera orchestra, we find that a tradition of extravagance was established during the baroque era. Addison's and Steele's descriptions of opera seria excesses in London are matched by illustrations of contemporary opera houses, showing crowded parterres and balconies and, more significantly, crowded orchestra pits. Typical of these pictures is the anonymous engraving of the interior of the Oper am Zwinger in Dresden around 1750. An enlargement of the portion of the picture containing the opera orchestra shows forty-five musicians squeezed together so tightly amidst candles and music racks that one wonders how they were able to play! The excitement of such scenes is palpable, and composers did not hesitate to take advantage of the large forces available in this medium of exaggeration.

In the classical period, Gluck's *Iphigénie en Tauride*, written in 1779 for the Paris Opéra, required a vast, colorful instrumentarium: piccolo, two flutes, two oboes, two clarinets, two bassoons, two horns, two trumpets, three trombones, timpani, and strings. Here is the orchestra of the future. It took almost thirty years for symphony scores to equal the size and variety of Gluck's ensemble. One does not find similarly extravagant forces in symphonies until Beethoven's last four works in that genre. We can observe an acceleration in the exchange between the opera and the symphony in the 1770s and 1780s, however—that is, soon after the classical symphony had been formally established as a genre. The exchange seems to have taken place chiefly at the wealthier courts in Mannheim, Vienna, Esterhaza, and elsewhere, where operas were produced in imitation of the large-scale productions of Paris and Italy and nonoperatic concerts were given alongside operatic events.

In 1775, just four years before Gluck's *Iphigénie en Tauride*, Haydn was able to request two oboes, two English horns, two bassoons, two horns, two trumpets, timpani, percussion, and strings for a performance of his opera *L'incontro improviso* at Esterhaza. His symphonies from the same period (Symphonies nos. 66–68) still rely on the basic eight-part ensemble, with two bassoons added. But his symphony orchestra was soon to grow. Haydn's increasing involvement with opera after 1775, through the composition of his own works as well as the arrangement and performance of pieces by other composers, undoubtedly broadened his views of the coloristic possibilities of the orchestra for symphonic writing. His symphonies of the 1780s and 1790s show new orchestral timbres, calling for more *concertante* wind and brass writing and "exotic" solo effects. This is especially true of the Paris and London works written for large, professional ensembles. One can speculate, too, that Mozart's experience with *Idomeneo, Die Entführung aus dem Serail, Le nozze di Figaro*, and *Don Giovanni* during the years 1780–1788 resulted in his increasingly ambitious scoring for his Viennese piano concertos, which go far beyond his Salzburg works in their use of coloristic, operalike techniques. (One can even observe a lively exchange of musical motives between *Le nozze di Figaro*, completed in May 1786, and the Piano Concerto in C Major, K. 503, written later the same year.)

Most of the "new" instruments added to the eight-part classical ensemble had long been members of the opera orchestra. This is true not only of the flutes, the bassoons (as melody instruments), and the trumpets (with timpani), but of the clarinets, the piccolo, the trombones, and exotic percussion instruments as well. Clarinets appeared around 1750 at the Paris Opéra and were slowly welcomed into the classical ensemble for their dark color. The piccolo was used on a tentative basis for special effects (such as the raindrops in the *La tempesta* movement of Haydn's Symphony no. 8 in G Major) before entering the symphony orchestra permanently in the nineteenth century. The trombones and exotic percussion instruments (such as the triangle and bass drum) had to wait until the late works of Beethoven and the *Symphonie fantastique* of Berlioz.

Special instrumental effects used in opera—*staccato* and *pizzicato* and the muffled tones of muted brass and strings—provided the classical orchestra with a battery of novel sounds. The *crescendo* and *diminuendo*, once credited to the Mannheim symphonies of Stamitz, have been more accurately traced to the operas of Jommelli and Rameau. And onstage and offstage bands used in opera for grandiose scenes demonstrated the effectiveness of divided instrumental forces, a technique adopted by Johann Christian Bach in his symphonies for double orchestra. Haydn may have been influenced by opera conventions when he decided to conclude his famous *Farewell* Symphony with its unorthodox coda, for the departure of the performers, one by one, is a truly operatic gesture.

The professional abilities of the players in the large opera ensemble also had a decisive impact. France, more than any other country, set the standard in this regard. The tastes of the French royalty were imitated by the upper classes throughout Europe, as is plainly seen in the proliferation of castles built on the French plan in Berlin (Sans souci), Vienna (Schönbrunn), and Schwetzingen (the summer palace of Elector Karl Theodor), to name but three. Musically, French aristocrats relied on ensembles composed of professional players. The orchestra of the Paris Opéra was one of the earliest and most influential. It established a pattern of professionalism that was followed in Paris by the orchestras of the Concert Spirituel and La Pouplinière's soirees and by groups in Dresden, Munich, Berlin, and elsewhere.

Of the large professional concert orchestras of the last half of the eighteenth century based on the opera model, those of the Concert Spirituel and the court in Mannheim were undoubtedly the most important. The Concert Spirituel dated back to 1725, when it was founded by Anne Danican-Philidor to provide music when the Opéra was closed for religious holidays. Initially the programs consisted of instrumental works and sacred pieces with Latin texts; secular compositions with French texts were introduced later. The ensemble grew steadily over the years, from thirty-eight players in 1751 (the first year for which statistics survive) to fifty-two in 1790. The players were professionals drawn from the large pool of skilled Parisian musicians. In the documents of the day, the members of the ensemble are divided into *quatuor* (strings) and *harmonie* (winds).

For the first fifty-nine years of its existence, the Concert Spirituel performed in the Salle des Suisses in the Tuileries of the Louvre. In 1784 it moved to the Salle du Théâtre and in 1789 to the Salle du Théâtre Italien. The *Mercure de France* described the alterations in the Salle des Suisses made by Philidor in order to accommodate the newly formed orchestra:

> Philidor has had constructed a type of tribune in the large room. It has been placed against the wall on one side of the chamber and measures ten feet high, thirty-six feet across, and nine feet deep. It is capable of holding sixty people and includes a small set of stairs so that it may be mounted easily. This tribune is enclosed by a balustrade enhanced with gold, of which the banisters, in the shape of a lyre, have been placed on a pedestal painted like marble. The wall against which this tribune stands has been done in the best taste. The painting, made by Lemaire on the sketches of Berain, draftsman ordinaire of the King's cabinet, represents an immense vista that is extremely pleasing. Twelve chandeliers and candles beyond number serve as lighting.

It is not difficult to see the influence of opera on the Concert Spirituel's home: the gold leaf, the painting by Lemaire, and the gaily lighted chandeliers were calculated to win the appeal of an audience weaned on the glitter of the Paris Opéra. In its sixty-five-year life, the Concert Spirituel offered audiences an extraordinary array of music. According to Constant Pierre's statistics, the orchestra (along with its chorus and visiting soloists) presented works by 456 different musicians. Michel Richard Delalande, Jean Joseph Mouret, and Pergolesi head the list of composers who performed most frequently. Haydn's compositions were played on 256 occasions, while Mozart's were heard on only fifteen.

While visiting Paris in 1778, Mozart was commissioned to write a work for the Concert Spirituel. The result was the Symphony in D Major, K.[6] 300a, the so-called *Paris* Symphony. Mozart attended both the rehearsal and the performance of the piece and described the proceedings in a letter (dated 3 July) to his father:

> I was very nervous at the rehearsal, for never in my life have I heard a worse performance. You have no idea how they twice scraped and scrambled through it. I was really in a terrible way and would gladly have had it rehearsed again, but as there was so much else to rehearse, there was no time left. So I had to go to bed with an aching heart and in a discontented and angry frame of mind. I decided next morning not to go to the concert at all; but in the evening, the weather being fine, I at last made up my mind to go, determined that if my symphony went as badly as it did at the rehearsal, I would certainly make my way into the orchestra, snatch the fiddle out of the hands of Lahoussaye, the first violin, and conduct myself! I prayed God that it might go well, for it is all to His greater honour and glory; and behold—the symphony began. Raaff was standing beside me, and just in the middle of the first Allegro there was a passage which I felt sure must please. The audience was quite carried away—and there was a tremendous burst of applause. But as I knew, when I wrote it, what effect it would surely produce, I had introduced the passage again at the close—when there were shouts of "da capo." The Andante also found favour, but particularly the last Allegro, because, having observed that all last as well as first Allegros begin here with all the instruments playing together and generally *unisono*, I began mine with two violins only, *piano* for the first eight bars—followed instantly by a *forte*; the audience, as I expected, said "hush" at the soft beginning, and when they heard the *forte*, began at once to clap their hands.

In spite of Mozart's caustic comments about the shoddy rehearsal, the orchestra of the Concert Spirituel enjoyed a reputation as one of the most proficient ensembles in Europe. It impressed through its size, its diverse repertory, and its professional execution. It was also one of the first concert orchestras to include clarinets on a regular basis, thus offering composers the opportunity to experiment with the timbre of the new

single-reed instrument. Mozart did not fail to take advantage of the clarinets of the Concert Spirituel, incorporating the instrument into his symphonic writing for the first time in his *Paris* Symphony.

In addition, the Concert Spirituel was known for the precision of the
string playing, a Gallic trait that we have already traced back to the
Vingt-quatre Violons du Roi. In the Concert Spirituel, the exactitude of
bowing was demonstrated through *le premier coup d'archet,* the strong
downstroke that was used to begin the *fortissimo* passage that opens so
many of the works written for the ensemble. The gesture became legendary in Europe, and even Mozart did not fail to observe it in the opening
allegro of his *Paris* Symphony. But he confessed secretly to his father (letter of 12 June 1778) that he thought the use of the device nonsense:

> I have been careful not to neglect *le premier coup d'archet*—and that is quite
> sufficient. What a fuss the oxen here make of this trick! The devil take me
> if I can see any difference! They all begin together, just as they do in other
> places. It is really too much of a joke. Raaff told me a story of Abaco's about
> this. He was asked by a Frenchman, at Munich or somewhere—"Monsieur,
> have you been to Paris?" "Yes." "Have you been to the Concert Spirituel?"
> "Yes." "What do you think of *le premier coup d'archet?* Have you heard *le
> premier coup d'archet?*" "Yes, I've heard *le premier* and *le dernier.*" "How is this,
> *le dernier?* What do you mean?" "But yes, *le premier* and *le dernier*—and *le
> dernier* actually gave me the more pleasure."

While the Concert Spirituel was a public venture, supported by tickets sold on a subscription basis, the Mannheim orchestra was a private
affair, financed by the Elector Karl Theodor, who spent some 35 million
florins on artistic projects over a fifty-five-year period. Karl Theodor was
a talented amateur musician, playing the flute and the cello reasonably
well. He was intent on making his court a center of the arts, and during
his stay in Mannheim between 1743 (when he became the elector) and
1778 (when Mannheim was forsaken as the electoral capital for Munich),
he assembled one of the best professional ensembles in Europe. By 1756
he had created an orchestra of fifty-six players. By 1782, the ensemble
included thirty-three strings (twenty-three violins, three violas, four cellos, three double basses), fifteen woodwinds (four flutes, three oboes, four
clarinets, and four bassoons), a large brass section (six horns and an
unspecified number of trumpets), and percussion. In terms of size, this
placed the Mannheim orchestra next to the opera orchestras of Milan,
Naples, and the Concert Spirituel.

Even more significant than size was the quality of the performers.

Numbering among the musicians were over a dozen gifted composers: in the "founding" generation, Johann Stamitz, Franz Xaver Richter, Ignaz Holzbauer, Anton Filtz, and Carlo Giuseppe Toëschi; in the second generation, Christian Cannabich, Franz Beck, Ernst Eichner, and Ignaz Fränzl; and in the twilight years, Karl and Anton Stamitz (sons of Johann Stamitz), Wilhelm Cramer, and Carl Cannabich (son of Christian Cannabich). The presence of so many composers in the Mannheim ensemble led Burney to utter his famous remark about the orchestra's quality: "There are more solo players, and good composers in this, than perhaps any other orchestra in Europe; it is an army of generals, equally fit to plan a battle, as to fight it."

In charge of this "army" was Johann Stamitz, a violinist appointed director of instrumentalists in 1750. To Stamitz must go the credit for breaking with the Italian tradition of laxity and instigating in its place a new regimen of discipline. By drilling the players both singly and in small ensembles, he was able to produce an orchestra whose precision was unmatched in its time, even by the Concert Spirituel. After Stamitz' death in 1757, his practices were carried a step further by Christian Cannabich, who insisted on uniform bowing and close observance of the score.

Under Stamitz and Cannabich the Mannheim ensemble became what might be considered the first modern orchestra, in terms of technique: it was a group of professionals, well trained, well rehearsed, and well commanded. Moreover, there was a steady international exchange of players with other professional orchestras. Stamitz and his sons, Toëschi, and others performed as guests with the Concert Spirituel and other ensembles. Mozart, on hearing the Mannheim orchestra for the first time, declared it "excellent and very strong." Burney, on his visit, complained of the tuning of the woodwinds, but otherwise gave the group a glowing appraisal, especially in its performance of symphonies.

> It was here that Stamitz, stimulated by the productions of Jommelli, first surpassed the bounds of common opera overtures...; it was here that the *Crescendo* and *Diminuendo* had birth; and the *Piano*, which was before chiefly used as an echo, with which it was generally synonymous, as well as the *Forte*, were found to be musical *colours* which had their *shades*, as much as red or blue in painting.

As we have noted, modern scholarship has shown that the Mannheim orchestra was not the inventor of the *crescendo*, as Burney claimed. And many of the orchestral gestures once credited to the Mannheim

school—the melodic sigh, the "rocket" (an upward shooting melodic figure), the use of primary and secondary themes in sonata form—have
been shown to originate with the Italian *sinfonie* of Jommelli, Galuppi,
and others. But the importance of the Mannheim ensemble remains
undiminished. Its precise attack, dynamic nuance, uniform bowing, and
polished playing created a new professional standard. The Mannheim
orchestra demonstrated the potential of the new orchestral style and the
"colours" of the idiom, as Burney put it. It inspired Haydn and Mozart
to consider compositional possibilities far beyond those that could be
realized by the versatile but mediocre ensembles available at Esterhaza
and Salzburg.

Although neither Mozart nor Haydn wrote a work for the Mannheim orchestra, both were quick to make demands appropriate to the
ensemble when they finally won the chance to compose for comparable
professional groups. For Haydn, this meant the Concert de la Loge Olympique in Paris and the orchestra of the impresario Johann Peter Salomon
in London; for Mozart, the professional orchestras in Vienna, Prague,
and elsewhere. Just as Bach looked with envy from Leipzig to the court
orchestra in Dresden, so Haydn and Mozart must have looked with
yearning to the Mannheim orchestra, with its brilliant capabilities. In retrospect, it might be called the first modern ensemble. Certainly Christian
Schubart's description of it points to the modern orchestra:

> No orchestra in the world has ever excelled the Mannheim. Its *forte* is a
> thunderclap, its crescendo a cataract, its diminuendo a crystal stream bab-
> bling away into the distance, its *piano* a breath of spring. The wind instru-
> ments are everything that they should be: they raise and carry or fill and
> inspire the storm of the strings.

THE RISE OF THE CONCERT AND MUSIC PUBLISHING

During the course of the eighteenth century, music moved slowly but
inexorably from the church and court to the concert hall. This movement went hand in hand with the shift in patronage from the private to
the public sector, a change that greatly affected the lot of composers. On
the one hand, composers were no longer bound to the ongoing demands
of a single, permanent employer; they were free instead to seek and
accept commissions as they wished. On the other hand, composers now
staked their livelihood on a fickle public, whose rapidly shifting tastes
and loyalties could suddenly leave a once-popular figure abandoned (as
Mozart learned in Vienna).

For the orchestra, the rise of the public concert meant emancipation from church and court, institutions whose financial limitations (in most cases) would have been restrictive. The wealthier churches and courts might have been able to afford a professional ensemble of forty or even fifty players, but anything beyond that would have been unfeasible. Public concerts, which a thousand or more people might attend, could support orchestras of a larger size. The movement of music into the concert hall also represented the separation of the concert from the church service and the opera performance. As a result, sacred and secular vocal solos, relics from the church and opera house, were eventually eliminated from concert programs in favor of larger orchestral works.

The concert life that flowered at Mannheim and Esterhaza was essentially private entertainment, a luxury financed by taxation. After the French Revolution, aristocrats were more hesitant to make such lavish expenditures. Public concerts were infinitely more democratic and reflected the rise of civic spirit that was a part of the classical era. Public concerts gained broad sponsorship in urban centers and appeared with increasing frequency as the century progressed. The Concert des Amateurs (1769) and the Concert de la Loge Olympique (1780) in Paris, the Harmonie Gesellschaft (1789) in Hamburg, the Hanover Square Concerts (1775) in London, or the Gewandhaus Concerts (1781) in Leipzig underline this pattern.

In Germany the transition from the *collegium musicum* to the public orchestra was principally a matter of scale and financing. The *collegium* was normally a small, amateur group with no permanent home. Its financing was casual: patrons were admitted for free or they were assessed a nominal fee or a contribution. At Zimmermann's Coffeehouse in Leipzig, one paid half a thaler to hear Bach's *collegium* when there was a special artist; otherwise, one paid nothing. Since the performers in the *collegium* were chiefly amateurs, substantial financial support was unnecessary. The orchestra for public subscription concerts relied more heavily on professional players, and it usually had a permanent home. Thus, it needed to be financed in a more systematic way, with tickets sold in advance, often on a series basis. A distinction in ticket prices enabled entrepreneurs to accommodate aristocratic patrons who did not want to sit with the common horde. But in return for charging admission, concert managers were obligated to provide the public with polished playing. In his advertisements for the Haydn concerts in London, Salomon assured potential subscribers that the performers would be "of the first rate" and backed up his claim by publishing a list of the most outstanding members of the orchestra.

The success of public ventures in the late eighteenth century led to the formation of orchestral societies in the nineteenth, such as the Gesellschaft der Musikfreunde (1812) and the Philharmonic (1842) in Vienna, the Philharmonic Society in Berlin (1826), and the Philharmonic Society in Hamburg (1828). These were stable municipal groups, formed to present orchestral music to a broad audience.

The rise of public concerts in large cities encouraged composers to travel, which in turn contributed to the internationalism of the new orchestral style. J. C. Bach ventured from Leipzig to Milan to London; C. F. Abel from Leipzig to Dresden to London; Gluck from Vienna to London and Paris; Haydn from Esterhaza to London; Mozart from Salzburg to Paris, Munich, Vienna, and other cities. In most cases, the composers traveled to towns where their music could be performed with professional finesse before receptive, knowledgeable audiences. The migration of composers from the provinces to large cities and from one country to another was unmatched in earlier times and helped to spread the new symphonic style over international boundaries. One could no longer speak of a French or Italian style, as had been possible in the baroque. The new orchestral idiom was international, with cosmopolitan gestures.

The demand for professional instrumentalists spurred the founding of conservatories such as the École Royale de Chant in Paris in 1784. At first, these institutions were patterned after the Italian *conservatori*, whose chief purpose in the eighteenth century was the training of singers for opera. By the nineteenth century, instrumental instruction had gained an even footing with vocal training. Institutions such as the Conservatoire de Musique (which succeeded the École Royale in 1795) in Paris or the Royal Academy of Music (1822) in London fostered a new generation of systematically trained orchestral players. The increasing availability of professional performers is reflected in the late orchestral scores of Mozart and Haydn and the symphonies of Beethoven, all of which require highly skilled players.

Concert halls, too, were needed for the new public orchestras. Initially, existing rooms were appropriated, such as the Salle des Suisses in Paris, Carlisle House in London, the Zuchthaussaal and the Kaiserhof in Hamburg, or Trinity Church in New York. But these adopted spaces usually proved insufficient. Subscriptions at Carlisle House, for instance, had to be limited to 400 in order to control the press of patrons. As a consequence, new halls were built: the Konzertsaal auf dem Kamp (1761) in Hamburg (a hall that attracted attention because it could be heated), the Hanover Square Rooms (1775) in London, or the Gewandhaus in Leipzig (1781). The Hanover Square Rooms, with a capacity of 800 to 900, enjoyed an illustrious history. They hosted the Bach-Abel concerts (which had been held earlier in Carlisle House) until 1782, the Professional Concerts of 1783-1793, the Salomon Concerts of 1786-1794, and other programs into the nineteenth century. During Haydn's visit in 1791-1792, over "1,500 entered the room," demonstrating that Hanover Square, like its predecessor Carlisle House, was inadequate for the large following that the orchestra was to attract.

The move of the orchestra from private into public hands had yet another result: the birth of "concert coverage." At first the reporting of concerts took the shape of formal announcements of upcoming events or recent programs, usually in local papers or journals. Johann Nikolaus Forkel's *Musikalischer Almanach für Deutschland* of 1782-1784 and 1789 represented a broader approach, outlining musical activities at courts throughout Germany. True music criticism, in the vein of Addison's early *Spectator* essays in London, appeared in the *Mercure de France* (1750) and the *Correspondence littéraire* (1753), both issued in Paris. One of the first journals devoted to appraising weekly events was Johann Adam Hiller's *Wöchentliche Nachrichten und Anmerkungen, die Musik betreffend* (1766), designed to reach a wide audience.

Reviews of concerts had the effect of making composers self-conscious. Mozart, during a stay in Paris, was quick to point out to his father that the *Courier de l'Europe* had recently reported the success of his *Paris Symphony*. Haydn's first concert in London received notice in the *Diary* and the *Morning Chronicle*. The first performance of Haydn's Symphony no. 93 in D Major (17 February 1792) was reported by the *Chronicle* as follows:

> His new Grand Overture was pronounced by every scientific ear to be a most wonderful composition; but the first movement in particular rises in grandeur of subject, and in the rich variety of air and passion, beyond any even of his own productions. The Overture has four movements—An Allegro-Andante-Minuet-and Rondo. They are all beautiful, but the first is pre-eminent in every charm, and the Band performed it with admirable correctness.

While such accounts seem perfunctory by later standards, they represent the beginning of public scrutiny of orchestral works. Such reports placed pressure on composers to write audience-pleasing novelties. In London the competition between Haydn and his student Ignaz Pleyel was spurred by the press and avidly followed by the reading public. Exposure to the public eye through concert reporting may help to account for the unusually high number of innovations in Haydn's *London* symphonies. Haydn confessed that in his Symphony no. 94 in G

Major (*Surprise*), he had used the "surprising" drum stroke in the *andante* specifically to keep ahead of Pleyel.

Late-eighteenth-century programs were much more of a mélange than those of today. Arias and choral pieces alternated with instrumental solos, chamber works, concertos, and symphonies. The program of the Concert Spirituel of 14 May 1780 ran as follows:

A symphony, by Amadeo Mozart
Venite sancte spiritus, by Jommelli
A concerto for harp, by {J. C.} Bach
Air Italien, by Sacchini
A new concerto for violin, composed and executed by Fodor
Te Deum, by Gossec
A new concerto for clarinet, composed and executed by Rathé
Air Italien, by Gluck

Three years later Mozart presented a subscription concert in Vienna that had a similarly varied makeup:

The Haffner Symphony {K. 385}
"Se il padre perdei" from *Idomeneo,* sung by Madame Lange
Piano Concerto in C Major {K.⁶ 387*b*}, performed by Mozart
Scena "Misera! dove son" {K. 369}, sung by Adamberger
Sinfonia Concertante in G Major {K. 320}
Piano Concerto in D Major {K. 175}, performed by Mozart
Scene "Parto, m'affretto," sung by Mlle. Teiber
Variations on "Salve tu, Domine" {K.⁶ 416*e*} and "Unser dummer
    Pöbel meint" {K. 455}, played by Mozart
"Mia speranza adorata" {K. 416}, sung by Madame Lange
The last movement of the Haffner Symphony

And Haydn's first Salomon Concert in London, on 19 February 1791, had the following contents:

An overture, by Rosetti
A song, performed by Signora Storace
An oboe concerto, performed by Mr. Harrington
A song, sung by Signor David
A violin concerto, performed by Madame Gautherot
A new grand overture, by Haydn
A song, sung by Signora Storace
A concerto for pedal harp, performed by Madame Krumpholtz

A song, sung by Signor David
A full piece, by Kozeluch

Haydn's biographer Albert Dies explained that Haydn's new symphonies were placed at the beginning of the second part of the concert rather than during the first because in England,

> the first act was usually disturbed in various ways by the noise of late-comers. Not a few persons came from well-set tables (where the men, as is the custom of the country, stay in the dining room and drink, after the ladies have left following the conclusion of the meal). Those arriving late took a comfortable seat in the concert room and were so gripped by the magic of the music that they went fast to sleep.

In the late eighteenth century the newly established orchestra stirred audiences and may be said to have started a concert industry, one requiring suitable halls, a corps of skilled instrumentalists, reviewers, and gifted composers. To keep this industry flourishing, an additional agent was necessary: publishers. As late as the third quarter of the eighteenth century, music was still disseminated chiefly by manuscript copy. Printing, through engraving or movable type, was commonly used for keyboard works, but for symphonies it was slow and very expensive. Copying, by contrast, was cheap and practical. It was cheap because trained scribes, raised in an almost feudal tradition, were available at low cost. At courts and monasteries, copyists were commonly employed on a full-time basis and listed on the roster of resident musicians (as can be seen from lists of court ensembles given in Forkel's *Musikalischer Almanach*). In large cities, scribes functioned as free-lance agents, offering copies of works they had available. Of this practice in Vienna Burney reports:

> As there are no music shops in Vienna, the best method of procuring new compositions is to apply to copyists; for the authors, regarding every English traveller as a *milord*, expect a present on these occasions, as considerable for each piece, as if it had been composed on purpose for him.... I was plagued with copyists the whole evening; they began to regard me as a greedy and indiscriminate purchaser of whatever trash they should offer; but I was forced to hold my hand, not only from buying bad music, but good. For everything is very dear at Vienna, and nothing more so than music, of which none is printed.

Years later Mozart came to distrust the Viennese scribes so much that he insisted on being present whenever his compositions were being copied. Copying by hand was practical, too, in an age in which the demand for new music was great and styles and tastes changed rapidly. The sta-bilization of the classical idiom and the establishment of a relatively stan-dardized eight-part orchestral ensemble made it more feasible, after 1770, for symphonies to be printed and promulgated on an international basis. Even so, classical composers may have hesitated at first to have their works published, for in a period without copyright, distribution by manuscript copy could be more lucrative than distribution by print. As Burney implied, it was possible for a composer (or scribe) to sell a fair number of handwritten copies of a composition and obtain a respectable payment for each before the work received wide distribution and moved out of his sphere of control. If a composer chose to print a piece, he received a single fee from the publisher and was then vulnerable to acts of piracy as the work circulated widely.

In the 1770s and 1780s the music-printing industry grew markedly in size and stature. The increasing concentration of populations in the larg-est cities made music printing a safer venture: distribution was easier and the possibility of large sales more probable. At first, the music-publishing industry was located chiefly in England, France, and the Low Countries. But by the end of the century, music publishers were ubiquitous. Among the most important printers of classical symphonies were Walsh, Brem-ner, Welcker, Forster, and Bland in London; Roger and Le Cene in Amsterdam; Huberty, Le Duc, and Sieber in Paris; Artaria and Torricella in Vienna; Breitkopf in Leipzig; and Simrock in Bonn.

If we look at the extant sources of Haydn's symphonies, we can observe a clear progression from manuscript to printed copies. The ear-liest symphonies were circulated chiefly in manuscript copies, which sur-vive today in Göttweig, Kremsmünster, Melk, and other monasteries. The middle works—from the 1770s at Esterhaza—began to appear more frequently in print, as Haydn's reputation grew and music publishing increased. Parts for Symphony no. 64 in A Major, for instance, were pub-lished by Bland, Forster, and Sieber, though they exist in a dozen hand-written copies from the time as well. (Classical symphonies were normally circulated in parts; orchestral scores were not generally printed until the nineteenth century.) By the 1780s, Haydn's works were international best sellers. Symphony no. 80 in D Minor was issued more or less simultane-ously in Vienna (Artaria), Berlin and Amsterdam (Hummel), Lyon (Guera), London (Forster), and Paris (Le Duc, as agent for Artaria). With the *London* symphonies, printing fully replaced manuscript copying as the principal means of duplication. Symphony no. 101 in D Major was published by almost a dozen firms by 1800, while less than ten hand-written manuscripts survive.

Mozart's symphonies did not equal Haydn's in popularity until the last years of the eighteenth century. They were not printed nearly as widely and have been passed down in far fewer manuscript copies. This seems to stem from the fact that they were much more difficult to perform than Haydn's symphonies—a phenomenon reflected in the program statistics of the Concert Spirituel cited above.

In the case of Haydn's symphonies, the picture of publication is telling. As the works were printed in ever greater numbers, Haydn's reputation abroad increased. His triumphant arrival in London would not have been possible had knowledge of his symphonies not preceded him in the form of printed editions. Conversely, as his fame spread, the demands for his works increased equally, making the symphonies a more attractive proposition for publishers. The financial stakes grew, and the problem of piracy became more acute. Approximately 150 "Haydn" symphonies were produced by falsifying Haydn's authorship; a good number of these were circulated in printed form.

Music printing, then, helped to spread the new orchestral style. It provided material for orchestral ensembles, and it encouraged composers to write publishable works. The immense appetite for orchestral pieces is demonstrated by the extraordinarily wide circulation of Haydn's real symphonies as well as the frequency with which new ones were fabricated.

THE EMERGENCE OF CLASSICAL STYLE

The orchestra, as a new institution emerging in the late eighteenth century, did not exist in a vacuum. It was highly dependent for its survival on the music written for its use. As long as this music remained vigorous and vital, the orchestra would also. The unusual popularity of the symphony and the rapidity with which the symphonic style spread across international borders toward the end of the century mirrors to a large degree the success with which the classical composers Haydn and Mozart realized the potential of the preclassical idiom they inherited.

By 1761, Haydn's first year with the Esterhazy family, the ingredients for a new style were at hand. The "orchestral" ensemble of eight or so well-blended parts was established. The singing *allegro*, drawn from Neapolitan opera, had prevailed over baroque counterpoint, marking a shift to homophonic texture. Periodic phrasing rather than *Fortspinnung* ("spinning out" in the baroque manner) was being used more and more as a means of extending musical materials. And a whole series of orchestral devices were being tried out.

The molds in which to cast these elements were available as well. Sonata form—with exposition, development (however rudimentary), and recapitulation (however unorthodox)—had been in existence for some twenty years. The three-movement symphony, derived from the Italian opera *sinfonia*, with its sequence of fast-slow-fast, was regularly employed by Sammartini, the sons of Bach, and others. The four-movement symphony, with added minuet and trio, was normally used by Georg Matthias Monn and Georg Christoph Wagenseil in Vienna and Johann Stamitz in Mannheim.

What stood in place, then, in 1761 was a popular, well-refined, but platitudinous style. Audiences were attracted by its new effects, and composers adopted it as the idiom of the future. But its virtues—naturalness and simplicity—were also its chief weaknesses: it lacked the depth necessary to sustain long-term interest. The preclassical style, with its *galant* foundation, was too superficial. We may wonder, in retrospect, whether the orchestra would have survived past the eighteenth century without the more sophisticated symphonic compositions of Haydn and Mozart.

To Haydn must go the credit of making the leap to classical style. During the Esterhaza years, Haydn reshaped the *galant* idiom, giving it substance through a series of remarkable innovations. As he proclaimed to Griesinger when summing up his Esterhaza tenure, these innovations stemmed from years of constant experimentation: "I was commended, and as conductor of an orchestra I could make experiments, observe what strengthened and what weakened an effect, and thereupon improve, substitute, omit, and try new things. I was cut off from the world, there was no one around to mislead and harass me, and so I was forced to be original."

Haydn's originality appears in the symphonies from this time, which exhibit an astounding array of fruitful ideas. On a formal level, he tried out a number of architectonic plans for the layout of movements: Italian *sinfonia* (fast-slow-fast, as in Symphony no. 19 in D Major), divertimento (fast-minuet-slow-minuet-fast, as in Symphony no. 7 in C Major), Viennese-Mannheim symphony (fast-slow-minuet-fast, as in Symphony no. 45 in F-sharp Minor), and others (slow-fast-slow-fast, as in Symphony no. 22 in E-flat Major).

Within movements Haydn tried various methods of enriching *galant* texture, from adding counterpoint (the fugal finales of a number of symphonies or the *al revescio*, or mirror-imitation, minuet of Symphony no. 47 in G Major) to using instrumental recitative (Symphony no. 7) and even Gregorian chant (Symphony no. 26 in D Minor) for melodic material. He experimented with subtractive orchestration (Symphony no. 45), cyclical techniques (Symphony no. 31 in D Major), and program music

(Symphony no. 8 in G Major, *Le soir*). The fruit of Haydn's inventiveness was the creation of a cosmopolitan style, one uniting the *style galant*, *Empfindsamkeit*, *Sturm und Drang*, baroque counterpoint, and Haydn's own sense of theater.

In terms of orchestration, Haydn's most important contribution may be the extraordinary *concertante* writing for both the string and wind instruments that occurs in his mature symphonies. It appears especially in the trios of minuets and in the theme-and-variation movements that became a hallmark of his late style. Looking at a portion of the theme-and-variation movement of Symphony no. 103 in E-flat Major (*Drum Roll*; Ex. 3), for instance, we see how delicately Haydn scores: at measure 135 the oboes carry the melody over obbligato bass figures in the bas-

Example 3. Haydn: Symphony no. 103 in E-flat Major (*Drum Roll*), movement 2, mm. 135–138

soons, horn chords, and pizzicato strings. The flute adds thirty-second-note embellishments. At measure 143 (Ex. 4), the upper strings, playing *arco,* join the oboes and flute in a *fortissimo* punctuated by arpeggios in the cello, downbeat chords in the brass and double bass, and accented timpani strokes. This scoring reaches back to baroque principles. But at the same time, it points forward to the modern orchestra. The use of delicate instrumental colors foreshadows Berlioz and Tchaikovsky.

Example 4. Haydn: Symphony no. 103 in E-flat Major (*Drum Roll*), movement 2, mm. 143–146

But an even greater legacy, perhaps, is Haydn's contribution to sonata form. For Haydn, sonata form became a drama, filled with tension and surprise. The truly symphonic histrionics one finds in Haydn's orchestral works stem not just from his deft manipulation of the musical fabric—the use of asymmetrical themes, monothematicism, false or encapsulated recapitulations. They come from his acute sense of timing, a feature that takes his sonata movements beyond the predictable gesture and into the realm of theater. In addition, his extension of "development" into other parts of sonata form (the bridges and closing sections, for instance) and into other movements (minuets and trios, for example) invests his pieces with a dynamic force not found in preclassical works.

The development section of the first movement of the *Drum Roll* Symphony is a case in point. Haydn develops the first theme, the second theme, and the closing theme, and introduces material from the slow introduction. There is syncopation, imitation, and silence. The immense scope of the development section is extended even further by a stormy digression away from the expected E-flat Major to A-flat Minor, followed by the unanticipated return of the drum roll from the introduction, which is used to announce the recapitulation. Such "plot twists," ingeniously planned and brilliantly executed, were beyond the abilities of a J. C. Bach, a Stamitz, or a Cannabich.

In the *Paris* and *London* symphonies, works written for professional orchestras, the experimentation of the early symphonies yielded to controlled innovation. The late pieces represent Haydn's crowning achievement in the realm of the symphony and served as repertoire for the new professional orchestra. Here was a style for all countries, with passages to please the instrumental players and to astonish the members of the audience. It is understandable why audiences demanded movements to be encored and why publishers attempted to produce even more Haydn symphonies through falsification. Piracy was to be expected where the treasure was so great.

Mozart's mature symphonies matched Haydn's in terms of drama and orchestral color but went beyond them technically. Mozart's works made unusual demands on the performers. They required a fully professional ensemble, and this may account for their infrequent performance during Mozart's lifetime. They did not appear in the Breitkopf Catalogues until the 1785–1787 supplement, and even then only two (K. 319 and K. 385) were listed. The Leipzig subscription concerts of 1786 included pieces by Haydn, Stamitz, Dittersdorf, and others, but not Mozart. The Concert Spirituel, as we have noted, performed Haydn 256 times and Mozart only 15. Mozart's unwillingness to compromise on matters of playability separated his orchestral works from normal concert fare.

Example 5. Mozart: Symphony no. 41 in C Major (*Jupiter*), K. 551, movement 1, mm. 131–143.

His father, Leopold, warned him about this matter twice during the preparations for the first performance of *Idomeneo* during the winter of 1780–1781 in Munich. The initial admonition came in a letter dated 4 December 1780: "Your music is always lost by a mediocre orchestra, because it is written too sensibly for all instruments and not so tritely as Italian music in general." The second came three weeks later, on 25 December, as Mozart began to prepare the orchestra: "Only try to keep the entire orchestra in good humor, by flattering them and without exception holding them to you through praise. For I know your method of writing: it demands uninterrupted astounding attention by all the instruments, and it is indeed no fun, when an orchestra must be pressed to such industry and attentiveness for at least three hours."

Mozart's special technical demands include split viola parts, large sounds from the string group (double stops, *crescendi* through the addition of instruments, unison or octaves in *fortissimo* passages), unusual rhythmic figures, syncopated entries, extremely fast passages, foreign keys and scales, obbligato wind parts, and long stretches without spots for resting. A good example of this type of sophisticated ensemble writing occurs in the development section of the first movement of the Symphony in C Major (*Jupiter*), K. 551, at measures 131–143 (Ex. 5), where the theme of "Un bacio di mano" (an aria Mozart had written for insertion into an opera by Pasquale Anfossi) is developed imitatively in E-flat Major. This type of writing requires great concentration on the part of the performers. More importantly, it demands a well-developed technique from the individual players and intensive rehearsal on the part of the group. Passages such as these appear throughout Mozart's mature symphonies and the piano concertos that served as his symphonic outlet in Vienna. The development sections of the outer movements of the Symphony in E-flat Major, K. 543; the Symphony in G Minor, K. 550; and the *Jupiter* Symphony are for neither the amateur nor the impatient professional. Without study and rehearsal they cannot be executed cleanly. It is undoubtedly for this reason that Mozart's mature symphonies gathered dust while Haydn's more approachable pieces circulated throughout Europe.

By the time Mozart's late symphonies were published, the orchestra was well on its way to becoming a public, professional institution ready to meet the challenges posed by such difficult scores. All that was wanting was the figure who would push technique to a new horizon, who would force instrument builders to produce more reliable instruments, who would compel ensembles to become more polished, and who would write works for which a conductor was no longer a decoration (as Haydn had been for his *London* symphonies). This figure, of course, was Beethoven. His symphonies, published from 1801 on, would bring the classical ensemble to maturity as the modern orchestra.

TABLE 1 Instrumental Distribution in the Major Eighteenth-Century Opera Orchestras

Orchestra	date	violin I	violin II	viola	cello	double bass	flute	oboe	clarinet	bassoon	horn	trumpet	timpani
Ansbach (Kammer und Hofmusik)	1782	12 (I+II)		3	5	2	2	3	3	3	4	?	?
Bentheim-Steinfurt (Court Orchestra)	1783	4	3	2	2	1	—	—	2	1	2	—	—
Berlin (King of Prussia)	1772	12 (I+II)		4	5	2	4	4	—	4	2	—	—
Coblenz (Hofmusik)	1782	13 (I+II)		4	2	3	3	3	2	3	4	2	1
Copenhagen (Court Orchestra)	1784	? (I+II)		2	2	2	2	2	—	2	2	?	?
Dresden (King of Poland)	1783	8	7	4	4	3	3	4	—	4	3	?	?
Esterháza (Prince Esterházy)	1783	10 (I+II)		2	2	2	—	2	—	2	2	?	?
Kassel (Hofmusik)	1782	5	6	1	2	2	2	2	2	—	2	2	—
Leipzig (Gewandhaus)	1781	6	6	3	2	2 (4)	2	2	—	2	2	2	1
Mannheim (Court Orchestra)	1777	10-11	10-11	4	4	4	2	2 (4)	2	4	2	?	?
Milan (Opera)	1770	14	14	6	2	6	2	2	2	2	4	2	2
Munich (The Elector's Orchestra)	1778	17 (I+II)		?	2	2	2	3	3	2	4	?	?
Naples (San Carlo Opera)	1770	18 (I+II)		?	2	5	?	?	—	?	?	?	?
Paris (Concert Spirituel)	1773	13	11	4	10	4	2	3 (5)	2	4	2	2	1
Paris (Opéra)	1773	22 (I+II)		5	9	6	2	5	1	8	2	1	1
Regensburg (Court Orchestra)	1783	? (I+II)		2	2	2	2	2	2	2	4	4	1
Vienna (Court Orchestra)	1782	? (I+II)		4	3	3	2	2	0	2	2	?	?

BIBLIOGRAPHY

Heinz Becker, "Orchester," in *Die Musik in Geschichte und Gegenwart* (1949–   ), Friedrich Blume, ed. Barry S. Brook, "Piracy and Panacea in the Dissemination of Music in the Late Eighteenth Century," in *Proceedings of the Royal Musical Association*, 102 (1975–1976). Charles Burney, *The Present State of Music in Germany, the Netherlands, and United Provinces*, 2 vols. (1773). Adam Carse, *The Orchestra in the Eighteenth Century* (1940; repr. 1950). Albert Christoph Dies, *Biographishe Nachricten von Joseph Haydn* (1810), Vernon Gotwals, trans. in *Joseph Haydn: Eighteenth-Century Gentleman and Genius* (1963). Hans Engel, "Mozarts Instrumentation," in *Mozart-Jahrbuch* (1956). Janos Harich, "Das Haydn-Orchester im Jahr 1780," in *Haydn-Yearbook*, 8 (1971).

Paul Henry Lang, *Music in Western Civilization* (1941). Jens Peter Larsen, *The New Grove Haydn* (1983); and "Zur Bedeutung der 'Mannheimer Schule,'" in *Festschrift Karl Gustav Fellerer* (1962). Christoph-Hellmut Mahling, "Mozart und Orchesterpraxis seiner Zeit," in *Mozart-Jahrbuch* (1967). W. A. Mozart et al., *The Letters of Mozart and His Family*, Emily Anderson, ed. (1938), 2nd ed., A. Hyatt King and Monica Carolan, eds. (1966). Constant Pierre, *Histoire du Concert Spirituel 1725–1790* (1975). Johann Joachim Quantz, *Versuch einer Anweisung die Flute traversière zu spielen* (1752), translated as *On Playing the Flute*, Edward R. Reilly, trans. (1966).

Gardner Read, *Style and Orchestration* (1979). H. C. Robbins-Landon, *Haydn: Chronicle and Works*, 5 vols. (1976–1980). Charles Rosen, *The Classical Style*, 2nd ed. (1972). Stanley Sadie, *The New Grove Mozart* (1983). Christian Schubart, *Deutsche Chronik* (1774–1791). Jack Westrup, "Orchestra," in *The New Grove Dictionary of Music and Musicians*, Stanley Sadie, ed. (1980). Eugene Wolf, "On the Origins of the Mannheim Symphonic Style," in *Studies in Musicology in Honor of Otto E. Albrecht* (1977). Christoph Wolff, "Aspects of Instrumentation in Mozart's Orchestral Music," in *L'interpretation de la musique classique* (1980).

Instruments and Their Use: Early Times to the Rise of the Orchestra

Gregory G. Butler

The wide array of instruments in the Middle Ages and the Renaissance and the colorful variety of sonorities they represent almost defy classification. Tracing the evolution of these instruments is a bit like trying to follow the densely interwoven threads of a bright, richly colored tapestry of the period. Non-Western cultures contributed many instruments to the Western instrumentarium, but European musicians were not content to leave the instruments in the forms in which they acquired them. On the contrary, they were constantly tampering with them, altering them or adapting them to instruments that had long been in use. The result is an almost bewildering variety of types and forms. The constant state of developmental flux, the unexpected twists and turns in the evolutionary paths taken by instruments, the disappearance of old instruments, and the appearance of new instruments form the substance of this essay.

STRING INSTRUMENTS

The principal string instruments of the ancient Greeks were the *kithara* and the *lyre*. The *kithara* was a larger, more powerful instrument played by professional virtuosos. Its sound chest was of wood, and its vertical arms often hollow; the lyre's sound chest was fashioned from a tortoise shell and its vertical arms were of solid wood. They may have found their way into northern Europe during the late years of the Roman Empire via Constantinople, perhaps carried home by the German soldiers who are known to have served in Byzantine armies. Certainly, it is clear from the "Allemanic lyre" that the lyre was used in Germany in the sixth century. There is evidence that this German lyre was played in Anglo-Saxon Britain by the second half of the seventh century, for fragments of such an instrument were found in the Sutton Hoo ship burial of around 670. This instrument is referred to in sources from the period variously as *rotta, chrotta, croud,* and, in modern times, the Welsh *crwth.* The instrument itself is a relatively thin, roughly rectangular piece of solid wood with somewhat rounded ends. The upper half of the instrument is pierced by a large oblong hole around which the body functions as a frame. As many as thirty strings (six is common) are attached either to a stringholder or directly to a nut at the bottom of the instrument, pass over a narrow bridge from which they are stretched over the opening, and are tightened by pegs stuck at right angles into holes across the top of the frame. The lyre is held by one hand, and the strings are plucked by the free hand with either a plectrum or the fingers.

Another string instrument of ancient origin is the *harp,* which is depicted as early as the eighth century in western European sources, in which it is almost invariably shown being played by King David. This is an instrument with a triangular frame, of which the diagonal side closest to the body is a resonating box sometimes shown with soundholes, the vertical side farthest from the body is the forepillar, and the more or less horizontal top member is the neck. A variable but relatively large number of strings are attached to the resonator by pegs or toggles and stretched vertically to attach to tuning pegs running the length of the neck. Both hands were used to pluck the strings. Such framed harps were small in comparison with the Renaissance harp and the present-day concert harp, and all were portable. The strings of both lyre and harp were tuned diatonically and were probably of gut, although metal strings may also have been in use. The lyre and harp were the bardic instruments par excellence, used by minstrels to accompany their spoken recitations. They may well have played solo preludes, interludes, and postludes during the recitation of sagas and lays and were undoubtedly used to accompany singing as well.

A third string instrument dating from classical and preclassical times appears with ever greater frequency in western European sources from the ninth century onward. This is the *psaltery.* Consisting of a shallow resonating box in any of a variety of geometric shapes, it usually appears without soundholes in earlier sources. A relatively large number of strings were stretched parallel to the soundboard and attached at either side by wooden pegs or metal pins. The instrument was held in the lap with the strings running vertically and pointing away from the body. It was plucked from either side by both hands. The psaltery was widely used up to 1500 to accompany singing and in ensembles, especially at feasts, but it was also used as a solo instrument.

The *monochord* is unique in having been in use continuously from the time of the ancient Greeks to the present. As it name suggests, it consisted of a single string stretched between two fixed bridges mounted at either end of a rectangular resonating box. The string was stopped at different points along its length by either a rod, a tangent, or a movable third bridge controlled by one hand while the other plucked a segment of the string with a quill. It was an instrument used for acoustic experiments by music theoreticians and for pedagogical purposes by choir masters. While it is of only passing interest in itself, the monochord is important, for from it later evolved the *organistrum,* which was in use from the ninth until at least the late twelfth century. The organistrum differed from the monochord in its form, since it was differentiated into a resonating portion and a neck. One player turned a crank at the resonating end of the instrument, causing a rotating wheel to rub the string so that it sounded continuously, while a second player stopped the string at various points along the neck by means of a key mechanism. The organistrum is often shown with more than one string, the strings sounding simultaneously, probably in parallel octaves or fifths. The use of this instrument seems to have been interchangeable with that of the organ, with which it is often confused in sources—that is, to sound pitches for the singers and act as a drone supporting the singing of chant.

The organistrum leads us to a discussion of stopped string instruments with necks. Several different lute- or guitarlike instruments had appeared in western Europe by the ninth century, all characterized by a broad "body," above which the strings ran and were plucked, and a narrower "neck," against which the strings were stopped. From iconographical evidence, these instruments seem in some cases to be carved out of a single piece of wood and, in others, to be hollow resonating boxes to which necks were attached. In the early history of these instruments a bewildering variety of shapes is depicted, but there seem to have been two basic types derived from the Arab *rabāb* and the Byzantine *lura (lyra).* The former came into Spain during the Moorish invasions beginning in the eighth century. It had a long narrow body with a belly of skin and a pegbox extending back at right angles to the neck and seems to have been confined to southern Europe. The latter was shaped like a pear cut in half longitudinally, with a vaulted back and flat soundboard. It seems to have been carved out of a single piece of wood, with no visible demarcation between body and neck, but rather a gradual narrowing. The fingerboard, when one existed, seems to have been simply a raised portion of the neck. The neck terminated in a flat pegholder. The rabāb usually had three strings; the lura, from two to six strings. Both were probably tuned in unisons, fifths, and octaves. In both types the strings were attached to endpins or a stringholder at the lower end, and at the upper end to tuning pegs inserted into holes at right angles to the pegbox. Both types are depicted with and without bridges. The use of these instruments in their early form is somewhat unclear, but an important use must have been as melody instruments, since the neck facilitated rapid changes of string length and made for greater overall agility in the playing of the instrument.

Another string instrument introduced by the Moors in their conquest of Spain and referred to in sources from the ninth century is the *lute* proper, the word deriving from the Arabic *el-ūd*. In early depictions it is shown as having a rather large oval resonator with a vaulted back and a belly pierced by at least one carved rosette. In contrast to the lura and the rabāb, the *Arab lute* had more strings, usually eight or nine, and they were attached at their lower end to a wide raised bridge glued to the soundboard. Since the necks are depicted as being relatively narrow, it is assumed that the strings were arranged in double courses. The pegholder projected back from the neck at a very sharp angle and was often open, with the tuning pegs inserted laterally from both sides into and across this opening, into which the strings fed.

Two events of momentous importance for the evolution of instruments in western Europe occurred in the tenth to eleventh centuries. The first of these was the spread of the bow from central Asia, first through Islamic lands and Byzantium, where the rabāb and lura were played with a bow by the tenth century. The bow seems to have appeared in Europe first in Spain and southern Italy, but its use spread quickly to northern Europe, where it became firmly established from the end of the tenth or the early eleventh century. The instrumental bow is a direct descendant of the hunting bow, a tree branch bent to form an arc and strung under tension with a length of sinew. As it was adapted for the playing of string instruments, rosined gut or hairs were knotted through or wound around the ends of the bow in such a way as to leave a handle at one end. By the end of the Middle Ages, built-up nuts had been invented to hold the hairs. In early depictions, the arc of these bows is quite large and the bows are unwieldy in appearance, but the bow was later to undergo considerable refinement.

The bow was seized on eagerly by musicians. The sound of plucked strings died away relatively quickly, but the bow allowed the sound of vibrating strings to be sustained for as long as it took to draw the bow across the strings. It also provided a nasal sonority rather than the metallic sonority of the plucked string, and allowed a large number of strings to be set vibrating simultaneously.

The bow was immediately applied to many plucked string instruments already in use in western Europe, notably the lyre, as well as the lura and rabāb types of necked string instruments. This necessitated certain structural modifications. In depictions of bowed lyres from this period, necks have been added to these instruments, influenced by the popularity of the necked string instruments in the ninth century as well as by the later advent of the bow. If all the strings on an instrument were to be sounded simultaneously the absence of a bridge was no problem. However, if only a single string was to be sounded, a curved bridge was necessary. Moreover, if a string toward either side of the bridge was to be bowed, the bridge had to be high enough so that the bow hair would not rub against the body of the instrument. Although the "waisted" shape of necked string instruments in which the sides of the resonator box are indented was in use before the introduction of the bow into western Europe, this feature greatly facilitated bowing, so that in time the waisted shape came to be encountered more and more in depictions of bowed string instruments. Both of these modifications, the raised bridge and the waisted shape, would have considerably altered the sonority of the instruments to which they were applied. All these string instruments continued to be plucked as they had been before the arrival of the bow.

The second event so decisive for the evolution of musical instruments in western Europe was the Crusades of the twelfth and thirteenth centuries. New instruments spread across Europe at this time, and thereafter certain features became standardized and certain basic types became established and accepted by the thirteenth century.

Foremost among the new bowed string instruments introduced at this time is the *fiddle*, which is first seen in Byzantine illustrations from the eleventh century. It was introduced into western Europe by troubadours traveling on trading routes through Byzantium on their way back from the East and by armies returning from the Crusades. The fiddle is depicted in a bewildering variety of forms and shapes—oval, elliptical, rectangular, and even spade-shaped, a type that was common in southern Europe. The bodies were often waisted for flexibility of bowing. The back of the fiddle may have been slightly rounded and, like the sides, was probably made out of hardwood, while the flat soundboard was probably of softwood. Soundholes were variable but C-shaped holes, one on either side of the strings, were most common in northern Europe.

The instruments are normally shown with five strings but could have anywhere from two to six, and their grouping indicates that they were strung in double courses. The strings were tensioned on tuning pegs inserted at right angles into a flat or concave pegholder or laterally into a sickle- or scroll-shaped pegholder bent back at a sharp angle to the fingerboard and secured at the lower end by a stringholder, a tailpiece, or endpins. In early depictions of the fiddle, a fingerboard is often absent, but on those with a bridge, the fingerboard is generally in evidence. If the bridge is straight, the strings must be tuned in consonant intervals in order to sound a concord when bowed together, but with a curved bridge, various different tunings are possible. In southern Europe, the fiddle was commonly held downward in the player's lap or on his knee with an underhand grip of the bow, but in the north it was usually held against the chest or shoulder with an overhand grip.

By the mid-thirteenth century the large fiddle, with an oval or elliptical body, flat back, and separate neck, had become the most common type. It is believed that up to this time the back and sides were carved out of a single piece of wood with a separate belly consisting of a thin piece of softwood but that thereafter the body was more and more frequently made of several pieces of wood. The thinner back and sides would have lightened the instrument considerably and rendered it more resonant. Skin bellies were common in the fiddles from the Iberian Peninsula but not popular in northern Europe, probably because skin did not hold its tension in the damp northern climate and produced a duller sound. At this time the bridges were more often curved and fingerboards more frequently carried frets, probably made of lengths of gut tied tightly around the neck. The frets were not indicators of finger placement for the player; rather, they altered the sound from the soft-edged tone of the unfretted stopped string to the hard-edged bite of the fretted stopped string.

During the same period, there appeared an increasing variety of bow sizes and shapes—long and thin to short and thick, almost straight to semicircular. The type of bow adopted in any particular case was probably dictated by the shape of instrument and bridge or by the type of music to be played (long bow for drones or slow-moving music, short bow for faster music). Short bows were probably more rigid and therefore of fixed arc, so that the tension of the hairs had to be regulated by the fingers or by a tensioning device. The greater arc of longer bows was probably maintained by the tautly stretched hairs, so that no tensioning beyond that maintained by bow arc was required.

The earlier lura and rabāb types continued to be in use during this period, both bowed and unbowed, waisted and unwaisted, but mainly in southern Europe. Both instruments contributed to the development of the traditional European *rebec* (often called *rubeba* or *rubible*) during the twelfth century. The rebec appeared in its established form late in the thirteenth century and by the fourteenth century had become firmly established in northern Europe. Like its immediate ancestors, the rebec was pear-shaped, had a vaulted back, and was carved out of a solid piece of wood, with little or no demarcation between body and neck. However, it was considerably narrower to facilitate bowing, and its body was more rounded at the bottom. The rebec, like the fiddle, was a versatile instrument that could play drone parts as accompaniment to a played or sung melody, or a fast-moving melodic part.

Various plucked string instruments appear in sources at the same time. The use of the plucked rebec, or *mandora*, indicates that players sounded their instruments according to their preference, some bowing and some plucking. The *citole* closely resembled the mandora but had a flat back. The *vihuela de mano* was at this time confined to the Iberian Peninsula. It was a waisted instrument, often with angular shoulders and a flat back, plucked with a plectrum. Elsewhere in Europe, a pear-shaped instrument of larger dimensions than the mandora was in common usage. The *gittern*, the northern European equivalent of the southern guitar, appears more and more frequently in sources in the course of the twelfth century. In its construction, the wing-shaped shoulders of the body betray its descent from the ancient Greek kithara, while the gradual deepening of the sides toward the base of the neck relates it to the citole. It was a massively built instrument, constructed from a single slab of wood. The gradual deepening of the body toward the neck end continued through the neck itself. A hole cut laterally through the length of the massive neck served to lighten the instrument and enable the left hand to grip the instrument and play on the fingerboard. A flat pegbox in early instruments gave way to one turned back, frequently terminating in an animal's head in which the tuning pegs were inserted laterally, as in the lute. The strings were arranged in three or four courses, either single or double. The gittern, like other plucked string instruments, is often depicted (with the harp and also with the fiddle) accompanying dancers.

The harp in its earlier form continued throughout the thirteenth and fourteenth centuries, although the soundbox had increased somewhat in size. But in the second half of the thirteenth century a new harp came into use. It was a far heavier instrument with a strongly curved forepillar, arched neck, and massive soundbox whose dimensions increased greatly toward its base. Although this instrument seems to have first appeared in England and become the domain of Irish harpists (hence the later references to it as the "Irish" harp), it is not clear where it first developed. The *Irish harp* is often supplied with "brays," L-shaped pegs by which the strings are attached to the belly and at the same time are in light contact with the strings, thus producing a buzzing sound. The number of strings runs from about a dozen to as many as two dozen in the Irish harp.

String instruments such as the lute and psaltery appear commonly in the thirteenth-century sources without noticeable changes in construction, except that around 1300 the pig's-head shape of the psaltery became predominant in northern Europe. Soon after the arrival of the fiddle in western Europe, the organistrum was adapted to it, enabling it to be played by a single person by means of a sliding key bar. The wheel was now turned by one hand while the other stopped the string. It is this adaptation of the organistrum, commonly called the *symphonie,* that evolved into the *hurdy-gurdy.*

Both the bowed lyre (or rotta) and the rebec, which disappear mysteriously from sources for some time, suddenly reappear in the second half of the fourteenth century. The fiddle still appears commonly in various shapes but seems to be growing larger, showing a bias toward lower pitches, just as the rebec did toward higher pitches. The lute continued on with its now standard ovoid shape, highly vaulted back, and narrow fingerboard, but one carved rose in the middle of the soundboard had become normal. The psaltery, now established in the pig's-head shape, began at about this time to be played with two light beaters. This hammered psaltery, or *dulcimer,* seems to have developed first in Germany. Except for more widely separated strings to allow for the heads of the beaters, it varied little from the normal psaltery.

A new bowed string instrument that appeared in the mid-fifteenth century was the *tromba marina,* a derivative of the monochord. It was a long, narrow resonating box with frets, over which a small number of strings, normally two, were stretched between bridges at either end. Fingered and bowed in much the same way as other bowed string instruments, it was well suited to playing drone parts.

Certainly the most important development among the string instruments at this time was the advent of stringed keyboard instruments. Since early plans and depictions of these instruments from the first half of the fifteenth century show them to have been already quite advanced in their construction, they must have developed in the previous century. There are many references to an instrument, the *chekker,* from the fourteenth century. This mysterious instrument, for which only a description and a set of drawings from the fifteenth century survive, was singled out as favored by the nobility.

Depictions from the first half of the fifteenth century show two other keyboard instruments. One of these closely resembles a monochord with a larger number of strings, to which a keyboard mechanism has been fitted along one of the long sides, parallel to the strings. That this early *clavichord* is referred to earlier in sources as the *monacordys* confirms that it was an adaptation of the monochord. The inner end of each key carries a metal tangent that projects upward from the end of the key. The keys are balanced over a fulcrum, so that when the outer end is depressed, the inner rises, bringing the tangent into contact with the string directly above it. The portion of the string to the right of the tangent is set in motion (the portion to the left is damped by a felt strip) and remains sounding until the key is released. Each of a number of double strings all tuned at the unison could be struck by the tangents of several keys singly. Each tangent touched its double string at a different point along its length, so that each key obtained a different pitch. The early clavichord differed from the monochord only in that with more than one string and a keyboard mechanism, it could play a succession of pitches quickly and could produce two or more pitches simultaneously so long as none of the intervals was smaller than a third.

At the same time there began to appear depictions of greatly enlarged psalteries that were too bulky to be held by the player and so were laid on a table. These instruments, adapted by the addition of a keyboard, appear to have been the first *harpsichords.* Their strings run parallel to the keys, away from the player instead of at right angles to the keys as in the clavichord, and each key is provided with its own string. The strings of the harpsichord are plucked by quills, instead of being struck by tangents as in the clavichord. When the key is depressed, a thin jack attached to the inner end of the key rises and passes between two adjacent strings. As it does so, the quill projecting at right angles to the jack plucks one of the strings. The quill is attached to the jack by a hinged tongue so that when the key is released it can return to its original position. The harpsichord at this time was a relatively large instrument, so that smaller *spinets* and *virginals* seem to have been later adaptations. Although the player did not have the same control over the strings as with the clavichord, the harpsichord's volume was greater, and it was more thoroughly polyphonic, since each key had its own string.

In the late fifteenth and early sixteenth centuries, decisive changes occurred in certain of the string instruments. This is particularly true of the lute, which at about this time adopted its classical Renaissance shape. The new lute was less ovoid and more pear-shaped than its predecessor. The back was somewhat less vaulted, and the highest point of the vaulting occurred not at the midpoint of the back but much lower down, just above the bridge. In addition, the neck of the new instrument was wider, to allow for a greater number of strings. A bass string course was added to the five courses of the older instrument, and the courses were doubled to give twelve strings. In the second half of the fifteenth century, the plectrum began to be discarded and the fingers were used to pluck the strings, so that polyphonic playing became more important. In its new form, the lute began to be identified as a courtly instrument for the playing of more cultivated, often serious music, both abstract solo music and song accompaniments. Thus, a repertoire especially for the lute grew up and began to appear in print.

The lute's counterpart among plucked string instruments was the *cittern*, played not with the fingers but with a plectrum. The small wings at the root of the neck derive from the gittern, and the tapering of the body toward the bottom and its general shape come from the citole. By the sixteenth century the gittern, like the lute, had six double courses of strings made not of gut but of wire, thus staying in tune longer. The frets were fixed and made of brass, since gut frets like those on the lute would have been cut through by the cittern's wire strings.

By the sixteenth century, the *guitar*, a Spanish instrument that had developed from the vihuela de mano, was becoming popular all over Europe. The earlier guitars had narrower, deeper, and slightly more waisted bodies than the vihuela. They were gut-strung for ordinary playing and wire-strung for playing with a plectrum, and were much louder than the lute.

An important development during this period was the growing use of chromaticism. Some instruments, such as the diatonic psaltery, had died out by about 1500, presumably because they could not play chromatic music. The clavichord and harpsichord soon acquired their traditional shorter chromatic keys, probably early in the fifteenth century. A second row of strings was added to many harps to enable them to play chromatic music.

Two new bowed string instruments appeared quite suddenly during the last quarter of the fifteenth century and soon came to a position of predominance. These were the prototypes for the bowed string instruments in the modern orchestra—the *viol* and the *violin*. The large, waisted fiddles held downward in the lap or between the legs and bowed underhand, which are depicted during the twelfth century, are often referred to as medieval viols. Rebecs had also been held downward in the lap and bowed underhand, but this method of playing seems to have died out in Europe by the early fourteenth century except in Spain, where rebecs continued to be played in this way. The new Renaissance viol appeared suddenly in the last quarter of the fifteenth century, the result of the application of Spanish rebec-playing technique to a new bowed instrument directly derived from the Spanish vihuela. This early Spanish viol had many of the features of the later, standardized form of the instrument—the same tenor size, fretted fingerboard, laterally inserted tuning pegs, central rose, C-shaped soundholes on either side of the strings—but the shape was closer to that of the vihuela, with its depth of body, flat belly and back, noticeably angular shoulders, and extremely long, narrow neck. By the early sixteenth century the body of the instrument had become deeper and had acquired a slightly arched belly, sloped shoulders, and a shorter, wider neck. The back, although still flat, bent in at the upper end toward the neck. At this time, the instrument had neither bass bar nor sound post, so that it had a thinner, more nasal sound than that of the baroque viol. Viols were almost always played in consort and, like lutes, were courtly, cultivated instruments. They were often taken up by amateurs, among them members of royalty. It is the bass member of the family from which the modern string bass is descended.

The culminating point in the long development of the medieval fiddle was the *lira da braccio*. Like the violin, this instrument had deeply inward-curving waists, rounded shoulders, slightly arched belly and back, S-shaped soundholes on either side of the bridge, and an unfretted fingerboard. However, the bottom of the body had rounded corners, and the pegs were inserted into a flat pegholder. Also, unlike the violin, the lira da braccio normally had seven strings, five running over the fingerboard and two drone strings along the side of the neck. It was once thought that the lira da braccio was the ancestor of the violin because they are so similar in appearance, but it has been established that early prototypes of the violin were in existence at the same time as the lira da braccio. As the early violin developed, it clearly derived many of its features from the lira da braccio and combined them with certain features of the rebec (the smoothly rounded sides at the bottom of the body and tuning pegs inserted laterally into a scroll-shaped pegholder), to produce an instrument that would satisfy the need for a treble instrument combining volume with agility. The viol, in contrast, was a large instrument with a softer sound, whose underhand method of bowing did not allow for such agile execution. The violin originally had three strings like the contemporary rebec but a larger, lira da braccio–sized body. However, it adopted its classical form in an astonishingly short time. Like the rebec and unlike the viol, the violin was a somewhat rustic instrument. With its louder sound, it appeared in the fields and taverns, and its use at feasts, dances, and other entertainments is widely documented.

WIND INSTRUMENTS

Like the string instruments, the few wind instruments in use in the early Middle Ages seem to represent remnants of classical antiquity. The *panpipe* consisted of a row of unholed flutes of cylindrical bore stopped at the lower end so that each would produce a different pitch. A melody was played by moving the mouth from one flute to another along the row. Panpipes were constructed from a series of tubes secured in a wooden case or a row of graduated bores in a single piece of wood. Short, open-ended *end-blown flutes* of cylindrical bore and four or five fingerholes along the length of the tube were common wind instruments of the period. As with panpipes, the air column was set vibrating by blowing air through a duct in the closed end of the tube. These end-blown duct flutes were constructed of cane, wood, or bone. Other wind instruments are depicted in iconographical sources from this period, but they cannot be identified with any degree of certainty. They may be reed instruments like the *bladder pipes*, which are seen later, or chanters or drones, like those employed later in the *bagpipe*.

Two types of *horn* commonly appear in depictions at this time. One is a short, curved instrument with fingerholes, probably made out of cow or goat horns. These were melody instruments and were hand-stopped to lower the pitch. The second type is a very long, curved instrument of conical bore without fingerholes, slightly flared at the open end; this instrument, known as a *beme,* was employed ceremonially for signals and fanfares. Most are so long and flare so widely that they cannot have been fashioned from animal horns. Often shown with bands possibly holding joints together, they were probably constructed from wood or metal. Very short horns from the period were also *signal horns,* used both for the hunt and on the battlefield. Some courtly instruments of this type made from elephant tusks and used for ceremonial or symbolic purposes still survive. All these signal horns were capable of only a few notes and were not intended for musical performance.

The *organ* had been used since Roman times, and the earliest sources, from the tenth century, indicate that it was exclusively a church instrument. The early organ was quite a large instrument in which bellows operated by the feet of organ blowers supplied air to flue pipes of various lengths. From descriptions of some really large organs—the one in Winchester in the tenth century, for example—it would appear that some organs had multiple ranks of pipes. All the pipes associated with one note sounded together, so that only full organ (with all ranks sounding) was possible. Sliders were pulled out to allow air into the pipes and pushed in to cut off the air supply, so that organ music at this time must have been slow-moving, either drone parts accompanying singing or simple signals. An illustration from the eleventh or twelfth century showing an instrument with a range of a diatonic octave would indicate that these early instruments had a limited compass.

As was the case with string instruments, a number of new wind instruments spread to western Europe from the Middle East during the Crusades to become strongly established by the twelfth to thirteenth centuries. One of the most important of these was the *shawm*, which is derived from the North African *ghaita* and Persian *surnā*. The shawm was a double-reed instrument, had a tube of conical bore pierced by fingerholes and a sharply flaring bell, and was made of a single piece of hardwood. Its mouthpiece consisted of three detachable parts—the staple, the pirouette, and the reed. The staple was a narrow, tapering brass tube that was inserted into the top of the bore. Over the staple was placed a vase-shaped wooden lip rest, the pirouette, with a cavity into which the top end of the staple protruded slightly. The reed was pushed onto this protruding tip of the staple. Since the player's pursed lips did not grip the reed (as in the modern oboe) but rested on the top of the pirouette, so that the freely vibrating reed was pouched in the mouth, the shawm could be blown at loud volume for a long time without fatigue. The use of the shawm in courtly and civic music, along with drums and trumpets, mirrors a Turko-Arab practice adopted in Italy at the time of the Fifth Crusade, early in the thirteenth century.

From early times, non-European cultures seem to have adopted various labor-saving devices for setting reeds in vibration with wind from a reservoir holding air under pressure supplied by the player's lungs. The simplest device was to breathe in through the nose, use the cheeks as an air reservoir, and blow out through the mouth. The difficulty in this method lay in maintaining a constant, steady air pressure. Another method adopted was to enclose the reed in a small reservoir in the form of a bladder, into which the player blew. Such *bladder pipes*, often supplied with chanters, can be seen in illustrations from the thirteenth century. The most satisfactory method by far was to attach around the mouthpiece of a reed instrument a bag made of an animal's stomach, to which air was constantly supplied through a tube. Using a larger bag as an air reservoir made playing far easier and eliminated the possibility of fluctuation in air pressure and the inevitable changes in pitch it caused. It seems probable that these bagged shawms and single-reed instruments were invented in the Middle East, because shawmlike instruments with and without bag attached are still played there. Illustrations of *bagpipes* in Spanish sources from the mid-thirteenth century depict instruments far more advanced and sophisticated than the primitive instruments of similar design from parts of Europe outside the orbit of Middle Eastern influence. The earliest bagpipes seem to have been without drone pipes, but later there appeared long conical drone pipes resembling trumpets or cylindrical drone pipes, either singly or in different lengths. These usually issued vertically out of the top of the bag, often resting on the player's shoulder. Sometimes the drones shared a common stock, a block with holes through it to which the outlet of the bag was attached, with the chanter, the fingered reed pipe of the instrument.

The end-blown duct flute described earlier continued into this period as the most popular type of flute. Two such instruments were often bound together side by side. They were blown at the same time, with one flute fingered by each of the player's hands, and could thus produce two different pitches simultaneously. Triple duct flutes also appear, although less commonly. Here, the third flute was unholed and acted as a drone pipe. Another type of end-blown duct flute, the *tabor pipe,* emerged at about this time. It soon became by far the commonest flute of its type in Europe. It had only three fingerholes located toward the open end of the pipe, two on the top for the first two fingers and one on the back for the thumb. Since the tabor pipe was of narrow bore, it could easily be overblown to obtain harmonics, and so, despite having so few fingerholes, it could still play all the notes of the diatonic scale plus a few chromatic notes. The tabor pipe was played with the fingers of the left hand while the right hand played on a small drum with a beater, the *tabor* (see below). This combination was the basic dance band from the thirteenth century onward.

Another type of flute, the *transverse,* or *side-blown, flute,* appears occasionally during this period. It was a relatively long tube of cylindrical bore open at one end with six fingerholes and an embouchure hole in the side in line with the fingerholes but near the closed end. It was the ancestor of the modern transverse flute.

The first depictions of a long, straight trumpet appear late in the eleventh century. These were the *būq* of the Saracen and the *nafīr* of the Moorish armies. This trumpet was never made in one piece but was constructed of sections of metal tubing. Decorative bosses strengthened the metal at the ends of these sections of tubing. The bore of these instruments was slightly conical and had a sudden flaring at the end, terminating in a wide bell. These were the imposing instruments of state of Moslem armies and became popular at once in European armies. The only other instruments of the trumpet family depicted with any frequency in the sources from this period are the shorter fingerhole horn and the short hunting horn.

Two types of small organ appear in the thirteenth century, the *portative* and the *positive organs*. The portative organ was small enough that it could be carried easily, usually supported by a strap over the player's shoulder, or placed in the player's lap when he was sitting. It usually carried a single rank of up to a dozen or so pipes. The bellows, either modified domestic bellows or more refined clapper bellows, fit onto the base of the instrument and were operated by the left hand while the right hand depressed the keys. The positive organ, a larger instrument, could be moved but not carried easily and was normally placed on a table. One person pumped a pair of bellows while another played on the keyboard with both hands. It usually had a single rank of pipes arranged in two rows, providing a range of two or more octaves. Both types of smaller organ were commonly provided with two long bass pipes at the treble end of the rank of pipes. These were probably drone pipes that were opened to sound not by depressing a key but by some sort of lever device. By the late fourteenth century the positive organ had grown in size, probably in order to accommodate two or possibly more ranks of pipes and the extra bellows and wind chests necessary for the added wind supply this necessitated. Some depictions show two ranks of pipes with only a single keyboard where the different ranks would be operated by stops, as in large church organs.

As for large church organs, the period from 1100 to 1450 was one of great activity as more organs were acquired in monastic churches in western Europe. The keyboard of spring-controlled or balanced keys, which made the smaller organs possible, was almost certainly applied to the larger instruments, probably by the twelfth century. Some depictions suggest that this keyboard had only one accidental for B-flat; others, that it had a twelve-note chromatic octave to allow the organ to be played in a number of different keys. Although reports of large organs in certain churches exist, they lack detailed descriptions and illustrations. By the end of the thirteenth century, organs had invaded the cathedral churches, where they were placed either on screens (as in England) or on an upper wall, but always near the choir. In late-fourteenth-century illustrations, organs are depicted with large bass bourdon pipes placed at the side of the instruments; they may have been played by a separate keyboard or even by pedals. After the middle of the fifteenth century, organs appeared with a second keyboard, used to operate different ranks of pipes. Ranks of pipes could now also be played separately or in various combinations, operations made possible by the stop. Each stop was connected to sliders by levers, and when the stop was drawn, these sliders, strips of wood pierced by holes, moved laterally so that the holes would coincide with the feet of the pipes in a given rank and allow the air from the windchests to enter the pipes. The greater number of windchests and bellows in these organs maintained the air pressure and large volume of wind required. In addition to retaining its earlier functions of signaling and providing drone accompaniments, the organ was now rendered more agile by the addition of the new type of keyboard, so that besides supporting slow-moving tenor parts, it may well have been used in the polyphonic treatment of sequences and the *Te Deum,* as later evidence would indicate. By the late thirteenth century, the organ probably alternated with the choir in mass settings.

Late in the fourteenth century, the tabor pipe and the two-handed end-blown duct flute continued much as before. Around this time, a longer end-blown duct flute with a beaked mouthpiece and small bell joint appeared. It had a thumbhole and seven fingerholes and was quite clearly the *recorder* in its earliest form. The small shawm described above remained the most common size, but by the mid-fifteenth century and probably earlier, the larger alto, tenor, and bass shawm had appeared.

What would seem to be a new reed instrument, the *hornpipe,* emerged in the mid-fifteenth century. It consisted of a cylindrical pipe along which fingerholes were bored. A single cane reed, like that used in the drone of the bagpipe, was inserted into the top end of the pipe, and a horn bell at the lower end projected the sound. The reed was enclosed by a smaller horn bell that served as a wind cap. The player blew into this wind cap, setting the reed vibrating without actually taking it into his mouth, as with the shawm, so that the reeds had a longer life without their playing characteristics undergoing any major alteration.

Both shawm and single-reed bagpipes continued into this period. Double-pipe instruments appear with one pipe played by each hand. It was during the fifteenth century that the bagpipe underwent a process of differentiation into the various national types of the instrument — English, Irish, Scottish, Flemish, and so on.

The *long trumpet,* still in common use, was unwieldy because of its extreme length, particularly when the player was walking in a procession. Trumpet makers thus began to bend these long trumpets, first folding them into S-shapes and later, into the more closely folded, flattened loop of the modern trumpet—with a middle yard connected by U-bends to the bell and mouthpiece yards. Sometimes the instrument was bent in continuous curves to produce a helical rounded shape. This instrument combined all the advantages of the long instrument, which could play at least up to the eighth and probably to the twelfth harmonic, with the convenience of the shorter but more acoustically limited horns. Thus it was that certain players developed the *clarino* technique of playing the high harmonics, possibly as early as the fifteenth, but certainly by the sixteenth, century.

Around the time the long trumpet was being bent, the *slide trumpet* was developed with a shanked mouthpiece that telescoped inside the first length of tubing to allow the instrument's length to be altered while it was being played. This type of instrument was used particularly by tower watchmen for the playing of hymns and also for the playing of higher parts of church music.

In the early Renaissance, there was a trend for musical instruments, especially the winds, to be made in families. At first, only two or three different sizes appeared, but through the sixteenth century the number increased steadily. In the late fifteenth and early sixteenth centuries, the transverse flute and recorder both added family members of different sizes. The recorder gradually developed its typical Renaissance form, with slightly beaked mouthpiece and gently flared bell. The longer instruments of the lower ranges required a key mechanism to extend the reach of the little finger in closing the hole closest to the open end of the instrument. To protect the key mechanism against damage, the keys were enclosed in a wooden capsule *(fontanelle)* pierced by a number of small holes. In very long instruments like the *bass* and *contrabass,* more than one key was required, and a bent crook with mouthpiece attached was necessary for blowing the instrument. The different sizes of shawm emerged during the same period, so that by the late sixteenth century shawms from descant to contrabass were in use. The key with *fontanelle* seems to have been added not only to the longer shawms but also to the shorter, and the bent crook of the longer recorders was also used.

The wind-cap principle discussed above in connection with the horn-pipe was applied at this time to new instruments. The most important of these was undoubtedly the *crumhorn (krummhorn).* That this instrument derived from the earlier bladder pipe discussed above is clear not only from its characteristic shape, with the gradual upward curve in the last third of the pipe's length, but also from the adaptation of the bladder into a widening of the bore to form a capsule enclosing the double reed. The bore of the crumhorn is cylindrical, not conical as in the shawm, and the reed is enclosed in a wind cap, so that it produces a buzzing sound rather than the loud, piercing tone of the shawm. The crumhorn, because of its cylindrical bore, could not be overblown, so its range was limited to one note over an octave. The wind cap was also applied to the shawm to produce an instrument called the *Rauschpfeife*. Later depictions of this instrument show it to have a more gradually flaring bell than the shawm. This instrument must have been relatively uncommon, for it appears only infrequently in sources from the period.

The long bass instruments of the wind families, even with the addition of crook and keys, were difficult and unwieldy to hold and play. One theory has it that the *curtal* was invented to avoid the difficulty of holding and playing the bass and contrabass shawms. The curtal is a double-reed instrument, like the shawm, in which two conical bores are drilled down one piece of wood so that the length of the bore is effectively bent back on itself, thus decreasing the length of the instrument by half. Others argue that the tone of the curtal is different from that of the shawm and that it should therefore be considered on its own as an independent instrument. Certainly, it is seen in smaller (*dulzian*) and larger (*fagott*) sizes. It is from the curtal that the modern *bassoon* developed.

The long trumpet seems to have diversified by the early sixteenth century into three fairly distinct types. These were the *field* (or *military*) *trumpet* with a wide bore; a longer instrument of noticeably narrower bore (*clareta*), the more cultivated instrument of the professional musician; and the *tower trumpet*, often a slide trumpet used by town musicians. The first two folded in overlapping (loop) shape, while the third was in the older S-shape. The military trumpet was used mainly for sounding signal calls on the battlefield and for fanfares and processional music. During the Renaissance, trumpet ensembles with drums were a symbol of a sovereign's importance, and large numbers of instruments were assembled. Because of the professional player's ability to reach higher and higher up through the harmonics, lipping the discordant ones into tune, the clareta was fast becoming a fully melodic instrument.

The slide trumpet was not agile enough to play fast melodies because the whole weight of the instrument had to be slid out and in, its extendability was limited by the player's reach, and the mouthpiece often wobbled as a result of the sliding action. These problems were solved by refolding the S-shaped tower trumpet so that the bell crook was lower down toward the bell and by making the whole of the mouthpiece section of the S-curve a telescopic slide by which the player could lengthen the tube. This slide mechanism allowed the instrument to play all notes, diatonic and chromatic, absolutely in tune as in the modern slide trombone. This improved slide trumpet, or *sackbutt,* is first mentioned and depicted in sources in the second half of the fifteenth century. Unlike the trumpet mouthpiece, which was flatter and smaller in diameter, the sackbutt mouthpiece had a hemispherical cap, a wide, sharp-angled throat, and a large diameter. The sackbutt also appears in different sizes in the sixteenth century, the larger bass size being equipped with a handle to allow the greater extension of the slide required.

Cornetts, descendants of the older fingerhole horn described earlier, were made of wood or ivory. There were two types—the *mute cornett,* a straight instrument with an integral conical mouthpiece, and the traditional *curved cornett,* with a detachable mouthpiece. The curved instrument could play softly or loudly; the mute cornett was always quiet in sound. Various sizes, from the *cornettino* down to *contrabass,* were made, the large sizes usually in serpentine shape. The cornett was the great virtuoso wind instrument during the Renaissance and, because it sounded remarkably like the human voice, was often used along with the sackbutt, to double various choral parts.

Although the short horn was used in all periods, the helically coiled horn came to the fore in the sixteenth century. Its mouthpiece was conical and less shallow than that of the trumpet, and its conical bore flared strongly toward the end to terminate in a much wider bell. Because of the more and more elaborate ceremony surrounding the hunt, these long coiled horns, which could play up to the eighth harmonic, were required.

PERCUSSION INSTRUMENTS

The percussion instruments depicted most frequently in the earliest Western sources are *cymbals* and *bells.* Cymbals were of two types—small cymbals attached to the fingers by leather thongs, one pair per hand, and larger cymbals closely resembling the Greek and Roman cymbals of antiquity. The latter were flat or hemispherical and played horizontally, one held in each hand. Cymbals were also mounted on tong clappers and played with one pair held in each hand. Bells were made of either brass or bronze cast into squared or rounded beehive shapes. Larger hand bells were shaken, one in each hand of the player, and tiny pellet bells could be attached to sticks in a cluster for use as rhythm instruments or attached to domestic animals or jesters' costumes to add to the noise. It is thought that the larger hand bells were used not only as general percussion instruments but also specifically as signaling instruments in the church.

The only depictions of drums from this early period show hourglass-shaped instruments suspended horizontally from a strap around the player's neck. Both open ends were covered with skin and were beaten by the bare hands. Another drum, the *tabor*, first makes its appearance in iconographical sources from the thirteenth century and is the most commonly depicted percussion instrument in later sources. It was a small, cylindrical side drum with a snare. The snare consisted of a length of gut strung across the front drumhead, which made a buzzing sound when the tabor was struck. The front and back drumheads were held on the frame by rope running from drumhead to drumhead. Leather buffs could be slid down each end of the rope to tighten the drumheads. In some depictions the beaters (short sticks) appear to have padded leather-wrapped tips. Normally, the tabor was beaten with the right hand while the left played on the tabor pipe, but large military tabors were beaten with both hands. As stated earlier, the pipe and tabor combination formed the basic dance band of the period.

Two other drums in use at this time, the *nakers* (*naqāra*) and the *timbre,* were brought back from the Middle East during the Crusades. The nakers, a small kettledrum, was widely used during the Middle Ages. Normally, two nakers were attached side by side and suspended from the player's waist. They were played with rather heavy, club-shaped beaters made of wood. The timbre is the forerunner of the later *timbrel* and the modern *tambourine.* It consisted of a circular wooden frame with a skin stretched across one side. The sides of the frame were pierced by slits holding small metal discs or cymbals that rattled when the drumhead was struck or the instrument was shaken. Like the tabor, the timbre was sometimes fitted with a snare.

The smaller bells and cymbals continued in use much as before, but series of bells graduated in size, suspended in a row from a frame, and struck by hammers appeared in the thirteenth century. Larger domed cymbals of fixed pitch, like those still in use in the Middle East, also appeared for the first time. In most illustrations they are held horizontally, one in each hand, and clashed vertically. A related instrument that also first appeared at about this time is the *triangle.* It consisted of a metal rod bent into a triangular or trapezoidal shape, often with rings on the lower horizontal bar. It rang when struck by a short metal bar, the rings prolonging the sound in a buzzing jingle.

In the fourteenth and fifteenth centuries percussion instruments remained basically unchanged. The nakers are more often depicted with snares, and there is some pictorial evidence that they, like tabors, could be muffled by means of a cloth fringe. A percussion instrument that appeared for the first time in early-fifteenth-century sources, if infrequently, is the series of *musical bowls* or *standing bells*. A series of graduated metal or glass bowls was set in a row on a table with the open side facing upward and was played with a metal rod, somewhat like *chimes*.

The large *kettledrums*, from which the modern orchestral kettledrums are directly descended, were introduced into the West by the Ottoman Turks during the fifteenth century, when they tried to overrun eastern Europe after their conquest of Constantinople. The Hungarians mounted these drums on horses in front of the saddle, one on each side. Kettledrums had spread to all the courts of western Europe by the early sixteenth century and, with the long military trumpets with which they were inevitably paired, became emblematic of military power. They were the first drums to be tuned to definite pitches, but for this, a more accurate tensioning mechanism was required. To this end, the drumhead was secured between a metal hoop, or collar, and the rim of the kettle. This hoop could be tightened accurately by nuts screwed onto threaded lugs fixed to the side of the kettle.

The early *side*, or *snare*, *drum*, another military drum from the period, is a descendant of the large military tabor and, like its ancestor, was used primarily to set the pace for marching soldiers. The *bass drum*, a very large side drum that also appeared first in the early sixteenth century, is an adaptation of the Turkish *tabl turki*.

The *xylophone* also appeared for the first time during the early sixteenth century. Cylindrical hardwood bars of graduated lengths were mounted on pads of straw tied to wooden struts. The bars were struck by beaters with spherical wooden tips. The earliest depiction shows a xylophone with twenty-five bars and a diatonic range of three octaves.

Less is known about the use of percussion instruments during the period under discussion than about the use of any other group of musical instruments. All that can be said with certainty is that they provided a rhythmic accompaniment for dance and other music.

USE OF THE INSTRUMENTS

Determining the use of the instruments described above poses formidable and even, in some cases, insurmountable problems. To begin with, very little secular music from before the twelfth century has survived, probably because it was largely improvised and aurally transmitted. Further problems are raised by the music that does survive, largely church music. It is so unclear and, at best, ambiguous in its notation that interpreters, both scholars and performers, cannot agree on its decipherment and transcription, let alone its interpretation. For this early music, and even for that written later on, when musical notation became clearer, basic questions as to which instruments played, and what and how they played, cannot be answered with certainty. Musical notation, even when precise, remains a system of shorthand for the player. That which appears on the page serves only as a guide. We know little about practices of improvisation during this period, since these were largely orally transmitted and often, within certain conventions, a matter of personal choice. We can be sure only that what is transmitted on the page is often just a skeleton to be fleshed out by the player and gives only a basic indication of what was actually played.

Up to the sixteenth century, there was little or no explicit indication of the instrumentation for a given piece of music. It is probable that the choice of instruments was relatively free and dictated largely by practical considerations such as the availability of instruments, place of performance, and balancing of sonorities. Parts were doubled freely, depending on the instruments at hand; and parts not written down, such as improvised accompaniments, drones, and percussion parts, were added freely. Instrumentation was "free" in the sense that it was probably also fluid. Instruments might drop in and out during a given performance, and the instrumentation usually changed from one performance to another.

A basic preliminary problem is the accurate reconstruction of these old instruments. It should be clear from the constant qualification adopted in their descriptions above that they were not at all standardized, that players and makers were constantly experimenting and tampering with them, and that their evolution was fluid and constant, moving often in unpredictable directions. Few instruments from before the fifteenth century survive, and those that do are usually damaged or incomplete, or have been altered from their original state by succeeding generations. In period sources, descriptions of instruments, their sound, their uses, and their performance are vague and imprecise, often subjectively colored or even distorted. What is more, it is often impossible to decide exactly what instrument is being referred to, since the nomenclature is often very confusing.

The best record of the physical form of instruments, the method in which they were played, the grouping of various instruments, and the circumstances in which they played is iconographical, painting and sculpture. These depictions, however, also pose problems. Depending on the artist's skill and musical knowledge, the depictions may be far from accurate. Even highly skilled artists may be working from memory instead of from live models or may distort the instruments as demanded by their concept of perspective or to suit the scheme of a given representation. Instruments, their players, and the circumstances of performance may be fancifully depicted to express an allegorical or symbolic theme. Pictorial glosses on biblical passages may give rise to inaccurate representations of actual instruments and to the invention of fictional instruments or artificial groupings of instruments.

If instruments cannot be reconstructed from the records available, how can we determine what they sounded like? Descriptions of their sound are, at worst, fanciful, and, at best, subjective. When instruments do survive, they are often "bad" instruments that are made of more inert materials like ivory and whose sound is not indicative of the instruments played by professionals, which were made of more perishable materials, such as wood. Even in cases where we have a "good" original instrument, the sonority produced now is to a large extent dependent on the player's technique, and we know little about period techniques. One important line of inquiry followed by researchers is to study the instruments and their sonorities; the playing technique and performance practices for known descendants of European art-music instruments; and the instruments of ethnic groups from Europe, North Africa, and the Middle East. But even here, the results not only fail to give a clear picture, but they also raise many questions. Given such obstacles, a discussion of the uses of early instruments must, under the circumstances, be incomplete and, to a high degree, qualified.

Although the records from the early Middle Ages are scanty, the professional musicians par excellence of the period seem to have been the bards and minstrels. They were often itinerant, traveling from one population center to another, but could be resident in a given establishment. The minstrel's role was an important one, for he kept alive the old sagas by his recitations and transmitted news in his lays. Both his recitations and songs were accompanied on lyre, harp, or psaltery. He would have been expected to play several other instruments and fulfill a number of musical functions besides providing accompanied recitation — among them, playing music for ceremonies, providing music for dancing at fairs and in taverns, and singing almost anywhere there were people to listen. Entertainers such as the jongleurs, acrobats, jesters, animal trainers, and jugglers had to be able to play music as part of their activities.

Simple end-blown duct flutes, drums, and cymbals would have figured prominently in such activities. It is not unlikely that a number of minstrels on occasion would have joined forces for large ceremonial spectacles or social gatherings. It seems clear from the sources that such musicians were considered low-class, vulgar, vagabond rogues or social outcasts.

The picture with regard to music in the church is equally hazy during this early period. The organistrum and monochord were used in the training of singers. We have fairly reliable reports of the use of organs in churches from the tenth century, but the role of the instrument is not clear. Organs may have been used for signaling only or for providing an accompaniment to the singing of chant as well. Because of the organ's clumsy mechanism, which depended on sliders, such an accompaniment would have been slow-moving. There is some indication that the organ may not even have been played on ordinary days but only on feast days. In the sources, *organ* and *organistrum* seem to be interchangeable, so that they may have performed much the same role. Bells may also have been used in the church as signaling instruments or for giving the pitch to singers at important points. That other instruments were played in the church at this early date is doubtful.

Both short and long horns were used as signaling instruments on the battlefield. The short horn was also used for sounding signals during the hunt, and special luxurious decorative instruments of this type, often made of ivory, served as ceremonial gifts or possessions among royalty and even as charters or deeds. The long trumpet may have been used in ensembles to perform ceremonial fanfares as well.

The ninth century saw the rise of polyphony and a flood of new instruments into western Europe from Moslem lands. We have much more evidence concerning the use of instruments from iconographical and literary sources.

The new instruments were taken up by the professional minstrels, who, as before, were often unruly, itinerant vagabonds. A new class of professional musician held respectable positions in noble households. Some of these musicians knew how to read music, most learned by rote tunes passed from one musician to another, but all were skilled improvisers. During Lent, when their duties were light, resident professionals often went to minstrelsy schools to improve their playing technique and add to their repertoire. They also often formed part of the noble retinue at state functions or on military campaigns. The art of the minstrels even spread into the noble class with the rise of the aristocratic professionals, the troubadour and the trouvère.

With a much wider variety of instruments available than previously for the performance of music with more than a single part, it is not surprising to see different instruments playing together in small groups. During this period instruments came to be divided into two groups, according to the volume of sound they produced—the *instruments hauts*, or loud instruments, and the *instruments bas*, or quiet instruments. With the exception of percussion and, later, cornett and sackbutt, these groups rarely ever mixed. Among the loud instruments were the shawm, bagpipe with shawm chanter, trumpet, short horn, fingerhole horn, pipe and tabor, and cittern. In the quiet instrument group were the harp, psaltery, fiddle, rebec, lute, portative organ, transverse flute, and bagpipe with single-reed chanter. The end-blown duct flutes, which sounded soft in the lower octave but loud when overblown, were placed in whichever group was appropriate. Percussion instruments were common to both groups. The loud instruments were used mainly for rough outdoor music, the quiet instruments being retained for more refined and intimate purposes indoors. These two divisions were to persist throughout the Renaissance.

In order to illustrate the use of instruments at this time in general, focus can be placed on an important instrument from each of the two groups. Perhaps the principal instrument from the loud group was the shawm. Not only could its piercing nasal sound compete with the trumpet in volume of sound, but it also was agile and highly versatile. It was used for military and courtly processional music, dance music, and street music. As they made their rounds, the watchmen, singly and in groups called *waits*, played on the shawm.

The most important among the quiet instruments, because of their great versatility, were the bowed and plucked string instruments with necks. Perhaps the leading instrument in this group was the fiddle. Much as the lyre and harp had earlier, the fiddle accompanied the singing of epic songs and played incidental music at feasts. Its widespread use in playing dance music—the *estampie, trotta, saltarello,* and *basse dance,* where it played either melody or drone—is documented. In the *basse dance* it may have provided the *cantus firmus.* In monophonic songs the fiddle might play an instrumental solo with or without drones or act as accompaniment to the voice by doubling it at a given interval, by playing parallel to it, by playing heterophonically around it, by droning, or by playing preludes, interludes, or postludes. Early in the period, it may have been used in church to double the voices in organum, conductus, and motet, or even in chant. Later, it might have played one voice in a completely instrumental performance, doubled a sung voice with or without ornamentation, or played a tenor in consort with other instruments and singers. The fiddle also played a prominent role in the incidental music performed in conjunction with liturgical and secular drama, where it is sometimes specifically called for in the text. As one of the quiet instruments, it was often played with other bowed string instruments, such as the rebec, or with plucked string instruments, such as the harp and the psaltery. In thirteenth- and fourteenth-century sources, it is often shown with portative organ or pipe and tabor. As further proof of its great versatility, the fiddle is also often shown with such loud instruments as shawm, bagpipe, or trumpet, not to mention percussion instruments, indicating that with all five strings sounding, it could hold its own in loud company.

The papal prohibition of instruments except for the organ in church during this period suggests that string and wind instruments, along with percussion, had crept into the church and were not easily to be banished. The organ and bells continued in their roles as church instruments but, in this later period, may have doubled vocal lines. The organ's ability to sustain tone may have been used in doubling slow-moving tenors in polyphonic music. Which instruments were prohibited and what they did before being banned remains open to conjecture, but the ban probably extended to all the instruments in the European instrumentarium, and their function in liturgical music was undoubtedly similar to that in the secular sphere.

Some instruments are repeatedly depicted with dancers, suggesting that they were favored in this capacity. These are pipe and tabor, gittern, fiddle, psaltery, and citole. The rebec, with its harsh cutting sound, was a rustic instrument prominent in taverns, at village revels, and in the fields. Its use at feasts, dances, and other social and courtly entertainments is widely documented.

Up to the thirteenth century, wandering minstrels, usually alone but occasionally in groups, constituted the principal force in European music-making. With the rise and growth of towns, the town musician now emerged as an important factor. During the day he sounded from a tower the hours on his instrument, usually a slide trumpet, and also played hymns. At night, making his rounds, he would often play on the shawm to assure the citizenry that their town was being patrolled. These town musicians attracted others to form town bands. To eliminate competition from wandering free-lance musicians, these town bands formed into guilds with restricted membership, regulations, an apprenticeship system, and pensions for retired members. They claimed, and enforced, their right to play on specific occasions. Their expanding functions required that they acquire proficiency not only on the loud instruments, which they had played originally, but also on a variety of other instruments as well. Thus, they were able to provide a group of loud instruments for a large municipal banquet, ceremonial procession, or street parade, or a group of quiet instruments for a small ensemble to play at a more intimate dinner or to accompany dancing.

Sovereigns had begun to retain minstrels in full-time residence at their courts. Later, along with maintaining a trumpet-and-drum corps for military and state occasions, they expanded their domestic, courtly musical establishments as well. These same sovereigns maintained court *capelle* ("chapels"), and although singers were the chief focus of these establishments, instrumentalists were eventually added to the musical staff to support the vocal forces. These musicians also would have performed many of the functions at court that the town bands were responsible for municipally—that is, playing for meals, various festivities, and the sovereign's private pleasure. This is the beginning of the court orchestra, a development of major importance in the evolution of the modern orchestra.

One important facet of the rise of court bands was the personal cultivation of music by the sovereigns themselves. As the ability to play instruments became a matter of cultural education and fashion among the nobility, various instruments took on a new function—that of satisfying the musical aspirations of the cultivated amateur. Certain instruments that acquired a courtly status were the lute, the new viol, and the new keyboard instruments.

Before the concept of homogeneous tone color took hold in the Renaissance, miscellaneous groups of instruments had been employed for ensemble music, chosen primarily on the basis of availability, convenience, and volume of sound produced. In the fifteenth century, different sizes of the same instrument began to be grouped together. Later in the fifteenth century, most of the different sizes, representing the various ranges, had been developed, thus making more instruments available. These families of instruments were grouped together in consorts to produce an evenness and homogeneity of tone color, which replaced the earlier casual mixing of contrasting sonorities. And so it is at this point, with the spread of the consort principle of grouping instruments, a principle so clearly in evidence in the makeup of the modern orchestra, that this chapter in the evolution of the orchestra comes to a close.

BIBLIOGRAPHY

Martin Agricola, *Musica instrumentalis deudsch* (1528; repr. 1896). Anthony Baines, *Woodwind Instruments and Their History* (1963); and, as ed., *Musical Instruments Through the Ages* (2nd ed., 1966). James Blades and Jeremy Montagu, *Early*

Percussion Instruments from the Middle Ages to the Baroque (1976). Alexandr Buchner, *Musical Instruments: An Illustrated History*, Bořek Vančura, trans. (1973).

Frederick Crane, *Extant Medieval Musical Instruments* (1972). Henry George Farmer, *Islam*, Musikgeschichte in Bildern, (n.d.). Gerald R. Hayes, *The Viols and Other Bowed Instruments* (1930; repr. 1969). Jeremy Montagu, *The World of Medieval and Renaissance Musical Instruments* (1976). David Munrow, *Instruments of the Middle Ages and Renaissance* (1976).

Hortense Panum, *The Stringed Instruments of the Middle Ages* (1939). Jean Perrot, *The Organ, from Its Invention in the Hellenistic Period to the End of the Thirteenth Century*, Norma Deane, trans. (1971). Gustave Reese, *Music in the Middle Ages* (1940); and *Music in the Renaissance* (rev. ed., 1959). Mary Remnant, *Music Instruments of the West* (1978). Raymond Russell, *The Harpsichord and Clavichord* (1959).

Curt Sachs, *The History of Musical Instruments* (1940). Johannes Tinctoris, "*De inventione et usu musicae*: Excerpts on Musical Instruments," Anthony Baines, trans., in *Galpin Society Journal*, 3 (1950). Sebastian Virdung, *Musica Getutscht* (1511; repr. 1970). Emanuel Winternitz, *Musical Instruments and Their Symbolism in Western Art* (1967).

Ensemble Music Moves Out of the Private House: Haydn to Beethoven

Michael Beckerman

The late eighteenth century was a period of transition for the orchestra. Fundamental economic and political changes in Europe, which were exemplified and exacerbated by the French Revolution and Napoleonic rule, had severely weakened the absolutist court, the primary institution in which the orchestra had developed, but the modern pattern of symphonic societies with varying mixes of state, private philanthropic, and public subscription support had not yet been established. In tracing the evolution of the orchestra from roughly the middle of the eighteenth century to the early years of the nineteenth, years that spanned all of Haydn's and Mozart's orchestral music and saw the beginnings of Beethoven's, we find little that was actually new in regard to the maintenance and performance setting of the orchestra. Virtually all of the institutions that were to determine the course of orchestral developments in the late eighteenth and early nineteenth centuries already existed in the middle of the eighteenth century, but near its end, new attitudes and political events brought about a significant shift in emphasis in the relative importance of these institutions. The strain between the old Europe and the new was clearly apparent in the fates of many orchestras. A period of tumultuous upheaval in some areas obliterated several orchestras, but a tendency to conservation in other areas resulted in virtual ossification of their orchestras. While beyond the bounds of revolutionary France orchestral music still occurred within the confines of the old institutions, a marked decline in the capacity of those institutions to support orchestras is apparent.

The essential evolutionary direction at this time was, broadly speaking, from private to public, but to suggest these as polarities between which orchestral developments can be traced would be a misrepresentation of the situation, because the distinction was not always clear. Even in the most traditional settings the difference between private and state function was frequently blurred, and the very nature of what constitutes the public in the class-stratified society of the eighteenth century is a complex question. Many orchestras and orchestral musicians also had multiple duties and functions; for example, the same musicians might perform in a sovereign's private chamber, in a court ceremony, and in the opera house. In such circumstances it is frequently difficult to tell where the line between public and private should be drawn.

Before considering the institutional and circumstantial relationships that affected the course of orchestral development in the late eighteenth century, it might be advantageous to list briefly the different settings in which orchestras performed. There were, first of all, the traditional court performances by orchestras whose musicians were in the private employ of a person of nobility. Such musicians were usually considered servants, being bound to the court by contract and more or less completely at the beck and call of the nobleman, who exercised such control that a musician risked imprisonment for even accepting another post without permission. The performances occurred in different places but usually in a large hall in the nobleman's residence, and the listeners were members of the court or the sovereign's invited guests.

A second performance setting was the academy. The term itself had many meanings in the eighteenth century, but it was frequently synonymous with *concert*. Rousseau's *Dictionnaire de musique* defines it as "an assembly of musicians or amateurs to which the French have already given the name *concert*." Even when the term is used in this specific sense, one must recognize that academies varied greatly from locale to locale, but they were in general halfway houses between private, or court, entertainment and public concerts. They flourished in towns, frequently in those in which there was no strong aristocratic social order; in that case, they were organized and supported by the upper bourgeoisie and the lesser nobility, who took great pride in them and considered them their own private means of entertainment. They were in essence private societies of prominent citizens who banded together for musical enjoyment with both music and setting not that different from that of a nobleman's chamber. Usually they were limited to members or subscribers, but occasionally the doors would be opened to all. Far from indicating a movement away from court practice, in many cases the academies represented the upper bourgeoisie's attempts to emulate the nobility.

In most cases it was impossible for the academy to maintain a retinue of professional musicians such as the wealthier courts could. The musical success of the academy was thus dependent upon the services of two types of musicians whose impact was only beginning to be felt in the late eighteenth century: the dilettante and the traveling virtuoso. When a virtuoso arrived in a city or principality, several options were open to his display of talent: he could hope to secure an invitation to perform at court, if such existed, and in the private academies. In addition, he might arrange a concert on his own. Since solo recitals were almost unheard of in the eighteenth century, this usually necessitated the cooperation of local musicians, be they professional or dilettante, to fill out the program and provide the necessary accompaniment, which was almost always an orchestra. An academy frequently provided the necessary organization intact. Regardless of whether the virtuoso concert was organized under the auspices of an academy, it was usually a true public concert, open to anyone with the price of a ticket and promoted with all the public relations know-how available to the eighteenth century.

Another concert setting was provided by the established public concert series. These existed in only a few places, and their concerts were relatively infrequent even where they did exist; but they acquired great prestige and served as a model for later developments. The two chief centers for such concert activity were London and Paris.

The orchestra had two other functions in the eighteenth century—to provide accompaniment for church services and at the opera. Of the two, the latter was by far the more important. This was often the principal function of the court orchestra, and many of the largest and most important orchestras were assembled specifically for that purpose. During the eighteenth century the orchestra assumed a much more prominent role in opera, especially in Germany, and many innovations and experiments in the use of instruments, particularly winds, may be traced to operatic practice. For instance, the first evidence of the orchestral use of the clarinet in France occurs in Rameau's operas *Zoroastre* (1749) and *Acante et Céphise* (1751), whereas Germany may not have encountered the instrument until 1758, when it was introduced at Mannheim. (Some evidence suggests it may have been used earlier in Germany.)

The principal steps in the evolution of the orchestra toward the modern public ensemble in the latter half of the eighteenth century occur primarily in northern Europe—in Europe's three largest cities, Vienna, Paris, and London. There were a number of large orchestras in Italy, particularly in the more prestigious opera houses, but they figure little in the historical development of the orchestral ensemble. Italian composers, interested mainly in the voice, provided only minimal orchestral accompaniment, leaving most of the innovations in scoring to the composers of northern Europe. The performance style in the opera houses was, according to contemporary accounts, loud and rough. As it was necessary for the performers to strain to make themselves heard above the noisy Italian audiences, any hints at subtlety or finesse were generally eschewed. There were exceptions, of course. At an academy in Milan, Charles Burney heard a small orchestra whose performance of Johann Christian Bach's symphonies was comparable to those of orchestras in London. But even Burney, whose prejudices toward Italian music were apparent, found the orchestral playing in the opera houses lacking in cultivation. And well into the nineteenth century, Spohr, Weber, and Berlioz all ridiculed savagely the Italian orchestras.

The general decline of the court orchestra in Germany forms an important chapter in the emergence of the orchestra as a public institution. The prestige and fortunes of German orchestras shifted constantly, reflecting a fluid political situation in which no one of Germany's constituent states was capable of domination. The tangled diplomacy and intermittent warfare of this period, which centered upon central Europe, resembled an extended chess game with one important constant—absolutism. Some rulers were more "enlightened" than others, but in all the German states, power was concentrated in the hands of one individual whose decisions regarding cultural issues were as all-encompassing and unappealable as his political ones.

As alien as this system is to the modern social order, it had considerable advantages for orchestral development, not the least being that a good orchestra could be assembled and, more importantly, maintained. Since an orchestral tradition as such was practically nonexistent before the eighteenth century, the stability necessary to discover the potential inherent in a tightly knit large ensemble, then to develop a musical style that exploited this potential, and finally to evolve and sustain the performance techniques requisite for the effectiveness of large-group playing could be provided only by the continuing long-term commitment of patronage. This was, of course, expensive, and the benefits were relatively intangible, especially when compared with other more obvious symbols of power and prestige, such as a lavish palace or a well-drilled military guard. As Germany was not prosperous in the eighteenth century, the maintenance of an orchestra especially depended upon the enthusiasm of a ruler who could, without having to worry about accountability, concentrate a significant percentage of his area's wealth upon a relatively narrow and seemingly frivolous pursuit.

The most important orchestras at midcentury were the court orchestras at Dresden, Mannheim, Berlin, and Stuttgart. The orchestra of the king of Poland at Dresden was, according to Johann Joachim Quantz, the best in Europe in the early eighteenth century (quoted in Marpurg, 1, 206). After 1734 it was under the overall leadership of Johann Adolf Hasse as kapellmeister, although Johann Georg Pisendel, who assumed the position of concertmeister in 1729, probably deserves much of the credit for its excellence. The division of responsibilities between the kapellmeister, who was primarily a composer and was in charge of vocal as well as instrumental music, and the concertmeister, who as principal violinist provided specific leadership of the orchestra, undoubtedly varied from locale to locale, but in the actual training and development of the ensemble, the role of the concertmeister should not be underrated.

The Dresden orchestra did not survive long as a first-rate ensemble. During the Seven Years' War (1756–1763), Dresden was occupied by Frederick the Great's troops, Saxony was taxed unmercifully to support his war efforts, and the Polish crown became an empty symbol. While the first partition of Poland, which virtually eliminated Poland from the map of Europe, did not occur until 1772, the Dresden court never recovered from the effects of the Seven Years' War, and Saxony permanently lost its place as one of the more important German states. When Burney visited Dresden in 1772, he found the orchestra in ruins, with most of the famous musicians, including Hasse, who went to Vienna in 1764, long since departed.

Nowhere are both the potential and the limitations of absolutism more apparent than in the fate of the orchestra in Stuttgart. Karl Eugen, the duke of Württemberg, and his successors rate as some of the most dictatorial and abusive monarchs in Germany at this time. Karl Eugen was educated at the Prussian court and brought home with him a desire to emulate the musical establishment of Frederick the Great. By offering him a particularly lucrative appointment, Karl Eugen was able to attract Niccolò Jommelli to Stuttgart in 1754 and provide him with the resources to build a great opera with its attendant orchestra. According to eighteenth-century accounts, the musical establishment during the years of Jommelli's direction was considered the finest in Europe. Karl Eugen was a profligate in more than music, however, and his opulent living soon began to have a deleterious effect upon the Württemberg economy. He was finally convinced by one of his mistresses to curtail expenses drastically before he brought the entire realm to ruin. Jommelli, sensing the impending difficulties, departed in 1769, and the Stuttgart court ensemble was drastically reduced. By 1772 it was, in Burney's words, "only a shadow of its former self" (2:36). In his autobiography Ludwig Spohr vividly describes the conditions to which musicians were still subjected in 1807:

> After the court had seated itself at the card tables, the concert began with an overture, followed by an aria ... the card players called out their "I bid," "I pass!" so loudly that nothing much could be heard of the music.... As soon as the King had finished his game, he pushed his chair back and the concert was broken off in the middle of an aria by Madame Graff, the poor lady having to stop with the last note of her cadenza still in her throat.
>
> At the theater, applause was forbidden unless the King himself applauded. The royal family however, because of the winter cold, kept their hands in muffs, and brought them out only when they felt the urge to take a pinch of snuff. At such moments, they also applauded, regardless of what was going on in the theatre.
>
> (pp. 66–67)

Of all the court orchestras in Germany, that which Karl Theodor, elector of the Palatinate, built at Mannheim is probably the most famous. Karl Theodor wished to emulate the court at Versailles just as Karl Eugen wished to emulate that at Berlin, and like Karl Eugen, he was willing to pay the price. And although Karl Theodor was in many ways no less dictatorial, his sincere enthusiasm for instrumental music in particular did much to secure the loyalty of his orchestral employees. As a result, the Mannheim orchestra attracted many outstanding players, and its virtuoso performances became celebrated throughout Europe.

The Mannheim orchestra did not suffer the drastic eclipse that befell the orchestras at Dresden and Stuttgart. In 1778, Karl Theodor became elector of Bavaria, which necessitated a move to Munich. He took his orchestra with him, but the economic and political situation in Munich necessitated some curtailment of expenses. So, while the Munich orchestra inherited the mantle of Mannheim, it lost some of its preeminence and had to await further developments in the nineteenth century to transform it into a modern ensemble.

The court orchestra was no less a doomed institution than eighteenth-century absolutism. This is particularly true of the many orchestras at the smaller courts, which were especially devastated by political change. If the court could withstand the military and political trend toward consolidation, it was usually able to do so only at the price of economic hardship and then usually only temporarily. The fates of four of the more prominent smaller court orchestras in the late eighteenth century may be taken as representative of a pattern that was duplicated many times over.

Kraft Ernst, count of Oettingen-Wallerstein in Bavaria, who took great pride in his ensemble and commissioned several symphonies from Franz Joseph Haydn, died in 1802. His heir, Ludwig, was still a minor, and so Ernst's wife, Countess Wilhelmine Friederike, was appointed regent. In spite of some clever political maneuvering, she could not retain the family estates, and the court underwent a steady economic decline. Most of the musicians had to be released within a year of her assumption of the regency, and in October 1807, she announced "that the entire *Hofmusik*, with the exception of those personnel standing in Livery, are released in order to find in the period of one year other service" (MacDonald, 68–69).

Ernst was lucky. Many of the smaller German courts had entered a period of steady deterioration long before Oettingen-Wallerstein. The dissolution of the Esterhaza orchestra in 1790 reflects similar, though less drastic, problems. Esterhaza had one of the largest incomes in the Austrian empire, yet almost immediately after the death of Prince Nikolaus, the new Esterhazy prince, Anton, released all of the musicians with the exception of the wind band, which was used for the hunt. Haydn and Luigi Tomasini were officially retained, although they no longer had any specific duties at Esterhaza. The move, which could be attributed to Anton's lack of interest in music, was undoubtedly financial. By the late eighteenth century the burden of maintaining a retinue of court musicians was sufficiently onerous that extraordinary interest and commitment on the part of the sovereign were required in order to justify the expense.

The Napoleonic Wars further destroyed many courts, either indirectly through increased economic hardship or directly through forced dissolution. The fate of Beethoven's sovereign in Bonn, Archduke Maximilian Franz, was typical. When the fall of Mainz in October 1792 appeared to jeopardize the entire west-bank area of the Rhine, Maximilian Franz decided to retreat from Bonn. He returned in April 1793, but by 1794 was forced to leave permanently, at which point the Bonn court of the elector of Cologne ceased to exist. The virtual end of the theater and the court orchestra, which was one of the larger ones of Europe, may be dated from Maximilian Franz's first departure in 1792.

Even more dramatic was the sudden end of the orchestra of the elector of Trier, which was located in southwest Germany, near the Luxembourg border. The electors Johann Philipp von Waldersdorff and Clemens Wenzeslaus had built this orchestra up to one of the largest private orchestras in Europe, comprising fifty to sixty players by 1790. A French army entered and pillaged Trier on 9 August 1794, and the entire court, including the orchestra, was permanently dissolved.

That the orchestras of the larger courts of Berlin and Vienna did not suffer the same eclipse as many of the smaller orchestras is attributable less to the greater prestige of these courts than to a combination of other factors: their presence in large urban centers, the multifaceted function of the orchestras, and a change in the nature of the patronage by which they were sustained. As these particular courts evolved into the centers of modern states, the orchestras evolved with them into state orchestras. They were still dependent upon government patronage but existed more within the public sphere, helping to build the cultural symbols by which the state defined itself.

The nature of this new role for the orchestra and the complexity of the relationship between state, public, and private endeavor are best reflected in the activities in the four most important cities of northern Europe: London, Paris, Berlin, and Vienna. Each of these cities was the capital of a powerful state by the late eighteenth century, and each was also a commercial, financial, and industrial center. By 1800, London, with almost a million people, was by far the largest city in Europe, twice the size of Paris, the second-largest city. Vienna and Berlin followed, respectively. All four cities underwent a substantial population increase in the eighteenth century, especially Berlin, which had only approximately twenty-five thousand residents at the end of the seventeenth century.

During the years in which Frederick the Great was crown prince and allowed to maintain his own residence, he assembled a small orchestra. Because of the opposition of Frederick's father, Frederick William I, to Frederick's musical activities, the orchestra performed only instrumental music—excepting an occasional aria—in Frederick's chamber. Once Frederick became king in 1740, he moved quickly to establish a royal opera in Berlin and built one of the largest and most spectacular opera houses in Europe. The orchestra itself was augmented from approximately twenty to forty players, and under the leadership of the Graun brothers—Karl Heinrich as kapellmeister and Johann Gottlieb as concertmeister—it was by midcentury considered the finest in Europe.

The orchestra's principal duty was to perform at the opera. Performances in the opera house were for the most part free and open to the public. When the opera house opened, Frederick had published in the papers a notice that the general public and soldiers would be admitted free, but in practice an invitation was usually required. This obstacle could be gotten around easily, however, the purpose apparently being to keep undesirables out. During the years in which the opera flourished under Frederick's patronage, the opera house was usually full.

The orchestra retained its courtly duties. The opera season lasted only from late November to the end of March, and throughout most of Frederick's lifetime, concerts in his chambers were almost a daily occurrence. Frederick took immense pleasure performing upon the flute, and by all accounts he was highly accomplished. He was also considered a skilled composer. The number of musicians performing with Frederick undoubtedly varied with the music that Frederick wished to play. Adolf Menzel's famous painting of a flute concert at the Sans Souci palace shows approximately a half-dozen instrumentalists accompanying Frederick, but when he wished to have a symphony performed—sometimes his own—the number would almost certainly have been greater.

The orchestra of Frederick the Great thus had both a public and a private function. Mirroring the extent to which Frederick retained despotic power over all aspects of Prussian life, even the public function was still almost completely dependent upon his tastes and whims. In later years, when Frederick was no longer able to perform on the flute, he seems to have lost interest in music in general. The effect this had upon the capital is visibly apparent; as Helm states, "Music in Berlin stagnated as the King lost his ability to perform adagios." The most obvious effect was upon the opera. In the last two decades of Frederick's life, little money was appropriated for the opera, the result being the recycling of costumes and productions and the employment of singers who were either past their prime or second-rate. The audiences were so sparse that Frederick would order entire companies of soldiers to attend simply in order to keep the theater warm. The resultant atmosphere was hardly conducive to inspirational performance.

The decline of the Prussian musical establishment began with the Seven Years' War, which in some ways was as hard on the conquerer as the conquered. Frederick was absent from Berlin most of that time, and the city was occupied briefly by Russian and Austrian troops. The war put a great strain on the Prussian economy, and Frederick was never as willing afterward to support his musical ensembles. Frederick's innate conservatism became more pronounced in his later years, and by the 1770s the Berlin orchestra was considered out of fashion, particularly in its lack of dynamic nuance and variety. Frederick made some attempt to revive his sagging musical establishment with the appointment of J. F. Reichardt as kapellmeister in 1776 and insisted that the orchestra be carefully rehearsed, but his steadfast refusal to allow the repertoire to be modernized resulted in an increasing sense of frustration in Reichardt, who took refuge in more and more extended leaves of absence. That Frederick allowed Reichardt's absences at all indicates the extent to which he was losing interest in his musical activities.

When combined with Frederick's conservatism and waning interest, the security of a state appointment, which originally had done much to ensure the stability of personnel necessary to allow the development of a unified ensemble, had an adverse effect upon the orchestra by the 1780s. Many of the better players had departed, and according to C. F. Cramer, those who were left were old and past their prime. In the meantime, other musical developments, particularly the new singspiel, or German comic opera, were attracting more Berliners. Frederick's tastes were decidedly Italian, however, and in a city such as Berlin, where the personal preferences of a single individual counted so strongly, it was difficult for any theatrical endeavor to thrive or prosper to any great extent without at least tacit royal approval, as long as Frederick was interested in what occurred on the stage. That the singspiel did as well as it did from the 1770s reflects both the extent to which Frederick's Italian tastes were no longer current and the fact that he no longer cared.

The political and social structure of Vienna differed from that of Berlin, principally in that Vienna had a larger and relatively more independent nobility. It is thus not surprising that, while a large retinue of musicians was attached to the elaborate court, the court orchestra was not nearly as influential an institution as in Berlin. Anyone investigating the orchestral situation in Vienna, however, does encounter a number of surprises. First is the paucity of records. Lists of orchestral personnel are scarce, and musicians and writers, such as Burney, Dittersdorf, and Mozart, who frequently discuss the musical life of Vienna in some detail, say little about the orchestras.

Second is the relative neglect of Italian opera for much of this period. Burney reported that in 1772 serious opera was virtually nonexistent in Vienna, although both the German and the French theater were thriving, each with its own orchestra, of which Burney thought highly. Burney suggests that the reason was economic, because the "frequent wars, and other calamities of this country," had so exhausted the public treasury. The reasons were not entirely economic, however. In the 1770s and early 1780s, Joseph II's wholehearted support of a German national theater further weakened the position of Italian opera. By the mid-1780s, however, Joseph II had mostly abandoned plans for a German national theater, and opera buffa was coming back into favor, a trend that was encouraged in the mere two-year reign of Joseph's successor, Leopold II.

Third is the relative paucity of public concert activity. There were practically no established concert series, and even subscription concerts by virtuosos were relatively rare. The several series of subscription concerts that Mozart gave in the early 1780s were actually atypical, attesting primarily to Mozart's reputation as a virtuoso. The only regular public concerts were those of the Tonkünstler-Sozietät, a group organized in 1772 to provide pensions for widows and orphans of musicians. In order to raise funds, they gave four concerts a year, two at Christmas and two at Easter, and virtually all of the best musicians in Vienna participated gratis in them. Kasper Riesbeck relates that four hundred musicians performed in one concert, a statement disputed by Eduard Hanslick, as the list of members contained only approximately 180. Mozart provides a more accurate and more detailed summary for one of the concerts in 1781. He says there were 180 members of the orchestra, which undoubtedly included the singers, and then, more specifically, that there were forty violins, ten violas, ten double basses, eight violoncellos, six bassoons, and wind instruments doubled an orchestra of at least eighty players (letters of 24 March and 11 April 1781). The concerts took place in the Kärntnertortheater.

The size of the orchestra does reflect one aspect of Viennese musical life—a high concentration of instrumentalists in the capital, many of whom were highly talented. Riesbeck observed that while there were not a great many virtuosos in Vienna, no other city could surpass it in terms of the quantity and quality of orchestral musicians, that "it is possible to enlist four or five large orchestras here, all of them incomparable" (Riesbeck, 275–276). The presence of so many musicians is due to the many private ensembles, which were both numerous and well supported. The size, diversity, and complexity of the Austrian Empire produced an usually large number of aristocrats who spent at least part of their time in Vienna, and the enthusiasm of the royal family for instrumental music encouraged the same among the aristocracy. It was this group of patrons that gave Viennese musical life its special tone, for while their resources were not always that of an Esterhazy, it was nevertheless desirable— almost socially imperative—to maintain some sort of instrumental ensemble. Consequently the size and composition of the ensembles varied greatly, from a minimal chamber group to a large orchestra, and employment opportunities were considerable.

Many of the upper nobility in Vienna have become well-known historically as patrons of Mozart or Beethoven, such as Baron von Swieten and the princes Lichnowsky, Lobkowitz, Kinsky, and Liechtenstein. Other members of the Austrian or Hungarian nobility who maintained private orchestras include the princes Hildburghausen, Schwarzenberg,

Grassalkovics, and, of course, Esterhazy. The sheer size of the aristocracy, the division of aristocrats between Vienna and their own private estates, and the tendency of many to bring only key players with them to Vienna and augment them with local musicians as needed resulted in a relatively fluid employment situation in the capital, more so than the conservative, aristocratic dominance of patronage would suggest. The genuine appreciation of instrumental talent found among the nobility further encouraged musicians to remain. Thus, while it would be some time before Vienna would catch up with cities such as London and Paris in the establishment of public orchestral activity, the situation and the attitude of the nobility that did support music were such that, once economic conditions warranted it, the resources for the transition existed.

Given the number and quality of orchestras present and the variety of settings in which they performed, Paris, more than any other city in Europe, stands out as a microcosm of eighteenth-century orchestral activity. And for scholars, much more source material about Paris exists than about most other cities, although it is uneven. Thus, we know a great deal about some orchestras and frustratingly little about others. Three types of orchestras may be identified: the theater orchestras; the private orchestras of the nobility, whose profusion reflects the active salon life of the latter days of the ancien régime; and the orchestras of the concert societies, whose prestige reflected the growing recognition and popularity of this more public type of musical setting.

It is ironic that in a state in which court ceremony was so intimately tied to governance, the king's orchestra (Musique de Roi) was in disrepute. Mozart's famous comment that "whoever enters the King's service is soon forgotten" (letter of 3 July 1778) reflects its general lack of prestige. The king himself was apparently not interested in instrumental performance, and the court atmosphere had become rigid and formalized. Where royal patronage did count, however, was at the Opéra, which could boast of the largest and one of the most innovative orchestras in Europe. The Opéra was under the Académie Royale de Musique, and like the opera in Berlin and Vienna, it was a state institution. The Opéra had a long and famous tradition, going back to the days of Lully under Louis XIV, and by the 1750s averaged around forty-five players, which was gradually increased to a high point of seventy-five in 1776. Between then and the Revolution it fluctuated between sixty-five and seventy-five. The prominence of ballet in the Opéra guaranteed an important role for the orchestra, and the general prestige of the opera house attracted composers of talent and imagination, who attempted many innovations in scoring.

Yet in spite of these circumstances, the Opéra orchestra did not enjoy a universally good reputation. In 1754, Rousseau criticized it on ten counts, which encompassed the ensemble as a whole, the musicianship of individual members, and the quality of their instruments (quoted in MacDonald, 404). In 1770, Burney visited the Opéra and discussed almost all aspects of the performance, including the composition (by Royer), the singing, the costuming, the decoration, and even the machinery, but was notably silent about its orchestra (2:19). The commentary of Rousseau and Burney must be taken circumspectly, however, as both were outspoken in their prejudices toward Italian and against French music. In 1757, Ancelet discussed the Opéra orchestra in some detail. He found that many of the musicians were competent, but because salaries were inadequate they neither kept their instruments in good repair nor took their duties as seriously as they should have (MacDonald, 406). Some years later, in 1776, Tommaso Tractta, in attempting to refute the criticism of the orchestra, confirmed the existence of the criticism. Traetta heard a performance of Gluck's *Alceste,* and according to the *Almanach Musical,* "he has praised aloud the orchestra of our Opéra, and he has asserted that this orchestra, of which he had heard considerable ill spoken, was composed of very able persons and that nowhere had he heard a better one" (quoted in MacDonald, 405).

The orchestras in the other theaters in Paris suffered the same problems as the Opéra, only more so. According to Ancelet, the orchestras of the Comédie Française, the Comédie Italienne, and the Opéra-Comique, which were all much smaller than the Opéra orchestra, were potentially fine ensembles, with some good players; but were hampered by lack of support from the management of the houses and, in the case of the Comédie Française and the Comédie Italienne, by a poor hall and music that, according to Ancelet, was boring to both musicians and public (MacDonald, 406).

The private orchestras of the nobility were generally smaller but were numerous and at times influential. Some of the more important ones belonged to the Prince de Condé, the Prince de Conti, the Baron Charles-Ernst de Bagge, and Alexandre-Jean-Joseph Le Riche de La Pouplinière. The latter did much to shape musical French taste in instrumental music in the middle of the eighteenth century. His salon was extremely popular, and even though his orchestra numbered less than twenty, La Pouplinière was willing to provide the support necessary to retain the best musicians possible and encouraged experimentation and the importation of new types of music. His efforts around midcentury, for instance, did much to nurture a taste among the Parisian elite for the newly developed German symphony. Unfortunately, like many court orchestras of the eighteenth century, La Pouplinière's was dissolved shortly after his death in 1762.

What set the musical life of Paris apart from that of other cities was its cosmopolitan atmosphere. Paris was still the cultural hub of Europe and acted as a magnet for merchants, intellectuals, artists, and aristocrats from many countries. Some visited only briefly; many remained permanently. Social life, which encompassed both the nobility and the upper bourgeoisie, was intense, and most salons welcomed anyone of birth, social standing, or talent. Traveling virtuosos were especially welcome in the salons, which often provided a springboard to a successful public concert appearance. This is precisely the way in which Mozart attempted to establish himself in Paris, his lack of success indicating that in the cut-throat atmosphere of the Parisian salons, more than pure artistic talent was often required.

Because of the relatively open nature of the salons, compared to the more tightly controlled atmospheres of many courts, and the penchant of the Parisian elite for excitement and spectacle, the distinction between private and public performance was relatively more blurred in Paris than elsewhere. Regular public concerts appeared earlier and were more firmly established than in any other city in Europe. As early as 1727, the German J. C. Nemeitz in his travel book *Séjour de Paris* could recommend that visitors to Paris indulge themselves in music if they had the inclination, for "one can attend the best concerts everyday with complete freedom" (quoted in Brenet, 167). Nemeitz also recommended music as an entree into the best Parisian society. The revival of the Concert Spirituel dates from 1725, and its concerts continued until the Revolution. At about the same time (1724), the Concert Italien was formed.

In the second half of the eighteenth century a number of concert series flourished, although some only briefly: the Concert des Amateurs (1769), the Concert des Associés (about 1770), the Concert d'Amis (1772), the Société du Concert de Émulation (1781), and the Concert de la Loge Olympique (1781), in addition to the Concert de la Société Académique des Enfants d'Apollon, which was founded in 1741. Of these, the Concert des Amateurs and its successor, the Concert de la Loge Olympique, were the most important. The extent to which these concerts were truly open to the public or were principally private academies varied, but most were open to all. The Concert Spirituel openly posted billboards throughout Paris announcing its concerts, and its two-tiered ticket prices (four livres for boxes, two for the pit) indicates that a relatively broad stratum of Parisian citizens or visitors attended (Brenet, 119, 132).

In considering the evolution of the orchestra in the late eighteenth century, it is impossible to separate concert orchestras from theater orchestras, because in both function and personnel they were closely related. While symphonies could form an important part of the concert programs, and were indeed enthusiastically received, the concept of a purely orchestral concert was nonexistent in Europe at that time. Virtually all concerts were potpourris, frequently designed as a showcase for one or more virtuosos, and the primary duty of the orchestra was to accompany them. Many symphonies still functioned like an opera overture as an introductory piece preceding the featured solo works on the program. Even in the 1790s the terms *symphony* and *overture* were still used interchangeably.

Personnel lists of some of the orchestras survive from the years after 1751, and they indicate that the orchestra of the Concert Spirituel consisted in large measure of musicians of the Opéra orchestra. This is not surprising, since the Concert Spirituel performed when the Opéra was closed, but it does underscore the importance of state patronage through such institutions as the Opéra. As the complaints about the low pay of musicians in the Opéra indicate, the economic life of an instrumental musician in Paris was precarious in the eighteenth century, and not even the salons, with their relatively small and in some cases improvised ensembles, could form a large or steady basis of support. The theaters, as the only institutions with constant and regular performances, provided the principal source of income that made possible the assemblage of enough musicians to allow an active orchestral concert life to burgeon. This is true not only of Paris but of all the large cities of Europe. The birth of the modern symphony orchestra was in the opera house more than the concert hall or the aristocratic chamber, and in some cities the connection still exists, as in Vienna, whose redoubtable Philharmonic spends most of its time in the pit of the Staatsoper.

In the late eighteenth century, concerts were given more frequently in London than in any other city in Europe. Christian Schubart particularly was struck by the activity in the 1780s. According to his account, the offerings were frequent and of high quality, and the opera stage was one of the richest in Europe. In addition, many lords and squires had their own private musical establishments, often with first-rate musicians.

Befitting its commercial and newly emerging industrial base, London became the center of an extremely competitive privately organized concert life, run mostly by foreign musicians and entrepreneurs eager to tap the largest market in Europe. No single prestigious organization in the city spanned the century (as the Concert Spirituel did in Paris), for most of its concert series were short-lived, the successful ones enjoying a brief enthusiastic reception before being superseded by other offerings more attractive to the relatively fickle public. The state of flux that characterizes London concert life fully reflects the dynamics of its rapidly developing society.

While the public orchestras received most of the attention, Schubart considered the royal orchestra, known as the King's Band, one of the best. He reported that Parliament provided a yearly stipend of £10,000 for its maintenance, not including singers, and that it contained between sixty and eighty persons, including some of the finest musicians in England. In examining the situation in London, however, we encounter much the same problem found in Vienna, a frustrating silence about the orchestras themselves. Thus, we know little else about the nature or the quality of performance of the king's orchestra. This silence is particularly noxious in relation to the orchestras of the important theaters and extends in large measure even to concerts in which one would expect more detailed accounts, such as the Haydn-Salomon venture in the 1790s. What is well documented is the nature of concert life—the types of offerings, the chambers in which they played, the audiences attending, and the organizations or individuals behind the concerts. This is actually the more valuable information, as the historical significance of the London orchestras has more to do with the forums in which they appeared than the nature of their performance.

That music in London flourished outside of the aristocracy is attributable less to a lack of interest by the nobility than to the extremely broad base of support provided by the variegated character of London society. This is nowhere more vividly illustrated than in the founding, in 1719, of the Royal Academy of Music (not to be confused with the conservatory of the same name, founded in 1722). Like similar groups in Paris, Vienna, and Berlin, the function of the Royal Academy was to produce opera, but unlike these other groups, it was primarily a private rather than a state venture. Even the name is misleading, for while the king was the principal patron and supporter, he was only one contributor of many, and his office exercised no particular authority in its governance. The Royal Academy was a corporation whose stocks traded on the London exchange and whose original subscription was bought up by the leading noble families as a business venture.

Public orchestral activity in London is closely related to the existence of two physical settings that were relatively new in the eighteenth century—the "pleasure garden" and the large concert hall. The pleasure garden dated back to the seventeenth century but reached its heyday in the eighteenth and may be considered England's most unusual contribution to the dissemination of music at this time. The two most important were Marylebone, established in 1659, and Vauxhall, established in 1661. Their significance as musical institutions dates from the 1730s, however. When Vauxhall was reopened in 1732 after renovation, it included an orchestra room, and evening concerts became a standard feature. Marylebone soon followed suit. These concerts featured a potpourri of instrumental and vocal numbers, like virtually all concerts in the eighteenth century, and the proprietors, especially those of Marylebone—Daniel Gough and, after 1763, Thomas Lowe—attempted to recruit the best musicians from the opera and the other theaters. While light vocal music tended more to be the featured attraction, the pleasure gardens did provide Londoners with an opportunity to hear orchestral music every night.

In the early eighteenth century, there were few physical spaces in London in which to hold public concerts. Several taverns took the lead by setting aside and equipping a room specifically for concerts, an arrangement still in force in the 1760s when Mozart visited London. In the second half of the century, a number of large halls suitable for concerts were constructed, the most important being the Tottenham Street Rooms (opened 1772), the Pantheon (1772), the Hanover Square Rooms (1775), the Freemasons' Hall (1776), and the concert room of the King's Theatre (1791). Other important rooms used earlier in the century included the Great Room of Hickford's Dancing School, Hickford's Room in Brewer Street (1739), and the Great Room in Spring Garden, in Dean Street (1751).

The availability of such spaces and the favorable responses of the Londoners to public concerts stimulated a number of enterprising musical ventures, the most important being the Bach-Abel Concerts of the 1760s and 1770s, the Professional Concerts of the 1780s and 1790s, and the Salomon Concerts of the 1790s. Typical of his time, Carl Friedrich Abel came to England as a royal chamber musician, but quickly realized that greatest opportunities for success in London came through public performance. In 1764 he teamed with J. C. Bach, and together they offered concerts regularly until just before Bach's death in 1782. The Hanover Square Professional Concerts were organized in 1783 to continue the style of concert begun by Bach and Abel, and they lasted until 1792, when they were forced to fold because of the competition from Salomon's concerts. Salomon began as a violinist in the Professional Concerts and broke away to form his own series beginning with the 1786 season. His great coup was, of course, bringing Haydn to London for the 1791–1792 and 1794 seasons.

One important factor shaping these developments was the sheer size of the halls and theaters in which the orchestras played. When Mozart gave his subscription concerts for the Lenten season in Vienna in 1784, he was delighted with an audience of 174, which filled the hall to overflowing, and would have considered anything over one hundred excellent (letters of 3 March and 20 March 1784). Investigation into the provincial academies in France in the early and mid-eighteenth century indicates that an audience of approximately one hundred was typical (Brenet, 179). The larger opera houses of Europe, the most important public setting for music for most of the century, could accommodate a much larger audience, however. The Schauspielhaus in Berlin, the home of the German national theater, which was built in 1774, seated twelve hundred people. The opera house in Dresden, the Hoftheater, originally built in 1716 and renovated in 1750, seated 814. When the King's Theatre in London was rebuilt in 1791, it seated three thousand three hundred, with dimensions of 90 feet from curtain to center box and a pit width of 62 feet. This may be compared to the Paris Opera House, opened in 1821, which, with dimensions of 82 feet and 42 feet, respectively, seated between 1,783 and 1,937 persons (depending upon the source), or Covent Garden Theatre, whose seating capacity for the eighteenth century is not given but which had dimensions of 63 feet and 50 feet, respectively. Burney indicated that the "German theatre" in Vienna, by which Burney probably meant the Kärntnertortheater, was approximately the same size as the Haymarket Opera House and that there were 120 boxes and 668 seats in the pit of the German theatre; thus, the Haymarket would have seated approximately one thousand. Burney also observed that the theaters of Florence and Milan were twice as large (2:85).

Many concert rooms, particularly in London, were comparable in size. According to some accounts, the Hanover Square Rooms measured 95 feet by 35 feet (length and width) and, according to others, only 79 by 32 (Robbins-Landon, 29); but various reports indicate it normally seated between eight hundred and nine hundred people and could hold as many as fifteen hundred. The Concert Room in the King's Theatre was even larger, measuring 95 feet by 46 feet, and the Freemasons' Hall 90 by 43. This compares with Hickford's Room, which was 50 feet by 30 feet and which was seldom used for music after 1780. For a special Handel commemoration concert, the Pantheon reportedly held sixteen hundred people, although that was more than could be accommodated comfortably. And for a concert of Mozart's at the Great Room in Spring Garden in June 1764, his father was surprised with an audience of two hundred, even though there was practically no time for advance publicity (letter of 8 June 1764).

The growth in the size of the orchestra in the late eighteenth century is clearly related to its presence in these much larger halls. A precise statistical analysis of orchestral size and instrumental distribution is impossible because necessary source information is frequently missing, and that which does exist can be unclear: for example, the lists of court ensembles frequently place all musicians together, including singers; do not indicate doubling on instruments, which was relatively common; or do not include some players, such as trumpeters. Furthermore, orchestras were at times augmented by amateurs, and some eighteenth-century accounts are either questionable in their reliability or, more frequently, simply not precise enough. Sufficient information does exist to establish an unequivocal relationship between the size of an orchestra and the size of the room in which it is performing.

Several scholars have attempted to synthesize what information there is into detailed lists or tables. The most complete are those of Adam Carse and Heinz Becker. Ottmar Schreiber has provided another, although it is limited to Germany. Other scholars have made more detailed studies of specific orchestras, such as Robert James MacDonald's year-by-year compendium of the theater orchestras in Paris. From all of this information it is clear that there was a considerable difference between the size of the typical court orchestra and the typical public orchestra. Most court orchestras averaged from fifteen to twenty-five performers, although a few, such as the Mannheim orchestra, were larger. Even the most well known, such as La Pouplinière's in Paris or Haydn's at Esterhaza, fall within this range. As mentioned earlier, the orchestra usually had multiple functions at the larger courts, frequently involving operatic performance in a large theater, and consequently the size of the court ensembles would reflect that.

Orchestras at public concerts tended to be somewhat larger. Haydn's orchestra for his Salomon Concerts, the largest orchestra that he ever had at his disposal, contained thirty-seven or thirty-eight musicians. The orchestra for the Concert of Ancient Music in London contained forty-three musicians in 1776, and the Gewandhaus Orchestra in Leipzig just over thirty. The orchestra for the Concert Spirituel was one of the largest for public concerts, fluctuating between fifty and fifty-eight in the 1780s and early 1790s. There is no precise information regarding most of the quasi-public orchestras in Paris, but eighteenth-century reports suggest that they were at least comparable in size to the Concert Spirituel orchestra.

The largest standing orchestras were the opera orchestras. The Paris Opéra orchestra reached a maximum of seventy-six musicians in 1776 but generally had between sixty and seventy in the last quarter of the century. Several theaters had orchestras of over fifty, including those in Naples, Milan, and Berlin. Most of the opera orchestras were somewhat smaller, ranging in size from twenty up to forty-five.

While the late-eighteenth-century orchestra was, on average, larger than the early-eighteenth-century orchestra, there is no specific correlation between date and size. Most orchestras that were well supported over a period of time tended to grow to a certain point and then either remain constant or decline slightly. The time frame in which this happened depended primarily upon the circumstances surrounding the orchestra; the extent of growth before a state of equilibrium set in depended primarily upon the type of orchestra it was. Many of the court orchestras, for instance, peaked early in the century, those at Mannheim, Dresden, and Stuttgart reaching their maxima by the 1750s. The various opera orchestras in Paris and the Concert Spirituel, for which there are detailed yearly records, peaked in the 1770s and then fluctuated only slightly. The reasons for a decrease in size could be several, the most important being economic or political. Then, too, once an orchestra reached a certain optimum number, which seemed to depend more upon the size of the hall than anything else, there was little artistic reason for augmenting it further, or if it had exceeded that which was necessary, some reduction could be made with little artistic sacrifice. Finally, it must be reiterated, many of the records are of such a nature that it is difficult to be certain of the exact number of performers for any given performance.

During the French Revolution a special type of grand festival musical celebration, involving huge choruses and orchestras, became popular. The most well known of these, the Fête de l'Être Supreme, held on 6–8 June 1794 in the Tuileries, had a chorus of two thousand four hundred singers and an oversized orchestra, with the refrains sung by the entire populace. This fashion for massiveness reached something of a peak in 1800 with a performance of Jean François Le Sueur's *Chant du 1.ᵉʳ Vendémiaire an IX*, at the church of Saint Louis des Invalides, which had been renamed the Temple of Mars during the Revolution. Le Sueur's work, a large dramatic scene, called for soloists, four choruses, and four orchestras.

The tendency for such grand spectacle was not unique to the French Revolution but may be traced throughout the eighteenth century. Schubart reported an opera performance in Prague in 1724 that involved over one thousand singers and instrumentalists, fifty keyboard accompanists, and four kapellmeister to maintain order. On a more reliable level, the Tonkünstler concerts in Vienna numbered probably one hundred and eighty performers. The greatest of these spectacles before the French Revolution, however, occurred in England, for the Handel commemoration, sponsored by the Society of Ancient Music, in 1784. There were performances in Westminster Abbey and the Pantheon, those in the Pantheon being somewhat smaller by necessity. Burney has left a detailed account of these performances, which included an orchestra of 250 players and a chorus of 274. Burney took great pride in the efforts necessary to include some unusual instruments, such as the large timpani tuned an octave below conventional ones, or the contrabassoon, whose performance technique had apparently been lost in England at the time. The festival was so popular that it was repeated until 1791, with the size of the assembled forces growing even larger. According to some reports, it included over one thousand performers by 1786 (Robbins Landon, 83).

While these types of concerts or festivals were clearly special occasions, they did suggest to the eighteenth century the power that only a large massed ensemble could bring. On a more conventional level, there is no question that large orchestras in large halls had an effect upon musical choices and musical style. Intricacies and nuances of an ensemble could be lost, and sheer power was necessary to produce an effect. Burney, for instance, describing a concert in the great hall of the Louvre in Paris, discusses the problems attendant upon the oboist Bezozzi trying to force his tone because of the size of the hall. It was inevitable that composers would start to compose works featuring the *tutti* ensemble. This point was recognized early in the century and is probably the origin of the distinction between the sonata and the symphony style. While many writers speak of the grandiose effects and the exalted character expected from the symphony, at least one connects these effects directly with the size of the hall. In a famous passage J. J. O. de Meude-Monpas discusses the problem of expression in the symphony:

> Generally the genre of the symphony is appropriate to places where grand effects appear to be necessary: in opera, a spectacle which can only be maintained by an intrinsic grandeur and the effects it produces, and in churches, as for example the arrival of the king. But in a chamber, it is something really awful—grotesquely big like the pictures from the Dome of the Invalides seen up close.
>
> (p. 194)

Theorists at midcentury distinguished between a chamber symphony and an opera symphony, but as the century progressed this distinction began to disappear. Johann Georg Sulzer reported that the opera symphony had taken on some of the qualities of the chamber symphony, which, called the *Konzertsinfonie,* has become the predominant type (2:1123). And Johann Adam Hiller simply stated that the chamber symphony should no longer be distinguished from the opera symphony (2:108).

As the symphony matured, particularly through the work of Haydn and Mozart, it is not surprising that it became identified more and more with public performance. When Mozart was asked to write a symphony for the Concert Spirituel in 1778, he was well aware of the importance of making a proper impression upon the audience, and according to his letters, he carefully calculated the effects (letter of 3 July 1778), just as Haydn did some years later in London. Haydn's last twenty-three symphonies were not written for Esterhaza: numbers 82–87 were written for the Concert de la Loge Olympique in Paris; numbers 88–89 for the violinist Johann Peter Tost, apparently for use in a series of public concerts in Paris; numbers 90–91, and possibly 92, for the French nobleman Comte d'Ogny; and the last twelve numbers, 93–104, for Salomon's concerts in London. The exact performance situation of numbers 90–91 is unclear, but the geographical distance between Haydn and Comte d'Ogny, the rapidity with which these works spread throughout Europe, and Haydn's willingness to sell the exclusive rights to Prince Oettingen-Wallerstein a year later suggest that Haydn had his eye upon a broader market in 1788 than Comte d'Ogny's private residence. And although the precise circumstances that occasioned Mozart's composition of his last three symphonies is still a mystery, it is likely they were intended for a series of subscription concerts. None of Mozart's last five symphonies— that is, none written after 1782—is known to have been written for a private estate. From the mid-1780s on, the symphony was a public event for both Haydn and Mozart.

Much the same is true of the symphonies of Muzio Clementi and of Beethoven. Clementi made no known attempts at symphonic composition until the mid-1780s, when he was engaged as composer and pianist by the Professional Concerts in Hanover Square, London. His first efforts were without question for this public forum. Beethoven did not complete a symphony until 1800, when he ventured his first public subscription concert, even though sketches that date back to his Bonn days indicate that the idea of writing a symphony was much on his mind.

This identification of the symphony with public performance closely parallels the emergence of the symphony as a preeminent genre. It was only in the last two decades of the eighteenth century that a symphony would typically become the centerpiece of a program that also featured singers and other virtuosos, and it was primarily in the large concert halls that the potential of the symphony became evident. J. C. Bach led the way with his symphonies in the Bach-Abel Concerts in the 1760s and 1770s, but it was Haydn's works that brought this tendency to fruition. The popularity of Haydn's symphonies in public concerts in both London and Paris was established long before his visit to London. Clementi found his symphonies being compared unfavorably with Haydn's in the mid-1780s, and in Paris in the late 1780s, Haydn's symphonies attracted the same kind of public attention they would receive in London. A review of the concerts of the Concert Spirituel in the *Mercure de France* in April 1788 observed that Haydn's symphonies were performed at almost all the concerts that year, and then singled them out especially for praise, noting not only Haydn's ingenuity at development but also the overall richness and sonority (quoted in Brook, 1: 337). In these concerts the orchestra assumed a prominence that it was not normally accorded at the time, and the very fact that Salomon would engage and feature Haydn specifically as a symphonic composer symbolizes the change in taste that occurred in the last two decades of the eighteenth century.

Underlying the proliferation of public concert life in the late eighteenth century and the orchestra's role in it is an important social trend—the tendency of the bourgeoisie to identify with the aristocracy. This happened for somewhat different reasons in England and France, but the outcome in each case was similar. In Molière's time, the bourgeois as stereotype was laughable in his values, pretensions, and affectations, but by the late eighteenth century the bourgeois had redefined himself to encompass the ideal of the *honnête homme*, the well-bred citizen, which in the seventeenth century was rooted in the aristocratic notion of gentility. In the eighteenth century the concept acquired a broader meaning. According to Darnton, "It suggested good manners, tolerance, reasonableness, restraint, clear thinking, fair dealing, and a healthy self-respect. Neither an aristocratic honor code nor a bourgeois work ethic, it expressed a new urbanity and marked the emergence of a new ideal type: the gentleman" (p. 139).

One problem that has plagued historians for many years has been the identification of the bourgeois. Recent historical studies have virtually demolished the older notion of defining the bourgeois through his economic base, as possessor of the means of production. There was a large group of citizens, however, who occupied an important position in the ancien régime, persons who had no inheritable claim to aristocracy but who, through pursuit of any of several professions, had acquired at least a moderate level of wealth. This wealth, rather than being further invested in capitalistic or industrial enterprises, was usually employed to purchase either property or office. The bourgeois could thus live off the rent and, in some cases, acquire minor titles of nobility.

Particularly since the nobility in France was frequently engaged in trade and manufacturing, the bourgeoisie found that it had much in common with the aristocracy, and in cultural matters the two groups were closely aligned. This alignment was most remarkably articulated by an anonymous writer who, in 1768, compiled a lengthy description of his city, Montpellier (quoted in Darnton, 116–143). He radically redefined the old concept of the three estates, with the clergy, who no longer mattered, being dropped entirely, and the bourgeoisie being established as the second estate. What is especially clear in this description is that in spite of the obvious distinction resulting from transmittable title between the first and second estates, in social and cultural pursuits the aristocracy and the bourgeoisie are closely identified and clearly distinguished from the third estate, which comprised the artisans, the domestic servants, and the general undesirables of society.

In each European country the relationship between the middle class and the aristocracy was unique, but these countries had one common denominator—in tastes and cultural preferences the second estate had much more in common with the first than with the third. Public concert life, where it existed, was supported by both the first and second estates, and the relative percentage of each depended more upon local demography than upon the nature of the musical events. What determined the presence of an active concert life was the existence of a large enough group of citizens willing and able to provide the financial support; whether these citizens were ennobled had little impact upon the nature of the concert activity.

Much more research about the relation between subscription and concert society records and the social character of eighteenth-century audiences is needed, but some examples can be cited which suggest that the movement away from private court entertainment to public concerts does not necessarily reflect a significant shift in patronage, at least in the eighteenth century. The list of subscribers for Mozart's Lenten concerts in Vienna in 1784 contains both aristocratic and nonaristocratic names, with a relatively large preponderance of nobility. The obviously bourgeois writer of the Montpellier description refers to the Music Academy with great pride, indicating that it was an institution in which all the leading members of both the first two estates participated. The Society of Ancient Music, founded in London in 1776, was strictly an aristocratic enterprise, its directors for many years being only of the upper nobility and its membership highly restricted. Beginning in 1785, George III patronized it, and as a result, strict protocol was observed: the musicians were in full-dress liveries; the king had a special state box, to which he was duly escorted; and only he could initiate applause or call for an encore. The concert in essence became a court performance. A similar development occurred at the Concert de la Loge Olympique when Queen Marie Antoinette and princes of the blood began to attend in 1786. And when Salomon announced what are probably now the most famous public concerts of the eighteenth century, the London concerts featuring Haydn, he had no doubts about his expected audience. On 15 January 1791, he placed the following announcement in the London papers: "HANOVER SQUARE. MR. SALAMON {sic} respectfully acquaints the *Nobility and Gentry*, that he intends having TWELVE SUB-SCRIPTION CONCERTS in the Course of the present Season" (Robbins Landon, 440; italics added).

Not everyone could be born into the nobility, but many could at least aspire to the status of gentleman in the late eighteenth century. This group of aspirants could no longer be ignored, and they formed the basis of support that not only would allow the orchestral ensemble its survival but would carry it to a level of prestige and a prominence hitherto unknown. The orchestra may be historically a creation of the older court system, but it came into its own only as it emerged into the public sphere.

BIBLIOGRAPHY

Heinz Becker, "Orchester," in *Die Musik in Geschichte und Gegenwart*, (1949–   ), Friedrich Blume, ed. Michel Brenet, *Les concerts en France sous l'ancien régime* (1900; repr. 1970). Barry S. Brook, *La symphonie française dans la seconde moitié du dixhuitième siècle*, 3 vols. (1962). Charles Burney, *An Account of the Musical Performances in Westminster-Abbey, and the Pantheon, May 26th, 27th, 29th, and June the 3d, and 5th, 1784, in Commemoration of Handel* (1785); and *Dr. Burney's Musical Tours in Europe*, vol. 1, *An Eighteenth-Century Musical Tour in France and Italy*, and vol. 2, *An Eighteenth-Century Musical Tour in Central Europe and the Netherlands*, Percy A. Scholes, ed. (1959). Adam Carse, *The Orchestra in the Eighteenth Century* (1940; repr. 1950); and *The Orchestra from Beethoven to Berlioz* (1949). Georges Cucuel, *Études sur un orchestra au dixhuitième siècle* (1913); and *La Pouplinière et la musique de chambre au dixhuitième siècle* (1913; repr. 1971).

Robert Darnton, *The Great Cat Massacre and Other Episodes in French Cultural History* (1984). Robert Elkin, *The Old Concert Rooms of London* (1955). Eduard Hanslick, *Geschichte des Concertwesens in Wien*, 2 vols. (1869–1870). Ernest

Eugene Helm, *Music at the Court of Frederick the Great* (1960). Johann Adam Hiller, *Wöchentliche Nachricten und Anmerkungen die Musik betreffend* (1766–1770). H. C. Robbins Landon, *Haydn: Chronicle and Works*, vol. 3, *Haydn in England: 1791–1795* (1976). Robert James MacDonald, "François-Joseph Gossec and French Instrumental Music in the Second Half of the Eighteenth Century," Ph.D. diss., University of Michigan (1968). Friedrich Wilhelm Marpurg, *Historisch-kritische Beyträge zur Aufnahme der Musik*, 5 vols. (1754–1778). J. J. O. de Meude-Monpas, *Dictionnaire de musique* (1787).

J. F. Reichardt, *Vertraute Briefe aus Paris*, 3 vols. (1804); and *Vertraute Briefe geschrieben auf einer Reise nach Wien*, 2 vols. (1810; repr. 1915). Kasper Riesbeck, *Briefe eines reisenden Franzosen in Deutschland* (1784). Jean Jacques Rousseau, *Dictionnaire de musique* (1768). Arnold Schering, *Geschichte des Instrumentalkonzerts bis auf die Gegenwart* (1905). Louis Schneider, *Geschichte der Oper und des Königlichen Opernhauses in Berlin* (1852). Ottmar Schreiber, *Orchester und Orchester-Praxis in Deutschland zwischen 1780 und 1850* (1938; repr. 1978). Christian Friedrich Daniel Schubart, *Ideen zu einer Aesthetik der Tonkunst* (1806; repr. 1969). Ludwig Spohr, *Autobiography* (1865; repr. 1878). Johann Georg Sulzer, *Allgemeine Theorie der schönen Künste*, 4 vols. (1773–1775).

Technical Development of Musical Instruments:
Strings

Nancy Groce

In the modern symphony orchestra the string section is the core around which all else circulates. The four string instruments found in the modern orchestra — violin, viola, cello, and double bass — are all members of the violin family and are technically defined as unfretted, four-stringed, bowed chordophones. A more homogeneous section than either the woodwinds, brasses, or percussion, the strings share a common history of musical and technical development. Yet, although string instruments were the first in the orchestra to be perfected in their modern form, there remain a mystique and fascination on the part of musicians and audiences alike about these instruments and their makers.

The modern orchestra typically employs about thirty-two violinists (divided into first and second sections), thirteen violists, thirteen cellists, and nine double bassists. The actual number of strings is, of course, modified depending on the requirements of specific compositions. Both the overall number of string instruments and their ratio to winds in the ensemble have been gradually increasing since the baroque era, when a somewhat more equal balance existed between sections of the orchestra.

Orchestral strings are arranged in a wide semicircle directly in front of the conductor. First and second violins are usually seated in a group to the conductor's left but sometimes are positioned to the conductor's left and right, respectively; violas are arranged in several rows immediately in front of the podium; cellos are situated to the conductor's right; and double basses form the last row or rows on the right-hand side of the ensemble.

As important as the role of strings is within an orchestra, this essay will focus on the technical development of the instruments rather than on their musical functions. Throughout the following discussion, readers should keep in mind that the term *violin* applies to all members of the violin family, as well as to its smallest member, the violin.

EARLY HISTORY

The earliest history of the violin family is filled with multiple possible ancestors, and thus, tracing the exact lines of instrumental evolution is difficult. Scholars now date the appearance of the modern violin to the earliest years of the sixteenth century. During the 1530s, three-stringed-violins began to appear in paintings of the Garofalo school at Ferrara. Early violins combined elements from several string instruments popular during this period, such as the fifth-interval tuning of the rebec and the graceful, rounded tripartite shape of the lira de braccio.

These features, based on concepts from older instruments and developed through experimentation, seem to have crystallized within a relatively short period in the region of Brescia, in northern Italy, around 1500. Interestingly, all four members of the violin family seem to have appeared at about the same time. This reflects the late Renaissance ideal of the *consort*, a multivoiced set of instruments of a single type, capable of producing homogeneous timbre and tone from the soprano to the bass. Even given the violins' sudden appearance as a family in a limited geographical area, it seems unlikely that a single craftsman was responsible for the invention of the instrument. It is more likely that the new instrument was a response to the musical demands of the era. It was fortunate that some of the finest luthiers (makers of string instruments) of all time lived and worked in northern Italy during the sixteenth and early seventeenth centuries, since this resulted in the standardization and perfection of the violin very early in its history.

THE VIOLIN

The sleek, elegant form of the modern violin is such a strong visual whole that it is difficult to distinguish the more than seventy individual parts in its construction. The basic parts are the body, the neck, and the strings. The body of a string instrument acts primarily as a resonating chamber, in which the tones, produced by the friction of the bow on the strings, are shaped, colored, and amplified; hence, the shape and dimensions of the body will determine the characteristic sound of an instrument. The body of the modern violin is divided into three sections, called *bouts*. The top and bottom bouts are rounded while the middle bout forms a waist that permits unobstructed movement of the bow at different angles. The average violin's body is 14 inches long and consists of an arched top plate, called the *belly*; an arched *bottom*, or *back, plate*; and side walls called *ribs*, which are usually 1.2 inches high. Unlike ribs on earlier string instruments, the ribs of a violin are slightly inset on the flat edges, or *tables*, of the top and bottom plates.

Luthiers prefer softwoods, such as European spruce, for the construction of the violin's top plate but hardwoods, such as maple, for the sides, back, neck, scroll, and pegbox. Fingerboards and tailpieces are almost always made of ebony.

The arching of the top and bottom plates greatly affects the sound produced by the instrument. Interior supports and linings such as the *soundpost*, a small vertical wooden shaft placed underneath the right foot of the exterior bridge, and the *bass bar*, a strip of spruce glued under the left foot of the bridge, help to transmit and shape the resonance of the strings.

The neck of the modern violin is usually 10.4 inches long. It is attached to the top block of the body and set at a slight downward angle away from the belly. The neck extends through the *pegbox*, which houses the pegs around which the strings are tightened, and terminates in a gracefully curved Ionian scroll. Occasionally, especially on older instruments, the neck ends in a grotesquely carved head.

Covering the neck of the violin is a smooth plaque of ebony known as the *fingerboard*. The fingerboard, which continues past the base of the neck, stops squarely about one-third of the way down the body. Players press, or "stop," strings against the fingerboard at specific points to obtain the string length necessary to produce the desired tone. Violinists must remember precisely where to stop the strings for each pitch, since the fingerboards of violins are "unfretted" (that is, they bear no markings, or "frets," like those on the guitar, to remind players where to place their fingers).

The members of the violin family have four strings. This number was standardized very quickly on the violin, viola, and cello, but double basses have at various times had three, four, five, and occasionally six strings. Violin strings are tuned in intervals of a fifth (g, d′, a′, e″ on the violin; c, g, d′, a′ on the viola; and C, G, d, a on the cello) except on the double bass, where the interval of a fourth (E′, A′, D, G) is used to help minimize extremely long reaches for the player's fingers. Strings are attached to the upper end of a fitted ebony plaque at the bottom of the instrument called a *tailpiece*. The latter is securely anchored to the bottom of the instrument by an *endpin*. Each string, having been secured to the tailpiece, is then strung over a maple *bridge* located between the *f*-holes, and then run parallel to the neck and over a small stanchion of wood or ivory, called the *nut*, located at the end of the fingerboard just below the pegbox. Finally, each string is wound around a tuning peg, a rounded pin of ebony or rosewood that can be turned so as to tighten the string until the proper pitch is reached. On modern instruments a secondary tuning device, called an *E-tuner* and located near the E string on the tailpiece, is used to fine-tune the violin's highest string.

Violin strings were originally made of twisted gut, but the tone produced by gut strings was often criticized for being "soft" and indistinct, and the strings slowly responded to newer and more sophisticated bowing styles. Around 1700, the lowest string on the violin began to be wound with silver wire to increase the string's volume and make it more responsive. This proved so successful that by the end of the eighteenth century the violin's two middle strings were also changed from gut to wound metal. The use of nonwound but metal E strings began in the nineteenth century; and by the early twentieth century few, if any, violinists played with gut strings.

Typical, if less critical, elements of the instrument include the two soundholes, called *f-holes* after their shape, which are cut into the top plates of all members of the violin family. The choice of shape seems to be largely traditional, although their placement can significantly affect the violin's acoustical properties. Another noticeable feature is the *purfling*, a line of inlaid wood or ivory almost at the edge of the top and bottom plates. More than merely decorative, purfling helps to prevent cracks and damage to the body of the instrument.

Finally, there is the chin rest. Although not technically part of the instrument, the chin rest has had a significant impact on how the violin and viola are now played. First introduced in 1820 by the German violin virtuoso Ludwig Spohr, the chin rest allowed the player's left hand freedom to move with more dexterity and speed. (Previously, a violinist or violist had supported his instrument against his arm, chest, or shoulder and placed his chin to the right or left of the tailpiece.) The chin rest was initially placed directly over the tailpiece in the middle of the instrument, but the left-side position used today quickly gained acceptance.

A word or two should be said about violin varnish, especially since so much of so little merit has been written on the subject. There seems to be no evidence that varnish can significantly improve the tone of a string instrument, although a poorly applied, thick coat can certainly prevent an instrument from sounding its best. Varnish acts to protect and beautify a violin, but the commonly held notion that the success of the instruments built by early master craftsmen such as Amati and Stradivari was due to a now-lost secret varnish formula is not true. Especially in the case of the Cremonan violin makers, impeccable workmanship seems to have had considerably more to do with the beauty of the instrument's tone than the varnish used.

THE VIOLA

The viola, the alto member of the violin family, is tuned in fifths at a fifth below the violin. The violin's size is in almost perfect acoustical proportion and relationship to its pitch, but that of the viola creates basic acoustical problems for the instrument. Theoretically, the viola should be one-third to one-half again as large as the violin in order to obtain proper acoustical results for its range. However, a viola that much larger than the violin would be impossible to hold and play as a shoulder instrument. Most modern violas are only one-seventh again as large as the violin, and thus, by remaining a shoulder instrument, the viola has been condemned to an acoustical limbo—forever attempting to balance the larger body required for acoustical success with the reality of physical manageability.

The history of the viola closely follows that of the violin. The name viola, like that of other members of the violin family, remains somewhat unclear in the earliest records. Because the term was often used in sixteenth-century Europe to designate any bowed string instrument, some musicologists have suggested that the viola is actually the oldest member of the violin family.

Historically, the length of the viola has ranged from 15 to 17.8 inches. Today, standard viola patterns vary from approximately 16.1 inches (the "alto" size) to 17.3 inches (the "tenor" size). The alto is a more playable size, but its low notes are said to lack richness and strength; the tenor sounds richer but is difficult to play.

Like the strings of the violin, those of the viola were originally made of gut, but over the last few centuries they have been replaced by wound and metal strings, which produce a larger, more powerful sound. Because of their weight, violas are held with their scrolls slanted at an angle to the floor, rather than parallel to it, but other playing techniques such as fingering and bowing closely resemble those of the violin.

During the sixteenth and seventeenth centuries, the viola was used for playing music in the alto and tenor registers. The preference of that era for smooth, homogeneous tone led to an emphasis on midrange instruments such as the viola, and small string ensembles commonly employed one violin, two violas, and a cello. In larger ensembles, such as the famous one at Saint Mark's in Venice, violas frequently outnumbered violins. This preference for violas explains why such large numbers of both alto- and tenor-size violas were produced before the middle of the eighteenth century, when musical fashions began to favor more pronounced melody lines.

Though fewer violas were produced during the late eighteenth and early nineteenth centuries, attempts to perfect the instrument continued. Most notable was Hermann Ritter's design for a "viola alto" in 1876. Its body, which measured 18.9 inches, did produce a significantly better tone, but its large size made it too difficult for most players to handle. A more successful design, one that combined better tone with playability, was introduced in 1937 by the English viola virtuoso Lionel Tertis. Known as the Tertis model, it remains popular with performers.

THE VIOLONCELLO

The bass member of the violin family, the violoncello, or cello, as it is more commonly called, is twice as large as the average violin, and its strings sound an octave below those of the viola. Technically, the cello is the bass, rather than the tenor, member of the violin family because the original tenor was a now-extinct "tenor violin," which in size and compass was halfway between the viola and the cello.

The cello, like the violin and viola, was first noted in the sixteenth century; but unlike other members of the modern violin family, its relatively deep ribs, shorter neck, and high back reflect the influence of the ancient lira da braccio family. Unfortunately, few early cellos survive, but evidence from extant instruments suggests that during the sixteenth century the size of cellos had yet to be standardized, some instruments had a fifth string, and holes were occasionally built into the back of an instrument so that it could be suspended around the player's neck for use in processionals.

Of all the members of the violin family, the cello had the hardest time establishing its rightful place in musical history because of stiff competition from its distant relative, the fretted, six-stringed *viola da gamba*. Although other members of the gamba family faded from popularity during the sixteenth and early seventeenth centuries, the tenor gamba, or viola da gamba, remained popular and coexisted with the cello for another century and a half. The gamba's popularity was based primarily on its social standing rather than its musical strengths, since—especially in England and the Low Countries, as Philibert Jambe de Fer noted in his *Epitome musicale* of 1556—the viol was esteemed as the instrument of a gentleman and the cello was deemed fit only for the commoner. Gradually, demands for a louder tenor part led to the replacement of the viola da gamba with the cello.

As with the viola, both larger and smaller patterns existed for the cello during the eighteenth century. Refinements made during the eighteenth century included a gradual thinning of the instrument's neck to facilitate fingering and the replacement of old-fashioned gut strings with lighter, more manageable wound strings. Floor spikes became standard, and players were no longer required to grasp the instrument between their knees, as they had had to do with the older viola da gamba. Fortunately, playing while standing or marching was no longer expected of players. By the end of the eighteenth century, the cello was ready to develop into an important orchestral instrument. J. S. Bach's six suites for solo cello (BWV 1007–1012) marked its emergence as a mature member of the string family. Later, concertos by C. P. E. Bach, Haydn, Boccherini, Schumann, Dvořák, Elgar, and Ernest Bloch would explore the complex beauty and musical capabilities of the instrument.

THE CONTRABASS OR DOUBLE BASS

The contrabass, or double bass, remains the least standardized member of the violin family. The only members of the family to be tuned in fourths (E', A', D, G)—which is done to make fingering of the large instrument easier—basses sound an octave lower than they are notated in orchestral scores.

Today, orchestral basses vary in length from 71 to 86.6 inches. The average body length of a modern bass is approximately 44.1 inches. Bass players distinguish between two main types of instruments: the *full bass*, usually of German make, with a body length of 44.1 inches, and the *three-quarter bass* of the Italian and French schools, which usually ranges from 44.9 to 46.1 inches. Some modern organologists, especially those in the German-speaking countries, further divide basses into five types: the quarter, half, and three-quarter sizes (all of which are referred to generally as *violone*); the smaller *Bierbass*; and the larger full-size bass. Outsized giant basses have also occasionally appeared. The German Hans Haiden reportedly built one around 1600; Praetorius described another in 1620. The French luthier Jean Baptiste Vuillaume experimented with several *octobasses* in the mid-nineteenth century, and the American John Geyer captured the record by designing a fifteen-foot-tall monster bass in 1889.

Written references to the double bass appear as early as the 1530s, and several Italian and German illustrations from the 1560s depict musicians playing violin-type instruments taller than themselves. Early basses occasionally reflected the strong influence of the rival gamba family, borrowing from the latter its flat, slanted back and sometimes its fretted fingerboard.

During the seventeenth century, basses were built with three, four, five, and even six strings. The popularity of the six-stringed bass seems to have endured longer in Germany than elsewhere. During the 1770s, Carl Ludwig Bachman of Berlin popularized a machine-screw tuning device that made possible much more accurate tuning, which had always been difficult because of the great tension exerted on strings the size and length of those of the bass. Bachman's innovation was the culmination of many attempts to facilitate tuning, among them a very early cogwheel device reported by Praetorius in 1620.

By the mid-nineteenth century, the demands of orchestral scores favored the use of the four-stringed bass. Nevertheless, three-stringed double basses were used in Italy, France, and England until the 1870s; and players are still experimenting with the instrument. Among the most recent innovations is the "C-string attachment," a device that lengthens the lowest string to produce the C below and thus extends the downward compass of the instrument. Automatic keying devices, like the one produced by the Frenchman Corbigny in 1839, are sometimes added to help bassists finger passages that would otherwise be "impossible to play." Of all the members of the violin family, the bass is the only one that is still evolving.

BOWS

Indispensable to the development of string instruments was the parallel development and refinement of the bow. Bows were perfected much later than the members of the violin family, and it might be argued that the full potential of many of the greatest violins was discovered only after the appearance of the modern bow in the nineteenth century.

The earliest violin bows had a convex curve (relative to the hair) like their medieval ancestors, rather than a concave curve like the modern bow. By 1700, this outward curve had been modified to an almost straight line. Still, bows of the classical period were shorter, thicker, and clumsier to handle than later bows. The new musical style of Mozart, Haydn, and other composers of the classical era demanded that string instruments sustain singing melody lines and perform increasingly intricate passages and such special bow-produced effects as *sforzando* and *martellato*. A lighter, more responsive bow was clearly needed.

Fortunately, the need for a better bow coincided with the appearance of the most famous of all bow makers, François Tourte, who, with the help and advice of other makers and musicians, introduced the modern bow in 1785. Working in Paris, Tourte standardized the length of the violin bow at 29.1 inches, lightened the head, designed a concave curvature of the stick, arranged the horsehair into a ribbon by using a ferrule to flatten it, and added a metal screw to the frog. Tourte-style bows were so successful that older styles were virtually abandoned. Unlike older string instruments, early bows could not be reworked to modern specifications, so most of the older bows were discarded and are no longer available for researchers to examine. The viola and cello bows are standardized at 29.5 and 28 inches respectively.

Double-bass players have yet to agree on a single type of bow. Presently, two styles are used for meeting the needs of those players who bow palm down and those who prefer playing palm up. The former prefer the "French bow" (28.5 inches), which is simply an enlarged version of the violin bow; the latter use a bow (29.5 inches) with a much higher frog, a bow introduced in nineteenth-century Vienna by Franz Simandl. The palm-up position, required by the Simandl bow, is more common in the United States and might be traceable to the grip used on the ancient viola da gamba.

THE GREAT VIOLIN MAKERS

The popularity and use of violins spread rapidly through Europe during the sixteenth and seventeenth centuries. By the middle of the sixteenth century, "schools" (that is, regional traditions) of violin making existed in France, Germany, and Poland. But it was in northern Italy, where the violin family had first appeared in the earliest years of the sixteenth century, that the making of the instruments came to full flower. The luthiers of this region appeared quite early in the violin's history and soon established a reputation for craftsmanship that remains unequaled. Within a generation, they were producing and exporting instruments that are still played and prized more than three centuries later.

One of the earliest master craftsmen whose history is known is Andrea Amati. Active during the 1560s and 1570s, Amati founded a school of violin making in Cremona that was to flourish for almost two centuries. Among his other contributions, he is credited with standardizing the violin's modern form by placing the *f*-holes in their present position. Amati received numerous commissions from the French court; records confirm that during the 1560s and 1570s, Amati constructed twelve small violins, sixty-two large violins, eight violas, and eight cellos for the court of Charles IX.

Another early maker was Gasparo (Bertolotti) da Salò, who founded a school of violin making at Brescia in the 1560s. His instruments are thought by some to be the most technically perfect of all early violins. Although da Salò's students included such famous makers as Giovanni Paolo Maggini, the Brescian school was relatively short-lived.

The instruments made by these early luthiers had approximately the same body dimensions as modern violins, but the amount of arching in the top and bottom plates of the body was less standardized. Fingerboards of early violins were considerably shorter, and necks were both shorter and wider, than on present-day instruments. The necks on all members of the violin family were straight and ran parallel to the instrument's body, rather than at a slight downward angle, since the short, light gut strings did not exert as much tension or force as the wound or metal strings on later violins. Also, since tension from the gut strings was fairly light, internal bracing of the violin was far less common. Bridges on early instruments varied considerably; but in general they seem to have been lower and thicker than modern bridges, and they were placed closer to the violin's tailpiece.

By the 1630s Cremona had begun to replace Brescia as the center of violin making. The school founded there by Andrea Amati was continued by his sons Antonio and Girolamo. As early as the 1570s, Cremonan violins were setting the pattern of violin making throughout Europe. Records from this period reveal that even in Paris, musicians were ordering violins *à la mode Crémone*.

Girolamo Amati's son, Nicola, is remembered today as the most accomplished, as well as last, of the Amatis. Nicola was an impeccable craftsman and renowed teacher whose apprentices included most of the famous luthiers of the following generation, including Andrea Guarneri and probably Antonio Stradivari. Nicola's "grand models" made during the 1640s, when he was experimenting with increasing the violin's tone and projection, were years ahead of their time. During the eighteenth century, violins made by Nicola were prefered to all others.

Other famous Cremonan makers of this period were the five members of the Guarneri family, whose most famous and last craftsman was Giuseppe Guarneri "del Gesù." From the 1720s to the 1740s Giuseppe built larger and more powerful instruments than other Cremonan makers and experimented extensively to improve his instruments.

The most famous of all makers was the Cremonan Antonio Stradivari (or, Latinized, Stradivarius). Working between 1666 and 1737, Stradivari is believed to have produced 1,116 instruments, of which 635 violins, 17 violas, and 60 cellos are known to be extant. Like other Cremonan makers, Stradivari experimented with perfecting the proportions of his instruments, turning briefly to a larger body size (the "Long Strad") about 1690 and then returning in 1698 to the classic proportions of his earlier period. Because Stradivari's instruments have been prized since they were first constructed, many examples of his work have survived. An interesting tradition associated with violins is the naming of famous instruments for their owners or for historical incidents connected with their past. Thus, when we refer to "classic" patterns of Stradivari violins, we can name specific instruments such as the Betts (1704), Viotti (1709), Parke (1711), Dolphin (1714), Allard (1715), Messiah (1716), Wilhelmj (1725), and Swan (1735). Stradivari also experimented with perfecting and standardizing violas, cellos, and other types of string instruments.

The real secret of Stradivari's fame, which was already well established during his lifetime, was his use of the highest quality raw materials and his absolutely flawless workmanship. As previously mentioned, Stradivari and his fellow Cremonan craftsmen achieved fame not through the use of a secret varnish formula but through a profound knowledge of their craft.

With the death of Stradivari in 1737 and the passing of his generation, northern Italy's unquestioned leadership in the production of fine violins began to wane. Outstanding luthiers were already appearing elsewhere in Europe. Jacob Stainer, for example, had founded a school in the Austrian Tyrol near Innsbruck in the mid-seventeenth century. The torch of great violin making, however, passed not to Austria but to

France, where in the late eighteenth century Nicolas Lupot, using Stradivari's instruments as models, transplanted the Italian instrument-making tradition to Paris.

THE NATURE OF INSTRUMENTAL DEVELOPMENT

Musicologists disagree about whether changes are made in musical instruments in order to keep up with the technical demands made of musicians by composers or whether technical advancement of instruments encourages composers to write increasingly difficult scores. Almost from their initial appearance in the sixteenth century, members of the violin family were capable of technically fulfilling far more than was being demanded of them by contemporary scores. Even as late as the beginning of the eighteenth century, string players were rarely required to shift their left hand higher than the third fingering position, and a few special bowing techniques would suffice for most pieces in the repertoire. This was soon to change.

With the dawn of the classical era, composers began to make an increasing number of musical demands that were to be reflected in the construction of the instruments. Classical compositions involved a much greater compass, and while earlier the string player had rarely used anything above the third position, the ability to play as high as the fourteenth position was now expected. And as the instrument's range was being extended, the standard pitch in western Europe was rising, by perhaps as much as a whole tone. Another musical development that was to have a great impact on the technical development of the strings was the new popularity of the concerto form, in which a single instrument is pitted against an entire orchestral ensemble. In addition to the larger compass, higher pitch, and more powerful tone demanded of string instruments by composers in the classical era, the democratization of European culture and art was moving orchestral performances from the intimacy of the court to the larger public concert hall of the bourgeoisie.

To deal with these changes, musicians required new, more powerful instruments with extended ranges and greater carrying qualities. Through experimentation, string-instrument players and makers discovered that by modifying, rather than revolutionizing, standard patterns, these new demands could be met. First, to meet the demand for a larger compass, each member of the string family was fitted with a slightly longer neck and a considerably longer fingerboard. On Cremonan violins, for example, fingerboards had usually been 7.5–8.3 inches long; by the late eighteenth century, 10.4 inches was standard. Also, both the neck and fingerboard were tapered slightly to permit easier fingering and shifting between positions.

The change from gut to metal or wound metal strings made it easier to tune up to the new, higher standard pitch; but it was soon discovered that the new, longer strings were putting a tremendous strain on the instruments. To compensate for this, the neck, which had previously been mortised into the body on a plane parallel to it, was now "thrown back," or angled down and away from the belly, by the insertion of a small wooden wedge between the body and the neck. To offset the negative effects of these changes, a slightly higher bridge was introduced; and to strengthen the body of the instrument, internal bracings, such as the soundpost and the bass bar, were significantly enlarged.

By 1800, all new instruments incorporated these changes, but instrument makers learned that older instruments could be easily refitted to meet the demands of the new music. Valued instruments, including those of the Italian masters, were modified in great numbers throughout the nineteenth century. In fact, no known Stradivarius violin exists with its original neck and fittings. Thus, many of our notions about the tone and playability of these legendary violins have been significantly altered by the work of nineteenth-century craftsmen. Ironically, many of the instruments made by the seventeenth-century masters and now owned by museums are again being sent to luthiers—but this time sent to have the nineteenth-century necks removed and the older features restored.

By the early nineteenth century, with the acceptance of the longer neck, metal strings, the Tourte bow, and the chin rest, the modern string instruments had been fully developed. Attempts to change and improve violins continued. Among the more significant were François Chanot's patent for a guitar-shaped violin in 1817 and, also that year, Félix Savart's experiment with a straight-sided trapezoidal violin.

The popularity of string instruments led to increasing demands in the early nineteenth century for modestly priced instruments suitable for students and amateurs. The demand, in turn, led to the growth of several regional schools, such as those of Mittenwald and Markneikirchen in Bavaria and Mirecourt in France, where networks of luthiers were organized to work systematically building violin parts that would later be assembled into instruments at large ateliers. Although many of the instruments produced by these schools were marketed under the slightly misleading label of Stradivari, Amati, or Guarneri, some of the instruments were quite well made.

The flexibility and beauty of string instruments make them the very backbone of the modern symphony orchestra. Despite occasional attempts to redesign and change the members of the violin family—for-example, Carleen Hutchins' experiments in the 1970s at building an eight-member string section that included intermediate sizes between the existing instruments—the technical development of the strings and their role in the orchestra are well established.

BIBLIOGRAPHY

Nicholas Bessaraboff, *Ancient European Musical Instruments* (1941; rev. ed. 1965). David Boyden, *The History of Violin Playing from Its Origins to 1761* (1965). Alexander Buchner, *Musical Instruments Through the Ages* (1956). Francis W. Galpin, *A Textbook of European Musical Instruments* (1937). Karl Geiringer, *Musical Instruments: Their History from the Stone Age to the Present Day* (1943).

William Henley, *Universal Dictionary of Violin and Bow Makers*, 5 vols. (1959–1960). W. Henry Hill, Arthur F. Hill, and Alfred E. Hill, *Antonio Stradivari: His Life and Works* (1902); and *The Violin Makers of the Guarneri Family* (1931; 1965). Sibyl Marcuse, *A Survey of Musical Instruments* (1975). Hortense Panum, *The Stringed Instruments of the Middle Ages* (1970). Joseph Roda, *Bows for Musical Instruments of the Violin Family* (1959). Curt Sachs, *The History of Musical Instruments* (1940). Boris Schwarz, *Great Masters of the Violin* (1983).

Technical Development of Musical Instruments:
Woodwinds

Nancy Toff

The history of the orchestral woodwind instruments is best compared to a sine curve, with alternating periods of stability and change. During periods of mechanical stability, the music developed; during periods of compositional stability, the instrumental mechanism evolved. Always, this phenomenon has been the result of interaction between the prevailing musical style and the instruments designed to play it.

In the seventeenth century, there was an exponential growth in the demand for woodwind instruments, to which makers responded with a period of intense design activity. In the eighteenth century, players learned to master the new instruments, composers wrote prolifically for them, and there was relative technological stability. In the nineteenth century the increasing sophistication of the orchestral repertoire demanded improved instruments, and so there was again considerable activity on the part of the makers. This time, however, a multiplicity of makers produced competitive models, products that they needed conscientiously to sell to potential purchasers; moreover, they had to create demand among musicians, particularly amateur players, often comfortable—even complacent—about customary eighteenth-century forms (or elaborations on them), despite their limitations, because of the difficulty of changing fingering systems. The composition of solo works for the woodwinds declined in the nineteenth century, however, even as those instruments found increased opportunities in the romantic orchestra. The combination of skilled design and effective marketing resulted, by the end of the nineteenth century, in another period of relative mechanical stability. The woodwinds achieved their modern forms (Boehm flute, Conservatoire or Sellner oboe, Conservatoire clarinet, and French or German bassoon), though national allegiances to particular designs marred the model of perfect homogeneity of design. This stability left twentieth-century players once again free, as were their eighteenth-century forebears, to concentrate on the ultimate mastery of their instruments and on the ever-increasing complexity of the music, which was itself spurred by the technical and acoustical capabilities of the instruments.

The technological progress of the woodwinds falls into five categories: mechanism; shape (particularly the internal dimensions and number of sections); tone-hole size and position; materials of construction; and, to a lesser extent, methods of manufacture. Modifications in shape, materials, and hole placement have been the result primarily of the need to improve intonation and projection (volume); mechanical changes enhance technical dexterity.

The basic acoustical operation of the woodwinds seems deceptively simple. The instruments produce different notes by altering the length of the air column or by using an upper harmonic as the note desired. They do so by means of holes bored in the length of the tube; the air-column length can be shortened by uncovering a succession of holes. For a diatonic scale, the sequence is simple; for a chromatic scale, however, nonsequential and therefore more complex combinations of hole coverings are necessary. Closing one or more holes above the uppermost open hole for a given pitch may provide a chromatic variation of that pitch. This procedure is known as cross-fingering or fork-fingering; and, as these names imply, they are more difficult to execute. For this reason, one of the prime goals of woodwind-mechanism designers has been to minimize the use of cross-fingerings. Their instrumentality is mechanism, designed, as Adam Carse wryly pointed out, "to remedy the shortcomings of the human hand; . . . keys are used to close note-holes where fingers are not available, to control holes which lie out of the reach of the fingers, or to close holes which are too large for the fingers to cover" (p. 46).

In the sixteenth century, the homogeneous string consort was the dominant instrumental ensemble, and the wind instruments were relatively dormant. The mid-seventeenth-century resolution of European civil wars and the assumption by Louis XIV of the full power of the

French throne in 1661 provoked a resurgence of artistic energies, new expressive ideals in music, and ultimately the revival of the woodwinds. When the winds reappeared, it was to add color to the string ensemble (as in Alessandro Scarlatti's opera *sinfonie*) and to provide character description in opera (for example, Robert Cambert's use of oboes in his 1671 opera *Pomone*). But the winds of the sixteenth century were inadequate to the demands of the music of the seventeenth. And thus the late seventeenth century saw the first major advances in woodwind technology: the division of the instrument into two telescoping pieces, which allowed the player to regulate its pitch in relation to other instruments; changes in the bore to produce a smoother, more pleasing tone; and corresponding changes in oboe and bassoon reeds.

Louis XIV wished to enjoy music and dance indoors as well as out—opera, under Lully's direction; ballet, which evolved from a component of opera to an independent art; and a new, intimately scaled chamber music (typified by the *Concerts royaux* of François Couperin). But of the existing instruments, only the violin and recorder were appropriately subdued; the noisy shawms and sackbuts were patently unsuitable. Thus, the need arose for new wind sonorities and for wind instruments with wider melodic ranges. The French court made a cult of pseudorusticity; and bagpipes and musettes, the favored instruments of peasants and their imitators, provided instrument makers with the experience and the technology to create more refined orchestral woodwinds. For instance, makers extended the concept of tenon-and-socket construction, used for musette pipes, to other winds; the short tenons that resulted simplified construction considerably, since they were easier to measure and ream. Moreover, by permitting makers to shape adjacent joints differently from one another, they allowed wider range and better intonation. Another feature transferred from the musette was the use of keys.

The first step toward mechanization of the woodwinds was the application of a single key, for D-sharp, to the flute by Jean Hotteterre about 1660. Hotteterre's flute had other innovative features as well: its body was conical, a scheme intended to eliminate the fifelike shrillness of its cylindrical predecessors. The conical bore also had a flattening effect, which allowed the fingerholes to be placed closer together, thereby reducing a previously uncomfortable reach. Similarly, Hotteterre reduced the size of the fingerholes.

Although the one-key flute remained the instrument of choice for more than a century, several minor modifications to the instrument were made during that span. Because the cork stopper was insufficient to remedy small changes in tuning, *corps de rechange* ("interchangeable bodies") gained currency about 1720. The instrument was divided into four joints, and the upper-middle was provided in from three to six different lengths for each instrument. The *corps de réchange* allowed the player to adjust to highly variable pitch standards. This technique was later used on the other woodwinds, as well. Johann Joachim Quantz, flute maker to Frederick the Great, made another innovation in tuning: a divided headjoint, joined by a tenon, which was the ancestor of the modern tuning slide.

The earliest form of the modern oboe appeared at the French court simultaneously with the one-key flute, making its first orchestral appearance in Lully's 1657 ballet *L'Amour malade*. It was descended from the treble shawm, a one-piece double-reed instrument with a wide conical bore and arbitrarily spaced fingerholes. The new instrument had three joints, a narrow conical bore, and more accurately spaced tone holes. Its most distinguishing characteristic was a set of twin holes for the production of certain chromatic notes; as a result, it had a fully chromatic two-octave compass if cross-fingerings were used and a wider dynamic range than the shawm. In its earliest forms, the oboe generally had two keys, a D-sharp key identical in function to that of the flute, and an open-standing "great" key that extended the range down to low C. Late in the seventeenth century an E-flat key was added. All three keys were playable by either hand. Perhaps the most important distinction between the shawm and the oboe was the latter's elimination of the *pirouette,* the metal tube that held the reed; its absence allowed the lips to control the reed more delicately and with greater refinement of tone. The oboe reed itself was wedge-shaped, as well as narrower and longer than that of the shawm. The oboe spread with spectacular speed; by 1674, French oboists had taken it to England, and it was soon adopted there for orchestral and military uses. By the early eighteenth century, the oboe had become a full-fledged member of orchestras throughout Europe.

The baroque bassoon derived from the Renaissance curtal or dulcian; Oxford's "Talbot manuscript" of 1685–1701, a major source for the study of instruments of the era, differentiates the one-piece *Fagot*, or curtal, from the four-piece *Basson*, or bassoon. Whereas the curtal was made of a single block of wood with two tubes bored within, the new bassoon had two separate parallel tubes: a wing joint (with six fingerholes) and an ascending long joint that ended in a bell, a novel feature that extended the lower range. These were joined at the bottom of the instrument by a U-tube. At the top was a crook, or bocal, a metal tube that held the reed. The early bassoon, like the curtal, typically had only two keys and was therefore not capable of producing a full chromatic scale.

The only entirely new woodwind instrument of the baroque was the chalumeau. A small ancestor of the clarinet, it resembled a soprano recorder but was equipped with a single reed. It had seven fingerholes, a thumbhole, and two keys. Because it was not overblown to produce a high register, its range was a mere octave and a half. Its utility was thus marginal, and its literature small; but it is important historically as the immediate ancestor of the modern clarinet.

The latter instrument, generally credited to Johann Christoph Denner of Nuremberg about 1700, took its name from the Italian term *clarinetto*, the diminutive of *clarino* ("clarion," a medieval trumpet), an etymology that denotes the similarity of its upper register to that of a trumpet. Denner's innovation was to move one of the chalumeau's key-covered holes and reduce its diameter so that the scale could be overblown by a twelfth (rather than an octave, as on the flute and oboe). The clarinet used a "speaker" key for the left thumb to bridge the gap between the lower and upper registers, something the chalumeau could not do. By the mid-eighteenth century, the clarinet, too, had become an established member of the orchestra.

In the mid-1700s, with the leadership of the Mannheim school in southern Germany, orchestral music became lighter, less constrained melodically, and replete with large-scale dynamic contrasts. As public concerts in large halls supplemented and ultimately superseded musical performances in private salons, instruments needed to become louder. Technical virtuosity was needed to lure the paying public, and wind instruments were needed to provide orchestral color. The clarinet in particular achieved greater prominence, not only in *allegros*, as orchestrated by the Mannheim school, but also in the slow movements of Beethoven and Schubert symphonies. The high, E-flat clarinet made its orchestral debut in Berlioz' *Symphonie fantastique*. Harmonically, music became more adventurous, and the baroque woodwinds were not always equal to the occasion: lacking extensive keywork, they were limited in the range of keys or tonalities that they could execute well; the flute, for example, was deficient in flat keys. Baroque woodwinds had been fully chromatic in their middle ranges but only diatonic in their upper and lower extensions. In the classic period, however, what had previously been regarded as "extra" notes became part of the instruments' normal range.

The major accomplishment of classic-era woodwind makers was the creation of supplementary keywork, which allowed tone holes to be placed in their proper acoustical positions while remaining accessible to the fingers. The results were numerous: the extension of range in both directions, enhanced flexibility of tonality, improved intonation (particularly in hitherto "distant" keys), increased technical facility (including choices of fingering for a given note), and greater uniformity of tone quality between registers.

The flute was the first of the woodwinds to receive extra chromatic keys. Shortly before 1760, the London flute makers Pietro Florio, Caleb Gedney, and Richard Potter added closed keys for G-sharp, B-flat, and F. Mounted in small wooden blocks, these keys were made of a sheet of brass with a solid leather pad; they rotated on brass pins attached to the flute tube through ridges in the wood. Because the reliability of these rather primitive contrivances was questioned by players—and with good reason—the keys did not become fully accepted until about 1785–1790. About 1774, some makers resuscitated the idea of the C footjoint, which had a brief vogue in Quantz's lifetime, and added keys for C and C-sharp. In 1782, a German flutist, Dr. J. J. H. Ribock, introduced a closed key for C^2; in 1786 Johann Georg Tromlitz devised a duplicate F-natural key, the "long F," which duplicated the action of the existing F key. But because it was operated by the left little finger, it eliminated the inevitable but unwanted slide from F to D or D-sharp. The resulting eight-key flute (also known as the Meyer system, old system, simple system, or German flute) remained the norm for much of the nineteenth century, even after the advent of the Boehm flute. Although ultimately superseded by the Boehm, it formed the basis for many non-Boehm competitors. There were also other, though comparatively less important, changes in flute design in the late eighteenth century: Potter's 1785 patent for keys with pewter plugs, to replace the square leather pads; a slight expansion of the footjoint bore, which increased the flute's volume; a similar increase in the size of the embouchure hole; and the adoption of the tuning slide.

The classic-period oboe, having become internationally accepted, became nationally differentiated. While French makers narrowed the bore and the reed (the reed also became longer) to make the tone sweeter and more refined and the dynamics more flexible, English makers aimed for a more robust sound. In comparison with the flute, the oboe was late to undergo mechanical elaboration, probably owing to its acoustical design; because the reed made it more susceptible to lip control, the oboe was able to compensate for certain difficulties of fingering and intonation without resort to mechanism. Nevertheless, by the late eighteenth century, the oboe had acquired an octave key to enhance upper-register note production. The standardization of the left-over-right hand configuration by this period not only made the duplicate E-flat key superfluous but also permitted additional keywork to be designed. Beginning at mid-century, the degree of ornamental woodwork declined, and the bell became more conical. The two-key oboe remained in use until about 1820.

The classic clarinet, with its relatively more durable single reed, to some extent usurped the popularity of the double-reed oboe. The clarinet was even less successful with cross-fingering than the flute was, and thus it was given a third key to produce the hitherto missing B-natural between the registers. It then acquired two more keys, for E-flat and C-sharp. This five-key instrument was the late-eighteenth-century standard, though a sixth key was also common—a trill key in England and a G-sharp key on the Continent. In one important regard, clarinet makers followed a different course from flute makers: rather than adding chromatic keywork to accommodate changes in tonalities, they provided alternate instruments, pitched in B-flat (for music in the keys of F, B-flat, and other flat keys); in C (for C, and sometimes for F and G), and A (for music in D, A, and other sharp keys). A few clarinetists, notably Anton Stadler, the Viennese virtuoso for whom Mozart wrote, had basset clarinets in A, with range to low C (rather than the usual E).

The classic bassoon had four keys, keys for E-flat and F-sharp having been added to the original two in the late eighteenth century. A major change was the widening of the bell, which increased the instrument's volume and endowed it with a more open tone quality. As with the oboe, national variations began to become apparent in bassoon manufacture. English makers, for instance, provided wider crooks than did some of their continental colleagues.

The trend toward mechanical elaboration of the woodwinds that had begun in the classic period continued with escalating force into the nineteenth century, attaining "quite remarkable elaboration in the romantic period," in the words of organologist Robert Donington. In this respect, the progress in the design and manufacture of the woodwinds paralleled that of the industrial revolution in general; it is not insignificant, therefore, that one of the most important figures in nineteenth-century woodwind history, Theobald Boehm, was active in the modernization of the steel industry. The mechanical and acoustical improvements in the design of the woodwind and brass instruments benefited from scientific advances in both acoustics and metallurgy.

The first quarter of the nineteenth century was pivotal: it encompassed the extensive and complex development of the older "simple-system" instruments, though that ironic label is a retrospective one and must not be taken too literally. Despite the addition of numerous keys, the late-classic instruments retained their antique appearance, with keys pivoted on pins. But in the first quarter of the nineteenth century, woodwind craftsmen made some strictly mechanical (as opposed to acoustical) innovations that were to have important consequences for later woodwind designs.

In 1806 the Paris flute maker Claude Laurent took out a patent for glass flutes. The use of glass is important only for its structural by-product, the rod-and-post method of key mounting. Laurent attached his keys to metal pillars or posts, which he soldered to a plate that was screwed into the glass tube. This configuration allowed the keys to fall more easily and reduced undesirable lateral play. The new key mounting also helped to encourage the use of new metals for the keys themselves; the new white bronzes (called German silver, *Neusilber*, or *maillechort*) were less expensive than silver but harder than brass. In addition, they were easily shaped and could even be cast, which was an inexpensive means of producing mass-market instruments.

In 1808 the Reverend Frederick Nolan obtained a British patent for ring keys, whereby a ring that surrounded an open hole simultaneously closed both that hole and another one. (Earlier keys and levers closed only one hole.) The ring-key principle is fundamental to the highly mechanized instruments developed later in the century. Early-nineteenth-century key pads also changed: makers found that using materials softer than leather, such as a sponge covered with a thin skin, sealed the tone holes more reliably. Their shape necessitated a shift from flat keys to cupped ones into which the pads could fit.

The second phase of nineteenth-century woodwind development, in the 1830s and 1840s, comprised changes in mechanism, materials, and bore design. The towering figure of this period was Theobald Boehm, a Munich flute maker who successfully combined several mechanical inventions of his predecessors with acoustical principles of his own discovery. His purely mechanical inventions, though they gained him the greatest fame, were actually secondary in importance. Boehm's borrowings were fourfold: large fingerholes (from the English flutist Charles Nicholson), though Boehm placed them according to acoustical principles rather than digital convenience; covering holes with keys in order to enable them to control distant holes and keys; the use of ring keys (Nolan); and open-keyed construction and the use of crescent-shaped touchpieces (H. W. Pottgiesser, 1803).

On Boehm's 1832 flute, the first true Boehm-system instrument, he made the tone holes as large as practicable. The logical extension of this principle was an open-key system (in which the keys were open-standing when at rest), which allowed full venting of the holes. In order to control the requisite fourteen holes with only nine fingers (the right thumb supported the flute), Boehm used Nolan's ring keys and horizontal rod-axles of his own invention. The fingering system that Boehm devised enabled the fingers to remain in their natural positions for all fingerings except for operating the trill keys and foot-joint keys.

Subsequently, several instrument makers made some mechanical improvements to the Boehm flute. Louis Auguste Buffet, a Paris instrument maker, moved all the axles to the near side of the flute, a more elegant arrangement than Boehm's. To do so, he invented the clutch, a rod-and-sleeve device consisting of overlapping lugs or pins. He also replaced Boehm's flat leaf springs with more delicate rotary-action needle springs. With his flutist colleague Victor Coche, Buffet devised a closed G-sharp key (patented 1839)—Boehm's open G-sharp being one of the prime obstacles to flutists', learning the new fingering—and, more important, a trill key for C-sharp/D-sharp in the second and third octaves, hitherto impossible on the Boehm flute. Another French flutist, Vincent Dorus, devised a different type of closed G-sharp key, based on two opposing springs; though hardly elegant, it helped ease players' transition to the Boehm flute.

In the 1840s Boehm returned to the drawing board and to the laboratory; he studied acoustics with Carl von Schafhäutl at the University of Munich and in 1847 unveiled a new model. It was made of silver, rather than wood, and its body was cylindrical. The head joint gradually decreased in diameter from top to bottom in what Boehm labeled a "parabolic curve," though the resemblance to a parabola was only in general shape, not in mathematical proportion. Boehm used padded, plateau (solid-top) keys rather than ring keys to cover the holes. Each key operated independently but was attached to the others in accordance with the Boehm fingering system. Boehm adopted the sleeves and rods of Buffet, attaching each key cover to its own sleeve and springing each open with a light needle spring; he linked the keys with clutches whose relative vertical positions could be adjusted by set screws. The only significant changes that the Boehm flute has undergone since 1847 are the introduction of the duplicate-hole closed G-sharp and of Giulio Briccialdi's B-flat thumb key, which places the B-flat lever about the B-natural key (a reversal of Boehm's design for the thumb keys), and the perforation of five keys by Clair Godfroy, Boehm's French licensee, now a common option known as the French model or open-hole flute. In 1844–1845, Boehm introduced the modern alto flute; it is essentially identical to the regular C flute except for the addition of an octave or speaker key (*Schleifklappe*).

The Boehm flute quickly became popular with professional flutists in France and England, and was manufactured in the United States as early as 1847. It garnered important prizes at industrial exhibitions in London (1851), Paris (1855), and Munich (1855), yet the instrument was slow to gain acceptance in the inventor's native Germany. The greatest objection to the Boehm flute there and elsewhere was the entirely new fingering system, which was difficult for players accustomed to the old system to learn in midcareer.

Work on the flute in the latter two-thirds of the nineteenth century corresponds to national allegiances: in Germany and elsewhere on the Continent work continued on the old-system cone flute, culminating in what seems to modern observers a mechanical absurdity, the Rube Goldberg–like "Reform flute" of Carl Kruspe, Maximilian Schwedler, and others. In England instrument makers worked on modifications of, and additions to, the Boehm flute; on entirely new instruments; and on compromise and combination models, which integrated Boehm and old-system features in a single instrument. Some examples of the latter category are the Card flute, which combined the Boehm right-hand mechanism for F-sharp with an otherwise old-system flute; the Carte 1851 flute; the Carte 1867 system (also known as the Guards' Model); Rockstro's 1852 conical adaptation of the Boehm flute, and several subsequent mechanical additions to it; the Pratten Perfected Flute (1852); and the Radcliff flute (1870).

The nineteenth-century oboe paralleled the flute in many ways but at a lag of some years. By about 1825 it customarily had a complement of ten to twelve keys. The thirteen-key oboe developed by Joseph Sellner in Vienna by 1825 became the basis of the standard instrument of central and eastern Europe for more than a century. Soon thereafter, the oboe began to develop in a different direction in France. Members of the Triébert family were responsible for the major French innovations, denoting the progress of their designs with a series of numbered systems: Système 2 had a half-hole plate, a brille ("eyeglass" ring-key mechanism), and a long E-flat key. Frédéric Triébert's Système 3 (ca. 1840) adopted the rod-axles of Boehm and a second octave key. Système 4 (ca. 1850) used a "butterfly key," a double-touched key with long axles between pillars to replace the long simple levers that had previously been used to control distant keys. Système 5 (1860) added a thumb plate to enhance movement across the octave break; Apollon Barret, a French oboist, altered the right-hand action in order to eliminate the thumb plate. Système 6 (ca. 1880), to which Lorée, Triébert's foreman, and the Paris Conservatoire professor Georges Gillet in 1906 added perforated finger plates (Système A6), became known as the Conservatoire model after the Paris school formally adopted it in 1882 and is the modern standard in France and the United States, although Système 5 also remains in use.

In 1844, Buffet, who had previously modified the Boehm flute, patented a design for the oboe based on Boehm's acoustical principles. Its large bore and tone holes and commensurately powerful tone, often described as "open," made it appealing to military musicians, but most French oboists disliked it. The London oboist A. J. Lavigne did use it, however, and made a number of design changes; one of his models was known as "old spider-keys." Some French makers, including Triébert, attempted to combine the Boehm mechanism with the conventional French oboe bore; this hybrid was attractive to doublers and had some pedagogical applications in England. Along with the mechanical development of the oboe, there were changes in the reed, which evolved from roughly a V-shape to a straight, narrow form.

As the nineteenth century began, the bassoon, like the other woodwinds, was an expanded simple-system instrument. It had from six to eight keys, including two new octave keys on the wind joint. In the second and third decades of the century, the bassoon took two divergent routes, French and German. In 1817 Jacques François Simiot of Lyons invented a removable metal U-tube to replace the cork as the connection between the two bores of the instrument. Another Frenchman, Jean Nicolas Savary, altered the bassoon's bore in order to make the tone more homogeneous; he also added seven keys. Instruments made to such specifications were favored initially in England as well as in France and were made principally by Triébert and Buffet in Paris, Mahillon in Brussels, and Key in London. Eugène Jancourt, professor of bassoon at the Paris Conservatoire, worked with Triébert and Buffet-Crampon on the development, by 1847, of a twenty-two-key model; with minor modifications, it became established as the standard French-model bassoon. Triébert experimented as well with a Boehm-system bassoon (1855), designed in collaboration with the Paris player A. Marzoli according to a schema provided by Boehm himself. It had larger than usual tone holes in acoustically determined positions and a complex mechanism to match; but ironically, its clear sound was considered not bassoonlike, and this factor, coupled with its mechanical complexity, doomed it.

Almost simultaneously with Savary's work, German woodwind makers were altering the bassoon into what would become, in the twentieth century, the world standard. Beginning in 1817, Carl Almenräder — dubbed the "Boehm of the bassoon" by organologist Curt Sachs — experimented with all facets of the bassoon's construction. He altered tone-hole size and placement and the relative lengths of the joints and added keys to increase technical facility and extend the range upward. He also adopted Boehm's rod-axles, post-mounted keys in place of the old saddles and stuffed pads, and connected keys with a pin through the inner wall of the double joint. His 1822 bassoon tutor provided instructions for an eighteen-key instrument with a full chromatic range over four octaves.

The negative effect of Almenräder's alterations was a harshness of tone quality, which seemed even more pronounced in comparison with the new French instruments. In 1831, Almenräder formed a partnership with Johann Adam Heckel, the first of a veritable dynasty of creative woodwind builders and the man responsible for refining Almenräder's work. Heckel succeeded in retaining the technical advantages of Almenräder's design while eliminating the roughness of its sound; he also made several mechanical improvements. One problem with the old instrument was that the fingers controlled only half the instrument, from the reed down to the bottom of the butt; the ascending tubing, from butt to long joint, to bell, was under the sole control of the thumbs. Heckel devised a rod to link the two parts of the instrument, which permitted a key on the far side to be operated by either a thumb or a finger. Heckel's son, Wilhelm, made further changes in bore and hole design and remodeled Simiot's U-tube. He made the instrument more watertight (1879) by lining the wing joint and descending tube of the butt with a layer of ebonite, a synthetic rubber, thereby preventing the lower sections from swelling as a result of accumulated moisture. By the 1880s the *Heckelfagott* was predominant in Germany and Austria.

Germany was also the site of the nineteenth-century development of the larger bassoons; these included the fifteen-key metal contrabassoon of Johann Stehle (1830s) and the *Claviatur-Contrafagott* (1845) of Carl Wilhelm Moritz, which was played from a keyboard. Heinrich Haseneier, in 1847, made the contrabassophone, a contrabassoon of double-dimension bore and wide tone holes, and Heckel, in 1879, made more conventional contrabassoons to low C, the model still in use.

The clarinet, like the flute, gradually shifted from the old system to the Boehm system. As the nineteenth century opened, the five- or six-key instrument, with the reed tied to the mouthpiece with cord and played against the upper lip, was the norm. About 1808, Simiot made an instrument with a number of important improvements: a speaker hole at the front of the clarinet, where it was relatively less susceptible to water blockage; a similar brass drainage tube in the left-hand thumbhole; a brass tuning slide; and a side key on the lower joint to give an in-tune, accurate B in the chalumeau register. In 1823 another French clarinetist, César Janssen, invented the roller key, a revolving cylinder that allows a finger to slide from one key to another without unwanted intermediate notes. Adolphe Sax added a low E-flat key that extended the lower range and was useful in transposing A clarinet parts for the B-flat instrument; other keys added by Sax (as many as twenty-four) made cross-fingering necessary only seldom. Sax's improved clarinet was manufactured and further modified by Eugène Albert and Charles Mahillon in Belgium; the Albert-system clarinet, as the model became known, was a staple throughout the nineteenth century in Britain and Belgium. Sax was also responsible for the invention of the bass clarinet in 1838.

Another major figure in the history of the simple-system clarinet was Iwan Müller, a clarinet virtuoso based in Vienna and Paris and the author of an influential tutor (ca. 1825). Among his improvements were the addition of seven keys (for a total of thirteen) to eliminate cross-fingering; the use of key pads made of animal intestines stuffed with wool, whose pliancy enabled them to close the tone holes more reliably than the old-style flat leather pads; and a metal ligature to clamp the reed onto the underside of the mouthpiece. (Up to then the reed had been tied to the mouthpiece with a cord, but since the reed was on top of the mouthpiece lay, the arrangement was gravity-proof, and a firm binding unnecessary.) The shift of the reed from the upper lip to the lower one, though it engendered no definitive change in the construction of the lay itself, was the most important change in clarinet playing in the nineteenth century. Müller's tutor recommended the downward position, which permitted a tongued staccato; at that time, German clarinetists were evenly split between the two systems. The Paris Conservatoire officially endorsed the downside reed in 1831, and by midcentury players everywhere in Europe except Italy agreed. Despite the loss of control over the high register, the tone was fuller, rounder, and warmer, and the articulation cleaner.

Another structural change in the mouthpiece was the growing tendency for makers to consider it a separate entity from the clarinet itself. Having earlier viewed it as an integral part of the basic instrument, they had limited themselves to the same materials used for the body, principally boxwood and ebony. Now, they felt free to experiment with other materials that were more resistant to the inevitable moisture generated by the mouth: they worked with harder woods, glass, ivory, and finally ebonite, the synthetic rubber that is now used almost universally.

In France, meanwhile, the modern clarinet was taking shape. This was the Boehm-system clarinet, patented in 1844, which was developed not by Boehm but by the clarinetist Hyacinthe Eleonore Klosé and Louis Auguste Buffet. The Boehm nomenclature referred not to the acoustical design—it did not adhere to the principle of full venting—but to the fingering system, with its chief characteristics, ring keys and rod-axles. A "full Boehm" clarinet, with additional keys, is the sole extant variation on the Klosé instrument; its popularity has been largely confined to Italy.

The last years of the nineteenth century were, for all the woodwinds,

a period of refinement: the addition of a few new keys of minor importance, such as extra trill keys, and experiments with new materials, such
as ebonite and plated metals. Like other industries, musical-instrument
manufacturing benefited from the progress of the industrial revolution;
assembly lines and interchangeable, mass-produced parts allowed instrument makers to keep pace with the expanding markets created by school
and community bands. By the beginning of the twentieth century, all
four woodwinds had attained their modern forms in all essential matters.
As a result, the current century has been one of mechanical stability.
Instrument makers have hardly been idle, however; they have devoted
themselves, as the historian E. A. K. Ridley put it so well, to materials and
microdimensions. Players had at their disposal instruments that were
mechanically efficient, flexible in timbre and volume, and reliable in intonation. That is not to say that players agreed with each other entirely on
what constitutes the ideal instrument. In the case of the flute, the silver
Boehm-system instrument has attained near universality, though many
British players persisted in using wood flutes into the second half of the
twentieth century. There have been numerous experiments with supplementary trill and vent keys, such as the "gizmo" for top C, but relatively
few major redesigns. The one large-scale (and long-term) attempt to correct defects in the Boehm flute is the Murray flute, in reality a succession
of some sixteen models—and at that, its inventor, Alexander Murray,
considers the Boehm "98 percent perfect." In the case of the piccolo, the
outstanding twentieth-century advance has been the use of the plastic
tube, which offers a tone quality not unlike that of the wooden instrument (the orchestral favorite), coupled with the durability and economy
of metal.

Most contemporary oboists use French instruments in the Triébert
tradition; the leading maker continues to be Lorée. In Austria and other
areas affected by the Viennese influence (Italy and the Soviet Union, for
example), the Sellner-style instrument held sway until the mid-1950s.
Overall, the technically flexible Conservatoire model has prevailed.

The modern player's choice of bassoon, similarly, has been governed
by national tradition. The French instrument has been favored in France,
Belgium, Spain, and Italy, and the German system in Germany, Austria,
and the Netherlands. In the United States, the German system has been
almost universally used because of the nineteenth-century immigration
of many German bassoon players; in Great Britain, the French system
was used almost exclusively at the beginning of the century but was
replaced by the German when it was later introduced by American players. There has been a rather interesting experiment with bassoon construction, the "logical bassoon" of the British neurophysiologist and

acoustician Giles Brindley. Brindley's objection to existing instruments was that the fingering for a given note was different in each octave. His 1967 design eliminated that difficulty; it used an octave key, connected to electrically powered logic circuits between the fingerplates and pads, to distinguish the registers. The instrument also includes a heating wire that regulates tuning and controls condensation. Other twentieth-century bassoon makers, working with the traditional instrument, have added new keys for trills, high notes, and alternate fingerings, as well as mutes, such as the internal butterfly valve designed by Nekhlyudov in the Soviet Union.

Modern clarinetists favor the Conservatoire model; the rather heavy "full Boehm" is used only occasionally, and the Albert system is extinct. The most recent innovation is actually an offshoot of the current interest in historical instruments: in 1983 the American virtuoso David Shifrin commissioned from Leonard Gulatta in Los Angeles a basset clarinet that would allow him to perform the Mozart clarinet concerto in its original version.

BIBLIOGRAPHY

Anthony Baines, "James Talbot's Manuscript: I, Wind Instruments," in Galpin Society Journal, 1 (1948); and Woodwind Instruments and Their History (1963). Philip Bate, The Flute (1969); and The Oboe (3rd ed., 1975). Theobald Boehm, The Flute and Flute-Playing, Dayton C. Miller, trans. and ed. (2nd ed., 1922; repr. 1964). Adam Carse, Musical Wind Instruments (1939; repr. 1965).

Horniman Museum, Wind Instruments of European Art Music, E. A. K. Ridley, ed. (1974). Edgar Hunt, "Some Light on the Chalumeau," in Galpin Society Journal, 14 (1961). Will Jansen, The Bassoon (1979). Oskar Kroll, The Clarinet, Diethard Riehm, rev.; Hilda Morris, trans.; Anthony Baines, ed. (1968). Lyndesay G. Langwill, The Bassoon and Contrabassoon (1971); and An Index of Musical Wind-Instrument Makers (6th ed., 1980). James MacGillivray, "Recent Advances in Woodwind Fingering Systems," in Galpin Society Journal, 12 (1959); and "The Woodwind," in Anthony Baines, ed., Musical Instruments Through the Ages (1961). Jeremy Montagu, The World of Baroque and Classical Musical Instruments (1979); and The World of Romantic and Modern Musical Instruments (1981).

F. Geoffrey Rendall, The Clarinet, Philip Bate, rev. (3rd ed., 1971). Richard S. Rockstro, A Treatise on the Construction, the History and the Practice of the Flute (2nd ed., rev. 1928; repr. 1967). Nancy Toff, The Development of the Modern Flute (1979). Jerry Lee Voorhees, "The Development of Woodwind Fingering Systems," D.M.A. diss., North Texas State University, 1971. Thomas E. Warner, An Annotated Bibliography of Woodwind Instruction Books, 1600–1830 (1967). Phillip Young, 2500 Historical Woodwind Instruments: An Inventory of the Major Collections (1980).

Technical Development of Musical Instruments:

Brass

Barbara Lambert

The brass section of a twentieth-century orchestra typically consists of trumpets, horns, trombones, and tubas. What are these instruments, how different are they from their predecessors, and how did they develop into what they now are?

The term *brass* was applied to musical instruments in this century to denote the class of instruments sounded by vibrating one's lips together into a cupped mouthpiece. The term is not accurate, simply because such instruments are not always made of brass. They are sometimes made of silver, ivory, bronze, nickel, or wood wrapped in leather. In this essay the term *brass instrument* is used to denote the method of making sound rather than the material.

MUSICAL AND ACOUSTIC PRINCIPLES OF THE BRASS

The orchestra requires the "musical" use of an instrument, or the ability to produce adjacent or stepwise notes in order to play melodies. Before brass instruments began to be "improved," only two of them could play melodies, the early trumpet and French horn, and this was possible only in their highest registers. The history of brass orchestral instruments is the development of the technology to make all types of brass instruments chromatic throughout their ranges.

There are three acoustic principles that define true brass instruments. (There is a subsection of this class that employs the same technique to sound its instruments but uses a different principle to play the various notes.) First, the entire length of the air column, from the mouthpiece to the flared bell that terminates the instrument, always fully vibrates when a true brass instrument is sounded. (Woodwind acoustics are different; the vibrating column of air in a woodwind is shortened or lengthened for each note by covering or uncovering fingerholes.) Second, all tones are part of the harmonic series of a specifically fixed tube length and permit no use of cross-fingering (woodwinds do). And third, different notes are obtained on brass instruments by overblowing (that is, using increased air pressure to reach higher notes). Woodwinds use this technique only to play the second and infrequently the third harmonics—an octave or a twelfth above a given note.

THE HARMONIC SERIES

The sequence of tones produced by overblowing a true brass instrument is called the harmonic series. The lowest note of the harmonic series, known as the fundamental, is the key in which the instrument is pitched. The successive notes in the series are always the same distance apart, no matter what the lowest note is. Figure 1 shows the harmonic series for an instrument pitched in the key of C. In addition to the actual note played, overtones, or "ghosts" of other tones, are present in varying degrees within each note of the harmonic series and affect the richness or ringing quality of the sound of that note.

The lowest note of the harmonic series, the "fundamental" (an octave below the normal range), is seldom used by brass instruments, because it is difficult or impossible to play except on orchestral tubas. The "easy" range to play on brass instruments is from the second or third "harmonic" (also called *note, tone,* or *partial*) to the sixth or eighth. These are widely spaced notes, not in a stepwise sequence. Simple military calls (such as taps) use the third through the sixth partials. They are usually

Figure 1. The natural harmonic series. (Note names assigned to 11, 13, and 15 are only roughly correct.)

played on bugles, but can be played on any instrument. From the seventh partial to the eleventh, the intervals are "diatonic," or stepwise in the pattern of a scale. From the eleventh harmonic upward, the range is "chromatic"; that is, every note is a "semitone," or half step, away from the adjacent notes (except between the thirteenth and fourteenth harmonics) and is available to skilled players. Highly skilled modern professional trumpet players usually do not play above the twelfth partial, because the technological development of brass instruments has made it possible to play chromatic notes and produce melodies in the lower registers. Further, various harmonics are either flat (the seventh, thirteenth, and fourteenth) or sharp (the eleventh) and require great skill to adjust. The pinnacle of brass instrument playing was attained late in the baroque period, from about 1700 to 1750, when players of "natural" trumpets and horns (the brasses that could produce the greatest number of harmonics without mechanical assistance) so developed their skills as to be able to play melodies on partials as high as the twenty-fourth.

THE CLASSIFICATION OF BRASS INSTRUMENTS

There are four principal families of true brass musical instruments: the trumpet and the trombone, which have cylindrical bores, and the horn and the bugle, which have conical bores. (One false type or subsection is the cornett/serpent.) A "family" is the generic grouping of types, while a "type" is a specific kind of instrument. Thus, within the family of horns are cornets, Wagner tubas, baritones, and so forth.

A tube's length, its structure (whether primarily cylindrical or conoidal), its diameter in proportion to its length (whether narrow, medium, or wide), and the shapes of the mouthpiece (funnel, cup, or a variation) and of the bell (whether conical, flared, or something in between) are the factors that distinguish families and types of brass instruments. Together they determine a family's characteristic sound, its compass (the outer limits of notes that can be played on it), and the range of each type within a family (whether, loosely, it is a soprano, alto, tenor, bass, or variation thereof).

TECHNOLOGICAL DEVICES

Various devices have been invented to enable a brass instrument to produce diatonic and chromatic notes. The early trumpet and French horn were alone among the brass in being capable of producing diatonic and chromatic notes, but few players of these "natural" instruments had the innate talent and highly practiced and refined skills to play them. Further, diatonic and chromatic notes could be produced only in the highest range of the two natural instruments; in their lower registers, wide intervals existed between the notes. These could be filled in only with the aid of a mechanical device.

The devices applied to brass instruments for chromatically filling in the natural intervals of the harmonic series are technically complex and function in different ways. In summary, they consist of four basic types and a technique. Each was applied to almost all types of brass instruments at one period or another for different effects, and each has its distinct advantages and disadvantages.

Slides are telescopic lengths of tubing that slide one within the other; they physically lengthen an instrument and consequently lower the key of the instrument's harmonic series. *Hand-stopping* is the technique of inserting the hand into the bell to shorten the length of the tube and thereby raise the pitch of a particular note by a semitone or tone. It also muffles the note's sound. *Crooks* are additional lengths of tubing that can be added or removed to change from one harmonic series to another. Changing the key of a harmonic series with crooks is a slow process because a player must stop and use both hands. Inserting a cold crook into an instrument warm from playing usually causes intonation problems until all parts reach the same temperature. Another risk is a loose crook, which can wobble or slip, causing cracked notes and bad intonation.

The *keys* covering the fingerholes allow the holes to be large in size and placed at greater distances apart than the human hand can cover or reach; they physically shorten the sounding length of the instrument when open and lengthen it when closed. This is particularly useful on the lower brasses that have especially long lengths of tubing, sometimes with wide diameters. The main drawback to keys is that when they are opened far above the bell, the sounding length of the tube is so reduced that the acoustic properties of the bell are ineffectual, and its ringing quality is lost. *Valves* mechanically and instantly change the total length of the instrument and the key of its harmonic series by adding or removing extra loops of tubing. Problems arise when two or more valve loops are used together; their total length is always less than that needed for correct intonation, resulting in a sharp note. Better-quality valved instruments are fitted with extra valves and loops to compensate for valve combinations.

PRE-NINETEENTH-CENTURY INSTRUMENTS

Although the first orchestras date from around 1600, brass instruments were almost never played in them until about 1700, except on special occasions. The trumpet was the only brass instrument used in the seventeenth-century orchestra. The social position of trumpet players was much higher than that of the other members of the orchestra, the sound of their instruments was inherently regal, and the guilds to which the players belonged strictly controlled where and when their services could be rendered. Consequently trumpeters played in orchestras only on the most important or formal occasions of the state, the military, and the church.

The natural or hunting horn was used primarily for ceremonial purposes during the hunt in this period. It did not blend well with other orchestral instruments; in the prevailing practice, players held the bell upward, maximizing its loud, penetrating sound in order to make it audible over the thunder of hooves and the baying of hounds. In the sixteenth and seventeenth centuries the horn was wound one and a half or two and a half times around, in a circle of quite wide diameter, so that when it was not being played it could be carried securely over a mounted player's head and one shoulder.

In about the mid-fifteenth century the trombone developed from a version of the trumpet with a slide, which enabled it to play adjacent notes and to play them absolutely in tune. Before this, it was associated with the church as an accompaniment to voices, probably because it was so "expressive" (it had a wide range of dynamic levels). Rarely found in purely orchestral works, the trombone was used mainly in opera and church orchestras until the early nineteenth century, when Beethoven began to use it in his symphonies.

In the seventeenth century, the only lip-vibrated instruments regularly included in the orchestra were those of the cornett/serpent family, also frequently used for vocal accompaniment. The family is the subsection of brass instruments that produces stepwise notes with fingerholes. The cornett family was never made of metal; rather, it was fashioned out of wood wrapped in leather to seal it or out of ivory. It had a very small cupped mouthpiece and a delicate, quiet sound; frequently it was likened to the human voice. As the trumpet came into use in the eighteenth-century orchestra, its range duplicated that of the cornett family and rendered the latter obsolete by midcentury. Only the bass member of the family, the serpent, survived into the nineteenth century—and then only in church ensembles and military bands.

By the late-baroque period, the orchestra consisted mainly of string and woodwind instruments. With the wane of the guild system, trumpets were gradually incorporated, and such composers as Bach and Handel began to score orchestral parts for them. The trumpet's useful compass was its highest, or "clarino," range. Although playing the instrument required exceptional talent, arduous training available only in guild apprenticeships, and constant practice, it was during this period that players attained the highest mastery of the trumpet. Nevertheless the inclusion of the trumpet in the orchestra, as well as that of the horn (usually to evoke pastoral hunting scenes), remained the exception rather than the rule. The only physical changes to the trumpet were the design and execution of more precise proportions, which assured players of better control over the upper partials, and a slight flaring of the bell, which somewhat increased its volume.

About 1750 a Bohemian horn virtuoso, Anton Hampel, discovered, or at least codified, a new technique for playing his instrument—hand-stopping. By inserting his hand into the bell, he could both muffle the volume of sound and raise a given harmonic by a semitone or whole tone, creating additional adjacent notes. To make it possible to reach the bell, the horn's wide diameter was reduced by coiling it three and a half times. This simple technique at once quieted its raucous sound and added notes to its compass; the horn immediately became the most important brass instrument in the classical orchestra.

By the beginning of the classical era, changes in the use of lip-vibrated instruments constituted the most important innovation. Composers, wanting more varied instrumental color, frequently wrote for trumpets and horns in an increased number of keys, which challenged performers and makers alike. The trombone during this period acquired a somewhat wider-flaring bell.

The slide had briefly reappeared on the trumpet in England and Germany in the late seventeenth century. In Germany the slide continued to be mounted somewhat unstably on the mouthpipe, as it had been in the fifteenth century. Nonetheless, this instrument seems to have been one of the types of trumpets for which Bach wrote. (Unfortunately no instrument of this type has survived; we have only contemporary depictions and descriptions of it.) In the late eighteenth century in London, the slide was again applied to the trumpet, this time in the back bow (the portion of the trombone's bore that curves round behind the player's ear), sliding toward the player's cheek and activated by a clock spring and later by elastic. Its function was to correct the intonation of the bad partials and to supply adjacent notes absent from the trumpet's harmonic series. Along with crooks, it remained in use in England until the end of the nineteenth century. To play in a greater number of keys and to produce stepwise notes, on a true brass instrument, a player had to be able to increase or decrease its total length. Up to then, the slide had been the simplest and most effective means to achieve this.

The standard key in which brass instruments were pitched was rising a tone in each musical period as mechanical and musical refinements were made. In the seventeenth century, for example, the trumpet was pitched in the key of C. By the beginning of the eighteenth century its pitch had risen to D; by the middle of the century, to E-flat; and by the beginning of the nineteenth century, to F. Because technology made it possible to fill in adjacent notes between otherwise quite wide harmonic intervals, it was easier to play higher notes on the lower, more widely spaced harmonics of shorter instruments, and so the trend was decidedly toward shorter instruments.

The next innovation was that of crooks and couplers. Crooks change the key of the harmonic series; the smaller couplers were combined with crooks to change the pitch by a whole or half tone, eliminating the need, expense, and awkwardness of many crooks (sometimes up to thirteen on a horn) formerly required for playing in additional keys. In the early seventeenth century trombones were the first type of instrument fitted with crooks; in the eighteenth century trumpets were similarly provided with crooks.

The search for a device to make brass instruments truly chromatic began around 1760 with the application of keys (or covers for fingerholes with levers, or "touches," operated by fingers). Keys were attached to trumpets, posthorns, and French horns. At the end of the classical period, the keyed trumpet was the standard orchestral instrument in southern Europe. (The natural trumpet, tuned a step higher to the key of F, remained the standard orchestral instrument in northern Europe.) Its advantage over the natural trumpet was that its keys enabled it to play all of the diatonic notes in the lower part of the compass and most of the chromatic notes. Its basically cylindrical bore retained the characteristic sound of the aristocratic natural trumpet. Both Haydn's and Hummel's trumpet concertos were specifically written for the keyed trumpet.

Other eighteenth-century attempts to make the trumpet chromatic were the stop trumpet (*Stopftrompete* in German) and the *Inventionstrompete*. The former's overall length was necessarily shortened by a pair of double bends so that a player could reach the bell for hand-stopping; the latter was a stop trumpet with a tuning slide.

NINETEENTH- AND TWENTIETH-CENTURY BRASS

During the nineteenth century, brass families, always less clearly defined than woodwind families, became even more confused by technological developments. Instruments that had once had a predominantly cylindrical bore, such as the trumpet, were redesigned with a predominantly conical bore; the reverse was true for the French horn. Further, the shape of an instrument became of no help in identifying the various types because once the pitch of an instrument is determined by its length, and the quality of sound by the combination of shapes of the various parts, the tubing can take any shape. Bells face forward or backward, up or down; the bore is wound round the body in a helical shape like a sousaphone, coiled tightly like some trumpets and horns, folded like the early trumpet, or stretched out straight. The shape has little effect on the instrument's morphology or acoustics. Nevertheless, the various shapes that a single type of instrument took in its history, and sometimes even within a particularly experimental period, have a great deal to do with the visual delight of a brass instrument.

Valves. The major achievement of the nineteenth century was the development of three-octave instruments into fully chromatic ones, primarily through the invention of valves. Technological development closely paralleled the growing musical importance of military bands. The results were that the four-octave, "true" trumpet family (which had the same proportions as the natural trumpet) was quickly replaced by three-octave valved bugles and cornets; tone quality was sacrificed for the ease and precision of duplicating the natural trumpet's notes and of doing so with a greater volume of sound. Valves on the horn eliminated the need for cumbersome, heavy, and expensive sets of crooks. And new forms of lower-pitched brass instruments were created out of the desire to have a greater variety of sounds and more-flexible sounds in the lower registers.

Valves, which revolutionized brass instruments, first appeared in Berlin about 1815. The valve is a mechanical device—an airtight chamber that connects the main body of a brass instrument to an auxiliary length of tubing—to increase or decrease an instrument's length instantly and at will. Three valves are usually provided: the first lowers the instrument's overall pitch by a whole tone; the second, by a semitone; and the third, by a tone and a half. When they are used together the pitch is lowered even further. Each pitch is the basis for an entire harmonic series of tones. Valves instantly make an instrument fully chromatic. A tuning slide attached to each valve loop adjusts the intonation of certain notes as well as the combination of valve loops, which have deficient proportions, producing a sharp note, until the slide corrects the intonation. Experimentation in the invention and development of valve mechanisms was diverse and profuse. Square valves, Stölzel valves, double-piston or Vienna valves, Berlin valves, and Périnet valves are the five principal types that emerged. Each was used on almost all types of brass instruments.

The *square valve* (with a square or rectangular cross section) appeared earliest. It was soon followed by the first truly successful version, the cylindrical piston valve, the *Stölzel valve,* named after the horn player Heinrich Stölzel, who introduced it in Berlin about 1815 and claimed to have invented it. The design was efficient, but its narrowness and the sharp bends of the air column tended to constrict the vibrating air and to affect adversely the quality of the sound. Also, the long stroke slowed down a player's technique. However, it was successful enough to have been used into the twentieth century.

The *double-piston,* or *Vienna, valve,* dating from the late 1820s, was the invention of Leopold Uhlmann. It comprises a short pair of pistons that work in tandem; one controls the entrance to the valve loop, and the other the exit from it. The pistons are smaller and shorter than other types, and the valve must be lifted rather than depressed; consequently, either the valve is mounted upside down or the instrument is turned upside down to play it. Such valves are still found on some types of brass instruments today.

The *Berlin valve,* or *Berliner Pumpe,* was created by Johann Gottfried Moritz and the bandmaster Wilhelm Wieprecht about 1835. It is musically efficient: the valve is short and has a wide diameter so that all passageways can be kept in the same plane, permitting a shorter, easier stroke and thereby improving the player's facility. It is easily identified visually by the fact that all four entry and exit tubes are brazed to the casing at the same level. Further, its single tubular piston is more durable than the Stölzel valve. Adolphe Sax pirated it in 1843 for his saxhorns, to which he also applied rotary valves. Berlin valves were widely used until late in the nineteenth century on bass instruments such as the tuba, and in northern Germany and Sweden into this century.

The *rotary valve*—or "conical turning-canister valve," as it was described in 1845 by Wieprecht—had appeared by the mid-1820s. In 1825, Nathan Adams of Lowell, Massachusetts, invented this type, but at the time, it failed to attract the attention it deserved. Here the piston is replaced by a rotor that turns in bearing plates at each end of a short cylinder. The rotors only have to turn 90 degrees to redirect the air into the auxiliary valve. The movement is exact, enabling a player to increase his facility, and the mechanism is easier to manufacture than that of a piston valve. Today, the French horn is the only type of instrument still using the rotary valve, even though many players think it is superior to the piston. In Europe, inventors associated with the rotary valve include Friedrich Blühmel of Berlin, Joseph Kail of Prague, and Joseph Felix Riedl of Vienna, the last of whom patented in 1832 the *Rad-Maschine,* the version of the rotary valve still used today.

The *Périnet valve* was introduced by the Parisian horn maker François Périnet in 1839. It is similar to the Berlin valve except that the piston is constructed more narrowly because none of the three ports lie in the same plane, as they do on the latter. It is the type of valve that predominates today.

Many other variations on these basic types have been invented to refine such details as the humps where one passageway transverses closely over another or to provide the full bore diameter throughout. *Peripheral mechanical devices,* such as independent and compensating pistons, or additional valves are sometimes attached to auxiliary lengths of tubing for the purpose of correcting the intonation of certain valve combinations.

The Horn. Concurrent with the development of valved horns was the invention of the omnitonic horn. This was a composite instrument, incorporating enough tubing for all the instrument's crooks between the body and bell. The earliest surviving example was built by a Parisian maker, J. B. Dupont, about 1815; the most successful, in 1824 by Charles Sax, father of the saxophone inventor, Adolphe. Advantages of the omnitonic horn were that the change of crooks was automatic and that the characteristic sound of the natural horn was preserved. Disadvantages were its heaviness and the necessity of using hand-stopping for nonharmonic notes, which restricted its dynamic levels.

By the mid-nineteenth century, the valved horn had won out over the omnitonic; nonharmonic notes could be played more easily and more loudly with valves; and more volume was becoming the norm. Schumann was the first important composer to write specifically for valved horn; other composers, such as Weber and Wagner, called for pairs of both hand and valve horns, exploiting the best features of each. Brahms, however, enamored of the dark, mysteriously romantic sonority of the hand horn, continued to write specifically for it.

Horns differed, too, from country to country. Austrian players still use the Vienna valve, invented by Leopold Uhlmann in the late 1820s. Although difficult to master, these valves are very sensitive and create a beautiful and distinctive tone quality unmatched by any other type invented after them. German horns were fitted with Riedl rotary valves, which had a rougher sound but were easier to play than the Viennese, and gradually they became standard.

Around 1898 the double horn was invented by Fritz Kruspe of Erfurt. It was a horn in F with an extra valve that cut out about a quarter of the tubing to convert it to a horn in high B-flat. This made the playing of higher notes easier on lower harmonics. In 1958, Paxman of London introduced a triple horn in F, high B-flat, and higher F, which took the principle even further.

French makers built instruments with narrower bores and smaller bells, which created a quieter sound reminiscent of the natural horn but ran the risk of missing notes. They were fitted with Périnet piston valves, which had a light fast action and unconstricted windways but lacked space for the additional windway needed to convert the single to a double horn. The French held to single horns with Périnet valves. The English used French instruments until the 1930s, when they switched to the German type, sacrificing a more refined sound for ease of playing and greater volume. The French and Viennese retained the hand-horn style of a separate crook between the horn and the mouthpiece. Players used only a few of the set of crooks, usually the high B-flat or A, in order to obtain some of the security of the double horn, if not the convenience.

Related to the horn is the Wagner tuba. Moritz and Wieprecht invented the bass tuba shortly after 1835. Because Wagner scored particularly characteristic parts for it in such works as *Der Ring des Nibelungen,* the instrument became known as the Wagner tuba. It is oval, the traditional German tuba shape, and is played with a horn mouthpiece by horn players. However, it has a wide buglelike bore and is reminiscent of the saxhorns, the bugle family that Adolphe Sax invented. Wagner tubas have a loud, rich sound and are pitched in the horn keys of F and B-flat.

The Cornet.   Another type of horn to which valves were attached was the cornet, known as the cornopean in England. Just before 1830, Jean Hilaire Asté, who called himself Halary after the firm he purchased, added the first valves to a B-flat posthorn, inventing the B-flat cornet. The cornet has the horn's mouthpiece and narrow conical bore; it sounds best in the upper registers, dull in the lower. Consequently, the lowest cornet range built is the tenor (or baritone).

The cornet's bore was shorter and narrower than the trumpet's and was conducive to a virtuoso technique, increasingly demanded by composers who were writing more-difficult parts for the trumpet in E-flat and F. Players gladly sacrificed the trumpet's tone quality for the agility and facility of the cornet. A set of crooks and shanks (small pieces of tubing usually inserted between mouthpiece and bore to tune an instrument to the same pitch as the others it is being used with) were retained to eliminate any need to transpose to another key. Performers chose to play the cornet over the trumpet, to the chagrin of conductors and composers, who, except for Berlioz (who did not like it but conceded to it), rarely wrote for it. In the nineteenth century it threatened the trumpet's very existence. Most types of valves were fitted to cornets, Stölzel's being the most common. Today, cornets are rarely heard, but the modern trumpet is so like the cornet (the trumpet's leadpipe is only slightly larger than the cornet's) that there is hardly any difference between the two.

The development of brass instruments is incomplete without mentioning the exceptional contributions of Adolphe Sax. Among his many notable designs are three families of valved brasses: cornets with narrow bores; saxotrombas with medium bores (the width somewhere between cornets and bugles; the modern valve trumpet derives from this group); and saxhorns with wide bores. Instruments by other makers are more difficult to group; suffice it to say that the narrower bores are cornets, and the wider bugles.

The Bugle. The wide-bored bugle was especially successful in the bass sizes, which had a rich, lush sound. They were the only ones admitted into the orchestra. In France about 1817, Halary added to his many inventions (including the B-flat cornet) the ophicleide, a bass bugle that initially had seven keys, although nine to twelve keys became standard. The ophicleide was intended to supersede the serpent, but the latter's use continued in church and military bands throughout the nineteenth century. The ophicleide, with its loud, clear, rich sound, supplanted it. Mendelssohn and Wagner both occasionally included parts specifically for ophicleide in their orchestras.

Valves were added to bugles too. Working with Berlioz, Adolphe Sax redesigned the bugle into nine sizes, naming them saxhorns. The bass tuba (later known as the Wagner tuba) was in fact a member of the bugle family. It had five valves (the fourth and fifth valves corrected the intonation of valve combinations) but a narrower bore and a bell that flared somewhat less than those of saxhorns. It is the tuba, however, that has survived as the standard member of today's orchestra.

The Trumpet. By the mid-nineteenth century, the valve system was standard for making trumpets chromatic. Valves produced a homogeneity of tone, considered a major advantage, and gave the player greater facility with slides and keys. Berlioz, Rossini, and Meyerbeer were among the first French composers to write for valved trumpets. To ease playing the increasingly difficult new parts on the F trumpet and to combat its replacement in the orchestra by the B-flat cornet, players adopted shorter B-flat or C trumpets. These diminished the chance of slipping or cracking notes by increasing the intervals between harmonics (easily filled in with valves), and performance was more secure. Proficiency was further increased by the alteration of the shape of the trumpet's mouthpiece and by the placement of the conical leadpipe between its mouthpiece and valves, which improved tuning. Nevertheless, the narrower-bore cornets persisted until the increasing volume of sound from the horn and trombone sections during the first half of the twentieth century mandated the use of the larger-bore trumpets for the sake of balance.

The revival of the music of Bach and Handel in the second half of the nineteenth century required playing the highest notes ever written for trumpet and sparked the development of "piccolo" trumpets. These trumpets were pitched in D above the B-flat trumpet and were half the length of the baroque trumpet in D; by the first decade of the twentieth century, they had reached B-flat or A, an octave higher. They eased the difficulty of playing the parts but produced a very different sound from the earlier instruments.

In more recent times virtuoso jazz trumpet players have had a decided influence on symphonic trumpet playing. They added a whole repertoire of special techniques, which composers then called for (such as flutter-tonguing by Richard Strauss in *Don Quixote*, 1897). These included a great variety of articulation; controlled vibrato produced by the chin and valve fingers, as well as the diaphragm; glissandos, rips, and smears played by partially depressing or using random valves; varying the sonority with the lips; and the use of a great variety of mutes. These are most clearly illustrated in the performances of such great jazz trumpet players as Roy Eldridge, Dizzy Gillespie, Miles Davis, Maynard Ferguson, and especially Louis Armstrong.

The Trombone. In the nineteenth century the trombone at last became a member of the orchestra. Its sound was very expressive, and it had a reserve of power unmatched by any other type of brass instrument, yet its use was still traditionally limited to the support of the bass and background music. Because more use was made of its low range than its high, there was never a tendency toward shorter instruments. Alto trombones were tuned to E-flat; bass trombones were tuned to F in Germany, E-flat in France, and G in Great Britain.

During this period, the pitch of the tenor trombone changed from A to the band pitch of B-flat, and chromatic slide positions replaced diatonic ones. German and French performers tended to play all orchestral parts on the tenor, changing mouthpieces for the alto and bass parts. To

further distinguish the sonorities of the different ranges, the alto trombone was built with a narrow bore, the tenor with a medium, and the
bass with a wide. The bass was also fitted with what performers call a
"plug," auxiliary tubing and a valve in its back bow to change the overall
pitch from B-flat down to F. The plug both increases the compass and
provides an alternative for long shifts. In the mid-nineteenth century the
bore diameter of the tenor widened to the same proportions as the bass,
and their bells increased in breadth, thereby increasing the volume.

Modern trombones have an even wider bore than those of the nineteenth century. Although this increases volume, it affects pitch and
reduces the harmonic overtones. Like the trumpet, the trombone fell
under the spell of jazz musicians, who added a variety of special effects to
its repertoire and expanded its use to solos. In addition, the tenor's range
has been extended, and slide technique has become even more flexible.
Although valves were added to the trombone, it has rarely been used in
this form in symphonic orchestras.

Brass instruments today generally can be said to have homogeneous
sonorities, whether within a single instrument's compass or among the
various types, no matter where or by whom they were made or are
played. This contrasts with the sounds of earlier instruments, which
reveal a decided difference in tone quality between types of brass instruments; within a given type, the sound quality differs from note to note,
instrument to instrument, and region to region. National differences
between playing styles also created distinct sonorities. In summary, one
might say that a unified sound characterizes the instruments of today,
whereas those of the past were distinguished by diversity and variety.

BIBLIOGRAPHY

Anthony Baines, "James Talbot's MS: I, Wind Instruments," in *Galpin Society
Journal*, 1 (1948); *Musical Instruments Through the Ages* (1961); *European and American Musical Instruments* (1966); *The Trumpet and Trombone* (1966); and *Brass
Instruments: Their History and Development* (3rd ed., 1981). Philip Bate, *The Trumpet and Trombone* (1966). Nicholas Bessaraboff, *Ancient European Musical Instruments* (1941; repr. 1965). Clifford Bevan, *The Tuba Family* (1978). Maurice Byrne,
"The Goldsmith–Trumpet-Makers of the British Isles," in *Galpin Society Journal*,
19 (1966). Adam Carse, *Musical Wind Instruments* (1939; repr. 1965); and *The
Orchestra from Beethoven to Berlioz* (1948).

Reine Dahlqvist, *The Keyed Trumpet* (1975). Robert E. Eliason, "Early American Valves for Brass Instruments," in *Galpin Society Journal*, 23 (1970). Horace

Fitzpatrick, *The Horn and Horn-playing and the Austro-Bohemian Tradition: 1680–1830* (1970). Francis W. Galpin, *Old English Instruments of Music* (4th ed., 1965). Eric Halfpenny, "William Shaw's 'Harmonic Trumpet,'" in *Galpin Society Journal*, 13 (1960); and "William Bull and the English Baroque Trumpet," *ibid.*, 15 (1962). Lyndesay G. Langwill, *An Index of Musical Wind-Instrument Makers* (6th ed., 1980).

Marin Mersenne, *Harmonie universelle* (1636; facs., 1963). Jeremy Montagu, *The World of Baroque and Classical Musical Instruments* (1979); and *The World of Romantic and Modern Musical Instruments* (1981). Reginald Morley-Pegge, *The French Horn* (1960). Don L. Smithers, *The Music and History of the Baroque Trumpet Before 1721* (1973). Daniel Speer, *Grund-richtiger Unterricht der musikalischen Kunst* (1687; 1697).

Romantic Composers Respond to Challenge and Demand

Alan Houtchens

Creative activity during the nineteenth century, as in every other his-torical period, was greatly influenced by social and political devel-opments, by general cultural and aesthetic trends, and by economic demands on artists and on the consumers of their art. The aim of this essay is to examine how some of those factors led romantic composers to cultivate further the forms, compositional styles, and instrumental tech-niques attendant upon the use of the orchestra. It will also be necessary to touch briefly on such matters as the influence of Beethoven's orches-tral technique on composers; the impact of Wagner on his contemporar-ies; and the effect of technological improvements in the construction and manufacturing of instruments, with special attention to the French horn and the piano.

Most composers of the time managed to function very well—though perhaps not always too happily—in a society racked by changes resulting from the spread of a new social-revolutionary spirit and from the rapid industrialization and urbanization of a vast part of Europe. Their posi-tion in this new society was much more similar to what it is today than to what it had been in the eighteenth century. Perhaps the most striking development was that composers for the first time could claim a truly professional status. All of their working hours could be devoted solely to musical activities—composition, performance, teaching, publishing, or writing about music. Concomitantly, they did not necessarily have to depend on a patronage system binding them in servitude to (usually) royal benefactors on a personal level.

Some perspective in this matter can be gained by considering the manner in which Julie Ritter, Otto Wesendonck, and King Ludwig II of Bavaria supported Richard Wagner. The relationship between the composer and his patrons represents a middle ground between Haydn's experience in his dealings with the Esterhazy family and the way in which the majority of nineteenth-century composers sought their livelihoods. Regardless of the station they may have had by birthright (here Mendelssohn, who was born into an especially wealthy, well-situated family, comes specifically to mind), there is no reason to believe that composers were other than workaday musicians simply trying to make a living.

THE COMPOSER AS CONDUCTOR

Since it was not possible to survive financially by concentrating on only one musical activity—least of all composing—many composers became associated with opera houses or independent large orchestras by serving as their directors and/or conductors. Others traveled throughout much of the world as guest conductors, laying the foundation for modern conducting and rehearsal techniques.

Trying to discharge adequately the duties of a full-time conductor while finding the energy and time to compose took a heavy toll. Mendelssohn found his rigorous activities as conductor of the Leipzig Gewandhaus Orchestra to be very draining yet also rewarding, as he wrote to Ferdinand Hiller:

> Two months of such constant conducting takes more out of me than two years of composing all day long; in the winter I hardly get to it at all here.... I often think I should like to retire completely and never conduct any more, but only write; but then again there is a certain charm in an organised muscial system like this, and in having the directing of it.
>
> (p. 274)

Part of the charm of working with an orchestra was that a composer could gain firsthand knowledge of the capabilities and sound qualities of each instrument and experiment with them in his own works. Bedřich Smetana regularly made corrections and improvements in scoring after conducting performances of his own compositions. Since he no longer could rely on this procedure after becoming totally deaf, some of his later scores are fraught with miscalculations in terms of balance and part-writing. The cycle of tone poems *Má vlast*, for example, has many awkward passages that have, on the one hand, discouraged conductors from programming the work in its entirety and, on the other, spawned hundreds of "retouchings" by those willing to struggle with the material. It was not until 1983 that a serious, concerted effort was made by some musicologists, conductors, and orchestral players to resolve these problems. The resulting practical performing edition (published by Supraphon) has helped to rekindle interest in a truly brilliant symphonic composition.

Especially during the first half of the century, the public wanted to hear new works. Adam Carse has demonstrated that, of the music played from 1830 to 1839 on the programs of the three great orchestral societies of the period (the Société des Concerts du Conservatoire, the Gewandhaus Concerts Society, and the London Philharmonic Society), between four-fifths and five-sixths was less than forty years old (pp. 7–8). Although no statistics are available, a similar preference probably existed with regard to opera productions, especially in Italy. Composer-conductors thus had the opportunity of becoming familiar with a vast amount of music composed by their contemporaries.

THE DEMANDS OF MUSIC PUBLISHERS

Even if a composer managed to get an orchestral work performed, there was no guarantee that it would ever be published. Consumer demand and the economics of the publishing business favored pieces for solo piano or for small ensembles that included the piano. Publishers were disinclined to accept orchestral compositions, and if they did, they found it more practical and financially rewarding to issue them in piano reductions only. Fritz Simrock, one of the principal publishers of the music of Brahms, Dvořák, and Max Bruch, expressed this position very clearly in a letter to Dvořák in 1890:

> If only I did sufficient business with your symphonies to be repaid for my enormous expense! But this is far from being the case! and I am thousands down on them. That is how it is—and nothing can change it. What use is it if I make money on one or six works and lose it again on four others? I can't carry on my business like that!...So unless you also give me small and easy piano pieces...it won't be possible to publish big works.
>
> (quoted in Clapham, 16)

Like many of his fellow composers, Dvořák rebelled at this attitude purely on artistic grounds. He did not necessarily want to write what was in vogue or thought to be marketable. Five years earlier, when the same subject had strained his relationship with Simrock almost to the breaking point, Dvořák had responded to similar arguments:

> If you take and consider all that you indicated in your last letter from a common-sense point of view, then we reach a very simple conclusion: not to write symphonies and large vocal and instrumental works, but only publish here and there some songs, piano pieces or dances and I know not what all: this, as an artist who wants to make his mark, I cannot do!
>
> (quoted in Šourek, 92)

THE IMPACT OF THE PIANO

The piano had an extraordinary impact on almost every aspect of musical life during the nineteenth century. The number of pianos in middle-class households increased as the instrument became more affordable, and composers could barely keep up with the demand for new works suited to the abilities of amateur musicians. As a result of improvements in its construction, materials, and design, the piano could stand up to the orchestra in terms of sonority and sheer volume, though it certainly could not cover an ensemble composed of a hundred players—or the screams of a faithless lover and her retinue being crushed to death in a collapsing steel-framed summerhouse. In his *Evenings with the Orchestra* (292–296), Berlioz had envisioned an instrument called the "orchestra-piano" that could be commanded by a single godlike artist and that was capable of producing powerful sounds of infinite variety.

Putting such fantasies aside, Berlioz and his contemporaries found the acoustic ideal of the piano to be spectacular enough. Since most composers played the piano—Berlioz was an exception—and many composed at the keyboard, its capabilities with regard to dynamics, counterpoint, and voice leading influenced them in their orchestral works. For example, the arpeggio figure that is first stated by clarinets and recurs throughout the orchestra in Mendelssohn's *Fair Melusine* Overture, regardless of whether it is idiomatic to the particular instruments involved, indicates that it was conceived with the piano in mind—or, at any rate, at the piano. Similarly, pianistic figurations and textures are very common in the orchestral music of Schumann and Brahms.

Carl Maria von Weber recognized that there could be a danger in working at the piano. His discussion of the matter as it appears in his uncompleted novel "Tonkünstlers Leben" provides insight into how a romantic artist typically viewed the act of creation:

> Life's problems seemed to weigh unbearably upon me.... Even the piano-stool, on which I had sat hoping to compose, seemed to have turned from my last resort into an object of sinister foreboding. The composer who finds the material for his work in that way is almost always poorly endowed from birth or on the way to entrusting his spirit to the commonplace and every-day. For these hands, these accursed piano-fingers, take on a kind of life of their own after years of practice to obtain mastery, and they become uncon-scious tyrants and despots over the creative faculty. *They* never invent a new idea, as all novelty is inconvenient to them. Secretly and on the sly, like the manual labourers whom they resemble, they cobble together whole works out of long-familiar, routine phrases. These almost look as though they were new, and because they sound well and flatter the ears which they have, as it were, bribed in advance, they are immediately accepted and applauded.
>
> The composer whose *inner* ear is the judge of his composition works in quite a different way. This inner ear is an amazingly able judge of musical shapes—something peculiar to the art of music and a sacred mystery which the layman cannot fathom.

(p. 322)

THE DEMAND FOR VIRTUOSITY

In keeping with the nineteenth-century view of the artist as a marvelous, superhuman being endowed with mysterious powers, a special premium was placed on virtuosity. Previously accepted limits of technical capabil-ity no longer were accepted. Concert societies gave top billing to those singers and instrumentalists who were known primarily for their tech-nical prowess, and their programs mainly included bravura arias, concer-tos, paraphrases, fantasias, quadrilles, potpourris, and other vehicles of virtuosity. Conductors who could lead a gargantuan orchestra and cho-rus without using a score were admired above virtuoso soloists. But per-haps the loftiest position of all was accorded to those conductors who were also composers. They were idolized as priests of a sacred muse.

Berlioz fantasized about a utopian town called Euphonia where the exalted art of music is nurtured under the despotic rule of a composer-conductor-director. After lesser deities—the various directors of rehears-als acting as prefects—have finished their preparatory work for a performance by working with each section of the orchestra and with the chorus and soloists separately, the whole is brought together:

> The grand ensemble next undergoes the composer's criticism. He listens from the upper part of the amphitheater, which the public will occupy; and when he finds himself the absolute master of this huge intelligent instrument, when he is sure that nothing remains but to communicate to it the vital nuances that he feels and can impart better than anyone else, the moment has come for him to become a performer himself. He climbs the podium to conduct.
>
> (p. 286)

This frenzied preoccupation with virtuosic display was reflected in the way composers wrote for this "huge intelligent instrument." Berlioz enthusiastically sought to expand the ranges of all the instruments and to make them more versatile, capable of producing new effects and sonorities. He was fond of assigning a specific role to a particular instrument and using it extensively in a soloistic capacity. A solo viola represents Byron's Childe Harold in *Harold en Italie*; Berlioz wrote the part expressly for Niccolò Paganini. Throughout the *Symphonie fantastique* various transformations of the *idée fixe* are rendered by a solo flute, oboe, or clarinet.

The same technique was developed by many other composers and was especially appropriate in opera. For example, Wagner clothed leitmotivs associated with specific characters, objects, or abstract ideas in distinct monochromatic instrumental garbs. Weber's fascination with the clarinet was a result of his association with the virtuoso Heinrich Bärmann, while Richard Strauss's style of writing for the horn reflects the impression made on him by his own father's playing. Liszt's piano paraphrases of operatic and orchestral works went far beyond being mere arrangements and established not only a new genre of composition but also a style of performance that is still pursued today, as exemplified by Vladimir Horowitz' rendition of Sousa's *Stars and Stripes Forever*.

The techniques displayed by virtuosic players were transferred not only to specific instruments but often to the orchestra as a whole. Berlioz' "Queen Mab Scherzo" from *Roméo et Juliette*, Mendelssohn's saltarello finale of the *Italian* Symphony, and the scherzo of Schumann's Second Symphony are three examples of a new genre of composition, the bravura showpiece for orchestra. Similarly, the intensely dramatic style of singing developed by the great virtuosos at midcentury, though rooted in the art of *bel canto*, provided new impetus to Meyerbeer, Wagner, and especially Verdi. In order to support and match this vocal style, they developed a kind of instrumental writing that took on a forcefulness and vigor hitherto unknown in opera.

Sometimes a composer's delight in virtuosity led him to overstep the bounds of artistic discretion. The last movement of Max Bruch's Violin Concerto in G Minor provides a good example. The rondo theme has an excitingly brilliant, gypsy flavor that is particularly well suited to virtuosic violin technique. Even though the woodwind and string players in practically any nineteenth-century orchestra were able to play this theme in the same manner as the soloist, it never seems to have occurred to the composer that having them toss fragments of it back and forth in the *tutti* sections would reduce the impact and effectiveness of the solo part.

REACTION TO THE VALVE HORN

It is not possible to determine whether this interest in virtuosity fostered improvements in the construction and design of musical instruments, or vice versa. Whichever the case, the new technologies that were applied not only to the piano but also to almost every orchestral instrument expanded composers' horizons in terms of timbre, range, and execution. This was especially true with regard to the woodwinds and brass. The instrument that benefited most from technological improvements and drew composers' attention perhaps more than any other was the French horn. The romantic instrument par excellence, it captured their imagination not only because of its rich, dark, mellifluous tone but also because specific associations had become attached to it: the hunt and, by extension, the forest and nature; the roebuck as a symbol of the cuckold; anything mysterious or exotic. Following the invention of the valve around 1815, which freed the horn from the fetters of a single overtone series, composers quickly assigned to the instrument an expanded melodic role in the orchestra.

Weber, whose hunting choruses spiced with lively horn calls in *Der Freischütz* became models of their kind, seemed eager to experiment with, and improve upon, novel techniques even on the traditional hand horn. In his Concertino in E Minor for horn and orchestra the soloist is required to sing into the instrument while playing certain notes in order to produce chords. Though the technique had been used before, Weber gave it an air of legitimacy. Berlioz wrote in his treatise on orchestration that one of the distinct advantages of the valve horn over its predecessor is that stopped notes can be achieved on all the notes of a scale. This statement may seem curious today—we are more appreciative of the fact that all the notes can be played open—but Berlioz' interest was in utilizing isolated stopped notes for specific coloristic effects.

In his enlarged and revised edition of Berlioz' treatise Richard Strauss pointed to Wagner's extensive use of the horn. There is no question that Wagner's orchestration would lose much of its characteristic color and excitement without the sound of this instrument. Following a practice established by Meyerbeer and others, he included four horn parts in his early operas, indicating that two of them could be played on valve instruments and two on hand horns. Actually, all of the parts can be executed on either instrument, and the use of valve horns undoubtedly depended on the availability of instruments and on players' preferences. In *Lohengrin,* Wagner manifested a decided preference for the new horns. He began writing for them exclusively in *Tristan und Isolde* and occasionally increased the number of parts to eight. Nevertheless, in the score of *Tristan* he took pains to issue a warning concerning their use:

> The composer feels called upon to recommend that special attention be given the treatment of the horns. The introduction of the valve has doubtless done so much for this instrument that it is difficult to ignore this improvement, although the horn has thereby suffered undeniable loss in the beauty of its tone, as well as in its powers of smooth legato. In view of this great loss, the composer, who is concerned with the preservation of the true character of the horn, would have had to refrain from employing valve horns, had he not learned that excellent performers have been able to eliminate these drawbacks almost completely by especially careful execution, so that it was barely possible to tell the difference in tone and legato. In expectation of a hopefully inevitable improvement of the valve horn, it is urgently recommended that the horn players study their parts in the present score with great care in order to find the proper application of the appropriate tunings and valves for all requirements of execution.

Brahms apparently never felt comfortable with the valve horn, arguing even more vehemently than Wagner that it could not produce the same kinds of tone qualities peculiar to the hand horn with its various crooks. Schumann, on the other hand, was fascinated by its capabilities. His later symphonic works show a special sensitivity to the instrument, and in 1849 he composed the first important solo piece for it, the Adagio and Allegro, Opus 70, as well as the brilliant Konzertstück for Four Horns and Orchestra.

Gustav Mahler was especially enamored of the horn's power, versatility, and penetrating beauty of sound, and he wrote magnificent solos for it in all of his symphonies and song cycles. The obbligato solo part in the scherzo of his Fifth Symphony is especially noteworthy because of the considerable intensity and dramatic impact that it adds to this central, pivotal movement. In the finale of his First Symphony he even directed all seven horn players to stand at the climax. Mahler had a flair for the grand theatrical gesture, and it is a pity that the closest he came to writing for the stage was to complete Weber's *Die drei Pintos*.

The technical demands on horn players made by Mahler and other composers almost surpassed human capability. An anecdote concerning Richard Strauss bears repeating, even though this particular version of it cannot be documented. During a rehearsal of *Ein Heldenleben* a member of the horn section could not play his part well enough to suit the composer and, when apprised of this fact, retorted, "With all due respect, Maestro, you may be able to play this passage on the piano, but I assure you it is quite impossible on the horn." Strauss replied that the poor fellow was in error: he himself could not play the passage on the piano.

DEVELOPMENTS IN OPERA

Opera provided fertile ground for the introduction of new or unusual instruments and for experimentation with novel orchestral techniques. Part of the reason lies in the fact that, even after the middle of the century, nearly all orchestras, especially those in Italy, were theater orchestras established principally to present opera. Concert performances were arranged by drawing personnel from the opera establishment and by renting the theater itself or whatever ballroom, hotel entertainment hall, or university commons might be available. Few concert halls were intended specifically as such, and still fewer halls of any kind had satisfactory acoustical properties or could accommodate a large orchestra, chorus, and audience. It was largely through the efforts of the concert societies and choral institutions, which had grown in number and size, that the situation improved as the century drew to a close.

In any event, many developments in the art of orchestration during the early nineteenth century took place in the world of French grand opera. Here an evenings's entertainment was expected to incorporate as much of the grandiose, the novel, the shocking, and the spectacular as possible, whether it came from the orchestra, the vocalists, the ballet troupe, or the stage machinists. Composers sought ways to provide contrast and variety in their scores and to titillate audiences with new sounds and modern techniques. Halévy was the first to use valve trumpets and horns in opera (in *La Juive*, 1835) and Meyerbeer was the first to use the bass clarinet (*Les Huguenots*, 1836). Important parts for the harp, for the English horn, and for percussion instruments hitherto not found in pit orchestras also began appearing in opera scores. Brass fanfares and diffi-cult solo passages for all the instruments—especially for the woodwinds, which in the hands of French players sound quite penetrating—were written to provide special brilliance and dramatic impact.

Auber, Halévy, and Meyerbeer were influenced, in turn, by such com-posers as Grétry, Cherubini, Méhul, and Le Sueur. The orchestral writ-ing in their "rescue" operas was especially worthy of imitation, for it matched the intense, suspenseful, and violent genre of opera, where the endangering situations, usually involving unjust imprisonment and last-minute rescues, mirrored everyday, real-life events during the French Revolution. This orchestral style likewise catered to the demands of a French public accustomed to ceremonial music composed specifically for outdoor fetes organized for national festivals and political rallies. Pieces for such occasions incorporated huge orchestral forces, military bands, and large choruses, usually of only male voices. Novelty and bombast were valued above profundity or musical quality.

Some of the finer coloristic touches in their scores also influenced composers like Beethoven, Berlioz, and even Brahms. Cherubini's *Les deux journées* (1800) is the first work of any kind to call for three horns in the orchestra instead of the usual two or four. Although Cherubini did not always give each of the horns an independent part, his practice anticipated that of Beethoven in the Third Symphony and in Leonore's "Abscheulicher, wo eilest du hin" in the first act of *Fidelio* (1805). Berlioz recognized that the advantage of having massive orchestral forces at one's disposal was not to use them all at once but, rather, to employ them sin-gly or in small groups to create exquisitely delicate instrumental combi-nations and to provide contrast. Brahms, who knew Méhul's work inti-mately, very likely was influenced by *Uthal* when he omitted violins from his own Serenade in A and the first movement of the *German Requiem*.

As an opera director, Carl Maria von Weber favored the French style. In Prague, for instance, he mounted 21 French operas (in a total of 191 performances) during the years 1813-1816, 30 German (but only in 141 performances), and a paltry 9 Italian works (70 performances). Most of the German operas either were fashioned directly on French models or were simply translations of them. Salieri's opera *Tarare* is included in the Italian count because Weber used Da Ponte's version of the libretto. Thus, the French repertoire clearly presented a stronger imaginative force to Weber than his native *Singspiel*, which was only in its first tentative stages of development. The articles he submitted to various newspapers in Prague and Dresden discussing the works of Nicolò Isouard, Pierre Gaveaux, Boieldieu, Charles-Simon Catel, and Nicolas Dalayrac indicate that he was especially attracted to these composers' brilliant, imaginative strokes of instrumentation and to their effective use of the orchestra to comment on the action.

Spontini and Rossini also had embraced this French operatic tradition when they composed for the Paris Opéra's multifarious orchestra. There is a distinct difference in style, for instance, between *Guillaume Tell* and Rossini's many earlier Italianate, Mozartean operas. Nevertheless, in all of his works the orchestra plays an important role, one that goes far beyond being mere accompaniment, not only in the arias and choruses but also in the accompanied recitatives. Rossini presented a challenge to other composers merely because of the extraordinary popularity that his operas enjoyed throughout Europe. This craze was so strong during the 1820s that if a composer was not willing to imitate Rossini's style there was little chance his operas would be performed.

Richard Wagner's operatic efforts from *Rienzi* to *Lohengrin* are firmly rooted in the French grand-opera tradition and are rather conventional in style of orchestration. The music dramas that followed—*Tristan und Isolde*, the tetralogy *Der Ring des Nibelungen*, and *Parsifal*—are more venturesome and had a greater impact on other composers. Wagner increased the number of wind instruments to enable multiple doublings and the homogeneous scoring of complete chords in every section of the orchestra, and as a consequence, he had to call for a much larger contingent of string players. In some works he wrote exceptionally prominent parts for the English horn and bass clarinet and added the bass trumpet, contrabass trombone, and tuba to provide support in the lowest register. He devised a new instrument, the Wagner tuba, which is made in two sizes, tenor and bass, and is designed to accommodate a French-horn mouthpiece. While freer-blowing than the horn, it has a more primitive, opaque tone quality.

Other operatic composers likewise called for enlarged orchestral forces to suit particular artistic needs. Their wishes usually could be fulfilled in performance, but there were exceptions. For the first production of *Kate and the Devil* (1899), for example, Dvořák was surprised to learn that the part for a contrabass clarinet he had written to give a ghoulish flavor to the scenes involving the devil Marbuel had to be omitted: the theater in Prague did not have such an instrument, and when one was sent from Paris, the clarinetist could not play it because he knew only the German fingerings.

The fact that Dvořák did not consult with the management of the

National Theater concerning the availability of a contrabass clarinet or of a player capable of executing the part serves to illustrate an important point: when conceiving their works nineteenth-century composers did not have to be as concerned as in earlier times about taking into account the size of a specific orchestra or the capabilities of its members. Most orchestral musicians were highly skilled, professional players. Many were trained in conservatories and had learned to play a single instrument very well instead of several only moderately well, as in the previous century. If there was an occasional shortage of good players, it was due to the ravages of war or—as Mendelssohn pointed out (p. 292) in his appeal for the establishment of a music academy in Leipzig—to the fact that young aspiring musicians preferred to take up the piano rather than an orchestral instrument.

THE SPIRIT OF NATIONALISM

It has been mentioned that the aesthetic framework of romanticism elevated the creative artist to a level approaching the divine. Wagner, more than any other personality, was viewed by many as nothing less than a god. He considered each of his music dramas to be a religious rite, and he was able to realize the construction of a new "temple" at Bayreuth, a theater designed to meet his own artistic specifications. Even Wagner's detractors could not avoid being influenced in some way by the man, his ideas, and his works. In many cases, positive developments resulted from opposition to his compositional style and artistic premises.

During the second half of the nineteenth century in France, composers reacted not only against the extravagances of grand opera but also against Wagner's music dramas. With the encouragement and support of the Société Nationale de Musique (founded in 1871), they strove to establish a modern style of music exuding atmosphere above all, specifically a French atmosphere, "without sauerkraut." Bizet provided a model in Carmen, where the orchestra takes on an expressive power born of transparency, lightness, fluidity, flexibility, and subtlety of color. Composers after him rarefied this manner to the extreme. One of the most striking passages in all of French music, for example, is that found at the end of the second movement of Saint-Saëns's Violin Concerto no. 3 in B Minor. Against a lightly orchestrated, pastel background, the solo violin and a clarinet in its lower register whisper the same rising and falling arpeggio figures over a tonic pedal. Harmonics in the violin part give the passage a marvelous timbre, and when this is combined with the sound of the clarinet at the distance of two and sometimes three octaves below, the total effect is unforgettable.

No German composer could have conceived such a light, airy, atmospheric sonority, one that mixes instruments from different families so exquisitely. Indeed, most nineteenth-century German composers did not break away from the traditional method of orchestration established by their predecessors, wherein the string section is used as the core, with the woodwinds and especially the brass serving to provide support and add variety. As late as the 1840s their reliance on the strings was reflected even in the format in which they wrote out their scores: the violins appear at the top, above the winds. This is in contrast to the layout used today, which became fairly well standardized in all countries except Germany by the end of the eighteenth century, wherein the instruments are arranged in the following order, from top to bottom: woodwinds, brass, percussion, strings.

Nationalistic composers in countries other than France also realized the usefulness of stressing not merely color in their works but local color. Spanish composers found popular folk dances and the sound and technique of guitar playing to be rich sources of inspiration. Their zarzuelas and guitar concertos, tone poems, and other symphonic pieces have a special flavor that derives in no small measure from their ability to translate these influences into orchestral terms. Russian composers, influenced by their own folk music and the special vocal quality cultivated by Russian basses, preferred orchestral textures in which the warm, virile tone color resulting from the massing together of the lowest-sounding instruments is contrasted with that "white," icy timbre characteristic of the high woodwinds, especially the flute and piccolo.

Similarly, the uniqueness of Dvořák's music can be attributed, in part, to certain features of his style of orchestration that reflect the characteristics of Czech folk music. These include the importance given to the woodwinds (especially the clarinet) and horns, often playing in thirds or sixths, with the traditional horn fifths; the light, transparent, outdoors quality; the occasional drones, melodic contours, and embellishments characteristic of bagpipe music; and the string writing, which occasionally takes on a gypsy flavor and is never as ponderous or consciously virtuosic as that of German or Austrian composers.

Most nationalistic composers found the orchestra as they knew it to be suitable for creating local color. Thus, instead of introducing bagpipes into their symphonic and operatic scores—for which a precedent already had been set by Lully, Boieldieu, and Meyerbeer—Dvořák, Smetana, and Janáček usually preferred to imitate their sound by using traditional orchestral instruments. Indeed, the basic conception of how an orchestra ought to be constituted remained remarkably unchanged throughout the nineteenth century, even though the many orchestras in Europe and America grew variously in size. Their "personalities" differed in subtle ways, according to the manner in which instruments were constructed or played and according to the sound ideal of each conductor. Several examples come immediately to mind. The tone quality produced by a Frenchman playing a narrow-bore French-made horn has always been strikingly different than that produced by a German using a wide-bore instrument. The French prefer a thinner, brighter, lighter, more "brassy" sound. French and Russian wind players have tended to use a considerable amount of vibrato, so that it is not difficult to distinguish the sound of their orchestras from German or Italian ones. As conductor of the court orchestra at Meiningen from 1880 to 1885, Hans von Bülow fashioned a distinctive sound quality and performance capability for that body by requiring all of his musicians to stand during performances and by insisting on the use of five-string basses, Hermann Ritter's larger alta violas, and pedal timpani.

COMPOSERS' RESPONSE TO CRITICISM

During the nineteenth century, music criticism became a significant force in the lives of composers and audiences. Beginning in 1808 with the musical columns written for the *Vossische Zeitung* in Berlin by J. C. F. Rellstab, general daily newspapers all over Europe devoted space to the musical arts. The reviews and informative feuilletons that appeared in their pages and in the several music journals served to educate an ever-growing number of amateur musicians and concertgoers. Even so, a gulf gradually developed between composers and lay audiences. Some composers—most notably Weber, E. T. A. Hoffmann, Schumann, Berlioz, Liszt, Wagner, Smetana, Hugo Wolf, and Tchaikovsky—turned to writing criticism themselves, as a means either of ensuring financial stability or of explaining their own artistic aims and gaining a following for them. It did not always help matters when Berlioz, Wagner, and Wolf, who were the most caustic among these composer-critics, regularly derided the public for its ignorance in musical matters and its lack of taste.

Berlioz was in turn bitterly attacked by P. Scudo, while Wagner and Wolf suffered under a torrent of criticism from Eduard Hanslick and Max Kalbeck. The exact nature or degree of influence that critics may have had on composers cannot always be ascertained, least of all with regard to the use and makeup of the orchestra. In Dvořák's case, we can feel reasonably certain that the pressure exerted on him by the highly influential music journal *Dalibor* played an important role in his artistic development, encouraging him to focus his patriotic fervor in specific directions. The ideas and aspirations of the Czech national revival took on an anti-German—and, in music, sometimes specifically anti-Wagnerian—stance, just as in France. When a few of Dvořák's vocal works were published outside of Bohemia by the German publisher Simrock with German texts and titles only, concern was expressed:

> We must observe with regret that so far Dvořák has not shown enough consideration for our musical heritage and our public to provide for the printing of Czech texts and titles in addition to the German. We are convinced—and it won't be long in coming—that the covetous Germans will be writing about our highly gifted Dvořák: "unser Dworzak"! If it matters to Dvořák to remain one of us—and we think it does matter—he should forestall any further unpleasant consequences while there still is time by vigourously standing up against the German publishers.
>
> (*Dalibor*, 2, no. 28 [1 October 1880], 222)

One of the "consequences" was that during the three months following this complaint nothing was published about Dvořák in *Dalibor*, whereas his name had previously appeared in almost every issue. Dvořák responded by notifying the editor in chief, Václav Juda Novotný, that henceforth he would make sure his vocal works were offered with the original Czech texts along with whatever translations were demanded. This experience must have made him even more determined in his resolve not to stray away from Slavic, and specifically Czech, subjects and to maintain the personal compositional style that he had developed during the 1870s.

Adverse opinions expressed not only publicly by Hanslick but also privately by such close friends as Hermann Levi, Franz and Joseph Schalk, and Ferdinand Löwe may have compelled Anton Bruckner to revise extensively many of his symphonies. We cannot fault him for being a perfectionist or for wishing to alter these works to suit a new and different conception of symphonic form, but it is difficult to understand why in some cases he allowed others to recompose entire passages and to perform them as authorized revisions. Most of these so-called corrections produce unfortunate results. They tend to obscure the clarity and brilliance of the original orchestration and fail to take into consideration that Bruckner's ideal of sound in the symphonies, which helps govern their formal design, grew out of his knowledge of the organ and the nature of its sound in a large cathedral.

In some cases, Bruckner himself made changes in orchestration and altered the internal proportions of his works to make them shorter, apparently in an effort to accommodate what he thought consumers of his music would prefer or be able to tolerate. In a tone conveying at once dejection and determination, he wrote to Felix Weingartner that he knew the original, longer version of the finale to his Eighth Symphony would ultimately be comprehended "only by a circle of friends and connoisseurs" (p. 130).

Like all creative artists, composers tend to be extremely self-critical, and Schumann presents a special case in point. With regard to matters of both form and orchestration in his large-scale symphonic pieces, Schumann initially felt incapable of surpassing the achievement of Schubert's Ninth Symphony (the *Great* C-Major); then, after suffering a mental breakdown, he was motivated by a peculiar inner drive to rework some of his earlier compositions. Charles Rosen has argued for a number of years that Schumann tamed the first versions, smoothing over certain harmonic novelties, rhythmic complexities, and piquant turns of phrase, very likely because he feared that these features might be taken as indications of his insanity. Rosen has concentrated on the composer's piano works, but a careful study of the various versions of his orchestral compositions, especially the Symphony no. 4 in D Minor (begun in 1841 and revised in 1851), would doubtless yield interesting results as well.

Brahms knew intimately the artistic and technical problems that Schumann had tried to solve in his D-minor symphony. He owned the autograph of the 1841 version and prepared a critical edition of it. His own approach to symphonic composition was influenced to a large extent by Schumann. It is doubly significant that Brahms chose the key of D minor for his first effort at composing a symphony and that it eventually became a piano concerto (no. 1). He struggled in the same way as Schumann did, not only with questions of form and the treatment of melodic material but also with techniques of orchestration. He wisely refrained from writing another symphony until he had reconsidered the artistic problems involved and had gained experience in writing for the orchestra with such choral works as the *German Requiem*, *Rinaldo*, *Alto Rhapsody*, *Song of Destiny*, and *Song of Triumph*.

AESTHETIC CONSIDERATIONS

Still to be examined are the more weighty philosophical, artistic, and aesthetic considerations that may have led nineteenth-century composers—

with perhaps the single exception of Chopin—to expend much of their energy in the composition of works for large instrumental forces. The intensity with which they devoted their attention to the orchestra cannot be explained merely as a response to public demand. Although average music lovers relished the bombastic festival overtures and solo concertos designed as vehicles for the display of virtuosity, their interest in new serious-minded concert works—secular or sacred—was much less than one would suspect judging from the large number of such compositions that were written.

The extreme popularity of opera and operetta provided a practical stimulus for composers to deal with the orchestra. But another important, less practical one seems to have impelled them to regard the orchestra in a special light: the prevailing conception of the "sublime" in music. In the *Dictionnaire des beaux-arts* (1806), Aubin Louis Millin's definition of the sublime as "the highest perfection of art" also included the idea that this art must have a monumentality, a grandiose nature that should "excite powerful impressions within the soul" and that "is essential whenever intellectual activity is to be stimulated or curbed" (quoted in le Huray and Day, 294-296). Typical of romantic thought is the notion that the sublime never can be experienced in perfection, just as the ideal never can be attained, the ineffable never spoken, divinity never achieved. It is the struggle for these things that is of paramount importance; and the greater the effort expended, the greater the reward.

Romantic artists felt that the attempt to express the sublime ought to be effected with the grandest possible artistic gesture, as Gustav Schilling clearly stated in his *Universal-Lexikon der Tonkunst* (1835-1838): "For something to be sublime it must be on a large scale: large *in itself*, in its power or in its extent or shape" (quoted in le Huray and Day, 472-473). Operatic, liturgical, and symphonic forms grew to such monumental proportions that the participation of a massive orchestral entity was required. Conversely, large-scale performing forces somehow fostered grandiose artistic conceptions with expansive formal structures.

To properly complete the mystical, sublime world view that Wagner had envisioned in the first of the librettos he penned for the *Ring* cycle, *Götterdämmerung*, he found it necessary to create three more; and in the process of setting all four to music he assigned to the orchestra a new and expanded role and size. Mahler told Jan Sibelius and Natalie Bauer-Lechner on separate occasions that he considered each of his symphonies to be a world unto itself, embracing everything. For him such a vision clearly required vast architectural designs and a correspondingly large performing apparatus. Even the most modestly orchestrated of Mahler's symphonies, the Symphony no. 4 in G Major, calls for a sizable and ingeniously variegated ensemble that excludes the trombones but incorporates an English horn, an E-flat clarinet, an enlarged percussion section, a harp, and a soprano soloist.

It is indicative of the romantic conception of sublimity that to Robert Schumann, who "discovered" Schubert's *Great* C-Major Symphony, the most appealing feature of the work was its "heavenly length." After hearing Mendelssohn conduct it with the Gewandhaus Orchestra in December 1839, he described it to Clara Wieck in the letter quoted below and in the following March published a very similar review in the *Neue Zeitschrift für Musik:*

> Oh, Clara, I have been in paradise today! They played at the rehearsal a symphony of Franz Schubert's.... The instruments all sing like remarkably intelligent human voices, and the scoring is worthy of Beethoven. Then the length, the heavenly length of it! It is a whole four-volume novel, longer than the choral symphony. I was supremely happy, and had nothing left to wish for, except that you were my wife, and that I could write such symphonies myself.
>
> (Walker, 279)

Schumann's reference to Beethoven and his Ninth Symphony introduces an interesting subject: the supposed challenge presented by the specter of that titanic artist to the next generation of composers. In his own lifetime and throughout the nineteenth century, Beethoven was viewed by writers, painters, sculptors, and musicians alike as one of the most imposing artistic figures of all time, and his works were considered achievements of almost unsurpassable perfection and power. The greatest compliment one could pay to a composer would be to describe him as the "successor to Beethoven." But even Schumann recognized the folly of thinking that all subsequent musical developments should—or even could—grow out of Beethoven's achievements. In his own case, the works of Schubert had greater impact. This also is true of Brahms, who, in any event, was slow to approach the composition of symphonies as a natural consequence of his own artistic development, not because he was in awe of the shadow cast by the figure of Beethoven. As regards achievements that could spawn new developments in orchestral writing, the fact remains that Beethoven did not bequeath as much to romantic composers as Haydn and Mozart had bequeathed to him.

Yet a few specific instances can be cited in which composers drew heavily from Beethoven's works, especially from the Ninth Symphony. For example, the opening movement of Bruckner's Third Symphony—

in whatever version—bears a remarkable likeness to the Ninth's first movement. It is in D minor and unfolds with what might be called the same dramatic gestures. These include the placement of and means of achieving climaxes; the contrapuntal complexities; and the use of extreme dynamic contrasts, sudden harmonic shifts, and striking changes of timbre. The overall formal design, which incorporates a characteristically weighty coda, and the breadth of its scope likewise strike one as being very Beethovenian. Other common features are the long-sustained pedals, the undulating ostinato accompaniment figures, and the "unison" statements of the first principal subject. It is also noteworthy that Bruckner placed the scherzo movements of his Eighth and (unfinished) Ninth Symphonies in second (not third) place within four-movement schemes and that the figure that begins the Eighth is very similar rhythmically to the opening motif of Beethoven's Ninth Symphony. Finally, it may not have been mere coincidence that Bruckner again returned to the key of D minor for his last symphony.

Perhaps the most significant responses to Beethoven's Ninth Symphony resulted from composers' attempts to come to terms with the aesthetic questions posed by the inclusion of voices in its last movement. Liszt's *Faust* Symphony and *Dante* Symphony both have choral finales, and Berlioz and Mahler incorporated vocal parts in a number of their symphonic compositions. But Beethoven's work also had an impact outside the realm of the symphony. It was reinterpreted, in a sense, by many romantic artists to suit their own aesthetic interests. The primary concern for them was the matter of the relationship of music to the other arts, especially to literature. Berlioz, Wagner, Mendelssohn, and E. T. A. Hoffmann, among others, felt that Beethoven had reached a point where a new liaison should be established between purely instrumental music and, ideally, all of the other arts, or, at least, between it and poetry.

Wagner attempted to solve the aesthetic problems presented by the notion of art-synthesis within the realm of opera, while Berlioz worked within the framework of the symphony; yet both composers considered the orchestra to be an extremely important tool for the realization of their artistic aims. Taking as his starting point what he thought constituted Greek tragedy, Wagner imagined a new kind of opera that would be an all-embracing, universal work of art (*Gesamtkunstwerk*, a term first coined by Hoffmann). In such essays as "Art and Revolution," "The Artwork of the Future," and "Beethoven," and in *Opera and Drama*, Wagner argued that the perfect work of art is drama in which all the arts—primarily poetry (speech), dance and mime (gesture), and music (tone), but also painting and architecture—are combined in such a way that the result has greater scope and expressive power than any one of its constituent arts taken singly. In this way "deeds of Music" are "brought to sight," as he wrote in "On the Name 'Musikdrama'" (5: 303).

Wagner conceived his music dramas in terms of the operatic stage, but since his compositional methods were firmly rooted in the German symphonic tradition, it was only natural for him to assign a special role to the orchestra. The musical means by which he was able to create a new world within opera included the systematic use of leitmotivs found principally in the instrumental parts and the manipulation of an enlarged performance apparatus to produce new textures and colors. In addition, partly in keeping with his ideas concerning the relationship of word and tone—to some degree in response to Beethoven's Ninth—and partly from his love for experimenting with timbres, Wagner added the human voice to his orchestral mass of sound. There are passages in his last music dramas, especially in *Tristan und Isolde*, where words serve merely as vehicles by which the singers add color to the orchestral texture, by which they can become drowned in oceans of harmony, to use Wagner's own metaphor.

Berlioz' conception of an all-embracing work of art seems to have been based on the fundamental premise that visual action presented on the stage can be replaced by action envisioned in the mind's eye—by imagination. This imagination must be guided in its course in two ways: by the knowledge and thorough understanding of either a program appended to the work or the literary sources upon which it is based; and by the music itself, which has phenomenally expressive, even pictorial, capabilities. Thus, the compositions that best reflect Berlioz' notion of art-synthesis are not his operas but those to which he applied, significantly enough, such descriptive terms as *légende dramatique, monodrama lyrique, symphonie dramatique,* or *épisode (de la vie . . .)*. These include *Roméo et Juliette, Symphonie fantastique* and *Lélio,* and *La damnation de Faust.* Here again the apparent disparity between a composer's fundamental compositional style and his aesthetic aims presents an interesting paradox. Berlioz' muse was strongly rooted in the Gallic vocal tradition, yet he worked toward a new symphonic conception.

Mendelssohn, Liszt, Tchaikovsky, Smetana, Dvořák, Mussorgsky, and Richard Strauss, among others, also added extramusical connotations to some of their purely instrumental works by appending programmatic titles or literary descriptions to them or, in the case of Mussorgsky's *Pictures at an Exhibition,* references to pictorial art. In addition, many composers wrote incidental music for plays. These extramusical sources frequently inspired them to treat the orchestra in new ways. Mendelssohn's

Hebrides Overture, for example, is awash with a vibrant, uniquely colorful splash of sound. The "special effects" that Strauss concocted to explicitly depict Don Quixote's escapades with a herd of sheep or with a windmill (Strauss devised a wind machine to suit the purpose) are only isolated examples of his brilliant use of an entity that, by the end of the nineteenth century, had become a veritable color machine.

It was, of course, against such attempts to be strictly pictorial that a composer like Erik Satie reacted by giving humorously absurd titles to his own works or by quipping—even though he knew Debussy's intentions were otherwise—that the most impressive part of "De l'aube à midi sur la mer" ("From Dawn to Noon at Sea," the first movement of *La Mer*) is the section at a quarter to eleven o'clock. Yet Satie himself composed programmatic music with perfectly serious intentions and in his own way was also a colorist in search of new ways of creating atmosphere. In his ballet *Parade* (1917), for example, he was able to make the orchestra speak as a representative of the mechanistic world about him, using not only traditional orchestral instruments but also typewriters, steamship whistles, and sirens. Such works belong to an age beyond the scope of this essay, but it is necessary to stress that, with regard to both the aesthetic and technical considerations pertaining to the use of the orchestra, they owe more to developments which took place during the nineteenth century than is generally assumed. To cite two final examples, Schoenberg's use of the orchestra as a vast palette of colors in the *Gurrelieder* or his treatment of a smaller group in the *Five Pieces for Orchestra*, Opus 15, would have been unthinkable without the *Symphonie fantastique*, *Tasso*, *Das Rheingold*, the *Tragic* Overture, Dvořák's *Carnival* Overture, or Debussy's *Nocturnes*.

BIBLIOGRAPHY

Heinz Becker, *History of Instrumentation*, vol. 24 of *Anthology of Music*, K. G. Fellerer, ed. (1964). Paul Bekker, *The Story of the Orchestra* (1936). Hector Berlioz, *Evenings with the Orchestra*, Jacques Barzun, trans. and ed. (1956). Anton Bruckner, *Gesammelte Briefe*, Franz Gräflinger, ed. (1924). Adam Carse, *The Orchestra from Beethoven to Berlioz* (1948). John Clapham, *Antonín Dvořák: Musician and Craftsman* (1966). Alfred Einstein, *Music in the Romantic Era* (1947). Peter le Huray, and James Day, eds., *Music and Aesthetics in the Eighteenth and Early-Nineteenth Centuries* (1981).

Kenneth B. Klaus, *The Romantic Period in Music* (1970). Paul Henry Lang, *Music in Western Civilization* (1941). Rey M. Longyear, *Nineteenth-Century Roman-*

ticism in Music (2d ed., 1973). Felix Mendelssohn, *Letters,* G. Selden-Goth, ed. (1945).

Reginald Nettel, *The Orchestra in England: A Social History* (1946). William S. Newman, "The Beethoven Mystique in Romantic Art, Literature, and Music," in *Musical Quarterly,* 69, no. 3 (1983). Brian Primmer, "Unity and Ensemble: Contrasting Ideals in Romantic Music," in *Nineteenth-Century Music,* 6, no. 2 (1982). Henry Raynor, *Music and Society Since 1815* (1976); and *The Orchestra* (1978). Walter Salmen, *The Social Status of the Professional Musician from the Middle Ages to the Nineteenth Century,* Herbert Kaufman and Barbara Reisner, trans. (1983), Otakar Šourek, *Antonín Dvořák: Letters and Reminiscences,* Roberta Finlayson Samsour, trans. (1954).

Richard Wagner, *Prose Works,* William Ashton Ellis, trans., 8 vols. (1892–1899). Alan Walker, ed., *Robert Schumann: The Man and His Music* (1972). Carl Maria von Weber, *Writings on Music,* Martin Cooper, trans., and John Warrack, ed. (1981). William Weber, *Music and the Middle Class: The Social Structure of Concert Life in London, Paris and Vienna* (1975); and "Mass Culture and the Reshaping of European Musical Taste, 1770–1870," *International Review of the Aesthetics and Sociology of Music,* 8, no. 1 (1977).

Orchestral Texture and the Art of Orchestration

R. Larry Todd

The modern symphony orchestra developed from the instrumental ensembles standardized in the middle of the eighteenth century. The fine details of this evolution still elude the grasp of scholars and will probably remain unresolved, but the idea that the Mannheim symphonists were the first to experiment with the gradation of orchestral dynamics at least may be put to rest; that technique appeared earlier, in the operas of Niccolò Jommelli from the 1740s and in Rameau's *Hippolyte et Aricie* of 1733. But other questions remain. At what point did composers adopt clarinets into the woodwind group, and when did they align the section into its customary pairings of instruments? How early did stopped horn notes appear in the orchestra? When exactly did the four-part string texture of early classical scores expand to five parts? These questions admit of no easy answers. But the general development of the orchestra from its modest origins to the institution we know today is more or less clear. Once the basic principles of contrasting and combined groups of wind and string instruments had been established, the inevitable process of experimentation with, and expansion of, orchestral resources—still continuing today—could begin.

As steady and irreversible as that process has been for more than two centuries, recognition of orchestration—the study of instruments and their use to create distinctive orchestral textures—as a discipline came relatively late. To be sure, instrumentation manuals began to appear with some frequency in the second half of the eighteenth century, especially in France, as detailed by Bartenstein (1971). The improvement of some wind instruments and the adoption of others encouraged the flow of new manuals to assist musicians eager to learn how to write for winds, among them Valentin Roeser's *Essai d'instruction à l'usage de ceux qui composent pour la clarinette et le cor* (1764) and Louis Joseph Francoeur's *Diapason général de tous les instruments à vent* (1772). This manual presents Francoeur's systematic discussion of the ranges and special properties of the winds—without differentiation between woodwind and brass—organized into chapters on flute, oboe, clarinet, horn, bassoon, trumpet, and the human voice. Instruments no longer in common use, such as the musette, are not treated, though Francoeur does include a chapter for the serpent, then primarily a musical participant in church processions. Francoeur argues that a niche should be found in the orchestra for this instrument, on account of its singularly strange sounds, a quality most suitable, he adds, for certain pieces in the pathetic manner (p. 71).

Francoeur's ultimately unsuccessful plea for the serpent contrasts with his influential and lengthy discussion of the clarinet, still a novelty in 1772 and not yet a regular member of the orchestra. After introducing the several available types, Francoeur suggests that composers write for a wind section of paired clarinets, horns, and bassoons. He adduces three examples of this larger wind ensemble, two of them drawn from works by Signor Stamitz (presumably Karl Stamitz). His brief commentary deals only with some practical suggestions—for example, that the horns not be overtaxed and that the second horn be allowed to sound the *basse fondamentale* (presumably a reference to Rameau's abstract bass line, designed to represent the roots of harmonic progressions). As if reluctant to discuss at length the possibilities of the wind sextet, Francoeur moves on to his next topic, the trumpet, somewhat summarily dismissed as "the most unpleasant and most limited" of the winds (p. 61). The *Diapason général,* in short, serves as a rudimentary primer about wind instruments. While there is a recognition of the different characters of the winds, there is no discussion of how to write for them in the orchestra of the time or, for that matter, of the string instruments, let alone their use in the orchestra.

Nearly sixty years separate Francoeur's treatise and a composition that drastically altered the course of orchestration—Berlioz' *Symphonie fantastique* of 1830. During this time the orchestra underwent profound changes. By 1772 the four-part string texture of the early classic orchestra, supported by a modest number of woodwinds and brass, had been firmly established. In the later symphonies of Mozart and Haydn the full wood-wind group of paired flutes, oboes, clarinets, and bassoons took final shape. And at the turn of the century, composers began to treat the brass section (generally paired horns and trumpets) as an independent group of instruments, not necessarily joined to the woodwinds. Beethoven but-tressed the brass by adding a third horn in the *Eroica* Symphony (1805), applied with spectacular effect in the *Trio* section of the third movement. Cherubini, Méhul, Spontini, and Weber (notably in *Der Freischütz* of 1821) took one further step by writing for four horns. Trombones, for-merly found in sacred or ceremonial music, played increasingly signifi-cant roles, too, in symphonies, as in Beethoven's Fifth Symphony (1808) or Schubert's *Great C Major* Symphony (written between 1825 and 1828 but not performed until 1839). The timpani, formerly joined to the brass section, enjoyed new independence as well, as in Haydn's Symphony no. 103 (*Drumroll*) of 1795. Finally, the string section grew in size, and five-part string writing became more and more customary.

With such expanded resources, composers began to exploit different types of orchestral textures. A major influence in this regard was opera. Composers of opera realized that the contemporary orchestra could be used for what has been termed an "expressive medium" (Charlton). Thus, in his overtures Rossini revived and experimented further with the orchestral crescendo, always carefully scored for maximum dramatic impact. Furthermore, David Charlton has suggested that certain recur-ring orchestral textures in eighteenth- and nineteenth-century operas represent specific topical ideas, such as "mutual affection or love, untrou bled by irony or premonition." And in the French operas of Le Sueur, Méhul, and Cherubini, orchestral color as a textural device took on a new significance. Two noted examples are the Ossianic operas, *Ossian, ou Les bardes* of Le Sueur (1804) and *Uthal* of Méhul (1806). Le Sueur included for his bards harp parts conspicuous throughout the opera, and Méhul opted for another orchestral solution, wittily related by Berlioz: "Méhul, to give the orchestration of *Uthal* a melancholy coloring of the cloudy, Ossianic kind, conceived the idea of using no strings but violas and cellos, the whole violin section being entirely omitted. The result of protracting this veiled timbre was a monotony more fatiguing than poetic, and Grétry, when asked about it, said frankly: 'I'd give a gold sov-ereign to hear an E string'" (1956, 352–353).

Such experiments in orchestration, of course, were not limited to opera. Two well-known examples from Beethoven's symphonies come easily to mind. In the second movement of the *Pastoral* Symphony (1808), Beethoven expanded the division of the string section, with solo muted cellos and pizzicato bass, to capture the effect of a gentle current in the "Scene by the Brook" in a way that a conventional string texture could not. Likewise the celebrated "wrong" entrance of the horn just before the reprise in the first movement of the *Eroica* stands as a bold textural experiment, one that many of Beethoven's contemporaries failed to understand (Ex. 1). The harmonic clash between the tonic and incomplete dominant harmonies, coordinated with the head motive in the horn *(pp)* and the string tremolo *(ppp)*, works like a subtle textural symbol of the idea of conflict that permeates the movement. Quite likely Beethoven had in mind here an orchestral imitation of the open-pedal effects he was then testing on the fortepiano, by which clashing harmonies blend together before a decisive point of tonal clarification, as in the opening measures of the *Rondo* from the *Waldstein* Sonata, Opus 53.

Example 1. Beethoven: Symphony no. 3 in E-flat Major *(Eroica)*, movement 1, mm. 390–399

Not surprisingly, the new techniques in orchestration did not gain immediate recognition in contemporary treatises, an indication again of the lapse between practice and theory. The passage from the *Pastoral* Symphony, for example, appears in Karl Czerny's *Treatise on Instrumentation*, the third volume of the comprehensive *School of Practical Composition*, Opus 600 (translated into English in 1848), in a curious chapter entitled "Of Unusual Combinations of Different Instruments." As if unconvinced by Beethoven's novel string texture, Czerny sounds this precaution:

> The employment of such effects, or the creation of new ones, depends on the fancy and the talent of the composer; who has merely to observe, that the same unusual combinations are only to be introduced rarely and with moderation, and also that the ideas which give rise to them are deserving of such means, by reason of their beauty and originality: for, otherwise, the hearers must regret to see them expended on ordinary, mean, or ugly thoughts.
>
> (p. 36)

These comments thus read almost more as an apology for Beethoven's passage than as a recognition of its novelty.

A radically different approach to orchestration obtains in Berlioz' *Grand traité d'instrumentation et d'orchestration modernes,* published as the composer's Opus 10 in 1843 (though originally released in article format in the *Revue et gazette musicale de Paris* in 1841 and 1842). In many ways Berlioz' work set the standard for the study of orchestration throughout the remainder of the century: on account of its comprehensive treatment of the instruments of the modern orchestra, its discussion of conducting, and its vision of the orchestra as a modern instrument capable of an inexhaustible diversity of effects. In his short preface to the *Traité* we gain some insight into Berlioz' view of the situation of his period. He notes the renewed interest in instrumentation, in contrast to the neglect it suffered in the eighteenth century, especially among those who opposed progress in music. From that dismal state of affairs, Berlioz draws a sweeping moral: enemies of true art have always impeded the natural course of progress. Thus, Monteverdi was criticized for introducing unprepared dissonances, though in time the new sonorities were widely acclaimed and, in turn, misused: "These musicians took a fancy for dissonant chords, as certain animals have a predilection for salt, prickly plants, and thorny shrubs." Theirs was "the exaggeration of reaction." As for orchestration — for Berlioz the art of using orchestral instruments to color melody, harmony, and rhythm or to produce novel effects independent of these elements—it, too, is at the point of exaggeration, but not yet fully mastered.

Berlioz viewed the modern orchestra as a progressively evolving instrument "capable of uttering at once or successively a multitude of sounds of different kinds; and of which the power is mediocre or colossal according as it employs the whole or a part only of the executive means belonging to modern music" (p. 240). In the closing pages of the *Traité* he outlined a utopian vision of a modern Parisian orchestra of some 467 instrumentalists and 360 choral members, its forces planned to ensure a proper balance but also to provide the composer with an untold number of new orchestral colors, textures, and harmonic effects. For some idea of the magnitude of the conception, the string section can be examined. Berlioz desired 120 violins (divisible into various groupings), 40 violas (of which 10 might play the viola d'amore, an instrument that had been revived by Meyerbeer in the opera *Les Huguenots* in 1836 and that Berlioz hoped to reestablish in the orchestra), 45 cellos, 31 double basses (in different tunings), and 4 octobasses (a three-string double bass with a range extending to the octave below the cello).

Berlioz advised that the whole enormous mass of 827 musicians be reserved for special moments of great breadth; the main advantage of this new orchestral colossus would be in its subgroupings and special effects. For example, a metallic percussive effect could be procured by joining 30 pianos with bells, antique cymbals, triangles, and sets of the Turkish crescent. Or 30 harps might be combined with the strings in pizzicato, forming by Berlioz' calculation a large-scale harp effect with 934 strings! In such ways the modern composer could generate an extraordinary richness of new colors formerly unimaginable—and presumably contribute to the progress of art.

Serving as an antidote to this ecstatic vision of orchestration is the down-to-earth view of Berlioz' contemporary and opponent François-Joseph Fétis. In the first volume of the *Revue musicale,* Fétis published in 1827 an article entitled "Des revolutions de l'orchestre." Fétis did not see the orchestral revolution in a positive light; quite the contrary, he asked, in a rather dour vein, "What are the natural bounds to the development of an orchestra?" He ascribed the new developments in orchestration to many factors: "the invention of new instruments, the disuse of many, the perfecting of others, and above all, the increased skill of performers;...the advancement of music, the necessity for novelty, the empire of fashion," and so on. Fétis then gave a thumbnail history of the development of orchestration. Pausing to consider Monteverdi's orchestra for *Orfeo,* he noted the assignment of individual instruments (for example, trombones for Pluto's infernal realm) but decided that the "effect of separating all these instruments must certainly have been meager in the extreme." Nor was there much improvement in later seventeenth-century opera, for "although the number of instruments was increased,...the accompaniment only followed the voice," yielding a "monotonous manner." The introduction of the flute and clarinets and the improvement of the French horn he viewed more favorably, as he did Haydn's treatment of the orchestra in his symphonies. But Fétis reserved the signal honor for Mozart, who "knew how to give to the instrumental parts a degree of interest hitherto unknown" and who "also knew how to stop at the exact point which it seems cannot be passed without injury to the air or fatigue to the senses."

The post-Mozartean orchestra posed a quandary for Fétis. Without commenting on Beethoven, he credited Méhul and Cherubini with improving the treatment of the horns—for instance, using four horns and stopped notes—but was taken aback by the orchestra of Rossini: "After borrowing from Mozart, Beethoven, Cherubini, and Méhul, their modes of producing effect,...he [Rossini] has himself advanced still further.... His compositions present the first examples of four violin parts, the formidable union of four horns, common trumpets, keyed trumpets, trombones, ophycleides, & c., all united for the accompaniment of particular movements." Ostensibly admiring Rossini's talent, Fétis was clearly disquieted by this orchestral upheaval: Rossini's effects are the product of an "abuse of means," and further, "the proportions of the orchestra are broken by the frequent use of such noisy instruments." Fétis is distressed to have "arrived at a point when an excess of effects is necessary, but which in the end prove detrimental to each other."

By a strange irony, Berlioz and Fétis thus agreed that orchestration had reached the point of exaggeration in the first half of the nineteenth century, but they drew utterly different conclusions. The progressive Berlioz saw the orchestra as a modern musical instrument capable of further development and improvement; the reactionary Fétis yearned to return to the classical ideal of the Mozartean orchestra. Berlioz welcomed the discovery of new effects and the invention of new instruments; Fétis sought to impose firm limits for the boundaries of modern taste. These two views offer convenient points of departure for the following discussion of orchestral texture as it evolved from the classical concept of orchestration as a structural device, to the romantic approach to orchestration as an expressive coloring agent, and to the neoclassical orchestration of the first few decades of the twentieth century.

TOWARD THE CLASSICAL IDEAL: THE ARTICULATION OF ORCHESTRAL TEXTURE

During the middle decades of the eighteenth century the eight-part orchestra, used often by Haydn and Mozart in their early symphonies, became the norm. Composers scored for strings in four parts (first and second violins, violas, and bass instruments, the latter including cellos and string basses), two oboes, and two horns. The bass line was frequently doubled by a bassoon part; a harpsichord continuo part, a vestige of baroque practice, was customary.

The core of this orchestra was the string section, ordinarily entrusted with the basic melodic and harmonic material. Early on, theorists affirmed the structural predominance of the string section. Thus, in the *Versuch einer Anleitung zur Composition* (1782–1793), Heinrich Christoph Koch lists the string parts as the four *Hauptstimmen* (principal voices), which should be "strongly supported (3:301)." In the *Musikalisches Lexicon* (1802), Koch again gives the strings priority, comparing them to a four-part chorus and noting that in the early symphonies composers either wrote for string orchestra alone or reinforced it with only a few wind instruments (p. 1386). In A. F. C. Kollmann's *Essay on Practical Musical Composition* (1799), the four string parts are compared to the parts in a four-part harmonic texture (pp. 17–18). And in the 1840s, when five-part string writing was more or less standard, Czerny could write, "The stringed instruments collectively are termed, in orchestral composition, the Quartett, in order to distinguish them from the wind instruments" (p. 5). Fétis reasserted the supremacy of the string section when he criticized Rossini's "noisy orchestras." For Fétis, Rossini's reinforcement of the wind section upset the natural balance of the orchestra, the basis of which "will always be the violins and the bass." Finally, at the beginning of the twentieth century, Richard Strauss suggested that the symphonies of Haydn and Mozart were essentially string quartets with added obbligato parts for wind instruments (p. 1).

Early classic composers arranged the four string parts in a variety of ways. In the simplest plan, the strings executed a unison passage with doublings at various octaves, or the first violins played the main thematic material, with the remaining strings aligned homophonically. In another alternative the second violins and violas were set against strong melodic and bass lines. In still another grouping, the violin parts engaged in imitative counterpoint with homophonic support from the lower strings, or the imitation involved three or four string parts. Very frequently the second violins doubled the first violins, and the violas the bass line, often at the octave. By this means the four-part texture essentially reduced to two parts, the structural outer voices, requiring the addition of winds or, in a movement without winds (such as a slow movement), the harpsichord realization to fill in the missing voices of the harmony.

The *Andante* of Haydn's Symphony no. 2 offers an instance of this last division. Dating probably from the early 1760s, the example looks back to the baroque, in its rhythmic superposition of a winding melodic line in sixteenth notes over a more slowly moving bass line in eighth notes. Haydn sustains this texture throughout the movement, and its continuity of affect is one more indication of baroque influence. Though there are not yet those frequent, marked changes in texture that became a hallmark of the high classic style, there are subtle changes in articulation (Ex. 2). Thus, the staccatos in measure seven interrupt the initial series of two-note slurs and mark the beginning of the modulation to the dominant, articulated by an alternation between four-note and two-note slurs. In measure eighteen, the sudden swerve to the minor dominant is joined with a fresh articulation of four-note slurs. In turn, a few measures later, when the dominant major returns, that pattern gives way to

Example 2. Haydn: Symphony no. 2 in C Major, movement 2, mm. 1–4, 7–11, 17–22

another. Changes in phrasing thus act in a small way to signify various structural points of the harmony, even though the basic string texture remains unchanged.

When departing from four-part string texture, early classic composers usually resorted to combinations of two or three parts; writing for five or more string parts was rare at this time. Examples of five-part writing usually reduce to simpler textures. Thus, in the slow movements of Symphonies nos. 14 and 16, Haydn's "five-part" string writing is in fact a reinforced two-part texture. First and second violins in unison are doubled an octave below by the cellos; violas double the bass line an octave higher. Only at some cadences does Haydn depart from this ordering, permitting the strings to engage momentarily in three- or four-part harmony. The doubling technique produces a richer, darker sound than that in the *Andante* of Symphony no. 2. In two examples from Mozart, five-part writing does obtain through the division of the violas *a 2*, though for the most part the violas either double the violins or other instruments (Symphony no. 22, K. 162: *Andantino grazioso*) or strengthen the harmonic accompaniment (Symphony no. 6, K. 43: *Andante*, also used in the duet "Natus cadit" from *Apollo et Hyacinthus*, K. 38).

The reduction of the string section to two or three parts is considerably more common. A good example of a two-part texture is the well-known opening of Mozart's Symphony no. 14, K. 114 (1771), for the first and second violins. Haydn's Symphony no. 16, from the early 1760s, also begins with a two-voice string texture, but one that suggests more an exercise in species counterpoint than it does the grace of Mozart's theme.

Composers had at their disposal a certain number of special effects for the string section. Among these were the string tremolo, employed to increase the sense of rhythmic energy, and two less common devices, the pizzicato and the mute. The last two occur almost always in slow movements, as in Haydn's Symphonies nos. 4, 16, 20, and 27 or in Mozart's Symphony no. 25, K. 183. Occasionally they are combined, as in Haydn's Symphony no. 27, a siciliano with muted violins and pizzicato violas and bass instruments (see also the slow movements of Mozart's K. 133 and 182). Occasionally pizzicato and arco writing appear simultaneously, as in the slow movement of Haydn's Symphony no. 20. An especially striking use of the mute, which suggested to Koch a *schwermütig* (melancholic character), occurs in the first movement of Haydn's Symphony no. 22 (*Philosopher*, 1764): muted violins play in unison with the lower strings an eighth-note bass line while fortissimo horns and English horns intone *alternatim* a choralelike melody.

In their early symphonies Haydn and Mozart often treat the bass and woodwind instruments as one complement of supporting wind instruments. Oboes and horns are the preferred instruments, though substitutions are found (thus, clarinets replace oboes in Carl Friedrich Abel's Symphony in E-flat, which Mozart copied in 1764, K. Anh. 109[1]), and sometimes a flute may be added to the ensemble. Ordinarily the winds fulfill one of three roles: they play simple chords to provide a harmonic backdrop to the more active strings, they double the melody of the violins (either exactly or in some simplified manner), or they perform short solo passages. Because of certain technical limitations, composers wrote for the natural horns of the period with considerable caution. Often these instruments sustain pedal points or play simple "horn fifths" or passages in which tonic and dominant pitches alternate. In minor-key symphonies, to enable the horns to participate in the secondary key area of the mediant, composers sometimes opted to add an extra pair of instruments tuned in the relative major key, as in Symphony no. 39 of Haydn or Symphony no. 25 (K. 183) of Mozart.

Generally wind solos are relatively short in length; their purpose seems to be to provide a brief contrast in color to the string section. In the first movements of Symphonies nos. 5 and 15 (early 1760s), Haydn features the horns briefly as solo instruments with the string accompaniment. In the *Adagio* of no. 5 the oboes play only a handful of notes; in the *Adagio* of no. 15 the oboes are silent throughout. More ambitious experimentation with the possibilities of the winds is evident in Haydn's symphonies from the later 1760s and from his so-called *Sturm und Drang* period (roughly 1760–1772). Solos for combinations of horns and oboes are present in the Symphony no. 21 (first movement) of 1764 and in the exceptionally fine Symphony no. 59 (*Fire*) of the late 1760's, where the wind complement is used in the finale to launch an extended orchestral crescendo.

For especially festive symphonies, composers might add two trumpets and a pair of timpani to the eight-part orchestra. In the early symphonies of Haydn and Mozart these inevitably play in forte passages, serving as points of harmonic and rhythmic punctuation, to further bolster the orchestral texture. Significantly, trumpets and drums almost always play together, not apart, a feature noted by Kollmann. This practice reflects the use of trumpets and drums in the military *Feldmusik* of earlier periods. Indeed, sometimes composers displayed the military character of the instruments, as Haydn did in his Symphony no. 69 of 1778, written in honor of Field Marshal Laudon. But on the whole the trumpets and drums played a subordinate, supportive role in the orchestras of the 1760s and 1770s.

These, then, were the resources of the mid-eighteenth century orchestra. Given an ensemble dominated by the string section and supported by the wind ensemble, composers could experiment with relatively few different textures. Kollman organized these into three categories: unisons, tuttis, and solos of various kinds. In unison passages, the winds play the same material as the strings, though at different octave doublings; also, the horns, because of their natural restrictions, play "where they serve best or else rest." In tutti passages, the winds may double the strings (as in the unison passages) or they may supply a homophonic support, taking the "chords of the thorough bass." Finally, in solo passages, "those passages where one or a couple of instruments have a predominant melody, though not of such a nature as solos in a Concerto," Kollmann offered several possibilities. In solos for one or two string parts, the winds may accompany in a chordal manner the other strings; and in a wind solo, the strings may offer the accompaniment. Throughout the discussion, Kollmann is careful to distinguish between *real* and *duplicate* parts—that is, between those essential to the basic four-part harmonic texture, generally the string parts, and those which are doublings or simplifications of *real* parts (pp. 18–19).

With these three textures, eighteenth-century composers could draw on two basic types of textural change. They could contrast textures, for example, by writing a solo passage after a tutti or a unison, or they could change textures gradually, by employing a crescendo or a diminuendo. A good example of textural contrast is the opening of Mozart's Symphony no. 24, K. 182, finished in 1773. In measures 1–18 alone, there are nine textural groups, alternating between forte (unison or tutti) and piano (string passages) in pairs of measures.

On a higher structural level, composers juxtaposed different textures in the minuet, where typically the minuet proper was scored for full orchestra and the trio for a reduced ensemble. And in some of his fast, lighthearted finales Haydn coordinated textural contrasts to demarcate broad formal outlines. The finale of Symphony no. 15, for example, falls into a large ABA pattern. The A section is orchestrated mainly as a tutti, but the B section, in the parallel minor, features strings in three parts. A more sophisticated experiment occurs in the finale of Symphony no. 2, cast in a rondo form ABACA. Here Haydn reserves the A section primarily for the tutti; the B section, marked piano, for strings in two and four parts; and the C section, marked pianissimo, for the strings and horns.

The experimentation in gradated dynamics around the middle of the century—popularized, if not first used, by the Mannheim symphonists— offered new possibilities for textural manipulation. The use of the crescendo by Stamitz and his contemporaries and then in such works as Haydn's Symphonies nos. 1 and 6 (where it depicts a sunrise) needs no review here. The reverse dynamics effect, the diminuendo, has prompted relatively little discussion, though it, too, represented an important tool for eighteenth-century composers. One example is the ending of Haydn's Symphony no. 23 (1764), where an eighth-note subject is stated piano by the strings, then pianissimo, and finally, after the insertion of some rests, reduced to a pizzicato chord and measure of rest. In this example Haydn restricted the diminuendo to the string texture. A more complex treatment is evident in the opening of the *Sturm und Drang* Symphony no. 39 in G Minor (1768). Here Haydn begins with a piano string texture supported by horns. A rest soon interrupts this, after which the violins continue by themselves before tapering to a measure of rest. The opening thus suggests a terraced type of diminuendo, a ploy all the more telling by the crunching forte tutti that soon follows.

Unquestionably the most elaborate and large-scale diminuendo was devised by Haydn in the finale of the celebrated Symphony no. 45 (*Farewell*) of 1772, the ulterior purpose of which was to win for his musicians a well-earned leave from Esterháza. The concluding *Presto* seems to operate as a normal finale until Haydn redirects the music from its "final" cadence to pause unexpectedly on the dominant. At this point, an *Adagio* in A major commences, and it is here that Haydn begins the gradual thinning of the orchestra. The first oboe and second horn are the first to depart, as the movement arrives at the new dominant, E major. Then, after the *Adagio* returns to A major, the bassoon, previously tied to the bass instruments, emerges briefly in a solo and exits. And toward the conclusion of the *Adagio* the remaining winds, second oboe and first horn, finish their parts. But still not content to conclude the work, Haydn writes a transition for the remainder of the strings, including a solo for double bass before it leaves as the music pauses on C-sharp major. Now the *Adagio* begins afresh, this time, though, in F-sharp major, with only violins, violas, and cellos. Through further reductions Haydn concludes with parts for first and second violins, which finish with mutes applied, the final stage of the diminuendo.

This systematic reduction in texture assists in defining the structure of the movement: winds and strings perform the first *Adagio* in A, the full string section, the transition to the second *Adagio*; and the strings in decreasing numbers, the second *Adagio* in F-sharp major. Such a bold and unique experiment is further evidence of Haydn's increasing interest in orchestration as a means of defining structure. He reaches here a new limit in the articulation of orchestral texture, which now audibly contributes to the formal plan of the music.

THE CLASSICAL IDEAL: ORCHESTRAL TEXTURE AS A STRUCTURAL DEVICE

The summit of classical orchestration is the two sets of symphonies Haydn wrote for Paris (nos. 82–87, 1785–1786) and London (nos. 93–104, 1791–1795) and the last four symphonies of Mozart (1786–1788). Three earlier examples from Haydn's symphonies, nos. 47 (1772), 61 (1776), and 62 (*ca.* 1780), enable us to trace the developments leading to this culmination; and the finale of Mozart's *Jupiter* Symphony, K. 551 (1788), stands as a superb example of the coordination of orchestral texture with formal procedures.

The years of Sturm und Drang have long been recognized as ones of critical changes for Haydn's instrumental music. Increasingly evident, too, is his new approach to orchestration. For a while Haydn continued to use the standard eight-part orchestra, though he began to experiment more freely with scoring techniques. In Symphony no. 47 (1772), for example, we find the older orchestra, but here the wind and string groups interact in a more nearly equal relationship. The work begins not with the customary string-dominated *tutti* or unison but with the opposition of the winds and strings. Haydn introduces the winds in four overlapping forte layers in the order of second and first horns and second and first oboes (Ex. 3). In measure 9, by inverting the oboe parts, he is able to create the illusion of a fifth wind entry, suggesting an expansion of the winds.

Example 3. Haydn: Symphony no. 47 in G Major, movement 1, mm. 1–12

On the other hand, the strings, marked piano, play the bass line in unison between entries of the winds. In short, the wind texture encroaches on the traditional primacy of the strings by introducing the main material of the movement.

Only four years later Haydn composed his Symphony no. 61 in D Major; by then the expansion of the eight-part orchestra was well under way. The woodwind complement for this work includes one flute, two oboes, and two bassoons (which do not necessarily double the bass line of the strings). Throughout the score signs of new orchestral techniques abound. For instance, in the slow movement Haydn ingeniously splits the cellos from the double basses for a false return of the opening (measure 65), a subtle hint about the deceptive nature of that passage. The finale contains a passage with separate parts for the bassoons (measure 93f.) and humorous injections by the oboes into the opening theme. The general trend in orchestration here is toward a greater independence of winds and strings, which may stand alone or in new combinations.

Increasingly, too, the alteration of texture coincides with formal subdivisions. Nowhere is this clearer than in the secondary key area of the exposition of the first movement. Here is a simple harmonic progression—not a new theme—deftly scored to achieve a contrast in texture (Ex. 4). Haydn desired a special effect and, to maximize the contrast, prepared the passage with three *tutti* chords and an unexpected fermata. What follows are four measures of eighth-note wind chords accompanied by pizzicato strings on the downbeats. The phrase is repeated, but this time the chords are sustained in the winds, while the flute plays a solo above them. Four measures later the flute solo is taken up by the strings, now marked *col'arco*. Had Haydn scored the same passage for strings, it would surely have lost its enchanting effect. Textural contrast, which identifies for the listener this striking passage, is the key to its success.

In the slow movement of Symphony no. 62, finished most likely around 1780, Haydn tightened further his control of texture. This movement has the same orchestra as Symphony no. 61 but is carefully and sparingly scored, a quality that highlights Haydn's newfound freedom in orchestration. He begins with a texture for muted strings in two parts. The second violins play an eighth-note triadic figure against a series of simple half steps in the cellos and the high range of the first violins (Ex. 5). Striking at the outset is the absence of a clear-cut theme; the opening sounds more like an introductory accompaniment. The sparseness of the texture is made more conspicuous by the inversion of the half steps and the severe leap from the cello to violins in measures 2 and 3. The four-measure beginning is repeated: the triadic figure appears now in the

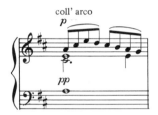

Example 4. Haydn: Symphony no. 61 in D Major, movement 1, mm. 41–49

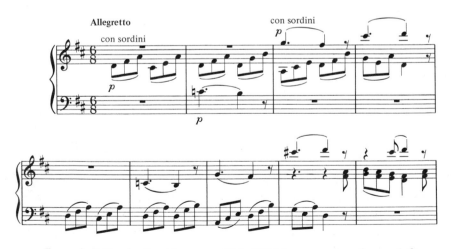

Example 5. Haydn: Symphony no. 62 in D Major, movement 2, mm. 1–9

cellos, and the half steps, in the violins. In measure 9 the texture thickens to three-part strings (violins and violas), and measure 13 has a third statement of the opening, now doubled by flute. The addition of the flute, the first entrance of a wind instrument, signals the modulation to the dominant, reinforced by the entrance of the cellos, producing four-part strings in measure 18. At measure 22, the midpoint of the first half of the movement, the remaining woodwinds enter along with the double basses; and six measures later Haydn adds the horns, thus completing the expansion to full orchestral tutti. In the closing section of the first half, the winds drop out, and Haydn concludes with strings alone.

The drastic reduction of melodic material—the movement is based principally on the triadic motive—encouraged Haydn to focus his attention on the orchestration, arguably one of the most successful examples from this period. Though the music is monothematic, its orchestration is not monochromatic; indeed, the masterful use of orchestration to define the structure remains one of its most noteworthy features.

By the 1780s, classical orchestration had reached its final stages of development, even though the size of the orchestra was not yet completely standardized. For example, clarinets appear more frequently in the works of Mozart than of Haydn, and five-part string writing was still in its experimental stage. Nevertheless, in such a work as the *Jupiter* Symphony, which has the same woodwind scoring as Haydn's Symphony no. 61 of twelve years earlier, Mozart broke decisive new ground in tying elements of orchestration to the formal process.

The fourth movement of the symphony is often cited for its combination of contrapuntal and sonata principles, bringing to mind such earlier works as the finales of Haydn's Symphonies nos. 13 and 70 and of works by others. Because of its complex structure, the movement afforded Mozart an extraordinary opportunity to treat the orchestration in a novel way. As is well known, he constructed the movement from four basic subjects (Ex. 6a), some of which play dual roles; specifically, the first

Example 6a. Mozart: Symphony no. 41 in C Major (*Jupiter*), K. 551, movement 4

and fourth serve also as the primary and secondary thematic ideas in the tonic and dominant. The second and third subjects, on the other hand, appear first in the bridge areas between the two thematic groups. By ordering his exposition into alternating sections for strings and full orchestra, Mozart uses the orchestration as one means of unifying this most complicated movement. Thus, the first theme (subject 1) appears in two piano string passages, the first one for a reduced string section (measures 1–8), the second an elaborated five-part fugato on the subject (measure 36ff.). The second theme (subject 4) appears likewise in a piano passage for reduced strings (measure 74ff.). Save for a short piano passage at the end, the rest of the exposition consists of forte tutti sections, in which subjects 2, 3, and 4 are treated in various canonic groupings.

The ne plus ultra of the *Jupiter* finale is usually thought to be the coda, the famous stretto in which all subjects are combined. While Mozart's contrapuntal perfection has inspired sufficient comment, his consummate orchestration is often overlooked. For this final climax Mozart again divides the strings into five parts by splitting the cellos from the double basses. By this means the string parts can double the five woodwinds available in the *Jupiter* orchestra, namely, one flute, two oboes, and two bassoons. But because Mozart has used only four subjects, yet is working with a five-part string-wind texture, he designs one more contrapuntal subject by combining bits of subjects 4 and 3 (Ex. 6b; see also measures 76–78). The stretto proper begins in measure 372, with two, three, four, and five voices as the five subjects enter in turn. During this portion the brass rests, while the bassoons and then flute and oboes intone the first subject. Every four measures Mozart rotates the subjects, yielding new combinations in invertible counterpoint. By measure 388, halfway through the stretto, all five voices are established, and this event is marked by two textural changes in the orchestration: the winds now double their respective string instruments, and the brass and timpani execute fanfares alternating between the tonic and dominant. The orchestration, in short, is just as carefully worked out as the counterpoint. It is indeed the summit of classical clarity, of orchestral texture allied with structural rigor.

Example 6b. Mozart: Symphony no. 41 in C Major (*Jupiter*), K. 551, movement 4

THE ROMANTIC IDEAL: TEXTURE AS AN AGENT OF EXPRESSION

In a March 1802 review in the *Allgemeine musikalische Zeitung,* a critic termed Haydn's instrumental music a "totally new type of romantic painting for the ear." The occasion for the review was the appearance of the oratorio *The Creation.* With its enlarged orchestra, augmented by an extra flute, a contrabassoon, and three trombones, Haydn produced a for-ward-looking masterpiece that has been termed "the most modern piece of music of its time" (Landon, 415). Indeed, parts of the oratorio antici-pate what we may call the romantic ideal in orchestration, in which tex-ture works as an agent of expression.

Contemporaries of Haydn were especially drawn to the overture, "The Representation of Chaos." In it Haydn set out to depict a formless void, and to do so, he drew upon extraordinary orchestral effects. Simply put, he rejected the standard techniques of classical orchestration in favor of textures less refined and more primeval in their effect. Tonally and harmonically this music indeed suggests a lack of structure: Haydn treats dissonances very freely, redirects cadential progressions to unexpected goals, and undermines a strong sense of tonal orientation. The music is gradually animated by a shifting assortment of rhythmic values, which ultimately return to the stasis of the beginning—a stark orchestral uni-son on C. There are metrical irregularities, too, as in the tied upbeats in measures 26ff. and measures 48ff., creating the impression of rhythmic chaos. But perhaps most striking of all is the orchestration and use of texture to capture the swirling void. Nowhere in his music did Haydn orchestrate in such a novel, expressive manner.

In this depiction of chaos Haydn stands classical orchestration on its head. The supreme clarity of Mozart's *Jupiter* Symphony, with its orderly orchestration, is contradicted here by a marvelously planned chaos, an order of disorder. To be sure, the string section still shapes the chaos, but its structural role is far less secure. The strings are muted throughout, but Haydn allows them to play at various levels from pianissimo to fortis-simo, creating unpredictable distortions of the dynamics, yet another sign of disorder. More striking, points of sound from the brass and winds, but in no particular order, impact on the string sonorities, like bits of matter accidentally colliding. Thus, in measure 6, a staccato triplet figure rises in the bassoon and then in the violas; two measures later, the trombones suddenly swell to cut through the texture momentarily. Per-haps a more striking example of this orchestration is in measures 31 and

32, where a glissandolike scale in the clarinet leads only to a dramatic drop of several octaves to a contrabass solo, followed in turn by a short figure in the flutes. This is expressive orchestration, organized for its coloristic effect, not for a structural purpose. Haydn treats single instruments or groups of instruments separately, not according to standard classical norms of orchestration.

Quite in contrast are the closing bars of the introduction, the famous passage where the chorus sings, "Und es ward Licht." For this act of creation Haydn marshals his orchestra to order. The strings remove their mutes, and the orchestra is strengthened by a third trombone and a contrabassoon. With these forces and a particularly bright scoring, Haydn in one dramatic stroke disperses the dark sonorities of his chaotic *Ur-Welt*. The whole orchestra unites here in a pulsating prolongation of a C-major harmony; the radiant, full-textured orchestra contrasts with the atomized scoring of chaos.

Just how much Haydn labored over his new orchestral conception is evident from the meticulous sketches he left for "The Representation of Chaos." First discussed in 1932 by Karl Geiringer, they were published in 1977 in full transcriptions (Landon, 357–373). They show quite clearly that the orchestration concerned Haydn from the start, for many of them are in full or nearly full score. In what was most likely the first sketch, Haydn began with a simple unison for violas and cellos, not the full orchestral tutti that we hear in the final version. In the next few measures he mixed strings and woodwinds. In other sketches, the unison for full orchestra or for violins, trumpets, and timpani is followed by passages for mixed strings and winds, with trumpets in the low register. Finally, in a sketch close to the final version, Haydn succeeded in separating the orchestral bodies. He began with a forte unison and continued with the strings alone, another forte unison, and the woodwinds. By this means he gradually isolated blocks of sound—or, as Landon has put it, he "dematerialized" the orchestration. The result was a new emphasis on orchestral color, which, to return to the 1802 review, gives the score a "remarkable, mysterious appearance."

The same phrase could have been used to describe parts of a composition contemporary with *The Creation*, Beethoven's Fifth Symphony, finished in 1808. The parallel passage here is the famous transition from the third movement to the finale. The similarities between this and Haydn's introduction are manifest, though they bear repeating. For the finale Beethoven adds trombones, contrabassoon, and piccolo; at the end of the introduction Haydn adds a third trombone and a contrabassoon. Both passages involve motion from C minor to C major, and in both an unusual orchestration plays a prominent role in the overall effect. Beginning in measure 324, Beethoven calls for triple piano strings to sustain the third A-flat–C doubled in octaves, while the timpani perform a pedal figure on C (Ex. 7). In measure 342 the timpani C becomes a dissonant fourth as the bass line descends to G. Now the violins etch the contours of the opening motive of the movement and begin to introduce diatonic pitches of the C-major scale. In the final stage, winds and brass enter in a crescendo as the dominant preparation erupts into the C-major finale.

This extraordinary music must have struck contemporary critics as a transformation from chaos to order, much in the manner of Haydn's introduction. We need only quote E. T. A. Hoffmann's famous review: the finale is "like radiant, blinding sunlight which suddenly illuminates the dark night"; the third movement, on the other hand, is marked by "premonitions of the realm of the spirits," and a "restless yearning"—for Hoffmann, the quintessence of romanticism. Similarly, a review in the *Allgemeine musikalische Zeitung* of June 1814 gives this interpretation of the transition from the third movement to the finale: "The dark entrance to the realm of spirits opens; its inhabitants draw forth and mingle among us.... A truly terrible darkness clouds the colorful realm of light and its creations. Then—Finale, C major—the sun joyously streams forth, and lost are the specters and fiends of the old night; light and clarity return, and all thrive with the most vibrant force of life."

What provoked this enraptured description is the dark, mysterious texture of the transition, punctuated by the timpani strokes. To return to Hoffmann: "Why the master allowed the dissonant C of the kettle-

Example 7. Beethoven: Symphony no. 5 in C Minor, movement 3, mm. 324–326, 339–343

drum to continue to the end is explained by the character he was striving to give to the whole work. The dull, hollow strokes, having the effect of a strange, frightening voice by their dissonance, arouse the terror of the extraordinary, of the fear of spirits" (p. 160). Beethoven achieved this largely by rejecting a conventional orchestration. The timpani pedal, at first the consonant third of the chord, becomes a dissonant ostinato, reversing its customary role; also, the low, muffled sound of the third A-flat–C and the lack of a stabilizing fifth in the sonority produce a hollow type of texture, a harmonic void. The juxtaposition of strings and timpani contrasts strikingly with the winds and brass, which act as an elucidating element, and finally the full orchestral tutti, in which C major emerges as the tonic. The passage thus depends for its effect on the manipulation of texture and its expressive consequences.

In short, Beethoven's symphonies continue the emancipation of orchestration from classical norms to satisfy the newer demands of expression. Some critical recognition of this development is apparent in an article by C. F. Michaelis, in the *Allgemeine musikalische Zeitung* in 1807, on the aesthetic character of musical instruments and their appropriateness for musical expression. Thus, flutes joined with other instruments are useful "especially in romantic music," and Haydn in his symphonies has proven that horns may be treated in "romantic and humorous" ways.

In the first few decades of the nineteenth century, the orchestra did not grow much in size beyond the forces required by the Beethoven symphonies. The augmentation of the brass by two horns and three trombones gradually became a standard, though some composers even resisted this. But the search for new textures and colors continued. Carl Maria von Weber, for instance, took pains to work out a specific combination of instruments for the Samiel chord in *Der Freischütz*: low strings (tremolo and pizzicato), coupled with the dark shades of the clarinet's chalumeau register and timpani strokes, all to prolong a dissonant seventh chord. This is but one example of a new trend in orchestration whereby the autonomy of the string section became more and more susceptible to the intrusion of other instrumental colors. As a result, instruments from different groups could generate mixed or blended textures.

The orchestral music of Beethoven and the operas of Weber worked a profound influence on the young Mendelssohn during the 1820s. By training a conservative musician, Mendelssohn nevertheless demonstrated a concern for tone color in his instrumentation. According to an account by Eduard Devrient, Mendelssohn tried an unusual experiment when he composed the *Reformation* Symphony, Opus 107, in 1830: instead of notating the melody and bass parts and then filling in the remainder of the score, he scored the entire movement, measure by measure, like an "immense mosaic." Though abandoned after only one movement, the procedure suggests again the increased prominence given to orchestration, which became increasingly part of the creative act of composition, not an afterthought.

Mendelssohn achieved a romantic orchestration most consistently in his concert overtures. The *Midsummer Night's Dream* Overture (1826), celebrated for its translucent, gossamer orchestration, and the *Fingal's Cave* Overture (1835), distinguished by its dark textures, are the most famous in this series. For the *Meeresstille und glückliche Fahrt* Overture (1828), Mendelssohn turned to a larger orchestra with the addition of a piccolo, contrabassoon, and serpent, instruments calculated to broaden the registral limits of the woodwind section. The score is filled with open-spaced chords, Mendelssohn's response to the vast expanses of water described in Goethe's poem. In a passage from *Meeresstille* (measure 29ff.) Mendelssohn wrote a series of chords for low strings and bassoons submerged beneath a pedal point in the violins some three octaves above. In the *glückliche Fahrt* episode, broadly scored chords (Ex. 8a and 8b) are propelled by a string tremolo and timpani roll. In this example, first and second violins are spaced one and one-half octaves apart, to allow wind instruments to fill out the texture in between, effecting a blend of the two groups.

Example 8a. Mendelssohn: *Meeresstille und glückliche Fahrt* Overture, mm. 29–37

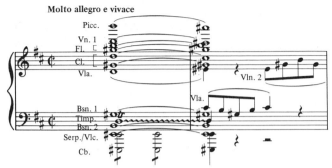

Example 8b. Mendelssohn: *Meeresstille und glückliche Fahrt* Overture, mm. 306–307

As large an orchestral conception as this overture represented for Mendelssohn, it scarcely approaches the demands made upon the orchestra by Berlioz. His scores contain innumerable novel instrumental effects, leading one to believe, with Richard Strauss, that Berlioz derived "his inspiration consistently from the character of the orchestral instruments" (Strauss, ii). The opening of the fifth movement of the *Symphonie fantastique*—that musical mélange inspired by events in the composer's life and literary sources as diverse as *Faust* and Thomas De Quincey's *Confessions of an English Opium Eater*—is but one example created by and for its orchestration. In the finale, describing the effects of an opium overdose, the hero dreams a nightmare of a witches' sabbath. The beginning is nothing more than a diminished-seventh sonority, enlivened by an unusual orchestration. First we hear muted strings *a 9* introduce the harmony with a tremolo. Cellos and basses unfold the interval of a tritone, and on the offbeats, two timpani tuned a third apart play the third and fifth of the chord, creating an indistinct, thudding sound. In measure 3, Berlioz directs the same harmony to the winds, which sustain it as the strings begin to move in short thirty-second-note cells before descending in parallel diminished harmonies. By measure 5 the passage reaches a C-major harmony, but any sense of tonal stability is undermined by the rumbling of the low strings (cellos and contrabasses divisi) in sextuplets, yielding a vaguely percussive, guttural sound even less distinct than the previous timpani strokes. Part of the brass and low woodwinds have some diminished chords and pause for eerie fanfares in high winds (which slide through an octave) and stopped horns. These are accompanied by sustained diminished-seventh chords in the low brass and wind (bassoons, trombones, ophicleide), and a roll on the bass drum marked *ppp*—the third and, as it is unpitched, least distinct of the three percussive effects. All four groups—woodwinds, brass, percussion, and strings—are thus represented in these opening measures, with some unexpected applications: the timpani play simultaneously, participating in the harmony, and low strings are exploited for their percussive character. Through the orchestration, Berlioz does his utmost to conjure up the macabre, and for him this required working with new and untested textural effects.

In the *Symphonie fantastique,* Berlioz exploded the boundaries of traditional orchestration and made possible the advances in his later scores, as in the "Tuba mirum" of the *Requiem* (1837), where he used four brass choirs and eight pairs of timpani which play complete harmonic progressions. For Fétis the *Symphonie fantastique* represented a cacophonic saturnalia, not music; for others who followed, it was a step further toward realizing the expressive potential of the modern orchestra.

Some measure of Berlioz' achievement in orchestration is indicated by the success of his *Grand traité,* which quickly became a standard text for composers and was updated by Richard Strauss in 1904. Just as Berlioz had begun with a short preface to set his treatise in historical perspective, so did Strauss add a short preface about developments in orchestration after Berlioz. He viewed Berlioz, in short, as the creator of the modern orchestra, the perfection of which awaited the monumental scores of Wagner.

Strauss distinguished between the symphonic orchestra, established by Haydn, Mozart, and Beethoven, and the dramatic orchestra, best suited for Wagner's new music dramas. The symphonic orchestra bore the stamp of chamber music, influenced by the string quartets of Haydn, Mozart, and Beethoven. Of more recent composers, Strauss found Schumann's and Brahms's scores to be pianistically conceived; only Liszt, he thought, breathed "new poetic life" into his orchestral music—a curious conclusion, since Liszt came to orchestration only in the middle of his career, and surely was influenced by his own mastery of the piano. But it was Wagner who, according to Strauss, combined the best of the symphonic orchestra with the new, expressive power of the dramatic orchestra. Strauss cited three technical points of Wagner's orchestration: the introduction of contrapuntal textures (equally divided, it should be added, among the winds, brass, and strings), a bold use of the new valved horn, and a virtuoso treatment of the other instruments.

The scope of Wagner's achievement is all the more striking when we consider the dynamic expansion of the orchestra during his career. He began with conventional double-wind orchestras in such early operas as *Die Feen* (completed in 1834 but not staged until 1888) and *Das Liebesverbot* (1836). *Tannhäuser* (1845) also requires winds in pairs but has an expanded brass section of four horns, three trumpets, three trombones, and one tuba. In *Lohengrin* (1850) and *Tristan und Isolde* (1865) Wagner expanded the winds to groups of three instruments, and in *Der Ring des Nibelungen* achieved quadruple woodwind scoring. The *Ring* also features a larger brass section, now with eight horns (four of them the so-called Wagner tubas), four trumpets (one a bass trumpet), four trombones (one a bass trombone), and one bass tuba. These fundamental changes in the orchestration made a decisive impact on Wagner's compositional methods, which have been studied in detail by Robert Bailey. Whereas Wagner employed a traditional two-stave format for his earlier sketches, he eventually began to add staves to his sketches, to take into account the larger, more complex orchestration of the later works. As a result, orchestral texture became increasingly bound up with the act of composition, in accordance with the general trends we have observed.

The beginning of *Die Walküre* affords one example of how Wagner used the new orchestra. The prelude, which describes a raging storm, unfolds as an orchestral crescendo-diminuendo. Before the curtain rises we hear an agitated string tremolo in the violins and violas an octave below. The cellos and double basses have a whiplike figure with sixteenth-note quintuplets and staccato quarters, which depict the lashing of the rain. Significantly, the cellos and basses play in unison, so that there are first only three registers, those of the violins, the violas, and the combined bass instruments. At measure 17, Wagner transposes the opening up a step to E, and here the basses begin to play an octave below the cellos, thus thickening the texture. In measure 37, Wagner reverses the direction of the figure; it now descends, and furthermore the quintuplet occurs on the last beat of the measure, in contrast to its earlier placement on the downbeat. This striking change accompanies another in the orchestration: Wagner introduces short fanfares in the horns and winds on E, which clash with the ostinato on D. In the next step, the bassoons and horns assume the string pedal point, and the strings play the storm figure in three-part imitation. This permits Wagner to introduce a new element, the thunder motive, and this is stated five times in the tubas, trombones, and trumpets, while the pedal points rise stepwise in the order D, E, F-sharp, and G. Finally, the winds and brass accelerate the sense of upward momentum with an ascending chromatic scale, and we reach the climax, a timpani roll on the dominant A. Now the strings drop out, and the thunder motive is given by winds and brass four times with successively thinner scorings. The storm figure returns in the basses, with a dominant pedal point in the timpani and a descent through transpositions on A, G, F-sharp, F-natural, E, and D. The timpani roll echoes the more agitated octave tremolo of the strings in the opening bars and prepares us for the first scene as the curtain rises. Through an expansion and contraction of orchestral textures and a careful coordination of instrumental massing, Wagner creates a sense of movement from the raging storm outside to the interior of Hunding's dwelling, where the action of the first scene takes place. In Wagner's hands, the orchestration is thus inseparable from the dramatic, expressive purpose at hand.

For Strauss, Wagner's scores constituted the alpha and omega of progress in instrumentation since Berlioz. This new type of orchestration left its mark on composers affiliated with the so-called Weimar school of Wagner and Liszt, such as Cornelius, Raff, and Humperdinck; on the symphonies of Bruckner and Mahler; on the tone poems and operas of Strauss; and on French composers who came under the Wagnerian sway (as Chausson did in his Symphony in B-flat of 1890). Rimsky-Korsakov, author of an orchestration treatise, termed the post-Wagnerian era the "age of brilliance and imaginative quality in orchestral tone colouring," a view borne out by the extravagant scores of the period (p. 1). Some idea of the new experimentation in tone coloring is evident in the openings of Bruckner's Seventh Symphony (1884) and Strauss's tone poem *Ein Heldenleben* (1899). The two passages, texturally very similar, have broadly arching bass melodies. Bruckner's melody begins with an unembellished form of an E-major arpeggiation stretched out over two octaves. It is doubled by a horn solo (measures 3–6), though the horn drops out as soon as the melody becomes chromatic. The accompaniment is limited to a tremolo in the violins. Strauss's scoring is considerably more daring. His E-flat major melody extends over some three octaves and is doubled throughout by a horn solo, regardless of chromatic excursions. In measure 17, Strauss repeats the opening but adds a tremolo accompaniment scored for four-part strings and five trumpets, resulting in a considerably denser mass of sound than in the Bruckner passage.

One example must suffice to illustrate Mahler's expressive treatment of the post-Wagnerian orchestra. The monumental finale to the Sixth Symphony (1906), well known for its hammer blows depicting the series of misfortunes in the composer's life, employs one of the largest orchestras in Mahler's music; it is here that he attempted quintuple woodwind scoring, surpassing the quadruple winds of Wagner's *Ring*. This sprawling movement is held together not only by the climactic hammer blows but also by the material of the opening, which returns three times to mark the development, recapitulation, and coda. Each of the four passages presents a sustained dissonant chord, though the scoring is artfully reworked in each case. The first, an altered 6–4–3 chord, uses woodwinds over a C pedal point. The intervening gap is filled by arpeggiations in the celesta and harps and by slowly rising tremolos in muted strings. For the second appearance, Mahler writes a softer, more conventional 6–4–3 chord; tuba, timpani, and bass drum are added, and horns make a brief melodic appearance. A few measures later Mahler invokes a pastoral setting by introducing cowbells, which are to create the effect of sounding from afar. Measure 520, marking the reprise, combines the sonority of the first passage with the bass note of the second; for this passage Mahler fills out the middle register with stopped horns and muted trumpets. Further, a timpani roll accompanies the bass pedal, and additional percussion instruments are introduced. Finally, in the coda (measure 774) the tonic note A is secured in the piccolo and, six octaves below, in the tuba; in between, Mahler scores a 6–5–3 chord for full orchestra, the densest of the four passages. This was to be the preparation for the final hammer blow, which, as is well known, Mahler removed. (Example 9 summarizes the basic dispositon of the four chords.)

No two works by Mahler require the same orchestra, an indication of the fundamental significance of orchestration in Mahler's compositional process. Vestiges of a double-wind orchestra appear in the 1893 version of the First Symphony, though Mahler had used triple winds in *Das klagende Lied,* begun in 1880, and soon worked with quadruple scorings. Similarly, following Wagner's example, he expanded the brass section, using ten horns (four offstage) in the fifth movement of the Second Symphony, and eight in the Third Symphony (completed in 1896). Perhaps most striking in Mahler's symphonies is the variety of percussion, which assume more and more an expressive purpose. Beginning with the complement of timpani, triangle, cymbals, bass drum, harp, and tam-tam in the First, there are, for example, glockenspiel, chimes, rute, and snare drum in the Second; a tambourine in the Third; sleigh bells in the

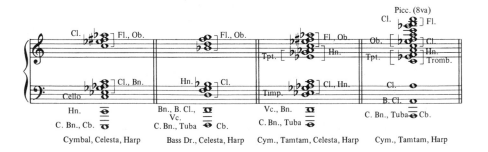

Example 9. Mahler: Symphony no. 6 in A Minor, movement 4, mm. 1, 230, 521, 774

Fourth; castanets in the Fifth; xylophone, hammer, and cowbells in the Sixth; guitar and mandolin in the Seventh; and harmonium in the Eighth. And each score, furthermore, has a different array of percussive effects.

The determined expansion of orchestral resources is just as evident in the works of Mahler's contemporary, Richard Strauss. In such pieces as the *Symphonia domestica* (1904), in which a quartet of saxophones is introduced, and *Salome* (1905), Strauss assembled enormous orchestras with an astonishing variety of instrumental effects. But probably the most notable in this line of development was Arnold Schoenberg's *Gurrelieder* (1913), based upon poetry of the Danish Jens Peter Jacobsen. In the woodwind section alone Schoenberg exceeded the quintuple orchestration of Mahler's Sixth Symphony. His score calls for 25 wind players (8, 5, 7, and 5, respectively, for the flute, oboe, clarinet, and bassoon families), a force equivalent to the size of Haydn's complete orchestra at Esterháza. There is a similar number of brass (10 horns, 7 trumpets, 7 trombones, and 1 tuba). In the percussion section we find 6 timpani and an imposing battery of other instruments, among them iron chains, used in Part 3 when Waldemar summons his vassals for their nocturnal ride in search of Tove. In this score, the post-Wagnerian age of orchestral splendor indeed reached a new limit.

REACTION AND REFORM

No less a figure than Richard Strauss sounded a cautionary note as he considered the dazzling orchestral opulence of his age: "The phenomenal sound combinations which a Berlioz or Wagner drew from the orchestra must not be misused. These masters used them for giving expression to unheard-of, great, poetic ideas, feelings and pictures of nature; they must not be reduced to the common property of bunglers, like a child's toy" (Strauss, ii–iii). Indeed, well before Strauss made this comment, conservative critics had begun to rail against the "misuse" of orchestral means. As early as 1876, the English theorist Ebenezer Prout vented his frustration at recent developments in orchestration in a passage of his *Instrumentation:*

> The besetting sin of the modern school for orchestration is the love of noise; and against this tendency the present is a suitable place to enter an earnest protest.... Two horns, two trumpets, and a pair of kettledrums sufficed for

many of the grandest inspirations of Mozart and Beethoven; but our modern composers think nothing of introducing on every occasion four horns,
two or three trumpets, three trombones, an ophicleide or tuba, and (as likely
as not), in addition to the kettledrums, the big drum and cymbals, triangle
and sometimes also side-drum....It is like using a Nasmyth steam-hammer
to kill a·fly. We are not protesting against the use, but the *abuse*, of these
instruments.

(p. 136)

Prout's censure is reminiscent of the views of Fétis, who had already
sought boundaries for the contemporary orchestra in 1828.

Composers such as Brahms, Dvořák, and Tchaikovsky were content
to work with conservatively sized orchestras, to produce "great effects
with small means," as Prout would have it. But theirs was not so much a
reaction against the newer developments of Wagner as a more cautious
continuation of the older symphonic tradition of Beethoven. Elsewhere,
though, we do find signs of reaction in orchestration against the Wagnerian standard. In Debussy's orchestral music, for which, as Adam Carse
has suggested, "such a word as *tutti* is hardly usable" (p. 324), there is a
marked tendency toward understatement and the use of the orchestra as
a symbolic, suggestive medium. The reaction against the Wagnerian line
of development took diverse forms after the turn of the century, as in
Strauss's *Ariadne auf Naxos* (1916), with its smaller, more intimate chamber orchestra, and Schoenberg's turn to smaller ensembles in the *Kam-
mersymphonie*, Opus 9 (1907), and other works of the period. In parts of
his Fourth Symphony, Mahler sought to imitate classical orchestration,
and Prokofiev turned to a double-wind orchestra in his famous *Classical
Symphony* of 1918. All of this could be viewed as a reaction against the
extravagant and brilliant orchestration of the post-Wagnerian era, which
was understood to have reached its historical conclusion in the early
years of the twentieth century.

That reaction led composers along many different paths, far too many
paths to explore here. A few examples drawn from the works of Schoenberg, Stravinsky, Bartók, and Webern, will suffice for our present
purpose. In the closing pages of his *Harmonielehre* (1911), Schoenberg
introduced the term *Klangfarbenmelodie* (tone-color melody) in an
attempt to isolate as a theoretical principle the practice of tone coloring
in orchestration. But whereas tone coloring had played a secondary
role—even if one gaining in importance—and had been regulated by
other musical (that is, harmonic or contrapuntal) or, in Wagner's and

Strauss's works, dramatic considerations, Schoenberg sought to establish it as an independent compositional principle:

> The distinction between tone color and pitch, as it is usually expressed, I cannot accept without reservations. I think the tone becomes perceptible by virtue of tone color, of which one dimension is pitch. Tone color is, thus, the main topic, pitch a subdivision. Pitch is nothing else but tone color measured in one direction. Now if it is possible to create patterns out of tone colors that are differentiated according to pitch, patterns we call "melodies," progressions whose coherence [Zusammenhang] evokes an effect analogous to thought processes, then it must also be possible to make such progressions out of the tone colors of the other dimension, out of that which we call simply "tone color," progressions whose relations with one another work with a kind of logic entirely equivalent to this logic which satisfies us in the melody of pitches. That has the appearance of a futuristic fantasy and is probably just that. But it is one which, I firmly believe, will be realized.
>
> (pp. 421–422)

Schoenberg's *Klangfarbenmelodie* bore important ramifications for orchestration, which the composer explored in the third of his *Five Pieces for Orchestra,* Opus 16, eventually subtitled *Farben,* written in 1909. In this atonal work Schoenberg harnessed the resources of a large orchestra (quadruple woodwind) to generate a slowly changing series of harmonic colors and textures, according to his idea of *Klangfarbenmelodie.* Similar experiments were made by Alban Berg in the third of his *Altenberg Lieder* (1912), in which a twelve-tone chord is gradually built up by the juxtaposition of different orchestral colors, and by Anton Webern in his arrangement of the *Ricercar a 6* from Bach's *Musical Offering* (1935), in which the famous subject is partitioned among several different instruments, again, as an experiment in tone coloring.

Quite a different direction was pursued by Stravinsky, who not only reacted against the "excesses" of Wagnerian orchestration but also sought to institute a reform. In his autobiography Stravinsky put forth these ideas on orchestration:

> This dangerous point of view concerning instrumentation, coupled with the unhealthy greed for orchestral opulence of today, has corrupted the judgment of the public, and they, being impressed by the immediate effect of tone color, can no longer solve the problem of whether it is intrinsic in the music or simply "padding." Orchestration has become a source of enjoyment independent of the music, and the time has surely come to put things in

their proper places. We have had enough of this orchestral dappling and these thick sonorities; one is tired of being saturated with timbres, and wants no more of all this overfeeding, which deforms the entity of the instrumental element by swelling it out of all proportion and giving it an existence of its own. There is a great deal of re-education to be accomplished in this field.

(p. 119)

For Stravinsky this re-education took shape in several scores in which he deliberately avoided writing for full orchestra, preferring instead to experiment with smaller, more manageable ensembles. These include the chamber settings of *Renard* (1922) and *L'Histoire du soldat* (1918), the use of only four pianos and percussion in *Les noces* (1923), or the restriction of the ensemble to wind instruments, as in the *Symphonies of Wind Instruments* (1921) or the Octet (1923). In these works Stravinsky reacted against the romantic cult of expression—indeed, against his own earlier efforts with mammoth orchestras, as in *Le sacre du printemps* (1913)—and emerged as a neoclassic formalist. The return to older musical values is especially apparent in the orchestration, which regained its previous function as a means of articulating structure. To accomplish this, Stravinsky worked toward a new austerity and formal purity, perhaps best exemplified by the *Symphony of Psalms* (1930), scored for winds (with no clarinets), brass, low strings (with violins and violas excluded), and percussion (including a harp and two pianos). Orchestral tutti are carefully controlled by Stravinsky, as in the opening and closing sonorities of the composition. In the first Stravinsky achieved a symmetrical distribution with closed triads at either end of the chord and open spacing between them (Ex. 10a). In the final sonority, Stravinsky omitted the fifth of the chord, instead doubled the root C in several octaves, and placed the third E at the very top (Ex. 10b). Such a pure, ascetic sonority brings to mind the composer's comment in his autobiography that "true sobriety is a great rarity, and most difficult of attainment."

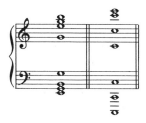

Examples 10a and 10b. Stravinsky: *Symphony of Psalms*, movement 1, opening sonority; movement 3, final sonority

While Stravinsky's *Symphony of Psalms* features mixtures of brass, winds, and percussion, Bela Bartók experimented with combinations of strings and percussion in his celebrated *Music for Strings, Percussion, and Celesta* (1937), a second example of the tendency toward classicizing reform. Bartók calls for two groups of strings to be placed on either side of the percussion complement, with double basses to the rear. The string orchestra is thus once again the core of the ensemble, as it had been in the eighteenth century, but Bartók exploits the percussion group and its interplay with the strings as a means of defining the structure of his music.

A good example is afforded by the first movement, planned as a fugue with textural changes demarcating its principal sections. Bartók orders the twelve entries of the subject (drawn from the rearranged chromatic notes of a major third) according to a symmetrical series of twelve statements about a tritonal axis: A, E, D, B, G, F-sharp, C, C-sharp, F, G-sharp, B-flat, E-flat. During the first seven entries the strings are muted. As they pass through the entry on C-sharp a timpani roll is heard, and the strings begin to disengage their mutes. The texture is worked up into a crescendo, with the twelfth fugal entry on E-flat (tritone from A) appearing in measure 45, the midpoint of the movement. As we approach the climax of the crescendo, Bartók introduces the cymbal, bass drum, and a timpani roll on A. Now he inverts the subject and reverses (with some abridgment) the order of transpositions. Mutes are gradually reapplied (measure 68f.), and with the reappearance of the initial statement on A, the prime and inverted forms combined (measure 78). The texturing here is especially exquisite: the two forms of the subject (A G-sharp F F-sharp G and A B-flat C-sharp C-natural B-natural) appear in the first and fourth violins some three octaves apart. The registral gap is occupied by the celesta, which plays a chromatic cluster highlighting the pitches D, E-flat, and E-natural—the three pitches not represented by the prime or inverted forms of the subject. All twelve pitches of the scale are thus present in this shimmering, magical passage. For the final bars of the movement, Bartók thins out the string orchestra, bringing the movement to a close on a unison A. As is evident, the percussion is used rather sparingly in the fugue but always as a means of marking the principal structural events: the prime and inverted series of the entries, and their combination.

A considerably more drastic economy of orchestral means is at work in the music of Webern. After using relatively large scorings in early tonal works, such as the idyll *Im Sommerwind* (written in 1904) and the Passacaglia, Opus 1 (1908), and in the atonal *Six Pieces for Orchestra*, Opus

6 (1913), Webern adopted smaller ensembles in his Symphony, Opus 21 (1929) and Concerto, Opus 24 (1935). The Symphony is the first orchestral work after his adoption of the twelve-tone method. Significantly, it is scored for four-part strings (without double basses), two clarinets (one a bass clarinet), two horns, and one harp, which plays very seldom. The result is a modern counterpart to the *sinfonia a 8*, ironically bringing us full circle to the modest forces of the early classic symphonists. In Webern's hands, orchestration became one means among many of regulating, with the utmost precision, the very fabric of the music. The first movement is a contrapuntal tour de force, a strict double mirror canon. By pairing instruments, Webern is able to control just as exactly the orchestration. Thus, clarinet and bass clarinet, first and second horns, first and second violins, and violas and cellos are grouped together as Webern weaves his contrapuntal strands. Since the harp is sparingly employed, it alone can stand for two contrapuntal parts.

Webern's technique produces a kaleidoscope of orchestral colors, all carefully presented in the framework of a binary sonata form. For instance, here is the distribution of one of the canonic pairs for the opening measures, which use prime and inverted forms (P-0 and I-0):

P-O: Horn 2 (4 pitches) Cl. (4 pitches) Cello (4 pitches)
I-O: Horn 1 (4 pitches) Bcl. (4 pitches) Viola (4 pitches)

Webern thus divides the rows to ensure equal emphasis of the three basic groups of brass, winds, and strings. For the continuation of the canon, the composer simply reverses the scoring for the next two rows, retrograde and inverted forms (R-3 and I-3), accomplishing a palindromic effect in the distribution of the instruments. Here is yet another sign of his meticulous control, rigorously extended to orchestration.

Stravinsky, Bartók, Webern, and others thus returned to an earlier ideal of orchestration as a structuring device, not as the expressive agent it had become in the nineteenth century. In their own ways, they formulated answers to Fétis's question of 1827 by establishing limits to the romantic quest for expressivity. Fétis had sought a "retrospective view of the past, not for the sake of giving up what we possess, but to enrich ourselves with what has been already given up too inconsiderately" (p. 197). As composers of the twentieth century have prepared their orchestral scores, they have either adopted that retrospective view in some way, attempted to continue the more brilliant and colorful orchestration inherited from romanticism, or struck out in new directions through the use of new instrumental and electronic media. Whether romantic opulence, Stravinskian sobriety, or some other style of orchestration will prove the most enduring has still to be determined.

BIBLIOGRAPHY

Robert Bailey, "The Method of Composition," in Peter Burbidge and Richard Sutton, eds., *The Wagner Companion* (1979). Hans Bartenstein, *Hector Berlioz' Instrumentationskunst und ihre geschichtlichen Grundlagen: Ein Beitrag zur Geschichte des Orchesters* (1939); and "Die frühen Instrumentationslehren bis zu Berlioz," in *Archiv für Musikwissenschaft*, 28 (1971). Heinz Becker, *History of Instrumentation*, Robert Kolben, trans. (1964). Hector Berlioz, *Evenings with the Orchestra*, Jacques Barzun, trans. (1956); and *Grand traité d'instrumentation et d'orchestration modernes* (1843; trans. 1855; see also Strauss entry). Paul R. Bryan, "The Horn in the Works of Mozart and Haydn: Some Observations and Comparisons," in *Haydn Yearbook*, 9 (1975). Peter Cahn, "Zur-Funktion der Hörner und Trompeten im klassischen Orchestersatz," in *Helmuth Osthoff zu seinem siebzigsten Geburtstag* (1969).

Adam Carse, *The History of Orchestration* (1925; repr. 1964). David Charlton, "Orchestra and Image in the Late Eighteenth Century," in *Proceedings of the Royal Musical Association*, 102 (1975–1976). Karl Czerny, *School of Practical Composition*, Op. 600, vol. 3, John Bishop, trans. (1848). Eduard Devrient, *My Recollections of Felix Mendelssohn-Bartholdy, and His Letters to Me*, Natalia Macfarren, trans. (1869; repr. 1972). F. J. Fétis, "Des revolutions de l'orchestre," *Revue musicale*, 1 (1827); translated in *Harmonicon*, 6 (1828). B. M. Fink, *Die Geschichte des Kontrabasses und seine Trennung vom Violoncello in der orchestralen Instrumentation* (1974). L. J. Francoeur, *Diapason général de tous les instruments à vent* (1772). Karl Geiringer, "Haydn's Sketches for *The Creation*," in *Musical Quarterly*, 18 (1932).

E. T. A. Hoffmann, "Recension" of Beethoven's Fifth Symphony, in *Allgemeine musikalische Zeitung*, 12 (1810); translated in Norton Critical Score of Fifth Symphony, Elliot Forbes, ed. (1971). Heinrich Christoph Koch, *Versuch einer Anleitung zur Composition* (1782–1793; repr., 1969); and *Musikalisches Lexicon* (1802; repr. 1964). A. F. C. Kollmann, *An Essay on Practical Musical Composition* (1799; repr. 1973). H. C. Robbins Landon, *Haydn: Chronicle and Works* 4 (1977). J. M. Levy, "Texture as Sign in Classic and Early Romantic Music," in *Journal of the American Musicological Society*, 35 (1982). Hugh Macdonald, "Berlioz's Orchestration: Human or Divine?" in *Musical Times*, 110 (1969). C. F. Michaelis, "Einige Bemerkungen über den ästhetischen Charakter, Wert, und Gebrauch verschiedener musikalischer Instrumente," in *Allgemeine musikalische Zeitung*, 9 (1807). S. Mikorey, *Klangfarbe und Komposition* (1982).

Ebenezer Prout, *Instrumentation* (1876). Nikolai Rimsky-Korsakov, *Osnoví orkestrovki* (1913); translated by E. Agate as *Principles of Orchestration* (1922). Arnold Schoenberg, *Harmonielehre* (1911); translated by Roy E. Carter as *Theory of Harmony* (1978). Richard Strauss, ed., *Instrumentationslehre von Hector Berlioz* (1905); translated by Theodore Front as *Treatise on Instrumentation* (1948). Igor Stravinsky, *An Autobiography* (1936). Egon Voss, *Studien zur Instrumentation Richard Wagners* (1970). Eugene K. Wolf, *The Symphonies of Johann Stamitz* (1981).

Why Conductors? Their Role and the Idea of Fidelity

Denis Stevens

Conductors and directors, whose duty it has been to mold, perfect, und bring to resounding life the performances entrusted to them from the earliest beginnings of music, whether worldly, religious, or ceremonial in character, remained for centuries in the same obscurity that envelops the majority of builders and architects. A conductor's role was essentially an impermanent one with a fleeting time-span of disappearing sounds. Their grand edifices, unlike those of their architect colleagues, resisted survival unless in the form of written signs and symbols. Up to the early years of the twentieth century, when recordings began to be made, the situation did not change, although the conductor as a musician in his own right (and not necessarily a composer-conductor as in earlier times) had placed a firm foot upon the podium of history by the latter half of the nineteenth century.

Originally conductors were time beaters—functional leaders, ready to use any legitimate technique to ensure cohesion of ensemble, unanimity of phrasing and dynamics, and the maintenance of discipline. Jerome of Moravia, writing on the performance of chant about 1275, recommended that the singers choose a conductor to whom they should pay diligent attention, following his precise directions in regard to notes and rests. A fourteenth-century psalter in the Bodleian Library depicts such a conductor, crowned as King David, author of the Psalms, using both hands for the purpose of delineating the melodic curve and its attendant expression. He may also have set the tempo for his choir of monks, for Conrad von Zabern, in his *De modo bene cantandi*, about 1475, distinguished between very slow, moderate, and fairly rapid tempos for high feasts, Sundays, and ordinary services, respectively.

If relatively few among modern conductors choose to dispense with the baton, their remote forerunners appear to have enjoyed a wider choice. Apart from purely manual gestures, there were stampings of the foot from time to time, which drew forth a complaint from Venceslaus Philomathes in 1512, and the use of the hand or a staff to beat time continuously, according to Johannes Vogelsang (1542). Juan Bermudo, in 1549, strongly objected to conductors who hit the music with their stick, of which a lighter and more graceful version was employed by the small but select number of women conductors then active.

One of these women, in all probability the composer-director Raffaella Aleotti, prompted Ercole Bottrigari to give us what is virtually the earliest description of a concert by a chamber orchestra—at the convent of San Vito in Ferrara, sometime between 1576 and 1586. After setting the scene, he praises the way in which the women instrumentalists quietly enter, standing or seating themselves at a large table (depending on which instruments they play), until finally "the Maestra of the concert sits down at one of the table and with a long, slender and well-polished wand . . . gives them without noise several signs to begin, and then continues by beating the measure of the time which they must obey in singing and playing" (Bottrigari, 58).

The nature of this account does not mean that the careful direction of music was rare, or that conductors (who are almost never mentioned in the kinds of source material that describe musical activities) were almost nonexistent. Since the composer, who was a singer, an instrumentalist, or both, would know most about the score and the intricacies of its performance, it was he who would be placed in charge as director. Although this might amount to no more than general supervision, in most instances it would also call for some conducting, cueing, and such expressive effects as may have been deemed appropriate to the composition or the occasion. Thus, the composer-conductor idea, far from being a recent feature of the musical world, probably arose in the Middle Ages and was certainly common in the Renaissance.

When music formed an essential part of any large theatrical venture, instrumentalists, choir, solo singers, and dancers had to be rehearsed and directed with the utmost precision. Consequently, a visible or audible conductor was an indispensable part of the team, no matter whether he functioned purely as a time beater (a tambourine or drum player appearing on stage in an *intermedio*, a musical entertainment inserted between acts of a play) or as a coordinator placed out of sight of the audience but well in control of the musicians and dancers.

The excellence of a theatrical ensemble in an *intermedio* in 1499 at Ferrara presupposes skilled and painstaking direction of a highly professional kind, if we can believe a letter from Giano Pencharo to Isabella d'Este:

> A group of ten peasants . . . having first entered leaping on to the stage in the fashion of a *moresca* . . . began with their tools to hoe the ground; and, always, every act, movement and measure kept to the tempo and the proportion of the playing, so that several men all seemed to be moved by a single spirit, according to the tempo of the musician.
>
> (Pirrotta, 50)

Berlioz, who made no claim to be a historian of music, was nevertheless not too wide of the mark when he guessed that Alfonso della Viola, a sixteenth-century Italian composer, not only composed but also rehearsed a music-drama based on the story of Francesca da Rimini. The point of the story is that Alfonso took his revenge on a parsimonious potentate by failing to conduct the sold-out performance at the Pitti Palace in Florence. This fiasco was supposed to have happened in 1557, in a city famous for its lavish and artistic entertainments. A genuine event, certainly one of the high points in the history of the *intermedio*, took place in the Uffizi theater on 2 May 1589, when a large number of musicians performed the opulently scored insertions designed especially for Girolamo Bargagli's comedy *La pellegrina*. The complexity of the choral and instrumental textures, climaxing in a composition for seven choirs, indubitably called for a principal conductor and possibly several assistants, one in charge of each group.

Similar arrangements governed the performance of polychoral music in the church, not so much for the psalms sung by alternating choirs (since it is now known that in general only a semichorus and a group of soloists were involved in day-to-day functions), but for the elaborate *concerti* written to celebrate major feasts or special events, such as the celebration of a victory, the reception of royalty, or a votive mass for an anniversary or a local saint.

Documents drawn up for the procurators of Saint Mark's, Venice, indicate that it was necessary for someone of ability who served in the organ lofts to beat time, as regulated by the maestro, who was often stationed on a platform at floor level, from which vantage point he directed the *ripieno* choir. So it would appear that up to the end of the sixteenth century, one or more conductors were essential for the satisfactory performance of any large composition.

THE CONDUCTOR'S ROLE

Any and every attempt to define the role of a conductor must necessarily depend on the period of history in question, the kind of institution sponsoring whatever music is being performed, and, to some extent, nationality. The virtuoso conductor as we know him today began to appear no earlier than 1840, when Louis Jullien astonished London with his showmanship, his massive instrumental forces, and his diamond tiepin. But conducting as a subtle and essential art began long before that.

Most composers had to learn the basic elements of the director's task for the simple reason that they knew most about the score and could best see to its realization and interpretation. This does not mean that all composers were good conductors. Despite their understandably strong desire to hear their music performed, they sometimes displayed an incontrovertible ability to get in the way of their own music, as did Schumann, Tchaikovsky, and Delius.

Even the word *conductor* could mean different things and different degrees of involvement. At one time he might have been no more than the organizer of a concert in which he took no actual part, while at another he might have directed it while seated at the harpsichord, piano, or organ. Yet again, he might have been the orchestra's concertmaster, influencing the proceedings by waving his violin bow or moving the scroll of the instrument up and down. Or he could even have been merely the accompanist at a song recital, although this use of the term was restricted to a relatively brief period in nineteenth-century London. Finally, he could have been the person beating time for the orchestra or choir, facing either his musicians or the audience.

As to his background and musical training, no single rule will suffice. Although many conductors have also been keyboard players, ranging in accomplishment from the rudimentary to the virtuoso (for example, von Bülow, Busoni, Bernstein, and Ashkenazy), others have excelled in orchestral instruments. Habeneck, Maazel, and Marriner were originally violinists; Monteux and Giulini, violists; Offenbach, Toscanini, and Barbirolli, cellists; Koussevitzky, a double-bass virtuoso. Gaubert played the flute; Colin Davis, the clarinet; and Kempe, the oboe. Nor are there lacking exponents of the brass and the percussion sections. Even vocalists have been known to step up to the podium, as in the case of Balfe, Lortzing, and George Henschel. The last was the conductor of the Boston Symphony Orchestra from 1881 to 1884. Extreme cases are those of Hans Richter, who played many instruments well, and Berlioz, whose abilities as flutist and guitarist were somewhat limited.

No matter what his field of specialization, the conductor has for the past century and a half been obliged to fill a role that is only partly musical. He may beat time efficiently or otherwise; he may inspire musicians or alienate them; and he may now and again manage to bring off a truly great performance. But his other activities and preoccupations spread over a wide field. He must, first and foremost, be capable of attracting audiences, for without them no concert-giving organization can survive.

The role of listeners in an auditorium may seem to be merely ancillary or mercenary, but it remains essential and vital to all concerned. Whether the desired end is achieved by admirable musicianship, a magnetic personality, a touch of the showman, or a blend of all three is not really important. What matters is that the conductor should be sufficiently impressive to draw in enough listeners to make the effort of the concert worthwhile.

A secondary and related role is that of artistic director, which the conductor normally assumes as part of his burden of office. It is he who is mainly responsible for building programs that are varied, colorful, and attractive to an audience of possibly undeveloped taste and experience in the symphonic repertory. He must include enough of the established classics to please the majority of his listeners and subscribers. But he must also show some degree of initiative in exploring other types of music, both early and modern, for without this the more well informed members of his audience may feel that they are not getting their money's worth.

A third role that falls to the conductor is one that is both time-consuming and to some extent distasteful, requiring him to participate in a good deal of socializing and fund raising. Only the greatest of the great can afford to maintain a safe distance from their supporters and bury themselves in seclusion without fear of being branded supercilious snobs. The average conductor is expected by his board members to attend lunches, teas, and dinners (not to mention cocktail parties), during which he must fraternize as gracefully as possible with those who make his concerts a financial reality. This is, of course, not so crucial a matter in Europe, where national and local governments play a much larger role in supporting the arts, but in America it is a reality that has to be faced.

A fourth role demands that the conductor be something of a scholar, for the days are long gone when it was possible to perform the classics in total ignorance of advances in editorial research over the past forty years. Scores should be carefully marked with improved readings and with the conductor's own preferences regarding interpretation. All these indications then have to be transferred to the orchestral parts by assistants and librarians, as a contribution toward the smooth running of rehearsals and an appreciable reduction in waste of time.

Finally, since no concert can be given without proper rehearsal, the conductor must fill to satisfaction the role of guide, disciplinarian, mentor, and inspirer of the blasé and the weary. Let him demand too much, and there will be little or nothing left for the concert. Let him relax, and the members of the orchestra may get the impression that he is not serious about the task in hand. The art of rehearsal, or of reaching out for perfection, still remains one of the most formidable to deal with and to understand.

CONDUCTORS IN REHEARSAL

A concert without a conductor is difficult to imagine, a rehearsal without a conductor impossible. The principle of government by a benevolent oligarchy may work in a chamber ensemble, but in the case of a full symphony orchestra, only one solution proposes itself, and that is monarchy. Only the most tyrannical of conductors descend into the dark realm of dictatorship, from which every sensitive orchestra revolts, preferring always the direction of a humane and understanding person whose knowledge and expertise are beyond question.

Some interest has been shown of late in penetrating the mystique of a great performance by lifting the veil usually cast over the rehearsal process. To this end, the principal violist of the BBC Symphony Orchestra, Bernard Shore, wrote a fascinating account of eminent conductors as seen through the eyes of an orchestral player, *The Orchestra Speaks* (1938). And starting in the mid-1950s there began to appear on various American and European labels (some noncommercial) a series of recordings made during rehearsals of orchestral, choral-orchestral, and operatic works in which the voices and rehearsal techniques of different conductors could be heard and studied. Such testimony from earlier ages can be found only with difficulty in the pages of memoirs, diaries, critical accounts, and even in literary works of a more general nature.

Walter Porter, an English pupil of Monteverdi, wrote a succinct description of the Italian master's attitude toward rehearsal in the preface of his *Mottets of Two Voyces* (1657):

> The Ignorant judge frequently by the Performance, not by the Composition; which caus'd that unparallel'd Master of Musick, my good friend and Mestro *Monteverde*, to vindicate a good Composition ill performed *to the Duke of Vennice*, affirming that had he been Rector Chori, he would have made that Song before judg'd bad, to have pass'd for good. So advantagious and necessary is the Judicious ordering and management of Musick. (Italics have been inserted by hand in the printed editions at Christ Church, Oxford).

The talkative conductor is no new phenomenon, and rarely very popular with his players, as may be seen in this passage from English dramatist Thomas Southerne's comedy *The Maid's Last Prayer* (1693), the speaker being the conductor, Sir Symphony:

> Come, pray, let's begin. O Gad: there's a flat note! there's art! how surprisingly the key changes! O law! there's a double relish! I swear, sir, you have the sweetest little finger in England! ha! that stroke's new; I tremble, every inch of me; now ladies, look to your hearts—softly, gentlemen—remember the echo—captain, you play the wrong tune—O law! my teeth! for God's sake, captain, mind your cittern—Now the fuga, bases! again, again! lord! Mr. Humdrum, you come in three bars too soon.

Johann Matthias Gesner, rector of the Thomas-Schule at Leipzig when J. S. Bach served as director of music, gives us an almost audibly evocative account of how much effort went into a rehearsal (or performance) of the Sunday cantata:

> If you could see him . . . doing what many of your citharoedists and six hundred of your tibia players together could not do, not only (like a citharoedist) singing with one voice and playing his own parts, but watching over everything and bringing back to the rhythm and the beat, out of thirty or even forty musicians, the one with a nod, another by tapping with his foot, the third with a warning finger, giving the right note to one from the top of his voice, to another from the bottom, and to a third from the middle of it—all alone, in the midst of the greatest din made by all the participants.
> (David and Mendel, 231)

Dr. Charles Burney, visiting the same city some years later, in 1772, attended a rehearsal of a singspiel by Johann Adam Hiller but was not unduly impressed by the composer's ability as a conductor:

> The instrumental parts went ill; but this was the first rehearsal, they might have been disciplined into good order, if Mr. Hiller had chosen to bounce and play the tyrant a little; for it is a melancholy reflection to make, that few composers are well treated by an orchestra, till they have first used the performers roughly, and made themselves formidable.
>
> (2:76)

Mozart was certainly no tyrant, but he felt bound to use audible persuasion when, at a rehearsal for a concert he gave at the Gewandhaus, Leipzig, on 12 May 1789, he found a few elderly members of the orchestra so sleepy that the fast movement of one of his symphonies was in danger of collapsing. Calling on them for greater speed and precision, he stamped his foot so violently that his shoelace broke—an occurrence duly noted at the appropriate point in the music by one of the viola players.

To some extent the results obtained by a conductor depend on the amount of rehearsal time available and his ability to make good use of it. When Wagner went to London in 1855 to work with the Philharmonic Society, he complained that too much was expected of him in too short a time. But the economic factor that played so great a part in London's musical life then (as now) was hardly a concern at the Berlin Court Opera in the time of Gaspare Spontini. Summoned to this prestigious post by Friedrich Wilhelm III in 1820, the Italian composer-conductor had already won a reputation for himself as a perfectionist and a stern disciplinarian, qualities that were to raise the standard of performance to an unprecedented level of excellence. Demanding up to eighty rehearsals for some of his operas, Spontini controlled his forces by moving his eyes rather than his head and by using a large baton for choruses and processions while a smaller one was always available for arias. His control over dynamics became legendary; the unanimity of his ensembles was without equal.

Michael Costa, another eminent Italian dedicated at first to the operatic repertory, became in 1846 the principal conductor of the Philharmonic Society in London and subsequently made his reputation as a symphonic interpreter. He knew how to command without bullying and tolerated no division of control among his forces. Under his baton, the tug-of-war between concertmaster and director vanished forever, and in his rehearsals no absenteeism was permitted. Discovering that fines acted as no deterrent, Costa warned his players that any future absences would result in canceled engagements, and from that moment on he was assured of an orchestra that was not only complete but punctually assembled.

A conductor capable of transforming an orchestra of tired and dispirited musicians into a body of energetic and fiery virtuosos must be ranked high among persuasive geniuses. An account of a rehearsal under Arthur Nikisch, written in 1905 by a member of the London Symphony Orchestra, proves what could be accomplished in this way, even when the players were exhausted after six hours of concentrated work. The symphony was Tchaikovsky's Fifth:

> Before we had been playing five minutes we were deeply interested, and, later, when we came to the big fortissimos, we not only played like fiends, but we quite forgot we were tired. For my own part I simply boiled over with enthusiasm. I could have jumped up and shouted—as a matter of fact when we reached the end of the first movement we all did rise from our seats and actually shouted because we could not help it.... He simply looked at us, often scarcely moving his baton, and we played as those possessed; we made terrific *crescendi*, sudden commas before some great chord, though we had never done this before.
>
> (Scholes, 1:390)

When Gustav Mahler was music director of the Vienna Opera in the early years of this century, his incessant demands for precision and expressive playing were backed up not only by painstaking rehearsals but also by his frequent invitations to individual players to come to his room and go over important passages on a kind of tutorial basis. His young assistant, Bruno Walter, knew the basic repertory so well that he could preside over a rehearsal without referring to a section letter or measure number—he simply sang a singer's part by way of a cue. The singer came in at once, and the orchestra quickly followed suit. Adrian Boult, who was present at the Vienna Opera when *The Marriage of Figaro* was in preparation, said that he had "never heard a rehearsal anywhere else where everybody taking part knew the work by heart" (1963, p. 42).

It was in 1956 that Walter's innovative recording of Mozart's *Linz* Symphony appeared: one side featured the complete performance, while the other three contained a lively and instructive account of all that went on during the rehearsals. Over the next two decades many more rehearsal records arrived to assuage the thirst of the curious, who could listen to the instructions, effusions, and anecdotes of Toscanini, Karajan, Beecham, Solti, Jochum, Kubelik, Monteux, Serafin, Boult, and Böhm. Possibly for the first time the general public was made aware that an immense amount of effort, time, and energy is spent in preparing a work for recording or performance. Nevertheless, in the final analysis it is not words, whether cajoling or commanding, that put fire into an orchestra but rather personality and charisma—an inner magnetism directed outward.

Despite the occasional appearance of conductorless orchestras (Moscow's Persimfans of 1922–1932, and numerous chamber orchestras directed from the harpsichord or by the concertmaster), the growing complexity of orchestral sources requires unified and unquestioned leadership. And it is basically in rehearsal that a conductor proves his worth. Some achieve fine results by exercising consideration for their players and politeness in their manner of speech, as did Nikisch, Monteux, Beecham, Boult, and many more; others resort to bad language (as did Charles Lamoureaux, whose rehearsals had to remain strictly private), outbursts of temper (Toscanini, Koussevitzky, Szell, and Reiner are legendary in this respect), or reliance on long and sometimes boring lectures, as in the case of Willem Mengelberg.

According to Bernard Shore:

> With all his dictatorial grip of his players, [Mengelberg] seems to need a similar grip on the part of his soloists in the orchestra. If he senses that responsive grip his hand becomes like velvet and at the performance he will himself respond to the player's expression and bring it to full bloom. But if he cannot obtain what he wants from an artist, he will be hard as iron and may seem to oppose rather than aid.... Long dissertations at rehearsals may be more trying, but there is always some truth in what he says, and though the time-table may go wrong, his rehearsals really are rehearsals.
>
> (pp. 124–125)

Reports and recordings of Toscanini's rehearsals indicate that while he was not alone in being a man in search of ultimate perfection, he may have achieved that aim more consistently than most. He was accustomed to working at white heat, and he spared neither himself nor his musicians. Yet he never wasted time and never made the mistake of rehearsing for his own pleasure. He did not appear to rely on any prearranged scheme, but he always knew what he wanted and how to get it. This enviable state of affairs derived principally from his unusual ability to concentrate on the essence of the music, forgetting the audience entirely and uniting with himself—in a bond that was at once mystical and electrifying—the players, whose art he knew so well how to inspire.

Toscanini's phenomenal memory, developed perhaps as a bulwark of defense against his nearsightedness, permitted him to rehearse and perform most of the repertoire without the aid of a score. Perhaps as a result, he was acutely sensitive to expression, and he brought it out of his players by asking them always to sing and then to sing more. Even the harmonies providing a cradle for some simple melody had to sound smooth and beautiful in a vocal way.

Of his conducting technique, Bernard Shore writes:

> There are two unique characteristics of his not otherwise very extraordinary stick. First is the magnificent sweep, which must be one of the most eloquent gestures ever made and which seems to hold all the threads of the orchestra and imbue them with life. Secondly, there is his not so apparent, but extraordinarily dynamic, almost magical preparation for his beats. The former holds audience and orchestra alike; in the latter only the orchestra can appreciate the wonderful anticipation of the beat. The most difficult change of tempo becomes, even to those farthest from him, clear and unmistakable just at the right moment.
>
> (p. 169)

Despite the vintage monaural sound of the Toscanini rehearsal records, the excerpts from *La Traviata,* the Overture to *The Magic Flute* (during which the Maestro slaps his own face in order to show that what he needs in the *allegro* is a smile), and the endless battling with basses and cellos in the recitative sections in the finale of Beethoven's Ninth Symphony provide a massive demonstration of energy, persistence, and devotion to the task in hand.

By some strange paradox, the greatest conductors sometimes fall short of a total command of the repertory. The music that they know and love shines forth time and time again in brilliant and moving performances, while works that may be intrinsically great tend to suffer because of some blind spot, some lack of basic comprehension. Toscanini once admitted that he did not feel quite comfortable with Mozart's *Figaro:* something in it eluded him, but what it was he did not know. Sir Thomas Beecham felt at odds with much of Beethoven and Brahms; with Bruckner and Mahler he had almost no contact at all. Yet his artistry and imagination sprang to life when he conducted Mozart, Haydn, Delius, and Sibelius, and there were lesser composers whose works he appeared to be able to improve out of all recognition.

A recording of rehearsals in Paris with the Royal Philharmonic Orchestra captures Beecham in one of his more relaxed moods, dealing somewhat nonchalantly with excerpts from Mozart's *Abduction from the*

Seraglio and two Haydn symphonies. His singing voice seems hardly capable of producing any results other than the purely risible, yet when the
orchestra phrases something he has tried to demonstrate, there is no
doubt whatever about the improvement. His musical mind is dominated
by the expressive line, a line not broken up and mangled by needless
accents, but flowing, mobile, and exultant in its leaps and persuasive in
its curves. These lines he coaxes skillfully from groups of players as well
as from soloists, using merely the hypnotic power of his eyes and an occasional creative gesture of the left hand or baton.

Beecham's remarkable gift has been summarized by Shore as "a consummate ability to express his inmost feelings through his personality.
He is never seen to labour under any difficulty, and though his actions
on the rostrum suggest to outsiders sometimes those of a ballet dancer
rather than a conductor, yet those very actions are a perfect expression
of himself." Shore goes on to affirm that "Beecham's stick describes all the
antics of an erratic firework. One moment it is motionless, his only movement a crooking of one finger in his left hand; the next, his whole body
is in furious action, with both fists threatening the orchestra. He breaks
every orthodox rule. No one else in the world could get away with it"
(pp. 39–40). The detailed account of his rehearsing the tone poem *Paris*
by Delius affords ample evidence of Beecham's power to evoke subtle
coloristic effects by the use of his own eloquent gestures and his sometimes jesting eloquence: "Gentlemen in the clarinet department, how can
you resist such an impassioned appeal from the second violins? Give
them an answer, I beg you!" (p. 45).

Few conductors have strayed into the realm of belles lettres, as Beecham did in his remarkable biography of Delius. Indeed, Arnold Bennett
surely had him in mind when commenting on a certain English conductor who is

> noted among orchestras for the beauty of his language at rehearsals. In fact,
> his remarks have been recorded *verbatim* by an orchestral player interested
> in literature. He said to the orchestra, in the way of guidance: "Sigh and die."
> He said: "Don't handicap the crescendo." He said: "I want a savage staccato."
> He said: "All this passage must be nice and manifold." He said to a particular
> player: "Weep, Mr. Parker, weep. (Mr. Parker makes his instrument weep.)
> That's jolly. That's jolly." He said, persistent in getting an effect: "Sorry to
> tease you, gentlemen." He said: "Now, side-drums, assert yourself."
>
> (p. 43)

If Beecham knew how to combine the elements of the impresario, the
showman, and the musician, he also adopted instinctively the correct atti-

tude toward the orchestra, individually and as a great ensemble ready to be molded into sonorous shapes. Players always gave their best for him, and they loved to work with him.

As conductor of more recordings with a greater range of style and period than anybody else, Herbert von Karajan ranks as one of the outstanding musicians of the century. Not only has he recorded the Beethoven symphonies several times over (and countless other works two or three times), he has also been consistently active in film and television, conducting and directing a wide spectrum of the operatic repertory on film, in addition to appearing in such television series as "The Art of Conducting," made with the Berlin Philharmonic Orchestra in 1966–1967. His concert schedule allows for little else in the way of ancillary activities, but he is such a master of his own timetable that he can achieve more in a day than most conductors could hope to do in a week. Like Beecham, he has magnetic appeal and a powerful personality, but in other respects the two men are quite dissimilar.

For Karajan, rehearsal is a serious, down-to-earth business in which everyone present is expected to maintain a high degree of professionalism backed up by the kind of concentration that he can apparently command at any time or in any place. His memory, like his conducting technique, is totally reliable, though on occasion he can throw caution to the winds while posing a problem for the strings, as one of the cellists in the Philharmonia Orchestra is quick to point out:

At one of his earliest concerts at the Albert Hall . . . he started the Tschaikowsky "Pathétique" with his eyes closed, facing away from the basses and dropping his hands very slowly. Somehow they came in and we were away. When, later, during a session he gave the wind a similar lead and Gareth Morris [principal flute] asked him when they were to come in, he said: "When you can't stand it any longer!"

(Beavan, 2)

A recording of one of Karajan's rehearsals of Beethoven's Ninth Symphony suggests an atmosphere of keen intensity underpinned by careful listening and observation. He talks a great deal and the musicians listen attentatively, only rarely interrupting for some vitally necessary question. There are no jokes. Everything is serious and everyone seems very much in earnest. Dealing with the cello and bass recitatives in the finale, Karajan asks for contrast above all, especially between the staccato notes and the normal ones: "The former are too colorless and the latter much too short."

Later he asks for a singing timbre, of dreamlike quality and feeling.

This kind of approach sometimes upsets English and American players, who prefer to be told whether to aim at loud, soft, or mezzoforte, yet there is no doubt about the splendid results of Karajan's detailed analysis of every note in a phrase. Of the D-major theme, every shade of meaning in its stepwise progression is discussed and tried out, first this way, then that: "Let the tone grow out of the D, and then back again: the connection between D and E must be softer, but place the center of gravity already on the E." When the *adagio* returns, great pains are taken with the balance of the divided violas and cellos, and the orchestra is constantly under fire for failing to observe the exact point at which a *crescendo* or *decrescendo* begins. Indeed, the entire rehearsal is an object lesson in extreme and conscientious thoroughness.

This same attention to detail is evident in Karajan's coaching of principal singers as he accompanies them on the piano. Elizabeth Harwood has said:

> He doesn't go over and over a passage, but suggests a way of doing it and asks you how it strikes you. For me it always seems so right, so musical and inevitable. He finds a form and a shape . . . he sees the end from the beginning. Unlike some other conductors he is never dogmatic about anything. If you want to do something out of the ordinary on the spur of the moment at a performance, you'll find that he's there with you. (*Records and Recording*, August 1978, 27)

There is little doubt that the perfection we have come to expect in modern performances, concert as well as operatic, derives partly from the very much improved standard of technique and execution among the performers, but in the main it stems from the authoritative control exerted by the conductor himself, within whose power it lies to bring off not merely good interpretations but great ones. The question remains, How did the modern conductor arrive at his position of lofty eminence?

A CHANGE OF DIRECTION

Until the early years of the seventeenth century, the conductor was usually in sole and undisputed control of his forces, excepting only polychoral music, which demanded more than one director. But the age of the *basso continuo* caused far-reaching changes, not only in creating a new polarity in musical texture—that of the soaring upper line (or lines) distantly underpinned by a bass part—but also in sowing the seeds of dissension between the musician at the harpsichord or the organ and the all-important first violinist, who (being somewhat more prominently in the limelight) began to regard himself as the true leader and director of the ensemble.

In some instances this division of control led to what might be described as a musical tug-of-war, and it was often difficult for the orchestra to decide whom to follow. As a general rule—and this, like others, was frequently broken—the harpsichordist held sway at the opera, while the violinist-leader commanded the orchestra in the concert hall. If the piece at hand was an oratorio and the composer happened to be Handel, the direction came from the composer presiding at the organ. Even so, the situation at any given performance was rarely as simple as might at first appear.

In church a director often reigned supreme because his visibility and audibility (if he hit the floor with his staff) were both needed in order to cope with the omnipresent problems of space and distance. When André Maugars described his impression of a polychoral service (1639) in the long and wide church of Santa Maria sopra Minerva in Rome, he gave prominence to the location of the choirs—two in the elevated organ lofts on each side of the high altar and eight others, four on each side of the nave on raised platforms facing each other. The problem of ensemble was solved as follows: "The leading conductor beat the measure for the main choir, accompanied by the best voices. With each of the others there was a man who did nothing but keep his eyes on the leading conductor, to conform his own beat to the leader's; in this way all the chorus sang in the same time, without dragging" (MacClintock, 118).

The acceptance in such circumstances of what was virtually a hierarchy led to the establishment of a comparable order of control in other spheres. If at the opera the harpsichordist served as the main source of control, this did not rule out the first violinist completely. In Benedetto Marcello's *Il teatro alla moda*, a brilliant satire on operatic conventions written about 1720, every aspect of the music and singing is dealt with except conductors. But the section reserved for violinist-leaders and other members of the orchestra reveals that nobody took much notice of the conductor, in all likelihood the composer seated at the harpsichord.

Satire aside, however, the system of dual control worked reasonably well, since each musician had his appointed task. The harpsichordist, whose main function was to play the *continuo* part, also deployed a number of subsidiary talents, such as giving the singers on stage their notes and cues, helping the orchestra in a similar way if there was any hesitation or unsteadiness, and generally supervising the artistic effort as a whole. His concertmaster would thus be free to concentrate his attention on the discipline and ensemble of the players.

Certain musicians blessed with facility on both the violin and the keyboard instruments, such as Mozart, were able at least to consider helping in one way or the other. When his *Abduction* was being given in Vienna in 1782, he found that the performance had a tendency to drag and, in consequence, decided to take his place at the keyboard and conduct it—that is to say, to play in such a way as to inspire the singers and orchestra to do better. There was no question of using a baton. But he had used the word *conduct* four years prior to this event, when in Paris attending one of the Concert Spirituel. He made up his mind that if the performance did not go well, he would mount the platform, snatch the fiddle out of the concertmaster's hands, and conduct the orchestra himself (letter to his father, 3 July 1778).

Some idea of the authoritative control enjoyed by the violinist-conductor may be gained from Johann Joachim Quantz's treatise on flute playing (*Versuch einer Anweisung die Flöte traversière zu spielen*, Berlin, 1752), in which he emphasizes that the source of control should be at the front of the orchestra, not further back where the *continuo* player usually sat. Quantz is therefore opposed to the opinion of C. P. E. Bach, who as a keyboard player naturally favored his own instrument.

There must have been problems with either method, since Quantz admits that good ensemble can be ensured only if the players memorize a few bars at the beginning of a movement, keep their bows close to the strings, and watch the principal violinist's bow. He adds the further caution that players who cannot see their leader should regulate their tempo by that of a neighboring violinist.

The same observation is echoed in a book of "truths about music" by an anonymous "German gentleman" (*Wahrheiten die Musik betreffend*, 1779), in which the section on orchestral direction warns against such evils as too much force from the *continuo* and basses, too much body movement and shrill playing from the violinist-director seated in his high chair, and an overabundance of straining and grimacing. The solution proposed is that the composer should direct from the harpsichord or piano, and the basses should follow him just as the leading violinist does. Indeed, control gradually passed to the keyboard player, who was soon to exchange the harpsichord for the richer sound of the piano.

Before this change of direction took place (and obviously it did so gradually, depending on the prevailing circumstances), there were indications that both the keyboard player and the violinist occasionally stopped playing, in order to give a visible sign with their hands, thus progressing slowly in the direction of the modern conductor. Yet the tension still existed between melody and harmony, as is shown by this extract from the *Jahrbuch der Tonkunst* (1796):

> The *Concertmeister* is in the position, as it were, of the front-rank man to whom the whole orchestra looks for guidance. But the *Kapellmeister* at the piano must sometimes stop playing in order to cut the air with both hands. It would surely be much better if the *Kapellmeister* left the conducting entirely to the *Concertmeister,* and occupied himself only with supervising the performance as a whole, and with seeing that the singers made their entries correctly. It would be a good thing if they studied the piece together and came to some agreement about the *tempo.* How easily things go wrong when two persons direct the performance, one at the piano and the other with the violin.
>
> (Carse, 1948, 295)

Dual direction not only caused problems in the establishment and maintenance of good ensemble, it offended members of the audience who came to hear the music rather than the audible time beating. An English musician who had heard Spontini conduct in Berlin admitted to some reservations regarding this exhibition of absolute control, yet he found it far preferable to the London scene, where one might experience the horror of a conductor clapping the beat with his hands while the first violinist stamped his version of the tempo by using his right foot as a pedal accompaniment. Musical journals reporting on London concerts in the late 1830s stress time and time again the unsatisfactory and tiresome results of divided direction: Henry Bishop was accused of flirting with the baton and the score while his concertmaster Nicholas Mori did the real work. It was even hinted that conductor and leader fought for the direction of the orchestra and that this state of affairs would continue until the movements of baton and bow reached the degree of simultaneity of a telegraph system. Divided control continued at the Philharmonic concerts until 1846, when Costa succeeded in unifying the orchestra under his sole command.

The uncertain state of leadership in London's orchestras and the number of years it took for the situation to be remedied may also have been due, in part, to the omnipresent cello and bass team of Robert Lindley and Domenico Dragonetti. These two men, incomparable virtuosos on instruments that could be seen as well as heard, formed a team so remarkable for its solidarity of musical purpose that weaker members of the group instinctively looked to them for leadership. Since some conductors were referred to in reviews as mere ciphers who were ignorant of whether they were three beats ahead of the orchestra or three beats behind, it is not surprising to find that players were in a state of almost continuous bewilderment. The marvel is that concerts continued to attract music lovers who were willing to overlook glaring blemishes for the sake of the works they wanted to hear.

In Germany, the change of direction came about in the 1820s, though not without a certain amount of experimentation and even misgiving. The pianists played fewer chords and beat time with their hands more frequently, while the violinists waved their bows but rarely allowed them to touch the strings. Felix Mendelssohn, a prodigy in so many ways, conducted the family orchestra with a baton from 1821 until 1824, and he also used this method of direction at his famous revival of Bach's *St. Matthew Passion* at the Berlin Singakademie in 1829. Nevertheless, conducting was still closely associated with beating time, leaving little scope for the finer points of interpretation. Mendelssohn's friend the baritone Eduard Devrient confessed to annoyance at continuous directing, while the violinist and composer Moritz Hauptmann, a longtime member of Ludwig Spohr's orchestra at Cassel, referred to "the cursed little white stick" and its ability to dominate a team of sensitive musicians who were perfectly capable of playing an opera with no more of a lead than was supplied by the *maestro al cembalo*.

The French composer André Grétry, in his *Mémoires* of 1789, suggests a compromise by which choruses and dances should be controlled by time beating, while arias deserved the kind of subtle accompaniment that could be given only by an entire orchestra listening intently to the singer and following the curve of every phrase, with no intervening conductor to complicate the situation. At the beginning of the nineteenth century, the Paris Opéra boasted a "conductor" armed with a wooden stick, yet this was used not for beating time but for prompting, so that everyone on stage would know when to come in. The first violinist was the musical emperor, and it was not long before his powers grew and his grasp over the orchestra, stage, and chorus became absolute. At this point he seldom played his violin (except to illustrate some special kind of attack or phrasing during rehearsal) yet continued to wield the bow in lieu of a baton, which makes one wonder how many valuable bows made by François Tourte were damaged or broken in the course of this period when a sliver of pernambuco wood and a few horsehairs ruled both pit and stage. The change to the baton came in the second half of the century, and even then with some reluctance.

The Italian scene was also slow to change. Up to midcentury, direction at La Scala, Milan, was in the hands of the first violinist, but he began to lose ground in the 1860s, when the man at the piano assumed the impressive title *maestro concertatore e direttore delle opera*. Despite what Berlioz saw in Naples in the early 1830s at the San Carlo Opera and despite his gloomy predictions for the future of Sicily, noisy violinists and directors did eventually give way throughout Italy to the composer at the piano.

One of the main objections, at first, to the visible gyrations of the opera conductor was the utterly distracting effect they had on the line of sight to the stage. Placed either near the prompter's box or, at a later period, in his now accepted position in front of the orchestra, the con-ductor could not help being seen, nor could he afford to cease moving his arms as some ventured to do in the concert hall. Weber, Mendels-sohn, Wagner, Habeneck, and Berlioz were among a select but influential number of musicians who stabilized the tempo and then folded their arms, allowing the orchestra to proceed on a kind of automatic pilot arrangement until it became necessary to revert once more to manual control. A few conductors of recent times, notably Sir Adrian Boult and Gennadi Rozhdestvensky, have occasionally been seen to adopt a similar method of temporarily (and effectively) relinquishing absolute sway over the orchestra. A well-established and sensitive ensemble should in any event be able to develop and maintain a built-in rhythmic pulse, proving that the earlier age of audible and continuous time beating was essentially one of preparation for the change of direction that altered the course of the history of conducting.

THE IDEA OF FIDELITY

Unless the composer is conducting, the conductor stands as the main link between the original score and its instrumental interpreters. That original score, if it exists, is likely to be more or less hidden in a national archive or a private collection of such treasures, its functional counter-part being a manuscript or printed copy, which may or may not be accu-rate. The idea of fidelity to a distant creative process thus becomes prob-lematic in direct proportion to these intermediary issues: the question of whether the conductor's score faithfully reflects the composer's thought and intent; whether the score implies possible liberties that might be taken in the process of a modern performance; whether in view of those possible liberties a conductor is justified in making changes of his own or ones he has borrowed from some other source.

Fidelity, whether high or otherwise, can be thought of in terms of scholarly accuracy in regard to notes, rests, dynamics, tempos, and all the other aspects that go into transforming a musical ideal into a page of full score. It can also be considered in the light of authentic sound, as in the timbre of modern instruments versus their older counterparts and the variations in pitch that such a choice may entail. But these are complex matters, not to be taken lightly by any conductor worthy of his contract.

First, insofar as the musical notation is concerned, the composer's autograph score may not necessarily conform to his later wishes, for composers are well known for their tendency to alter their original ideas after having had the opportunity to listen carefully to the resounding results. They make changes, they invite the criticism of friends and colleagues, and they modify orchestration for reasons of expediency. Fidelity is therefore relative and depends to a large extent upon the interpreter of a score, who may or may not reflect the composer's wishes. Editors have a habit of making changes on their own initiative, and some conductors (who sometimes imagine themselves to be editors) do exactly the same. Musicologists, too, have been known to alter the sequence of scenes in an opera or to add or subtract material, by virtue of the discovery of manuscript fragments belonging to a bygone age.

It is simple to maintain that one composer could not orchestrate and therefore his manner of scoring should be changed to conform with some mysterious and undefined norm or that another had a poor idea of musical form and so his scores should be cut and pasted and transmogrified into something he himself never imagined. Not all composers suffer in this way, but the number who do is larger than the general public might be aware of.

George Bernard Shaw, in a letter to Sir Henry Wood (17 October 1941), had this to say about a much-performed Beethoven overture:

> The lower half of the classical orchestra is so weak that a moving bass cannot be heard against a chord held by the full wind. The No. 3 *Leonora* is repeatedly spoilt by senseless blares during which the figuration of the cellos and double basses is completely lost. I have not heard a note of them since I played piano duets with my sister 60 years ago. Elgar agreed and said that there is a Belgian trombone with five valves which could do it. Coates thinks that bass saxophones could; but I doubt if any woodwind can. One of my uncles played the ophicleide: and though Berlioz called it a chromatic bullock, it had more character than the tubas and was as flexible as a piccolo. It was a gigantic bugle with keys instead of valves. A bass piano with thick strings and steel hammers might be useful. Anything for Beethoven's sake.
>
> (Wood, 103)

Shaw was as usual overstating his case, but the fact remains that many conductors have touched up scores, ancient and modern, with or without the approval of the composer. Some, it is true, repent in their old age, as Felix Weingartner did over his youthful recommendations regarding the rescoring of Beethoven. On being asked some question about the book in which he enumerated those ideas (*Ratschläge für Aufführungen klassischer Symphonien*, 1906) Weingartner replied, "You have that book of mine on re-scoring Beethoven? Then please will you go home and take it from your shelf and put it into your waste-paper basket?" (Boult, 1963, 56).

The vast majority of any audience is unaware of the preparatory work that assists in bringing to their ears a faithful version of the scores on any given program. Even if the conductor's score happens to be authentic, the orchestral parts in the library or on hire may not correspond to what he wants, especially if he is making a guest appearance. With the help of librarians or other assistants, his corrections and markings must be transferred one by one to the fifty or more separate orchestral parts the players will use. Fortunately, if corrected editions are not available, there are books, articles, and journals that list the most egregious errors in printed classical scores. Some idea of the seriousness of the situation may be conveyed by the fact that a fully corrected and annotated edition of the Beethoven symphonies by Igor Markevitch is only now being published, more than a century and a half after the composer's death. Reliable editions of Haydn's symphonies are now available, thanks to the scholarly research of H. C. Robbins Landon, but not all conductors go to the trouble of using them. The same is true of other classical and modern scores. Much depends not only upon the availability of materials but upon a real interest in them and a desire to incorporate their improvements into such sets of parts as an orchestra may possess.

It is unquestionably the role of the conductor to make the best possible use of all this new knowledge and research, and in certain circumstances he should also be concerned with another aspect of fidelity: that of timbre and the use of instruments appropriate to the period of the music. From a purely practical point of view, an orchestra must be so constituted as to perform with modernized instruments or with those that have been modified to sound as they might have in earlier times. Not merely the string section and their bows come under this heading but also the entire wind section and the percussion. It is not possible in normal circumstances for the same body of players to change from one set of instruments to another, so all concerts with programs that cover a time span of more than a century are bound to compromise in the matter of authentic timbre and pitch.

Complete authenticity is ruled out by the very nature of history. One can claim to give a performance of a Mozart symphony using a corrected score and parts, a set of instruments approximating as nearly as possible those in use in Mozart's day, and pitch and tempos as close as possible to those he might have used when directing a performance. But what of the quality of the playing? Many of the composer's letters indicate that the standards of performance in Paris or Salzburg were sometimes below par, and if this fact is admitted, it follows that any "authentic" modern performance should seek to reproduce those very blemishes that Mozart had to put up with. If we do not reproduce the original, warts and all, there is a risk of failure in this difficult matter of accuracy. Yet the errors in playing, the slipshod ensemble, and the insistent noise of the director are all part and parcel of true fidelity.

The perfect conductor does not exist, even though many have claimed to communicate only the essence of the works they interpret, leaving aside all the dross of tradition, the emendations of editors, and the emotional clutter of others less talented or clairvoyant. Mendelssohn was much admired in his day, and he knew how to draw the best from his orchestra, but that did not prevent his tempos from erring occasionally on the rapid side. During his five years as conductor of the Meiningen Orchestra, Hans von Bülow transformed a competent court orchestra into an ensemble of the highest caliber, yet his musical sympathies, though wide, fell far short of what might now be considered desirable. When Hans Richter conducted in London and Manchester, he was considered to be the greatest living exponent of his art, but his idea of fidelity was essentially Germanic, and he had little sympathy for the scores that began to appear in the early twentieth century.

Arthur Nikisch, famed for his sensuous balance of orchestral tone and his musical flexibility, shunned absolute fidelity in matters of tempo, preferring always a type of directorial rubato that enabled him to give the impression that each performance was an improvisation, a totally new event. In an entirely different group, Weingartner shunned new readings and orchestral rubato, yet he abandoned one aspect of fidelity in his many rescorings of the classics, at any rate during his youthful career. It is worth noting that Boult, an admirer of Weingartner and a pupil of Nikisch, felt that in questions of fidelity one of the most experienced of his British contemporaries led the way: "Wood excelled in giving a clear performance of a work and putting it over so faithfully that one could go away and think it out for oneself afterwards and not have another mind in between one and the work, as one might have with Furtwängler or Beecham" (1963, 61).

Yet perhaps the idea of fidelity can be carried too far. The reproduction of a printed score in terms of sound cannot be purely mechanical, and in any event there is too much of a mechanical element in music to be ignored in modern times. What one wants and needs most in an interpretation exceeds the confines of mere fidelity, for the best conductor can move our hearts as well as our intellects.

BIBLIOGRAPHY

Peter Beavan, *Philharmonia Days* (1976). Arnold Bennett, *Things That Have Interested Me* (1921). Hector Berlioz, *Les soirées de l'orchestre* (1852), translated by Jacques Barzun as *Evenings with the Orchestra* (1956). Ercole Bottrigari, *Il desiderio*, Carol MacClintock, trans. (1962). Adrian Boult, *A Handbook on the Technique of Conducting* (1921); and *Thoughts on Conducting* (1963). Charles Burney, *The Present State of Music in Germany, the Netherlands and United Provinces* (2nd ed., 1775). Adam Carse, *Orchestral Conducting* (1929); *The Orchestra in the Eighteenth Century* (1940); and *The Orchestra from Beethoven to Berlioz* (1948).

Hans T. David and Arthur Mendel, eds., *The Bach Reader* (1945). André Grétry, *Memoires* (1789). Carol MacClintock, ed., *Readings in the History of Music and Performance* (1979). Nino Pirrotta and Elena Povoledo, *Music and Theatre from Poliziano to Monteverdi* (1982). Walter Porter, *Mottets of Two Voyces* (1657). Johann Joachim Quantz, *Versuch einer Anweisung die Flöte transversière zu spielen* (1752), translated by Edward R. Reilly as *On Playing the Flute* (1966). Max Rudolf, *The Grammar of Conducting* (1949).

Hermann Scherchen, *Handbook of Conducting* (1933). Percy Scholes, *The Mirror of Music*, 2 vols. (1947). Bernard Shore, *The Orchestra Speaks* (1938). Thomas Southerne, *The Maid's Last Prayer* (1693). Richard Wagner, *On Conducting* (1887). *Wahrheiten die Musik Getreffend* (1779). Felix Weingartner, *Weingartner on Music and Conducting* (1969). Henry J. Wood, *About Conducting* (1945).

The Public for Orchestral Music in the Nineteenth Century

Peter Anthony Bloom

For chronologists, the nineteenth century is a precise historical unit of a hundred years. But for those who would consider its cultural history, its borders must be taken to be the great political and social upheavals at the end of the eighteenth century and the beginning of the twentieth the French Revolution of 1789 and the outbreak of World War I in 1914. Its interior partitions are the restoration of the monarchy in France (1815), the European uprisings at midcentury (1848), and the Franco-Prussian War (1870). These were the events—there were others, of course—that shaped the lives of the Western Europeans with whom we are concerned, and the historical accounts, old and new, that we have of the period.

If the establishment of a time frame for our endeavor requires subtlety, so too does the limitation of our subject matter, for orchestral music includes not only the symphony but also the concert overture, the concerto, and even music with vocal components—such as the "Royal Hunt and Storm" from Berlioz' opera *Les troyens*.

But the problems of definition posed by the terms *nineteenth century* and *orchestral music* pale before those associated with *the public,* for which a definition such as "the general body of mankind" or "the people" will not do. In the words of Hector Berlioz, "It would require a book and more to encompass a truly scientific study of the strange multitudinous creature, half just and half unjust, half rational and half freakish, ingenuous and cunning, enthusiastic and cynical, profoundly susceptible yet sometimes surprisingly independent which goes by that name" (Cairns, 410). Like a pendulum that swings eternally under the combined action of gravity and momentum, the public is now the recipient, now the generative force of artistic endeavor.

Convenient formulas have often been used to describe the nature of the public. For the music of the eighteenth and nineteenth centuries, the formula used to be something like the following: (1) Until the eighteenth century, classical music provided refined entertainment for a small, privileged, and aristocratic class, whose members were the great patrons of the art. (2) In the eighteenth and nineteenth centuries, as a result of social reform, industrial development, international trade, and increased economic well-being, the middle classes, or bourgeoisie, increased in numbers, power, prestige, and influence. (3) By the nineteenth century, with more leisure time available, these middle classes, in imitation of their aristocratic forebears, attempted to patronize and appreciate classical music. (4) Concomitantly, composers began to consider, in different and sometimes opposite ways, the relatively unsophisticated tastes of the new mass audience. Some turned inward and wrote in isolation for their intimate circles or for posterity. Some turned outward and wrote with broad strokes in the effort to touch or convert the widest possible public. Robert Schumann belongs to the former category: he explicitly stated that he did not wish to be understood by everyone. Franz Liszt belongs to the latter category, insofar as the pyrotechnical operatic fantasies that he composed and performed were guaranteed to impress even the most innocent of musical observers. Januslike, some composers were lured by public acclaim yet uncompromisingly faithful to their deeper musical impulses. Richard Wagner falls into this category, theorizing about a music for all the people while creating music dramas that—in form, instrumentation, and especially harmony—were on the cutting edge of musical modernity and thus available, in reality, to a restricted few.

The four items of this formula require further explanation. The patronage system of the eighteenth century, which cast musicians in the role of glorified servants, did offer certain undeniable advantages, among them secure employment (given correct behavior) and musical understanding from an instructed public. The career of Franz Joseph Haydn demonstrates the patronage system at its best. Employed for nearly half a century by one of the wealthiest families in Europe, the Esterhazys, Haydn treated his masters and their upper-class guests to a rich and varied diet of symphonies, quartets, and a host of other works, each more original than the last. The very regularity of his audience caused Haydn to search out ever more novel means of expression, all the while counting on their understanding of the basic elements of his articulate and refined musical language.

Haydn went before the public by reason of his office. But as soon as composers went before the public as artists who were individually responsible for concert arrangements and remunerated on an ad hoc basis, the intellectual and financial balance between composer and consumer shifted. Mozart was the first great composer to challenge the patronage system. Unhappy with his employers in Salzburg, he went off to Vienna and began to put on subscription concerts for his own benefit. He was only partially successful and spent the later years of his short life in continuous financial embarrassment. Haydn diagnosed the cause of his loving friend's failure as simply the lack of an appropriate patron—not as the lack of talent, obviously, and not as the lack of an understanding public. Mozart himself was not anxious to secure the blessings of a patron, and attempted to make a living by other means. In his famous letter of 28 December 1782, Mozart shows his sense of the importance of a sympathetic public, writing to his father about three newly composed piano concertos (K. 413–415) that had some things in them that would satisfy the demands of connoisseurs and others that would please the less well versed members of the audience, though they would not be aware of the reasons for their pleasure.

Beethoven, by philosophical conviction and physical necessity, would bid farewell to the eighteenth century's notion of patronage and move the relationship between artist and amateur to another plane. His creative lifetime spans the period of the French Revolution and the Napoleonic Empire; his work embodies the spirit of those days of glorious battle. But if the political history of the nineteenth century was in part a reaction to the work of the fiery French emperor, the musical history of the nineteenth century may be seen as a continuous glorification of the work of the great German composer.

Any inquiry into the nature of the public for instrumental music in the nineteenth century is as much a sociological as a musical one. In the United States the sociology of music has not had a large number of practitioners. Elsewhere, musical sociologists have dealt primarily with the music of the twentieth century, and some, faced with contemporary division between so much serious art music and the broad musical public, have offered the solution of socialist or Marxist realism, advocating an art that reflects society as it is, materially or economically speaking, and as it should ideally become. Of those who have developed the field of musical sociology in a nondoctrinaire manner, none is more prominent than Theodor Adorno, the German philosopher and musician who died in 1969. Adorno's ideas are not easily classified, because in the effort to explain the "consumption" of culture in industrialized society, he became hostile to all systems of thought. But his notion of society's relation to musical objects appears comforting to the musician who would undertake the study of the public, for it seems based on the assumption that audience reaction is apt to be determined primarily by the objective structural features of the musical composition and by the adequacy of the listener's musical understanding. Adorno ridicules research into such questions as whether middle-income urban housewives between the ages of thirty-five and forty would rather hear Mozart or Tchaikovsky; he minimizes the importance of differential analyses of composers' family backgrounds, since "the social standpoint which an individual occupies is not directly translated into the tone language." And he emphasizes the special difficulties of measuring relationships between music and social class. Chopin, after all, clearly preferred the intimate soirees of high society to the extroverted stages of the public concert and wrote music that is, if anything, eminently aristocratic. But his music is now exceedingly popular—familiar to millions of all social strata.

These difficulties must be overcome, however, for

> if we listen to Beethoven and do not hear anything of the revolutionary bourgeoisie—not the echo of its slogans, the need to realize them, the cry for that totality in which reason and freedom are to have their warrant—we understand Beethoven no better than does one who cannot follow the purely musical content of his pieces, the inner history that happens to be their themes.
>
> (Adorno, 62)

It is this insistence on the inner life of the work of art, as well as the outer life of the period of its composition, that makes Adorno so important and attractive a musical philosopher. Some of his principal beliefs have been effectively summarized in an article in 1976 by Rose R. Subotnik. They include the notions that Western art has tended toward increasing autonomy from society; that the more autonomous the work of art, the more deeply it embodies the most profound social tendencies of its time; and that proper analysis can decipher the social meaning of artistic creation so as to criticize art and society simultaneously. Such complex precepts, based on the notion that the manifold contradictions of society are precisely what cause society to evolve, require much reflection.

Adorno's ideas do provide us with a logical focal point, for at the heart of his view of middle-period Beethoven is that of a unique musicohistorical moment when the artistic interests of an individual and those of a society genuinely coincided. The old-fashioned patronage system was coming to an end as Haydn's career moved into its final phase, and the privileges of the class that operated the system were being challenged by increasingly more widely disseminated philosophical notions of liberty and equality.

> For the first time composers were confronted with the anonymous marketplace. Without the protection of a guild or of a prince's favor they had to sense a demand instead of following transparent orders.... [The public's] need for entertainment turned into one for diversity in the compositions ... [and led to] that dynamic relation of unity and diversity which constitutes the law of Viennese classicism.... Social compulsions under which music seems to be placed from without are absorbed by its autonomous logic and the need for compositional expression, and are transformed into an artistic necessity.
>
> (Adorno, 208)

That "dynamic relation of unity and diversity" is the hallmark of the sonata principle itself: the key conflicts and thematic contrasts of mature music of the classical period, held together by the gravitational pull of a strongly asserted central tonality (and thus essentially different from the unified affections of earlier times), embodied the later eighteenth century's desire for divertissement. And Beethoven's music gained acceptance with relative ease both because it seemed to promote the notion of rapprochement between the individual and society and, in Subotnik's phrase, because it answered a generally felt need for the right to self-assertion.

Whose need in particular? Who, at the time, heard the social polish of the rococo gleaming in Mozart, the official zeitgeist singing in Rossini, or the bourgeois revolution rumbling around in Beethoven? These are things not learned from Adorno, who seemed to prefer to decipher the nature of society from the nature of music while paradoxically emphasizing the reciprocity of the two. Adorno was a critic's ideologue, not a data collector. Nonetheless, his work, with its apparent attentiveness and sensitivity to harmonic nicety, contrapuntal intricacy, and structural complexity—this in the context of a larger, openly moralistic world view of art and society that, if nothing else, heightens the human significance of music—is something that anyone investigating the "public" must consider. It was instrumental music's ability to evoke the infinite that led it to the fore in the nineteenth century—and that leads modern scholars,

consequently, to distinguish its public from others. From the poetic effusions of Wackenroder, Tieck, and E. T. A. Hoffmann, through the writings of Balzac, Sand, and Berlioz, to the philosophical speculations of
Schopenhauer, Hanslick, and Nietzsche, "absolute" instrumental music,
after centuries of playing. second fiddle to the vocal repertory, was seen
to have the awesome and mysterious power to articulate the ineffable.
Sounding from the apex of all nineteenth-century art was music, and
heard as the highest manifestation of that art was instrumental music—
music realized by players and composed of tones unencumbered by singers and essentially freed from words.

In "Beethoven's Instrumental Music," Hoffmann spoke of the "infinite longing" awakened by the symphonic genre and of the relative poverty of vocal music, which could only re-present emotions defined by
words; he spoke of the realms of the colossal and the immeasurable that
were opened by instrumental music, "the most romantic of the arts—one
might say, the only purely romantic art—for its sole subject is the infinite" (quoted in Schaffer). In 1820, Ludwig Tieck spoke similarly of vocal
music as "only a qualified art" and of instrumental music as "independent
and free": "It prescribes its own laws, it improvises playfully and without
set purpose, and yet attains and fulfills the highest; it simply follows its
own dark impulse and in its dallyings expresses what is deepest and most
wonderful" (Blume, 185). In the poetic hands of a master, wrote Richard
Wagner in 1850, instrumental music becomes "the sounds, syllables,
words, and phrases of a language which could express the unheard, the
unsaid, the unuttered" (Strunk, 151). And a few years earlier, Hector Berlioz wrote in the preface to the score of his dramatic symphony *Roméo et
Juliette*:

> If, in the famous garden and cemetery scenes the dialogues of the two lovers,
> Juliet's asides and Romeo's passionate outbursts, are not sung, if the duos of
> love and despair are given to the orchestra ... it is because the very sublimity
> of this love made its depiction so dangerous for the composer that he had
> to give his imagination a latitude that the positive sense of the sung words
> would not have allowed him, and he had to resort to instrumental lan-
> guage—a language more rich, more varied, less limited, and, by its very unlit-
> eralness, incomparably more powerful in such circumstances.

To these citations one could add many more in order to show the
especially high regard in which instrumental music was held by certain
sophisticated nineteenth-century thinkers—though not without running the risk of muddying the waters, for Wagner was, after all, a com-

poser of operas (though he did write program notes for the Beethoven symphonies that emphasize their purely musical qualities); and in his own mature works, the drama is carried as much by the orchestra as by the singers. If Berlioz was an even stronger advocate of instrumental music, his program notes for Beethoven are especially pictorial and suggestive. Furthermore, all commentators on Beethoven—from the accounts of Beethoven's contemporaries Ferdinand Ries and Anton Schindler, through those of midcentury by the theorist A. B. Marz and the biographer Alexander Oulibicheff, to the volume (1898) on the symphonies by the author of the famous musical dictionary, Sir George Grove—took his music to be about something, and certainly something more than the purely musical relationships of its parts. Needless to say, concert programs did not all of a sudden eschew vocal music: the ascendancy of instrumental music in the real world was a gradual process indeed.

The strongest philosophical advocate of instrumental music was surely Arthur Schopenhauer, whose treatise *The World as Will and Idea* has a good deal to say about the relationship of music to the essence of life. No doubt thinking of Beethoven, Schopenhauer wrote that "music is ... not an image of the appearance, or rather of the adequate objectification of the Will, but a direct image of the Will itself, and thus presents the metaphysic to all physicality in the world, the Thing-in-Itself of every phenomenon" (Burbidge and Sutton, 48). In other words, music is a microcosmic version or an extracted quintessence of the macrocosm— the whole world in miniature.

Could the art of music be exalted more highly? And is Schopenhauer's thinking about the special status of music in any way representative of the thinking of the public? We know he influenced Richard Wagner. But did he influence Joseph Prudhomme, the fictional symbol of bourgeois conformity created by the writer Henri Monnier? Do the writings of other philosophers, poets, and composer-critics of the nineteenth century speak for those who listened but did not record the nature of their musical appreciations? By speaking here of only the public for orchestral music and by excluding the public for opera, the vast majority of listeners are clearly removed from consideration—the admirers, devotees, fans, buffs, and fanatics of Italian opera composers from Rossini to Verdi and Puccini, of German opera composers from Weber to Wagner and Strauss, of French opera composers from Auber to Offenbach and Massenet—and an elite is singled out. The word *elite* is a loaded one, for societies are riddled with elites of all sorts: hereditary, governing, economic, and military. These may or may not overlap with cultural elites. Indeed, determining if they do is part of the purpose of this volume. Suffice it to say that if there were any music-loving readers of Schopenhauer in the nineteenth century, they would more likely be found in the concert hall than in the opera house—perhaps.

Had Beethoven found satisfactory librettos and librettists, he, too, might have devoted more of his efforts to opera. As it turns out, he became the Holy Spirit of nineteenth-century orchestral music, a guide and teacher to countless generations, a mighty compositional hero with a worldwide public that continues to grow to this day. "If there had not been a Beethoven, I could never have composed as I have." These words, reputed to have been pronounced by Richard Wagner (Lockwood, 90), might have been spoken by all who came to know his art. It is to Beethoven that our attention is now turned—Beethoven, whose music was the raison d'être of so many European concert societies that appeared at the time—and to Beethoven's Vienna, the great center for music of the high classic period.

Having established himself in Vienna as a virtuoso pianist of considerable distinction with the assistance of certain important personalities (he was the protégé of a wealthy aristocrat and a pupil of Franz Joseph Haydn), Beethoven could not continue to perform in public after his deafness, of which he first seems to have become aware in 1801, became severe. Unlike Mozart, who seems to have almost spurned publication, Beethoven was thus compelled gradually to abandon his career as a performer and to earn a livelihood by selling his music to the highest bidder. His dealings with publishers—borrowing large sums of money and delaying repayment, offering works as yet unfinished, promising the same work (finished or not) to two or more publishers—were hardly scrupulous, but his situation was urgent. "I am obliged to live entirely on the profits from my compositions," he wrote to a friend in 1817. "Since the onset of my illness I have been able to compose only extremely little and therefore have been able to earn only extremely little" (Anderson, letter no. 778).

Fortunately for the composer, publishers were always anxious to have his works. Almost all Beethoven's music appeared in print during his lifetime and, at his death, only a few minor or fragmentary manuscripts were found unpublished. His public consisted in part, then, of the customers of his publishers. His publishers included the Bureau des Arts et d'Industrie, Artaria, Breitkopf and Härtel, Cappi, Diabelli, Hoffmeister, Nägeli, Peters, Schlesinger, Schott, Simrock, and Steiner, but we know little about their customers. Customers there were, of course. By 1828, one year after Beethoven's death, seven impressions of the Fifth Symphony had been made from the Breitkopf and Härtel parts and some seven hundred copies had been distributed (Kinsky, 159).

If specific names of his admirers cannot readily be found in the archives of his publishers, they can be found, at least in limited numbers, in the dedications of his works. Here we find a list of those persons—mostly members of the Viennese nobility—to whom Beethoven owed gratitude; from whom he hoped for favors; with whom he felt it his right, by talent and inclination if not by birth, to associate; and for whom, in a literal sense, he wrote his music. The dedicatees of the nine symphonies, Baron van Swieten, Prince Lichnowsky, Prince Lobkowitz, Count von Oppersdorff, Prince Rasumovsky, Count von Fries, King Friedrich Wilhelm III of Prussia, form a distinguished company. Their biographies comprise a basic chapter in the study of Beethoven's public.

A number of specific names can also be found on the list of subscribers to Beethoven's first Viennese publication, the Piano Trios Opus 1—by which opus number he quite deliberately hoped to launch his public career as a composer. This list includes "the cream of the Austro-Hungarian nobility" (in the words of H. C. Robbins Landon, who reproduces the document). The number of subscribers (123) is impressive, since the highest nobility in Vienna consisted, roughly, of one hundred families. Among the names here are many that are familiar in the Beethoven literature, including Waldstein (of the *Waldstein Sonata*, Opus 53), Rasumovsky (of the *Rasumovsky* String Quartets, Opus 59), and Archduke Rudolf (of the *Archduke* Trio, Opus 97). These were the individuals who supported Beethoven's endeavors by paying for his dedications and for the right to perform the music he published; they also paid, presumably, for tickets to his concerts.

The three earliest performances of the *Eroica* Symphony tell us something of the changing nature of the public for orchestral music at the time. The first reading of the symphony took place in the palace of Prince Lobkowitz, in August 1804, in a room only 54 feet long and 24 feet wide. In December of that year it was played again at the home of a wealthy banker named Würth. Finally, in April 1805, it was given at the Theater an der Wien. In other words, it was played first to a small circle of nobles, then to a group of wealthy businessmen and their aristocratic friends, and finally to a much broader public that included all of those who could afford the price of a ticket. It was premiered by a private orchestra in the private home of a private citizen and was shortly thereafter performed in a public theater originally designed for the opera. For the latter event the court officials noted that such music was a favored diversion "of the higher and middle orders" and that "even the lower orders" had become interested. Such was no doubt the case at the several subscription concerts that Beethoven organized in Vienna, for his own benefit, during the first decade of the nineteenth century.

What were these concerts like? Today's audiences would find them both enormously varied and enormously long. The program of the first public concert that Beethoven gave for his own benefit, at the Burgthea-ter on 2 April 1800, included a late Mozart symphony, excerpts from Haydn's *Creation,* and his own Septet, First Symphony, and First Piano Concerto. Beethoven also improvised before the public, something for which he was especially renowned. In 1808 when he obtained use of the Theater an der Wien after a considerable amount of difficulty (for it was nearly always in use), he rather overeagerly presented almost all of his recent music: the Fifth and Sixth Symphonies, the Fourth Piano Con-certo, excerpts from the Mass in C, the Scena and Aria "Ah! perfido," and—after an improvisation at the piano—the Choral Fantasy. This pro-gram lasted well over four hours, but little is known of the financial ben-efits the composer was able to reap from this concert and from the others he gave at the time.

After 1809, by a system of patronage that was apparently free from all the preceding century's restrictions, Beethoven's economic security was guaranteed by an annuity, paid to him by three aristocratic friends, Prince Lobkowitz, Prince Kinsky, and Archduke Rudolf. According to Beethoven's student Carl Czerny, Prince Lobkowitz, a violinist, and his brother, Count Moritz, were great connoisseurs who had taken the lead in persuading the high Viennese nobility to support the young composer from Bonn. Prince Kinsky (whose sudden death in 1812 threatened the continuation of the annuity) was a most generous patron, though we know little of his personality, and Archduke Rudolf, the youngest brother of Emperor Franz I, was a gifted pianist and Beethoven's last stu-dent. Though untypical in their generosity, these men may typify the instructed Viennese music-lover of the period, men exclusively from the "educated classes," as Beethoven's first biographer Anton Schindler put it, "who by inclination and breeding assigned music its place among the disciplines." These were the connoisseurs for whom Beethoven presum-ably wrote his own brand of *musica reservata*—the *Quartetto serioso* Opus 95, for example, which the composer held back from publication for five years, saying to the Londoner Sir George Smart, no doubt because of the complex demands it made on the listener, that it was never to be per-formed in public.

Such noble patronage was most blatantly demonstrated during what may have been the high point of Beethoven's public career. On 29

November 1814, a concert was given in the Redoutensaal, with music by Beethoven, before two empresses, the kings of Prussia, Württemberg, and Denmark, and almost all of the participants in what was one of the most brilliant international gatherings of the century, the Congress of Vienna (September 1814–June 1815). In attendance were Czar Alexander I of Russia, Tallyrand of France, Castlereagh of England, Metternich of Austria, Hardenberg of Prussia, and more. If this famous Congress quelled the threat of Napoleon and of domination by a universal monarchy, it likewise marked the point of origin of Beethoven's reputation as a dominant and universal composer. The obvious irony is that the work occasioned by the Congress and by Beethoven's desire to incorporate in music the historical events of the waning years of the Napoleonic era, a work that was regularly repeated during 1814—when more than half of all the concerts Beethoven gave for his own benefit in Vienna took place—was more bombastic than brilliant and more hollow than heroic. This work was the *Battle Symphony* or *Wellington's Victory*, a potboiler that was included on the program along with Beethoven's monumental Seventh Symphony.

The powerful rulers of Europe had certified his fame and had launched his legend for posterity, and yet Beethoven's immediate popularity began to wane. The heroic style of the middle period, which had fueled the high expectations of the revolutionary era, was in a way exhausted—or no longer needed, for the Viennese were retreating from Beethoven's categorical imperatives to the greater security of Biedermeier comforts, operatic opulence, and the delights of the dance. In his penetrating study of the composer's life, Maynard Solomon, attributing much of Beethoven's fame to the support of the Viennese aristocracy, which had for so long been devoted to music, traces his momentary fall from grace to the death, emigration, or estrangement from the composer of Kinsky, Lichnowsky, Lobkowitz, Rasumovsky, and other princely patrons and to the decline of their personal musical establishments. At the core of Beethoven's public, aside from a number of doctors, lawyers, and other professional men, was that traditionally elevated minority of rulers, nobles, generals, and artists who by their breeding and training were equipped to appreciate both the force and the finesse of his music.

Such a conclusion is only slightly modified by the names of the signatories to a famous letter written to Beethoven in February 1824, requesting a public performance of, among other works, the "new flower" that grew among the garlands of his "glorious, still unequalled symphonies"—the Ninth. Among the thirty signatories regretting Beethoven's retirement from public life and demanding his aid in establishing "a new sovereignty of the true and beautiful" were members of the nobility, pub-lishers, businessmen, court officials, artists, and amateurs. The audience at the premiere of the Ninth Symphony, which took place on 7 May 1824, in the Kärntnertortheater, was described by A. W. Thayer, the first great biographer of Beethoven, as exceptionally large and peopled by Bee-thoven's friends and most of the finest artists in the city. Though all reports say that this public was a most appreciative one, Beethoven him-self was greatly displeased with the concert's financial yield. In spite of the humanitarian message of the choral finale of the symphony, he alleged—not for the first time—that he had been cheated. And perhaps there is a larger significance to this sort of accusation. In earlier times composers had depended for their security on one wealthy prince or a few, but in the changed economic circumstances of the period after the Congress of Vienna, with the concomitant reductions of the fortunes of many of the great landowners, composers were compelled to depend more and more on entrepreneurs, directors, managers, and middlemen in general. The possibility for deception, if not petty thievery, was thus distinctly increased.

Had it not been for his deafness, Beethoven might well have contin-ued throughout his lifetime to give public concerts, for his own benefit, as a pianist. It is also possible that he would have taken a post as kapell-meister of the musical establishment of one of the great families or at the imperial court, fulfilling the composing, conducting, and performing obligations of such a position as Haydn, for example, had done before him and as Weber, Spohr, and Wagner, among others (though with dif-ferent contractual obligations), would do after him. Beethoven, however, was forced to become a composer occupied only by the creation of his own music. Though it became the model for many who followed, his divorce from the overtly functional role in society that other composers had played was in fact necessitated by illness.

Even if Beethoven had become associated with it, the kapellmeister system had, sooner or later, to break down, as wealth passed from the landed aristocracy to the owners of capital—to those who, in the age of invention and industrialization, began to wield ever greater power and influence in behalf of their own class. Such persons—unlike their aris-tocratic forebears, for whom musical training was considered natural and even necessary—may or may not have had an education or an interest in the arts. Obviously, the economic history of Vienna in the first part of the nineteenth century—the cycles of inflation, rising prices, and cur-rency devaluation that followed the wars and the occupations—is related to the musical history of the period. But the death of Beethoven in 1827 did not by any means spell the death of music in Vienna.

Franz Schubert, born twenty-seven years after Beethoven, though dead only one year after him, was able to live entirely from his musical compositions—from honoraria paid to him on a onetime basis by a number of Viennese publishers. The public apparently clamored for Schubert's lieder, part-songs, piano music, and ecclesiastical works. Otto Biba reports that Schubert's position in Vienna, far from a poverty-stricken one, was instead a rather celebrated one, the envy of his contemporaries. But if Schubert's chamber music was popular, played by famous artists such as the violinist Ignaz Schuppanzigh and others at salon concerts and informal occasions, including the *Abendunterhaltungen* (evenings of light music by the Gesellschaft der Musikfreunde), his orchestral music was not. For psychological reasons that remain unclear, Schubert seems actively to have discouraged public performances of his symphonies. Those that were performed during his lifetime were heard only within the walls of private homes. The prominent Viennese violinist Otto Hatwig, who himself supported a sizable orchestra (seven first violins, six seconds, three violas—among them Schubert—three cellos, two basses, and winds in pairs), gave a good number of Schubert's earliest efforts in the symphonic genre.

Who attended the Hatwig concerts? Who comprised the public for Schubert's orchestral music? Here the archives are relatively detailed: wealthy merchants and manufacturers, government officials and civil servants, university professors and schoolteachers, wholesalers and retailers, and members of Schubert's own circle—musical amateurs, young people from cultured homes, poets whose writings Schubert set to music (Johann Mayrhofer, Eduard von Bauernfeld, and Franz von Schober), painters (Moritz von Schwind and Leopold Kupelwieser), students, and a small group of professional musicians.

Even if Schubert had been anxious rather than reluctant to give large-scale performances of his orchestral works, he might still have found it difficult to produce them, since there was no suitable hall in Vienna specifically designed for symphonic concerts before the Gesellschaft der Musikfreunde opened its own in 1831, three years after Schubert's tragically early death. Prior to that, theaters designed primarily for opera or for ballroom dancing (the Burgtheater, the Theater an der Wien, the Kärntnertortheater, the Redoutensaal) were hired by musicians as the calendar permitted—not often, as Beethoven learned—and were used for concerts of symphonic music played by pickup orchestras composed of trained amateurs and free-lance professionals. Of the public for the famous concerts given by the Gesellschaft der Musikfreunde itself, founded in 1812 for the advancement of music in all its branches by a devoted society of amateur musicians, Ignaz von Mosel said, "Here one saw counts next to tradesmen, high officials next to civil servants, Ph.D.'s next to students, and in the soprano and alto sections {women were not pemitted to play in Viennese orchestras}, aristocratic ladies next to middle-class women—all taking their places with the sole ambition of contributing to the success of the whole" (quoted in Biba, 1980, 87). Those mentioned here include nobles, professional men, and bureaucrats, but not peasants, artisans, and unskilled workers—not "innkeepers, cobblers, and tailors," as Beethoven once snarled—for of the latter's existence, Beethoven, Schubert, and their circles may have had little awareness indeed.

By the third decade of the nineteenth century, then, with the decline of the connoisseur aristocracy that had nurtured so much Viennese classicism, the box office situation, dependent in part on the entrepreneurial skills of the composer, had begun to look a little like that of today. The composer's desire for experimentation was reinforced by that segment of the Viennese public which clamored for novelty, but it was challenged by that segment most comfortable with familiarity. The systematic non-acceptance of the unfamiliar begins its long history in music in the post-Beethoven era. In nineteenth-century Vienna gradually more diverse audiences began to appreciate Beethoven's symphonies as paradigms of heroism and the victory over adversity, while creating the misleading impression that the man himself was a champion of the people. Thus, there is considerable irony in Beethoven's continued popularity during the reign of the fathers of the waltz, Johann Strauss, Sr., and Joseph Lanner. Indeed, like the Viennese café, the Viennese waltz, with its lush melodies and lively rhythms, provided a musical escape from everyday existence.

The Vienna that served as capital to those widely varying territories and peoples united by their common obedience to the Hapsburg monarch, the Vienna of Franz I, Ferdinand I, and Franz Josef I, was in its outward stability conducive to conservative and orderly tastes—the Metternich system—in the arts. No composers of the stature of Beethoven or Schubert challenged that system in the post-1830 generation; Vienna would have to wait for the permanent arrival of Johannes Brahms, in the 1870s, to hear their true musical successor. Meanwhile, as the need for regular professional performance of orchestral music became gradually apparent (the Gesellschaft der Musikfreunde consisted on principle of amateurs and did not begin a professional concert series until after 1860; and the Concert Spirituel held at the Church of Saint Augustine, though professional, was infrequent), the seeds were sown for the birth of the Vienna Philharmonic Orchestra, which took place in 1842. The growth of this young ensemble was slow—only a few annual concerts were given in its early years—and it was periodically interrupted, by the revolutions of 1848 and other social upheavals. But after 1860, the revitalized orchestra moved from the Grosser Redoutensaal (a large ballroom in the palace, built in 1740 and used successfully for concerts by Beethoven, Berlioz, and others) to the Kärntnertortheater, and, a decade later, to its newly built (and present) home, the Grosser Musikvereinssaal.

This orchestra, the most fully professional orchestra to develop in Vienna in the nineteenth century, played for a distinguished series of conductors, including Otto Dessoff, Hans Richter, and Gustav Mahler. It introduced the concert music of Wagner, Liszt, Bruckner, and Dvořák to the Viennese public. But the greatest champion of symphonic music in the post-Beethoven period, the man who demonstrated that it was still possible to write symphonies after Beethoven, was Johannes Brahms. His Second (1877) and Fourth (1885) Symphonies were premiered in Vienna, and the First (1876) and Third (1883) also became regular fare at the Philharmonic.

It is not surprising that Brahms, whose public career was launched by a fervently laudatory article from Robert Schumann, should have become a controversial figure. His composing, conducting, and performing had made him a figure of international renown by the time he decided to settle permanently in Vienna. (His income, largely from the sale of his publications, was considerable.) Controversy stemmed from his role as the favorite of Eduard Hanslick, the Viennese music critic whose opinions nearly dominated that city's musical life. Hanslick's bête noire was Richard Wagner, who mocked the critic (and thus raised his ire) in creating the personage of Sixtus Beckmesser—learned, but pedantic—in Die Meistersinger von Nürnberg. For years Hanslick did what he could to praise Brahms at the expense of Wagner and more importantly, to advance "absolute" instrumental music into the limelight traditionally occupied by opera.

Hanslick was a critic of the public as well. For him, the audiences of the Vienna Philharmonic, to the extent that they applauded the works, for example, of Anton Bruckner—a Wagner idolater and thus in the camp of the enemy—were little worthy of respect. In fact, Bruckner's symphonies, with their Schubertian melodiousness, Beethovenian principles of construction (vastly expanded, if not bloated, to Wagnerian lengths), and overtly Wagnerian instrumentation, represent the culmination of the nineteenth-century Viennese symphonic tradition. The history of the critical reception of Bruckner's symphonies provides an excellent view of the fin de siècle Viennese public for orchestral music. The Philharmonic refused to play the First Symphony, which its players found wild and daring; the Second seemed nonsensical and unplayable to the orchestra at first glance but nonetheless received at its premiere a standing ovation from both audience and orchestra; the Third, again deemed unperformable, occasioned whistles, catcalls, a mass exodus, and an unpardonably harsh review from Hanslick. And so it went for this simple, insecure, and remarkably gifted composer, who had innocently strayed onto the political battlefield by dedicating his Third Symphony to Wagner.

Indeed, toward the end of the century, Vienna was peopled with Beethoven idolaters and partisan Brahmsians, devoted Brucknerites and militant Wagnerians—overtly nostalgic advocates of the music of the past and adamant proselytizers for the music of the future. In fin de siècle Vienna art occupied a high place in the scale of bourgeois values. Culture became "democratized," as Carl Schorske puts it, as a result of the "aristocratization of the middle class." But of strictly orchestral music Schorske and most such historians have little to say. They concentrate instead on vocal and dramatic music. A number of artists in fin de siècle Vienna, faced with a society that was straining for coherence, delivered messages of liberation and destruction that were too precise for the expressive vagueness, revered in certain corners, of instrumental music. The major-minor tonal system, developed and used for over two centuries by composers in Western Europe, was similarly straining for coherence and rebirth, and such straining, made audible, is magnificently expressive in the orchestral works of Bruckner, Mahler, and Richard Strauss. These composers were faced with a technical dilemma concerning the harmonic system—the musical drama of the departure from and return to a single tonic chord, or single tonic note, was played out—but they all appeared regularly before the public. The solution to the dilemma proposed by Arnold Schoenberg and his circle was an intellectual triumph. But the elimination of tonality that resulted from their egalitarian method of composition, in which all notes of the chromatic scale are considered equal, the so-called twelve-tone system, would please a limited public indeed.

Though it might not have been his preferred destiny, Hector Berlioz became the chief exponent of orchestral music in France in the first three-quarters of the nineteenth century. "Beethoven being dead, only Berlioz can make him live again," wrote Niccolò Paganini in 1838 in words both apt and prophetic. Indeed, both Beethoven and Berlioz figure prominently in the revitalization of concert life in France in the post-Napoleonic period. There was of course a native French school of symphonic composition in the eighteenth century, though no one composer achieved the status of Haydn or Mozart. Symphonies and concertos were played as fillers on essentially vocal concert programs. And concerts themselves took place only when the lyric theaters were not putting on their regular attractions.

Concert life in France was revitalized in the early nineteenth century partly through the work of one of the great champions of the music of Beethoven, the violinist-conductor François Antoine Habeneck. He joined the orchestra at the Opéra as a section violinist in 1804, became concertmaster and assistant conductor in 1817, served as general director of the Opéra between 1821 and 1824, and then served as principal conductor from 1824 to 1846. He was also first violin in the orchestra at the French court and professor of violin at the Paris Conservatoire, whose fine student orchestra he directed from 1806 to 1815. Habeneck's enthusiasm for Beethoven, whose symphonies he read both with the student orchestra at their public concerts and with the Opéra orchestra at their occasional symphonic concerts, led him to establish a professional concert orchestra of his own—the Société des Concerts du Conservatoire.

The Société, of which today's Orchestre de Paris is the direct descendant, was born in 1828; Habeneck was the conductor, Luigi Cherubini, director of the Conservatoire, was the honorary président, and the French government of Charles X was a moderately generous financial sponsor. Members of the orchestra, originally selected from the best orchestras of the capital city, were gradually recruited from the ranks of the Conservatoire's alumni, with current students filling in the back sections of the string sections as needed. Each spring six concerts were given, at two-week intervals, in the Grande Salle of the Conservatoire. The organization, democratic in principle but ruled with an iron hand by its founding director, became the first great professional symphony orchestra in France and one of the leading orchestras of the world at the time.

What seems to have been most remarkable about this new orchestra was the formidable precision of the ensemble. Most orchestras in Europe at the time would have only one rehearsal prior to a concert performance. But the Société des Concerts usually had five or more—so many, in fact, that Cherubini was upset by the interruptions such rehearsals caused in the school's weekly schedule. Nevertheless, the orchestra's concerts showered glory upon the Conservatoire and produced unanimous approval from a variety of critical observers: F. J. Fétis, the critic whose enthusiastic review of the opening concerts in 1828 proclaimed a "great day in the annals of French music," Felix Mendelssohn, who wrote to his family about the orchestra's tremendous character and zeal, and Richard

Wagner, whose eyes were opened by this orchestra to sonorous possibilities of which he had never even dreamed.

Habeneck's addiction to Beethoven made the Société's repertory a new and experimental one in the early years, when Beethoven himself was considered a daredevil; but continued performances of the works of the three masters of high Viennese classicism made the repertory a decidedly conservative one by midcentury.

The legislation that established the Société and the organization's charter say little about the public expected to attend the concerts, though in the hallowed French tradition, a large number of individuals—government officials, theater directors, professors at the Conservatoire, and a host of others—were all entitled to receive free passes. Tickets, priced from two to nine francs, were relatively expensive; and season subscriptions, a new concept in the nineteenth century, soon became nearly impossible to obtain. Indeed, they were passed down, from father to son, like so many rare objets d'art. "New listeners," as Jeffrey Cooper puts it, "were all but shut out."

The Grande Salle of the Conservatoire had a capacity of approximately one thousand. At the time of its inauguration in 1811, a weekly journal deplored the ferocious heat of the place, which rendered the enjoyment of music there practically impossible. Furthermore, "the ladies complained bitterly about the problems of displaying their elegance and finery from the loges. An overly bright illumination revealed the little mysteries of the toilette so essential to the creation of a fresh appearance" (quoted in Chantavoine). Comments about the lighting, heating, and other accoutrements of public auditoriums were common in the Parisian press of the time and suggest that listeners' concerns were by no means all musical. But many listened with great devotion, as Antoine Elwart later reported, like the members of a congregation of which Beethoven was the supreme pontiff.

Of the public's intelligence, we have a number of reliable witnesses, among them the young Felix Mendelssohn, who visited Paris in 1831 and 1832. He described the sort of genuinely curious dilettante often found in artistic circles—the sort of person who might have read Fétis's little book on music appreciation, *La musique mise à la portée de tout le monde* (*Music Explained to the World;* 1830), with its revealing subtitle: "A succinct presentation of everything necessary to discuss and evaluate this art without ever having studied it." If a person wished to attend concerts at the Conservatoire but was not instructed in music, he was well advised to make the pretense of having instruction, which itself requires guile, if not intelligence.

Thanks to the many volumes of lists of subscribers that are preserved at the Bibliothèque Nationale in Paris, the public of the Société des Concerts can be studied in close detail. The lists contain the names of aristocratic families from the ancien régime, nobles from the empire and the restoration, bankers, businessmen, and military officers. If they do not contain the names of artists and writers familiar to us, it is because these individuals—frequently in attendance—were usually invited by wealthy boxholders and permanent subscribers. The poet Alfred de Vigny was invited by Countess Marie d'Agoult, Liszt's celebrated mistress, for example; George Sand was invited by the editor François Buloz; others, such as critics or friends of the performers, were admitted with special passes. We also have the lists of the subscribers to Pierre Baillot's series of chamber music evenings in Paris in the 1820s and 1830s—some five hundred names in all. This was an elite sanctuary and perhaps a microcosm of those who attended orchestral concerts, a society of aristocrats and a devoted corps of amateur and professional musicians. Baillot, the most distinguished French violinist of his day and a credible rival to Paganini, seems to have worshipped two trinities at these concerts: the classic one of Haydn, Mozart, and Boccherini, and the contemporary one of Cherubini, George Onslow, and Mendelssohn. Beethoven, whose music Baillot advanced more as an editor of printed music and as a violin teacher than as a performer, was the god of the several quartet societies directly spawned in France by Baillot's own.

Because the lists of subscribers for the one official concert series in earlier-nineteenth-century France, that of the Société des Concerts, survive with some precision the nature of its public can be identified. But no lists survive for the concerts given by Hector Berlioz, who, as a result of the growing conservatism of musical officialdom and his own radical inventiveness, was all but excluded from performance by the Société des Concerts, as well as by the Paris Opéra. He had to develop his own means of putting his work before the public. For this reason Berlioz, without prior wish or intention, became one of the first great conductors and concert impresarios in the modern sense of the word. Again out of necessity, he became a music critic. And it is from his critical writings—his collected essays, his memoirs, and parts of his collected correspondence— that we learn a good deal about concert-giving in France and elsewhere in the Western musical world where Berlioz traveled, gave concerts of his own, and observed.

Obviously, to give a concert himself, Berlioz had first to prepare the music. This meant not only putting the final touches on new compositions or making revisions in those already performed but also copying out the parts or correcting those copied by others. He then had to obtain the use of a concert auditorium—no mean feat in Paris, where the selection was not large. Next came the hiring of players one by one, with no contractor other than himself. Since he could count on no more than one full rehearsal, he invented the sectional rehearsal and went to the players, individually or in small groups, to teach them their parts. This procedure led to Berlioz' great respect for, and many friendships with, Parisian instrumentalists and to the detailed knowledge he would later impart in his treatise on orchestration written in 1843. Finally, as the day of the concert approached, there was the publicity to attend to, including writing preview articles himself and persuading friends to do likewise. Here, of course, he was to make good use of the influence he wielded as a journalist at a time when readership—and thus the power of the press—was on the increase.

Berlioz, on the podium, inspired in his orchestra great energy and devotion as he guided them through demanding programs and complex scores of unprecedented difficulty. When he introduced his symphony with solo viola, *Harold in Italy*—still a challenge even to virtuoso orchestras—it was the last item on a program that included a concert overture, two songs for soprano and orchestra, a trio from an opera, a fantasy for piano and orchestra, and an excerpt from another symphony. Such a variety of symphonic music interspersed with vocal excerpts and virtuoso showpieces—the typical program of the time—was a recipe sure to attract the public, so long as a famous soloist was on hand as well. But such programs demanded important financial resources, since then, as now, famous soloists were very highly paid and taxes on concert receipts were considerable. Setting ticket prices was a tricky business—too low and expenses might not be covered, too high and the house might be empty. For nine francs—the highest-priced ticket—a French soldier in 1830 had to work about two weeks, and a laborer, about one week; for nine francs a music lover could buy Fétis's book *La musique mise à la portée de tout le monde* (and receive a franc and a half in change) or four copies of a piano-vocal score of "La Marseillaise"; the pension Berlioz received from the French government as a winner of the Prix de Rome was worth just under nine francs a day; for a regular newspaper article, he would receive more than ten times that amount.

Berlioz never became wealthy as the result of his musical activities and lacked official support. His music should have been a staple of the repertory of the Société des Concerts, which could have offered him material, institutional support; he should have been given a teaching post at the Conservatoire, in orchestration or conducting, but was offered the honorary post of librarian. For two seasons, 1850 and 1851, Berlioz did head what might have become a second regular Parisian concert organization and a major boon to instrumental music, the Grande Société Philharmonique de Paris. But after some half a dozen concerts in the second season and in spite of the generosity of several aristocratic backers, financial exigencies and other matters caused the enterprise to fold. Thus, in midcentury Paris, the death of music that Berlioz had lately predicted (in the preface to his memoirs, written in London in 1848) seemed in part to have occurred. The Société des Concerts remained the sole institution for the support of the orchestral repertory. And its repertory was a decidedly conservative one, appreciated by a "musical patriciate," as Elwart put it, and inimical to the innovations of any young composer wishing to pursue instrumental music.

This situation contrasts markedly with that obtaining in London and in a number of smaller European cities and towns that Berlioz visited and reported upon. In Paris, orchestral music began to regain its earlier status around 1861, when Jules Pasdeloup began his series of Concerts Populaires at the Cirque d'Hiver and made classical music availble to the less affluent members of society by presenting it at prices less than half of those at the Conservatoire and in the unpretentious neighborhood of the Boulevard du Temple. Indeed, the critic for the *Revue et Gazette Musicale* wrote of Pasdeloup's opening concert (which featured music by Weber, Mendelssohn, Beethoven, Haydn, and Méhul) that what was to be judged was not so much the artists and the music but rather the public itself: "The question was whether the large number would be of the same opinion as the small—whether massive and sophisticated masterpieces would be understood by a multitude that had never before been able to approach them" (Bernard, 150). The critic did not answer the question he posed. Berlioz, in his review for the *Journal des Débats*, reports that the public listened religiously, silently, and attentively to works "whose real value this audience can never appreciate, but whose grand form and content astonish and excite in it veritable transports of emotion" (Bernard, 151).

Pasdeloup's series of popular concerts endured until 1884, when competition from several new series directed by Charles Lamoureux, Edouard Colonne, and others caused a decline in attendance. But it was not only competition that hurt Pasdeloup; it was also the insufficient technical prowess of his performances and his own lack of interpretive imagination. The very public that showered Pasdeloup with praise at the beginning had become sufficiently knowledgeable, or so it seems, to condemn him. Did Pasdeloup's public diminish simply because it was attracted by novelty or advertising to go elsewhere? Or because it was genuinely disappointed with his performances? Did other organizations take root because the public appeared in quantity? Or because their performances were of higher quality?

Such questions often arise in this sort of inquiry, and they take a variety of forms. Clara Schumann's concert repertory, for example, shows a kind of progression from the pure glitter of the virtuoso pianist—composers Herz, Moscheles, and Pixis—to the more substantive music of Beethoven, Chopin, and Robert Schumann. Was Clara Schumann responding to improved public taste, as some have suggested? Or was she simply responding to her own artistic development?

For Pasdeloup, political issues seem also to have played a role in the diminution of his public: because of his insistence on the classic German repertory (the six most often played composers at his concerts were Beethoven, Mendelssohn, Haydn, Mozart, Weber, and Wagner), Pasdeloup was dubbed a German agent. And if, after the Franco-Prussian War, a journalist could write, "The music of Wagner is for us no longer a question of art, it is a question of public order. It is no longer up to the critic to judge it; it is rather up to the Prefect of Police" (quoted in Bernard, 1971, 176), then indeed repertory, and musical affairs in general, had distinctly entered into the political arena. As German troops moved into Paris in 1871, Camille Saint-Saëns founded the Société Nationale de Musique, with its motto *Ars Gallica*. As Richard Wagner laid the foundation of his empire, French composers experienced a renewal of their native energies.

Concert life in cities other than Vienna and Paris can be examined using Berlioz as a guide. Beginning a long-contemplated series of extensive travels toward the end of 1842, he remained an itinerant musician, frequently seeking fame and fortune abroad as well as refuge from misunderstanding at home, until shortly before his death in 1869. The places he visited and subsequently described in letters and in articles for Parisian newspapers and journals include all of those centers of Europe and Russia where the professional performance of orchestral music was more or less possible: Áachen, Baden-Baden, Berlin, Bordeaux, Bremen, Breslau, Brunswick, Brussels, Cologne, Darmstadt, Dresden, Frankfurt, Gotha, Hamburg, Hannover, Karlsruhe, Leipzig, Loewenberg, London, Lyons, Mainz, Mannheim, Marseilles, Moscow, Pest (soon to become part of Budapest), Plombières, Prague, Riga, Saint Petersburg, Strasbourg, Stuttgart, Versailles, Vienna, and Weimar.

This list suggests that in France there were a few cities outside of Paris capable of mustering forces adequate for the performance of scores as complex as Berlioz'. In addition to those on the list, Dijon, Lille, and

Montpellier heard at least one concert overture by Berlioz; indeed, it was by his overtures that Berlioz became widely known as an important com-poser of instrumental music. But in none of these French cities was there a regular professional orchestra dedicated to the performance of essen-tially symphonic music. The same can be said of Brussels, which in cer-tain ways was a cultural offshoot of Paris. But what of all those German towns, large and small, that welcomed Berlioz during his travels, some on more than one occasion?

Most prominent on the list, perhaps, is Leipzig, the city of Bach's maturity and long a center of musical importance. The tradition of instrumental performance there dates from the seventeenth century, but it was with the building of a new concert hall, the Gewandhaus, at the end of the eighteenth century that concert life in Leipzig was given a focal point for music both old and new. During the years of Felix Men-delssohn's tenure as conductor (1835–1847), the Gewandhaus Orchestra reached new levels of professionalism and introduced important sym-phonic music by Schubert, Schumann, and Mendelssohn. In later years the orchestra gave major performances of new music by Brahms, Wagner, Grieg, and Tchaikovsky. During his visit there in 1843, Berlioz found a strongly opinionated but not unknowledgeable public—a public that enjoyed a rich musical life of opera and choral music, the benefits of a music conservatory, and some of the most important international music journals of the century, including Robert Schumann's *Neue Zeitschrift für Musik*.

In Berlin, where at the court of Frederick the Great music had played an exceptionally prominent role, symphonic music in the nineteenth century was performed at occasional concerts given by the court or opera orchestras or by private orchestras put together by local musicians. One such musician, Benjamin Bilse, founded the organization that would become the antecedent to the Berlin Philharmonic, whose famous nine-teenth-century conductors included Joseph Joachim and Hans von Bülow. Berlioz, who knew two of the directors of the royal opera house, Spontini and Meyerbeer, found music everywhere in Berlin; and he found the art universally respected and even worshipped by king and people, rich and poor, professional and amateur (instruction in music had long been compulsory in public education in Berlin). Indeed Fried-rich Wilhelm IV's passion for music, as well as that of his son, the future emperor of Germany, and his wife, only reinforced the pervasiveness of musical culture in Prussia. Nevertheless, in the mid-nineteenth century, there, as elsewhere in German-speaking lands, vocal music and opera reigned supreme.

In the Saxon capital of Dresden, where the young Richard Wagner held his first important post as kapellmeister of the court opera and orchestra, regular subscription concerts were introduced only in 1858, after several earlier attempts to do so by Carl Maria von Weber in 1821 and by Wagner in 1848. In 1843, when Berlioz visited the city, he found the richest combination of musical resources he had as yet encountered in Germany. And he found a socially mixed and discerning public that, in his memoirs, he chose to differentiate from others:

> The *Fantastic Symphony* was much less well received by one section of the audience. The smart elements, headed by the King of Saxony and the court, were not amused (so I was told) by the violence of its passions and the pensiveness of its reveries and all the horrid fantasmagoria of the finale; I believe the Ball and the Scene in the Country alone found any favour with them. The ordinary public simply let itself be carried along by the current of the music, and it applauded the March to the Scaffold and the Witches' Sabbath more warmly than the other three movements. But it was quite clear that this work, so well received in Stuttgart, so perfectly understood in Weimar, so keenly debated in Leipzig, was in its whole musical and poetic ethos largely alien to the inhabitants of Dresden, and disconcerted them by being so unlike the symphonies they were used to. They were more surprised than charmed—not so much moved as dazed.
>
> (p. 302)

Berlioz had given his concerts in the opera house in Dresden, and they were exceptional events on the calendar. After the construction of an independent concert hall, the Gewerbehaussaal, in 1870 (which became home to the Dresden Philharmonic), purely instrumental concerts in Dresden—as in other European cities that witnessed the construction of suitable auditoriums—became quite normal. Indeed, the history of public concert life is obviously bound to the history of public concert halls: when the orchestra, not the singer, is the protagonist, then the physical setting must be appropriately recast.

In Weimar, where musical activities at court were directed at midcentury by Franz Liszt, musicians enjoyed the enlightened patronage of the Grand Duchess Maria Pavlovna, daughter of the Russian czar and a student of one of Liszt's predecessors, the pianist-composer Johann Nepomuk Hummel. Such patronage, together with the general enlightenment of the city where for so long Goethe had held forth, made possible a great succession of avant-garde performances, including Wagner's *Tannhäuser* and Berlioz' revised *Benevenuto Cellini*. For Berlioz, who was received throughout the country with respect, admiration, and, sometimes, as in Brunswick, citywide enthusiasm, Germany was thus a land of attentive and unprejudiced audiences, a "bounteous second mother to all the sons of harmony." His opinion was soon to be shared by music lovers everywhere.

In Pest, where regular orchestral concerts were given after 1836 by the Society of Musicians and after 1853 by the Philharmonic, Berlioz fueled Hungarian nationalism with a performance of his *Rakoczy March*. (After 1869, Liszt became the leading musical figure of the Hungarian capital and permanently established its position as a center of musical activity.) In Prague—site of some of Mozart's greatest successes in the 1780s—there was no regular concert organization until 1840, when both the Cecilienverein and the Zofin Philharmonic were formed. Berlioz conducted the latter during his visit in 1846; he found a lively feeling for music among all classes of Bohemian society and noted that because of the low ticket prices he had set for the theater, even peasants attended his concerts and seemed to have appreciated them.

In Moscow, where music was long associated with only the aristocratic milieus, concert music was performed but rarely, and only when the lyric theaters were either closed or unoccupied. In 1860 the Moscow branch of the Russian Music Society began a series of symphonic concerts under the baton of Nikolai Rubinstein, first director of the Moscow Conservatory, but before that time only celebrated performers were known to produce and direct their own orchestral concerts. Indeed, as Berlioz so hilariously recounts in his *Memoirs*, nonperforming conductors, for the citizens of Moscow (where he spent three weeks in 1847), were rare birds indeed.

Saint Petersburg, the Russian capital, was considerably more sophisticated. A regular concert orchestra, the Saint Petersburg Philharmonic Society, was founded as early as 1802 and gave concerts open to the public in the Assembly Hall of the Nobility. Orchestral concerts were also given in the private mansions of wealthy aristocrats, of course: Beethoven's symphonies, for example, were first performed in Russia at the palace of Count Wielhorsky; and it was another Count Wielhorsky who welcomed Berlioz to the city in 1847. Berlioz' concerts, like those given there by Liszt, Clara and Robert Schumann, Wagner, and other artists, employed experienced, professional players and were received with enthusiasm by a bejeweled public and a diamond-studded imperial court.

Despite the genuine musical talent and awareness he found on his travels, Berlioz was compelled by something inexplicable and deep in his nature to return permanently to the French capital. He did not make an effort to return to Italy, where he had spent time in the early 1830s as winner of the Prix de Rome in composition, for the concert life in that country held no attraction for a composer of his particular abilities. Indeed, though a small quantity of instrumental music was composed in Italy in the nineteenth century, it received little support from the public and none from the leading Italian composer of the period. In letters to the Scala Orchestral Society and to other friends and acquaintances, Giuseppe Verdi, surely speaking for many, made his position on orchestra music perfectly clear: "Why, in the devil's name, must we in Italy produce German art? ... We cannot, indeed I say we must not, write like the Germans, nor the Germans like us" (p. 205). Verdi saw increased attention to instrumental music as potentially ruinous to the Italian lyric theater. He refused the presidency of the Milan Orchestral Society in 1879 precisely because he was "averse to this kind of thing." He even criticized Puccini for having larded his operas with too many symphonic elements.

The one place Berlioz visited on five separate occasions between 1847 and 1855, the one place he might have remained and eventually been able to call home, was London. Unlike Paris, which had only one fine concert society through much of the nineteenth century, London had several. The oldest, the Philharmonic Society, founded in 1813 as a kind of competitor to another series that began in the 1770s, the Concerts of Ancient Music, survived not because of a series of famous conductors but rather on the strength of a series of famous soloists and a number of important commissions (among them that for Beethoven's Ninth Symphony). The New Philharmonic Society, founded in 1852 as a direct competitor to the old, endured only until 1879. These orchestras, both of which Berlioz conducted in the 1850s, followed directly opposite paths vis-à-vis the public: in 1856, the New Society transferred its concerts from the spacious Exeter Hall (with a capacity of three thousand) to the smaller Hanover Square Rooms (with a capacity of nine hundred), raised its ticket prices, and thus rendered its audience more exclusive. In 1869, the old Society moved from these same Hanover Square Rooms to the larger St. James's Hall (with a capacity of two thousand one hundred), lowered its ticket prices, and thus drew more socially varied audiences. Meanwhile, the one-shilling promenade concerts of Louis Jullien attracted regular audiences in London for nearly twenty years. To some, Jullien was a progressive democratizer; to others, he was no better than the vulgar crowd to which he played.

London provided a significantly growing market for numerous composers, conductors, soloists, and orchestral players. As the economist Cecil Erlich has written, the demand for music, as for other cultural goods, was augmented in general by growing urban populations, growing numbers of those earning more than susbsistence-level wages, and growing numbers of those with at least some leisure time. The London musical public grew from the mysterious forces of social emulation, from aspirations to snobbery, and from desires for respectability. Those who pursued serious musical entertainment, whether for aesthetic pleasure, self-improvement, or prestige, increased the scope of the system and in a self-regenerative manner brought music to an ever-wider segment of the population.

In *Howards End* (1910), E. M. Forster gives us a glimpse of a part of the fin de siècle British public:

> It will be generally admitted that Beethoven's Fifth Symphony is the most sublime noise that has ever penetrated into the ears of man. All sorts and conditions are satisfied by it. Whether you are like Mrs. Munt, and tap surreptitiously when the tunes come—of course, not so as to disturb the others; or like Helen, who can see heroes and shipwrecks in the music's flood; or like Margaret, who can only see the music; or like Tibby, who is profoundly versed in counterpoint, and holds the full score open on his knee; or like their cousin, Fräulein Mosebach, who remembers all the time that Beethoven is "echt Deutsche"; or like Fräulein Mosebach's young man, who can remember nothing but Fräulein Mosebach: in any case, the passion of your life becomes more vivid, and you are bound to admit that such a noise is cheap at two shillings.
>
> (Chap. 5)

Forster has his party go to a concert at the Queen's Hall (an auditorium built in 1893 with a capacity of two thousand five hundred) to hear an overture by Mendelssohn, the Beethoven Fifth, and, after intermission, Brahms's *Four Serious Songs.* The writer's half-German Schlegel family, and the aspiring clerk Leonard Bast, who dipped into literature and attended concerts quite clearly to establish his gentility, were no doubt the sort of persons who would meet at an orchestral concert in Victorian or Edwardian London. They and other educated listeners would surely agree that on listening to Beethoven's Fifth Symphony "the passion of your life becomes more vivid."

In the United States, concert societies developed first in Boston and Philadelphia, later in New York and elsewhere, in emulation of European taste and sophistication. Repertory, artists, and even concert manners were entirely European. Indeed, the hospitality afforded to European musicians, in terms of employment opportunities and standards of performance, is an extraordinary phenomenon. For confirmation of the predominance of foreign musicians in the United States one need only think of the conductors of the great American orchestras: Barbirolli, Giulini, Koussevitsky, Ormandy, Rostropovich, Solti, Szell, Toscanini, and more. It is as though the American public could understand and appreciate European art music only as interpreted by European artists.

The New York Philharmonic Society, founded in 1842 and now the oldest American orchestra in continuous existence, was modeled on several European concert organizations, including its namesake, the Philharmonic Society of London. This orchestra, like others that developed in the metropolitan areas of the eastern United States and in certain other cities—Cincinnati and New Orleans, for example, where there were large European immigrant populations—had first to create a public for orchestral music and subsequently to develop that public's listening habits and tastes in symphonic music.

Some of this kind of music education would take place in New York at the open rehearsal—an idea generated by the management to give the public a chance to increase its understanding and enjoyment of works played. But in spite of such efforts, pure orchestral music did not always fire the American listener's imagination, as was noted by the authors of the Philharmonic Society's Sixth Annual Report: "We are living in a community where considerable prejudice exists unfavorable to music in its highest state of cultivation, more particularly to instrumental music" (quoted in Mueller, 42). The management determined that more vocal music had to be included on the orchestra's programs, "in order to satisfy the demands of those ... who would not without it have been persuaded to contribute their support." The fledgling American public, major donors and ticket buyers alike, seems not to have hesitated to make demands on those who would otherwise have prepared concerts more in accordance with the dictates of art than of finance.

That public received written enlightenment from, among other sources, John Sullivan Dwight's music journal, founded in 1852 for the purpose of developing higher standards of musical excellence and taste. But Dwight, whose idol was Beethoven, was rather more of a musical democrat than Robert Schumann, for he wished to plant Beethoven's works in the hearts and minds of the broadest possible segment of the American public. In Europe, Schumann was often preaching to the converted.

The evidence suggests that in the United States, audiences appeared at orchestral concerts as much to demonstrate a kind of exclusiveness as to manifest their elevated economic status. This was nothing new. But the lack of a historically refined, aristocratic musical tradition in the United States seems to have led to a greater receptivity among the populace to the urgings of impresarios such as P. T. Barnum and his imitators. Showmanship, no matter how shallow, became especially crucial to artistic success.

Gatherings at which music was performed in the early nineteenth century often served another, sometimes more fundamental purpose—as an accompaniment to conversation, dancing, dining, or display. Concert-hall decorum, with its demand for quiet attentiveness and concentration, is a relatively recent phenomenon. But the European tradition that also permitted the expression of displeasure (cries and whistles and other varieties of circus behavior) seems, oddly enough, never to have caught on firmly in the American concert auditorium. This may be explained by the greater politeness one might wish to demonstrate in the face of something essentially foreign. In any event, American audiences listening to indigenous American music—black spirituals, blues, ragtime, jazz, swing, and folk music from the seas, mountains, and plains—were and are far more relaxed and far more participatory.

There is another great source of information about the public for orchestral music, the music itself. Composers, like painters, writers, and all artistic inventors, must pose to themselves, in one form or another, as a part of the creative process, the question of who constitutes their audience. They may pose the question more or less consciously or explicitly and manipulate their musical style more or less subtly, in accordance with the preference and instruction of eventual listeners or with the dimensions of the various places of performance. But pose the question they must.

Mozart and Haydn seem usually to have thought highly of their listeners. Their humor, for example, A Musical Joke or the Joke Quartet, poses the expectation that they had for their audiences, for these jokes to be appreciated, since the jokes require a basic understanding of the rules of the major-minor tonal system and an understanding of the fundamental role played in all classic music by regular, periodic phraseology. The story of Beethoven's anger at his neighbor's identification of a "wrong" horn entry in the Eroica Symphony, apocryphal or not, is again suggestive of what he would have hoped for by way of listener understanding. Berlioz' own premeditative techniques—the systematically rising cadential patterns in the "Pilgrims' March" of Harold in Italy, for example, or the careful reversal of the contrapuntal roles of chorus and orchestra in the "Funeral March" of Roméo et Juliette—mark that composer's dependence for appreciation upon the highly sophisticated listener. Bruckner's foursquare repetitiveness or Tchaikovsky's symphonic music for the dance, to say nothing of Richard Strauss's wind machines and bleating sheep, suggest less reliance on the auditor's intelligence.

And what of the sometimes blurred distinction between orchestral and chamber music? For example, Beethoven's *Grosse Fuge,* which was the original finale to his String Quartet in B-flat Major, Op. 130, was long played orchestrally, and the composer himself arranged his Second Symphony for the trio of violin, cello, and piano. Indeed, in the nineteenth century, the arrangement was a great leveler of genres as well as of people: "Here music works the miracle which is generally attributed only to love," wrote Ignaz von Mosel in the Vienna of 1800. "It levels all ranks—the aristocracy and the bourgeoisie, landowners and their tenants, employers and their employees; all sit at a single desk, and in the harmony of sound forget the disharmony of their social positions" (quoted in Antonicek). Arrangements, as well as original solo and ensemble pieces, were likewise central to the fare offered by the music publishers of the period. In fact, the study of music publishing and the musical public go hand in hand. In the first part of the century new audiences were reached with newly economical editions of music produced by the newer processes of lithography and movable type. Once considered an irrelevancy or a nuisance by some eighteenth-century composers, publication became both an honor and a necessity for many nineteenth-century composers; and the publishing business, formerly artisanal, became an industry.

It is clear that the subject of the public for orchestral music encompasses sociological, philosophical, analytical, and economic issues. Close investigations of a quantitative sort may clarify one or another corner of the problem, but will probably not vitiate the broad truth of the formulaic generalizations set out at the beginning of this essay. The public for art music in concert did indeed grow during the nineteenth century from causes both obvious and obscure, and it has continued to grow in our own.

Berlioz, who considered the symphony orchestra "the finest achievement of modern art and the truest manifestation of what we mean by music today," in the opening of À *travers chants* defined music as follows:

> Music is the art of moving, via combinations of sounds, the emotions of intelligent persons gifted with exclusive and cultivated organs of hearing. To define music in such a way is to assert that we do not believe, as others would claim, that music is made for everyone. Whatever the conditions that bring music into being, whatever the means it employs for its effect—simple or complex, calm or energetic—it has always been evident to the impartial observer that, because a large number of individuals are able neither to feel nor to understand its power, these individuals *were not created for music,* and, consequently, that *music was simply not created for them.*

BIBLIOGRAPHY

Theodor Adorno, *Introduction to the Sociology of Music*, E. B. Ashton, trans. (1976). Theophile Antonicek, Program Notes for Archiv Recording 2533-136. Jacques Barzun, *Berlioz and the Romantic Century* (3rd ed., 1969). Ludwig van Beethoven, *Letters*, Emily Anderson, trans. and ed. (1961). Hector Berlioz, *Memoirs*, David Cairns, trans. and ed. (1975). Elisabeth Bernard, "Jules Pasdeloup et les Concerts Populaires," in *Revue de musicologie*, 57 (1971). Otto Biba, "Schubert's Position in Viennese Musical Life," in *Nineteenth-Century Music*, 3 (1979); and "Concert Life in Beethoven's Vienna," in *Beethoven, Performers, and Critics*, Robert Winter and Bruce Carr, eds. (1980). Friedrich Blume, *Classic and Romantic Music*, M. D. Herter Norton, trans. (1970). Peter Burbidge and Richard Sutton, eds., *The Wagner Companion* (1979).

Jean Chantavoine, "L'Ancienne salle du Conservatoire," in *Bulletin of the Association pour le 150ᵉ Anniversaire de la Société des Concerts du Conservatoire* (1978). Jeffrey Cooper, *The Rise of Instrumental Music and Concert Series in Paris, 1828-1871* (1983). Ronald L. Davis, *A History of Music in American Life* (1982). Edouard Deldevez, *La Société des Concerts, 1860 à 1885* (1887). Antoine Elwart, *Histoire des Concerts populaires de musique classique* (1864). Cyril Erlich, "Economic History and Music," in *Proceedings of the Royal Musical Association*, 103 (1976-1977).

Eduard Hanslick, *Music Criticism, 1846–99*, Henry Pleasants, ed. (1950). Georg Kinsky, *Das Werk Beethovens* (1955). H. C. Robbins Landon, *Beethoven: A Documentary Study* (1970). Lewis Lockwood, "Eroica Perspectives: Strategy and Design in the First Movement," in *Beethoven Studies 3*, Alan Tyson, ed. (1982). John H. Mueller, *The American Symphony Orchestra* (1951).

R. Murray Schafer, *E. T. A. Hoffmann and Music* (1975). Anton Schindler, *Beethoven as I Knew Him*, Donald MacArdle, ed., and Constance Jolly, trans. (1966). Carl Schorske, *Fin-de-siècle Vienna* (1981). Leo Schrade, *Beethoven in France* (1942). Maynard Solomon, *Beethoven* (1977); and "Beethoven's Tagebuch of 1812-1818," in *Beethoven Studies 3*, Alan Tyson, ed. (1982). Oliver Strunk, ed., *Source Readings in Music History: The Romantic Era* (1965). Rose R. Subotnik, "Adorno's Diagnosis of Beethoven's Late Style: Early Symptom of a Fatal Condition," in *Journal of the American Musicological Society*, 29 (1976); and "The Historical Structure: Adorno's 'French' Model for the Criticism of Nineteenth-Century Music," in *Nineteenth-Century Music*, 2(1978). Giuseppe Verdi, *Letters*, Charles Osborne, trans. and ed. (1971). Richard Wagner, *My Life*, Andrew Gray, trans. (1983). William Weber, *Music and the Middle Class* (1975).

The Main Forms of Orchestral Music

Elaine R. Sisman

Works for orchestra have always been the most prestigious of all forms of instrumental music. Partly because of their size and "public" nature, and partly because of the growth of both of these aspects over the last 250 years or so, the principal orchestral genres have also been in the forefront of stylistic change.

The main forms of orchestral music are the symphony, the concerto, the overture, and the symphonic poem. Additionally, orchestral suites were popular in the baroque period and reappear in the twentieth century, and composers as great as Mozart have written charming and functional but generally lightweight dance music. Each form has its own array of subgroups as well. The word *concerto,* for example, covers *concerto grosso,* solo concerto, and concertos for two or more soloists, while it overlaps with the symphony in the *symphonie concertante.* Then there are program symphonies, or multimovement programmatic works that cut across the boundaries of symphony and symphonic poem.

Distinctions can be made between types of orchestral music in two major areas: works in several movements (for example, symphonies, concertos) as opposed to single-movement works (overtures, symphonic poems), and works with programs or descriptive intentions as opposed to nonillustrative, or "absolute," music. These two sets of distinctions do not necessarily correlate with each other, although programmatic orchestral works are often in a single movement.

Confusion still surrounds the terms *form* and *genre*. *Genre* normally refers to a type of work whose name is an indication of the performing forces employed, as in the symphony and the concerto, and often the place of performance and subject matter, as in opera and oratorio. Form, on the other hand, popularly carries with the meaning of *genre* but also a more particular meaning—that of the organizing pattern or principle operating within individual movements in any given genre. Forms that one finds in symphonies, for example, may include theme and variation; rondo; minuet and trio (itself a composite of binary forms); ternary, or ABA, form, the paramount sonata form; and all sorts of hybrid combinations. Even programmatic works in the "symphonic poem" genre may embody certain more abstract musical forms, such as sonata and rondo, and indeed, they usually do so. Most works before the twentieth century rely on, or at least refer to, certain time-honored conventions of musical organization. The remainder of this essay will maintain these distinctions between genre and form.

SYMPHONY

The rise of the symphony was nearly coextensive with the rise of the classical style in the eighteenth century. The symphony also was an outgrowth of the establishment of concert life and the emergence of a musical public during the 1730s, when symphonies (sometimes called overtures on concert programs) were nearly always used to open and close concerts. The rest of these concerts usually featured virtuosic soloists (singers or instrumentalists) who were more often than not the motivating force behind the concert in the first place. Occasionally a concert initiated by a composer would feature more than one of his symphonies—for example, Mozart's concerts of 1 April 1784 in Vienna (*Linz* and *Haffner* Symphonies).

Scholars are still debating the specific origins of the symphony. One commonly accepted notion finds its roots in the Italian opera overture, the so-called *sinfonia avanti l'opera,* which, after being standardized by Alessandro Scarlatti in the 1680s, was always in three sections, with a fast-slow-fast ordering. At some point, perhaps as early as the 1730s, the *sinfonia* was separated from the opera to which it belonged, and was performed separately as a "concert symphony." Evidence includes manuscript copies of symphonies by Giovanni-Battista Sammartini, which include no reference to their original status as overtures. Presumably, the increasing number of concerts made more freestanding instrumental works necessary, and the role of symphonies as "overtures" to the concert as a whole made natural the appropriation of actual overtures. Yet the mechanism by which this exchange of genres took place has never been fully or adequately explained; it is perhaps something of an overstatement to say that the Italian opera sinfonia "gave way" to the independent symphony.

Another plausible theory finds the origins of the symphony in the concerto, specifically in the *ripieno concerto* of the early eighteenth century. These pieces are written for an orchestra that acts in a dual capacity both as full complement and as individual sections of soloists (*concertino*). This seems a fruitful line of investigation. Possible links between the symphony and the orchestral suite may be more remote, especially since symphonies nearly always followed a pattern of movements much different from those of the suite. Terminology is, of course, completely unstandardized in sources from the period; it is sometimes not clear from the sources even whether a piece labeled *sinfonia* is for orchestral or chamber performance.

The rise of the symphony in different European centers—most notably Vienna, Mannheim, and Paris—has been well charted in recent years. We now have a fair picture of the work and styles of the principal composers in these centers and their contributions to the genre. The theory, first propounded by Hugo Riemann, that the composers of the Mannheim school originated many aspects of the symphony and the classical style has now been fully refuted. Some Mannheim techniques even had Italian models. Yet, contributions to the genre by Mannheim composers such as Johann Stamitz include frequent use of a four-movement symphonic plan (as opposed to the three-movement Italian model), brilliant orchestration with much soloistic use of winds, and a celebrated style of performance honed with flashy devices like the famous "Mannheim crescendo" and "rocket" fanfare themes.

The four-movement symphony—the earliest example of which is often credited to Georg Matthias Monn in Vienna for his D-Major Symphony written in 1740—became standard by around 1770, although three-movement works continued to appear. After his Symphony no. 30 of 1765, Haydn no longer wrote three-movement symphonies, and all but Symphony No. 60 (*Il distratto*) are in four movements. In Mozart's symphonic output, Italian and Viennese influences are displayed in his use of the three- or four-movement plan, respectively; here, the only anomaly is the Symphony no. 38, K. 504 (*Prague*), a fully mature "Viennese" symphony without a minuet.

Throughout the nineteenth century, the four-movement plan was standard, with such notable exceptions as Beethoven's *Pastoral* Symphony, Berlioz' *Symphonie fantastique,* Schumann's *Rhenish* Symphony, Tchaikovsky's Third Symphony, and Mahler's Second, Third, Fifth, Seventh, and Eighth Symphonies. (All of these are in five movements, except for Mahler's Third and Eighth, which are in six and two, respectively.) In the twentieth century, symphonies in more than four movements have been written by Vaughan Williams and Shostakovich, among others, while many composers have gone back to an arrangement of three movements.

As eighteenth-century treatises on composition, by such theorists as Joseph Riepel and Heinrich Christoph Koch, began for the first time to approach instruction by focusing on genres and forms, the symphony emerged as the locus of normative formal patterns. In fact, an examination of the discussions in such treatises of first-movement form in the symphony is one way of charting the development of what the nineteenth century termed *sonata form,* the most important new formal structure of the classical period. Some modern writers go so far as to say that in the first movements of eighteenth-century symphonies one can trace the rise of the classical style itself.

Eighteenth-century treatises show that the first-movement form could be best explained in harmonic terms. The first section opens in the tonic, modulates to the dominant, and closes there; these harmonic areas may be articulated with contrasting thematic material, but themes are less forcefully described by theorists. The second section comprises two different periods of harmonic activity: the first continues the modulation, moving from the dominant to the relative or mediant minor, and perhaps touching on a few other keys along the way. The second part of the second section returns to the tonic, and restores most of the material of the first section, now all in the tonic key, where the movement ends. This threefold division within two large sections was ideal for a dramatic ordering of tonal presentation, conflict, and resolution.

Calling first-movement form *sonata form,* later writers labeled these three parts *exposition, development,* and *recapitulation,* terms so familiar that it is unlikely that they will ever be satisfactorily replaced, despite their inaccuracies. (Koch's terms "first principal period," "second principal period," and "third principal period" never really caught on.) Nineteenth-century writers concentrated on the thematic contents of each section, giving rise to a recipe for mixing first and second themes with a dash of modulation, spicing with a "thematic development," and rising inevitably into a full recapitulation. This recipe was modeled on Beethoven, and made the eighteenth-century composers look inadequate:

after all, Haydn often did not have a different second theme, Mozart did not have "enough" development, and many other composers had "incomplete" recapitulations. Recent studies have begun to reassert the validity of looking at eighteenth-century structures on their own terms.

For the slow second movement, the same form as that of the first movement was most popular, but with fewer phrases and less expansion and connective tissue. Occasionally these movements were in rondo form, and Haydn wrote a fair number of theme-and-variation second movements. (Koch states that Haydn was the first composer to introduce the theme and variations into the symphony.) Indeed, Haydn created a number of original designs for his symphonic slow movements, especially alternating variations on two themes and an ABA form with development, which were then taken further by Beethoven.

The minuet and trio, the symphony's only apparent debt to the orchestral suite, was the standard form for third movements in four-movement symphonies. Haydn's and Mozart's minuets are richly scored and often either humorous or passionate. Toward the end of his life, however, Haydn remarked that he wished someone would invent a "really new minuet"; the inevitable alteration of two binary forms apparently was wearing thin for him. Beethoven's fast tempos (all but the Eighth Symphony are *allegro* or faster), new structures (abandonment of binary form in the Fifth Symphony scherzo, frequent fugatos, extreme expansion of the second part of the binary in the Third and Seventh Symphonies, sonatalike expansion in the Ninth Symphony), and explosive effects (sudden *tuttis*, shocking climaxes, novel use of timpani) in his symphonic scherzos may be seen as Haydn's answer.

Finales often took the form of the first movement, with a more four-square opening theme (as in the finale of Mozart's Symphony no. 40 in G Minor), but more popular were romping rondos. Haydn and Mozart sometimes combined these two into a hybrid later called "sonata rondo," a form that was described but not named around 1800. Ideally suited to ending a symphony, the sonata rondo featured a square opening theme, often with repeats, that leads into the rest of the exposition, with a second theme in the dominant; a return to all or part of the opening theme in the tonic, in rondo fashion; a development section or an episode with a new theme; and a recapitulation, with the second theme returning in the tonic. The main theme might reappear one final time, and this appearance might occur in the coda. Both Haydn and Mozart started working with this structure in the 1770s, with their most famous examples appearing somewhat later (for example, Mozart's *Haffner* Symphony, K. 385, of 1782, and many finales of Haydn's *London* symphonies).

Almost any of Haydn's *Paris* or *London* symphonies might be taken as paradigmatic of the popular yet sophisticated classical symphony. His Symphony no. 101 (*Clock,* 1794), for example, begins with the dark, minor-key gestures of his typical slow introductions, employing figures that will reappear in the main theme of the movement. Employing two similar themes in the exposition of the opening *presto,* Haydn nonetheless maintains their individuality in the development, adding contrapuntal complexities to the second theme that return with it in the far-from-literal recapitulation. The slow movement, with its "ticking" accompaniment, is a rondo with varied and reorchestrated returns of the main theme and a relatively freely structured middle section. The minuet and trio are each given a distinct profile: the former features elided phrases and strongly contrasting themes, while the latter features solo flute and bassoon over a deliberately monotonous string accompaniment. The finale is one of Haydn's most masterful hybrids. After the typical binary theme, the remainder of the exposition follows, with a closely related second theme. A return to the theme before the development heralds a sonata rondo, here with the added twist that the return is varied and embellished. And when the theme comes back after the development, it takes the form of a fugato, followed by a coda. Thus, the exposition is never "resolved," in terms of sonata-rondo form, yet the movement combines sonata, rondo, variation, and fugue without sacrificing coherence.

A Mozart symphony, on the other hand, is less likely to have a slow introduction; it may have as many as four different themes in the exposition (as well as a host of individual motives, as in the *Prague* and *Jupiter* symphonies); its development section will often recombine those motives in several circle-of-fifths progressions; and its slow movements and finales tend to be more oriented toward sonata form. Perhaps Mozart's most exciting symphonic movement, the finale of the Symphony no. 4l, K. 551 (*Jupiter,* 1788), perfectly sums up all of the stylistic possibilities of the late eighteenth century in a synthesis of *galant* and more "learned" (fugal) styles. The reconciliation of the classical style of motivic counterpoint and the baroque-style fugal counterpoint is fully realized in a sonata movement with a fugal passage in the exposition, double fugue in the coda, and four main thematic motives that are recombined throughout.

With Beethoven, the length and relative weight of symphonic movements changed dramatically. His first two symphonies retain the proportions of Haydn's *London* symphonies, changing only the slow introduction so that it moves without pause into the opening *allegro;* in fact, the first theme of his First Symphony seems to conflate the themes of Mozart's *Jupiter* and Haydn's no. 97. But his *Eroica* (1805) is gigantically conceived; its first movement is substantially longer than the latest and longest ones by Haydn and Mozart. In its thematic and harmonic expansiveness, complex development, and level of dissonance, the movement makes a self-conscious statement about its place in the history of music. All the stories about Napoleon and the French Revolution connected with this work only add to its epic nature. And the finale is given new stature, balancing the first movement in length, complexity, and long-range planning. The finale of the *Eroica* takes on Haydn's alternating variation form (indeed, the whole classical variation tradition) and strikingly transforms the relationship between the two themes (a melody and its bassline) before the end of the piece. That the melodic theme, similar in design to the opening theme of the first movement, ends up in the bass during its last and most triumphal statement provides the symphony as a whole an almost narrative thread.

This type of narrative-thematic thread comes back again and again in Beethoven's Symphonies no. 5 (struggle giving way almost palpably to triumph), no. 6 (this time made explicit with programmatic titles for each movement), and no. 9 (made explicit by the choral finale's text). In the last, of course, the finale shatters all formal precedents and is almost a four-movement symphony in itself. It also led to the inclusion of vocalists in a number of later symphonies by Liszt, Mahler and others, and helped Wagner to justify his synthesis of the arts. Composers in succeeding generations also looked to the unprecedented motivic concentration of the Fifth Symphony's first movement and the linking together of its scherzo and finale; the dramatic character and relatively free structure of the scherzos; the large-scale, static repetition of lyrical motives in the *Pastoral*; the rhythmic unity of the Seventh Symphony; and the mysterious opening (found in many of Bruckner's symphonies) and overwhelming affirmations of the Ninth.

In the nineteenth century, the enormous reputation of the Beethoven symphonies, as well as the increasing size of orchestras and concert halls, put symphonies in the spotlight and caused critical response to individual symphonies to be writ large. In fact, the symphonic literature became an aesthetic battleground; the symphony's purpose and meaning were constantly debated. Beethoven emerged as the great precursor or archetype and was hailed, paradoxically, by both sides in the aesthetic debate as the progenitor of "absolute" and "program" music (the latter stemming mainly from the *Pastoral*). It is often considered appropriate today to divide nineteenth-century composers into "conservatives" (or classicists) like Mendelssohn, Schumann, and Brahms, and "radicals" like Berlioz and Liszt. The former were interested in retaining classical models for the formal design of each movement, while the latter cultivated program music and claimed that the symphonic repertoire needed an extramusical or poetic dimension, thus obviating the use of traditional forms; an early standard-bearer was Berlioz' *Symphonie fantastique* (1830). Yet this apparent dichotomy badly oversimplifies the many stylistic tendencies running through the nineteenth century. And recent research has begun to stress the narrative aspects of "conservative" music and the formal aspect of "radical" music (Newcomb; Kaplan).

Several lines of thought may be isolated in the development of nineteenth-century symphonic style. First is the approach that champions development in its Beethovenian sense—a full exploration of motivic shapes, textures, and harmonic relationships. Then, the many melodies of the Mozart model yield, through Schubert's lyricism, to the appearance of long, closed melodies with an associated episodic style, even in development sections where sequences may be juxtaposed. Finally, the use of thematic transformation—in which always recognizable melodies are presented in different contexts, normally based on a program—often results in looser structures based on juxtaposition, repetition, and alternation.

More than one of these approaches may appear in the works of a single composer. Mendelssohn's Symphony no. 4 (*Italian*, 1833), for example, employs considerable repetition of themes and motives, along with a certain degree of formal freedom (a theme introduced in the development of the first movement comes back in the recapitulation) but its movements are traditionally separated and utilize various techniques of contrapuntal development. Schumann's Symphony no. 4 (1841, revised 1851) is a fully cyclic work, without breaks between movements, in which four themes return, transformed, in several of the movements; it also features formal freedom (a monothematic first-movement exposition is followed by two new themes in the development), along with more traditional developmental procedures.

Both Brahms and Bruckner aspired to carry on the Beethovenian tradition, and each also adopted the kind of lyricism favored by Schubert, yet the results are strikingly different. Brahms's symphonies are the epitome of various developmental techniques (Schoenberg later used the term "developing variation"), even in the expositions and in some cases throughout entire movements (Symphony no. 4), and even in those movements with gorgeous lyrical melodies. Bruckner, on the other hand, who took on a number of Wagnerian devices in his symphonies, created much more loosely structured and expansive works, featuring extensive repetition of themes, choralelike episodes, and alternation of thematic sections, especially in the slow movements (Symphony no. 4 is a good example).

Berlioz' *Symphonie fantastique,* a work of exceptional importance with, however, few direct imitators, amalgamated several different symphonic tendencies. Undeniably influenced by Beethoven's *Pastoral,* its vastly expanded and vivid orchestration immediately made it a landmark work: audiences had simply never heard that kind of sound before. In his essay on Berlioz' symphony, Schumann attempted to make his contemporaries understand it by referring to all the traditional forms with which it could be associated, and indeed, the first three and perhaps even four movements can be so understood. Only the *idée fixe* and the finale still remain objects of criticism, since they require the detailed program provided by Berlioz to be fully appreciated. Yet the *idée fixe,* unaltered in each movement except for rhythm and affect (though truncated in the third and fourth), fits into the lyrical conception in all but the finale. This movement juxtaposes various thematic fragments in preparation for the ultimate arrival of the witches' dance, the principal theme of the movement, which is then worked out with several contrapuntal overlays that allude at times to traditional developmental procedures.

The "program symphony" of Berlioz led to Liszt's works within that genre and to his invention of the "symphonic poem," to be discussed later. And this genre in turn fueled the aesthetic debate between the "radical" forces of Liszt and Wagner, on the one side, and the self-styled keeper of the Beethovenian flame, Eduard Hanslick (and, reluctantly, Brahms), on the other. Hanslick, in *The Beautiful in Music* (1854), wrote that music must express only "musical ideas"—in his most famous phrase, "The essence of music is sound and motion." He rejected the notion that the poetic dimension is primary. Wagner, in a well-known letter written in 1857 in defense of Liszt's symphonic poems, answered Hanslick indirectly by upholding extramusical values and lauding the new and freer non-recapitulatory forms that resulted. The Hanslick side stressed theme, development, and form, the Wagner-Liszt side poetry, melody, and transformation. In a sense, leaving programmatic implications and personal styles aside for the moment, the differences between the two factions centered mainly on the nature of the melodies chosen, the extent to which they are either repeated and presented in different contexts or undergo development, the building of either tightly knit or more episodic structures, and the "splashiness" of the prevailing orchestral sound. Tchaikovsky, then, with his high level of repetition, episodic sonata-form structures (especially in the long, unrelated second themes), and colorful orchestration, continues the Lisztian ideals, even while writing four-movement symphonies whose underlying programs were never made explicit. (In letters, however, he frequently refers to the "content" of his symphonies.) Mahler's symphonies, on the other hand, combine novel orchestral effects with a truly developmental style, even when traditional forms seem to be expanded dramatically. The first movement of his Symphony no. 4 (1901), for example, may be thought of as having two expositions and two recapitulations; it is certainly thematically rich and developmentally diverse.

After Mahler, the symphony was virtually abandoned by Germanic composers, although Hindemith was later to return to it. Composers of the "second Viennese school" either eschewed the genre altogether (Berg) or wrote chamber symphonies (Schoenberg and Webern, the latter a two-movement work titled Symphony). The richest centers of symphonic composition were in Russia, with Prokofiev and Shostakovich; in Scandinavia, with Sibelius and Nielsen; in France and later America, with Stravinsky; in England, with Elgar and Vaughan Williams; and in the United States, with Ives, Copland and Sessions, among others.

Many of these works are in some sense "neoclassical," using elements of traditional tonal organization, contrapuntal development, and sometimes a rich but newly deployed orchestral palette. Diatonic themes may be harmonized chromatically (Prokofiev, Symphony no. 5) or unexpectedly consonant interludes may surface between more dissonant thematic statements (Shostakovich, Symphony no. 5). Recognizable variants of sonata form are often present, with development sections that are lengthy and rhythmically active. Yet the lively and varied rhythmic language often acts as a substitute for other organizational features, especially in Stravinsky, whose symphonies tend to be nondevelopmental, juxtaposing various rhythmic ostinatos (as in the Symphony in Three Movements, 1946). While most composers continued writing in multi-movement formats, even explicitly referring to older forms, a number of works comprising one movement or several movements in one have been written in the twentieth century. As many writers have noted, the multiplicity of styles in this century precludes acceptable generalizations beyond a certain point. But the very prestige and tradition of the symphony have tended to work against it, and composers have often shied away, preferring a kind of one-movement format related to the symphonic poem or "multipiece" formats related to the suite. Or the tradition itself might be invoked to create self-parodying references that call attention to stylistic discontinuities, as in Luciano Berio's Sinfonia (1968), the third movement of which contains quotations from many works

embedded in the frame of the third movement of Mahler's Second Symphony, together with spoken and chanted vocal fragments of a literary,
politically relevant, or merely nonsensical nature. But the lengthier formal continuities normally implied by the label *symphony* are more often
avoided entirely.

CONCERTO

As an orchestral genre that features an opposition or contrast between a
soloist or small group of instrumentalists and a larger instrumental aggre-
gate, the concerto has flourished since the late seventeenth century, amid
ever-changing interpretations of the relationship and precise makeup of
those two groups. The twelve *Concerti grossi*, Opus 6, of Arcangelo Corelli (published posthumously in 1714 but written as early as the 1680s)
are the earliest examples of pieces for string orchestra and *continuo* that
present a *concertino* solo grouping (two violins and cello), derived from
the trio sonata, against the backdrop of the full string body, the *tutti* or
ripieno (originally referred to as the *concerto grosso*). Writings by George
Muffat, who heard Corelli's concertos in the 1680s, suggest that the solo
group was considered paramount. Modern writers sometimes refer to the
pieces as "orchestrally amplified trio sonatas" (Hutchings, 1980).

The first eight of Corelli's Opus 6 are written in the format of the
concerto da chiesa (church concerto), with fast and slow movements alternating, while the other four are in the more suitelike format of the
concerto da camera (chamber concerto), with movements based on
dance forms; however, the two types are not always completely
distinct. The most well-known is undoubtedly his *Christmas* Concerto,
no. 8, with its dramatic and rhetorically persuasive introduction, compelling contrapuntal slow first movement, lyrical aria in second place, and
the moving *Pastorale* at the close. Corelli's masterful use of suspensions
in the solo violins and exciting or spacious *tutti*-reinforced cadences are
among the hallmarks of his style.

Giuseppi Torelli's *Concerti grossi*, Opus 8 (published in 1709), introduced many traits that became standard practice with Vivaldi and later
writers of concertos. Torelli used a three-movement fast-slow-fast ordering of movements, much like the early symphony, and fully half of his
collection comprises solo concertos for violin and orchestra, featuring
elaborate figurations for the soloist. Form in the outer movements tends
to use the *ritornello* as a structural device: the *ripieno* is given the primary thematic material, which recurs between statements of similar or

contrasting ideas by the *concertino*. The Corelli concertos were very loosely structured by comparison. In Torelli's Opus 8, no. 7, for solo violin and orchestra, the *ritornelli* in the first and third movements are fugal, while the solo sections introduce ever more varied, elaborate, and rhythmically active figures.

Handel adopted the Corelli model, writing concertos with varying patterns of tempo and structure. He also employed the trio-sonata *concertino* of two violins and cello in his twelve dramatic *Concerti grossi*, Opus 6 (1739), and he was probably the first to write concertos for the organ. Handel often included fugues in his concertos, and *ritornello* form as the structural focal point. His orchestra is fuller and more varied than Corelli's, calling in some cases for wind instruments.

Vivaldi, on the other hand, took the Torelli model, and Bach received it in turn from him. The sheer numbers and popularity of Vivaldi's concerto output have made him practically the locus classicus of the baroque concerto. His first collection, *L'estro armonico*, Opus 3 (published in 1712), already reveals important facets of his style: long motivic *ritornelli*, parts of which recur between solo sections, elaborate figurations for solo violins, clear modulatory schemes, many sequences, and occasional motivic interpenetration of *ritornello* and solo material. A good example of these characteristics is the first movement of the Concerto for Two Violins in A minor, Op. 3, no. 8. Freer in structure are some of his more programmatic concertos, such as the *Four Seasons*, from Opus 8. He also wrote many solo concertos, including pieces for bassoon and piccolo.

Most of J. S. Bach's concertos come from his Cöthen years (1717–1723) and include solo concertos for violin and harpsichord, the Concerto in D Minor for Two Violins, and the six *Brandenburg* Concertos. Of the latter, three are traditional *concerti grossi* with different solo groups (nos. 2, 4, 5), while the three others are *ripieno* concertos, in which the orchestra is divided into sections, or even sections within sections, that play "against" each other. In each of the *concerti grossi*, one instrument in the solo group receives extra prominence: in no. 2, in which the *concertino* consists of trumpet, flute, oboe, and violin, the trumpet stands out in virtuosity and brilliance, and in no. 4, with a *concertino* comprising two recorders and violin, the violin is most conspicuous. Partly because of its proleptic harpsichord cadenza, the *Brandenburg* Concerto no. 5 in D Major has often been singled out for special mention. Its solo group (flute, violin, and harpsichord) always plays imitatively and sequentially, engaging in imaginative interplay between the motivic treble instruments and the figural harpsichord. The *tutti's ritornello*, on the other hand, provides brief, homophonic waystations on the exciting journey of the first movement. After the lyrical slow movement, in which only the solo instruments play—and in which the harpsichord again has a dual role as *continuo* player and motivic participant—the finale, in ABA form, features new ways of ordering solo and *tutti* in its fugal outer sections.

Although many composers wrote concertos for a wide variety of instruments in the middle of the eighteenth century, posterity has given greatest recognition to the keyboard concertos of Bach's third son, C. P. E. Bach. And research has shown that the theorist Heinrich Christoph Koch probably used C. P. E. Bach's concertos as a model for his descriptions of first-movement concerto form. Because there is a fair amount of terminological and conceptual confusion surrounding this form, it may be helpful to present Koch's simple formulation, which is, as was his description of symphonic first-movement form, given in harmonic terms. He saw three principal solo periods, which correspond to the three main periods of the symphony, surrounded by four *ritornello* sections. The first *tutti* is in the tonic (although it may contain a passing modulation); the first solo period modulates from tonic to dominant; the second *tutti* is in the dominant; the second solo moves to one or more related keys; the third *tutti* effects a transition from a cadence in a related key back to the tonic, where the third solo period returns with its material from the first period; the final *tutti* reiterates the tonic (with space for a cadenza). Within each solo section, the orchestra may bring in *ritornello* phrases. (Koch always refers to the orchestra as "the *ritornello*" and makes clear that *ritornelli* are of secondary importance to the solo sections.)

The terminological difficulty becomes acute in the classical period, when the concerto fully takes on the sonata style. It has become popular to adapt sonata-form terminology to concerto first-movement form, so that the opening *tutti* is called the "first exposition," the solo entrance and modulation the "second exposition," and the following sections proceed apace, with the recapitulation summing up both of the expositions. The problem with this idea, as Donald Francis Tovey recognized, is that the term *exposition* seems absurd for the opening *tutti*, a section that usually does not modulate and the themes of which may or may not return in the soloist's exposition. In other words, as Tovey pointed out, it really is a *ritornello*, not an exposition. Perhaps a good way around this problem would be to refer to the "opening *tutti* section," and to "subsequent *tutti* sections," which do, after all, appear in the expected places.

Mozart's piano concertos, the pinnacle of the genre in the eighteenth—and perhaps any—century, always find new and inventive solutions to the problem of classical concerto form. Piano concertos were

Mozart's "characteristic creation," according to Alfred Einstein, and as most of them were written for his own subscription concerts, they were the showpieces of his career in Vienna in the 1780s. They feature elegant and often virtuosic solo parts and present both dialogue and opposition between the protagonists, with dramatic ordering of tone colors and textures. Especially significant is the new prominence given to the wind instruments from the B-flat Major Concerto, K. 450 (1784), on. Second-theme groups are typically shared between piano and winds. The piano's statements of themes are continuously varied (the state of some of the autographs shows that figurations were frequently changed), and the concertos encompass forms ranging from theme and variations to sonata-rondo types, to simple ABA structures in middle and final movements. In the first movements, Mozart's *tutti* themes may bear little or no relation to the themes of the solo exposition, as in the C-Minor Concerto, K. 491, or there may be real parallelism between *tutti* and solo, as in the G-Major K. 453. Indeed, part of the drama of the C-minor work is in the tension created between the opening *tutti* motive, which always retains its identity, even in rhythmic and melodic transformations, and the more lyrical solo themes, which always give way either to figurations or to the *tutti* motive itself.

At the same time that Mozart was writing his concertos, a kind of hybrid of concerto and symphony was making its presence felt, particularly in France, although adherents included Mannheim composers, J. C. Bach, and even Mozart and Haydn. The *symphonie concertante* is similar to the *concerto grosso* only in its use of a solo group of instruments; in format, structure, and style, it more closely resembles the classical concerto. Beautiful melodies, two or more instruments simultaneously showing off virtuoso capabilities, popular rondo finales—these features combined to make the *symphonie concertante* the rage of Parisian concert life. The term *symphonie concertante* is applied today principally to works that used the name.

With Beethoven's concertos, we enter a period in which composers began to write fewer works, but at the same time to give each one a sharply individual profile. Even though he continued to explore devices already used by Mozart, Beethoven interpreted them anew. For example, he begins the Piano Concerto no. 4, Opus 58 (1806) with the piano; Mozart had introduced the piano into the opening *ritornello* in his Concerto in E-flat Major, K. 271 (1777). Beethoven then gives the orchestra the sequel on the same pitches but in an unexpectedly remote key: the effect is extraordinary. And in the same concerto, Beethoven introduces themes that modulate within themselves each time they proceed; Mozart had already experimented with such themes in his G-Major Concerto, K. 453. But now Beethoven begins the finale with a modulating theme, so that the movement begins in the "wrong" key. And he links the second and third movements together with a transition, as he also did in his Fifth and Sixth Symphonies and the Violin Concerto. His concerto slow movements sometimes appear to "speak"—either through ethereal figurations, as in the Violin Concerto and Third Piano Concerto; or else nearly literally, in the Fourth Piano Concerto, which Liszt likened to Orpheus taming the beasts of hell.

Nineteenth-century composers in many cases dispensed with an opening *tutti* section, creating instead a "confrontation" between soloist and orchestra, which are thus on an equal footing from the beginning. Though the soloist would sometimes simply have an opening flourish and then subside (using the precedent of Beethoven's *Emperor* Concerto), Mendelssohn's G-Minor, Schumann's A-Minor, and Brahms's B-flat Major piano concertos, among others, present an almost symphonic opposition right from the start. A symphonic parallel is also suggested by the four-movement scheme of Brahms's B-flat Major Concerto. The appearance of a scherzo in second position reassigns the weight of the movements: the first movement, with its famous horn call, now becomes broadly lyrical, with the piano and orchestra sharing the same material, while the scherzo has true symphonic intensity. The slow movement continues the formal expansion of the ABA structure that Brahms had already explored in many other works and introduces another *concertante* soloist to balance the pianist. In the Violin Concerto, a solo oboe gave out the lovely melody of the slow movement; here it is a solo cello, and the cello and piano emerge as equal partners at the close. Finales still tend to be rondolike in structure, with foursquare themes and expansive codas, and are often given a special character, as in the "Hungarian" finale of the Violin Concerto.

Another type of romantic concerto is the virtuoso showcase. Of course, technological advances in the instruments went a long way toward giving soloists a better chance of competing with an orchestra, especially in the spotlight of fiendish figurations. While the difficulties of the works by Brahms or Schumann should not be minimized, technical display "for its own sake" was routinely avoided in their works, in favor of thematically based figurations. But in works like the violin concertos of Paganini and the piano concertos of Liszt and Tchaikovsky, the almost demonic capabilities of the soloist come to the fore. This tendency derives in part from the combination of brilliance and poetry in the solo writing of Chopin's two piano concertos. Liszt's First Piano Concerto recycles and transforms its themes, while those in Tchaikovsky's concertos are merely repeated. Liszt's model spawned many imitators.

The twentieth-century concerto is as diverse as the twentieth-century symphony, and traditional forms are as frequently in evidence. Some composers have maintained classical opposition between soloist and orchestra, with sometimes ferocious solo writing (Prokofiev, Shostakovich); others have harkened back to the more continuous give-and-take of the baroque concerto (Stravinsky, Berg, Sessions); and still others have attempted not only to reinterpret or redirect the relationship between solo and *tutti* but to find new ways of deploying the *tutti* elements themselves (Bartók, Carter). Stravinsky's Violin Concerto (1931) bears a self-conscious resemblance in style to Bach's solo and double violin concertos; in his *Dumbarton Oaks* Concerto (1938) the relationship to Bach's *Brandenburg* Concerto no. 3 is explicit. Berg's Violin Concerto (1935) is a quasi-programmatic meditation on the death of Alma Mahler's daughter, and though written using the twelve-tone method, it utilizes tonal elements (a Bach chorale). Elliott Carter's Double Concerto for Harpsichord and Piano (1961) divides the orchestra into two groups, one for each soloist, in a witty reassessment of the nature of the genre. Bartók's Concerto for Orchestra (1944) returns at times to older ideas about *concertante* instrumental writing and traditional forms; the first movement has a clear sonata structure with a "mirror" recapitulation, divides its themes between different solo instruments or groups, and has a development section that announces itself dramatically, as in "tradition-oriented" twentieth-century symphonies. Most modern concertos are marked by a brilliant polyphony and formidable technical difficulties.

OVERTURE

The word *overture* has come to be applied to works in three categories: the single- or multimovement composition played before an opera, oratorio, or ballet; the single-movement prelude to a nonmusical dramatic work; and the single-movement concert work detached from its original context (if it ever had one) and performed alone. The first meaning applies from the seventeenth century to the present, while the second and third stem primarily from the nineteenth century. (When a three-movement overture was detached from the larger work in the eighteenth century, it was often called a symphony. Because terminology was so free in the eighteenth century, however, symphonies and suites were sometimes called overtures.) The overture might be divided into two types, based on function: the "dramatic," meaning those intended to precede a staged musical work, and the "concert," for freestanding works from a literary work or play (Temperley).

Baroque dramatic works generally began with either a French or Italian overture. The French overture, standardized by Lully in the seventeenth century, consists of two linked sections, slow and fast, the slow part being a series of stately gestures and flourishes featuring dotted rhythms, ending on a half cadence, with the following fast section normally imitative or fugal in style. Purcell and later Handel favored this form; well-known examples are the former's overture to *Dido and Aeneas* and the latter's to *Messiah*. The Italian overture is a three-movement piece with a fast-slow-fast ordering; the finales were frequently dancelike in character. A typical mid-eighteenth-century Italian-type overture is George Christoph Wagenseil's to his opera *La clemenza di Tito* (1746), which also is known on its own as a D-Major Symphony. The brightly scored opening *allegro* has considerable thematic differentiation, the lyrical *andante* is in the relative minor, while the concluding *presto* is a short, binary piece in triple meter.

With the late eighteenth century came the standardization of the overture as a one-movement work, most often in sonata form and sometimes with a slow introduction. Mozart and Haydn both stopped writing three-movement overtures in the 1770s. In many cases, the overture led immediately into the first scene, and a special concert ending had to be provided for separate performance. Beginning with Gluck and continuing with Mozart, overtures featured a few essential musical ideas from the opera (as in *Don Giovanni*, in which the overture's introduction returns in the Stone Guest scene, and *Così fan tutte*, 1790, the overture to which contains the punchline of the opera). Haydn's oratorio *The Creation* (1801) opens with a fully programmatic orchestral introduction, the "Representation of Chaos," an extraordinary departure in the history of the overture.

Beethoven was the first composer to write overtures for occasions that traditionally had called for symphonies: the emperor's name day (*Namensfeier*, 1815) and the opening of a theater (*Die Weihe des Hauses*, 1822). Particularly significant in these cases was the concept of a concert overture with no programmatic associations; the latter even contains a double fugue. He also outdid previous composers, albeit unintentionally, by providing so many overtures (four in all) to his much-revised opera *Fidelio* (1805). But perhaps his most well-known overtures are those to the nonmusical dramas, *Coriolan* (1807, a play by Collin, not Shakespeare) and Goethe's *Egmont* (1810). In fact, Beethoven also wrote incidental music to *Egmont,* following the stunningly dramatic overture with four entr'actes, two songs, and three more orchestral movements. These include the final triumphal *Siegessymphonie,* which recalls the close of the overture.

Mendelssohn's concert overtures are held in much higher esteem than most of his symphonies, and two of them are indeed splendid. The overture to *A Midsummer Night's Dream* was composed in 1826, when the composer was only seventeen, long before the rest of his incidental music to Shakespeare's play. Effectively contrasting the different "levels" of the story with sprightly, high-register fairyland music, hunting horns and regal chords for the duke, lyrical melodies for the highborn lovers, and buffoonery for Bottom, the piece nonetheless proceeds in an elegant sonata form. All of these moods are echoed in the later incidental music. And in Mendelssohn's *Fingal's Cave,* or *Hebrides,* Overture (1830), the agitated waves lap around the first theme group but give way to a transcendent second theme (the greatest melody he ever wrote, according to Tovey). Indeed, this juxtaposition of a rhythmically active section with a supremely lyrical one provides the most pungent of the many special pictorial and programmatic effects Mendelssohn aimed for in his overtures.

Composers continued to write overtures throughout the nineteenth century, in many cases inspired by Mendelssohn's example. As in the past, some of these were inspired by dramas (Wagner wrote an overture to Goethe's *Faust,* for example), others were evocative in a more general way (Brahms's *Tragic* Overture), while still others were occasional pieces with brilliant effects (Tchaikovsky's *1812* Overture). Some overlap begins to occur in the middle of the century between the overture and the new genre that Liszt dubbed the symphonic poem. In the second half of the century, many composers of one-movement programmatic or descriptive works preferred to use Liszt's designation for what they previously would have called overtures. Yet there were exceptions, and some preferred to create their own labels. For example, Tchaikovsky called his 1870 *Romeo and Juliet* overture an "overture-fantasy" after its last revision in 1880.

SYMPHONIC POEM

Liszt coined the term *symphonische Dichtung* to describe his one-movement orchestral works that were born of poetic ideas and aspired to a unique synthesis of the literary or visual and the musical. The principal technical means he used to accomplish this was thematic transformation, the presentation of a single theme in different contexts with suitable rhythmic and affective alterations. His symphonic poems were constructed in several linked sections with differing tempos, keys, and themes. Wagner was delighted that Liszt rid himself of the tyranny of the recapitulatory forms, creating new forms governed instead by the dramatic development of the subject at hand. Wagner also recognized that the roots of the genre lay in the overture and in Berlioz' program music.

Liszt began writing symphonic poems during his Weimar period (*Les Préludes*, written 1848); within six years Hanslick's treatise on the primacy of "absolute music," *The Beautiful in Music*, arrived and the stage was set for the ever-increasing polemics between the Liszt-Wagner and Hanslick-Brahms factions. Although the genre of symphonic poem did not survive as such much past the first quarter of this century, the controversy has continued. The most enduring problem is the most vexing: Can music be about something? (An excellent recent examination of this question is contained in Jacques Barzun's 1980 article.) Tovey's answer was, "It is always characters and moods that are successfully portrayed, while chronology is useless and the illustration of incidents is apt to be ridiculous unless it contrives to be witty" (1956, 170). One could then argue that since many of Liszt's symphonic poems do not attempt to portray incidents but precisely "characters and moods," then he succeeds, especially in *Les Préludes*, with its loosely connected series of episodes alluding to the life cycle. Curiously, the dramatic or pictorial overtures of Beethoven and Mendelssohn never seem to excite the ire of the absolute-music faction, nor does Mendelssohn's constant reliance on extra-musical imagery ever weaken the assertion that he was a "conservative" composer.

The introduction by Liszt of the symphonic poem had two immediate consequences. The first was the proliferation of such pieces, especially outside Germany, by such composers as Smetana, Dvorak, members of "The Five" and Tchaikovsky in Russia. The second was the transferral of some of its traits, such as the linked-movement scheme and thematic transformation, into normally multimovement genres, such as Liszt's own piano concertos and Cesar Franck's Symphony in D Minor. But, of course, thematic transformation was hardly an innovation of Liszt; he acknowledged his debts to Berlioz' *Symphonie fantastique* and even composed his own "program symphonies," the *Faust* and *Dante* symphonies.

Two of the best and best-known symphonic poems are Smetana's *The Moldau (Vltava)* and Tchaikovsky's *Romeo and Juliet*, which offer quite different approaches to the genre. Smetana's musical depiction of the course of a river in his native Bohemia carries a detailed program about the joining of two small streams into a larger river, the hunting horns and peasant dances heard on its banks, nymphs dancing by moonlight, and swirling rapids, until the mighty river flows past Prague into the Elbe. As imagery, the music is unsurpassed. Yet the wealth of detail never obscures the thematic unity of the piece, which is in effect a loose rondo with several reiterations of the principal river theme, and with rhythmic reminders of that theme running throughout the episodes.

Romeo and Juliet, on the other hand, bears only the Shakespearean title and the associations it implies, and is constructed in a kind of sonata form. And yet those associations are clear: the choralelike slow introduction evokes the character of Friar Laurence, the agitated first theme depicts the feuding families, and the lyrically episodic second theme represents the young lovers. Although the connection with sonata form is a loose one, the development does contrapuntally work out the inevitable clashes between the intensifying feud and the friar's attempts to solve the insoluble. The recapitulation then contains further juxtapositions of the vengeful families and the friar's futile efforts, leading to a funeral procession and the joining of the lovers after death. All of this can be read into the piece without recourse to a more explicit program than that provided by the title; indeed, it might be argued that *The Moldau* is equally clear without Smetana's program. Both pieces describe and represent extramusical ideas, the one full of pictorial allusion and nationalistic emotion, the other an exposition of situation and unfolding of dramatic conflict.

Clearly either piece would "work" without program or title, but whether the extramusical dimension and the poetic inspiration are necessary for a complete appreciation is less clear. Hanslick allowed that one could hear in the Beethoven symphonies "impetuousness and struggle, unsatisfied longing and defiance, all supported by a consciousness of strength," yet these characteristics are not necessarily representative of specific ideas or incidents; as Beethoven himself said, the *Pastoral* symphony was "more the expression of feelings than tone-painting." The difference between representation and expression is a crucial one in this context.

Later symphonic poems continued the trends established earlier, although the only significant body of such works were Richard Strauss's tone poems (the term he preferred). Filled with the sweeping, effervescent orchestral color that was his hallmark and that demanded virtuosity, especially from the brass and wind sections, these works combine more or less detailed programs with loosely applied traditional forms. *Don Juan* may be associated with sonata form, *Till Eulenspiegel* with rondo, and *Don*

Quixote with variations, and yet the pieces are at the same time episodic and narrative, with frequent transformations of their main themes. *Don Quixote* also presents an interesting combination of genres, in that it features a solo cello and viola; the first programmatic work to give some of the spotlight to a single solo instrument throughout had been Berlioz' *Harold in Italy* (1834), a "symphony with viola obbligato."

Debussy's programmatic music merits special comment. His *Prélude à l'après-midi d'un faune* (1894), evoking the fleeting moods and images of the Mallarmé poem, creates a delicate tracery of tone colors and textures. Despite the subtle chromatic and whole-tone nuances, the piece introduces a quasi-Wagnerian melody in the middle. But designation for Debussy's other orchestral music is problematic. The *Nocturnes* (1901), for example, are a kind of set of "characteristic pieces for orchestra," and yet no other model but the symphonic poem suggests itself as appropriate. Similarly, *La Mer* (1905), subtitled "Three Symphonic Sketches," may be thought of as three related symphonic poems or as a program symphony with descriptive titles.

The question of genre in one-movement orchestral works of the twentieth century is a tricky one because composers continue to give pieces vague designations (like "symphonic sketch") and because scoring becomes more unusual. Can Charles Ives's *The Unanswered Question* (1906) be considered a symphonic poem? It is certainly based on a program, yet its rather small ensemble is hardly "symphonic," but rather small and spatially conceived. Roger Scruton considers the idea of program music in the early part of the century to have been crushed under the weight of its own pretensions, as expression and representation gradually become indistinguishable in programmatic works. It might be argued that Stravinsky, as one of several composers who reacted against romantic ideals and abandoned program music, nonetheless continued to write representational works in the form of ballet scores such as *Le sacre du printemps*, *Apollo*, and many others.

SUITE

The origins of the suite, which in the baroque period was a series of pieces mostly based on dance forms and unified by their tonality, are in the fourteenth century. By the mid-seventeenth century, suites for keyboard and for various small instrumental combinations were being written throughout Europe. Perhaps the earliest suites written for a large body of instruments were those performed by the Vingt-quatre Violons du Roi, which performed at court entertainments in the mid-seventeenth century. It is not always clear, however, just what kinds of ensembles played at other entertainments of this period. But even at this early stage, suites were often created by extracting pieces from ballets and other large works; Lully, for example, wrote practically no suites per se, but arranged or had made dozens of suites of dances from his orchestral music. This practice, after more than a century of disuse, came back in favor in the nineteenth century, when most suites were made up of extracted pieces from ballets (Tchaikovsky's *Nutcracker* Suite being the best known).

The high points of the baroque orchestral suite are the four suites of Bach (which he called "overtures") and the two collections by Handel, the *Water Music* and *Music for the Royal Fireworks*. The first and fourth of Bach's suites were probably composed at Cöthen, while the second and third date from the later Leipzig period, perhaps for use by the *collegium musicum* that Bach directed between 1729 and 1737. Each one begins with a French overture, in which the fast section is a fully drawn fugue, although in no. 4 the counterpoint is more lighthearted. The scoring for each suite is different: in addition to string orchestra with *continuo*, the first has two oboes and bassoon; the second, a solo flute; the third, three trumpets, timpani, and two oboes; and the fourth, three trumpets, timpani, three oboes, and bassoon. The sequence of dance movements after the initial overture changes as well; suites nos. 1 and 2 each have seven movements, while nos. 3 and 4 have five, and each has at least one dance movement unique to itself.

Bach approaches the style of Handel's suites most closely in the two with trumpets and timpani, but even here characteristic differences are apparent, Bach's textures, even to the spacing of chords, being consistently denser and more complex. The charming flute solos of the B-Minor Suite are in a style similar to that of Telemann. In the finale to this suite, the *Badinerie*, the flute embellishes the simple line played simultaneously by the violin. Bach's Suite no. 3 is perhaps the most famous, at least in part because of the air that was later arranged as the "Air on a G String" and in part because it has the most brilliant scoring of the four.

Handel's *Water Music* is probably his most immediately appealing instrumental composition. Yet there are real difficulties in establishing the original sequence of the twenty-one movements. Tempo indications and dance types are often not present in the extant sources. The three suites making up the *Water Music* were composed at different times, though all were probably performed during a royal procession on the Thames in 1717. The Suite in F Major is scored for two horns, two oboes, bassoon, and strings, that in D major for two trumpets, two horns, two oboes, bassoon, and strings, and that in G major for recorder, flute, and strings. Only the F-major suite, the longest of the three, has a real French overture. The most frequently performed is the D major, with its regal melodies and festive alternations of trumpets and horns. This piece makes up most of the extracted *Water Music* Suite that is most well known today.

The *Fireworks Music* was written to honor the peace at Aix-la-Chapelle in 1749, and it thus includes movements called *La Paix* and *La Réjouissance*. Calling for massive forces of wind and brass, it was later reorchestrated by Handel with added strings. While more coherent than the sprawling *Water Music*, it lacks some of that music's melodic sweep.

The orchestral suite virtually disappeared after the baroque period, as its place in the repertoire was taken over by larger genres like the symphony. Composers still wrote sets of dances, but such works were purely functional pieces for balls and other gatherings and tended to be all of one kind; throughout his career Mozart wrote many sets of minuets, German dances, and contredanses, but none of these sets constitutes a suite. A few composers wrote suites in the nineteenth century, for various instrumental combinations; Massenet wrote eight for orchestra.

In the early twentieth century the orchestral suite experienced a resurgence in popularity, partly as a result of neoclassical ideals. Composers began to write suites in the style of, or as an homage to, earlier composers (such as Ravel's *Le tombeau de Couperin*, a 1917 piano work that he orchestrated in 1919), or in many cases took over the earlier works wholesale (Respighi's *Ancient Airs and Dances*, 1917–1931). Programmatic suites also appeared (although Holst admonished that his orchestral suite *The Planets*, 1918, contained no program music), but here the term *suite* did not usually appear in works' titles.

It is uncertain whether modern multimovement pieces that fall into no other category may be considered suites by default or if the dance component of earlier suites must still be present. The problem of the traditional tonal unity of suites in a posttonal age must also be considered. Can Schoenberg's *Five Pieces for Orchestra*, Opus 16 (1912), and Webern's *Five Pieces for Orchestra*, Opus 10 (1926), be considered suites? Each piece in each set explores tone colors and textures through atonal means, and in that sense both sets are unified in approach. A recent study by Jonathan Dunsby has perhaps offered a solution to the genre problem in these cases, by suggesting that groups of pieces published together be examined to see if they are "multi-pieces" or "collections," the former with and the latter without some integral connection. Discussions of orchestral genres in the twentieth century all run aground on precisely the same issues.

MISCELLANEOUS ORCHESTRAL PIECES

Few compositions for orchestra that fall outside of the major categories were written before the nineteenth century, although one finds the occasional single concerto movement—a *Konzertstück*, fantasy, or rondo—from Mozart's time on. Brahms's *Variations on a Theme by Haydn* (1873), probably the first really well-known independent set of variations for orchestra, inspired others to write such works, some of which feature a soloist. Among the latter are Tchaikovsky's *Variations on a Rococo Theme* (1876) for cello and orchestra and Franck's *Symphonic Variations* (1886) for piano and orchestra. Many sets of variations have been written for orchestra in the twentieth century (Reger, Schoenberg, Webern, Dallapiccola, Nono, Britten, Carter).

The fantasia for orchestra, a related type, also has roots in the nineteenth century (for example, Schumann's Fantasia for Violin and Orchestra); a well-known example is Vaughan Williams' *Fantasia on a Theme by Thomas Tallis* (1910). But most compositions for orchestra in the twentieth century are outside the major classifications. Many are highly individual, in a sense inventing their own categories. Orchestral music in this century has been written in a host of unconventional formats, making precise formal definitions impossible.

BIBLIOGRAPHY

Gerald Abraham, *A Hundred Years of Music* (4th ed., 1974). Jacques Barzun, "The Meaning of Meaning in Music: Berlioz Once More," *Musical Quarterly*, 66 (1980). Barry Brook, "The Symphonie Concertante: An Interim Report," *Musical Quarterly*, 47 (1961). Louise Cuyler, *The Symphony* (1973). Jonathan Dunsby, "The Multi-Piece in Brahms: *Fantasien*, Op. 116," in Robert Pascall, ed., *Brahms: Biographical, Documentary, and Analytical Studies* (1983). Walter Frisch, *Brahms and the Principle of Developing Variation* (1984). David Fuller, "Suite," in *New Grove Dictionary of Music and Musicians*, edited by Stanley Sadie (1980).

Arthur Hutchings, *The Baroque Concerto* (3rd ed., 1973); and "Concerto," in *New Grove Dictionary*. Owen Jander, "Beethoven's 'Orpheus in Hades': The *Andante con moto* of the Fourth Piano Concerto," *Nineteenth-Century Music*, 8 (1985). Richard Kaplan, "Sonata Form in the Orchestral Works of Liszt: The

Revolutionary Reconsidered," *Nineteenth-Century Music*, 8 (1984). H. C. Robbins Landon, *The Symphonies of Joseph Haydn* (1955). H. C. Robbins Landon and Donald Mitchell, eds., *The Mozart Companion* (1969). Jan LaRue, Nicholas Temperley, and Stephen Walsh, "Symphony," in *New Grove Dictionary*. Anthony Newcomb, "Once More Between Absolute and Program Music: Schumann's Second Symphony," *Nineteenth-Century Music*, 7 (1984). Leslie Orrey, *Programme Music* (1975).

Ursula Rauchhaupt, ed., *The Symphony* (1973). Charles Rosen, *The Classical Style* (1972); and *Sonata Forms* (1980). Roger Scruton, "Programme Music," in *New Grove Dictionary*. Edwin J. Simon, "The Double Exposition in the Classical Concerto," *Journal of the American Musicological Society*, 10 (1957). Oliver Strunk, *Source Readings in Music History* (1950). Nicholas Temperley, "Overture," in *New Grove Dictionary*. Donald Francis Tovey, *Essays in Musical Analysis: Concertos* (1936); *The Forms of Music* (1956); and *Symphonies and Other Orchestral Works* (repr. 1981). Homer Ulrich, *Symphonic Music* (1952).

The Orchestra in Opera and Ballet

Katherine T. Rohrer

Though many music lovers today think of the orchestra primarily as a concert organization, for roughly the first century and a half of its existence it served almost exclusively to provide music for stage works. In the sixteenth century, large ensembles of wind and string instruments were included in the lavish productions of *intermedii*, which were performed between the acts of plays given on ceremonial occasions at the Florentine court. The first large opera orchestra was that for Claudio Monteverdi's first opera, *L'Orfeo* (1607); the score calls for about forty players. The first permanent orchestra is thought to have been the string ensemble in the service of the king of France, Les Vingt-quatre Violons du Roi, established by Louis XIII by 1626 and later directed by Jean-Baptiste Lully.

At times in their histories, opera and ballet have been twin arts; in France, certainly, the popularity of dance shaped the structure of opera from its very beginnings through the nineteenth century. The orchestra is an essential contributor to both forms. Instrumental music—not only in its affective or emotional content but also simply through its variety of timbres—is crucial to the development of dramatic atmosphere and tension. Just as a modern film score can tell the audience when to prepare for a shock, the operatic score can tell the audience what to feel or even indicate that the characters are feeling something different from what they are saying. The ballet score, besides providing music to accompany the dance, joins with the dancers' gestures and movements to narrate the drama.

Throughout the development of opera the orchestra has not only accompanied singers but has also contributed on its own, in overtures, ballets or other dance sequences, descriptive pieces (depicting, for example, storms, sunrises, and battles), marches, wedding music, funeral music, and stage-band music. Through Richard Wagner's compositional innovations, the orchestra has also become entrusted with the role of narrator; especially in the long and episodic *Ring des Nibelungen*, the leitmotivs help to provide continuity and clarity within the complicated plot.

Ballets are included in the operas of many composers—Monteverdi, Lully, Gluck, Mozart, Rossini, Verdi, and Wagner among them. But the full-length romantic ballets of the nineteenth century tended to attract a different group of composers, those who were willing to subjugate musical independence to the requirements of choreography. Ballet scores by Adolphe Adam, Alois Minkus, and Léo Delibes still hold a place in the repertoire; but even first-rank composers such as Tchaikovsky, Stravinsky, and Prokofiev are better known for their ballet music than for their operas. The diminishing role of dance within twentieth-century opera is paralleled by the increasing practice of choreographing independent dances to instrumental music not originally intended for that purpose, as in the plotless ballets of George Balanchine and Jerome Robbins set to the music of Chopin or Mendelssohn.

THE SEVENTEENTH CENTURY

The birth of opera in the last decades of the sixteenth century was by no means the beginning of stage music in Italy. Besides incidental music for spoken dramas and music in pastoral plays and madrigal comedies, a musical production called an *intermedio* was performed between the acts of plays, reaching elaborate proportions on festive occasions. Such productions were recorded in Florence from 1539 onward. Most famous are the six *intermedii* performed with Bargagli's comedy *La pellegrina* (May 1589) as part of the celebrations for the wedding of Grand Duke Ferdinand de' Medici and Christine of Lorraine. Among the composers contributing to these *intermedii* were Jacopo Peri and Giulio Caccini, who later became pioneers of opera. The instruments in the orchestra included violin, viola da braccia and viola da gamba, violone, lute, guitar, chitarrone, harp, recorder, cornett, trombone, and harpsichord.

While both Peri's and Caccini's operas on the text *Euridice* (1600) were apparently accompanied only by small string ensembles, Monteverdi's *L'Orfeo* (1607) returned to the large Renaissance orchestra of the *intermedii*. Two items that contribute to the success of this work in modern revivals are its many short but lively dance sections (mainly the *ritornelli* in strophic songs) and its colorful use of instrumental timbres, including the careful manipulation of different *continuo* instruments for the various characters and scenes, as well as the virtuosic writing for pairs of violins, recorders, cornetts, and a double harp in the great central aria "Possente spirto" of the third act. The association of trombones with supernatural elements in the underworld scene of the fourth act was a convention that would reappear throughout the next two centuries.

Most records indicate that the orchestras of midcentury Venetian opera were on the small side and may frequently have consisted only of strings. Scores like Cesti's *Pomo d'oro* (1667), which calls for violins, viols, trumpets, cornetts, trombones, flutes, bassoon, violone, regal, cembalo, and "gravi organo," were the exception rather than the rule. Yet much uncertainty remains about the instrumentation of the more typical works. Some scholars believe that the Venetian manuscript of Monteverdi's mature masterpiece, *L'incoronazione di Poppea* (1642), which is very short on instrumental parts other than those for the *continuo*, is an accurate reflection of the way in which the piece would have been presented; others think it must be a rehearsal score and that lost instrumental parts should therefore be reconstructed in order to create a more authentic performance.

In France, the dominant stage genre for the major part of the century was the *ballet de cour*. More than five hundred of these entertainments were produced at the French court between *Circé, ou le ballet comique de la reine* (1581), thought to be the first true example of the genre, and the death of Louis XIII in 1613. The musical components of these works included *récits*, narrative portions usually sung by a solo voice; *entrées*, individual dances that corresponded to the entrance of a unified group of dancers who often impersonated, for example, farmers, monsters, provincials, or Turks; and *grands ballets*, danced by the nobles and sometimes by the king. The genre continued to thrive during the reign of Louis XIV, whose chief musician, Jean-Baptiste Lully, was himself a dancer.

Lully's *Ballet d'Alcidiane* (1658) was performed by an orchestra of more than eighty instruments, including thirty-six violins, flutes, viols, harpsichords, guitars, lutes, and theorbos. It is also notable for its overture, which displays the characteristic dotted rhythms and fugal second section of the French overture, which was to reign for almost a century.

The French operatic genre, *tragédie lyrique* or *tragédie en musique*, was molded by Lully to combine elements of Italian opera and French dramatic and dance traditions. The popularity of the *ballet de cour* ensured the presence of numerous dance movements in the opera; other instrumental sections, all called generically *symphonies*, accompanied dramatic action. Lully's scoring relied on a distinction between the *grand choeur* (*ripieno*) and *petit choeur* (*soli*), the latter consisting of probably ten instruments, including two violins, two winds (the same performers doubled on flutes, recorders, oboes, and bassoons), and *continuo* instruments, including cello, theorbo, and harpsichord. This group often accompanied solo airs. The full contingent consisted of five-part strings, six to eight players of the aforementioned wind instruments, and an occasional trumpet and kettledrum. The three middle string parts were performed by violas.

The discipline and precision of Lully's orchestra became famous throughout Europe. He was a demanding conductor, not above breaking a violin when its player could not meet his musical standard.

THE EIGHTEENTH CENTURY

In the early eighteenth century, the sprawling baroque opera was subjected to its first official reform, as extravagances of plot were trimmed to produce the *opera seria*. Primarily a string of recitatives accompanied only by *continuo* (*recitativo semplice*) and solo arias, the opera seria was enlivened by imaginative scoring, especially in the works of Handel. Later in the century opera seria yielded to some influences from the *opera buffa*, the comic opera, which had developed out of the two-act comic intermezzo.

In France the brilliant dance traditions of the *opéra-ballet* continued, while the debut of Jean-Philippe Rameau as an opera composer at the age of fifty with *Hippolyte et Aricie* (1733) transformed the languishing *tragédie-lyrique*. Rameau's string writing, reflecting changes that had occurred around 1720, reduced the texture from five parts to four. His orchestral innovations mainly center around the use of wind instruments: he wrote numerous obbligato bassoon parts, exploited the non-Lullian sounds of the horn and piccolo, and introduced the clarinet to the orchestra at the Opéra. Because of the wholesale reorchestration of many scores in the old complete edition of Rameau's works, a full assessment of his powers as an orchestrator awaits the publication of a new critical edition, now in progress.

The French integration of plot, dance, and music received a stronger dramatic focus at the hands of Christoph Willibald Gluck, whose operatic reforms redressed some of the infelicities of opera seria. Among the guidelines set forth in his 1769 preface to *Alceste* is the stipulation that the overture should set the mood of the drama. Gluck's noble and simple style was hardly innovative in its use of the orchestra, although he did occasionally employ specific instruments for extramusical purposes. His orchestration was fanatically admired by Hector Berlioz, who took a number of examples in his *Grand traité d'instrumentation* (1843) from Gluck's operas.

Gluck's operatic reform was paralleled by a like-minded movement in ballet—an attempt to make the dance more expressive by unifying music, gesture, and plot—undertaken by the choreographers Jean-Georges Noverre and Gasparo Angiolini. Gluck collaborated with Angiolini on the ballet *Don Juan* (1761); the trombones associated with the Stone Guest in this score reappear in Mozart's *Don Giovanni* (1787).

George Frideric Handel used a wider variety of instruments in his operas than contemporary opera seria composers and employed them in endless combinations of independent lines and vocal and instrumental doublings. The basic baroque orchestra of strings, oboes, bassoons, and *continuo* was enlarged in most of his operas through the addition of one or more flutes, recorders, horns, trumpets, cornetts, or chalumeaux (a precursor of the clarinet); the harpsichord of the *continuo* might also be joined by theorbo or harp.

In his book *Handel and the Opera Seria* Winton Dean argues that Handel's use of instrumental color reflects deliberate aesthetic choices. Supportive evidence for this assertion can be found in abundance in *Giulio Cesare* (1724). Cleopatra's arias, for example, are distinguished as much by their instrumentation as by their dramatic type. The seductive "V'adoro pupille" uses a lush, concerto-type scoring, with a solo group of oboe, strings, theorbo, harp, and bassoon. Her lament "Piangerò la mia sorte," in contrast, exploits the plaintive low register of the transverse flute. Cleopatra's big scene in the third act, in which her declining fortunes are finally reversed, includes a chain of movements that rely heavily on instrumentation for their effect. As the apparently defeated queen prepares to take leave of her faithful servants, a doleful F-minor *adagio* is played by solo oboe and strings. The heightened dramatic intensity of the following monologue calls for recitative of the *accompagnato* type (that is, accompanied by instruments other than those of the *continuo*). Suddenly Cleopatra and her maids hear the sounds of battle, represented by rapid string and oboe passages. Caesar rushes in, announces his victory in *recitativo semplice*, and departs, leaving Cleopatra to exult in the bravura aria "Da tempeste." Her virtuosic vocal part is matched by a brilliant solo violin line; the bright E-major tonality (eminently suited to strings) contrasts sharply with the F-minor that opened the scene.

In addition to the long *ritornelli* that appear in da capo arias, purely instrumental passages in Handel's operas include marches, dances, sinfonias (to accompany dramatic action), processions, and, of course, overtures. Handel normally used the French type of overture, which he scored for four parts (oboes and bassoons presumably doubling the violins and basses); but he also usually added another movement or two, frequently a binary-form dance scored more lightly for two trebles and bass.

The products of Mozart's twenty-odd years as an opera composer reveal not only his own stylistic growth but also a maturation of orchestral technique that in some cases followed, and in others led, general developments of the period. Mozart's operas of the 1770s are fairly consistent in their instrumentation of double flutes, oboes, and bassoons, a brass section of pairs of horns and trumpets, timpani, and four-part strings. According to custom, when the bassoons were not given their own lines, they played along with the cellos and double basses on the bass line. Similarly, the flutes customarily doubled the oboe line when not otherwise employed. The violas frequently had no independent part, simply playing *col basso* at the octave.

In his mature operas, Mozart dispensed with most of these conventions, taking greater control over orchestral coloring by providing independent lines for each instrumental group. Beginning with *Idomeneo*, the great opera seria of 1780, he added clarinets to his opera orchestra. From this date trombones also began to appear when required by supernatural or ceremonial situations: the oracle in *Idomeneo*, the Stone Guest in *Don Giovanni*, and the mystical circle of priests in *Die Zauberflöte* (1791). The piccolo is used for the storm music in *Idomeneo*, along with the "Turkish" instruments of *Die Entführung aus dem Serail* (1782)—triangle, cymbals, and bass drum. The magical instruments that play so important a role in *Die Zauberflöte* included a regular flute, a keyed glockenspiel, and a piccolo, which stands in for Papageno's reed pipes.

Other unusual isntrumental demands in Mozart's operas include clarinet replacements: two examples are the bassett horns used in Constanze's aria "Traurigkeit ward mir zum Lose" in *Die Entführung*, and a bassett clarinet, pitched a major third below the regular B-flat clarinet, for the obbligato part in Sesto's "Parto, parto, ma tu ben mio" from *La clemenza di Tito* (1791). And while pizzicato strings are used to represent Cherubino's guitar in *Le nozze di Figaro* (1786), Don Giovanni's serenade, "Deh vieni alla finestra," requires a real mandolin.

Mozart's early operas begin with the three-movement Italian overture or *sinfonia*, which developed in late-seventeenth-century Naples and became standard throughout Europe by the mid-eighteenth century. As did his contemporaries, Mozart eventually abandoned the last two movements of the fast-slow-fast group and expanded the opening *allegro*, usually employing sonata form with or without a development section. The overture to *Die Entführung* replaces the development with a C-minor *andante* episode that presages the first vocal number in the score, Belmonte's arietta, which is magically transformed to C major. Sketches show that Mozart originally intended to include a similar minor-key episode in the overture to *Figaro*. This was to be a *siciliano* in 6/8 time positioned right before the recapitulation; the four measures that are crossed out in the autograph show an opening for solo oboe and pizzicato strings.

While some of the overtures (*Così fan tutte*, 1790; *Figaro*) are complete entities, ending with a cadence in the tonic, others (*Entführung*; *Don Giovanni*) end with a transition directly into the first scene and thus need to be provided with a different ending for concert performance. Many of the overtures include one theme or motive that appears later in the opera: in addition to the example of the *Entführung* overture mentioned above, others include the chords eventually to be set to the words "Così fan tutte" in that opera; the *dreimalige Akkord*, or three sets of triads, that are a central Masonic symbol in *Die Zauberflöte*; and, in the most dramatically effective example, the use of the hair-raising D-minor music associated with the Commendatore as a slow introduction to the full sonata-form overture to *Don Giovanni*. This use of thematic material from the body of the opera was expanded by Beethoven, for example, in the *Leonore* Overture no. 3 and by Weber in *Der Freischütz*, overtures that still retain sonata form. The technique was also used in shorter preludes, for example, the curse motif in Verdi's *Rigoletto*, and became the guiding principle in the looser medley or potpourri overtures that characterized nineteenth-century comic opera or operetta and later served to introduce Broadway musicals.

A few specific examples of Mozart's orchestral technique must be mentioned. In *Die Entführung*, Constanze's famous bravura aria "Martern aller Arten" is a breathtaking piece of work not only for the soprano but also for the orchestra, which here features flute, oboe, violin, and cello as *concertante* soloists. The interplay between the voice and the solo instruments reminds us of another fine example, the "Et incarnatus" from the C-Minor Mass of about the same period.

Perhaps the most famous Mozartean orchestral tour de force is the dance scene from the first-act finale of *Don Giovanni*. As the guests gather for the party, a stage orchestra of two oboes, two horns, and strings is twice heard trying out its dance tunes. When the dancing begins in earnest, not one but three stage orchestras provide the music, and it is in their coordination that Mozart truly dazzles. The first orchestra strikes a stately triple-meter minuet for Donna Anna and Don Ottavio. As these two try to keep an eye on Don Giovanni, he invites Zerlina to join him in a contredanse (in duple meter) played by the second orchestra, which has just finished tuning up. In order to distract Zerlina's angry boyfriend Masetto, Leporello whirls him away in a sprightly *Teitsch* (German dance) in 3/8 time. Now all three dance bands are playing at once, a miracle they sustain for fourteen measures before Zerlina's screams break the spell and return control to the main orchestra.

THE NINETEENTH CENTURY

The last master of classical opera buffa, Gioacchino Rossini, also contributed to opera seria the compositional conventions that would dominate Italian romantic opera until midcentury. After Rossini, Italian opera was dominated by the long career of Giuseppe Verdi.

The Opéra in Paris entered a new era of magnificence and influence with the development of "grand opera," a five-act extravaganza featuring complicated plots, crowd scenes for the chorus, spectacular ballets, and a fresh exploration of instrumental color via its large orchestra. Solo writing for winds and brasses was newly cultivated. The great French virtuoso of orchestration, Hector Berlioz, applied his skills most impressively in his problematic but incomparable *Les Troyens* (1858).

In Germany the role of orchestral music in creating dramatic atmosphere was expanded in the works of Carl Maria von Weber. Richard Wagner assimilated French grand opera, German romantic opera, and his own philosophy about the goals of art in a series of overwhelmingly effective music dramas. He expanded the size of the orchestra not only by adding (and even inventing) wind and brass instruments but also by increasing the population of the string sections.

The nineteenth century was a crucial time in the history of dance. It saw the development of the romantic ballet, a full-length plotted work that featured exotic, supernatural, or tragic elements and was much more the spinning of a tale in movement than a compilation of entertaining dances. With the growth of pointe technique, the ballerina became the focus of the art.

Although the historical importance of Rossini may lie primarily with his influence on the development of serious Italian opera in the nineteenth century, his reputation is based on his comic operas, chiefly *L'Almaviva, ossia L'inutile precauzione*, better known as *Il barbiere di Siviglia* (1816). Equally beloved are Rossini's many opera overtures, which have been a staple of the concert repertory for over a century and a half. These overtures usually take the shape of a sonata-form movement without development. A slow introduction is typical, as is the delegation of the first theme to the strings and the second to the winds. The second theme group also usually contains the famous Rossini crescendo, created through the repetition of a simple phrase—usually of two or four measures and alternating tonic and dominant harmony—with ever increasing numbers of instruments, registral spread, and dynamic level.

The crescendo appears in many numbers of *Il barbiere* but never with greater effect than in Don Basilio's aria "La calunnia." The technique is used here not merely to create mounting excitement but to illustrate the text. As the orchestral crescendo builds up in seven distinct stages, Basilio describes the course of slander, from a tiny breeze of a whisper to "an explosion like the shot of a cannon." His aria has a sly double purpose: in the plot, to convince Doctor Bartolo to let him put about some damaging lies about Count Almaviva; and for the delectation of the experienced Rossini audience, to describe in words one of the most delicious of the composer's orchestral techniques (Gossett).

Rossini was responsible for the crystallization of certain forms for arias, duets, larger ensembles, and finales that became the standard in Italian opera for at least half a century. The role of the orchestra in the structure of these forms is considerable. For instance, the typical large scale Rossinian aria begins with an orchestral introduction (comparable to the opening *ritornello* of a baroque da capo aria), which includes an exposition of the first or second thematic idea of the aria and ends on a well-articulated full cadence. *Il barbiere* includes five arias and two finales that begin in this manner; the introductions range in length from eight measures to forty-three in Figaro's "Largo al factotum," though here the singer actually joins the introduction with a bit of offstage humming. This kind of instrumental introduction was adopted in turn by Bellini, Donizetti, and Verdi, who parodied it in the oddly truncated opening to "La donna è mobile" (*Rigoletto*).

An important function of the orchestra in Rossini's comic works is the provision of an instrumental melody against which buffo declamation can take place, particularly in finales. Vocal dialogue set against a backdrop of instrumental melody is a technique that served many different styles of nineteenth-century operatic composition. Another central feature of Rossini's comic style that relies heavily on orchestral definition is the clear-cut, headlong rhythmic drive characteristic especially of the finales. In one passage of the *stretta* of the first-act finale of *Il barbiere*, for instance, each beat of the measure is assigned to a different group of instruments—the first to a trombone, the second to the horns, the third to the clarinets, and the fourth to the piccolo and sistro (a percussion instrument of the glockenspiel type)—creating a rapidly alternating sparkle on top of the racing voices and strings.

The orchestra of *Il barbiere* is not a large one, though the score does call for two piccolos in addition to two flutes. Three notable additions to the percussion section are the aforementioned sistro, the guitar (which by itself accompanies the Count's second, successful serenade to Rosina), and the piano (required for the music-lesson scene, where it is used in conjunction with the orchestra). The piano might also have been used in place of the harpsichord for the accompaniment of recitatives.

Giuseppe Verdi was first and foremost a dramatist. Despite his traditionally Italian orientation toward vocal rather than instrumental beauties, he knew well how to make his orchestra an active contributor to dramatic effect. In his early works Verdi adapted his orchestration to the particular attributes of his singers; for instance, during the writing of *Ernani* in 1843, he was unwilling to begin the orchestration until the piano rehearsals had begun. But at least by the time of *Rigoletto* (1851), he had begun to think of important instrumental motives in terms of their characteristic scorings.

Unlike Wagner, Verdi was no great experimenter in terms of the composition of his orchestra, which in its basic form consisted of strings, flute and piccolo, two oboes, two clarinets, two bassoons, two trumpets, four horns, three trombones plus cimbasso (a bass brass instrument), timpani, bass drum, and other percussion as needed. Later Italian works add a third flute and English horn; those originally intended for Paris add cornets and two extra bassoons, which were available there. In addition, certain operas call for special touches of color, such as the straight trumpets in *Aida* or the mandolin and bagpipes in the second act of *Otello*.

Rigoletto reveals not only conventions inherited by the composer but also the inventiveness of scoring that emerged in operas of his middle period. The opera begins not with a full-scale overture in modified sonata form (such as that of *Luisa Miller*) but with the most concise of preludes, centered on a single musical idea: the motive of Monterone's curse, which is so important to the drama that Verdi originally intended to entitle the work *La maledizione*.

The grave and spine-chilling effect created by the brass fanfare at the opening and the *tutti* climax with wailing strings is then immediately dissipated by the sound of flippant dance music as the curtain rises. This is the *banda* (stage band), that collection of independent musicians which invaded the opera houses not only of Italy but also of Paris (where Adolphe Sax, prolific inventor of musical instruments including the saxophone, directed the *banda* in midcentury). The composition of this group changed from place to place, so that Verdi never orchestrated its music but instead provided a two-stave score to be fleshed out as appropriate. The *banda* music that opens *Rigoletto*, like that in the first act of *La traviata*, provides a background of melody against which Verdi writes lively declamation for his singers. The technique of combining orchestral melody with what is in effect a replacement for recitative is familiar from the works of Rossini. Another example from *Rigoletto* occurs at the beginning of the famous third-act quartet, "Un dì, se ben rammentomi." In a similar way, the introduction of the assassin Monterone is accomplished with a melody for solo cello and double bass in octaves, accompanied by lower winds and strings and by the dialogue between Rigoletto and Monterone.

In brilliant contrast to the dark orchestration of this mysterious and unsavory encounter stands Gilda's music in the next scene, particularly the fine woodwind introduction to her aria "Caro nome." Another notable passage is the accompaniment of flutes and pizzicato string arpeggios to Gilda's invocation of her dead mother—a scoring that will return poignantly at her own untimely demise.

The Duke's famous canzone "La donna è mobile" parodies two conventional techniques of earlier nineteenth-century Italian opera (including Verdi's own works): mindless oompah-pah accompaniment and the practice of starting an aria by having its opening phrase played by the orchestra—which here chooses a comically inappropriate pitch upon which to halt.

Perhaps the most famous instrumental music in the opera is that of the storm scene in the third act. From its odd, evocative opening with open-fifth chords in the lower strings and a single high oboe pitch above, through its pictorial devices of rapid flute and piccolo figures for lightning and a chromatic humming chorus for the wind, to its pitch of musical excitement at the dizzily hurtling trio as Gilda rushes in to her doom, the scene is a showcase for Verdi's most imaginative orchestral scoring up to that date.

Another storm scene marks Verdi's final period, one of astonishing development and revealing of a musician whose capacity for invention remained fresh even into his old age. *Otello* (1887) opens without overture or prelude of any kind. The terrifying storm that threatens the doomed hero is depicted by a rich variety of orchestral activity, including both old and new effects—the lightning of *Rigoletto* alongside a sustained cluster of three notes, each a semitone apart, to be played on the organ. The love duet that closes the first act contains another example of the reminiscence motive (like Monterone's curse in *Rigoletto*). The kiss, which is but a stage direction in Shakespeare, is given verbal expression by the librettist Boito; the soaring sequential melody accompanying Otello's breathless request for "un bacio... ancora un bacio" will return only once, to literally stunning effect, in the last measures of the opera.

This duet shows a kind of orchestral writing that would have been inconceivable in the operas of Verdi's earlier years. Its major characteristic is the rapidity with which the scoring changes to create instrumental coloring appropriate to the words of the lovers. To effect the transition between the angry scene in which Otello breaks up the fight and the coming ecstatic nocturne, Verdi reduces the orchestral forces, first to solo winds and then to a single solo cello, which is joined by three others to open the duet, "Già nella notte densa." Desdemona's entry is accompanied only by muted violins and violas, until she reaches the word *rammenti*. The world of memory is then opened by a giant registral expansion into a three-and-one-half-octave C-major chord, given added articulation by a harp arpeggio. As the duet continues, each new line of thought producing a new orchestral color, unity is ensured by a frequent reliance on tremolo figures in both strings and winds, and by the reappearance of the four solo cellos at the end.

Carl Maria von Weber's *Der Freischütz* marks a significant point for the growing importance of the orchestra in the creation of operatic atmosphere, though the composer's choice of instruments per se is unexceptional. The brass section consists of four horns, two trumpets and three trombones, with timpani, and though the standard woodwind contingent is expanded only by two piccolos, these play a rather important role. They are introduced first in the villain Caspar's drinking song, "Hier im ird'schen Jammerthal." Their saucy figure, all in high-register thirds, of trills and octave leaps decorated with grace notes, is then transferred with chilling effect to the bravura aria that follows, in which Caspar shows his evil hand to the audience. The piccolos' only other appearance is in the Wolf's Glen scene. With the exception of a brief appearance at the opening of the scene, they are reserved for the wildest passage, the frightful natural (and supernatural) terrors that accompany the casting of the seventh and last bullet—the one that will go where the Devil directs it.

This scene is famous precisely because of its romantic atmosphere: the combination of virtuoso stage effects and highly evocative orchestral and vocal writing cannot fail to thrill the audience. The mournful F-sharp-minor tonality is established by tremolo strings and clarinets in thirds in the low part of their register—the sign of the demonic Samiel, who was thus announced while slinking around the stage during the hero Max's aria in the first act. An offstage chorus utters unearthly whoops. The actual casting of the bullets is a melodrama, in which spoken dialogue—here, primarily Caspar's counting of the bullets—is combined with the music. Each bullet is accompanied by a different scenic effect, for which Weber created deliciously descriptive music. A wild boar crashes across the stage to a careening diminished-fourth figure in the bassoons and double basses; the four horns, bassoons, and trombones announce a ghostly troop of hunters; the full orchestra creates a ghastly storm to finish the scene.

This last musical idea is one of several from the opera to make its way into the overture. Also included are Samiel's clarinet thirds, the syncopated C-minor figure that accompanies Max's premonition that he is beset by dark powers, and the triumphant C-major tune that first appears in Agathe's second-act aria and returns to seal the happy ending of the story. This overture is not a potpourri, however, but a big sonata-form movement complete with slow introduction. Most of Weber's overtures are attractive enough to have outlived their operas.

Richard Wagner is the composer who immediately comes to mind in any consideration of the orchestra in operatic works. Not only in his expansion of the dimensions of the orchestra, both in numbers of strings and in numbers and types of winds and brass, but also in his use of instrumental music to further the drama, Wagner was the great innovator of his century. Some have argued that the orchestra is more important than the singers in Wagnerian opera, and that the action of the drama is more clearly spoken by the music than the text. In Donald Jay Grout's judgment,

> he was original in placing the orchestra at the center, with the essential drama going on in the music, while words and gesture furnished only the outer happenings. From this point of view his music dramas may be regarded as symphonic poems the program of which, instead of being printed and read, is explained and acted out by persons on the stage.
>
> (p. 411)

The use of leitmotivs, or "leading motives," to narrate the drama is the technique most frequently associated with Wagner's orchestral writing. The association of these short, characteristic motives—often defined by their orchestral color as much as by their pitch and rhythmic content—with characters, objects, concepts, dramatic situations, and emotions is clearly helpful in holding together such a sprawling concoction as *Der Ring des Nibelungen*. But the identification of the leitmotivs tends to stifle serious analysis of the composer's musical language. A better approach is to consider the contribution of the instrumental music to the emotional progress of the drama. Of one thing the listener can be sure: in no sense can the orchestra be construed as a mere accompanist to the singers.

Wagner's operas contain long stretches of purely instrumental music. Like previous works, they begin with overtures or preludes, and some (notably the Paris version of *Tannhäuser*) include dance music. But there are also long internal instrumental sections, such as "Siegfried's Rhine Journey" in *Götterdämmerung*, and even fairly sizable passages in which the characters are fully engaged but simply not talking. One such is the music in the first act of *Tristan und Isolde* immediately following the drinking of the love potion. Isolde has just proclaimed "Ich trink sie dir!" to the motive of the rising minor sixth and successive falling half steps first introduced by the cellos as the opening notes of the prelude. As she drinks, a *fortissimo tutti* chord dissolves into the same haunting wind sonority that followed in the prelude, adding the four-note rising chromatic line to the aforementioned cello motive. The long instrumental passage that follows is essential to the expression of the intense emotions of the two characters; mere gestures cannot suffice. The music combines material from the prelude with new effects, including tremolo strings crescendoing on a harsh diminished-seventh chord and a harp entering with a delicious F-major arpeggio on a deceptive cadence that only partially alleviates the tension of the moment. At this point, the lovers find their voices, crying each other's names to bits of motives that we already know in their instrumental forms.

The opening of the second act is especially noteworthy for its instrumental requirements. The score calls for six horns, and "more if possible," behind the scenes, as well as the four in the orchestra. Wagner uses these forces to depict the departing hunting party of King Mark, but also to show us something of Isolde's mental state. While the cautious Brangäne can still hear the distant horns, her impatient mistress hears only the burbling of a spring created by shimmering alternating-third figures in clarinets, second violins, and violas against sustained pitches in the first violins—divided into four sections—and the bass clarinet. Thus, two competing groups of instruments describe alternate realities on at least two levels: the foreground of natural sounds of hunting horns and water, and the background of Isolde's real-world marriage to Mark and her spirit-world bond with Tristan. She closes her mind to the threatening horns, dashing the torch to the ground as she banishes the harsh light of earthly existence and embraces her night of love.

An important example of the use of instruments on stage is the English-horn part in the third act. The shepherd who is keeping watch for Isolde's ship plays a mournful, chromatic song—the "alte Weise," or ancient melody, on which Tristan reminisces in his delirium. The actual arrival of the ship is announced by a happier and simpler tune. Wagner insisted that the first melody, because of its difficulty, be played behind the scenes by the regular English-horn player, but he thought that the second could be handled either by another English horn (after the first player had returned to his duties with the rest of the orchestra) or perhaps on a "specially built simple natural instrument."

Memorable creations of instrumental color are sprinkled throughout the Wagner canon. Two popular favorites—chronologically close but at opposite ends of the timbral palette—are the overture to *Tannhäuser*, with its rich, resonant opening for horns, clarinets, and bassoons, and the prelude to the first act of *Lohengrin* (1848), which uses four solo violins with the rest divided into four parts to create a shimmering curtain of sound. The music of each passage is associated with an element of the drama (the pilgrims, the Holy Grail), and in each case the musical content is inseparable from its orchestral color. The opening of *Das Rheingold* (1854), itself a prelude to the *Ring* drama, is an extended orchestral meditation on a single E-flat triad, and one of the most original evocations of water in Western music.

The quintessential Wagnerian ensemble is the *Ring* orchestra, whose dimensions are worth recording here. The number of strings required totals sixty-four: sixteen first violins, sixteen seconds, twelve violas, twelve cellos, and eight double basses. Woodwinds are quadrupled except for the bassoons, which number only three. Wagner suggested a specially constructed alto oboe as a stronger replacement for the English horn. The brass section shows the greatest expansion: eight horns, four of which double on tenor and bass Wagner tubas (actually bass horns); an additional tuba (contrabass); three trumpets and bass trumpet; three trombones and contrabass trombone. The large percussion section includes two pairs of timpani, triangle, cymbals, tenor drum, glockenspiel, and gong. The orchestra is completed by six harps. Well over a hundred players are required in all.

While the nineteenth-century musical scene in Italy and Germany was spread among numerous cultural centers, opera and ballet in France continued to be centralized in the capital. The Opéra, besides being home to the finest ballet company in Europe, produced grand opera (which had to have sung recitative). The Opéra Comique, the more progressive of the two institutions in the latter part of the century, accepted works with spoken dialogue, and hence was the original home of Bizet's *Carmen* (1875).

According to Richard Strauss, "If you want to learn how to orchestrate ... study the score of *Carmen*." Bizet's masterwork, despite its deceptively popular nature, is an astonishing achievement in subtle, economic, yet richly atmospheric scoring. The composer relies principally upon the strings, adding woodwinds and brass for special effects. Much of the score is therefore extremely clean and transparent. Extensive use of pizzicato further lightens the string-based texture. This is perhaps intended to imitate the sound of the guitar and add to the Spanish atmosphere of the piece.

The orchestral *tutti* is rare in this score; it never accompanies solo singing, for Bizet was always careful to avoid overbalancing the voices. In the overture and its source music in the fourth act, the *tutti* is used to create a blatant, overstated sound associated with the crowds of the bullfight. The first and main part of the overture, *allegro giocoso*, is in rondo form, using the opening idea of the fourth act's "Quadrille des toréros" as its *ritornello*. Both this passage and the two that serve as contrasts—the F-sharp-minor section and Escamillo's F-major theme—are structured in eight-measure phrases, further reinforcing the popular nature of the music. The holiday spirit of the overture changes abruptly in the second section, *andante moderato*. Against the background of tremolo violins and violas, an ominous D-minor motive with an augmented second is played by unison cellos, clarinets, bassoons, and cornets. This motive is variously associated with Carmen, the doom she brings upon herself and Don José, and fate. It reappears on a carefully limited number of occasions, most notably in the card duet in the third act and at the end of the opera.

In this final scene, the deadly combat between Carmen and José is played out against the music of the bullfight, performed offstage by the chorus, two cornets, and three trombones. The orchestra in the pit concentrates on the fate motive and also poisons the final repetition of the toréador music with its insinuating half steps.

Bizet uses instrumental color to depict his characters' conflicting spheres of existence. The raucous scoring of the overture represents not only the crowds who populate the bull ring but also the relatively sunny and uncomplicated character of Escamillo. The military side of Don José's life is first depicted in the march and chorus of children in the first act.

At its opening, the bugle call of an offstage cornet is answered by one in the orchestra. The march tune itself is introduced by two piccolos (as fifes) and cornet, accompanied by pizzicato strings. The flute, which is associated with Carmen in her opening number, the "Habañera," is effectively used to speak for her in the "Chanson et Mélodrame" that follows. Zuniga (speaking, not singing) questions the gypsy about her role in the cigar-factory fight, but Carmen refuses to answer, instead singing an impudent melody, "Tra la la la la, coupe-moi." As Zuniga presses on with his interrogation he is mocked by the little tune, first played by the flute and later taken up in turn by a solo violin, a clarinet, and cellos.

The clash between Don José's military obligation and his attraction to Carmen is embodied in a most original manner at the opening of the long duet in the second act. As Carmen sings and dances for him to the accompaniment of castanets and pizzicato strings, two cornets from backstage sound a retreat, summoning José to rejoin his troops. The two disparate musical ideas join in a remarkable counterpoint, and the mesmerizing gypsy works away at her suitor's will, reducing him to inarticulate cries of "Carmen, pitié! O mon Dieu! Hélas! Ah! tais-toi!" The moody José later recovers himself enough to sing one of the great tenor arias of the repertory, "La fleur que tu m'avais jetée." The accompaniment includes high divisi violins and ecstatic arpeggios in the harp and clarinets but also, most notably, the very first appearance in the score of the English horn, the singular tone of which at once announces the aria and perfectly describes the mournful temperament of Don José in love.

Throughout the opera, the instrumental writing does much to reinforce the all-important rhythmic verve of the music. In addition to providing its delicate and sophisticated accompaniment to the voices, the orchestra also has a chance to shine in three colorful entr'actes.

The troubled history of Modest Mussorgsky's *Boris Godunov*, the flawed masterpiece of nineteenth-century Russian opera, has been due in part to the composer's alleged incompetence as an orchestrator. Both the first and second versions of the score (completed in 1869 and 1872, respectively) were originally rejected for performance by the theater management to which they were submitted. After the premiere in 1874, the work received a middling success before being withdrawn from the repertoire in 1882. At this point the work's admirers began to harass it. Rimsky-Korsakov feared that the *Boris* would disappear permanently from the stage unless improved by himself. (Indeed, his zeal encompassed more than just this opera; he declared in 1896 that he would feel satisfied "only after having revised the whole of Mussorgsky's output.")

Under the guise of repairing the "poverty of orchestration" in the original score, Rimsky-Korsakov rewrote much of the piece entirely, changing melody, harmony, scoring, and dynamics at will. He inserted some newly composed passages and changed the order of the last two scenes. Rimsky-Korsakov's version was the one favored in opera houses until recent years, when the cruder harmonies and less polished surface of the original score came to be preferred by many.

Mussorgsky's original orchestration is indeed simple in the extreme but hardly as inept as has been claimed. His biographer M. D. Calvocoressi cites a study by the Russian scholar Gliebof which concludes that the composer's "technical errors are no more numerous than those which composers with far greater experience commit; and a good many of these are due to the novelty of his conceptions and the difficulty of carrying them out at that time." Yet composers continued to be drawn to the score with their own pens in hand. Karol Rathaus altered Mussorgsky's orchestration for a Metropolitan Opera production in 1952. Shostakovich produced a version that was performed in 1959. He worked from Mussorgsky's vocal score and then compared his own scoring to that of both Mussorgsky and Rimsky-Korsakov; when either of these had a version he preferred to his own, he substituted it. In some cases he wrote for instruments not present in either of the other scores.

In Shostakovich's assessment, Mussorgsky functioned well when orchestrating soft passages (such as the scene in Pimen's cell, often singled out for its evocative scoring), but because of his lack of training, he was at a loss with the climaxes, loud passages, and orchestral *tutti*. Yet the coronation scene, with its crashing bells and gongs, and the part of the St. Basil scene in which the crowds cry to Boris for bread are two of the most dramatically effective moments in Mussorgsky's original score.

The birth of the romantic ballet may arguably be traced to a specific work of grand opera, Meyerbeer's tremendously successful *Robert le diable* (1831). The third act contains a famous ballet scene in which Robert, the son of a demon, is set upon by a band of ghostly and debauched nuns. The supernatural atmosphere was greatly aided by the existence of gaslights, which had been installed in the theater just a few years previously. The mother superior of this wayward order, Maria Taglioni, was featured the next year in *La sylphide*, usually counted as the first romantic ballet. (Two scores to this work survive: the original by Jean Schneitzhoeffer, and a second one by H. S. Løvenskjold, which was choreographed by August Bournonville.)

The ballets from this period that have survived into our own century are *Giselle* (1841; choreography by Jean Coralli and Jules Perrot, music by Adolphe Adam) and *Coppelia* (1870; choreography by Arthur Saint-

Léon, music by Léo Delibes). The scores of these works are surprisingly attractive despite their enslavement to the four-measure phrase. The demands of the choreography placed a premium on sharp, clearly defined rhythms; colorful instrumentation was essential for interest and variety. The romantic interest in exoticism and local color inspired the inclusion of dances like the mazurka, czárdás, and bolero in *Coppelia*.

For most modern music lovers the high point of nineteenth-century ballet music is the work of Peter Ilyich Tchaikovsky. Though not a ballet specialist like Minkus or Cesare Pugni, both of whom provided much of the music required by the Imperial Ballet in St. Petersburg, Tchaikovsky was persuaded to meet the stringent requirements of the genre in three scores: *Swan Lake* (1876), *The Sleeping Beauty* (1889), and *The Nutcracker* (1892). The first was written for the ballet company of the Bolshoi Theater in Moscow, in collaboration with the ballet-master Julius Reisinger. The others were undertaken at the urging of I. A. Vsevolozhsky, director of imperial theaters in St. Petersburg from 1881, who brought together Tchaikovsky and the influential choreographer Marius Petipa. Petipa was a central figure in the creation of a Russian national ballet so glorious that St. Petersburg supplanted Paris as the international leader in the art.

Tchaikovsky felt that *Swan Lake* had been a failure (a judgment that may have been true then but that has certainly been reversed) but believed *The Sleeping Beauty* to be his finest score. Though the musical invention in this work is infinitely richer than that of contemporary ballet specialists, it is still clearly crafted in response to the demands of the choreographer. The composer attempted to provide Petipa with exactly what he required and adapted his symphonic mode of thinking to the conventional numbers of which a classical *ballet d'action* was composed. He suppressed his penchant for rhythmic complexity (a variation in 5/4 time was originally suggested by Petipa, not Tchaikovsky, and was cut before the first performance) and concentrated on the melodiousness, highly contrasted orchestral coloring, and short-winded construction that was thought to make a work danceable.

The long score, divided into a prologue and three acts, includes an introduction, numerous scenes of mimed action, independent dance movements (like the famous waltz in the first act), and a number of classical variations—each set consisting of an introduction, from four to six brief numbers for individual dancers or groups, and a coda. The composer uses specific themes to characterize the good and bad forces in the story. The entrance of the Lilac Fairy is preceded by a soaring compound-meter, F-major melody announced by harp arpeggios and accompanied by soothing repeated chords, while the evil fairy Carabosse is succinctly portrayed by a grating, prickly staccato theme utilizing chromatically generated dissonances. Each theme not only recurs at appropriate moments in the score but also gives birth to other music, expanding the worlds of the two competing powers.

As in earlier nineteenth-century ballets, the use of obbligato instruments is essential to the style, especially in solo variations. An unusual, though not unprecedented, feature in the third act is the addition of the piano to the orchestra for the *pas de quatre* for the four fairies. These variations are particularly colorful in their scoring: featured instruments include the horn for Gold, bells and piano for Silver, pizzicato strings for Sapphire, and triangle for Diamond.

THE TWENTIETH CENTURY

The late nineteenth century produced one of opera's most successful practitioners, Giacomo Puccini. A hallmark of this composer's style is the reinforcement of his irresistible melodies by orchestral doubling. This technique produces an occasional page in his scores in which the whole orchestra appears to be playing in unison. For instance, at the reprise of Butterfly's "Un bel dì," the vocal melody is doubled by flutes, oboes, English horn, clarinets, bassoons, horns, and all the strings except the double basses. The only accompanimental material is a pair of notes offered by two trombones.

Another interest of Puccini's was the evocation of atmosphere. He made a special trip to Rome to listen to the church bells, the sound of which he incorporated into the third act of *Tosca* (1900). He studied books about Japanese and Chinese music while composing *Madama Butterfly* (1904) and *Turandot* (1926). *Butterfly* includes a few exotic percussion instruments but mainly relies on melodic and harmonic means for its oriental flavor.

A composer with an entirely different approach to melody was Claude Debussy, whose one completed opera, *Pelléas et Mélisande* (1902), is unique in its approach to musical drama. The dialogue—lifted virtually intact from Maurice Maeterlinck's play—is uttered in extremely restrained recitative or arioso style throughout. The orchestral part supplies a continuous musical background to the declaimed drama, functioning rather like the theater organ at the silent movie (though in a very different style). Unlike Puccini's orchestra, which slavishly doubles the vocal part at lyrical climaxes, Debussy's seems almost completely detached from the singers' lines. At the same time, it provides the essential expression of the characters' emotions as well as the evocation of place and scene so central to the feel of this work. Forest, castle, sea, fountain, as well as fear, jealousy, confusion, and remorse, are all given life by the brief melodic fragments and shifting colors of the orchestra.

Debussy was extremely sensitive to timbre and sought in this work to avoid muddy mixes and heavy doublings (for which he criticized Wagner) and to attain a purity and aptness of tone color. Though its orchestra is virtually the same as that of *Tristan*, *Pelléas* is executed with a clearer and more delicate palette. Remarkable effects include the passage directly preceding Mélisande's death in the fifth act, in which a trumpet playing *pianissimo* blends magically with low-register flutes and eleven-part divisi violins and violas.

The shady, elusive scenes of the drama are linked by orchestral interludes, a device that had been occasionally practiced by Wagner in the *Ring* but that is here a principal organizational feature. Some of the interludes were lengthened by Debussy in response to the need for sufficient time to change the scenery. These instrumental passages maintain dramatic tension with the slightest of means: in the reticent language of *Pelléas*, a single quiet timpani roll or an unsettling chord progression in the horns is enough to create suspense.

Wagner's principal heir was Richard Strauss, who wrote his major operas after having achieved a mastery of orchestration through the composition of tone poems. With the exception of *Guntram*, his first effort, all of Strauss's operas postdate *Don Juan*, *Tod und Verklärung*, *Till Eulenspiegel*, *Also sprach Zarathustra*, *Don Quixote*, and *Ein Heldenleben*. The operas are full of originality and virtuosity in their scoring. At their best they are unrivaled in their use of the orchestra to enhance the drama, but sometimes the level of detail creates the impression of a kaleidoscope that changes too rapidly for its beauties to be grasped.

Strauss used orchestras of all sizes in his operas (thirty-seven instruments in *Ariadne auf Naxos* and over a hundred in *Salome*), but even the smallish ones hardly sound like the classical orchestras they resemble. Strauss's compositional technique of layering leitmotivs and other short figures in constantly changing orchestral groups creates a glittering mosaic surface only occasionally relieved by broadly expressed lyrical melodies.

Fauré called *Salome* (1905) "a symphonic poem with vocal parts added"—the same judgment that Grout made of Wagner's music dramas. The leitmotivs in this opera include associations of particular scorings with characters or events in the drama. Jochanaan is accompanied (in his less rabid pronouncements) by six horns, sometimes joined by four trombones. In contrast to this rich, dark sound are the long, reedy clarinet trills that first appear in connection with Herod's rash promise to Salome.

Other stunning orchestral effects include the eerie, pinched middle-register B-flats played by solo string basses as Salome listens while the prophet is executed.

The orchestra is most notable for its large woodwind and percussion sections. The score calls for two oboes, English horn, the newly invented Heckelphone (a bass oboe pitched one octave below the regular oboe), and no fewer than six clarinets. To the timpani, triangle, cymbals, glockenspiel, and gong of the *Ring* orchestra, Strauss adds three other drums, tambourine, xylophone, castanets, and celesta. A harmonium plays offstage at the opening of the opera, an organ at the end.

The one lengthy instrumental passage in this long one-act opera is the "Dance of the Seven Veils," in which Strauss takes fullest musical advantage of the orientalism of his subject. Here, without competition from the voices, the orchestral writing can be best enjoyed.

The relationship between voices and instruments is treated in quite a different way in *Intermezzo*, the comic opera of 1923 that Strauss based on a stormy event in his own marriage. The orchestra is relatively small — the string section is roughly half the size of that of *Salome* and the woodwinds come only in pairs — and is therefore less threatening to the well-being of the singers, particularly because Strauss carefully arranged the orchestra's part not to interfere with the vocal lines. Yet the instrumental component in this work is in some ways more important than in any other Strauss opera, for two reasons. Most obviously, the scenes that make up the drama are connected by eleven orchestral interludes. But Strauss also assigns to the orchestra the major emotional content of the drama, for the text is set almost entirely as recitative (much of the remainder is spoken). In a long preface to the published score, the composer comments on his experience with trying to balance the instrumental and vocal components of his operas, and says this about the present work:

> In none of my other works is the significance of the dialogue greater than in this bourgeois comedy which offers very few possibilities for the development of cantilena. By constant and careful refinement, the symphonic element has been reduced often to no more than a suggestion; even with imprecise dynamics it can no longer be an obstacle to the vocal part, so that the completely natural speech, taken from and imitating everyday life, can be clearly understood both in the whole context and in its individual words. The lyrical element, representing the emotional experiences of the characters, reaches full expression mainly in the longer orchestral interludes. The singers have no opportunity for extended cantilena until the closing scenes of the first and second acts.

The peculiarly translucent quality of the scoring may be the result of a much-divided string section, which occasionally splits into as many as twelve parts. But many fine details of instrumentation, revealed in a reading of the score, are imperceptible in performance.

The greatest twentieth-century achievements in the operatic genre to date are Alban Berg's *Wozzeck* (written 1917–1922) and *Lulu* (written 1928–1935), the latter now available in its three-act form with the orchestration of the third act completed by Friedrich Cerha. For the first of these, Berg chose and ordered fifteen scenes from a total of twenty-six left by the early-nineteenth-century playwright Georg Büchner. These fifteen scenes are arranged into three acts, five to an act, each of which is unified by an overall formal scheme: Act 1 consists of five character pieces, each describing one of the persons in the drama; Act 2 is a symphony in five movements; Act 3 is a series of six inventions. The scenes within each act are divided by prominent orchestral interludes. The most important of these, which falls between the last two scenes of the opera, is given special status as a separate component in the formal scheme. This is the "Invention über eine Tonart," the shattering passage in more or less D minor that, after recapitulating many leitmotivs from the preceding action, brings the drama to its tragic climax in one *tutti* dominant-tonic cadence.

Among the orchestral changes rung by Berg in *Wozzeck* are one scene scored with the same instruments as Arnold Schoenberg's Chamber Symphony no. 1; a dance band on stage for Act 2, scene 4; and a honky-tonk piano beating out the rhythm that is the subject for the invention of Act 3, scene 3.

Some commentators have suggested that the formal plan of *Wozzeck* was necessary because Berg's atonal harmonic language could not supply the structure normally available through tonal means. Yet his next opera, *Lulu*, though theoretically completely structured through its twelve-tone organization, also shows a large-scale formal plan that relies on schemes from the past. In George Perle's analysis (based on written indications in the score), the first act contains a sonata-form movement; the second, a rondo; and the third, a theme and variations. The constituent sections of each plan are distributed throughout the movement, divided from one another by other numbers (in the eighteenth-century operatic sense) to which Berg himself drew attention by labeling them such things as "cavatina," "aria," and "chorale."

The big orchestra of *Lulu* is colored by especially prominent parts for harp, piano, and vibraphone. The three clarinets are joined by alto saxophone and bass clarinet. Act 1, scene 3, entitled "Ragtime" in the score, employs a large jazz band offstage. This rowdy collection of nine wind and brass players (including sousaphone), banjo, piano, strings, and percussion, alternates with, and eventually joins, the regular orchestra.

In a remarkable musical and dramatic innovation, Berg uses as the very keystone of his work a brief film accompanied by orchestral music. The events of the film—showing Lulu's arrest for the murder of Dr. Schön, her trial, imprisonment, release to a mental hospital, and escape— are paralleled by an orchestral palindrome. At the reversal of Lulu's fortunes, the music turns around—audibly, on a piano arpeggio that freezes at the top and then descends—and proceeds in literal retrograde back to the point where the film began (and now ends).

Much of the towering impact of Berg's operas is created by the ability of his dissonant, searing musical style to express the emotions raised by the harrowing events of the drama. His rich expressionistic language, full of ecstatic beauties as well as horrors, vividly portrays the raw and sometimes surrealistic tragedies of opera's greatest antihero and antiheroine.

Pride of place in the works of Igor Stravinsky must go to the ballet scores. The young Russian composer first came to public notice through his music for *The Firebird*, a ballet produced by Sergei Diaghilev for the 1910 Paris season of the Ballets Russes. The imaginative orchestration of this work owes much to Rimsky-Korsakov, Stravinsky's teacher, though some of the notable effects were original. Stravinsky continued his work for Diaghilev with *Petrushka* (1911) and *The Rite of Spring* (1913). *Petrushka* began its existence as a piece for piano and orchestra; the prominent role for piano in its second scene is a legacy of this origin. The large orchestra is used with special effectiveness in the crowd scenes at the fair, when numerous separate short motives assigned to different instruments are combined in a noisy, bustling *tutti*. Contrasting textures include an unaccompanied flute solo for the Magician and a jaunty dance for the Ballerina accompanied only by a cornet and a snare drum. A peasant plays a pipe (clarinets in high register); the growls of his bear are heard in the tuba. Scene changes are accomplished to the sound of the snare drum and tambourine.

This inventive approach to scoring is continued in *The Rite of Spring*, which, in its rhythmic complexity and dissonant harmonic language, far exceeds even its bold predecessor. The program of the original ballet, rather disastrously choreographed by Nijinsky, concerned a ritual human sacrifice in pagan Russia. The unexpected noises that the composer coaxed out of his instruments helped to create the prehistoric aura of the work. The orchestra was the largest for which Stravinsky ever wrote: quintuple woodwinds, eight horns, five trumpets, three trombones, two tubas, a large percussion section, and strings. It omits the harps, piano, celesta, and xylophone that contributed much to the characteristic sounds of *Firebird* and *Petrushka*.

The introduction opens with the eerie sounds of a solo bassoon in high register. In this showcase passage for woodwinds, instruments are added in such a way that each characteristic tone color is audible within the texture, though the level of activity accelerates rapidly. Another remarkable wind sound is later achieved through the use of the alto flute as a bass instrument; at one point it doubles a melody two octaves below the high E-flat clarinet while static flute and clarinet trills provide the accompaniment.

A complete reversal of Stravinsky's instrumental language is found in his *Apollon musagète*, a neoclassical work of 1928 (and the first product of a long and fruitful collaboration with the choreographer George Balanchine). In this ballet, scored only for six-part string orchestra, timbral contrast is scrupulously avoided. In other works, the composer called on the forces of the eighteenth-century orchestra. The ballet *Pulcinella* (1920), based on music attributed to Pergolesi, omits clarinets and percussion and divides its strings into solo and *ripieno* groups. The Mozart-inspired opera *The Rake's Progress* (1951) revives *recitativo semplice*, accompanying it with keyboard (in some performances realized on piano, in others on harpsichord). In neither of these works is the composer's use of instruments circumscribed by eighteenth century style, however; Pergolesi would not have written a duo for trombone and double bass, nor Mozart a passage of recitative accompanied by two bassoons.

Trends in later twentieth-century theater music have tended to reflect the tastes of those who buy the tickets. Avant-garde musical styles have not made much of a place for themselves on the stage. The directors of ballet companies and opera houses are a conservative lot, and though they may be willing to present challenging new pieces, they cannot keep in the repertoire works that an audience will not support. Of all Prokofiev's theater music, only the late full-length ballets *Romeo and Juliet* (1936) and *Cinderella* (1944) have had lasting success in their complete forms; these are neoromantic scores, owing more to Tchaikovsky than to Stravinsky. Aaron Copland's ballets *Rodeo* (1938), *Billy the Kid* (1942), and *Appalachian Spring* (1944) contain attractive but hardly difficult material. Of the operas written since 1940 that appear to be holding ground, most look to the past in their musical style and their operatic conventions.

A prominent example of this phenomenon is *Peter Grimes* (1945), by Benjamin Britten. Its design must have been carefully calculated by the composer to combine the best of old and new operatic procedures. As in *Wozzeck* the story opens, without an overture, *in medias res*. As in *Pelléas* the score contains a number of evocative interludes that describe both natural and psychological phenomena. Effective use is made of the off-stage chorus (as in *Madama Butterfly*). A stage band (familiar from *Don Giovanni* to *Lulu*) makes an obligatory appearance in the third act. As in *Carmen*, the English horn is reserved for an important dramatic moment—here, the discovery of the missing apprentice's jersey.

If the sources are eclectic, the formula is nevertheless successful; especially for English-speaking listeners, *Peter Grimes* is a dramatic triumph. The overall orchestrational style is rather dense—a quality that was to change in Britten's later works—but several instruments are singled out for specific dramatic purpose. The fine scene that juxtaposes a church service and Ellen's one-sided conversation with the boy uses an organ along with real chant melodies for the worshippers. In the second act, the beat of Hobson's tenor drum turns the villagers into a lynch mob. When the townspeople arrive at Grimes's hut, just after the boy has fallen to his death, the seeming order and innocence of the scene are belied by an eerie ostinato figure for the celesta. Grimes's final demented monologue is punctuated not only by the spectral cries of the chorus but also by an offstage tuba masquerading as a foghorn.

As the proportion and importance of instrumental music in opera has grown in the post-Wagnerian era, the practice of preparing concert versions of such music has increased. Overtures and ballet suites are joined in the symphonic repertoire by the "Polonaise" from *Boris Godunov*, the suite from Prokofiev's *Love for Three Oranges*, and the "Four Sea Interludes" from *Peter Grimes*. Two purposes are served: concert programs are enriched, and music from stage works that might otherwise rarely be heard is salvaged for composer and listener alike.

BIBLIOGRAPHY

James R. Anthony, *French Baroque Music from Beaujoyeulx to Rameau* (1978). Janet E. Beat, "Monteverdi and the Opera Orchestra of His Time," in *The Monteverdi Companion*, Denis Arnold and Nigel Fortune, eds. (1968). Philip Brett, *Benjamin Britten: Peter Grimes*, Cambridge Opera Handbooks (1983). Julian Budden, *The Operas of Verdi*, 3 vols. (1973–1981). Peter Burbridge and Richard Sutton, eds., *The Wagner Companion* (1979). M. D. Calvocoressi, *Modest Mussorgsky: His Life and Works* (1956). Mary Clarke and Clement Crisp, *Ballet: An Illustrated History* (1973). William L. Crosten, *French Grand Opera* (1948).

Winton Dean, *Georges Bizet: His Life and Work* (1965); and *Handel and the*

Opera Seria (1969). Edward J. Dent, *Mozart's Operas* (1947). Philip Gossett, "Rossini," in *New Grove Dictionary of Music and Musicians*, Stanley Sadie, ed. (1980). Donald Jay Grout, *A Short History of Opera* (8th ed., 1965). Arthur Jacobs, "Will the Real Boris Godunov Please Stand Up?" *Opera*, May 1971.

Michael Kennedy, *Richard Strauss* (1976). Robert Orledge, *Debussy and the Theatre* (1982). George Perle, *The Operas of Alban Berg*, 2 vols. (1980-1985); and "Lulu: The Formal Design," *Journal of the American Musicological Society*, 17 (1964). Gabriella Biagi Ravenni and Mosco Carner, "Puccini," in *New Grove Dictionary*. Graham Sadler, "Rameau and the Orchestra," *Proceedings of the Royal Musical Association*, 108 (1981-1982).

Carl B. Schmidt, "Antonio Cesti's *Il pomo d'oro*," *Journal of the American Musicological Association*, 29 (1976). Richard Strauss, Preface to *Intermezzo*, Elisabeth Davies, trans., in program notes to EMI recording IC 165-30 983/85; SLS 5204; LC 0233 (1980). Nicholas Temperley, "Overture," in *New Grove Dictionary*. Eric Walter White, *Stravinsky: The Composer and His Works* (2nd ed., 1979). John Roland Wiley, *Tchaikovsky's Ballets* (1985). Lesley A. Wright, "A Musical Commentary," in *Carmen: Opera Guide* (1982).

The New Conception of "The Work of Art"

Michael Beckerman

One area of musical studies where even fools fear to tread is the search for the ultimate meaning of music. Metatheories aside, some of the thornier problems relating to the question of meaning in the nineteenth century can be explored by referring to several measures taken from the fourth movement of Berlioz' *Symphonie fantastique*. Entitled "March to the Scaffold," this movement includes the following as part of its program:

> The procession moves forward to the sounds of a march, now somber and ferocious, now brilliant and stately, during which the muffled noise of heavy footsteps follows without transition upon the noisiest outbursts. At the end of the march, the first four measures of the *idée fixe* reappear like a last thought of love interrupted by the fatal blow.

The primary musical idea associated with the march is a descending figure in the lower register (Ex. 1).

Conventional ways of dealing with program music focus on the relationship between this musical figure and an actual scene presumed to be in the composer's mind when the work was written. In this particular case, there is a not altogether atypical problem: we know that this march was originally written not for the *Symphonie fantastique* but for a never-

Example 1. Berlioz: *Symphonie fantastique,* movement 4, mm. 17–25

completed opera called *Les francs juges* and was transferred in its entirety by the composer into the symphony.

But even if we could ignore this problem and assume that there is a real and valid kinship between literary image and musical score, it is almost impossible to discover how that relationship ought to function. Are we supposed to imagine a ragged figure, bound and shackled, actually walking in time to the music (Berlioz himself?), or do we optimally re-create only the ambiance of such a scene, drawing on such films as *A Tale of Two Cities* to provide us with the proper visual symbols of the French Revolution? Should the music function as a kind of sound track for our imagination, or do both music and story act upon us simultaneously but independently?

Let us proceed to an even more notorious and specific instance in the same movement where the "meaning" of a particular passage ought to be exceedingly precise—the presentation of the beginning of the *idée fixe* depicting the beloved, and the execution of the poet, as described in the passage above. This material was tacked on to the conclusion of the march from *Les francs juges* and was created specifically for the symphony. Generations of music-appreciation students have thrilled to the ghastly pizzicato that purportedly represents the rolling head of the decapitated poet (Ex. 2).

Berlioz has actually asked us to imagine something quite complex. The *idée fixe* has been, if anything, associated with the beloved; if it "evokes" anything at all, it is her image. "Cutting off" the *idée fixe* readily allows us to imagine not the poet's execution but rather that of the beloved. The rolling head presents problems as well. Which came first, the musical image or the program? Does Berlioz use the pizzicato figure to "depict" a rolling head, or is he using the program as an excuse to write the kind of music he wants, or is he merely alluding to his favorite instrument, the guitar?

These are knotty questions. The difficulty of articulating and even

Example 2. Berlioz: *Symphonie fantastique*, movement 4, mm. 111-113

discussing the notion of program is compounded when one acknowledges multiple types. In the *Symphonie fantastique* itself there are manifold levels of programmatic relationship, from the onomatopoetic (sounds of thunder), to the symbolic (the *idée fixe*), to the narrative (the execution). Even a seemingly simple aural image such as the sound of the English horn in the third movement is powerfully diverse. On a basic level, the instrument may be considered an "actor" playing the "role" of a shepherd's pipe. The pipes themselves may function as a pastoral image on still another level of abstraction, rich in allusion, and may even suggest the isolation of man in nature or, more specifically, of the poet in nature.

However difficult it is to pin down any question of meaning in relation to the program, we must realize that the idea of meaning in the
nineteenth century in no way depends on the existence of a program.
The two measures that follow, for example, both contain diminished
chords (Exs. 3 and 4). The first example is from the storm sequence in

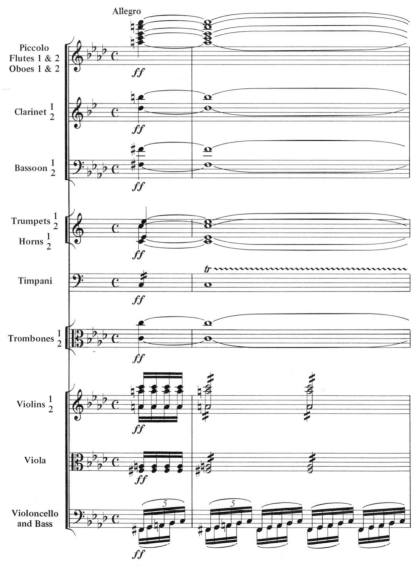

Example 3. Beethoven: Symphony no. 6 in F Major (*Pastorale*), movement 4,
mm. 106–107

Example 4. Beethoven: Symphony no. 5 in C Minor, movement 1, mm. 390–392

the fourth movement of Beethoven's Sixth Symphony and is doubtless somehow related to thunder. The second example is "merely" a part of the development section of Beethoven's Fifth Symphony. If one were to view meaning solely in relation to a program, the first example would have to be considered more "meaningful" than the second, since we ostensibly know what it is supposed to represent. Of course, it is impossible and even absurd to try to prove such a statement. In fact, from a cultural point of view, there would seem to be a consensus that the Fifth Symphony is somehow more "meaningful" than the *Pastoral*; and it might follow, however absurdly, that any passage in it has therefore "more meaning."

This brings us to the larger issue of the debate between absolute and program music. Just as we must distrust conventional attempts to divide music cleanly into programmatic and absolute categories, so too must we resist the impulse to argue, as Jacques Barzun has done, that all music is programmatic. Barzun's definition of *program* as "any scheme or idea, general or particular, that helps to determine the course of composition" (p. 3) is all well and good; but if we accept the notion that everything is more or less programmatic, it is merely a semantic division and we are still left with the task of making distinctions between types of programs. Finally, we must realize that the explicitness of the program is in no way related to the "meaningfulness" of the work.

Of course, positing such levels of program is hazardous, especially since composers are not always clear about the genesis of their ideas. We have already noted that the "March to the Scaffold" was composed before the program was written. The same may be true for Liszt's *Les préludes* (we are not yet sure). Mily Balakirev changed the program of his symphonic poem now known as *Russia* several times, while Tchaikovsky wrote to Nadezhda von Meck about the "secret" program of his Symphony no. 4. In addition to these after-the-fact, altered, or secret programs, we may posit a whole series of categories of works actually written with an extramusical idea in mind and offered to the public with a written program.

As the search for musical meaning continues, it becomes ever more difficult. Our best guides are often thought to be composers, who, after all, should know what they are doing. But there are two fundamental problems. First, despite their exalted status in the nineteenth century, composers are not entirely reliable. Like the rest of us, they sometimes say things they do not mean, and mean things that remain unsaid. For example, in discussing the origins of atonality, Schoenberg said in different places that the resolution of the dilemma of the dissolution of tonality "came upon me unawares" and that it had "been generating in my mind for several years." Which is correct? Both? Neither? On which statement would we wish to base a theory of creativity? Composers are often fiercely caught up in the events and duties of their lives and can make notoriously bad witnesses.

But there is a second problem, which looms even larger when exploring the issue of musical meaning. How can we possibly know—even if we believe that a composer has expressed himself clearly and honestly— what the real relationship between ideas about creativity is to the creative act itself? Even if we believe that Berlioz honestly thought he was depicting, suggesting, or evoking the sufferings of an artist in the *Symphonie fantastique,* what does that really tell us about the most profound and therefore most compelling aspects of his thought, and what does it tell us about the nature of his musical language? It is all too easy for broad theories of meaning to lure us into the realm of metaphysics, where actual musical works become hazy, shadowy, almost unnecessary things.

CHANGING PERCEPTIONS OF MUSICAL MEANING

Fortunately, even though it is impossible to discuss the nature of musical meaning without tying oneself and the subject into knots, it is possible to distinguish changes in attitudes toward the issue of musical meaning. Of course, we must realize at the outset the simple fact that all music has always been considered "meaningful" in some way. From Plato, through the medieval theorists, to the Renaissance and beyond, philosophers and musicians have speculated on the significance of music and on the manner in which it communicates. The idea of the program is hardly unique to the nineteenth century. One may cite such effects as Janequin's evocation of the battle of Marignano; the dissonant drunken revels in Biber's *Battalia;* the *Gall-Stone Operation* of Marin Marais; and the thunder, lightning, birds, and brooks in Vivaldi's *Four Seasons* as evidence. Furthermore, there has always been an obvious programmatic aspect to opera and oratorio. One could certainly argue that the overture to Mozart's *Don Giovanni* is a piece of program music and that Haydn's depiction of chaos in *The Creation* is closely related to the later development of the tone poem.

Yet there are very real changes in attitudes toward both music and musical meaning around the beginning of the nineteenth century that formed the basis of lively aesthetic debates in the second half of the century. First, we see a growing cult of instrumental music. Friedrich von Schlegel wrote that "all pure music must be philosophical and instrumental," while Johann Gottfried von Herder stated that "music has developed into a self-sufficient art sui generis, dispensing with words." Furthermore, there is a mandate stressing the relationship between the musical work and the inner working of the human spirit. Schopenhauer asserted that music "reproduces all the movements of our innermost being but quite divorced from phenomenal life, and remote from its misery," while Hegel maintained that "music rises to the level of true art only when the sensuous element of sound in its innumerable combinations expresses something which is suitably spiritual." The idea that music "expresses" something was so taken for granted that Mendelssohn could even argue that "a piece of music that I love expresses thoughts to me that are not too *imprecise* to be found in words, but too *precise*."

These ideas are representative of a virtual obsession with musical meaning in the nineteenth century that had tangible results. Not only do we see the rise of the program symphony in the work of Berlioz, Liszt, and others, but we also witness the invention of a whole new genre with the symphonic poem. In addition, even scrupulously absolute music came to be considered ultimately programmatic, albeit on a different level. Yet these changing attitudes toward the musical work did not result simply from an abstract philosophical premise; the reasons for the transformation are numerous and varied, and include sociological, political, and purely aesthetic factors. Even though these multiple "explanations" in reality overlap, it is most appropriate to explore them individually.

MUSIC AND THE ROMANTIC MOVEMENT

The simplest explanation for a change in the "meaning of meaning," as Barzun called it, is also the most general and the most challenging: that is, the relationship of music to the fundamental ideas of the romantic movement. A satisfactory definition of *romanticism* is as difficult to come by as a precise articulation of *meaning*, but a sampling of contemporary approaches at least reveals some common touches. Peter Lichtenthal called "romanticism" the "overwhelming enhanced by the pleasant and attractive," Gustav Schilling said that "romantic art springs from man's attempt to transcend the sphere of cognition; to experience higher, more spiritual things, and to sense the presence of the ineffable," while Baudelaire cryptically stated that "romanticism is neither a choice of subject, nor exact truth, but a way of feeling." Thus, romanticism may be considered a movement concerned with modes of feeling and expression, preoccupied with the unknown, and absorbed with a perpetual longing and displacement in time and spirit. The generalized physical search for the unknown and unknowable found an outlet in a fascination with faraway places and ancient times, while the quest for the spiritual unknown led to mysticism and the supernatural. There was a belief among the leading figures of the period that only art—particularly poetry and music—could express this new way of feeling.

An example of the ability of art to express the ineffable can be found in Goethe's novel *The Sorrows of Young Werther*. It is a moment representative of a certain type of nineteenth-century ethos, but one that nowadays cannot fail to evoke a smile. The self-absorbed Werther is standing next to his beloved Lotte after a storm: "She stood leaning on her elbow, her eyes searching the landscape; she looked up at the sky and then at me. I saw her eyes fill with tears; she laid her hand on mine and said: 'Klopstock'" (entry for 16 June 1771). In such telling moments of longing and desire then, only Klopstock, a poet of turgid odes, could fill the void.

In this realm of expression music occupied a special position. Not only was it considered "the most romantic art," but all music was thought to be "in its innermost essence romantic" (Schilling). Many thinkers felt that music was the only medium able to bridge the gap between the knowable and the unknowable, between material and spiritual reality. Perhaps this is the reason that of all the arts, music is the one on which romanticism made the most profound impact. Indeed, while one stops speaking of romantic literature and painting by midcentury, the romantic era in music seems to swallow up the entire nineteenth century.

Nevertheless, this romantic way of thinking was so pervasive in 1829 that F. R. de Toreinx complained, "Nowadays one cannot pass for an intellectual without being a Romantic; and who would wish to be thought an idiot?" Stendhal even went so far as to say that "romanticism was the art of pleasing one's contemporaries while classicism was the art of pleasing their grandparents."

In spite of this spate of quotations concerning romanticism and music, it is impossible to determine precisely the way a literary and philosophical movement interacts with the creation of musical works, since the musical world has its own characteristic and somewhat arcane set of traditions and practices. Yet it seems clear that the concerns of the so-called romantic composers were nearly identical to those of philosophers and artists in other areas. Such composers as Schumann, Berlioz, Liszt, and even Mendelssohn expressed themselves through the fashionable metaphors and images associated with the romantic movement. It would seem that on the most fundamental level the change in attitude toward musical meaning, toward what music is capable of expressing, is bound up with the intellectual climate of the early nineteenth century.

For this reason music can be said to have become "more meaningful" in two ways. In the first place, the value ascribed to music by the culture itself became enhanced by its position as a kind of mediator between the cognitive and noncognitive aspects of human thought. In the second place, independent instrumental music began to be explicitly used to evoke or suggest moods, places, activities, and even dramatic action. It is possible to see the rise of the symphonic poem, for example, as a reflection of such relationships. Carl Dahlhaus says that one of Liszt's aims was to "mediate between music and a traditional culture which was primarily literary and philosophical." He sees program music therefore as the music of an era "when experience was shaped by reading and when literature as a subject was scarcely less important than the subject itself." Thus, according to Dahlhaus, music aimed to be meaningful in the same way that a novel or a poem was meaningful.

MEANING AND THE MARKETPLACE

Despite this demonstrable yet elusive relationship between music and the romantic movement, there are other reasons for this concentration on musical meaning that are both sociological and commercial. One of the areas now enjoying the greatest popularity in musicological studies is the field of musical patronage. For reasons unclear, the study of patronage has been considered prestigious when associated with the music of earlier periods and to be a rather desultory branch of the sociology of music when discussed in nineteenth-century terms. But there is an important connection between changing systems of patronage and the preoccupation with musical meaning.

In 1781, after a series of squabbles, Mozart formally ended his employ with the archbishop of Salzburg, and he was literally kicked out of the royal residence by Count Arco. Though there still remains a great deal of work to be done in order to more accurately describe the changing role of the musician at the beginning of the nineteenth century, it is possible to interpret this historic kick as a symbolic event, heralding the new area of the "free artist." Whether or not there was actually such a creature as the free artist remains to be seen, but it is certain that between roughly 1780 and 1820 there was a drastic shift in the patronage system as it affected composers and musicians in general. The French Revolution completely destroyed the court system in that country, while many of the minor duchies and kingdoms in German-speaking lands either disappeared or declined in influence. It was no longer the aristocrats who could be counted upon to support the artists but rather the paying customers in the expanding arena of the public concert.

If the composer's support was almost entirely in the hands of a paying public, he had to do two things. First, it was critical that he convince this audience that purely instrumental music was worthwhile and had value—in short, that it was worth paying for. Second, as part of this process, it was of the greatest importance to speak with this audience, to communicate in some way with this mass patron, to become involved with it, even to argue with it.

The first point is perhaps the more critical, since changing systems of patronage also resulted in the transformation of the idea of function in relation to the musical work. After all, public concert music at the beginning of the nineteenth century was devoid of function in the usual sense. It was not to be danced or marched to, it was not to accompany liturgy or ritual, and it was certainly not to be played as background to ceremony or dinner conversation. If audiences were to be asked to sit quietly in a large room and merely pay and listen, they had to be convinced of the inherent value of the product. It had to be entertaining yet somehow transcend mere entertainment.

The genre most often used to communicate with this mass patron was the large orchestral work. Is it not curious that we have almost no programmatic chamber music? Other than some enigmatic comments in Beethoven's String Quartets nos. 15 and 16 and quotations of songs in Schubert's chamber works there is almost nothing; no genre of the "program quartet" or "trio poem."

Even though many keyboard works of the early nineteenth century can be loosely thought of as programmatic, a distinction must be made between the generalized extramusical allusions found in so-called character pieces and the more elaborate descriptive or narrative "programs" found in symphonic music. While piano character pieces could suggest a wide variety of images with great nuance and subtlety, it was orchestral music that became the main line of communication between a composer and his larger audience, and in it the question of meaning was asked and answered most often. One of the earliest and most explicit communications of this nature occurs in the final movement of Beethoven's Ninth Symphony when the "reciting" violoncellos and double basses dismiss the themes of the first three movements in favor of the D-major melody, implying, not so subtly, that the very simplicity of this "Ode to Joy" is the ideal way to communicate with the entire audience.

The program of the *Symphonie fantastique*, written less than a decade later, reveals an even greater desire to communicate with a larger public and was, at the same time, a clear bid for publicity and notoriety. Such a lurid program, delivered into the hands of the audience, could indeed be a way of attracting paying customers. Since the spectators had been conditioned by their experience of opera to look for, and follow, narrative elements, why not give them similar structures and incidents in symphonic works?

There is another aspect of this process that is perhaps not quite so metaphysical. As the composer lost the financial security of the aristocratic patron he gained, almost in Faustian exchange, a kind of power he had never dreamed of. After all, if meaning was to be a fundamental element of musical presentation, the composer, who created the work, must be some kind of metaphorical god, since he alone is possessed of the key to understanding the total significance of the work. Thus, the composer was able to create for himself a new kind of mystique, which could even add to the success of a work as audience members debated its importance.

MEANING AND WILLFULNESS

Though all of the above may be true on one level, it also seems clear that the program and the constant allusions to meaning could have other, more deceptive sources and purposes. The simple fact is that composers are musicians first, and if they are great composers, their imaginations are primarily musical. The composers themselves may not even be fully aware of this and may not even realize that they are merely using the idea of "meaning" in order to free themselves to write the kind of music they wish to write. No matter what Liszt, Wagner, Schumann, and Berlioz said (and no matter what we say), it is most probably their musical thinking that interests us and their ability to use and create musical language that is most compelling.

The process by which composers were able to free their imaginations remains to be traced, but we know that figures such as Berlioz, Liszt, and Wagner often insinuated weird new effects into their works and claimed, via a program, that they were somehow related to a character, a thing, or an event. In a way, this softened the break with the past that was one of the hallmarks of nineteenth-century music, as composers were able to create the impression that their novel, and often unpalatable, musical innovations were the result of an external rather than an internal logic.

This was critically important for the romantic composer, who was living in an age when one had to be distinctive and original to survive. Yet, paradoxically, it was also the age of the audience as mass patron. How did one reconcile the need for originality, which might result in provocative and even unpleasant sounds, with the need to please and communicate with an audience? The program was an ideal way to accomplish this. If the artist was to be a success, it was critical that he should not antagonize the entire audience, unless he was somehow cultivating the rather ambiguous succès de scandale. If the composer wished to employ new sonic combinations in orchestral music and thus violate conventional norms, it was important that this should not seem willful, that it somehow be linked to an event, an idea, or a thing that would justify it.

This circumstance made it possible for the program to function as a kind of smoke screen for harmonic or orchestral experimentation. Examples 5–8 are several passages that certainly would have been considered outré, if not completely unacceptable, in works without a program. The first of these is not merely a dissonant collection but the introduction to a fearful witches' sabbath; the second is part of a battle in Liszt's *Battle of the Huns*; the third is not simply a crude contrabass rumble but Alberich turning himself into a dragon; and the final one is a rush of sound associated with the rapids of the River Vltava (Moldau) in Smetana's cycle *Má vlast* (*My Homeland*). Though traditional models of the program assert that the composer creates new musical images to match extramusical ideas, it is equally possible that some composers used extramusical ideas as an excuse for violating conventional "rules" of composition.

One piece of evidence that supports this contention is the almost total lack of programmatic usage in the works of more conservative composers. Schumann, Mendelssohn, and Brahms were certainly no less concerned with musical meaning than their avant-garde contemporaries, yet they tended to avoid the program in their orchestral works. At most, as in a work like Mendelssohn's *Fingal's Cave* Overture, there is an allusion to extramusical ideas but never a fully formed setting or explanation. Considering his remarks about the expressive precision of music we would hardly expect any explicit programmatic devices from him. Schumann went even further when he wrote, "If some composer presents us with a program *before* his music is performed, I tend to say: 'Let me hear first of all whether it is beautiful, and then afterward your program will please me too.'"

NATIONALISM

A related development, which first asserted itself around the beginning of the century, also played a role in determining attitudes toward meaning and music. The idea of the primacy of the nation-state can be traced back to antiquity, but the Napoleonic Wars ushered in a self-conscious period of national awakening that led to the revolutions of 1848 and

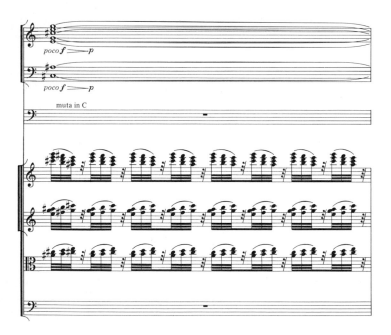

Example 5. Berlioz: *Symphonie fantastique,* movement 5, mm. 1–5

ultimately to the creation of modern Europe. Music became associated with nationalist movements on multiple levels, and composers now known as nationalists should often be more properly called realists, orientalists, folklorists, and even impressionists. Yet even as we discuss the aspects of nationalism that do affect the creation of musical works, we must be aware that much of what occurs in so-called nationalistic music is still determined, to at least some extent, by the more general factors outlined above. The composer who is allegedly involved in incorporating national images into his music because of "love of country" may also be doing so to communicate with a mass audience or seeking to use the struggles of the nation as an excuse for writing a particular dissonance. We must always keep in mind that even the most patriotic composer is capable of using the nation for his own ends.

It is probable that a man walking in the environs of Prague around 1800 would have identified the various features of the landscape as trees, rivers, and towns, while the same man walking in the same spot fifty years later might have spoken of Czech trees, Czech rivers, and Czech towns. This new attitude involves one of the critical aspects of any nationalist philosophy: the perception on the part of a group of people that the geographical unit in which they live is somehow part of a unity. Furthermore, it was thought that all the elements that constituted this

Example 6. Liszt: *Battle of the Huns*, mm. 237-240

Example 7. Wagner: *Das Rheingold,* scene 3

unified nation—historical, cultural, political, linguistic, and geographical—coalesced and gave rise to a kind of national essence.

Nationalism, at least in a hypothetically pure sense, was a philosophy
and a political movement that created a total sensibility—a "Czechness,"
"Russianness," or "Germanness"—for the nation based on its diverse elements. It also involved a complex process whereby this national sensibility and the elements that had created it were in a continual state of
mutual redefinition. To put it simply, the Norwegian nationalist creates
an image of his nation based on a synthesis of Norwegian folk music,
Norse mythology, the landscape of the fjords, the climate, and so on. Yet
once this vision is created, it alters the manner in which folk music, myth,
and panorama are perceived, and this new perception in turn redefines
the sensibility itself.

Example 8. Smetana: *Má vlast: Vltava* (*The Moldau*), mm. 307–311

Though that which we wish to examine is a fluid and even slippery phenomenon, we must realize that the nationalist impulse played an important role in defining musical style and concepts of musical meaning by the nineteenth century, since composers in virtually every European country, along with historians, poets, and philosophers, were influenced and motivated by the issue of national style.

In Russia, Balakirev's revisionist platform turned the philosophically phlegmatic Glinka into the father of Russian music. By their incendiary polemics, the gifted young Balakirev and the critic Vladimir Stasov were able to force friends and enemies alike to deal with the issue of national music. Of course, the absolute clarity of this national vision cannot be taken too seriously. As mentioned earlier, Balakirev changed the program of *Russia* several times to keep pace with his own changing world view. Nevertheless, nationalist ideology was clearly a motivating force in Russian music of the nineteenth century.

The nationalist impulse stressed the revival of the nation's past glory and linked it with a movement toward a future where that glory would be rekindled, a future that would redeem an unsatisfactory present. The past was often evoked by the use of ancient modes or even actual pieces of ancient music. The national essence, which we have mentioned as the sum total of the nation's elements, functioned as a kind of "eternal present," which was embodied in the folk song. Thus, the use of folk songs or a stylized folk idiom acquired a symbolic significance in addition to its purely musical value.

One of the most famous programmatic works of the century can easily be approached in terms of its preoccupation with national significance. Smetana's *Vltava (The Moldau)* uses the image of a flowing river as a symbol of national unification. There are several types of water imagery, from the opening sextuplets, which represent mountain brooks, to the familiar tune that (according to the program) represents the broad river, to the slow trills that represent the rippling sound of the river at night, to the metaphorical rapids that conclude the work. In addition, the folk-stylization of the "wedding scene" reflects the eternal present of rural Czech culture, while the well-known Vyšehrad theme ostensibly evokes the deeper recesses of Czech history. It is noteworthy that the means used to evoke national character are not necessarily nationally distinctive. Thus, while the wedding party in *Vltava* is represented by a stylized Czech dance, the Vyšehrad theme, a symbol of Czech self-determination, is a rather commonplace harmonic progression: I–VI–V^6–I (Ex. 9) By such devices composers throughout Europe and the United States used orchestral music as the primary way of expressing ideas about the nation.

Example 9. *Smetana: Má vlast: Vyšehrad*, opening

THE MUSIC OF THE FUTURE

The association between the program and the avant-garde is most clearly seen in the compositions of Liszt and Wagner, who created an almost absolute equation between musical phenomena and extramusical states. In his preface to *Album d'un voyageur* (later reshaped as *Années de pèlerinage*), Liszt articulates his fundamental attitude toward musical expression:

> As instrumental music progresses, develops, and frees itself from its first bonds, it tends more and more to take on an ideal quality of the kind that is the perfection of the plastic arts; it tends more and more to become not a simple combination of sounds but a poetic language, more apt perhaps than poetry itself to express all that which transcends within us our customary horizons, all that which escapes analysis, all that which relates to the inaccessible depths of imperishable desires and longings for the infinite.

With the creation of the genre of the symphonic poem Liszt capitulated to the romantic tendency to ascribe eternal significance to almost everything connected with the creative process and to espouse an approach to the program often based on a tenuous connection between it and the work itself.

Though it has become increasingly clear that Liszt is one of the critically important musicians of the nineteenth century, it was Richard Wagner who more than any other figure was responsible for changing contemporary attitudes toward music and the way it was perceived. As such, no matter what one might think of the quality of his works, Wagner may be the only artist in Western history whose influence is impossible to overestimate. Though not known as a composer of independent orchestral works, he forged the most potent and enduring link between abstract musical ideas and the literary image; and in this process the orchestra was his main ally.

In Wagner's writings and works we see outsized examples of all the tendencies and views previously mentioned. For example, we have seen the obvious connection between changing attitudes toward music and the philosophy of romanticism. Wagner seized on the most notable characteristics of romanticism, enlarging and synthesizing them. The romantic fascination with longing and death becomes, in *Tristan und Isolde,* a virtual monument to them; the tendency to dwell on the mysterious and faraway leads to Venusberg, Nibelheim, and Klingsor's enchanted castle.

Earlier in the century composers made the first tentative efforts toward self-conscious communication with their mass patron. Wagner communicated with the audience on a grand scale, not only through his massive music dramas, employing an enormous orchestra, but also through the thousands of pages of articles, notes, and commentary that accompanied them. No artist—not even George Bernard Shaw—was more eager to articulate his reasons for every aesthetic choice. For example, the assumption that the orchestra could communicate ideas by itself is outlined in an almost axiomatic manner in this manifesto from *The Artwork of the Future:* "The orchestra indisputably possesses a *faculty of speech,* and the creations of modern instrumental music have disclosed it to us."

Other composers may have used extramusical ideas to mask an intentional break with the past. Wagner goes one step further in this romantically tinged disclaimer from *A Communication to My Friends:*

> It thus could no more occur to me to rack with willful outward canons the musical form that sprang self-bidden from the very nature of these scenes, to break its natural mold by violent grafting in of conventional slips of operatic song. Thus I by no means set out with the fixed purpose of a deliberate iconoclast to destroy...the prevailing operatic forms of aria, duet, and so on; but the omission of these forms followed from the very nature of the stuff.
>
> (pp. 267–268)

Hence, Wagner's break with the past was to be seen not as a willful assault on accepted tradition but as a carefully argued necessity, arising out of obvious historical developments.

Although Wagner's impact was clearly international, he was also one of the preeminent nationalistic composers of the century. Wagner fulfills all the interests and characteristics of the so-called nationalist composer: the use of national historical events and legends, the veneration of national song, the preoccupation with the nation's future, the creation of a kind of eternal present, and ultimately the primacy of the nation-state. All of these are gathered together in his declaration of German art in "German Art and German Policy":

> Universal as the mission of the German folk is seen to have been, since its entrance into history, equally universal are the German spirit's aptitudes for art; the rebirth of the German spirit, which happened in the second half of the preceding century, has shown us an example of the activation of this

universality in the weightiest domains of art; the example of that rebirth's evaluation to the end of ennobling the public spiritual life of the German folk, as also to the end of founding a new and truly German civilization.

(p. 443)

Wagner's philosophy may be considered the epitome of an extremely self-conscious (and self-aggrandizing) attitude toward musical meaning. On the one hand, he outlined a quasi-political artistic program (the unification of the arts, the glorification of Germany, the artwork of the future, universal drama), and on the other hand, he provided a series of musical symbols and motives, which he manipulated to produce an immediate effect or linked with long-range harmonic movement to create quasi-narrative musical metaphors, notably in *Tristan und Isolde*. Indeed, it has become a commonplace to assert that *Tristan und Isolde* may be considered as much a large programmatic orchestral work with obbligato singing as it is an opera.

Not content to master the present, Wagner attempted to re-create the past through the power and magnetism of his writings. His discussions of Haydn and Mozart and his revisionist description of Beethoven's artistic development turned the history of music into a series of incidents paving the way for himself. Not content to actually visit with Beethoven in a fictional essay and lay claim to the dawning of the romantic age, he reached back all the way to ancient Greece in order to reveal parallels with his own efforts.

In a sense, Wagner reached into the future as well, for our entire society thinks about the relationship between musical and extramusical phenomena in a basically Wagnerian manner. Certainly the way we have been conditioned to respond to music in film, television, and such new media as music videos would tend to support such a conclusion. The equation between discrete musical figures and events, states of mind, and characters has become a virtual truism.

REMINISCENCE OF LISZT: THE WORK OF ART

In 1840, Josef Danhauser painted a "Reminiscence of Liszt" set in a Paris salon. Liszt is seen in youthful profile improvising at the piano; Countess Marie d'Agoult sits huddled at his feet. Behind him, in neat composition, are Victor Hugo, George Sand, Alexandre Dumas *père*, Rossini, and Paganini. On the far end of the piano, near an open window, stands a ridiculously oversized bust of Beethoven, dominating a third of the painting. The seven mortals are almost shrouded, while the head of Beethoven seems to exude a celestial glow. This work is one of the most telling pieces of nineteenth-century iconography, for it documents the composer's change in status from artisan to artist, from mortal to god. There is no doubt that the value ascribed to musical works increased markedly in the first decades of the century. Since, it was argued, music represented "eternal" things, it acquired a new kind of significance. The more significant a thing is, the more it is thought to be worth preserving. But because one cannot easily preserve an ephemeral substance, one must transform it into a thing, something concrete. Thus, Beethoven's head is not only enormous, a tribute to the value of the composer's music; it is also fixed in stone as an object of awe and worship.

By the middle of the nineteenth century the compositions of Beethoven and of those who followed were considered not functional but, rather, almost aggressively nonfunctional; their "function" was to be works of art. Paradoxically, as the actual purpose of musical compositions became less and less clear, their identities seemed to become ever more concrete in the minds of critics and audiences. During this period the substances known earlier as music or musical compositions became canonized as works of art, while the creators of such works became canonized busts on countless mantels and pianos, fulfilling the role of icons in a society obsessed with the loss of religion and the significance of art.

BIBLIOGRAPHY

Jacques Barzun, "The Meaning of Meaning in Music: Berlioz Once More," in *Musical Quarterly*, 66, no. 1 (1980). Carl Dahlhaus, "Program Music," in *Esthetics of Music*, William W. Austin, trans. (1982). Alfred Einstein, *Music in the Romantic Era* (1947). Joseph Kerman, "A Few Canonic Variations," in *Critical Inquiry*, 10, no. 1 (September 1983); and *Contemplating Music* (1985). Peter Kivy, *The Corded Shell: Reflections on Musical Expression* (1980). Lawrence Kramer, *Music and Poetry: The Nineteenth Century and After* (1984).

Peter le Huray, and James Day, eds., *Music and Aesthetics in the Eighteenth and Early Nineteenth Centuries* (1981). Edward Lockspeiser, *Music and Painting* (1973). Leonard Meyer, *Emotion and Meaning in Music* (1956). Richard Norton, *Tonality in Western Culture* (1984). Leon Plantiga, *Romantic Music* (1984). Henry Raynor, *A Social History of Music* (1972); and *Music and Society Since 1815* (1976). Charles Rosen and Henri Zerner, *Romanticism and Realism* (1984).

Walter Salmen, ed., *The Social Status of the Professional Musician from the Mid-*

dle Ages to the Nineteenth Century (1983). Rita Steblin, A History of Key Characteristics in the Eighteenth and Early Nineteenth Centuries (1983). Richard Taruskin, "How the Acorn Took Root: A Tale of Russia," in Nineteenth Century Music, 6, no. 3 (1983). Richard Wagner, A Communication to My Friends, and "German Art and German Policy," William Ashton Ellis, trans., quoted in Albert Goldman and Evert Sprinchorn, eds., Wagner on Music and Drama (1964). Piero Weiss and Richard Taruskin, Music in the Western World (1984).

The Rise of the Classical Repertoire in Nineteenth-Century Orchestral Concerts

William Weber

The overarching significance of nineteenth-century orchestras lay in their building of a museumlike classical repertoire. The word *classical* here, as throughout the essay, does not refer to the classical or classic style of the late eighteenth and early nineteenth centuries. It instead denotes the performance of music of any previous period that forms part of a canon of great works, as is usually meant by the term *classical music*. Orchestral concerts established the authority of most of the key composers in the modern canon of musical taste: first Haydn, Mozart, and Beethoven; then Bach, Schumann, and Mendelssohn; and finally Wagner and Brahms. The orchestras acted as musical kingmakers; at their concerts a pantheon was formed. Their concerts also became some of the most central civic and national rituals in the industrial age, grandiosely celebrating high art and the new social order. As arrogant as they were conservative, the orchestras retreated from contemporary music in the course of the century and, in so doing, established some of the key principles of modern musical taste.

The tradition of revering classical masters was founded during the eighteenth century. The orchestras did not initiate this tradition, for in most countries important tendencies toward that kind of repertoire appeared independently. Orchestral programs were not strictly symphonic—that is, dedicated to instrumental works alone. Vocal music (opera, oratorio, song, and sacred music) remained at the heart of the orchestral repertoire down to the end of the nineteenth century. Finally, the list of great composers went far beyond the names of Haydn, Mozart, and Beethoven. However central that trinity was to the musical canon, it was accompanied by a great number of composers—from Carl Maria von Weber to Giovanni Battista Viotti, and on to Étienne Henri Nicolas Méhul. References to the programs of the major orchestras are derived from the histories by Foster (the Philharmonic Society of London), Elwart and Deldevez (the Society of Concerts of the Conservatoire of Paris), Perger (the Vienna Philharmonic), and Dörffel (the Gewandhaus Concerts of Leipzig).

Browsing through the progams of the early orchestral concerts brings many surprises—arias from Haydn's operas, for example, appeared in the Gewandhaus Concerts as late as the 1860s—and makes generalization suspect. But a few patterns do emerge, primarily in Leipzig, Vienna, Paris, and London—the cities whose orchestras were the most central to European musical life for the greater part of the nineteenth century. This essay will first discuss the eighteenth-century antecedents of the classical repertoire, then sketch out the main periods in the development of orchestral programs, and finally look in greater depth into the leading concert series in these four cities.

EIGHTEENTH-CENTURY ANTECEDENTS OF THE CLASSICAL REPERTOIRE

Music had no canon of great work from the past prior to the eighteenth century. A *canon* is a body of works that are defined as the summit of achievement in an artistic field; they are studied and emulated by practitioners and honored in ritual and iconography. Pieces of music sometimes remained in performance a fairly long time—a number of sixteenth-century *chansons*, for example, were reprinted in successive editions for over a century. But that did not amount to a formal corpus of great works such as had long been established in poetry and sculpture. This situation began to change during the eighteenth century, as both the classical tradition in literature and the structure of musical life underwent fundamental transformations and as the performance of old works began to a significant extent.

While we usually think of the nineteenth-century classics as instrumental, those of the eighteenth century were chiefly operatic and sacred. Since instrumental music was regarded as aesthetically inferior to vocal, it could hardly have provided the basis for the rise of a great musical canon. Moreover, vocal and instrumental music had been so closely related to each other in the evolution of style and genre that neither could have taken an independent path. Even though instrumental music earned a new stature during the early nineteenth century, its links with the longer and more formidable tradition of vocal music remained strong, and the two traditions worked together during the rise of the classical repertoire.

In France the operas of Jean-Baptiste Lully and many of his successors (most prominently André Campra and Jean Joseph Mouret) persisted in the repertoire of the Paris Opéra until the 1770s. Moreover, the Concert Spirituel, the city's central concert series, included sacred works from the turn of the eighteenth century in its programs of vocal and instrumental music. While this repertoire of *la musique ancienne* disappeared completely after that time, it established a tradition of revering great composers in the nation's history, which was continued by the performance of Gluck's operas after his death in 1787 through the 1820s. The city's leading orchestra, the Society of Concerts of the Conservatoire of Paris, was established upon this tradition in 1828 and offered occasional excerpts from the operas of Lully, Rameau, and Gluck.

A parallel to the French repertoire could be found in Prussia. At the Berlin Opera the works of Carl Heinrich Graun and Johann Adolph Hasse were kept in performance from their original production in the 1740s up to the death of Frederick II in 1786. Excerpts from their operas and sacred works were performed by the Gewandhaus Orchestra in Leipzig and at concerts in Berlin and other cities in the late eighteenth century. Indeed, some of these pieces were performed at the Gewandhaus well into the nineteenth century.

A repertoire of old music first developed in Vienna at the private concerts of Baron Gottfried van Swieten in Vienna during the 1770s and 1780s. Gathering together the musical intelligentsia of the capital city, he offered works by Handel and J. S. Bach. During the first half of the nineteenth century, these concerts were followed by private performances of Renaissance and baroque music organized by the high Austrian civil servant Raphael Kiesewetter and by the city's most classically oriented orchestral series, the Concert Spirituel. Here sacred works figured more significantly as the starting point of the classical tradition than was the case in France or Germany.

But the country in which the performance of old music went the farthest during the eighteenth century was England. There the earliest tradition of performing old instrumental works as classics developed, with the concertos of Arcangelo Corelli becoming standard fare at the more than one hundred music societies found throughout England in the course of the century. Best seen as the English parallel to the German societies usually called *collegia musica,* these societies built up a repertoire of *concerti grossi* by Corelli, Handel, Francesco Geminiani, and Charles Avison that persisted in some places well into the nineteenth century. Much of the music of Henry Purcell also remained in performance. His anthems and *Te Deum* were done at summer music festivals by cathedral choirs, and songs from his theater music became a standard part of many singers' concert repertoire.

The most self-conscious interest in old music throughout the eighteenth century was fostered by London's Academy of Ancient Music. For about fifty years after its founding in 1726, it offered a repertoire consisting almost entirely of vocal music focused upon masses and motets of the sixteenth and seventeenth centuries, most prominently those of Giovanni Palestrina, madrigals of the same vintage, and a fair number of more recent works. Though this was a unique repertoire, only parts of which persisted in public concerts, the Academy began a tradition of performing old music that was expanded on a broader plane by the Concerts of Ancient Music after its founding in 1776. The Academy, which lasted until 1796, then adapted its repertoire to that of the Concerts of Ancient Music. (Its programs are found in the Bibliothèque Nationale, in the Leeds Public Library, and in the collection of Christopher Hogwood.) This series drew together the repertoire of old works that had grown up independently of either organization in the course of the eighteenth century—the concertos of Corelli, the madrigals of the sixteenth century, the theater music and sacred works of Purcell, opera arias by Hasse and Jommelli, and, most important of all, a broad representation of Handel's music.

These concerts were an important starting point for nineteenth-century orchestral concerts, since they utilized an ensemble of forty players along with a chorus of the same number and included baroque concertos as an essential part of their repertoire. Their organization as an annual series of subscription concerts also laid down an important social precedent for later orchestral concerts. Indeed, the Philharmonic Society was formed in 1813 as an upper-middle-class alternative to the aristocratic Concerts of Ancient Music and was thereby deeply influenced by them. It also borrowed from their repertoire, offering works by Pepusch, Graun, Hasse, and Jommelli, as well as some less well-known arias of Handel.

But despite these elements of continuity, the orchestras founded in the four major cities during the first half of the nineteenth century took the emerging classical tradition in a new direction. Whereas the old works performed regularly during the eighteenth century had varied from country to country, from this time on they became increasingly oriented toward a common body of great composers—Haydn, Mozart, and Beethoven most essentially. Though the core of this repertoire was Austrian or German, reverence for it spread throughout Europe and eventually all over the Western world, becoming a highly cosmopolitan tradition.

This repertoire also took on much richer intellectual trappings than did its predecessors. There had been little aesthetic discussion of the old works performed during the eighteenth century, and the only place a comprehensive canon of great works was definitely established was England. During the first half of the new century, the cult of Beethoven became a powerful interest among romantic writers, and music a central topic in aesthetics. The "canonization" of the great works came about in this intellectual context; while it was not accomplished overnight, the status of music in culture rose to an entirely new level.

To understand how this came about, the way in which programs were put together must be studied. In the great majority of cases, programs were governed by strict conventions regarding how different genres and performing forces were employed. These conventions tended to change only very gradually. Orchestras in different countries did, of course, adhere to somewhat different practices, determined by variations in national taste and available performing resources—especially the existence of a chorus regularly on call. But basic principles were followed in all countries: no two pieces of the same genre (opera arias, say, or concertos) would appear back-to-back, and vocal and instrumental works would usually alternate. If two vocal pieces appeared together, they normally would be in different genres—an aria and an oratorio chorus, for example. Another convention dictated that an overture or a symphony (perhaps just the first or last movement) would open a concert. The symphony had grown out of the opera overture during the middle of the eighteenth century, and this practice suggests that the two genres continued to be linked in people's minds.

The most important innovation in program format achieved by the end of the eighteenth century was a focus on single long works, usually symphonies. At the beginning of the century, most programs included eight to ten pieces of short or moderate length; the only long compositions were oratorios or sacred works, many of which were presented in segments, with other pieces intervening, or even in succeeding concerts. At the Gewandhaus, for example, the programs from the 1780s through the early 1800s always offered the following sequence in the first half: an overture, an aria, a concerto or solo number, and a vocal or choral finale from an opera or an oratorio. The sequence of the pieces played after the intermission would be almost the same.

Thus, composers were not the focal point or the organizing principle within concert programs. People looked forward chiefly to hearing a sequence of types of music, rather than works by specific persons. Indeed, in many cases composers were not cited on the sheets given to people as they entered a concert hall. A performer would simply introduce a new solo number by himself or one of his colleagues, or a singer would announce the numbers to be sung.

The symphonies of Beethoven broke down the traditional rigidity of programs. In 1807, Beethoven's *Eroica* Symphony was introduced as the opening work in the second half, followed only by one opera aria. This symphony was presented in the same manner anywhere from one to three times every season for several decades. In due course the performance of other long compositions—Beethoven's other symphonies, those of Ludwig Spohr and Peter Winter, and eventually those of Schumann and Berlioz—further dramatized leading symphonic works in an emphatic way. (An index of works performed at the Gewandhaus can be found in Dörffel; the programs themselves are available only in the Museum der Geschichte der Stadt Leipzig.)

Behind this innovation lay the romantic idea of genius—the glorification of personal artistic genius as the lamp from which imagination would spring. In focusing a program upon a single major work, the composer was thus elevated in a manner rarely done before. Romanticism also smashed the strict social customs that had subordinated the composer to tradition. With the reshaping of programs, the masterpieces of the classical repertoire became the focal point of the concerts. By the 1880s it was conventional to feature a major symphony, by one of the dead master composers, in the second half of the program. Formats in general had become far more varied and flexible than they had been at the start of the century. Art was now free from traditional social bonds.

Yet the dominance of the symphonic repertoire in orchestral concerts ought not to be exaggerated. At least in the first half of the century, a substantial portion of the public remained skeptical of these works, finding them too abstract for their taste and preferring instead opera arias and concertos in a lighter vein. In Leipzig, as in many other places, the Beethoven symphonies were usually followed by an aria or a choral finale, probably to keep people from going home early. Moreover, shorter symphonies were still played at the start of a program; thus, they were heard at a disadvantageous time—while people were getting settled in their seats. Vocal music remained an integral part of almost all orchestral series, being eliminated only in the cheaper and less prestigious concerts, where the cost of hiring soloists and a chorus was prohibitive.

It is therefore something of a distortion to speak of the great orchestras exclusively as "symphony" orchestras. Orchestral programs were designed to please a variety of tastes, not simply the people who wished to hear the great symphonies. The role of absolute music has been exaggerated in the history of these concerts, as well. According to this notion, instrumental works are the pinnacle of musical taste, and music must be understood strictly on its own terms rather than on those of a literary text. This idea was not a powerful intellectual force in musical life until the middle of the nineteenth century. During the 1820s and 1830s Beethoven's music was still discussed in poetic or even explicitly programmatic terms. The aesthetician Eduard Hanslick put the idea of absolute music into the center of aesthetics in the 1850s, but it nonetheless was still not applied strictly to the programs of the major orchestras.

THE EVOLUTION OF THE REPERTOIRE

The first major period in the evolution of the classical repertoire occurred between the deaths of Mozart (1791) and Beethoven (1827). During this time a process began in all orchestral programs by which works were kept in performance much longer than was formerly usual. Few works were revived after long disuse. The predominant tendency was to keep works in the repertoire after the death of a composer. Nor was the process inherently historical. While the growth of the study of music history as a scholarly discipline contributed to the building of a canon, it did not help to further generate the canon and, if anything, went in the opposite direction.

The most important idea established during this period was that Haydn, Mozart, and Beethoven were the greatest of the masters. Charles Rosen has traced the formation of this great triad to as early as 1810, chiefly through reviews of Beethoven's works. That Beethoven was elevated into the musical pantheon before he died illustrates how the process of canonization was not a search for history but for eternal standards of taste—which then became part of history. Concern for the taste of the present was the main motivation for investing authority in the past. Only in the early twentieth century did a sharp discontinuity come about between past and present in musical taste.

The orchestras were the most important place where the musical trinity of Haydn, Mozart, and Beethoven became institutionalized. In Leipzig performance of works by Mozart and Haydn continued unbroken in the Gewandhaus Concerts after their deaths. In London, the Philharmonic Society and, in Vienna, the Society of Friends of Music (Die Gesellschaft der Musikfreunde) and the Concert Spirituel took up the works of Mozart and Haydn from the 1810s. In Paris orchestral concerts by students at the Conservatoire offered these pieces in the same decade. The Concert Spirituel paid the fullest attention to this trinity, for in 1824 a concert was devoted exclusively to the music of each of the three great masters.

The music of Haydn, Mozart, and Beethoven nonetheless played differing roles in these concerts. Beethoven was known most of all for his symphonies, which became the sine qua non of virtually all orchestral concerts for the rest of the century. Yet the different genres in which he wrote were represented more equally than was the case with Haydn or Mozart. His concertos and overtures were often performed, as well as excerpts from *Fidelio*, songs and concert arias such as "Adelaide" and "Ah! perfido," his incidental music to *The Ruins of Athens,* and his oratorio *Christ on the Mount of Olives.* Moreover, his piano sonatas sometimes appeared on these programs, as well as some of his chamber works, performed either by a quartet or in orchestral transcription. Because so many different genres of Beethoven's music were presented, Beethoven acted as the integrating force in this repertoire, binding together the music of the other great composers, rather as works by Handel did in London's Concerts of Ancient Music.

Mozart, however, was known first and foremost as a vocal, especially operatic, composer. Though his symphonies sometimes opened programs, they were less common and were placed less prominently than those of Beethoven. Mozart was mainly represented by arias and scenes from *Don Giovanni* and *Figaro.* Performances of excerpts from the other operas varied considerably from place to place. At the Gewandhaus Concerts, for example, excerpts from *La clemenza di Tito* and *Così fan tutte* appeared almost as often as those from the two best-known operas. His motets and *Requiem* were also frequently performed. But his concertos were given strikingly little attention by some orchestras (the least by the Philharmonic Concerts, and the most by the Gewandhaus). All in all, Mozart was not a cult figure as Beethoven was then or as he himself has since become.

Haydn's music rivaled Mozart's in the frequency of its performance at most orchestral concerts. At the Paris Conservatoire, for example, by midcentury his symphonies were played twice as frequently as those of Mozart, and two of his oratorios, *The Creation* and *The Seasons,* were used for ceremonial occasions by almost all orchestras. While London's Philharmonic Society neglected him to a particular degree, the Leipzig Gewandhaus offered a remarkably diversified selection of his music, bringing forward opera selections and movements from sacred works that are rarely performed today. Thus, it was Beethoven's role that was special; Haydn and Mozart took secondary places, despite their seeming equality in the pantheon.

The canon in orchestral concerts went far beyond the musical trinity. During the first half of the century orchestral programs included a rich array of works by composers active between 1770 and 1820, and in some cases even earlier. While many of the pieces were eventually dropped from the repertoire, at any one time there were a large number of works approximately fifty years old by composers now little known. The closer the programming in these series is studied, the more impressive is the variety of works that lasted for a significant period of time.

The earliest composer found on all orchestral programs was Handel. His music persisted in two different ways. One was a vehicle for celebration: his oratorios, odes, and masques were presented on festive occasions, often linked to a charity. The Gewandhaus Orchestra offered these works at its annual benefit for the poor fund; the Society of the Friends of Music presented an annual oratorio festival in a large hall. The best-known choruses from *Messiah* and *Judas Maccabaeus* were often used to close concerts on a festive note. The second role given to his music was more of an artistic one, for on a significant number of occasions, orchestras performed arias from his less well-known oratorios and from his operas. At the Philharmonic Society of London almost half of the vocal numbers by Handel performed in the orchestra's first one hundred years were excerpts from his operas with Italian texts. A similar tendency is evident at the Gewandhaus Concerts after 1850, where there appeared numbers from *Giulio Cesare, Rodelinda, Rinaldo,* and such little-known oratorios as *Semele, Susanna,* and *La resurrezione.* The Vienna Philharmonic likewise offered arias from *Ezio* and *The Choice of Hercules* in the 1860s. Even the Paris Conservatoire orchestra, whose programs were usually not terribly adventurous, presented an aria from *Ezio* in 1854.

Gluck, like Handel, was an important figure in the orchestral repertoire throughout the century. Gluck's operas had a longevity that was quite unusual in the genre, for they were revived in London up to about 1815 and remained on stage in Paris until the 1820s. His arias and vocal scenes were generally more common than his overtures. Though his music did not appear as often in concerts as did that of Handel and Mozart, the regularity of its appearance with all the major orchestras and its relative age compared to most of the repertoire suggest a particular respect paid to Gluck. Because of the dramatic impact of his operas in Paris in the 1770s, he became enshrined in the French national musical tradition. The continuing performance of his arias constituted an important link with the eighteenth century. Though his later operas were the most commonly represented, especially those written or adapted for the Paris Opéra, arias from his earlier works did appear upon occasion. For example, one from *Ezio* was given at the Vienna Philharmonic in 1865.

Another major member of the musical pantheon was Carl Maria von Weber. Though ultimately elevated to a less exalted plane than Haydn, Mozart, and Beethoven, his works rivaled theirs in frequency of performance. His admirers constituted a broader public than did theirs, for, like Mendelssohn, he remained popular among both learned connoisseurs and the general public. His opera overtures were quite fashionable, being among the few works by then dead composers heard at benefit concerts in Paris. In addition, his concertos became vehicles for prominent virtuosos, and his opera arias were frequently performed as well—for example, at the Gewandhaus they outnumbered his instrumental works. After his death in 1826, he was eulogized as being on a level close to that of Haydn or Beethoven. In London the Philharmonic Society played Handel's "Dead March" from *Saul* and Mozart's *Requiem* in his honor.

For several generations a host of composers from the late eighteenth and early nineteenth centuries were found on programs in France and Italy as well as Austria and Germany. Not only did pieces from the middle of the eighteenth century by Hasse, Graun, and Jommelli occasionally appear but also many by composers of the next generation or so—Sacchini, Sarti, Vogler, Cimarosa, Paisiello, Méhul, Winter, Viotti, and Andreas and Bernhard Romberg. Cherubini deserves particular mention; arias from his operas composed just after the turn of the century were central to the repertoire of most orchestras and related in interesting ways to the Gluckian tradition. Similarly, the overtures of Méhul were found in the programs of almost all the major orchestras until the last quarter of the century, as were Viotti's violin concertos and Vogler's overtures and sacred works.

But even though a growing repertoire of old works was in place at orchestral concerts by the time of Beethoven's death, the modern canon of musical masterworks was as yet only partially discernible. While the names of Haydn, Mozart, and Beethoven were already revered as a unit, there was only a vague sense of a complete canon of great works surrounding them. It was during the two decades after Beethoven's death, the second period in this essay, that a self-conscious sense of this repertoire as a canon was established. This was a critical point in the development of the classical repertoire, since by traditional expectations it would have been about this time that the music of the generation of Haydn and Mozart should have dropped out of performance. What most distinguished this period from the former one was the militance with which the emerging canon was defended; the idea of classical music now became a cause.

The militance of taste for the classics was a reaction against the intense commercialism of musical life during this period. The growth of publishing and concert-giving for a mass public brought about a rash of simplified editions of the most recent and popular opera arias and virtuoso numbers—mostly to be played at salons, the cocktail parties of the time. The orchestras accordingly stood outside the mainstream of musical taste; popular attention was focused upon revivals of Rossini's operas, upon the *bel canto* singing in the operas of Donizetti and Bellini, and upon the virtuoso pieces of superstars like Franz Liszt, Sigismond Thalberg, and Henri Herz. Even though Haydn, Mozart, and Beethoven were generally considered the most distinguished composers in recent history, their works were seen by many to be approachable only by connoisseurs, not by the general public.

The more serious musicians and amateurs therefore turned to the classics to combat salon music, which they thought was degrading popular taste. They were not interested in old music but rather wanted to establish taste upon loftier, firmer, and less modish principles. Much the same tendency had stimulated some of the eighteenth-century cults for old music. In England especially, the idea of ancient music arose in large part in opposition to the fast pace of musical life in the dynamic English commercial economy.

The musical canon began to take on its own language and symbols within this context. The word *classical* had been used occasionally in England in the late eighteenth century as a synonym for *ancient music*, and German critics of the 1810s and 1820s sometimes used it to honor the works of Haydn and Mozart. But during the 1830s the term became standard in almost all European countries to designate the canon of great works. In 1832, for example, a writer in the *Revue musicale* declared, with some exaggeration, that people were either "classicists or Rossinists." And in 1842 the pamphlet announcing the formation of the Vienna Philharmonic Orchestra called for classical music.

Orchestral taste during this period might better be described as conservative rather than reactionary. The officials who chose the programs did not turn their backs on all music of their time. Some of them—the leaders of the Philharmonic Society of London especially—commissioned new works of a serious nature from Schumann, Mendelssohn, and Spohr. Nor were fashionable operatic or virtuosic pieces entirely absent, since the officials generally tried to appeal to a public broader than simply the connoisseurs who knew Beethoven's symphonies by heart. At the Philharmonic concerts in London, for example, arias by Donizetti were frequent, and such virtuosos as the violinist Camillo Sivori appeared fairly often.

Nonetheless, in the decades before 1850, orchestras were slowly building up a standard repertoire of classics, taking few chances on young composers. While their repertoire was usually seen as an idealistic force in musical life, some commentators saw it leading in a less fortunate direction. As early as 1839, for example, a French magazine writer criticized the Conservatoire orchestra for playing so much music of Beethoven and his contemporaries and specifically for turning down a new symphony offered them by the German composer Franz Lachner.

It was during the period 1848–1870 that orchestras and their classical repertoire moved into the center of musical life. When musical life resumed after the revolutions of 1848–1849, there was a serious trend in public taste that favored the orchestras and the classical repertoire. The public seemed tired of the musical razzle-dazzle of the earlier period; it seems to have wanted something more substantial than vocal or technical display. A new generation of virtuosos, most prominently Henri Vieuxtemps, Joseph Joachim, and Anton Rubinstein, began playing the concertos of Mozart and Beethoven (as Liszt had done), and their performances became feature attractions.

During this period orchestras grew from private concert societies into national cultural institutions. The revolutions had something to do with it, since the performance of oratorios served as a powerful ritual of social unity. The rapid pace of the industrial revolution contributed further to this process, creating a need for new kinds of civic celebration. The canon of great works emerged among the most important bastions of high culture in the new industrial society, providing high-minded art as a counterpoise to the increasingly aggressive profit-seeking in the marketplace. Urban growth played a part as well, since big new concert halls were put up in all major cities. In Vienna, for example, the Musikverein was built by the Society of the Friends of Music with funds from the state. While during the 1840s the Society's orchestra had been a little-known amateur ensemble, its professionalization and shift to the new hall placed it in the center of the musical world.

The classical repertoire changed in several important respects. One was the growing prominence of overtures, arias, and full scenes from operas made popular from the 1820s through the 1840s. However much the proponents of the German symphonic masterworks were antipathetic to the most popular operas of those decades, pieces from these works appeared in the programs of most of the orchestras. Rossini was the composer most often chosen, and Bellini the least, even though his *Norma* was frequently excerpted. Donizetti's and Meyerbeer's arias became staples of many orchestras for the rest of the century. Thus did the tradition of operatic repertoire in orchestral concerts evolve from the initial interest in Handel, Hasse, and Gluck, to Mozart, Paisiello, and Cimarosa, and then to composers of *bel canto.*

A much newer element in the repertoire was music of the Renaissance and the baroque. Aside from the music of Handel, works in the baroque style were a rarity in orchestral programs before 1835. Bach was the first major figure whose music was revived. Though a few earlier performances are to be found, the Bach revival began most prominently with Mendelssohn's 1829 performance of the *St. Matthew Passion* in Berlin, where, with several of his students, C. P. E. Bach had kept alive the study of his father's music. The orchestras were able to join this movement because they made use of diverse instrumental resources—choruses, solo players, and chamber groups, as well as the orchestra itself. Bach's concertos, fugues, and dance suites were the most commonly performed, either by chamber players or in orchestral transcription. The Gewandhaus led the way with performances of his choral works—not only arias from the Passions but also from little-known cantatas.

The Bach revival set off a much broader movement for early music at orchestral concerts, eventually reaching as far back as the sixteenth century. Here again, choruses played a central role. Psalm settings by Alessandro Stradella were presented by virtually all the major orchestras; the concertos of Tartini were common; and vocal works by Luigi Rossi were given in Paris, Vienna, and Leipzig. The Conservatoire went the farthest in this direction. It offered music not only by these composers and the French national figures Lully and Rameau but also *a cappella* pieces by such sixteenth-century composers as Orlando di Lasso, Giovanni Palestrina, Costanzo Festa, and Tomás Luis de Victoria. The Gewandhaus Orchestra had almost as strong musicological interests, offering works by the same composers and works by Alessandro and Domenico Scarlatti and Michael Praetorius.

The baroque revival functioned in part as a return to the eighteenth-century origins of the classical repertoire. It increased the number of performances of Handel's music, especially of his opera arias, and revived interest in works of the early classical period by Jommelli, Hasse, and Graun. Moreover, the performance of sacred music by the orchestras grew to some degree out of the tradition of musical learning dating from the early seventeenth century, usually called the *stile antico*. Though the *stile antico* was originally only a set of compositional rules associated with the vocal style of Palestrina, it engendered the performance of sacred polyphony first in eighteenth-century England and then in early-nine-teenth-century France, Germany, and Austria. It also continued to play an important role in music education.

This is not to say that pieces of baroque and Renaissance music were frequent at orchestral concerts. Nowhere were they offered more than a few times each season, and much of the public was not interested. But the revival of old music was so unusual that these few instances were necessarily very significant. Even though the main repertoire did not derive from historicist interests, this later addition to it was a major force in the growth of the historical study of music.

Even though opera selections and early music brought a new variety to the orchestral repertoire after midcentury, in other respects the pro-grams became considerably more standardized. The enshrining of the master composers throughout Europe brought about a greater homoge-nization of the repertoire. While during the early 1830s most of the orchestras honored a fair number of local composers (both living and dead) who had no international reputations, by the 1870s they increas-ingly played music by the same core of dead master composers. The pro-cess of critical scrutiny had reduced the number of composers since the turn of the century, and the growing proportion of works by the masters had allowed only a few composers to make their names in orchestral music. All of which added up to an increasingly narrow and rigid focus upon the musical canon, at the expense of new music.

A crisis in the acceptance of new music began during this period. Whereas at the start of the century it was unusual for works by dead composers to occur more than occasionally on concert programs, by the 1870s none of the major orchestras devoted more than a third of their annual repertoire to the music of living composers, and the proportion was often smaller. As the orchestras came into the focus of musical life they came to uphold an increasingly backward-looking musical taste that resisted advanced styles. Admittedly, they still performed a great deal more contemporary music than orchestras do today (only 10 percent of the works performed by the more forward-looking orchestras in the 1980s were by living composers), and the gap between composers and their public was still much less. But the roots of the present-day situation of new music are in this period, and the orchestras were the leading force behind the retardation of taste.

Since the orchestras came under intense pressure by composers to perform their works, they developed the custom of holding trial performances of new works, usually only for a few guests. The practice is evident as early as the late 1810s at the Philharmonic Society of London, and almost all major orchestras had adopted it by 1850. Since only a few pieces played at the trials were performed publicly, the sessions functioned as an insidious way by which the orchestras wielded power over composers while granting them some opportunity to hear their own works.

The Wagnerian movement launched a bitter ideological attack against orchestras during the 1850s. Led by the *Neue Zeitschrift für Musik* in Leipzig and Franz Liszt in Weimar, the Wagnerians attacked the Gewandhaus Orchestra and all such institutions for their increasing concentration on the established masters and their resistance to forward-looking works. The Wagnerians were answered in equally vicious terms by Eduard Hanslick and François Joseph Fétis, who in effect set themselves up as the interpreters and guardians of the musical canon performed at orchestral concerts. While neither Wagner nor the Wagnerians rejected the great works as models, they developed an ideological defense of new music that is still powerful. They shifted their attention away from established orchestras to form their own performing institutions dedicated to new music and to the less well known classics.

Ironically, Wagner himself owed much to the orchestras for the diffusion of his music. Prior to the 1880s his works appeared far more frequently in concerts than in opera halls, in large part because of his role as one of the most important conductors of the repertoire as a whole. Despite the controversiality of his operas and the ideas in his essays, which made his reputation in the first place, excerpts from his music had become a staple at most orchestral concerts by the time of his death in 1883. Bayreuth, too, was to become a musical museum.

Another major development during the middle of the nineteenth century was the establishment of new concert series for audiences less affluent than the wealthy subscribers to the major orchestras. A series of this kind called the Euterpe had been in existence in Leipzig since the early 1830s. Low-priced concerts started in London's Crystal Palace after its reopening in 1854; and the Popular Concerts of Jules Pasdeloup, begun in Paris in 1861, were followed by those of Édouard Colonne in 1873 and Charles Lamoureux in 1881. All of these concerts formed around the basic classical repertoire. Though few of them were able to present a chorus, common in the older series, solo vocal works—opera excerpts especially—were frequent in most of the newer series.

These concerts also paid greater attention to new music than did the elite orchestras. Though we ought not exaggerate how far they went in this direction (as their promoters tended to do), most of them welcomed some young composers and performed works by the avant-garde followers of Liszt and Wagner. The performance of controversial new works provided these orchestras an opportunity to get themselves into the public spotlight and to draw a public that was not as intolerant of new music. These series did not have a mass audience, strictly speaking. Many of their listeners were middle-class people who were fairly well educated musically—the clerk who would bring his well-worn pocket scores of the Beethoven symphonies. In gathering this public, the popular orchestral concerts played a significant role in the advancement of new music during the late nineteenth century.

THE ORCHESTRAS

Leipzig. Leipzig was the only one of the four major cities with an orchestral history spanning the eighteenth and nineteenth centuries. The Gewandhaus programs show how the classics came to dominate the repertoire, as can best be seen in the percentage of works by living and dead composers as it evolved between the 1780s and the 1870s. During the years 1781–1785, only 13 percent of the works presented were by dead composers; 84 percent, by living composers; and 3 percent, unidentifiable. By the period 1820–1825, these numbers had changed to 23 percent, 75 percent, and 2 percent, respectively, for during that time the music of Mozart and Haydn, among others, remained in performance. (These figures have been derived from Dörffel.) No compensation has been made for the length of works, because that is too problematic an adjustment and because some people must have been interested chiefly in the brief opera arias. In any event, such an adjustment would make the shift to works by dead composers look even more drastic.

From the 1810s on, the percentage of works by dead composers was to rise about 10 percent every decade. This gradual change emerged as an institutional process rather than as the work of any specific musical figures—Mendelssohn especially. Between 1828 and 1834 the proportion by dead composers had risen to 39 percent and that for the living had dropped to 60 percent. Between 1837 and 1847 (while Mendelssohn was music director) the figures had changed to 48 percent, 50 percent, and 2 percent, respectively. The triumph of the classics at midcentury is evident in the figures between 1850 and 1855: 38 percent, 61 percent, and 1 percent, respectively; and finally between 1865 and 1870: 76 percent and 24 percent. Thus, between 1820 and 1870 the power of the present and the past had become exactly reversed—moving ineluctably from the living to the dead.

The changes in the Gewandhaus programs are particularly interesting because, as a small city (103,000 people in 1870, compared with 3.25 million in London), the central concert series fulfilled the needs of audiences that in the capitals went to various concerts. Its public was therefore more diverse in taste than in larger cities, and from the 1820s to the 1850s there was a running conflict within the public over the relative prominence of the great symphonies versus the opera and virtuoso literature. The victory of the former over the latter is evident as well in the programs for the *Extra-Concerte*, events sponsored by individual performers but licensed by the orchestra. As can be seen particularly well in the evolving repertoire of the pianist Clara Wieck, these concerts shifted essentially from dazzling virtuoso works to classical chamber works between the 1830s and 1860s.

The victory of the classics came in part because the leading virtuoso performers, such as Joachim and Rubinstein, made them popular. By reviving interest in the concerto, especially the works of Mozart, Beethoven, and Weber, they gave the classical-music repertoire a glamour that became essential to the maintenance of its public. This happened in part because new operas were rather less in vogue after the middle of the century, compared to the period of intense popular interest earlier in the century. The focus of public attention accordingly shifted to some degree from opera stars to the great performers at orchestral concerts—and classical works benefited accordingly. The more idealistic members of the public objected to the popularity of the performers, seeing it as a compromise upon the integrity of the classical concerto. But they had to admit that the virtuosos were responsible in no small part for the acceptance of the classical repertoire by the public at large.

The remarkably early date at which the Euterpe concerts grew up alongside those of the Gewandhaus demonstrates how large and diverse a musical world there was in Leipzig. Begun informally in 1824 and made public after 1830, the Euterpe series had a mixed amateur and professional ensemble and charged half as much as its august competitor. During the 1830s the series took up the classical repertoire in a manner similar to the Gewandhaus, but there was no regular chorus and lieder were substituted for operatic arias. From the start the series outdid the Gewandhaus by offering the works of contemporary composers (Peter von Lindpaintner, Konstantin Julius Becker, and Niels Gade, for example), by presenting works by Berlioz frequently, and by giving numerous local composers the chance to have their pieces played. As the series grew during the 1840s it began to add recent Italian operatic arias but did not lose its contemporary German repertoire.

During the 1860s the Euterpe became a showplace for the music of the faction surrounding Liszt and Wagner. Not only was their music performed but also works by such Wagnerians as Hans von Bülow, Robert Volkmann, and Karl Goldmark. Still, though the series provided an important counterpoise to the conservatism of the Gewandhaus concerts, it did not have the high performing standards or international reputation by which to become a powerful force in the Wagnerian movement. The rest of its repertoire resembled that of the Gewandhaus fairly closely; it too participated in the baroque revival, offering arias from Handel's *Semele* and *Choice of Hercules* and from the chamber music of Bach and Tartini.

When one considers the repertoires of these two orchestras, it becomes clear that Leipzig was one of the most interesting musical cities during the nineteenth century. Though its performing standards did not measure up to the competition in Paris and Vienna, no other orchestras outdid those of Leipzig in the fascinating variety and richness of both classical and contemporary repertoire.

London. The programs of the Philharmonic Society of London were similar to those of the Gewandhaus Orchestra in their fairly considerable length (usually six to ten works) and in the variety of genres and performing forces. But unlike the Gewandhaus, the Philharmonic concerts offered a classical repertoire from their very start, since the performance of old works had developed so far in England during the eighteenth century. In its very first seasons, the proportion of works by dead composers was close to that of the living. The orchestra regularly played symphonies of Haydn and arias of Mozart, as well as many works by other middle- and late-eighteenth-century composers. The Rossini craze of the 1820s briefly disturbed this balance between new and old, but in the late 1830s the proportion of the classics in the repertoire began growing again, and by 1870, music by living composers made up only a quarter of the pieces performed. A further change came about during the last quarter of the century, when Sir Arthur Sullivan focused his programs upon a striking amount of contemporary English music—probably more than was found at any other of the major orchestras.

The Philharmonic differed from the orchestras in the three other major cities in its social base. The Leipzig Gewandhaus, the Paris Conservatoire, and the Vienna Philharmonic orchestras all commanded publics from the highest social classes; subscription tickets to these concerts were usually passed down between generations in wills. But while the Philharmonic Society originally admitted subscribers by nomination within its board, as was the norm in all such series, it never had an aristocratic following, and during the 1830s it lost many of its most prestigious subscribers. By the 1840s anyone could buy a subscription at will, as was not the case with any of the other leading orchestras. Accordingly, in 1845 an exclusive series of chamber-music concerts was established called the Musical Union, offering programs almost entirely from the classical repertoire. Thus, the Musical Union became London's most prestigious classical-music series.

The programs of the Philharmonic Society were the slowest to lose the rigid format found at the start of the nineteenth century. The almost invariable sequence in each of the two parts of a concert during the first half of the century was a symphony, an aria or song, a chamber-music piece or concerto, a second vocal number, and finally an overture or a symphony. The Philharmonic concerts did not have a chorus, probably because the Concert of Ancient Music, for several decades its competition, was so noted for its singers from the Chapel Royal and from the leading municipal choirs. During the 1850s the number of works on each program began to decrease somewhat; piano solos replaced chamber works, and the second part of a concert sometimes became focused upon a single major work—though still generally followed by an aria. It was only after the 1880s that the Philharmonic Society followed the example of other orchestras by shortening programs and limiting the second part to a major symphony.

The records of the Philharmonic Society show particularly well how the standard classical repertoire became sacrosanct in the middle of the century. In January 1855 its directing board wrote Wagner that "the primary object of the Philharmonic Society has been, from the beginning, the cultivation of orchestral music by the performance of standard works of that class; and this object has been for a half a century so constantly adhered to, that the subscribers regard the introduction of those symphonies and overtures which have gained European celebrity as indispensable in every concert" (Papers of the Royal Philharmonic Orchestra, Letter to Richard Wagner, 29 January 1855). Visiting soloists played under the same restrictions—never more than one solo work per concert.

The New Philharmonic Society, which attempted to challenge the established series between 1854 and 1856, departed only in limited respects from its rival in setting programs. The performance of oratorios by British composers was its major innovation. One observer remarked, "Compositions like Mr. Horsley's *Joseph*, Mr. Pierson's *Jerusalem*, and Mr. Macfarren's *Leonore*, however triumphant a single performance, aided by friendly audiences and propitiated critics, may seem, are quite powerless to launch a new society into the open sea of permanent success" (*Atlas*).

Musical events held at the permanent site of the Crystal Palace in Sydenham after 1854 evolved from band concerts to an imposing series of weekly classical-music concerts. Though much less well known than the Pasdeloup and Colonne concerts in Paris, they must be regarded as just as important both socially and musically. Their programs resembled those of the Philharmonic Society in their fairly considerable length, regular offerings of Beethoven and Mozart symphonies, and the frequency of operatic selections (some nights being devoted exclusively to opera). A tendency toward popular repertoire carried on, however, in the performance of English ballads, as was not the case at the Philharmonic. The component of English music was fairly strong, but probably not featured as centrally as was the case of its counterpart in Paris.

Vienna. Professional orchestral concerts were founded by far the latest in Vienna. Although the Vienna Philharmonic was formed in 1842, it gave no more than two programs per year until its reconstitution in 1860. Prior to 1848 the Society of the Friends of Music and the Concert Spirituel each presented four concerts a year, but neither commanded much public attention, and each one came close to collapse at some point in this period. By principle the Society included only amateur players in the ensemble of about eighty-five and therefore had weaker performing standards than that of the Concert Spirituel, where professionals occupied some of the principal chairs.

The Society's programs were focused on recent works, much in the manner of late-eighteenth-century concerts; they did not suggest a canon as did those of the Philharmonic Society in London. Their usual sequence was a classical symphony, an aria, a solo instrumental number or concerto, an overture, and an opera finale or a cantata movement. Though the opening symphonies were usually by Mozart or Beethoven, the programs featured instrumental works by Spohr, Hummel, Kalkbrenner, Moscheles, and Mayseder but—given the amateur soloists usually involved—not the more challenging works of Thalberg or Liszt.

The programs of the Concert Spirituel, however, developed a purer classical repertoire than any other orchestral concerts in the first half of the century. Essentially a spin-off from the Society of the Friends of Music in 1819, the Concert Spirituel was designed to feature a higher level of repertoire and performance than was to be found with the Society's ensemble. Before the death of Beethoven almost half the works performed were by dead composers; after that time, virtually three-quarters were by dead composers. The programs' focus upon sacred music gave them a distinctly learned tone. The chorus came from the choir of the Augustinerkirche, where Franz Gebauer, music director of the concerts in the 1820s, was choirmaster. Only one work of sixteenth- or early-seventeenth-century polyphony is known to have been sung (Allegri's *Miserere* in 1835) and no pieces by J. S. Bach seem to have appeared. But masses, motets, and oratorios by Handel, Haydn, Mozart, and Beethoven were joined by those of other composers revered for their compositional craft—Pergolesi, Marcello, Graun, C. P. E. Bach, Vogler, Albrechtsberger, and the more recent Gebauer, Ignaz Mosel, and Éduard Lannoy (Gebauer's successor at the concerts). The absence of any recent opera selections, in favor of arias by Mozart and Cherubini, also gave the series an austere character.

Actually, these programs seem remarkably modern in format when compared with those of the Philharmonic Society of London or the Leipzig Gewandhaus during the first half of the century. Since few opera or solo virtuoso numbers were done, it was unusual for more than five works to be performed, and single movements from symphonies or concertos were uncommon. The concerts were touted as the model of artistic high-mindedness. One observer compared them to the "profane" benefit concerts; another saw them as "a dam . . . by which to set a bulwark against the pressure of today's awful taste for musical gaudiness and exaggeration" (*Allgemeine musicalische Zeitung*).

After the revolutions of 1848, the mood of Viennese musical life changed more drastically than in any of the other major cities. Little was left of the giddy, hypercommercial state of musical activity; the number of concerts declined, and even the most fashionable virtuosos began playing Mozart and Beethoven. "All of the capital's concert life has changed fundamentally in the last ten years," said one commentator, for "no more tumults of virtuoso concerts, but rather great instrumental and vocal presentations, have taken root as the high point of the season. Indeed, the ungodly proliferation of concert promotions has given way to the present flood of 'classical' taste" ("Zehn Jahre aus dem wiener Musikleben").

The Society of the Friends of Music was a leading force behind the new order of concerts. In 1850 the Society made the amateur ensemble essentially a private gathering and established a professional orchestra as the basis for its four annual public concerts. These concerts offered much more of the international and classical repertoire; the works of living local composers became uncommon, and the programs focused on the most revered of the classical composers, now including Schubert, Mendelssohn, and Schumann. In 1861 the series was expanded to six concerts, two of which were devoted to oratorios or sacred works, often Bach's Mass in B Minor and Beethoven's *Missa Solemnis*. The Society thereby made more prominent the annual oratorio festival it had presented every year since its inception, drawing upon conservatory students and wealthy amateurs for the chorus. The revolution played no small role in encouraging these grand rites. As was the case in Leipzig as well, the tradition of paying homage to the musical masters provided an important vehicle for pulling society back together again.

After its reconstitution in 1860, the Vienna Philharmonic adopted the most modern program format and the strictest symphonic focus found in any of the major orchestras. It never developed a chorus, and the performance of vocal works gradually declined in frequency, probably because the Friends of Music (whose public seems to have overlapped the Philharmonic's considerably) focused its repertoire upon large choral works. The baroque revival was thus weaker there than elsewhere, though instrumental works by J. S. Bach, Stradella, Handel, and Rossi were presented. Most important of all, as at the Concert Spirituel earlier, the Philharmonic concerts rarely included more than five pieces and tended to focus upon a single major work after the intermission—without the traditional concluding aria or scene that hung on elsewhere. The elite audience that gathered Sundays at 11 A.M. got home to an early lunch.

For all their austerity, the Philharmonic concerts were not especially reactionary in regard to new music. While the directors did not take many chances on unknowns, by the 1880s the programs had a healthy representation of works by such composers as Brahms, Bruckner, Raff, Henselt, Kässmeyer, Dvořák, Smetana, Massenet, and Richard Strauss. What hindered the dissemination of new music in Vienna was the absence of any low-priced and musically adventurous series such as existed in all the other major cities. The Society of the Friends of Music and the Philharmonic worked in tandem to obstruct the rise of such an organization; musically, Vienna was a closed society. It was not until 1899 that the Vienna Concert Orchestra, later named the Vienna Symphony, was founded with such ends in mind.

In Vienna orchestral concerts were thus weak in their development throughout the nineteenth century. The symphonic classics were accessible to a very small group of people—during the first half of the century to devotees of the two amateur orchestras, and in the second to the prestigious subscribers to the Philharmonic and the Society of the Friends of Music. The late date at which cheaper concerts arrived in the city was a factor in the social and artistic radicalism of Viennese composers by the end of the century. The followers of Arnold Schoenberg declared their independence from the general public and began building their own performing institutions, most prominently the Society for Private Musical Performances, just after World War I. In the elitism of the Philharmonic and the Friends of Music, the roots of this artistic rebellion can be found.

Paris. The orchestra of the Conservatoire of Paris, founded in 1828, was by far the most resistant to new music. During its first two decades under the founding director, François Antoine Habeneck, the names of contemporary composers recurred fairly often—George Onslow, Henri Brod, Charles Dancla, and Auguste Franchomme. Yet as early as 1840 the directing committee began limiting new works and trial performances. In the decade after Habeneck left his post in 1847, the percentage of works by living composers declined to somewhere between 10 percent and 15 percent—that is, one piece at every other of the dozen concerts each season. Even at that, most of these works were by composers no longer active—Rossini, Auber, Meyerbeer, and Berlioz. In the early 1860s the committee gave up all leadership in new music; it announced that it would not entertain any requests for performances but would instead solicit works only from a few well-established composers.

A certain purism can be seen in the programs of the Conservatoire orchestra. The city's role as international tastemaker and center of the music-publishing business stood behind this tendency, causing classical-music concerts to keep as far as possible from the world of salon music. The programs generally excluded the arias of Donizetti and Bellini, and almost all arias from recent works, offering instead the older arias by Gluck, Mozart, and Rossini and orchestral selections by Wagner. Curiously enough, operatic choruses by the leading opera composer Meyerbeer were done fairly often. A strong emphasis upon sacred music also lent these programs a learned character, rather like that of the Viennese Concert Spirituel. The seventy-member chorus was involved in several pieces on each program and usually closed the concert. A similar tendency is evident in the limited attention paid to the concerto in the second half of the century. Not only were the piano concertos of Mozart rarely performed, but also new works in the genre appeared only about once a season during the 1860s and 1870s, a period when the genre was so important elsewhere.

Compared with the Euterpe in Leipzig, Paris' popular orchestral concerts took a nationalistic rather than a factional approach to leadership in new music. Jules Pasdeloup began this tendency, first while directing a series of orchestral concerts by students of the Conservatoire during the 1850s and then as head of his Popular Concerts after 1861. "They were so numerous," said an observer after Pasdeloup's death in 1887, "the composers for whom Pasdeloup was a veritable providence, drawing them out of obscurity, performing their works, and making them known among the public" (*Feuilleton du moniteur universel*). Though not always constant in his attention to each of these composers, he figured in the rise to fame of Jules Massenet, Vincent d'Indy, Georges Bizet, Augusta Holmès, and Édouard Lalo. Though supporting few foreign composers, he nonetheless championed Wagner in the face of French nationalism.

Édouard Colonne began his series, initially called the Concert National, in 1873 in the wake of defeat by Germany. He oriented the orchestra's new works toward French composers and achieved considerably higher performing standards than did Pasdeloup. It is indicative of the mood of the time that Pasdeloup tried to compete with Colonne for several seasons by labeling the two halves of his programs "classical" and "modern" (though padding the modern section with numbers by Rossini and Meyerbeer).

Yet the repertoire of all of these orchestras was rooted in the classics. During the first three decades of the Colonne Concerts, for example, works by living composers amounted to only 35 percent of the compositions selected and 28 percent of all performances of these pieces. The same composers dominated as at the Conservatoire—Beethoven, Mozart, Haydn, Weber, and Mendelssohn. The baroque revival was also apparent in Pasdeloup's performances of instrumental pieces by J. S. Bach, Tartini, and Rameau; string quartets were done in transcription in the same fashion as at the Conservatoire. Still, the programs at the Popular Concerts differed from those of the Conservatoire in the absence of a regular chorus and the infrequency of solo vocal, especially operatic, pieces. The concerto played a much more significant role here, both classics and new works, and there was a more diverse symphonic repertoire. The Pasdeloup concerts, for example, often presented the symphonies and suites of Franz Lachner.

CONCLUSION

During the nineteenth century, orchestral concerts laid down a canon of great works that became the most important such repertoire in musical life. By comparison, the opera houses of Europe were slower and less self-conscious in building a canon; though the works of Rossini and Donizetti remained on stage, they did not attain so lofty a cultural role as the symphonies of Beethoven and Mendelssohn. Chamber-music concerts, though focused upon many of the same composers as the orchestras, played a less public and more specialized role in the shaping of taste. The most drastic change in taste at orchestral concerts was the enshrining of the great symphonic works. Here instrumental music acquired a central place in musical taste for the first time, and the idea of "absolute" music established its primacy in musical aesthetics.

Yet we must remember the diversity of nineteenth-century orchestral programs. They were not limited to the symphonic literature, for they also included operatic selections, oratorios, songs, and chamber works. The public was equally diverse; the symphonies were not everybody's cup of tea. Though by the end of the century repertoires had become considerably more homogenized in respect to composers and works represented, many programs would seem strange to us today because of the number of short pieces offered, the amount of vocal music, and the variety of composers represented. These traits came out of the eighteenth century, out of the early period in public concerts, and it was not until well into our century that they were to disappear.

BIBLIOGRAPHY

Allgemeine musikalische Zeitung, 17 March 1821. *Atlas,* 9 December 1854. J. Peter Burckholder, "Museum Pieces: The Historicist Mainstream in Music of the Last Hundred Years," in *Journal of Musicology,* 2 (1983). Adam Carse, *The Orchestra from Beethoven to Berlioz* (1948); and *The Orchestra in the Eighteenth Century* (1940). Colonne Concerts, *Trente ans de concerts, 1873–1903* (1903). Jeffrey Cooper, *The Rise of Instrumental Music and Concert Series in Paris, 1828–1871* (1983).

Arthur Dandelot, *La Société des Concerts du Conservatoire de 1828 à 1897* (1898). Édouard Deldevez, *La Société des Concerts du Conservatoire de Musique, 1860 à 1885* (1887). Albert Dörffel, *Geschichte der Gewandhausconcerte zu Leipzig* (1881–1884). Antoine Elwart, *Histoire de la Société des Concerts du Conservatoire imperial de musique* (2nd ed., 1864); and *Histoire des Concerts Populaires de musique classique* (1864). *Feuilleton du moniteur universel,* 17 December 1894. Myles Birket Foster, *History of the Philharmonic Society of London, 1813–1912* (1912).

Eduard Hanslick, *Geschichte des Concertwesens in Wien* (1869–1870). George Hogarth, *The History of the Philharmonic Society of London from Its Foundation, 1813, to Its Fiftieth Year, 1862* (1862). Joseph Kerman, "A Few Canonic Variations," in *Critical Inquiry*, 10 (1983). Reginald Nettle, *The Orchestra in England: A Social History* (1946). Hans-Joachim Nosselt, *Das Gewandhausorchester: Entstehung und Entwicklung eines Orchesters* (1943). Richard von Perger, *Denkschrift zur Feier des ununtergebrochenen Fünfzigjährigen Bestandes der Philharmonischen Konzerte in Wien* (1910). Richard von Perger and Robert Hirschfeld, *Geschichte der k. k. Gesellschaft der Musikfreunde in Wien* (1912). Philharmonic Society of London, Papers on Permanent Loan, British Library, London.

Society of Concerts of the Conservatoire of Paris, Papers in Bibliothèque Nationale, Paris. Vienna Philharmonic Orchestra, Papers in Archive of the Orchestra, Vienna. William Weber, *Music and the Middle Class: The Social Structure at Concert Life in London, Paris and Vienna, 1830–1848* (1975); "Mass Culture and Reshaping of European Musical Taste, 1770-1870," *International Review of the Sociology and Aesthetics of Music*, 8 (1977); and "Wagner, Wagnerism and Musical Idealism," in David C. Large and William Weber, eds., *Wagnerism in European Culture and Politics* (1984). K. W. Whistling, *Der Musikverein Euterpe zu Leipzig, 1824–1874* (1874). "Zehn Jahre aus dem wiener Musikleben," *Recensionen und Mittheilungen über Theater und Musik*, 6 (1860).

Music In Relation to the Other Arts: The Critical Debate

Jane F. Fulcher

In a sense, the critical debate in Europe over the nature and thus the appropriate boundaries of content or meaning in instrumental music bisects the nineteenth century. Significantly, the debate erupted most intensely after the revolutions of 1848–1849, in the wake of, and partly brought on by, the political and cultural rupture marked, for it was then that the ambiguities inherent in romantic musical theory surfaced baldly and polarized by entering the context of social and cultural issues. Thus, interlaced with cultural theory as well as with professional and personal antagonisms, the traditional questions of musical aesthetics posed themselves in strident new terms. The interlocked questions of the most desirable way to listen to music and the preferable tendencies in musical style elicited new attitudes and an ideologically charged response.

To understand these developments, we must trace them systematically on a number of different levels, beginning with the ambiguities implicit in romantic musical thought. These we may examine most clearly in the writings of Robert Schumann, whose immediate successors were responsible, in part, for launching the critical debate. Our attention must focus on the question of why the positions became opposed, on the personal, professional, and cultural confrontations that now converged, on the terms and arguments of each side, and on the reality of what was being said—using words that have since changed in sense. Despite the rhetoric or disclaimers of several of the figures involved, the issue that fundamentally divided the positions was the social function of music—that is, the role that music was now to serve in European civilization, in light of the new cultural era that the revolutions in Europe had ineluctably ushered in. Thus, we shall examine the proponents, as well as the opponents, of the "music of the future" and the complex manner in which both "progressive" and "conservative" tendencies interacted in both.

To understand the debate completely we must not concentrate exclusively on the synchronic element—that is, on the simultaneous developments occurring in causally interacting cultural spheres. The issues must be followed diachronically and traced from Germany and Austria into France, where they became imperative after 1870, for the question of musical representation or appropriate musical content is one that came to divide positions in the late nineteenth century. These issues vitally affected not only the music of Brahms, Wagner, Liszt, and those who came after them but also several generations of composers in France. Here, too, it involved a struggle for power within the major institutions of musical life, becoming an obstreperous debate in which the professional stakes were high.

The theories and writings of Robert Schumann embody the legacy of romantic thought about music and the seeds of the critical debate to follow, for the subtle argument characteristic of the romantic theorists concerning expression and perception in music became, in Schumann, ambiguities and vacillations. Instrumental music, according to Schumann, as well as to Hegel and E. T. A. Hoffmann, was quintessentially a medium for the expression of the elusive realm of inner life. But the ambiguous issue was a question of who was expressing, the composer or the listener, and the way in which the creative and perceptive acts relate.

For Hoffmann, music expressed the composer. It was an artistic transcription of the innermost self, but one that was inherently vague, being separate from the external or sensual world. In music the self was transcribed into pure and inimitable artistic terms, and hence a content was indeed present, but it was not by nature precise. Music, for Hoffmann, was simultaneously transcendental and personal, expressing the composer's feelings but through reference to an infinite realm:

> When we speak of music as an independent art, should we not always restrict our meaning to instrumental music, which, scorning every aid, every admixture of another art, gives pure expression to music's specific nature, recognizable in this form alone? ... Music discloses to man an unknown realm, a

world that has nothing in common with the external sensual world that surrounds him, a world in which he leaves behind all definite feelings to surrender himself to an inexpressable longing.

Have you ever so much as suspected this specific nature, you miserable composers of instrumental music, you who have laboriously strained yourselves to represent definite events? How can it ever have occurred to you to treat after the fashion of the plastic arts the art diametrically opposed to the plastic? Your sunrises, your tempests, your... *"Bataille des trois empereurs,"* and the rest... were surely quite laughable aberrations....

In song, where poetry, by means of words, suggests definite emotions, the magic power of music acts as does the wondrous elixir of the wise, a few drops of which make any drink more palatable and more lordly. Every passion... is clothed by music with the purple luster of Romanticism, and even what we have undergone in life guides us out of life into the realm of the infinite.

(Strunk, 5:35)

Music, then, is a mediator between two realms of man's experience, its function relating to its special force as a metaphorical or poetic language. For this reason, Hoffmann condemns the tendencies he sees in instrumental music to make its expression more specific, thus violating its inherent nature. Against these unhealthy trends, Hoffmann pits the work of Beethoven, who, he claims, first exploited music's abstract and yet referential language: "Mozart and Hayden, the creators of our present instrumental music, were the first to show us the art in its full glory; the man who looked in it with all his love and penetrated its innermost being is Beethoven" (Strunk, 5:36). Composers like Beethoven, according to Hoffmann, were able to transcribe "all the music of his innermost self," but to communicate it in abstract terms.

Certainly, Beethoven did play a pivotal role in defining musical content as both personal or specific and universal or abstract: he himself supposedly indicated that an understanding of his Piano Sonata in D Minor, Op. 31, no. 2, could be induced by a reading of Shakespeare's play *The Tempest.* And the late quartets, such as Opus 135, carry references to a private content or significance that served as the composer's inspiration for the music. For Hoffmann, great composers inscribed a content in their works, one that emanated from the most profound recesses of their inner being but one that was nevertheless translated into an indirect language accessible to the listener through his own interpretive act. Hence he speaks of "all the wonderful, enchanting pictures and apparitions that the composer has sealed into his work with magic power" and that may be "called into active life."

Hegel further developed the idea that the content the composer invests in his music is accessible to the perception of the listener in an indirect way. For Hegel, this occurs not through active interpretation but rather through an almost unconscious act of identification:

> Music is spirit or soul, sounding without mediation for itself alone and find-ing satisfaction in its self-recognition.... It transforms the momentary state of affection in the inner self into one of self-recognition, into a free intro-spection, and in this way liberates the heart from oppression and suffer-ing....The special task of music is that, in presenting any content to the mind, it presents it neither as it is latent in consciousness as a general con-cept, nor as definite external form offers itself elsewhere to observation...but rather in the way in which it becomes alive in the sphere of "subjective inwardness." ... If we refrain from new intellectual analysis and listen with-out restraint, the musical art work absorbs and carries us along with it.
> (Strunk, 5:109)

For Hegel, music, in inviting identification with the composer's feel-ings and hence self-recognition on the part of the listener, naturally com-bines two processes, for perception of music is not an intellectual matter or rational process but an absorbing identification, a natural empathy with its significance. This aspect of Hegel's thought was to become trou-blesome for Schumann, and soon after, it became a central point in the controversy between Eduard Hanslick and Franz Liszt. As Edward Lipp-man has noted, the writings of Schumann confront the problem of the distinction that can or cannot be made between the effect of music and its stimulus. The kind of act that listening should be—active and intel-lectual, or passive—is here integrally linked to the issues of what it is that music communicates and precisely how it does it.

The question of content raised further ambiguities in Schumann's thought and led to the troublesome issue of correctness of interpretation. For Schumann, instrumental compositions did contain a definite con-tent, the result of the specific environmental influences working on the composer. And hence, by implication, "among the interpretations that may exist there will be one that is uniquely sufficient." Indeed, for Schu-mann, the task of criticism, its most essential function, was to get at the content of a work. Thus the role of the new poetic criticism that Schu-mann employed was "to educate the public to the most significant prop-erties of music."

The nature of these properties became yet another troublesome point, causing Schumann to encourage certain programmatic tendencies and yet to criticize others. The ideal, for Schumann, was characteristic music, as distinguished from the explicitly descriptive or pictorial. Characteristic music, for Schumann, and music in general, for Hegel, represented not the the circumstances of life but rather the states of the soul. The "character," then, was not explicit, and yet it was perceptually clear, a disposition obtruding itself so that no other interpretation was possible. Indeed, the basis of its appeal was its very elusiveness, mysterious ambiguity of character, and the challenging vagueness that is inherent in the creative process itself.

Content, for Schumann, was in no way antipathetic to the demands of form. Schumann saw content, even more explicitly than Hegel, as generalized feeling and mood; thus, if music restricts itself to the kind of content to which it is suited, it can be referential and yet satisfy on its own terms. As a result, Lippman observes, Schumann was apparently often unsure or contradictory about the content of his own instrumental compositions.

And so the question of the necessity of programmatic guides for the listener was a subject on which Schumann oscillated and attempted to make fine distinctions. In some cases he was uncertain as to whether guides to the meaning of his works were required; in others he vacillated over how realistic or detailed a program should be and whether or not the listener should employ it.

In his famous review of Berlioz' *Symphonie fantastique*, Schumann took a firm position with regard to what he perceived as the negative effects of explicit programs. As Lippman explains, "Schumann finds fault here not with the practice of composing to a program, but with making the program public, and indeed with the exposure of any of the circumstances of creation." According to Schumann, a program meant that the content of the work, its essential character, was not self-evident, as it should be. Moreover, an explicit program thwarted or restricted that which Schumann valued so highly, the independent poetic fantasy of the listener.

Schumann's fine distinctions and points of subtle equivocation did not survive his death, nor did their rarefied aesthetic context. After 1849 the question of what music should signify or contain and the relation of music to the listener assumed a decidedly new tone. The events of 1848–1849 in Europe posed the overarching issue of how to interpret their implications for the social and cultural future. The revolutionary events might have marked an aborted yet inevitable and rightful revolt, suppressed by the forces of order but capable of being ignited again. Or they might rather be a frightening aberration, a symptom of cultural decay, the direct result of the spread of democracy and the increasing political force of the masses.

For Wagner and Liszt, it was the former interpretation that shaped their social and musical thought. For them, 1848–1849 had unleashed the suppressed power of the people or, as Carl Schorske has stated, of the new "social material" with which to make society whole. And so the spread of music to the people and acceptance of popular modes of peception was, to them, an inevitable and healthy development to be encouraged by musicians.

Schorske has observed that Wagner's enemies now became "the philistines of his own burgher class and the rationalistic, absolute state." Since these two forces, the traditional enemies of the creative German intellectual, were the upholders of convention supported by reason, they became Wagner's targets. Wagner's goal accordingly became the release of the suppressed communal consciousness through a drama that would "cut through the external realities of an age of false authority and materialism" (Schorske, 221 ff.).

If reason figures prominently as a target in Wagner's polemics about the music drama, it similarly became the nemesis in the writings of Liszt. For him, not just opera but instrumental music existed to combat this pernicious force and serve the future of mankind. In his article on Berlioz in 1855, Liszt makes the theoretical reasons for this contention clear: "Only in music does feeling, in manifesting itself, dispense with the help of reason and its means of expression, so inadequate in comparison with intuition." Or, as Liszt otherwise stated, music's advantage is "its supreme capacity to make an inner impulse audible without the assistance of reason." It was within this context that Liszt approached the question of the content of music and its relation to the listener.

Liszt's argument was subtle and cast in the traditional terms of aesthetic debate. Its pupose was to establish that the direction he proposed was a progressive step forward; that he was merely encouraging or directing an existing force, which he perceived as a natural consequence of the way music communicates. Significantly, in his argument Liszt drew on Schumann's theories in a selective way, combined with ideas from Wagner as well.

Like Schumann but unlike Wagner, Liszt steadfastly maintained that objective elements did not lie within the proper sphere of musical language. Rather, if such phenomena are to affect the soul they have to be translated into musical terms, or, as he phrased it, "into music's own mysterious language." And Liszt, like Schumann, stressing the representative content of a composition, firmly believed that some interpretations of a piece were more correct than others. Yet unlike Schumann, Liszt did not hold that the content should be self-evident, and he stressed the importance of guiding the listener's perception of the work. Hence the need for the program, which was for Liszt "any foreword in intelligible language added to a piece of music, by which the composer intends to guard the hearer against an arbitrary poetical interpretation, and to direct his attention in advance to the poetical idea of the whole." But the program should not be a narrative guide to the specific events of the work; it should merely indicate "the spiritual moments which impelled the composer to create the work" (Niecks, 277).

Thus, Liszt employed a wide variety of programmatic techniques, and as Max Harrison has noted, few of his programs make use of narrative, unlike those of Berlioz. Since Liszt did not believe that music could describe objects, he held that the program should only "put the listener in the same frame of mind as would the objects themselves." He attempted representation only in an oblique sense, for "by suggesting the emotional reality of things, music could indirectly represent them." Accordingly, Liszt's piano work *Harmonies poétiques et religieuses* (1834) is prefaced by two paragraphs from Lamartine's *avertissement*; but in the case of the symphonic poem *Ce qu'on entend sur la montagne* (1849), the composer prefaced the score with Victor Hugo's entire poem. Indeed, Liszt is said to have first written the symphonic poem *Les préludes* (1848) and then sought the appropriate poem to capture his inspirational moment.

Although not all of Liszt's symphonic poems were inspired by literature (*The Battle of the Huns* of 1857 was inspired by a Kaulbach painting), the composer's approach, as well as his impetus, was primarily literary. He attempted no less than a transcription from literature. In this regard, Liszt was apparently influenced by Hugo, in terms of both theory and approach to style; clearly Liszt espoused Hugo's dictum that literature was the true "modern art," according to the Hegelian progression of the "self-unfolding idea of beauty." For Hugo, it was literature that provided the new principle of authorization for art, and thus he demanded that all the arts henceforth attempt to approach its condition (Drexler, 332). And so, according to Liszt, "Music in its masterpieces tends more and more to appropriate the masterpieces of literature. What harm can come to music … if it attach itself to a species that has sprung precisely from an undeniably modern way of feeling?"

In architecture, the outcome of this philosophy was the use of a descriptive syntax of forms, instead of coherent architectural orders, producing an architecture that could be "read." In music, the literary model resulted in the primacy of content over form and a stress on techniques that have analogies with specific verbal meanings: music, theoretically, was to attain the descriptive range of language, an ideal practiced by Wagner in the leitmotiv.

Unlike Schumann but like Berlioz, Liszt held that music generated by literature could be written on a large scale. Liszt went beyond Berlioz' attempt to imbue instrumental music with greater specificity and thus coherence by merging it with literature. Berlioz had sought to loosen the internal structure of the symphony and to maintain coherence through programmatic detail; hence, he used the symphony to express ideas generally considered to be outside the proper boundaries of instrumental expression. As Harrison observes, in works like *Harold in Italy* Berlioz was able to make a distinction between the feelings of Harold and the external circumstances of the story. Berlioz thus introduced a distinction into the category of representation of objects in the world.

Berlioz and Liszt sought new ways of renewing symphonic form, above all by exploiting its inherently associative elements. Both refused to adhere to any formal or schematic outline that bore little relation to what they wished to express. Finally, both composers allowed a program to dictate important decisions, but it was Liszt who renounced even a nominal adherence to traditional form. He openly abjured the principle of accommodation of program to form, going beyond previous attempts to give music the specificity of literature; he sought an alternative that involved a complete transcription of expressive techniques from one medium into another.

In works like *Ce qu'on entend sur la montagne* Liszt attempted to capture the content as well as the force and style of Hugo's magisterial poem. Sensitive to the pace at which the poem unfolds, to Hugo's free structure, to his vivid new imagery, color, and rhetorical power, Liszt sought analogues, for all of these aspects, as well as content, dictate the composer's choices of key and of the nature, presentation, contrast, transformation, and development of themes. Hence, exposition and development remain, but in no way analogous to sonata form, for Liszt does not restrict himself to the traditional events or oppositions it supposes. As Niecks observes, for Liszt all purely musical or formal considerations are subordinate to the action. And since, for Liszt, content is the determining factor of form, every composition will assume its own unique shape.

Liszt vociferously decried the so-called classical approach to musical form, or rather his own distorted view of what it comprised. To him, it signified inviolable rules concerning the return and development of themes, as opposed to a freer governance by a guiding poetic idea. Instrumental music, with the exception of Beethoven and Weber, he claimed, was "laid out squarely after a symmetrical plan that may be ... measured in cubic feet." Indeed, according to one of Liszt's supporters, Hans von Bülow, Liszt and his school advocated "the artistic emancipation of content from schematicism."

In his innovations, Liszt was not acting without precedent, although he carried certain established tendencies to perhaps their extreme conclusion. And although Liszt invented the term *program music,* he freely acknowledged that he had not inaugurated the idea. For Liszt, Beethoven was still the great originator, although Liszt, like Wagner, acknowledged that Beethoven had not been fully conscious of his own innovations. Liszt saw himself as simply making explicit a new ideal for symphonic music foreshadowed in the work of Beethoven, and followed by Mendelssohn, Schumann, Weber, and Berlioz. Since the growing associative tendencies and potential of instrumental music were increasingly incompatible with traditional form, Liszt thought he was merely shifting the crucial balance, for program music now renounced any claim to purely formal coherence and simply sought to be understood by its program.

For Liszt, this line of innovation was both inevitable and healthy, being but a tendency inherent in music that was now flowering in a new social context: "And for this reason, the poetic solution of instrumental music contained in the program seems to us rather one of the various steps forward which the art has still to take, a necessary result of the development of our time, rather than a symptom of exhaustion and decadence" (Strunk, 5:119). As further proof, Liszt pointed out that "the custom of providing instrumental pieces with a program has already found such acceptance with the public that musicians cease to struggle against it, regarding it as one of those inevitable facts." And in support of this claim, he cited the Belgian critic François Joseph Fétis, who, in consternation over the situation, had remarked, "Fine instrumental music must reckon with a much smaller number of competent listeners than opera.... [Such an audience] will never listen to a symphony without outlining a program for itself during the performance." Hence, Liszt argued, "Is it not evident from this that it is merely a question of officially recognizing an already existing power with a view to allowing it greater freedom of action and assisting it in the removal of liabilities?"

There is no simple reason why the critic Eduard Hanslick found Liszt's ideas deeply disturbing and repellent. Rather, a confluence of factors—ideological, professional, and personal—were responsible for pitting Hanslick and Brahms against the parties of Wagner and Liszt. The reaction of the former to 1848 was far different from that of the latter, partly because of personal experience and early background. The most important factor is that both Hanslick and Brahms attempted to assimilate themselves to the very social groups that Wagner so acidulously condemned. For both were outsiders, Brahms in the bourgeoisie and Hanslick in the Austrian state bureaucracy.

Hanslick had grown up in Prague, the son of a music teacher and library cataloguer of Bohemian peasant background who was enabled to marry the daughter of a Jewish banker through the winning of a lottery. After moving to Vienna and receiving his law degree, Hanslick entered the Austrian bureaucracy, first in the Ministry of Finance and then in the university department of the Ministry of Education, continuing his musical interests and writings. He published *Vom musikalischen Schönen (The Beautiful in Music)* in 1854. The book was an amazing success, winning him instant recognition. Hanslick soon mounted in the academic hierarchy and established himself not only there but as an official representative and administrator for the state, traveling widely throughout Europe.

There seemed to be an inherent affinity between Hanslick's aesthetic position and the particular aesthetic ideal promoted by both university and state. Both saw in Hanslick's synthesis a doctrine eminently appropriate for official authorization, for it was not only Hanslick who sensed a need for "something more elevated and substantial" in the musical life of Vienna in the wake of 1848. As Schorske has explained, the "haute bourgeoisie" that ruled Vienna was now characterized in part by its moralistic inclination: "Morally it was secure, righteous, and repressive; politically it was concerned for the rule of law. It was initially committed to the rule of mind over body." Despite the open attacks he launched on the moralistic elements in music, Hanslick's emphasis was, in fact, on the moral potential of the art. Music, for Hanslick, does have a spiritual force and thus a social end, but through its formal, sublimating properties, not through its elemental force; hence, Hanslick explicitly denounced the "older systems of aesthetics," which underrated the sensuous element and subordinated it to "morality." Here, as his argument later makes clear, Hanslick was referring to the ancient Greek system and to the theory that music can "enervate, effeminate, and benumb" its listeners. The moral influence of sound, then, he equated with mere physical conditioning, as opposed to what he referred to as the spiritualizing function of music.

As Hanslick then proceeded to argue, the wrong kind of moral influence in music is particularly dangerous among the lower classes, which are inherently subject to it, for "as the physical effect of music varies with the morbid excitability of the nervous system, so the moral influence of sound is in proportion to the crudeness of mind and character. The lower the degree of culture, the greater the potency of the agent in question" (p. 94). It becomes clear, moreover, by a careful reading of the entire discussion, that he is specifically referring to the dangers of Wagner and Liszt; as musical demagogues, they were especially dangerous for the masses, since "mankind is much more easily impressed by elemental forces in a primitive state of culture than later on, when intellectual consciousness and the faculty of reflection have attained a higher degree of marturity." The masses, he argued, lack the necessary preparation for aesthetic appreciation, thus indulging in music's elemental properties, "reveling in sensation and emotion" (pp. 91, 97).

Hanslick saw Wagner as a composer who encouraged such a descent to mere sensation, not only among the lower classes but also among the more socially elevated listeners who simply gave in to their baser impulses: "In the indolent and apathetic attitude of some and the hysterical rapture of others, the active principle is the same—delight in the elemental property of music." He thought that "to be the slave of unreasoning, undirected, and purposeless feeling, ignited by a power which is out of all relation to our will and intellect, is not worthy of the human mind. If people allow themselves to be so completely carried away by what is elemental in art as to lose all self-control, this scarcely redounds to the glory of the art, and much less to that of the individual." If beauty is the result of the "untrammeled working of the human mind on material susceptible of intellectual manipulation," this is because the emotions are not a source of knowledge. Hanslick's aesthetic and social theories were firmly rooted in an epistemology: reason, the source of knowledge, is also the source of the beautiful in art.

Hanslick's ideal was the opposite of Wagner's tyrannical, visceral art, which demanded complete and passive surrender on the part of its audience: it was the ideal of intelligent gratification, implying that music ought to be listened to in a specific way, actively engaging the listener's mind. And so, on numerous occasions, he made abundantly clear the particular kind of listening or audience response that he wished to oppose: "Instead of closely following the course of the music, these enthusiasts, reclining in their seats and only half-awake, suffer themselves to be rocked and lulled by the mere flow of sound.... For their ears the aesthetic criterion of intelligent gratification is wanting" (pp. 90–91).

For Hanslick, and typically of the academy and bureaucracy of which he was ostensibly an ally, the proper response to music required an appropriate preparation. The right faculties were to be engaged in the musical experience, made conscious, if it was to meet the ideal standard of objective response: "The spiritual force of music can only be attributed to the definite beauty of musical form as the result of the untrammeled working of the human mind on material susceptible of intellectual manipulation" (p. 127).

Hanslick's terminology in the treatise that made him famous is a curious blend of the language of moral injunction and that of traditional philosophical aesthetics. He stresses the praise of pure beauty amid trenchant comments on contemporary cultural decline, and in certain other of Hanslick's writings the rationale behind this juxtaposition emerges. "Pure beauty," the realm of the rational, the disinterested, the controlled, is a kind of "redemption," a quality that, as Peter Gay pointed out, Hanslick invoked in his praise of Brahms. In describing his personal experience of hearing Brahms's Sextet in B-flat Major immediately after having heard a performance of fragments from *The Ring* and *Tristan und Isolde*, Hanslick exulted, "We thought ourselves suddenly transported into a world of pure beauty." He goes on to exclaim, "It sounded like a kind of redemption."

Such music, for Hanslick, helped redeem man from self-absorption: it "sublimated and disciplined," leading man into a purer realm, with a socially salubrious effect. There is an analogy here between Hanslick and Fétis, who sought similar musical values, although within a different ideological framework. For Fétis, writing in 1852 at the start of the Second Empire, the role of music was "to transform sentiments and passions into sonorous harmonious images." In accordance with Fétis's roots in utopian socialist aesthetics, such harmony was to serve to balance man's ever-competing faculties: it was thus in restoring balance to the spheres of sensation, emotion, and reason that music could prepare man as a social being to become part of the harmonious whole.

It was through his praise of Brahms that Hanslick expressed his own specific goal of a quasi-religious redemption, through an art that engendered the right kind of response. As Eric Sams has observed, both in music and in people, Hanslick "admired above all integrity of craftsmanship as of purpose, and clarity of communication." If music was not an expression of the composer's feelings or soul, it was symbolic of his character—a Platonic symbol that both represented and instilled. Here, too, there was an analogy with the contemporary conservative position in France, and particularly with the Platonism of writers like Fétis.

But in praising Brahms's personal character, training, or academic authorization, Hanslick was indeed following the precedent already established by Robert Schumann. In his famous article that brought the young

Brahms to public attention, Schumann already attempted to link the composer to the mystique of the great classical masters: "His name is Johannes Brahms, and he comes from Hamburg, where he has been working in silent obscurity, trained in the most difficult theses of his art by an excellent teacher who sends me enthusiastic reports of him, recommended to me recently by a well-known and respected master" (Taruskin and Weis, 362). For Hanslick, Brahms was a demanding composer whose music appealed to the intellectual faculties, and as Gay observed, he remarked that Brahms "is not among those who obligingly meet you halfway." Indeed, Brahms became, in part through Hanslick's rhetoric, a modern classic, coming later in his career to be grouped with the venerable masters, Bach and Beethoven.

Brahms, of course, was patently ambivalent toward such an appellation, finding it at once compatible with his professional interests and a rhetorical misrepresentation. The son of a street and dance musician who had later in life married his housekeeper, Brahms, throughout his career, quested for assimilation into the middle class. And as Gay observed, Brahms "provoked no salacious scandals such as those marking the life of Liszt; he made no move to compete with Wagner in prophesying a new religion for art. Brahms sought financial security, practiced innocent pleasures, enjoyed decent company; he was a slave to the ethic of work, much like a bank clerk or a shopkeeper."

Brahms saw himself as a man of the people, and moreover, of the German people, since people and patriotism were to him the same thing. Brahms understandably resented the attempt on the part of Wagner and Liszt to root their theories in a conception of the people that stressed their healthily instinctual nature. The question of the past as well as the future of German music hence became a particularly sensitive issue for both Hanslick and Brahms. It was in this context that the critical rupture at last took place, ignited finally by personal friction as well as professional sparks.

This antagonism and its concomitant polarization of aims occurred not immediately but gradually, as a result of converging events. In the beginning of Brahms's career, the circle around Liszt and Franz Brendel was rapidly becoming influential and hence already demanding obeisance. When Brahms went to Leipzig for the performance of his Piano Concerto in D Minor, he knew that a visit to Liszt and Brendel was expected of him, yet he avoided it. But when Brahms's work failed in Leipzig, their vehicle, the *Neue Zeitschrift für Musik*, chastised the Leipzig public, thus creating an overture of friendship to Brahms. Soon after came the unfortunate declaration by Brahms and his professional allies that was to widen the chasm of misunderstanding and professional resentment.

In March 1860, Brahms, Joseph Joachim, Julius Grimm, and Bernhard Scholz signed a declaration that conclusively dissociated themselves from the principles of Liszt and his school. This was perhaps a response to the fact that Brendel, in June 1859, had engaged in highly provocative public propaganda on the part of his school. To celebrate the twenty-fifth anniversary of the founding of the *Neue Zeitschrift für Musik,* he organized a convention of musicians in Leipzig, most prominently attended by Liszt's supporters. It was here that they launched the propagandistic Allgemeine deutscher Musikverein (German Musical Society), which appropriated the future of German music. Abjuring the label *music of the future* as an insidious misrepresentation, Brendel boldly proposed to replace it with the "neo-German school," for "the Italian-influenced epoch of the Viennese masters is the period of classicism, of the equal supremacy of idealism and realism. Beethoven once more clasps hands with the specifically German North and inaugurates the Neo-German School" (Taruskin and Weis, 384–385). This was clearly a provocation, since, as Gay has incisively noted, Hanslick "could not permit the Wagnerites to monopolize the future by monopolizing the past."

The effect of their declaration was to be made impressive by the number of signatures appended, and indeed, Brahms and Joachim circulated it privately with this aim. But in what was perhaps a cunning act of sabotage, someone prematurely slipped the declaration to a prominent newspaper in Berlin. The result was that it appeared with only four signatures, causing immediate public ridicule of the hapless individuals involved.

Hanslick's conflicts with the neo-German school were both ideological and personal. Well known are Wagner's vitriolic remarks about Hanslick's supposed Jewish ancestry and his pointed attack on the critic in the portrayal of Beckmesser in *Die Meistersinger.* As with Brahms, these personal injuries marked the final rupture after a period of cordial disagreement between the two schools. Even in 1854, when Hanslick explicitly rejected Wagner's theories, there was as yet no personal antipathy involved. But attitudes were to change dramatically when, in 1862, Wagner came to Vienna to give several readings of his text for *Die Meistersinger.*

This was a moment of struggle for professional power and for the future of German music. As Gay observes, Hanslik was a dangerous reviewer, "the feared music critic of the *Presse,* a learned lecturer on music at the university, and the sociable acquaintance of everyone who was anyone in music." This was a significant reversal, for as Gay observed, at the start of Hanslick's career in the 1850s,

> Liszt, Wagner, and their allies were moving to engross strategic posts in the musical world; they were beginning to edit respected periodicals, conduct famous orchestras, launch dependable followers.... Liszt and his disciples made an effective bid for the sympathetic attention of the public by parading their compositions as music that had broken with a dying tradition and was pregnant with new vitality.... The *Zukunftsmusiker* saw themselves as Beethoven's rightful heirs and their adversaries as mere epigones.
>
> (p. 267)

But Wagner renewed this line of attack in the changed context of the 1860s and, above all, in the thinly veiled portrait of Hanslick in *Die Meistersinger*. His insulting characterization of Hanslick as the worst kind of reactionary was bound to arouse indignation on the part of the now powerful critic. As Hanslick freely avowed in his preface to the seventh edition of his book, the libretto was written and then revised against the background of the intensifying critical debate:

> When I wrote this treatise, the advocates of the "music of the future" were loudest in their praise of it, and could not but provoke a reaction on the part of people holding opinions such as I do. Just when I was preparing the second edition, Liszt's "Program Symphonies" appeared, which denied to music more completely than ever before its independent sphere.... Since then, the world has been enriched by Richard Wagner's *Tristan, Nibelungen Ring*, and his doctrine of the infinite melody, i.e., formlessness exalted into a principle—the intoxicating effect of opium manifested both in vocal and instrumental music, for the worship of which a temple has been specifically erected by Bayreuth.

Although cast in traditional aesthetic terms, Hanslick's argument throughout the book is linked directly to his ideological and personal debate with Wagner and Liszt. Perhaps the key statement that reveals his line of argument most completely is an observation concerning the theories of the opposing side: "The proposition that the feelings are the subject which music has to represent is due partly to the theory according to which the ultimate aim of music is to excite feelings" (p. 20). He then proceeded to argue that for a number of cogent reasons music is inherently incapable of directly arousing such a response: it cannot, by nature, depict or incite anything precise or specific, for this is contrary to the very principles characteristic of the art: "In reality there is no causal nexus between musical composition and the feelings it may excite, as the latter vary with our experience and impressability." He conceded that music is capable of representing or imitating objective phenomena, but it is not capable of conveying the specific feelings they arouse. The subject of music had to be something intrinsically musical and not simply a translation of a subject into musical terms.

It was clearly Liszt's specific claim that music should approximate the condition of literature and thus employ its expressive means that so aroused the dissension of Hanslick. As Hanslick stated explicitly, "The conviction is daily growing that each individual art can be understood only by understanding its technical limits and inherent nature." He noted the development of a tendency to see the laws of beauty for each art as inseparably associated with the individuality of the art and the nature of the medium.

Even more specifically opposed to the rhetoric of Wagner and Liszt is Hanslick's contention that "music can never be elevated to the rank of speech." To buttress his argument, he traced what he considered the essential error behind this contention from the theories of Rameau and Rousseau through the ideas of Wagner. Moreover, he claimed that the doctrine of his opponents was "not so much the fruit of original speculation as the enunciation of traditional convictions that have gained great popularity." As illustration, Hanslick cited the major baroque theorists, focusing on their basic conviction that music must imitate nature in order to move the understanding and thus induce the desired passions in the listener.

For Hanslick, music was not, as Wagner contended, a language of the specific: it is incapable of conveying emotions, things, persons, or ideas. Music cannot be said to contain any linguistic features and is thus in no sense an analogue of literary art. For Hanslick, as for Hoffmann, instrumental music was the highest form, for it alone is the embodiment of music's true uniqueness as an art: "Instrumental music alone ... produces unalloyed musical beauty," and it alone is the "pure absolute art of sound" (Gay, 273).

Hanslick's position is not an easy one to categorize, for like that of Schumann, it embodies a subtle balance that can easily be upset. Hanslick did concede, as Gay observed, that musical pleasure was "very much a matter of feelings, but its vocabulary, its grammar, its means of expression and communication were all its own." Further, Hanslick averred

> that one may legitimately assign to music descriptive epithets normally laden with emotional content ... as long as one employs these adjectives in their

musical connotations alone. But when one insists, as most aestheticians have insisted, that music expresses feelings with which the listener identifies and may come to share, one misunderstands activity for passivity, mistakes the importation of one's feelings into music for the reception of feelings from music.

(Gay, 270)

This was the very point of ambiguity faced by Schumann, on which Hanslick, in defense of his ideal, takes a polemical stance.

Against the theories of Hegel and Hoffmann, Hanslick argued that neither the expression of the composer or his epoch is sealed into his music. Gay observed,

> The historian viewing a work of art may discover in Spontini "the expression of French imperialism," in Rossini "the political restoration," but the student of aesthetics must restrict himself to the examination of the works themselves.... [Hegel] quite unconsciously confounded the point of view of art history...with that of pure aesthetics, and attributed an explicitness to the music which, as such, it never possessed.

And, Gay further observed, Hanslick's theory, unlike Hegel's, shifted "the weight of analysis from the producer and the consumer of the music to the music itself" (p. 271).

As several commentators have noted, to label Hanslick a formalist because of certain superficial resemblances is a patent misnomer. Eric Sams observed, for example, that Hanslick's "central admission of music as metaphor or symbol makes a significant concession." And he also pointed out that Hanslick's basic position is closely related to that of the philosopher to whom the work was dedicated, Robert Zimmerman. Zimmerman was himself a disciple of Johann Friedrich Herbart, who was apparently the first to stress that, as Gay put it, "music is a solely sonorous form with no significant content or expression other than the sound it makes; it can neither convey specific concepts nor express specific feelings." But Hanslick's position was not identical with that of either of these theorists, and hence, his stress on form cannot be equated simply with their formalism. As Gay pointed out, the force of Hanslick's subtle qualifications was unfortunately lost in his pithy, often quoted formula that music is "sounding, moving form." This and other extractable statements, taken out of context, helped, as Gay observed, to launch "the myth of his formalism" (p. 273).

Having examined the broader context of Hanslick's so-called formalist language, we can see the subtle blend that took place within his theories and the way in which he marshaled arguments developed by contemporary aestheticians in the service of an ideological position. Undoubtedly, distortion characterized both sides of the critical debate, and it has endured tenaciously, to the detriment of Hanslick and Brahms. Gay has discussed the modernist element in both of these figures and the misconstrual of their achievements resulting from the false polarities we have formed. As Gay pointed out, Hanslick's stress on aesthetic auton-omy was a distinctly modernist idea, contrary to our picture of him in most writings today; but Gay went on to qualify that even if one rejects the patent distortions of him, Hanslick remains essentially a traditionalist or a defensive critic. The paradox of Hanslick's ideas is that although he developed and marshaled them for a socially conservative end, they introduced a new conceptual—later radical—departure. Born in defense of civilized values, as conceived by a specific social class, Hanslick's theo-ries introduced new conceptions that were seminal to later departures.

As Sams pointed out, "His emphasis on autonomy and structure pre-pared the ground for such analysts as Schenker and Reti—at the same time his acknowledgment and identification of the metaphorical and symbolic aspects of music found fruitful development in the theories of Suzanne Langer and others." And if, as Edward Lippman observed, "feel-ing was brought into the orbit of the symbolic nature of art," Hanslick's theories provided a departure. Hanslick, then, in spite of his socially and culturally defensive stance, falls into the larger progressive tendency that Lippman sees in the later nineteenth century: to consider "feelings con-nected with music as virtual or fictional rather than realistic copies, and as dynamic and changing in their course."

This larger tendency in musical thought entered France in the late nineteenth century under a very different set of conditions. The question of instrumental music and the development that it ought to follow is one that, for a number of reasons, became of great moment in France after 1870. In the wake of the devastation caused by the Franco-Prussian War and the Commune, instrumental music in the Third Republic experi-enced its first efflorescence. With the stringent financial pressure attend-ing the political trauma of these years, the traditional dominance of opera over musical life briefly and abruptly ceased. The most important insti-tutional innovation conceived to implement the new ideal of the culti-vation of serious instrumental music was the Société Nationale de Musique Française. Even more so than the other concert-giving organi-zations flourishing in France, the Société Nationale became the matrix for innovation. But for this very reason, it was also soon to become the nexus for opposing conceptions of the appropriate objectives of new French instrumental music.

The initial ideals of the organization bore a striking resemblance to those that we have seen as characteristic in Germany, in the party of Hanslick and Brahms, for although in a very different context, the new Société Nationale was to stress the importance of stylistic probity: seriousness, sincerity, and elevation of purpose. But in France this ideal was in evident reaction to what many perceived as the triviality and frivolity of musical life during the Second Empire. And German influence was unquestionably strong, as it was in many spheres of French culture in the early years of the Third Republic. In music the goal was to meet German composers on their own ground in the context of serious traditional, or "academic," forms.

In France the return to traditional forms of absolute instrumental music was perceived not as conservative or defensive but rather as an exploration—a liberation from routine. The discovery of different conventions led concomitantly to what French musicians happily acknowledged as a reawakening, at last, of French composers to tradition. Without a complete loss of moorings, composers were free to break away from the narrow restrictions so long imposed by a circumscribed, aesthetically stifling musical establishment. They were no longer forced or willing to make facile concessions to popular taste and hence looked to the alternative materials being discovered in the classical past.

In France, unlike Germany, the return to conservative or classical musical forms was in no way pitted against the exploration of new programmatic ideals, for French composers discovered simultaneously the instrumental forms of the German present and past, seeing new formal rigor and ingenuity as inherently compatible qualities. Composers like Camille Saint-Saëns, one of the leaders of the Société Nationale, hence experienced no polarization as in the case of Brahms and Liszt, for form was a vehicle of expression, to be explored extensively together with the values of line and color or with the new conceptions of melody and orchestration.

And yet a division was to arise within the Société Nationale. The confrontation arose over the question of innovation in form as opposed to content and, in the latter case, the specific innovations of Wagner. The slowly growing tensions in the Société Nationale led finally to a truculent split between Saint-Saëns and Vincent d'Indy. The latter, together with César Franck and opposed to Saint-Saëns, came to advocate the ideals and techniques of Wagner, even within the traditional forms. While

Saint-Saëns was heavily influenced by the symphonic poems and techniques of Liszt, he nevertheless came to reject Wagner's theories and certain of his innovations. For d'Indy and Franck, however, the traditional as well as contemporary forms could accommodate the advanced technical knowledge that they perceived in Wagner's work.

If the debate over musical content that we have seen in Austria and Germany repeated itself in a different context in the 1880s in France, it was in the next generation of composers, those maturing in the 1890s, that the question of meaning and content in instrumental music assumed new urgency. In the generation of Claude Debussy, the new values of formal ingenuity or formal design began to be called into question and were challenged by other values. With Debussy began the exploration of a new kind of musical logic, which includes a new musical content as well as a new approach to the definition of form.

It is in light of the previous generation, the members of the Société Nationale and the professors of the Paris Conservatoire, that Debussy developed his distinctive aversions. Above all was the emphasis on formal design, particularly on academic forms, which fostered in Debussy a strong reaction to schematicization. In this respect, Debussy's rhetoric, in many points, resembled that of Liszt, particularly in his condemnations of the rigidity of traditional forms. The extent to which Debussy's approach resembled that of Liszt, and hence may properly be called program music, is a far more difficult question. This depends on what we can include as program music or as the kind of musical representation we consider characteristic of it.

According to Max Harrison, "In the strictest sense programme music does not include music that is merely expressive, imitative, or evocative"; he proposed that "it is doubtful even whether Debussy's La Mer is a description rather than an evocation of its subject." For Harrison, the impressionism of Debussy and Ravel is not program music proper but rather an evolution from it. He pointed out that Debussy often placed his titles not at the beginning of his pieces but rather at the end, for he apparently did not believe that a knowledge of them was essential to understanding. Rather, the titles were intended to indicate merely an expressive atmosphere.

Debussy's theories of musical meaning were different from Liszt's, being far closer to those of the contemporary French symbolists than to those of Hugo. Music, for Debussy, was in no way related to rational language; rather, it captured that which language was powerless to express. Hence, musical content could not be seen in terms of simple analogies, although it could invoke other modes of expression synesthetically. Music embodied a unique and ineffable vagueness, and its particular strength was the way it could stimulate reverberations in the soul. Thus, it was the Wagner of the symbolists that so integrally affected Debussy, a composer whose music subtly insinuated itself into the listener's consciousness. In this light, we can see why Debussy was so hostile to the use of leitmotivs, conceived as explicit representations of properties outside music.

Like Hanslick, Debussy considered music a distinct mode of communication, bearing no relation to the properly linguistic aspect of speech. Hence, he, too, denounced Rousseau's theories for the same reasons as the Austrian critic and similarly, to use Lippman's phrase, recognized "the separate status of musical feelings." Both fit into the tendency Lippman sees in the fin de siècle to stress the indefinable character of musical feelings and to remove them from the realm of human feeling. And as he points out, this tendency was, in part, responsible for the "appreciation of new types of musical logic" that gradually arose and took hold.

In this context the debate concerning the proper nature of instrumental music can be followed to Erik Satie, who rejected the music of the so-called Wagnerian fog together with what he caustically termed the impressionist mist. With Satie in the twentieth century another of Hanslick's seeds developed—the rejection of music that assaults, insinuates itself, or moves around the listener. We see then a return to a stress on music that could be actively grasped by the mind and yet still retain its autonomy or its distance from linguistic features.

From the nineteenth into the twentieth century, then, the larger conceptual tendency was to grant autonomy to musical communication, to stress music's specific expressive means, and to concede that it can be inspired by the other arts while maintaining its own language and logic. And so, paradoxically, it was, to a great extent, the conservative defenders of the past who laid out the future of musical thought.

BIBLIOGRAPHY

Heinz Becker, "Johannes Brahms," in *New Grove Dictionary of Music and Musicians*, edited by Stanley Sadie (1980). Martin Cooper, *French Music from the Death of Berlioz to the Death of Fauré* (1951). Arthur Drexler, ed., *The Architecture of the École des Beaux-Arts* (1977). Jane F. Fulcher, "Meyerbeer and the Music of Society During the Monarchy of July," *Musical Quarterly*, April 1981; "Wagner,

Comte, and Proudhon: The Aesthetics of Positivism in France," *Symposium*, Summer 1979; and "Music and the Communal Order: The Vision of Utopian Socialism in France," *Current Musicology*, Summer 1979.

Peter Gay, *Freud, Jews, and Other Germans* (1978). Eduard Hanslick, *The Beautiful in Music*, edited by Morris Weiz (1957). Max Harrison, "Programme Music," in *New Grove Dictionary*. Arthur Hervey, *French Music in the Nineteenth Century* (1903). Hans Gunter Höke, "Programmusik," in *Musik in Geschichte und Gegenwart*. Edward A. Lippman, *A Humanistic Philosophy of Music* (1977) ; and "Theory and Practice in Schumann's Aesthetics," *Journal of the American Musicological Society*, 1964.

Friedrick Niecks, *Programme Music in the Last Four Centuries* (1907; repr. 1969). Henry Pleasants, ed., *Vienna's Golden Years of Music, 1850–1900* (1950). Eric Sams, "Eduard Hanslick," in *New Grove Dictionary*. Carl E. Schorske. *Fin-de-Siècle Vienna: Politics and Culture* (1980) ; and "The Quest for the Grail: Wagner and Morris," in Kurt H. Wolff and Barrington Moore, eds., *The Critical Spirit: Essays in Honor of Herbert Marcuse* (1967). Oliver Strunk, *Source Readings in Music History*, vol. 5 (1965). Richard Taruskin and Piero Weis, eds., *Music in the Western World* (1984).

The Twentieth Century and the Orchestra as Museum

J. Peter Burkholder

The orchestral music of the twentieth century is distinguished by an unprecedented diversity in aesthetic, style, and technique, ranging from the familiar to the bizarre, from imitation of ancient styles to experimentation with new resources, and from immediately accessible pieces to compositions of unrivaled complexity. Yet beneath the varied surface of modern music lies a hidden unity. Composers as different as Schoenberg and Sibelius share not a common musical language but a common problem and common strategies for solving it, and the diversity of their music is itself a necessary part of their response.

The principal fact with which composers of our century have been confronted in writing for the orchestra is the retrospective nature of the orchestral repertoire. Even before Brahms had written his First Symphony, the orchestra had been transformed from an operatic accompanist and a courtly amusement into a museum for the display of great works of art from the past. The orchestral music of Haydn and Mozart was ephemeral when it was written, each symphony, overture, or concerto receiving very few performances over a brief period. Yet by the middle of the nineteenth century that same music had been revived and granted immortality among the first "classics" of the orchestral repertoire. Once the concept of classical music was established, in analogy to the classics of literature or the visual arts, the music of composers other than

Haydn, Mozart, and Beethoven was gradually added to the canon. This included not only the more recent music of Schubert, Mendelssohn, and the first generation of romantic composers but also the older music of Bach and his contemporaries and predecessors. "New" music began entering the classical repertoire on two fronts: living composers sought to add their own music to it, and music historians sought to revive the forgotten music of past generations.

Composers in the late nineteenth century and throughout the twentieth century have aspired to the same immortality for their music. In their quest to achieve it, they have had to compete with the music of the past for performances and for the affection of players and listeners. It is a contest in which the reigning champions have an overwhelming advantage, for the orchestral repertoire is very crowded and the classics have enormous prestige. It is in this struggle with the great music of the past that modern orchestral music has been shaped and formed.

THE ORCHESTRA AS A MUSEUM OF ART

The modern concert hall may be likened to a museum, where natural wonders or man-made artifacts are taken from their native habitats and mounted for display to an admiring and curious public. Taking an item out of its context and placing it in a museum changes our perception of it, as Marcel Duchamp demonstrated in 1913 when he chose a factory-made bicycle wheel at random from among hundreds like it, set it on a pedestal, titled it *Bicycle Wheel,* and exhibited it as a work of art. It is no longer available to be used but only to be looked at; indeed, we are forced to pay attention to it in a way we would not have when it was part of our everyday environment. The armor, costumes, musical instruments, furniture, and home furnishings in the Metropolitan Museum of Art in New York have similarly been mounted for display as objects to be admired, making it impossible for them to serve their original functions. Often the pieces least suited to a practical function—the ornate ceremonial armor appropriate for parades but too heavy for war, or the Frank Lloyd Wright chairs whose beauty is matched by the discomfort they cause the sitter—become the most admired in the museum. The aesthetic side of these objects, which was in most cases a secondary concern in their creation, is now primary. Enshrined in an art museum, they have become art.

The same is true in the realm of music. In the modern concert hall, the "classical" music we hear has been taken out of the context for which it was created, stripped of its original purposes, and fitted out with new ones. For instance, Bach's *St. Matthew Passion,* while still a piece of religious music, is no longer liturgical. It plays no part in religious ceremonies, is rarely performed by small church choirs like the one for which it was written, and is no longer presented only on Good Friday, the one day of the church year for which it is liturgically appropriate. Instead, it is now performed year-round by large amateur and professional ensembles and is heard not by congregations at religious services but by concert audiences. It has shed its original function to adopt new ones, offering amateur singers a chance to sing with others, offering an aesthetic rather than a religious experience to the listener, and offering performers and listeners alike a chance to touch and be touched by an artwork that has become one of the defining icons of European civilization. It no longer offers the experience shared by its first hearers, and in a sense it is no longer the same piece of music; it cannot be, for we are different people with very different expectations of it.

The standards of the concert hall, like those of other museums, are at odds with the standards of everyday life. Bicycle wheels work better when they are not attached to pedestals; comfortable chairs are not designed just for their looks; the most serviceable church music is brief and simple in comparison to Bach's *St. Matthew Passion.* In the art museum, we are concerned not with practicality but with aesthetics: we approach the art before us with attentive concentration, and we evaluate each work according to how richly it rewards us for our trouble. The best concert music repays that concentration not only once but again and again, no matter how frequently we rehear it and no matter how intently we study it. Clearly, most of the music written in any age will not stand up to such intense concentration.

Success in the orchestral museum demands qualities different from those needed for success in other spheres. This is music that is not merely entertaining, not merely spectacular, and not associated with any particular ritual, except perhaps the social rituals of concertgoing. Museum music is music as pure art, art for its own sake. In the concert-hall museum, no matter how many others may be in the room, each of us encounters the music alone, seeking an individual aesthetic experience. The museum intensifies our experience of a work of art, visual or musical, by directing all our attention to it, away from ourselves and our fellow viewers or listeners. The museum is a place in which we take our art very seriously indeed.

THE ORCHESTRAL MUSEUM AS A PATRON OF NEW MUSIC

While all museums preserve the past, not all cultivate the new. Some record and preserve a tradition without seeking to augment it. Zoos keep animals of all kinds, including endangered species, but do not attempt to evolve new species; natural history museums do not create new kinds of rocks or plants. Folk ensembles in southeastern Europe preserve the music, dances, costumes, and other folk arts of peasant cultures that have essentially been destroyed, where the rituals that gave meaning to those arts have largely disappeared. Similar ensembles in Western Europe and America seek to revive the music, dance, and related arts of Europe from the eleventh through the nineteenth centuries, reconstructing their sound and style as faithfully as possible. While such ensembles inevitably change the tradition they seek to preserve, they would no more invent new pieces than lexicographers would invent new words. Other museums, such as museums of science and technology, record change but do not themselves promote it; for example, London's Toy Museum preserves toys from many countries and eras, including new ones, but the new toys are developed for the marketplace, not for the museum. Again, there are parallel institutions for music: the Smithsonian Institution, for instance, supports festivals and recordings that preserve American folk and popular music just as it is, documenting its changes as well as reviving forms of popular music from earlier eras.

Art museums are different, and the orchestra is a kind of art museum. Although usually arranged on historical lines, art museums are fundamentally ahistorical. Aesthetic experiences are personal and immediate, encountered in the present moment; they have no history, although they may be shaped by a person's previous experience. The history of an artwork interests us precisely because the work of art is not simply an historical artifact but a living one. We learn about Rembrandt not because his life interests us but because his work interests us, and we believe that knowing the facts of his life or the manner of his brushstroke may help us understand his art. Similarly, in the concert hall, we enter into the music we hear with complete concentration on the aesthetic experience. We may know when and why it was created and first played, but its history concerns us only as a way to refine our expectations of the work and its performance: we expect certain things of Beethoven, others of Bach, still others of Wagner, and we can prepare ourselves for pieces we have never heard and for the music of composers we do not know by placing them in the framework of the familiar. Other than as preparation for hearing the music, a piece's history really does not matter. We are there to experience the piece for its own sake, and no amount of historical interest can compensate for a work's lack of aesthetic appeal.

By their very nature as collections of living artifacts divorced from their original historical contexts, art museums encourage the production of new works to hang on their walls next to the masterpieces of other eras. Art museums, therefore, not only preserve a tradition, but promote and influence it. Indeed, just as the folk arts of Macedonia emerged from a particular culture, art museums themselves form a culture for the creation of new art, art with no other purpose than to be displayed in a museum alongside other art, providing the stimulus for new individual aesthetic experiences.

As a kind of art museum, the modern orchestra invites the creation of new music, but of course on its own terms. New music for orchestra must behave like music that is already in the repertoire, meeting the expectations of performers and audiences for orchestral music just as a new work in any other tradition must meet the expectations of the culture that produces it. In one sense, this is no different from the situation in past centuries, for the music in the current repertoire has always influenced the shape of new orchestral music. What is different now is that such an overwhelming proportion of the music is decades or even centuries old. A composer in the eighteenth century, like a Tin Pan Alley songwriter in the early twentieth century or a rock band in the 1960s, wrote for a market with a constant thirst for novelty, and old pieces fell out of the repertoire as quickly as new pieces came along to replace them. But in the modern orchestral market, it is the old pieces that constitute the repertoire, and new works cannot hope to replace them, only to join them. The core of the repertoire changes slowly, if at all; the last major body of work added to the canon was the Mahler symphonies, which were finally admitted into full partnership only half a century after their composition. Only peripheral works leave the repertoire, and the newest entries, whether newly written or just revived, remain the most peripheral. Competition for acceptance into the repertoire has intensified with each generation over the past century and a half, until the chance of a new orchestral work joining the permanent repertoire seems very remote indeed.

The slow progress of much modern music in establishing itself in the repertoire cannot simply be attributed to the number and quality of the works already there. What is expected of modern orchestral music has become so difficult to achieve that the museum curators and the musical public no longer agree on which new pieces belong in the repertoire or even on the criteria for making choices.

THE PROBLEM OF COMPOSING FOR THE MUSEUM

If it is to find a place in the museum's permanent collection, new orchestral music must meet the expectations of performers, audiences, and critics for how orchestral music should act, as defined by how music in the existing repertoire does act. This presents the composer with an interesting but sometimes contradictory set of demands: lasting value, links to tradition, individuality, and familiarity.

By definition, the classical repertoire consists of "classics," pieces of lasting value that withstand repeated rehearings. The more central a work is to the repertoire, the more often it is performed. The most successful pieces, such as the symphonies of Beethoven, still offer fresh rewards long after they have become familiar. Many compositions fail this test: purely functional works, like Beethoven's German dances, often have little interest as concert music; occasional pieces, such as Beethoven's cantatas on the death of Emperor Joseph II and the accession of Leopold II, are usually as ephemeral as the occasions they celebrate; and pieces such as Beethoven's *Wellington's Victory*, in which superficial razzle-dazzle masks an almost complete absence of content, quickly lose their charm and can survive only as curiosities. These compositions receive occasional modern performances not because of their own merit but simply because they are by a composer whose symphonies, sonatas, and string quartets have become a central part of the classical repertoire. While they contributed to Beethoven's critical and financial success during his lifetime, they add little or nothing to his status in the museum, because they have little enduring value in their own right.

Thus, the first and most important problem confronting the composer who seeks a place for his compositions in the orchestral repertoire is to create musical works of lasting value, works that reward many and frequent rehearings and so have the capacity to become classics. As we will see, judging which pieces meet this criterion is a matter of no little difficulty.

Not every "classic" is part of the museum repertoire. There is no denying that *La Marseillaise, Dixie, The Stars and Stripes Forever*, the score to the film *Citizen Kane*, and *Sergeant Pepper's Lonely Hearts Club Band* are all classics of their genres, musical works of lasting value that stand up to repeated rehearings, but they are not considered to be classical music. The classical repertoire is not just music that is of enduring value or is old but "art music" as the museum defines it. Any candidate for admission to the repertoire, no matter what its age or origin, must be recognizably part of the tradition of Western art music. Recent utilitarian and popular music is normally excluded. This is ironic, for many pieces that were originally utilitarian or part of popular culture, from medieval dances through the operas of Verdi, have been included in the collection and now form part of the tradition of art music; only popular and functional music of more recent vintage seems to be beyond the pale.

The need for a new work to demonstrate links with the classical tradition tends to exclude not only new popular music but also art music that seems too radically innovative. To its first hearers, much of the music of Schoenberg and Webern seemed to have nothing whatsoever in common with the Bach, Beethoven, and Brahms to which they were accustomed and thus was not recognizably a part of the tradition of Western music at all. The composers countered with lectures and articles designed to prove how intimately their music was linked with the past and how logically it resulted from past developments in the history of music. In order to establish their credibility as candidates for acceptance into the classical repertoire, these composers had to demonstrate what their music shared with the music that was already familiar to performers and audiences, taking to lectures and articles when the musical relationships that were so obvious to them were not recognized by the musical public.

Thus, the second important problem confronting the composer of new orchestral music is to demonstrate how his music is like the music already in the repertoire. When this is not readily apparent in the music itself, composers and their disciples resort to polemic. This is one reason that so many modern composers take to print in words as well as in notes.

The requirement that new music recognizably take part in the tradition of classical music limits the freedom of contemporary composers, but it is balanced by a corresponding limit on the other side. New music cannot be too similar to music that is already in the repertoire, or it will be ignored. Why listen to an imitator of Beethoven when we can hear Beethoven? New music must be both traditional and innovative, like the music of the past, yet different from it—a neat and not altogether simple conundrum.

Indeed, one of the most remarkable traits of works that have entered the permanent repertoire is that each composer's music, and to a certain extent each piece, is seen as distinctly individual. In the concert-hall museum, it is common for music from all periods to be presented side by side, stripped of the social functions and historical contexts that gave rise to the differences between Vivaldi and Beethoven, Haydn and Schumann, or even Handel and Bach, and all that seems to distinguish one composer from another is musical style. All of the music in the repertoire now serves as concert music, experienced in the same ways by the same audiences, and the stylistic variety from one work to the next is a source of pleasure. The great composers are esteemed for the strength of their personalities, and their most distinctive music is the most highly prized. If new music is to compete with theirs, it must have an equally distinctive personality.

Thus, a composer of new music for the orchestral museum must find a distinctive personal style that sets his music apart and makes it recognizably his own. Each generation of modern composers has responded by reproducing the diversity of the existing repertoire in their own time, creating music that sounds as different from that of their contemporaries as does the music of composers writing in very different eras. Indeed, the music of Scriabin, Reger, Rachmaninoff, Schoenberg, Ives, Ravel, Falla, Ruggles, and Dohnányi, all born between 1872 and 1877, is as diverse in style and technique as was the entire orchestral tradition at the time they were born. The variety of styles has multiplied with each succeeding generation of composers, until the very concept of style no longer seems useful for comparing one composer's work with another. The resulting absence of stylistic consensus among modern composers makes the twentieth century unlike any previous period in Western art music and unlike any other tradition among the musical cultures of the world.

The problem of familiarity is the hardest to solve. The classical music that is already in the repertoire is, by definition, familiar and well loved. Even when we hear a piece of classical music from the eighteenth or nineteenth century for the first time, we are likely to know other works by the same composer or by his better-known contemporaries, so we will at least be already acquainted with the style. But new music is by definition as unfamiliar as classical music from those centuries is familiar, and when composers must stake out an individual style in order to distinguish themselves from their predecessors and contemporaries, the style they adopt may be unlike any idiom we know. The more unfamiliar a piece is in style, sound, and aesthetic, the more likely it will be difficult for listeners to understand and enjoy on first hearing; the less enjoyable or comprehensible a work is on first hearing, the less likely it will receive the repeated hearings that will allow it to become familiar and well loved.

The stylistic diversity of twentieth-century music exacerbates the problem, for our familiarity with one modern composer's work will as likely confuse us as help us in approaching the work of another. Knowing the music of Steve Reich, for instance, is no preparation for encountering an orchestral work by Elliott Carter for the first time. As a result, learning how to listen to modern classical music is much harder than learning how to approach the music of any other era; ironically, the very distinctiveness the museum demands of each composer makes it more difficult for modern music as a whole to appeal to a wide audience. Knowing other kinds of contemporary music is also of little help, for the strong links that once united art music, dance music, popular song, and musical theater have been broken. Only slowly, as the sounds and textures of modern classical music find their way into music for films and television, does this isolation begin to break down.

To compete with the familiar and beloved classics on their own ground, new compositions must be in some respect familiar and lovable, making use of well-known musical styles and gestures and speaking in a language that listeners can understand. While this places obvious limits on a composer's novelty and individuality, it also provides a creative tension between the familiar and the unique that can be one of the greatest pleasures of classical music, particularly since the mid-nineteenth century. The tension between immediate appeal and lasting value tends to be harder to calculate; if the balance is not right, a piece may enjoy brief success before disappearing into oblivion, or may find an enduring but tiny cadre of enthusiasts.

CRITERIA FOR SUCCESS

These four demands are challenging enough in themselves, but what makes the task of the modern composer so formidable is that there is no clear-cut method of determining if they have been successfully met. When composers sought to please a patron, to make money, or to achieve immediate popularity, they knew soon after their music was performed whether they had succeeded. Although each new piece was a gamble, they could learn from past successes and failures. Their experience of what pleased and what sold allowed them to predict what would succeed in the future, and they could shape their new music accordingly.

Modern composers have no such control over their success. Their expectations of immortality, by definition, cannot be realized in their lifetimes. They cannot learn from their own past successes in achieving lasting value and cannot apply their experience to their own new compositions. The entire corpus of music they compose is a gamble whose result they will not know.

Unable to predict their future success from their own experience, modern composers have turned to the experience of past composers for guidance. Unfortunately, the historical record only demonstrates the unpredictability of fame. The selection of pieces for the permanent repertoire has been somewhat capricious, depending not only on intrinsic quality, for which there are no agreed criteria, but also on concert politics, publicity, influence, and accident: Franz Schubert, Gustav Mahler, and Charles Ives might be as obscure today as Cipriani Potter, Franz Schreker, and Leo Ornstein, had not later generations of critics, composers, conductors, and performers enthusiastically promoted their music.

Some of the great composers in the current repertoire, including Handel, Haydn, Beethoven, and Verdi, achieved great fame and popular success in their own lifetimes. Some modern composers, from Richard Strauss to Philip Glass, have likewise sought and gained a wide audience in their own time, hoping that current popularity might predict lasting acceptance—though they are well aware from the examples of Dittersdorf, Salieri, Hummel, Spohr, Raff, and countless other once-famous composers that contemporary renown is no guarantee of immortality. Other great composers, from Bach to Mahler, had relatively modest reputations as composers during their lifetimes and found a wide audience only after their deaths, largely through the efforts of a few committed partisans. Recognizing that popularity can be ephemeral, most prominent modern composers have opted for this second path to immortality, seeking to write music that, whatever its appeal or lack of appeal to a wide audience, will be rich enough to attract a small coterie of disciples devoted to keeping it alive. While not exactly proclaiming unpopularity as a virtue in new music, these composers make clear that it is no vice; meanwhile, by making their music rich enough to attract the devoted fans who will (they hope) become its advocates, they virtually guarantee that many listeners will find it impenetrable.

The measure of success for new music becomes not its popularity, which becomes irrelevant, or its immortality, which composers cannot know, but its intrinsic value. But there are no universally accepted criteria for intrinsic value in a piece of music. Indeed, the very notion of intrinsic value in music is philosophically suspect, for artworks no less than other human artifacts acquire value because of their usefulness and attractiveness to human beings; their value is instrumental, not intrinsic, but based on the experience they occasion. The only way to evaluate new music is to compare it directly to the great music already in the repertoire, whose high value is universally accepted, and demonstrate that it exhibits to a high degree the same qualities that are valued in the classical masterpieces—whatever qualities the critic, composer, or listener may esteem. A modern composer naturally seeks to exemplify in his music the qualities he finds most precious in the music he admires. In a way, he becomes the sole judge of his own success.

EMULATION AND PROGRESS

The four demands delineated above—lasting value, links to tradition, individuality, and familiarity—would not be so difficult to meet and the criteria for success would not be so vague if the repertoire of Western classical music were not so heterogeneous. Creators in other musical traditions, such as jazz, bluegrass, or the classical musics of Asia, work within a prevailing style; familiarity and links to tradition are assured by their materials, and they achieve individuality through their distinctive approaches to the general style. The same was true of European composers in the eighteenth and early nineteenth centuries, who wrote music in the prevailing styles of their own eras for audiences who knew little of the music of earlier generations. But the repertoire of European classical music, by definition, has no common style. It is not a unified body of work from a single artistic tradition, like the classical music of Persia or the genre painting of the Netherlands. Instead, like the works displayed in an art museum, it is a collection of works created over the course of several centuries by artists in many regions representing many different styles and approaches. Verdi's music has much less in common with Vivaldi's than it does with the popular music of its own day, yet both are considered classical music, as is music in countless other styles from different eras, nations, and composers. In this respect, Western classical music is unique among musical cultures, creating unique problems for its composers. There is no prevailing style on which the modern composer can put his stamp. Instead, there are many different styles, each so closely identified with a composer, school, or period that none is immediately available to a contemporary composer who wishes to write original music. The originality that the master composers achieved through innovation within the common style of their own time can be achieved by the modern composer only through other means.

What holds the classical repertoire together despite its extreme diversity of style and origin is the notion that the pieces in it are the products of a single evolutionary process and represent individual stages of this process. While this interpretation is very much open to question, it has proven to be an idea of tremendous power, serving to organize the history of Western classical music into a coherent pattern, providing a rationale for the coexistence of music from many different periods within a single repertoire and suggesting to younger, historically self-conscious composers what their place in the panorama of music history might be.

In the early years of the conscious formation of the classical repertoire, it fell to the new field of music history to rationalize the collection, to explain what all those very different pieces from very different eras had in common and in what sense, despite radical disparities of sound, style, and aesthetic, they were all part of one tradition. Nineteenth-century music historians offered varying accounts, but most shared the themes of autonomy and progress. First, music was seen as an art or science developing on its own principles, shaped by fundamental laws of nature and aesthetics. Thus, its history could be studied as an autonomous stream, independent of political or intellectual currents, and with little concern for music's social functions, except as they imposed limitations on the freedom of music in any age to fulfill its innate destiny. This view of music history corresponded to (and perhaps helped to establish) the new function of musical compositions as autonomous artworks to be admired for their own sake. Second, the idea that music developed independently of wider historical forces raised the question of why it should change at all, and the notion of progress provided the explanation. The history of music was conceived as the development over time of musical techniques and aesthetics to a point of perfection, variously placed in the present, recent past, or future, and each great composer took his place in a long chain of influence, learning from the example of his forebears, refining and improving their techniques and introducing new ones, and serving as a model for those who followed. According to this view, music evolved like a scientific discipline: new techniques were seen less as inventions than as discoveries, as if there were one true way to write music that was gradually revealed through the contributions of individual composers. In such a view, innovation itself was part of a composer's greatness, if his discoveries were valid extensions of the known laws of music (determined in part by whether they were adopted by other composers); at the same time, past discoveries continued to be valued and were synthesized with the new, guaranteeing the continuity of the tradition.

Composers of new music for the museum, as well-informed students of their art and its history, naturally thought of themselves in similar historical terms. They took older composers as their models—not as past composers had actually lived and worked, writing constant streams of ephemeral music for immediate use, but as the museum and its curators had reconstructed them. Since the history of music was seen essentially as a history of musical styles and procedures, composers considered themselves to be making a contribution to the technical and stylistic progress of music, a task requiring not only the creation of a unique personal idiom but also the discovery of new devices in order to match the greatness of past innovators.

Considered in these terms, the solution to the problem of composing for the musical museum was readily apparent: a new composition must take its substance from the classical tradition while adding something new, combining emulation of the past with progress toward the future. Certainly, dependence on any one classical style would result in music with too little of its own character to be successful. But since the entire tradition was available to be emulated, sounds, techniques, and textures from different eras could be synthesized in a new work, linking it to the past without making it sound like any music ever heard before. In juxtaposing old elements in new ways and developing new techniques based on old procedures, composers wrote music that was at once traditional and innovative, classical in aspiration and inspiration yet wholly individual. Emulation and progress were not antithetical but were two sides of the same coin.

SOMETHING OLD, SOMETHING NEW

Arnold Schoenberg was the quintessential modernist, knowledgeable about past music, self-conscious about his relationship to it, and obsessed with his position in music history. His music exhibits this blend of emulation and progress in a characteristically extreme fashion. He made clear in his writings that for him the great music of the past was great precisely because it was new:

> There is no great work of art which does not convey a new message to humanity; there is no great artist who fails in this respect. This is the code of honor of all the great in art, and consequently in all great works of the great we will find that newness which never perishes, whether it be of Josquin des Prés, of Bach or Haydn, or of any other great master.
> *Because: Art means New Art.*
>   (pp. 114–115; emphasis in original)

Thus, for Schoenberg, the very newness of his music was, paradoxically, part of his emulation of the classical masters. Yet despite its newness, Schoenberg considered his music to be intimately linked to the German tradition in aesthetic and technique. He regarded the German classical masters from Bach to Reger as his mentors and claimed to have written "truly new music which, being based on tradition, is destined to become tradition" (p. 174).

Schoenberg's solutions to the problem of writing music that was like the music of the classical masters yet different from it were ingenious and are characteristic of modern composers in general. His orchestral music may be divided into three groups, each exhibiting a different strategy in this regard: (1) in terms of technique, by extending procedures derived from earlier music to new extremes; (2) in terms of structure and shape, by creating pieces whose substance entirely depends upon nontraditional techniques (usually derived through extension from earlier procedures) yet which establish strong analogies to classical models at every level from surface gestures to core structural principles and overall form; and (3) in terms of style, by borrowing not only structural devices and formal patterns but even stylistic clichés or actual compositions from the past and overlaying them with recognizably modern stylistic traits. Naturally, these three strategies are not mutually exclusive, nor are they limited to Schoenberg. Indeed, they are the most common strategies modern composers have utilized in their reconciliation of tradition with innovation, and they underlie a great deal of the orchestral music of the twentieth century. Thus, they merit examination in some detail, both in Schoenberg's own music and in the works of other composers.

The tonal orchestral works of Schoenberg's first period—*Verklärte Nacht* for string sextet (1902, arranged for string orchestra in 1917), the symphonic poem *Pelleas und Melisande* (1905), and the two *Chamber Symphonies* (no. 1, 1907, arranged for full orchestra in 1922 and 1935; no. 2, begun 1906 and finished 1939)—and the *Five Pieces for Orchestra* (1912), the sole orchestral work from his free atonal period, are highly individual works that take to new extremes traits common in earlier music: complexity of counterpoint; saturation of the texture with thematic and motivic material; constant variation of ideas; inequality of phrase lengths; displacement of rhythmic patterns and accents; novel instrumental sounds and techniques; use of timbre to highlight motivic relationships or as a means of organization in its own right; and, in general, a severe economy of means in pursuit of a rich network of relationships. None of these originated with Schoenberg, and he carefully attributes them to his "teachers" in the German classical tradition. His dependence on these techniques makes his music like that of the past, yet his music sounds very different from his models; indeed, these links to the past become more abstract and less immediately audible as Schoenberg's music develops and as he takes these common traits to their logical extremes.

In this process of intensifying common elements of the nineteenth-century tradition, Schoenberg is typical of his generation. The music of the early twentieth century is very diverse, but it is paradoxically united in the common themes of extremism and idiosyncrasy. The hour-long second movement of Mahler's Eighth Symphony (1910) and the fifteen-second-long fourth movement of Webern's *Five Pieces for Orchestra*, Opus 10 (written 1913, premiered 1926) are examples not of contradictory trends within music but of the same trend toward extremes. Nor is the hothouse chromaticism of Richard Strauss's operas *Salome* (1905) and *Elektra* (1909) contradicted by the smooth tonality of his *Der Rosenkavalier* (1911); even in the earlier operas, blistering dissonance alternates with blissful diatonicism, as Strauss portrays emotional extremes through the most extreme contrasts tonal harmony can offer. The tone poems of Debussy and Scriabin and the early ballets of Stravinsky extend the search of Berlioz, Rimsky-Korsakov, Mussorgsky, and Wagner for new musical and orchestral resources to the point that the very structure of pieces like Debussy's *La Mer* (1905) and Stravinsky's *Rite of Spring* (1913) depends as much on new scales, new chord types, new means of establishing pitch centers, and orchestration and timbre as stuctural devices as on more traditional motivic and tonal organization. All of these composers extend and exaggerate traits common to classical music, serving to make their own work innovative and distinctive while linking it intimately to the existing repertoire.

The same chemistry has worked for later generations, who have responded as often to their modernist predecessors as to the older classical heritage. The sound-masses of Edgard Varèse derive in part from the static or slowly changing blocks of sound in much of Debussy and in Stravinsky's *Rite of Spring*, but in works like *Intégrales* (1925) and *Arcana* (1927) he attains a monumentality wholly unlike his models. Since World War II, composers for orchestra such as György Ligeti (as in *Atmosphères*, 1961) and Krzysztof Penderecki (as in *Threnody for the Victims of Hiroshima*, 1960) have blended orchestral effects inspired by electronic music with the tradition of novel timbres built upon the pioneering work of the early modernists. In his Variations for Orchestra (1956), Double Concerto for Harpsichord and Piano with Two Chamber Orchestras (1961), Piano Concerto (1967), and Concerto for Orchestra (1970), Elliott Carter simultaneously reached back to classical genres and entirely transformed them in terms of a modern language that synthesizes the achievements of Schoenberg, Stravinsky, Ives, and Varèse in the realms of pitch, rhythm, and texture with his own contributions: gradual changes of meter and tempo, forms based on cycles and slow processes of evolution, and a personal vocabulary of expressive gestures. Like Schoenberg, each of these composers bases his innovations on the innovations of the past; their progressivism is predicated on their emulation of the classical masters and finds its meaning solely in terms of the classical tradition.

Schoenberg's second solution for reconciling new ideas with old models can be seen in his development, around 1921, of the twelve-tone system and its use in his orchestral works: Variations for Orchestra, Opus 31 (1928), Accompaniment to a Cinematographic Scene, Opus 34 (1930), the Violin Concerto (1940), and the Piano Concerto, Opus 42 (1942). The fusion of old and new in these works is in one sense obvious: using the new twelve-tone language, Schoenberg re-creates the familiar tonal genres of variations, film or program music, and the concerto. While the substance of his music is entirely new, its surface has all the expected gestures of romantic music, including shifting moods, dramatic climaxes, cadenzas and virtuoso passages, and classical forms. Some references are even more specific: his orchestral variations resemble those of Brahms in their sharp contrasts of style, tempo, and figuration, and his Piano Concerto gathers four movements into one unbroken stream, harking back to both Brahms's Second Piano Concerto, which is the only major piano concerto in four movements, and to Liszt's First Piano Concerto, whose three movements are played without pause, whose middle movement is really two (*adagio* and *scherzo*), and whose final movement recapitulates the concerto's opening theme, as does Schoenberg's finale.

But Schoenberg's reinterpretation of the past extends far beyond traditional forms and gestures to permeate his use of the twelve-tone technique as well. Schoenberg pairs each transposition of the original form of a tone-row with a transposition of the inverted form, whose hexachords are complementary (that is, the last six notes of either form are the same as the first six of the other, but in a different order). Together with their retrogrades, each such pair uniquely defines a tonal field, just as the diatonic chords in a key uniquely define that key, and there are twelve possible transpositions of this twelve-tone complex, just as there are twelve major and minor keys. The theme of the Variations uses two such related rows and their retrogrades and is stated in its original transposition in all but one of the variations; this consistency holds Schoenberg's twelve-tone variations together in the same way consistency of key unifies tonal variation sets. In other twelve-tone works, Schoenberg made explicit the analogy between his tonal fields and the keys of the tonal system in various ways: by using only rows from one transposition at a time, just as tonal music is in one key at a time; by changing transpositions, just as tonal music changes keys; by treating one transposition as a "tonic" associated with major structural events, such as statements of the principal theme and the beginning and end of the work; by establishing transpositions of secondary importance for the presentation of thematic material, in analogy to the secondary key areas in classical forms; and by restricting his use of some transpositions to transitional passages, just as classical tonal works may touch many keys briefly but emphasize only a few. Using this analogy, Schoenberg could reproduce the flexible structure of his tonal models in every respect, including not only rhythm, phrasing, and gesture but also tonal polarities and the expectation of tonal resolution. Here, the observation that the new in Schoenberg's music is part of his emulation of the past is quite literally true.

Schoenberg's development of the twelve-tone system has been one of the most influential innovations in modern music, precisely because it offers a system as flexible and complete as tonality itself. As might be expected of an era that requires individuality for success, every major composer who has adopted twelve-tone procedures has used them in an entirely personal way. Berg's approach in his second opera, *Lulu* (written 1929–1935), and his Violin Concerto (1936) accommodates tonal effects within the twelve-tone system by including triads, scale segments, and diatonic melodic elements in his rows. Moreover, both of these pieces, like Berg's non-twelve-tone opera *Wozzeck* (1925), refer constantly to earlier models in their use of stereotyped melodic and rhythmic gestures and archetypal forms from the music of the eighteenth and nineteenth centuries. Webern's music is condensed and self-reflective where Berg's is expansive. Webern's twelve-tone works, including the Symphony, Opus 21 (1929), Concerto for Nine Instruments (1935), and Variations for Orchestra (1940), while laid out in classical forms such as sonata, rondo, and variations, are full of canons and palindromes, their rows and themes based on manipulations of small melodic cells in a concentration of ideas that Webern learned from studying Renaissance music, notably that of Heinrich Isaac.

Since World War II, composers such as Milton Babbitt, Pierre Boulez, and Karlheinz Stockhausen have shunned direct references to the past in favor of further systematization, extending the twelve-tone system to include serial organization of rhythm, timbre, and dynamics. Their music is deeply influenced by the history of the musical language yet is entirely novel in structure and sound—and, of course, wholly unlike. In a way, these composers have applied Schoenberg's first strategy, that of intensifying existing procedures, to serialism, a product of his second strategy. Some younger serial composers have returned to classical forms; Charles Wuorinen, for instance, has written symphonies, two piano concertos, a concerto for amplified violin and orchestra, several concertos for soloist and chamber ensemble, and other works in classical genres. The variety of music produced using some facet of serial procedures can be gauged by comparing the music of Roger Sessions, Luigi Dallapiccola, Nikos Skalkottas, Elizabeth Lutyens, Humphrey Searle, Bruno Maderna, and Luigi Nono with that of each other and of the composers already named; even among these composers, there is no prevailing "style," only individual idioms shaped by their common heritage.

Other composers, while not adopting serialism, have evolved theoretical systems of comparable rigor and flexibility for their own music. Paul Hindemith opposed the twelve-tone system as being unnatural, creating as an alternative a harmonic language based on simple diatonic intervals and on tonal relationships derived from the overtone series. Olivier Messiaen's music exploits systematic melodic modes, bird calls, rhythmic patterns adapted from Hindu theory, and chords and chord progressions based on the upper partials of the harmonic series, to achieve a distinctive idiom. In the music of Iannis Xenakis, large gestures are built up from the accumulation of many small events determined through mathematical models, particularly probability theory. In their efforts to create modern analogues to the tonal system, these and other composers demonstrate their conviction that new systems are necessary if new music is to match the classical masterworks in logic, power, originality, and comprehensibility.

Schoenberg's third solution to the problem of creating music that is like the music of the classical masters yet different from it is, in a sense, the most radical and ingenious of the three. In his Concerto for Cello and Orchestra in D Major (1933), freely adapted from a harpsichord concerto by the Viennese composer Matthias Georg Monn, and his Concerto for String Quartet and Orchestra in B-flat Major (1933), freely adapted from the Concerto Grosso, Opus 6, no. 7, of Handel, Schoenberg reshaped his models into works that could only be Schoenberg's, marked on every page by his distinctive signatures: special effects in the solo strings such as harmonics, tremolos, mutings, bowing on the bridge or with the wood, and a varied vocabulary of articulations; use of orchestration and added pitches to emphasize motivic relationships; rhythmic displacements; enhanced counterpoint; and a complex network of musical ideas overlaid on the simple structure of his models. This music is obviously like eighteenth-century music because it takes its very fabric from the past and because composers of that era, notably Handel, also indulged in such free reworkings. Yet, at the same time, it is wholly modern; Schoenberg does not borrow from the past but rather possesses it, obliterating the earlier composer's personality with his own.

Stravinsky earlier had accomplished the same feat in his ballet scores *Pulcinella* (1920), based on music attributed to Pergolesi, and *The Fairy's Kiss* (1928), based on songs and piano pieces by Tchaikovsky. Stravinsky changed his models as little as necessary to accommodate his distinctive style of ostinatos, superimposed layers of sound, dry and percussive writing for strings and winds, diatonic harmonies other than triads, "wrong" notes and offbeat accents, and textures that alternate with and interrupt each other without transition. Webern's 1935 orchestration of the *Ricercare* from Bach's *Musical Offering* is even more restrained; without changing a note, Webern puts his own stamp on the piece by redistributing each entrance of the fugal subject among several instruments in ways exactly analogous to the canonic entrances in his own concerto and symphony, producing the *Klangfarbenmelodie* ("melody of tone colors") that is so typical of Webern and so untypical of Bach and highlighting motivic relationships, latent in the original, of the sort that underlie Webern's own music.

In contrast to Webern's restraint, Paul Hindemith's *Symphonic Meta-morphoses of Themes by Carl Maria von Weber* (1944) is even freer than Schoenberg's reworkings but demonstrates a remarkable reconciliation with the earlier composer's style. Lukas Foss's *Baroque Variations* (1967, on pieces by Handel, Domenico Scarlatti, and Bach), the third movement of Luciano Berio's *Sinfonia* (1968, based on the third movement of Mahler's Second Symphony), Mauricio Kagel's *Variationen ohne Fuge* (Variations Without Fugue, 1972, on Brahms's *Variations and Fugue on a Theme by Handel*), and Hans Werner Henze's *Il Vitalino raddoppiato* (1977, on the chaconne for violin and *continuo* attributed to Tomaso Vitali) are all highly individual reworkings in the same vein, transforming their models by addition, omission, reordering, and superposition. Henze's piece, in which he inserts one or two original variations after each of Vitali's, is a perfect metaphor for the work of the modern composer, who spins variations on the classical tradition, setting his contribution beside that of his predecessors, aiming not to displace them but only to join them in the repertoire, asking of his audience an understanding of how his new music reflects the past. The metaphor is also ironic: modern orchestral music is often played in the middle of concert programs, sandwiched between warhorses, so audiences must sit through it, however unwillingly.

None of these compositions are typical of their composers—one can get away with this sort of thing only once or twice. But evocations of archaic styles are extremely common in modern music, ranging from Prokofiev's imitation of Haydn in his *Classical Symphony* (1918) and Hindemith's resurrection of the forms, gestures, and aesthetic of Bach's *Brandenburg* Concertos in his *Kammermusik* series (1922–1928) to Hugo Distler's choral music modeled after that of the baroque composer Heinrich Schütz and Carl Orff's neomedieval *Carmina Burana* (1937) and neoantique *Catulli carmina* (1943) for voices and orchestra. Indeed, neoclassicism, broadly defined as the revival of sounds, techniques, and stylistic features identified with preromantic music, has been more influential in twentieth-century composition than any other movement. It is so important because it provides such flexible solutions to the demands of the museum: links to the past are obvious, yet composers may choose their models from many different eras, and the combination of style traits from past music with a composer's own idiosyncrasies is almost guaranteed to create music unlike any heard before, freshening the clichés of each era through their juxtaposition. Neoclassicism resolved the dilemma of the modern composer as surely as did the twelve-tone system, and, while not as obviously novel in its musical language, had the undeniable advantage of speaking to a much wider audience in a language it could understand.

For Stravinsky, neoclassicism solved a double problem, for he had to compete over his long career not only with the masterpieces of earlier generations but also with his own early success. He won his reputation with the three ballets that are still by far his most popular works, *The Firebird* (1910), *Petrushka* (1911), and *The Rite of Spring*. In the last of these, Stravinsky established a dry, rhythmically obsessive style that was to give all his later music a distinctive signature. Faced with the problem of writing new music without repeating himself, Stravinsky turned to the past for renewal, beginning with *Pulcinella*. The result of his "collaboration" with Pergolesi was quite different from its models, clearly Stravinskian, and yet very different from his own earlier music. Most of his later music depends on the same principle of integrating his personal style with another to which it is essentially alien, whether that be Bach's *Brandenburgs* in the *Dumbarton Oaks* Concerto (1938), the symphonic idiom of Haydn and Beethoven in the Symphony in C (1940), the operatic Mozart in *The Rake's Progress* (1951), medieval music in his *Cantata* (1952), or popular styles in his *Tango* (1941), *Circus Polka* (1944), and *Ebony Con-*

certo (1946) for clarinetist and jazz band. Even Stravinsky's adoption in his last period of the structural principles of serialism, after the deaths of Schoenberg and Webern had made that most modern of procedures in a sense an artifact of another age, may be seen in this light.

Other composers have also sought to renew classical music by infusing it with ideas from other traditions. In general, their music is classical in its fundamental techniques and aesthetics, extending common procedures of the past, and it absorbs from other traditions primarily surface features of style. Jazz has been a frequent source of new ideas, not only for Stravinsky but also for Darius Milhaud in his ballet *La création du monde* (1923) and many later works, George Gershwin's *Rhapsody in Blue* (1924) and his other "classical" pieces, Leonard Bernstein's *The Age of Anxiety* (Symphony no. 2 for piano and orchestra, 1949), and many others. Asian music has been an important influence on American composers such as Colin McPhee, Lou Harrison, and Harry Partch and, of course, on Asian composers working in the Western tradition, such as Japanese composers Toru Takemitsu and Toshiro Mayuzumi.

Both Béla Bartók and Charles Ives achieved a distinctive and successful synthesis of the classical tradition with another. Neither was a "folkloristic" composer, smoothing out folk materials to fit classical forms and harmonies; instead, the two traditions are fully integrated without compromising the integrity of either. Bartók synthesized his classical heritage with peasant music from southeastern Europe and Turkey by emphasizing both the points of contact, including pitch centers, scalar melodies, motivic repetition and variation, and phrase structure, and the elements from each tradition that make it most distinct from the other: from classical music, elaborate contrapuntal and formal procedures like fugue and sonata; from peasant music, modal scales, ornamentation, dissonance, folk instruments or imitations of their timbres, and complex meters and rhythms. In his late orchestral music, such as *Music for Strings, Percussion, and Celesta* (1937) and Concerto for Orchestra (1944), the modality and complex rhythms of peasant music and the forms of classical music are so completely abstracted from their sources that the music sounds little like folk music and nothing like that of any other classical composer.

In *Three Places in New England* (written 1903-1914, premiered 1931), the *Holidays Symphony* (written 1904-1913), the *Orchestral Set no. 2* (1915), and the Fourth Symphony (written 1909-1916, premiered 1965) Ives devised novel forms, based on the traditional classical procedures of variation and development, that use American tunes as their source material. The tunes are more often paraphrased than quoted, never left unchanged, often transformed beyond recognition; the last movement of *Three Places in New England,* for instance, spins a long melody of ravishing beauty out of a simple gospel hymn tune that is never stated in its original form. Even if one recognizes none of the tunes, this music sounds distinctly American because of its melodic sources; even if one recognizes none of the common procedures of European art music that are its foundation, this music could be nothing but classical concert music.

The music of Bartók and Ives is important not only because it blends the classical tradition with another, although that is an important part of its appeal, but also because these composers solved in unique ways the same compositional problems as Schoenberg, Debussy, and Stravinsky, extending the heritage of nineteenth-century art music to new extremes. Neither Bartók nor Ives founded a national school or spawned successful imitators, despite the renewal of the classical tradition that their music represents, but the intense originality and individuality that has made their music impossible to imitate has won it success in the modern concert-hall museum.

A few composers have attacked the problems posed by the concert-hall museum by refusing to play the game. Their most prominent spokesman is John Cage, who has suggested that contemporary music is and ought to be "adding to the disorder that characterizes life (if it is opposed to art) rather than adding to the order stabilized truth beauty and power that characterize a masterpiece (if it is opposed to life)" (p. 46). Pieces created through chance operations, like Cage's *Music of Changes* (1951) for piano, certainly do not express the personality of the composer, as museum pieces are expected to do. Indeterminate pieces, like Cage's Concert for Piano and Orchestra (1958), can hardly become classics, because they are different at each performance; in this work, the number of players, the coordination of parts, which pages are played and in which order, and even how the notation is to be translated into sound are all left to the performers to determine. This is music that is purposeless, which is not to say it is useless: Cage intends it to open our ears to the purposeless and beautiful sounds around us, to extend our aesthetic sensibilities beyond the picture frame and beyond the museum walls to embrace everything we experience. Cage's vision of music embodies both the good-natured anarchism of everyday life and the discipline and cooperation that for him are the hallmarks of the ideal society. His is perhaps the most thorough and consistent philosophical challenge the museum of classical music has faced since its inception.

THE PROBLEM OF POPULARITY

The most "modern" of modern composers, from the twelve-tone Schoenberg to the neoclassic Stravinsky, have solved the conundrum of writing
musical works of lasting value for display in the orchestral museum by
posing the question primarily in terms of musical technique. Their music
is indeed of lasting value, at once richly traditional and remarkably novel
and individual, rewarding many rehearsals and thorough study of their
scores. These are the composers favored by historians committed to a
music history in which progress in musical technique is the overarching
theme, by critics concerned with the new and unique, by theorists interested in the complex development of musical language, and by connoisseurs who can follow the elaborate commentary on the past that forms
the core of modern music. These are the composers who figure most
prominently in the textbooks and critical literature on modern music.
And these are the composers whose music audiences tend, with a few
exceptions, rather not to like.

The conundrum of creating musical works of great and lasting value
is not to be solved only on the safe ground of musical technique. What
made the music of Haydn, Mozart, and Beethoven so popular in its day
and keeps it popular still was not its techniques per se but its double
appeal, to the musically learned for its structure and intelligence and to
the general audience for its tunefulness and emotional expressivity.
These two groups unite in endorsing Bach, Beethoven, and Brahms as
great composers but for different reasons, and the success of modern composers in winning over the musical elite is no guarantee that audiences
will join the chorus of praise, now or in the future. The lay listener
demands different things of the music he loves, and much modern music
fails to provide them. For the mass audience of classical music lovers,
Schoenberg's twelve-tone music is not tuneful, Stravinsky's neoclassical
music is not expressive, and most of the modern music that the critical
establishment most deeply respects is too unfamiliar and confusing to be
heard as beautiful, melodic, or moving.

For these listeners, another group of twentieth-century composers for
orchestra is far more important than the composers mentioned thus far.
These composers are equally modern in outlook, although not so novel
in sound; like other composers of their time, they recognize that to compete with the classical masters, they must write distinctive music of lasting
value that continues and yet renews the tradition, and they aspire to a
place in the permanent repertoire. But these composers are more aware

than their somewhat elitist peers of the importance of speaking in a language listeners understand. They write music in which the layman's values of tunefulness and expressivity are paramount. Theirs is the music of the modern romantics, composers who are considered conservative in style and are often associated with national schools: Puccini, Respighi, Sibelius, Nielsen, Rachmaninoff, Shostakovich, Kabalevsky, Khatchaturian, Delius, Vaughan Williams, Holst, Britten, Bloch, Copland, Barber, and many others. The music of these composers has demonstrated not only immediate appeal but also a remarkable staying power. This cannot be because the concert audience cannot tell schlock from substance; it must be, instead, that there are indeed new things to be said in the classical vernacular. If anything, it is more difficult to speak with an individual voice in the common language of tonal romanticism than in an idiosyncratic style, and the great tonal composers of the century have been as concerned with establishing their distinctive musical personality as their peers. They write in a conservative tradition of concertos, symphonies, ballets, and tone poems, and in that tradition their works have a character all their own. If the music of twentieth-century tonal composers were to fall out of the repertoire, something distinctive and irreplaceable would be lost, as sure a test of success in the museum as there is.

In the long run, perhaps the most enduring modern music will be that of composers who have appealed to both the learned and the mass audience, such as Mahler, Debussy, and the young Stravinsky. Like Haydn, Mozart, and Beethoven, these composers appeal to these two competing constituencies on very different grounds, combining the complexity, depth, and novelty expected by the connoisseur with the tunefulness, expressivity, traditionalism, and immediate appeal expected by the average listener. It is not an easy juggling act, but even today it is not impossible, as demonstrated by the recent successes of David Del Tredici, Steve Reich, and Philip Glass. It remains to be seen whether the concert audience will become as enamored of Schoenberg, Webern, Carter, and the modernist mainstream as is the critical establishment. It may yet happen; the most obvious difficulties of dissonance and unusual sounds have diminished over time, and orchestras and audiences are seeking a more varied repertoire. But if lay listeners embrace the modern masters, they will do so on their own terms.

BIBLIOGRAPHY

Theodor W. Adorno, *Philosophie der neuen Musik* (rev. ed., 1972), translated by Anne G. Mitchell and Wesley V. Blomster as *Philosophy of Modern Music*

(1973). Reinhold Brinkmann, ed., *Die neue Musik und die Tradition* (1978.) J. Peter Burkholder, "Brahms and Twentieth-Century Classical Music," *Nineteenth-Century Music*, 8 (1984); and "Museum Pieces: The Historicist Mainstream in Music of the Last Hundred Years," *Journal of Musicology*, 2 (1983). John Cage, *Silence* (1961). Michael Kowalski, "The Exhaustion of Western Art Music," *Perspectives of New Music*, 21 (1982–1983). Ernst Křenek, "Tradition in Perspective," *Perspectives of New Music*, 1, no. 1 (1962).

Samuel Lipman, *Music After Modernism* (1979). Leonard B. Meyer, "Innovation, Choice, and the History of Music," *Critical Inquiry*, 9 (1983). Robert P. Morgan, "Secret Languages: The Roots of Musical Modernism," *Critical Inquiry*, 10 (1984). James Parakilas, "Classical Music as Popular Music," *Journal of Musicology*, 3 (1984). Henry Pleasants, *The Agony of Modern Music* (1955). Hans-Peter Reinecke, *Das musikalisch Neue und die neue Musik* (1969). John Rockwell, *All American Music: Composition in the Late Twentieth Century* (1983).

Arnold Schoenberg, *Style and Idea*, Leonard Stein, ed. (1975). Rudolf Stephan, et al., *Zwischen Tradition und Fortschritt. Über das musikalische Geschichtsbewusstsein* (1973). Leo Treitler, "The Present as History," *Perspectives of New Music*, 7, no. 2 (1969). Anton Webern, *Der Weg zur neuen Musik*, Willi Reich, ed. (1960), translated by Leo Black as *The Path to the New Music* (1963).

Musicology and the Rise of the Independent Orchestra

Jon W. Finson

/ / The science of music [musicology] is coeval with the art of music,"
Glen Haydon once asserted (p. 4), and the interaction between
the orchestra in its various guises and modern musicology provides a
particularly good case in point. The beginnings of musicology in its modern manifestation are usually traced to the period around 1600, when the
great systematic treatises by men like Michael Praetorius, Marin Mersenne, and Pietro Cerone appeared. Though these authors contributed
very little directly to the formation of the autonomous orchestra as we
now know it, their interest in organology helped to lay the foundation
for the modern ensemble and deserves at least brief mention here. The
orchestra that dominates modern musical life in so many western European cultural centers is more intimately connected with historical musicology. Musical scholars of the late eighteenth and nineteenth centuries
heavily influenced the concept of the symphony orchestra and its literature. As musicological activity became increasingly centered in academic
institutions during the twentieth century, the discipline assumed
another, advisory role in the life of orchestral institutions. Throughout
all of these changes, however, musicology has consistently taken part in
the structure of Western instrumental music.

THEORETICAL ROOTS

That many of the early printed musicological treatises deal at great length
with instruments may seem merely the result of their authors' relentless

encyclopedic intent. Cerone in *El melopeo y maestro* (1613), Praetorius in *De organographia* (1618), Mersenne in *Harmonie universelle* (1635–1636), and Kircher in *Musurgia universalis* (1650) discuss instruments known only by rumor (from Greek mythology or the Old Testament) as well as theoretical instruments like the monochord. Nevertheless, these authors possessed a sincere and inordinate curiosity about mechanical matters, including the production of sound by machines. Vocal music is still the predominant art music in these treatises, but the new organologies reflect an acceptance of instrumental music without which the present estate of the orchestra would be unthinkable.

If the early organologies did nothing else, they disseminated information about the various kinds of available instruments and asserted the importance of this knowledge. Early musicologists organized instruments into vocal families from which the modern orchestra was selected: the symphony orchestra is the ultimate broken consort (that is, an ensemble of mixed instrumental families). Notions of historical teleology do not apply here, of course; neither Praetorius, nor Mersenne, nor Kircher aimed even remotely to create the modern orchestra. But the history of the orchestra exhibits incremental development, with musicology publicizing the variety of instruments and their newfound respectability.

Aside from cataloging the kinds of instruments, the early organologies seem most concerned with tuning and temperament. We now take standardization of pitch for granted, though it was not well established until the end of the nineteenth century and even today varies slightly from one ensemble to another. But much musicological energy was expended between 1600 and 1800 trying to resolve or at least explain major discrepancies in pitch. Praetorius prefaces his discussion of individual instruments by saying, "We must know from the beginning that the pitch of organs as well as of other musical instruments varies quite often, for in olden times concertizing and making music with all kinds of instruments at the time was not common, and the wind instruments were made and tuned by instrument makers quite variously, one high, another low" (p. 14). The convention in Praetorius' time still involved discrepancies of several semitones between *Chorton* and *Kammerton,* and he seems content to instruct composers about the differing transpositions rather than to propose a new system.

The most ingenious solution to the lack of standard pitch came from Mersenne, who puts the whole problem on a scientific basis. Each composer, Mersenne suggests, should record the frequency of the first melodic note in the manuscript or print of each piece. Thus, were the performer to use modern pitch in this hypothetical example, an air for flute beginning on the A above middle C would feature the "pitch signature" 440, signifying the number of vibrations per second needed to produce the first note. Unfortunately, Mersenne did not convince his contemporaries to adopt this most rational procedure, and the question of standardized pitch remained. Nonetheless, writers like Mersenne needed to recognize and publicize the problem before agreement on a solution could be reached. An international orchestral culture would be impossible without the attention first called to this dilemma by early organologists.

Temperament, the relationship of notes within the scale, presented an equally troublesome problem for early instrumentalists and organologists. Almost all early organologies begin with a consideration of the proper distance between various notes in the octave. Kircher, for instance, begins his study of instruments with the division of a string into those proportionate lengths that generate certain kinds of intervals (3:2 will produce a perfect fifth, 4:3 will produce a perfect fourth, and so on). This preoccupation reflects to some extent an ancient theoretical tradition associating music with mathematics and astronomy. But these mathematical considerations also had a practical application in the tuning of mundane instruments and their use in ensemble. Scipione Cerreto, Praetorius, Mersenne, and Cerone were all concerned with the compatibility of instruments gauged according to their temperaments. Gambas, as fretted instruments featuring equidistant semitones (equal temperament), would not fit well with harpsichords in meantone temperament, where the semitones were not equidistant. Similarly, winds varied in temperament from town to town, from instrumental family to instrumental family (recorders, shawms, trumpets, and so forth), and even within those families.

In their solutions to the myriad problems of temperament, early musicologists were more concerned with the compatibility of instrumental pairs than with large ensembles. Mersenne alone mentions a substantial ensemble, one composed of violins, whose unfretted strings allow an infinitely adjustable temperament (making them the logical basis for a large orchestra). The combination of large wind and string groups in a single ensemble was not susceptible to general solutions in the sixteenth and seventeenth centuries. Instead, adjustments were made whenever a large ensemble was formed, and this activity could only summon the vaguest of comments from organologists. Even though large orchestras were not their specific concern, early musicologists began to provide the theoretical groundwork for arranging large assemblages of instruments.

Musicology in the eighteenth century continued many of the early studies. We find organologies like Filippo Bonanni's *Gabinetto armonico* (1722) and Joseph Majer's *Museum musicum* (1732), as well as encyclopedic dictionaries like Sébastien de Brossard's *Dictionnaire de musique* (1703) and Johann Gottfried Walther's *Musikalisches Lexicon* (1732), all of which give more or less detailed information about instruments.

Eighteenth-century authors also added a new practical bent to organology: many of their descriptions of instruments specify their use in ensembles. And in tutors such as that by Johann Mattheson orchestral instruments are often discussed. *Das neu-eröffnete Orchestre* (1713), a treatise devoted mostly to composition, includes a section listing the instruments encountered in orchestral settings and their appropriate functions. Mattheson's interests lie in the utility of particular strings and winds, not in an encyclopedic account of real and fictional instrument. He does discuss tuning and temperament, though these subjects no longer loomed as large as they did in the previous century.

The orchestral ensemble that appeared in early-eighteenth-century musicology bears some evidence of standardization. The heart of the orchestra was clearly the violin family (Mattheson calls them the *corps de bataille* in the *Vollkommene Capellmeister* of 1739) plus a keyboard instrument and often the lowest member of the viol family (violone). Winds were added according to availability and taste and with an eye to the problems of temperament. The tutors must have been particularly influential in promoting standardization, for they purvey much advice on this point; even Johann Joachim Quantz, writing a method for the solo flute player (1752), concerned himself with the proper constitution of an orchestra. The early-eighteenth-century writers speak mostly of orchestras in the church or in the theater—that is, those that provide the accompaniment for singers. Vocal music was still the ideal, and the orchestras at the small independent German courts and at the Concert Spirituel in Paris received little attention.

MODERN MUSICOLOGY

The late eighteenth and nineteenth centuries saw increased emphasis on music history as part of musicology and on the importance of the orchestra as an independent musical institution. Neither music history nor the orchestra was new, but both underwent a significant change in status as the result of social change. And both became, for various reasons, the darlings of the professional middle class (engineers, lawyers, teachers, doctors, and others holding higher degrees), which was slowly attaining power. Both music history and the independent orchestra served in their own ways as symbols of status for the professional middle class. And for this reason, musicologists (who were often lawyers, engineers, or doctors by training in the early years of academic musicology) had much to say about the aesthetic underlying the orchestra and its literature. By the same token, orchestral artists often contributed to musicology as a symbol of the scientific progress so dear to the professional middle class, which often founded and maintained independent symphonies. Both musicologists and orchestral performers helped to establish the notion of a "classical," as opposed to a "popular," music, around which the professional middle class rallied.

The new prominence of music history (it replaced both practical and speculative theory as the main musicological activity) at the end of the eighteenth century owed much to the new aspirations of the professional middle class. Charles Burney wrote signally at the beginning of his *Musical Tours*, "Music has indeed ever been the delight of accomplished princes, and the most elegant amusement of polite courts: but at present it is so combined with things sacred and important, as well as with our pleasures, that it seems necessary to our existence" (p. xxvi). Members of the professional middle class were not noble by patent or pedigree, but they could at least participate in the aristocracy of culture and the intellect. They naturally sought to foster an art that transcended the social status of its creators and audience, an art with an enduring ability to address the human condition rather than with the mere novelty of fashionable style. The measure of endurance was the "test of history"—or at least the potential for survival—and the assaying agent was the intellect trained (usually at the university) to discern a body of "classical masterworks." Thus, the roles of music historian and music critic were combined, and writers like Burney, who held a doctorate of music from Oxford, engaged in both historical and journalistic enterprises. Similarly, much nineteenth-century musicological activity was recorded in general music journals. By this means the knowledge of music history and of "classical" music became the property of the professional middle class, helping to legitimize its aspirations to social equality.

The new emphasis on music history also entailed certain moral values that served the professional middle class. Burney, for instance, writes in the dedication of his *History of Music* that the "science of musical sounds ...may be with justice considered as the art that unites corporal with intellectual pleasure, by a species of enjoyment which gratifies sense,... and which, therefore, the Great may cultivate without debasement, and the Good enjoy without depravation" (1:9).

Not only did acculturation in the fine arts benefit the scholar or reader morally, but the study of the history of high culture led to a sense of those pluralistic values espoused around the turn of the nineteenth century by the liberal professional class. These professional people tended as a group to favor democratic politics governed by a written constitution that mediated between the various interests competing in a pluralistic society, the assumption being that such pluralism was healthy. Historians of high culture reinforced the value of plurality, suggesting that many different styles of music reflecting diverse values from several periods might reasonably coexist in concert life, subsumed under the label "classical music." Anton Thibaut, by vocation a professor of law and by avocation an influential aesthetician (Schumann was one of his disciples), wrote of artistic plurality in 1824, "One deprives oneself of the greatest pleasure in music when one assumes that one style or one master can obliterate all the others. For each has its own magic, as a rule, and a perfected music is inextinguishable precisely because it can excite, purify and ennoble the intellect and heart in all respects" (p. 176).

Yet another benefit derived from the study of "classical" culture was the promotion of progress. Again, Thibaut observes, "Never has it been so generally recognized as now, that historical study and familiarity with the available classics should be the foundation of all well-grounded knowledge. For sure progress can be made only if one seeks to promote the good with new zeal, instructed by the teaching of others" (p. 1). In short, the study of cultural history, including music history, came to bear almost religious connotations. Cultural historians not only helped the professional middle class to gain new status but also became priests of a discipline that fostered the virtues of plurality and progress.

The fate of the independent orchestra was bound to that of the professional middle class for more mundane reasons, partly economic in nature and partly in default of any other large musical institution to absorb the social energies of this class. Opera had traditionally been associated with court theaters; and even where "public" opera houses existed, they were often dominated by aristocratic societies that underwrote their enormous costs. Sacred vocal music had been the province of the church. The independent orchestra carried no such connotations because it had been practically nonexistent during the first three-quarters of the eighteenth century. Even great orchestras were appended to vocal groups. Burney says of the Mannheim orchestra, for example:

> It has not been merely at the Elector's great opera that instrumental music has been so much cultivated and refined, but at his *concerts,* where this

extraordinary band has "ample room and verge enough," to display all its powers, and to produce great effects without the impropriety of destroying the greater and more delicate beauties, peculiar to vocal music; it was here that Stamitz, stimulated by the productions of Jommelli, first surpassed the bounds of common opera overtures.

(2:35)

Dependent orchestras had generally accompanied singers on stage or in church. The independent symphony, then, could serve without stigma as a major cultural institution for an anticlerical professional class vying for power with the nobility.

The independent orchestra also fit the more limited financial means of professionals. As organizers and subscribing members of philharmonic societies, people of moderate resources could support an orchestral season, whereas only the financial backing of the court or the very wealthy could underwrite the opera. In their most inclusive manifestations, orchestral societies provided a meeting place for the aristocracy and the professional middle class, but the organizations were largely dominated by the latter—a complexion that many retain to this day.

The only problem with the independent orchestra as the focus of the professional middle class's cultural energy was the lack of a proper repertoire. Music historians could point to classical vocal music, either sacred or secular, from the long period of vocal predominance, but the dances, concertos, and opera overtures of bygone years seemed somehow too trivial to be enshrined in this way. (In a later phase of music history these pieces would resurface, as we shall see.) Establishing a classical orchestral repertoire enlisted the aid of musicologist-critics, just as music history and theory attracted the talents of composers and conductors.

The selection of the Austro-Germanic symphony in preference to other candidates (such as the French *symphonie concertante*) as the foundation of the repertoire was the result of complex factors. The German-speaking lands, with their small cities, were more likely to support orchestras than to excel in opera. And the symphonies of Beethoven, the most admired nineteenth-century composer of instrumental music throughout western Europe, promoted a powerful cult surrounding the German symphony. Most important was the extraordinary energy expended by the German professional class in raising absolute music to a preeminent position among the arts. "That the concept of absolute music ... originated in German romanticism," Carl Dahlhaus writes of this phenomenon, "that it owed its pathos [that is, the association of music "absolved" from texts, program, and functions with the expression of notion of the "absolute"} to German poetry and philosophy around 1800, was perceived even in France" (p. 9). The symphony was simply the grandest manifestation of absolute music.

Using Beethoven as the ideal for their romantic view of the symphony, music historians and critics applied the aesthetic system developed for him to the works of Mozart and Haydn. The resulting historical distortion imputed far more importance to the symphonies of Haydn and Mozart than their authors could possibly have imagined, while demoting Haydn's operas or Mozart's opere serie to second- or even third-class status. Haydn's and Mozart's symphonies could then be portrayed as progressing logically toward a Beethovenian summit, and by this line of reasoning, a distinguished historical repertoire of orchestral music became immediately available. (Almost no trace of such a tradition appears in Burney just a few decades before.)

Thus the so-called classical literature emerged in the music journals of the time, like Athena sprung from the head of Zeus. E. T. A. Hoffmann, a lawyer by profession, expounded the accepted view as early as 1810 in his famous review of Beethoven's Fifth Symphony:

> Haydn and Mozart, the creators of the new instrumental music, first reveal this art to us in all its glory; he who gazed upon this art with a more perfect love and penetrated its innermost being is—Beethoven. The instrumental compositions of all three masters breathe the same romantic spirit in which lies the same inner comprehension of the particular essence of the art.
>
> (p. 632)

Hoffmann clearly implied that Beethoven had inherited a Viennese tradition, and this historical notion includes the concept of a music eternally relevant by virtue of its transcendent spirtuality. His comments were not the mere fantasies of a novelist; rather, they entailed a precise technical analysis of Beethoven's symphony in musicological terms.

Many articles in German periodicals of the time held a similar view. Ernst Ludwig Gerber, a noted music historian, asserted in "A Friendly Presentation About Developed Instrumental Music, Especially About Symphonies," that "unquestionably, this manner founded by Haydn of writing symphonies on one main idea, which has also been followed by Mozart, Beethoven and many other German masters, is the *non plus ultra* in the new art, the most lofty and excellent thing in instrumental music" (p. 457). The establishment of the Austro-German classical tradition required incessant repetition of the Viennese litany.

Later German musicologists cemented the repertoire of classical absolute music to the notion of progress. Adolf Bernhard Marx, originally trained in law, sketched such a history of symphonic music in 1855, first confirming the Viennese point of departure: "A definite line of progress is outwardly quite prominent in those works of Beethoven which apparently tread the selfsame paths of his predecessors, Mozart and Haydn" (p. 77). Marx then proceeded to the newest inheritors of progressive tradition:

> What our masters created here [in the symphony] has produced its effect everywhere, and has called forth the most delightful new generation in Schumann, Schubert, Mendelssohn and Gade.... Among the symphonists who succeed Beethoven, we must include Hector Berlioz above all. What draws our attention to him ... is the structure of his orchestra. One must read his *Cours d'instrumentation*, distinguished by its complete technical insight and poetic understanding of particulars, and his other publications to see how he conceives of orchestral construction.
>
> (p. 124)

Music historians continued to comment on the modern scene because they felt obligated to place new music in relationship to the past. In this way musicologists not only added to the body of orchestral repertoire but also influenced the music retained in the standard corpus. By 1854 the most extreme view of absolute music had been definitively articulated by Eduard Hanslick in *Vom Musikalisch-Schönen*, and the complete dominance of instrumental music had been achieved. Hanslick, an erstwhile lawyer and worthy scholar-critic, did much to establish the reputation of later symphonists, among them Brahms and Mahler.

Much the same relationship between musicology, music journalism, and the independent orchestra existed elsewhere in Europe. In England, for instance, William Ayrton, first music director of the Philharmonic Society, edited the *Harmonicon*, a journal dedicated to contemporary criticism and short essays on music history. As music director of the society, Ayrton chose its repertoire (leadership of orchestras and other ensembles was left to the appropriate musicians), and the programs during that first year of 1813 concentrated heavily on the symphonies of Haydn, Mozart, and Beethoven, a practice observed in subsequent years. Again Beethoven led the way to the Viennese classics. The Philharmonic Society began to request works from Beethoven, and one such petition resulted in the British premiere of the Ninth Symphony.

Much like their German counterparts, later British musicologists maintained close ties to the independent orchestra throughout the nineteenth century. Sir George Grove, originally trained as a civil engineer, managed a series of concerts competing with the Philharmonic Society, in his capacity as secretary of the Society of Arts and then as secretary of the Crystal Palace. Grove wrote program notes for the orchestral concerts that were given under the direction of August Manns and in 1896 published a book devoted to Beethoven's symphonies. In England as in Germany, such books served to consolidate the newly invented classical repertoire for the independent orchestra. Grove ends his treatise on Beethoven thus: "There can never be a second Beethoven or a second Shakespeare. However much orchestras may improve and execution increase, Beethoven's Symphonies will always remain at the head of music as Shakespeare's plays are at the head of the literature of the modern world" (p. 399). Such statements invoke all the aesthetic criteria connected with the movement toward historical scholarship, and they effected the swift establishment of a standard orchestral literature.

In France, unlike Germany and England, the independent orchestras were organized by professional musicians rather than by a board of directors of some society's subscription concerts. François-Joseph Fétis, the prominent French critic and musicologist, wrote in 1830:

> It is unfortunate that the lack of institutions here limits the careers of composers to dramatic music.... The symphony is completely neglected, because a musician who attempts to write one cannot succeed either in publishing his works or in having them heard. Nature would be laboring in vain to have a Haydn or a Beethoven born in France; such talent would be better hidden in the milieu of the capital than a diamond in the bowels of the earth.
>
> (p. 145)

Fétis is exaggerating here, for he knew well that Habeneck had successfully organized an orchestra at the Conservatoire specifically to perform Beethoven's symphonies. Indeed, Fétis edited Beethoven's symphonies for publication in France, and he wrote several long reviews comparing the Philharmonic Society in London to the Conservatoire concerts in Paris. Perhaps Fétis simply meant that France lacked the large number of smaller orchestras found in Germany.

French musicologists shared their German colleagues' belief in progress, applying it to the technique of the orchestra itself rather than to its literature. For Fétis the orchestra was the acme of modern innovation:

> All parts of music have been subject to period variation; but none has undergone such great changes as the composition of the orchestra. These

changes have had many causes: on the one hand, due partly to the invention of new instruments, the abandonment of many others, the perfection of some, and above all due to the development of the players' abilities; on the other hand, due partly to progress in music, the need for novelty, boredom with simple things, and the rule of fashion.

(p. 272)

The interest of musicologists like Fétis in the independent orchestra and its literature was partially responsible for an increase in the number of French ensembles during the nineteenth century. At first they were formed by individual conductors following the previous French model. Jules Pasdeloup and Édouard Colonne established their own orchestras around midcentury, playing literature mostly from the Austro-Germanic school. Charles Lamoureux would follow in 1897, combining his interest in the orchestra and in early music. The musicologist Julien Tiersot pointed to the founding of the Société Nationale de Musique in 1871 for the promotion of French instrumental compositions as the greatest single event in late-nineteenth-century French musical culture. The Société was especially devoted to orchestral works, taking the Philharmonic Society of London as its model. Musical progress in France, as elsewhere, was associated largely with the independent orchestra and its literature. German musicologist-critics, aided by their English and French colleagues, finally established the primacy of the orchestra throughout western Europe, save for the operatic bastion of Italy.

In light of the active influence of musicologists on the independent orchestra, it is not surprising to find prominent orchestral composers taking an active part in historical and theoretical musicology. The Leipzig school played a particularly important role in historical musicology. Robert Schumann was an important symphonist and prime advocate of the German symphony:

> When a German speaks about symphonies, he speaks about Beethoven: he considers the two words as one and indivisible; they are his pride and joy. Just as the Italian has his Naples, the Frenchman his Revolution, and the Englishman his merchant marine, so the German has his Beethovenian symphonies; because of Beethoven he forgets that he cannot boast of a great school of painters, and he wins in spirit the many battles forfeited to Napoleon; he may even dare to place Beethoven on the same plane as Shakespeare.
>
> (p. 1)

Schumann promoted the work of Gustav Nottebohm and developed a predilection for Bach, conducting both the St. John and St. Matthew passions in Düsseldorf with great success. Schumann's friend Mendelssohn also combined talent as a symphonic composer and orchestral conductor with a profound interest in the works of Bach. Julius Rietz, one of Mendelssohn's successors as conductor of the Gewandhaus Orchestra, carried on the Leipzig tradition, both editing Mendelssohn's complete works and serving as secretary of the Bach Society for five years.

The most prominent heir of the Leipzig school was Brahms. Again we find a prodigious symphonic talent stemming from an interest in absolute music combined with a keen historical curiosity. Brahms engaged in making editions of earlier masters, and he even sat on the board of *Denkmäler der Tonkunst in Österreich*. This musicological bent directly affected his works for the orchestra. For example, Brahms deliberately modeled his early orchestral serenades, Opus 11 and Opus 16, on Mozartean cassations. Though their musical language is peculiarly Brahmsian, the allusion to the eighteenth century is clearly transmitted in the multiple movements including archaic minuets. Such historical allusions also found their way into the last movement of the Fourth Symphony in the form of a chaconne with a ground bass taken from Bach's Cantata 150, "Nach dir, Herr, verlanget mich."

References to the history of music permeate the orchestral literature of other nineteenth-century composers. The most obvious example is Louis Spohr's *Historical* Symphony (1839) with movements imitating, respectively, the style of the "Period of Bach and Handel, 1720," the "Period of Haydn and Mozart, 1780," the "Period of Beethoven, 1810," and finally the modern period. Stylistic references also appear in Grieg's orchestrated version of the suite "From Holberg's Time." Even Tchaikovsky would participate in the historical trend, especially in his Fourth Suite (1887), entitled "Mozartiana" and based on that composer's music.

The theoretical side of musicology also enlisted the talents of orchestral composers. Most prominent among them was Berlioz, whose *Grand traité d'instrumentation et d'orchestration modernes* (1843) became the standard European text. Berlioz (yet another potential member of the professional middle class, who forsook medicine for music) expressed most directly in his letters from Prague the familiar notions concerning musical progress. The Paris Conservatoire should teach, in his opinion, instrumentation, conducting, new instrumental techniques for violin and viola, and new instruments, including bass clarinet, saxophone, bass tuba, valved cornet, and percussion—in short, all those instruments that accompanied "advances" in the symphony orchestra. Berlioz' list ends with yet another suggestion:

A comprehensive conservatoire, bent on conserving the significant facts and worthwhile achievements handed down from the past and various revolutions through which the art has passed, would necessarily have a chair in the history of music, which would ensure that the works of our predecessors were studied and known, not only by means of oral and written instruction but also by the example of meticulous and authentic performances of the appropriate masterpieces. One would not then find students, even talented ones, who, so far as their awareness of the noblest works of great composers still living is concerned, are as unenlightened as Hottentots. The general taste of musicians would be transformed, their whole conception of music would become larger and more serious, and in the ranks of the profession artists would at last outnumber artisans.

(p. 404)

Berlioz, like many prominent music journalists, associated both the orchestra and music history with progress and the interests of the professional middle class.

ACADEMIC MUSICOLOGY AND HISTORICISM

The twentieth century has witnessed the widespread establishment of musicology in major universities and, consequently, a change in the role played by musicologists in the life of the independent orchestra. Scholars have increasingly abandoned their activities as critics in favor of more systematic research and writing, and with minor exceptions their direct influence on public taste has waned. Paradoxically, musicologists have gained a greater hold on the orchestral repertoire, perhaps because their status as experts has been more highly respected by performers. As a result of musicological academicism, the function of the orchestra as a museum has intensified. Far from being an unhealthy development, the more historically oriented modern symphony has made an increasingly wide variety of material available to composers as well as a greater number of performing styles available to players and listeners.

Ethnomusicology, which deals with music falling outside of the Western classical purview, has exerted a surprising influence on the vocabulary of orchestral music, with the most profound effects appearing after the institutionalization of ethnomusicology during the twentieth century. Indeed, few prominent orchestral composers actually participated in ethnomusicology: Bartók, most notably, contributed scholarship on Hungarian, Romanian, and North African folk songs. Many of his symphonic pieces, including the *Dance Suite*, the *Music for Strings, Percussion, and Celesta*, and even the *Concerto for Orchestra*, show the influence of his ethnomusicological work. Ethnic materials are reflected in the originality of rhythm and melody as well as in his novel use of orchestral instruments.

Stravinsky's involvement with ethnomusicology, though limited to private collecting, also had a profound impact on his early ballet music, which has become the property of the independent orchestra. Because folk music prompts a kind of orchestral color intensely interesting to modern concert audiences, *The Firebird, Petrouchka,* and *The Rite of Spring* have all been transfigured into part of the classical literature for the independent orchestra, eclipsing their status as ballets. The same might be said of Falla's *Three-Cornered Hat* as well as of Copland's *Rodeo, Billy the Kid,* and *Appalachian Spring.*

The activity of ethnomusicologists is also reflected in symphonic compositions. This phenomenon began in the late nineteenth century with the symphonies of Dvořák, Tchaikovsky, and Mahler. Indeed, at the beginning of that century Thibaut had advocated the acceptance of certain kinds of folk music into the classical canon. Little did he suspect that composers like Copland, Vaughan Williams, and d'Indy would incorporate this notion into the classical genres. The expansion of orchestral literature and instrumental technique through the introduction of ethnic material falls under the rubric of "musical progress."

Historical musicology in its traditional guise of philology has also exerted a profound influence on orchestral literature in the twentieth century. Some of this influence took familiar nineteenth-century forms, usually explication of orchestral music in books for amateurs. Examples include biographies like Guido Adler's monograph on Mahler (1916), so important to the establishment of that symphonist in the standard repertoire. (Adler even helped Mahler publish some of his first symphonies.) Other instances include Donald Tovey's analytical essays on symphonic music, based on his avocation as conductor of the Reid Orchestra in Edinburgh. Though the nineteenth-century tradition of disseminating musicological criticism in journals for the amateur has not generally endured, some scholars have contributed to the large industry for record liners. David Cairns's notes for albums of Berlioz' orchestral works and H. C. Robbins Landon's notes for the complete Haydn symphonies provide listeners with thorough and expert information.

The theoretical branch of musicology has contributed much toward the neoclassical movement in twentieth-century orchestral music. Much of the codification of musical style and structure occurred during the nineteenth-century, but it was employed by twentieth-century composers as diverse as Walton, Copland, Piston, Hanson, Vaughan Williams, and even Henze to produce symphonies structured along the lines of the

German classical stereotype. Sometimes the adoption of historical structure also entailed explicit reference to earlier styles, as in Prokofiev's *Classical* Symphony or in the writings of Parisian composers between the two
world wars. The studies of theorists and analysts facilitated such neoclassicism, but it is also true that the excellent ears of composers like the
Stravinsky of *Apollo* proved to be the most sensitive musicological tools.

The research of musical philologists has resulted in the literal borrowing of newly exposed (or reexposed) material. Some composers have paid
homage to music history by borrowing themes from early composers, as
in Britten's *Young Persons' Guide to the Orchestra* (Purcell) and
Hindemith's *Symphonic Metamorphoses* (Weber). On occasion other composers have adapted early music through elaborations, reharmonizations,
and reorchestrations. Examples include Stravinsky's use of Pergolesi in
Pulcinella and Respighi's use of Rameau in *The Birds* and Renaissance
dances in *Ancient Airs and Dances*. And some composers and conductors
have simply provided fanciful reorchestrations and transcriptions of
older music for modern orchestra, like Mahler's arrangements of Bach
suites or Sir Hamilton Harty's versions of Handel's *Water Music*.

In this continuum a number of independent chamber orchestras
arose after World War II specifically to perform on modern instruments
the texts of baroque composers unearthed by the copious research of
musicologists. Performances during the 1950s and 1960s by groups like
the Chamber Orchestra of the Saar or the Bath Festival Orchestra had
few pretensions about historicity; they regarded early orchestral literature
exactly as philologists had presented it—as a series of note texts representing only relative pitch and duration. Nonetheless, such performances
added a substantial amount of new music to the repertoire exactly when
recording companies were seeking new material. This activity constituted
the important first step in bringing much neglected orchestral repertoire
before Haydn to public attention. Such expansion of the literature
resulted not only from philological work but also from the many musicological catalogs of early composers' outputs.

Musicologists soon realized that orchestral scores assume a context
that must be understood in order to maintain the classical literature in
any semblance of its historic form. Two related branches of musicology
have contributed to our notion of context, thus changing the variety and
nature of orchestral literature radically. One of these is organology, the
study of musical instruments—important to early musicology, as we have
seen, but much neglected in the eighteenth and nineteenth centuries.
The second is the study of performing practice, which has so changed
and continues to change what we hear in our concert halls.

The rebirth of organology began in Germany and Great Britain during the first part of the twentieth century. During the previous century, early musical instruments resided in the collections of art museums, where they were regarded as specimens of the woodworker's craft. Several pioneers in the field saw them in a different light, a point of view best stated by Francis Galpin, who wrote after his retirement:

> Neither purse nor inclination led me to pay fancy prices for mere *objets d'art*, though many beautiful, historic, and decorative examples came across my path and have been incorporated in the general scheme. To me a musical instrument is a thing of life, something that will speak to us and reveal the hidden secrets of its sound. Therefore I made every effort to secure specimens that were playable or could be rendered so.
>
> (quoted in Bessaraboff, xxiii)

Galpin himself published a prominent treatise, *Old English Instruments of Music* (1910), and after his death in 1945 an organological society bearing his name began publication of a yearbook dedicated to his work. In Germany scholars like Curt Sachs pioneered in ethnic organology and later in historical organology with *The History of Musical Instruments* (1940). This musicological activity prompted several instrument builders to take an interest in early instruments. Men like Arnold Dolmetsch studied the history of instruments in order to fashion replicas. Though musicologists continued to study old instruments after World War II, most of the expert knowledge about their construction now resides in the workshops of craftsmen who produce excellent copies of historical examples.

The scholarly study of performing practice has lagged just slightly behind the interest in organology. The pioneering works in this field began with basic issues of philology and then moved beyond them to the interpretation of the text. Arnold Schering wrote in 1931, "The question 'How should old music be performed?' can be raised on two accounts. One arises from purely academic curiosity, in so far as the correct answer determines any formal, stylistic and aesthetic appraisal of the music from a particular time. The other arises from the particular intention to realize the sound of any kind of older music" (p. 1). Scholars have been slow to view performing practice as essential to understanding a musical text. More than twenty years after Schering, Thurston Dart still needed to suggest, "The musical system *must* be heard if it is to have significance, for though the written symbols can be understood visually, they are merely a highly stylized representation of the music and not the music itself" (p. 12). The increasing importance of performing practice to both scholars and players has finally given rise to a journal devoted solely to this issue. *Early Music*, first published in January 1973, seeks to "provide a link between the finest scholarship of our day and the amateur and professional listener and performer" (p. 1).

In the realm of the orchestra, the first research on early performing practice appeared in books like Charles Sanford Terry's *Bach's Orchestra* (1932) and Adam Carse's *The Orchestra in the Eighteenth Century* (1940). Terry puts his case quite simply: "Bach's usage and characterization of his instruments is the major theme of these pages. Of all the Masters whose art has continuing and unabated vogue, he especially spoke through voices silent in the modern orchestra" (p. xi). The orchestra proves ideally suited in many ways for pursuing historic performing practices, because the sound of old orchestras can be reconstituted in part by purely mechanical means. If the right number of players with correctly constructed instruments can be assembled, part of the desired end has been achieved. Questions remain concerning how to play the instruments and how to interpret the musical notation—issues not to be brushed aside lightly—but the details of physical construction provide some security for instrumentalists. Nevertheless, these early attempts to promote historical performing practice reinforce the special status of the orchestra for musicologists. There is still no comparable book detailing the practical considerations in performing early opera. The orchestra continues to constitute the most appropriate forum for musical "progress," which means in this case historicism in performance.

The musicological work on the orchestra by Carse and Terry before World War II took some time to be realized by performers. In the 1960s, chamber orchestras composed of modern instruments slowly gave way to performance on original or authentic (that is, historically accurate) instruments in orchestral ensembles. Groups playing such instruments included the Concentus Musicus, the Collegium Aureum, and later the Academy of Ancient Music and the Bach Ensemble. The ensembles are often directed by musicologist-performers like Nikolaus Harnoncourt, Christopher Hogwood, Jaap Schröder, and Joshua Rifkin. In their work we can hear realized the musicological goal of stylistic plurality. More music than ever is performed today in "authentic" renditions, and the resulting enrichment of musical culture through the vehicle of recordings has assumed major proportions.

Musicology will continue to play an important role in the life of the independent orchestra, which will follow the new custom of employing academics in advisory capacities. Scholars like Steven Ledbetter at the Boston Symphony and Michael Steinberg at the San Francisco Symphony have traditionally written program notes; but their expertise will be increasingly sought on matters of performance, and it will be essential for major orchestras to retain such experts as their repertoire grows larger. For instance, Neal Zaslaw of Cornell University has provided the musicological research for a recording of all of Mozart's symphonies by the Academy of Ancient Music. In his substantial program notes, he suggests a reappraisal of Mozart's pieces, observing that they were not as important to the composer as nineteenth-century scholars had supposed. The eighteenth-century symphony, according to Zaslaw, represents a light artistic gesture. This revisionism will not remove Mozart's symphonies from the standard repertoire, nor will it diminish our appreciation of them, but it will change they way in which we perform them.

In their advisory capacities, musicologists will have the power to expand the symphony repertoire even further. This process has already been intimated in the extensive edition of lesser-known eighteenth- and nineteenth-century symphonies published under the general supervision of Barry S. Brook. Though this series appears only in the form of scores, without parts, the works are bound to be recorded and performed, relieving our somewhat monotonous orchestral diet. We will hear at last the French and Italian symphonies eclipsed by contemporary Viennese works, as well as the work of the lesser-known German composers like Spohr and Franz Lachner.

The independent orchestra is a museum today because it was conceived as such during its formative period two centuries ago. Musicologists have been influential in the life of the orchestra because they helped establish and maintain the repertoire of classical music in its changing manifestations. The independent orchestra and the notion of a classical music grew up at about the same time, and both have been traditionally associated with a kind of musical "progress."

The historical trends brought to the modern orchestra by musicology should not be viewed as antithetical to the promotion of the contemporary literature. Rather, the creation of new symphonic literature serves the same end as the retention of older pieces: increased variety for the public. Musicology has promoted diversity, not uniformity, in the orchestral literature. We may expect that in their new advisory positions with modern symphony orchestras, musicologists will advocate the works of new orchestral masters just as they did in the nineteenth century.

BIBLIOGRAPHY

Hector Berlioz, Memoirs, David Cairns, trans. (1969). Nicholas Bessaraboff, Ancient European Musical Instruments (1941). Charles Burney, A General History of Music, 2 vols. (1935); and Dr. Burney's Musical Tours in Europe, Percy A. Scholes, ed., 2 vols. (1959). Adam Carse, The Orchestra in the Eighteenth Century (1940). Pietro Cerone, El melopeo y maestro (1613). Scipione Cerreto, Della prattica musica vocale et strumentale (1601). Carl Dahlhaus, Die Idee der absoluten Musik (1978). Thurston Dart, The Interpretation of Music (1954).

François-Joseph Fétis, Curiosités historiques de la musique (1830). Myles B. Foster, History of the Philharmonic Society of London: 1813–1912 (1912). Ernst Ludwig Gerber, "Eine freundliche Vorstellung über gearbeitete Instrumentalmusik, besonders über Symphonien," in Allgemeine musikalische Zeitung, 15 (1813). George Grove, Beethoven and His Nine Symphonies (3rd ed., 1962). Eduard Hanslick, Vom Musikalisch-Schönen (1854). Glen Haydon, Introduction to Musicology (1941). F. T. A. Hoffmann, "Sinfonie pour 2 violons,... par Louis van Beethoven," in Allgemeine musikalische Zeitung, 12 (1810). Athanasius Kircher, Musurgia universalis (1650).

Adolf Bernhard Marx, Die Musik des neunzehnten Jahrhunderts und ihre Pflege (1855). Johann Mattheson, Das neu-eröffnete Orchestre (1713); and Der vollkommene Capellmeister (1739). Marin Mersenne, Harmonie universelle, Roger E. Chapman, trans. (1957). Michael Praetorius, Syntagma musicum, vol. 2, De organographia (1618). Arnold Schering, Aufführungspraxis alter Musik (1931). Robert Schumann, "Neue Symphonieen für Orchester," in Neue Zeitschrift für Musik, 11 (1839). Charles Sanford Terry, Bach's Orchestra (1932). A. F. J. Thibaut, Über Reinheit der Tonkunst (3rd ed., 1851). Julien Tiersot, Un demi-siècle de musique française (1918).

Twentieth-Century Composers Return to the Small Ensemble

Bryan R. Simms

The ideal of sound pursued by late romantic composers was typically realized by the large orchestra. Symptomatic of the profound change in musical style that occurred at the beginning of the twentieth century is the widespread abandonment of this ideal. A new conception arose in its place that found its expression in small instrumental ensembles.

A notable preference for small orchestras emerged suddenly in the first decade of the century: 1906 saw the completion of "chamber symphonies" by Arnold Schoenberg and Ernst Toch, the earliest works in this new genre. The cultivation of the chamber orchestra reached its height in the years immediately following World War I, and by the late 1920s the large orchestra began to regain a measure of its former popularity. The small orchestra, nevertheless, has remained to this day a major rival of the full orchestra as a medium for instrumental compositions.

The rise in popularity of small orchestras went hand in hand with a renewed emphasis upon traditional genres of chamber music. It also signified an enthusiasm for new musical types and instrumental combinations. Among the former were works for voice and instrumental ensemble, symphonic music for chamber orchestra, chamber opera, dramatic recitations, puppet theater, and other diminutive works for the stage. Unlike the classical orchestra, the reduced orchestra of the twentieth century did not develop a standard instrumentation. Diversity of sound has, in fact, been as much a part of modern orchestrational practice as has the use of smaller numbers of instruments. In general, the percussion have increased in prominence and the woodwinds and brass have rivaled or outstripped the strings as the foundation of the orchestra.

In this essay we shall focus upon works for small orchestra (with and without voices) and chamber works for unusual combinations of instruments composed in the first half of the twentieth century in Europe and America. We shall seek the major causes of the preference for these new instrumental media and conclude with a survey of the literature.

PRECEDENTS IN THE NINETEENTH CENTURY

Several developments in the orchestral music of the nineteenth century prefigured the turn to smaller media. The genre of the orchestral serenade underwent a revival in the later nineteenth century in works by Brahms, Dvořák, d'Indy, Saint-Saëns, Richard Strauss, and Tchaikovsky. These composers returned to the serenade as a vehicle for chamber orchestra, in the manner of Mozart's Viennese serenades. Brahms's Serenade in D Major was originally scored for strings and only five winds, and his Serenade in A Major calls for a small orchestra without violins. Dvořák's Serenade in E Major and Tchaikovsky's Serenade in C Major are for string orchestra. Strauss's Serenade in E-flat Major for thirteen wind instruments is modeled upon Mozart's Serenade in B-flat Major, K. 361.

Composers of the early twentieth century continued to favor the serenade and related types such as the sinfonietta, suite, divertimento, and capriccio. All of these works display the lightness of spirit of the classical serenade and utilize ensembles ranging from small orchestra to various chamber groups. Serenades in a neoclassical vein were written in the first half of the twentieth century by Alfredo Casella, Jean Françaix, Arthur Honegger, Bohuslav Martinů, and Darius Milhaud. Max Reger's Serenades, Opus 77a (1904) and Opus 141a (1915), are chamber trios, and his Serenade, Opus 95 (1906), is for small orchestra. Schoenberg's Serenade, Opus 24 (1924), for seven instruments and baritone, a work that in part employs serial methods of composition, prefigures his wholly dodecaphonic works in its clarity of rhythm and classicizing tendencies in structure and overall form.

The sinfonietta in the twentieth century is related to the serenade in size of ensemble and lightness of tone. The first important work in this genre was Rimsky-Korsakov's *Sinfonietta* (1884) on Russian themes, which inspired Prokofiev's *Sinfonietta* (1915). The latter piece uses an orchestra of classical proportions, to which Prokofiev also returned in his *Classical* Symphony (1918). The sinfoniettas by Janáček (1926) and Reger (1905) are for large orchestra; but others by Britten, Cowell, Hindemith, Martinů, Milhaud, Poulenc, and Roussel call for less sizable forces.

Other isolated works for small orchestra written in the later nineteenth century were models for twentieth-century composers. Probably the most influential of these among German and Austrian modernists was Wagner's *Siegfried Idyll*. This vividly programmatic work—a birthday greeting from Wagner to his wife—is scored for five woodwinds, three brass, and strings. In its first performance at Triebschen on Christmas morning of 1870, only fifteen players were used, a number that allows the work's linear-contrapuntal texture and mottled colors to be best appreciated. It was an important precedent for the highly polyphonic chamber symphonies of Schoenberg and Franz Schreker.

An intermediate stage between the large romantic orchestra and the small orchestras favored by early-twentieth-century composers is clearly in evidence in the orchestral works of Debussy and Mahler. Debussy wrote for an orchestra of moderate size, which he used with great refinement and understatement. His instrumentations varied according to the image that he attempted to represent. In the *Nocturnes* (1901), for example, the gray coloring of "Nuages" is suggested by its ensemble of woodwinds, horns, and strings; the brilliant revelry of "Fêtes" by the addition of a band of trumpets, trombones, tuba, and percussion; and the mysterious seascapes of "Sirènes" by the unexpected appearance of a female chorus. In soft or lightly scored passages, Debussy rarely doubled important melodic lines, preferring instead the unmixed colors of solo instruments. He greatly favored the woodwinds, which, more often than not, are the principal bearers of melodic material.

Among Mahler's many innovations in orchestration was his tendency to use the full orchestra only at isolated or climactic moments. He preferred to deploy heterogeneous subdivisions of the full ensemble, in which a minimum of doubling is employed. His economical style of orchestration was especially influential upon the works for small orchestra by Schoenberg. In a lecture on Mahler in 1912, Schoenberg commented, "What first strikes one about Mahler's instrumentation is the almost unexampled objectivity with which he writes down only what is absolutely necessary" (p. 463).

CIRCUMSTANCES AND MODELS FOR THE RETURN TO
THE SMALL ORCHESTRA

What conditions led composers to the small ensemble? Egon Wellesz spoke to this question in *Die neue Instrumentation*: "It is a singular fact that the appearance of cultural phenomena can be explained by several causes without the possibility of giving priority to one or the other. Thus, it is scarcely possible to determine whether the appearance of the chamber orchestra came more from economic necessity of the period or from a sudden inner renunciation of the large orchestra" (p. 30).

Certainly, the "inner renunciation" to which Wellesz referred is at the root of this movement. It is a renunciation that took the form of a common and widespread rebellion against romantic overstatement, stemming from a desire among composers of all Western nationalities for less, rather than more, simplicity rather than complexity, and for clarity rather than clutter. This new artistic stance was most pronounced in post–World War I France, where a common distaste for Wagnerian rhetoric was shared by many of the younger composers. Jean Cocteau wrote in "Le coq et l'arlequin," "A poet always has too many words in his vocabulary, a painter too many colors on his pallette, and a musician too many notes on his keyboard." German composers also sensed that Wagnerian overstatement was contrary to the taste of the new century. In his essay "Die neue Oper," Kurt Weill wrote:

> The musical development of recent years had led initially to the realization that people must withdraw as much as possible from the sphere of influence of Richard Wagner. . . . Complete renunciation of any external or inner "program," intentional avoidance of large orchestral forces, limitation of the means of expression in favor of an intensification of the inner powers of expression, instinctive ties to the style of the masters of *a cappella* music and the pre-classicists, finally, a nearly fanatical preference for chamber music— these were the characteristics of this development.

The renunciation of which Wellesz spoke was also an orchestrational solution to the demands of new musical styles and aesthetic objectives. The preponderantly linear conception of music embraced by many early-twentieth-century composers was not congenial to the large orchestra, nor was the desire for unmixed, soloistic timbres. Stravinsky, for example, settled upon an orchestra of four pianos and percussion in *Les noces* (1923) because it suited the idiom of that work: "perfectly homogeneous, perfectly impersonal, perfectly mechanical," he wrote in *Expositions and*

Developments (p. 134). The cool objectivity sought by the French neo-classicists—the *netteté extraordinaire* that Satie praised in the music of Stravinsky—was not musically feasible with the romantic orchestra. Instead, these composers produced a series of works for small orchestra and chamber ensemble. Schoenberg was led to the chamber orchestra because it best conveyed the economy, clarity, and precision that he valued in music. "My goal has been for some time," he wrote in "Interview mit mir selbst" (1928), "to find for my orchestral structures a form such that the fullness and saturation of sound shall be obtained only through the use of relatively few voices."

Wellesz also mentioned economic necessity as a factor in the shift away from the large orchestra. In fact, economics was only one of a large number of external conditions that catalyzed the rise of smaller ensembles. Also of importance were the new sounds being introduced by popular music, the tastes of important musical patrons, the revival of baroque musical styles, and the emergence of radio and film as important media for new musical works.

Economic restrictions were, to be sure, a central consideration in the rejection of large orchestras, especially in the period following World War I. The instrumentation of Stravinsky's *L'Histoire du soldat*, for example, was due in part to Stravinsky's plan to tour Swiss towns with this work following the war. But, as the composer wrote, the chamber orchestra of *L'Histoire* was also selected for artistic reasons: "The shoe-string economics of the original *Histoire* production kept me to a handful of instruments, but this confinement did not act as a limitation, as my musical ideas were already directed toward a solo-instrumental style" (1962, 102–103).

Economic deprivation was a significant consideration in postwar Germany and Austria. The repertoire of Schoenberg's Society for Private Musical Performances, founded in 1918, demonstrates how such restrictions guided this important concert organization toward the development of a distinctive literature for chamber orchestra. Before it succumbed in 1922 to Austria's disastrous inflation, the Society generated a significant number of arrangements for chamber orchestra. Works of all kinds were performed by the Society, but since it was financially unable to hire a large orchestra, arrangements of pieces for smaller forces were used. Alban Berg wrote in a prospectus of the Society (September 1919): "Since the Society today does not yet have the means to perform them [orchestral works] in their original shape, they can be played for now only in specially made arrangements for four to eight hands. The performance of these arrangements is given great emphasis."

In its first season of concerts, all orchestral works were performed in arrangements for one or more pianos. But, beginning in the fall of 1919, leaders of the Society increasingly made arrangements for a chamber orchestra consisting of four or five strings, one or two pianos, harmonium, and a few winds and percussion. By 1912 the number of such arrangements had greatly increased, thanks to the efforts of Erwin Stein, who worked tirelessly as an arranger and promoter for the organization.

The importance of arrangements in the repertoire of the Society also reflected Schoenberg's predilections and his belief that the essence of an orchestral work could usually be preserved—even enhanced—by a smaller medium. He wrote in the "Interview":

> Coloristic changes serve, while animating the expression, to clarify the musical idea. That is their principal function; it is even possible to annul, as it were, the colors and to reduce the dynamic intensity of my works, to make (in a word) transcriptions of them for piano; and if one day we arrive at an age of musical intelligence alert enough to do without the props of a complete materialization, great pleasure will be taken in transcriptions.

Of great importance to the shift in favor of small ensembles was the influence of popular music, especially the bands that accompanied music hall or variety shows and, after 1918, American jazz bands. The influence of popular music was another aspect of the rebellion against romanticism that inspired so many of the stylistic directions of the early twentieth century. The jazz band represented a *Kleinkunst,* or popular art, that modern composers increasingly used to supplant romantic high art. Cocteau's aphorisms are again instructive: "The music hall, the circus, and American negro bands fertilize an artist just as life does. . . . The café-concert is often pure; the theatre is always corrupt."

The earliest model for the small ensemble adopted by twentieth-century composers was the variety-show band. This type of orchestra is evoked in Schoenberg's *Nachtwandler* (1901), in which the voice is accompanied by piano, piccolo, trumpet, and drum. The instrumental resources, text, and style of this work parody the music of the contemporary *Brettl,* a forerunner of German cabaret.

Schoenberg also availed himself of popular idioms in *Pierrot lunaire* (1912), in which verse by Albert Giraud is recited to the accompaniment of five instrumentalists. It is very likely that Schoenberg's choice of this medium and the recitation, which he called *Sprechstimme,* were influenced by early German cabaret. Nachtlicht, the first important Viennese cabaret based on French models, opened in 1906; it was reorganized a year later and renamed Fledermaus. The main entertainer in both establishments was the French-born *diseuse* Marya Delvard. The *diseuses* of French cabaret delivered their poetry in a dramatic style mixing song and recitation. Delvard may well have been in Schoenberg's mind as he worked out the part of Pierrot, especially since she was known for her portrayal of morbid images akin to those of Giraud's poetry. The first performance of *Pierrot* (Berlin, 1912) found the reciter Albertine Zehme in costume and the band hidden from view behind a screen. The description of a 1904 Berlin performance by Delvard by the critic Alfred Kerr is strikingly similar: "The composer Hannes Ruch writes an easily remembered singsong with a few instruments in accompaniment. The performer stands apart before a gray cloth; behind it, the music is played.... Fräulein Marya Delvard sings a song of child murderers in sallow green lights" (p. 345).

Evocations of American jazz bands were extremely common among composers in France, where jazz became instantly popular after World War I. Milhaud's ballet *La création du monde* uses a chamber orchestra with saxophone and an enlarged complement of percussion. The affinity of this score with American jazz is heightened by its pungently dissonant polyphony and its use of "blue notes," or lowered third and seventh-scale degrees.

Stravinsky imitated the jazz band in *L'Histoire du soldat* and *Rag-Time* (1918), in addition to several later works written expressly for dance orchestras. Regarding *L'Histoire*, the composer wrote in *Expositions and Developments* (103–104):

> My choice of instruments was influenced by a very important event in my life at that time, the discovery of American jazz. . . . The *Histoire* ensemble resembles the jazz band in that each instrumental category—strings, wood winds, brass, and percussion—is represented by both treble and bass components. The instruments themselves are jazz legitimates, too, except the bassoon, which is my substitution for the saxophone. . . . Jazz meant, in any case, a wholly new sound in my music, and *Histoire* marks my final break with the Russian orchestral school.

Stravinsky's imitation of the jazz band was followed in the 1920s in works by numerous other European composers, including Arthur Bliss's *Rout* (1922), Hindemith's *Kammermusik No. 1*, Opus 24, no. 1 (1922), Frank Martin's *Fox Trot* (1925), Martinů's *Jazz Suite* and *Le jazz* (both 1928), and works by Kurt Weill, including *Die Dreigroschenoper* (1928), *Das Berliner Requiem* (1928), *Happy End* (1929), and *Der Aufsteig und Fall der Stadt Mahagonny* (1930).

Serious composers in America in the 1920s were also quick to ally the small orchestra to evocations of jazz, as in Copland's *Music for the Theatre* (1925) and Adolph Weiss's *American Life* (1930); the original version of George Gershwin's *Rhapsody in Blue* (1924) called for piano and jazz band. The popular American theater orchestra was imitated in a series of works by Charles Ives after about 1900. Ives's customary flexibility of orchestration, in which a line may be taken by any one of several instruments, also stems from his youthful experiences as a keyboard player in theater orchestras. As a note to the first edition (in *New Music*, January 1932) of his *Set of Pieces for Theatre or Chamber Orchestra*, Ives described this medium:

> The make-up of the average theater orchestra of some years ago, in the towns and smaller cities, in this part of the country, was neither arbitrary nor a matter of machinery. It depended somewhat on what players happened to be around. Its size would run from four or five to fifteen or twenty, and the four or five often had to do the job of twenty without getting put out. Sometimes they would give as much support "during the rescue" as the whole town band. Its scores were subject to make-shifts, and were often written with that in mind. There were usually one or two treble Wood-Winds, a Trombone, a Cornet, sometimes a Saxophone, Strings, Piano and a Drum—often an octave of High Bells or a Xylophone.

Musical patrons in the twentieth century have been powerful influences in the movement toward small media. The most important in the history of early-twentieth-century French music was American-born Winnaretta Singer, the Princess Edmond de Polignac. Daughter of the sewing machine magnate Isaac Singer, she lived primarily in Paris, where she married Prince Louis de Scey-Montbéliard and, following a divorce, Prince Edmond de Polignac. In the 1880s and 1890s she was a devoted Wagnerian, and she helped to introduce her friends Gabriel Fauré and Emmanuel Chabrier to performances of Wagner's music at Bayreuth. About the time of World War I, she commissioned a series of pieces in smaller media, many of which received their first performances in her private salon. She wrote in her memoirs, "My intent at that time was to ask different composers to write short works for me for a small orchestra of about twenty performers. I had the impression that, after Richard Wagner and Richard Strauss, the days of big orchestras were over and that it would be delightful to return to a small orchestra of well chosen players and instruments."

Her first important commission was Stravinsky's *Renard* (1922), a pivotal work in his transition from music for large orchestra to his more economical neoclassicism of the 1920s. She subsequently commissioned Satie's *Socrate* (1920) for small orchestra and four sopranos and Manuel de Falla's *El retablo de maese Pedro* (1923) for chamber orchestra and puppets, based on a scene from Cervantes' *Don Quixote*. Commissions followed for pieces by Germaine Tailleferre, Jean Wiéner, Karol Szymanowski, Darius Milhaud, Francis Poulenc, Nicolas Nabokov, Kurt Weill, and Jean Françaix.

Falla's use of the harpsichord in his *Retablo* was intended no doubt to please his patron. The princess and her second husband were greatly fond of this instrument and of baroque music in general. The appearance of harpsichord in this work initiated a series of pieces in which this instrument was used, including Falla's own *Concerto for Harpsichord, Flute, Oboe, Clarinet, Violin, and Cello* (1926); Poulenc's *Concert champêtre* (1929) and *Suite française* (1935); and Martinů's Harpsichord Concerto (1936).

America's greatest patron of chamber music in the early twentieth century was Elizabeth Sprague Coolidge. Her commissions were most often for string quartets, but they also led to new pieces in more diverse chamber media. Examples of the latter include Honegger's *Concerto da camera* (1949) for flute, English horn, and strings; Ravel's *Chansons madécasses* (1926) for soprano, flute, cello, and piano; and Roussel's Trio (1929) for flute, viola, and cello. Works intended to be premiered in a small auditorium in the Library of Congress donated by Mrs. Coolidge were of necessity diminutive in medium. These include ballets, among them Aaron Copland's *Appalachian Spring* (1944), originally scored for thirteen instruments; Hindemith's *Hérodiade* (1944) for eleven players and reciter; and Stravinsky's *Apollon musagète* (1928) for string orchestra.

The Swiss conductor Paul Sacher has been an influential force in European music for chamber orchestra through his commissions on behalf of the Basel Chamber Orchestra and the Collegium Musicum Zurich. The Basel Chamber Orchestra was founded by Sacher in 1926 and dedicated to the performance of orchestral music from both the baroque period and the twentieth century. By 1950, Sacher had commissioned nearly one hundred new works for small orchestra. These include Bartók's *Music for Strings, Percussion, and Celesta* (1937) and Divertimento for String Orchestra (1940), Honegger's Symphonies no. 2 (1942) and 4 (1947), Strauss's *Metamorphosen* (1946) for twenty-three solo strings, and Stravinsky's Concerto in D (1947) for string orchestra. Other works were forthcoming at Sacher's invitation from Alfredo Casella, Wolfgang Fortner, Jacques Ibert, Ernst Křenek, Frank Martin, Bohuslav Martinů, and Michael Tippett.

The revival of interest in earlier musical styles that underlay the neo-classic movement in Europe between the world wars brought with it a powerful motivation for composers to return to the smaller orchestras of the age of Vivaldi and Bach. Baroque revivalism among European composers was prefigured by Richard Strauss in his operatic collaborations with Hugo von Hofmannsthal. In the original version of *Ariadne auf Naxos* (1912), an opera of this name is interpolated into a spoken version of Moliére's farce *Le bourgeois gentilhomme*. Strauss evokes in his music an atmosphere of the seventeenth century through a small orchestra of thirty-seven players. Although these limited resources were required by an early plan to perform the work in Max Reinhardt's Kleines Deutsches Theater in Berlin, Strauss kept the same small orchestra in subsequent versions of the work: namely, the independent opera *Ariadne auf Naxos* (1916) and the incidental music to Moliére's play (1918).

The sonority of Bach's orchestral suites and *Brandenburg* Concertos is imitated in numerous neoclassical works for chamber orchestra of the 1920s and 1930s, including Hindemith's *Kammermusik* nos. 2–7 (1922–1928), Martinů's *Tre ricercari* (1938) and *Concerto grosso* (1941), and Stravinsky's *Dumbarton Oaks* Concerto (1938). Hindemith's *Kammermusik* consists of a series of concertos for piano, cello, violin, viola, viola d'amore, and organ, each accompanied by an ensemble of twelve to twenty-five players. These pieces usher in Hindemith's neoclassical period of composition with their busy polyphony, unemotional objectivity, and traditional structures. Baroque polyphonic textures and violinistic figuration were imitated in Stravinsky's *Dumbarton Oaks* Concerto, which the composer modeled upon the *Brandenburg* Concertos of Bach. In this piece for fifteen instrumentalists, Stravinsky adopts the genre of the orchestral concerto, which is found in the first, third, and sixth *Brandenburgs*.

Artistic arrangements of baroque music are numerous in the literature for chamber orchestra between the world wars. The prototype of such compositions is Stravinsky's *Pulcinella* (1920), an arrangement of music attributed to Pergolesi, which Stravinsky scored for voices and an orchestra of thirty-three. This work created a vogue for similar ballets and dance suites, including Casella's *Scarlattiana* (1927); Strauss's *Tanzsuite aus Klavierstücken von François Couperin* (1923) and the related *Divertimento nach Couperin*, Opus 86 (1943); Poulenc's *Suite Française*, based on music by Claude Gervaise; and Respighi's *Antiche danze ed arie per liuto* (three sets: 1916, 1923, 1931) and *Gli uccelli* (1927). Anton Webern's 1935 arrangement of the six-voice Ricercar from Bach's *Musical Offering* calls for an orchestra of sixteen. Its kaleidoscope of fragmented instrumental colors distinguishes it from the neoclassical arrangements of Webern's contemporaries.

SURVEY OF THE LITERATURE

The survey that follows will cover a selection of works for chamber orchestra, songs accompanied by small instrumental ensembles, and dramatic music using small orchestra written by major European and American composers from 1900 to 1945. Since there is no broad agreement on the size of a "chamber" orchestra, this survey will be limited arbitrarily to works for fewer than about thirty-five instrumentalists that do not fall into the traditional genres and instrumentation of chamber music. (A more detailed list of works for chamber orchestra, excluding those with voice, is found in Saltonstall.)

Germany and Austria. Schoenberg and his circle of composers were the modernists in Germany and Austria most devoted to the small orchestra. For Schoenberg this medium was superior to the large orchestra because of its greater clarity and precision. "Lucidity is the first purpose of color in music, the aim of the orchestration of every true artist," he wrote in "Eartraining Through Composing" (1939). Schoenberg's works for small orchestra are closely related to his composition of chamber music. "Since I was educated primarily by playing and writing chamber music," he wrote in "Composition with Twelve Tones" (1941), "my style of orchestration had long ago turned to thinness and transparency."

Schoenberg's cultivation of chamber ensembles was most intense during the period of his transition from tonal to atonal composition. Between 1905 and 1912 he wrote his Chamber Symphony no. 1, the beginning of his Chamber Symphony no. 2, the ensemble song *Herzgewächse*, and *Pierrot lunaire*. During these years he also composed several works for chamber orchestra that were left incomplete or unpublished. Among these are the ensemble songs *Stelldichein* (1905) and *Still so ist* (1906) and three untitled chamber-orchestra pieces composed in 1910. Schoenberg returned to the chamber orchestra in the early 1920s, at the beginning of his period of twelve-tone composition, in his Serenade and his Suite, Opus 29 (1927).

For practical reasons, Schoenberg also felt obliged to continue writing for the large orchestra. He attributed the persistence of the large symphonic orchestra in the twentieth century to the fondness of Americans for the monumental. In the "Interview," he wrote slightingly, "If it were not for America, we in Europe would be composing only for reduced orchestras, chamber orchestras. But in countries with younger cultures, less refined nerves require the monumental: when the sense of hearing is incapable of compelling the imagination, one must add the sense of sight."

Alban Berg was persuaded by Schoenberg to use a small wind ensemble (thirteen instruments) in his Chamber Concerto for piano and violin (1925), a work dedicated to Schoenberg. Berg also used the orchestra of Schoenberg's Chamber Symphony no. 1 (fifteen solo instrumentalists) in Act 2, Scene 3, of *Wozzeck* as a tribute to his mentor.

Anton Webern made a dramatic shift to the medium of voice (or chorus) and small instrumental ensemble at the time of his activities in Schoenberg's Society for Private Musical Performances. Between 1918 and 1926 he completed seven consecutive opus numbers (13–19) for these resources. Their instrumentation and contrapuntal texture were initially attributable—as Webern remarked in correspondence with Schoenberg—to his study of *Pierrot lunaire*. But Webern's enthusiasm for ensemble songs must also have been stimulated by the Society's performances of Stravinsky's *Pribaoutki* and *Berceuses du chat*. Webern wrote to Berg on 9 June 1919, "Stravinsky was magnificent! These songs are wonderful. This music moves me completely beyond belief. I love it especially. The cradle songs {*Berceuses*} are something so indescribably touching. How those three clarinets sound! And *Pribaoutki*. Ah, my dear friend, it is something really glorious" (quoted in Moldenhauer).

All of Webern's orchestral music except his Passacaglia, Opus 1 (1908), and Six Pieces, Opus 6 (1913), is for small orchestra. His Five Pieces, Opus 10 (1913), uses nineteen players; the Symphony, Opus 21 (1929), and Concerto, Opus 24 (1935), each use nine. The Variations, Opus 30 (1940), and the arrangements of Schubert Dances (1931) and Bach's Ricercar are for small orchestra.

Arrangements for chamber orchestra made by members of Schoenberg's Society for Private Musical Performances were often collaborative projects begun by less experienced colleagues and later revised by senior members of the organization or begun by Schoenberg and completed by assistants. Their instrumentation varied, but normally these arrangements used some or all of the Society's ensemble of string quintet, pianos, harmonium, and a few winds, brass, and percussion. Their exact number is not ascertainable, because of the abrupt cessation of concerts in December 1921 and the subsequent dispersion of manuscript materials. It is reasonably certain that chamber-orchestra arrangements were completed for all of the following seventeen pieces (those that have been published are so noted):

Bruckner, Anton: Symphony no. 7 in E Major. Arranged by Hanns Eisler, Karl Rankl, and Erwin Stein. Score and parts: Arnold Schoenberg Institute (Los Angeles).

Busoni, Ferruccio: *Berceuse élégiaque*. Arranged by Erwin Stein. Score and parts: Arnold Schoenberg Institute. Published by Breitkopf and Härtel, 1973 (arrangement erroneously attributed there to Schoenberg).

Debussy, Claude: *Prélude à l'après-midi d'un faune*. Arranged by Benno Sachs. Score and parts: Arnold Schoenberg Institute. (The attribution of this arrangement to Hanns Eisler on Deutsche Grammophon 2531 213 with the Boston Symphony Chamber Players is erroneous.)

Mahler, Gustav: *Lieder eines fahrenden Gesellen*. Arranger unknown. Parts: Arnold Schoenberg Institute.

Mahler, Gustav: Symphony no. 4 in G Major. Arranged by Erwin Stein. Location of score or parts unknown.

Reger, Max: *Romantic Suite*. Arranged by Rudolf Kolisch. Score privately owned; parts: Arnold Schoenberg Institute.

Schoenberg, Arnold: Five Pieces for Orchestra, Opus 16. Arrangement begun by the composer. Full score with autograph annotations: Arnold Schoenberg Institute. (A related chamber-orchestra arrangement attributed to Felix Greissle was published in 1925 by C. F. Peters.)

Schoenberg, Arnold: *Die glückliche Hand*. Arranged by Anton Webern. Location of score or parts unknown.

Schoenberg, Arnold: Six Orchestral Songs, Opus 8. Arranged by Hanns Eisler, Josef Rufer, and Erwin Stein. Score to songs nos. 1, 2, and 5: Arnold Schoenberg Institute.

Strauss, Johann, Jr.: *Lagunenwalzer*. Arranged by Arnold Schoenberg. Location of score or parts unknown.

Strauss, Johann, Jr.: *Rosen aus dem Süden*. Arranged by Arnold Schoenberg. Autograph score: Harvard University. Published by Belmont in 1974.

Strauss, Johann, Jr.: *Schatzwalzer*. Arranged by Anton Webern. Score: Berlin, Preussischer Kulturbesitz.

Strauss, Johann, Jr.: *Wein, Weib und Gesang*. Arranged by Alban Berg. Score: Berlin, Preussischer Kulturbesitz.

Webern, Anton: Five Pieces for Orchestra, Opus 10. Arranged by the composer. Score privately owned.

Webern, Anton: Six Pieces for Orchestra, Opus 6. Arranged by the composer. Score privately owned.

Zemlinsky, Alexander von: "Und kehrt er einst heim" and "Die Mädchen mit den verbundenen Augen" from the Maeterlinck Songs, Opus 13. Arranged by Erwin Stein. Score and parts: Arnold Schoenberg Institute.

Zemlinsky, Alexander von: *Psalm 23*. Arranged by Erwin Stein. Score and parts: Arnold Schoenberg Institute.

Although the chamber orchestra of the Society was devoted primarily to arrangements of modern music, it also led to at least one noteworthy original composition: Fritz Heinrich Klein's *Die Maschine: Eine extonal Selbstsatire*. This was the winning entrant in a competition for new music for chamber orchestra sponsored by the Society in 1921. It was published two years later in a version for piano four hands under the nom de guerre *Heautontimorumenus* (Vienna, Carl Haslinger). The work is of interest primarily for its use of a form of twelve-tone composition; one passage is entirely made of a succession of transpositions and inversions of a twelve-tone row. Klein presented a copy of the piano version to Schoenberg with this inscription: "It is the same Machine which came into your beloved hands in the summer of 1921 as a score for chamber orchestra, on the occasion of the competition of the Society for Private Muscial Performances."

At this time Schoenberg was concerned that the development of the twelve-tone principle be credited ultimately to him alone, especially since he feared that other systems of composition, such as the "tropes" of Josef Matthias Hauer, might be confused with his method and seen erroneously as its historical precedent. Therefore, beneath Klein's inscription, Schoenberg wrote:

> Not so. In Webern's hands, who told me about it but was not able to interest me in it. I doubt if I had this in my hands, but more especially that I looked at it, and certainly that I knew what it represented.
>
> In any case, he has fundamentally nothing in common with twelve-tone composition: a compositional means which had its discrete precursor in "working with tones," which I used for two or three years without discovering the twelve as the ultimate necessity.

Franz Schreker's *Der Geburtstag der Infantin* (1908) was perhaps the earliest twentieth-century ballet using chamber orchestra. Schreker lim-

ited himself to a small ensemble of strings on account of the circumstances of the work's first performance: the opening of the Secessionist
exhibition of 1908 in a small Viennese gallery designed by Josef Hoffman.
Schreker revised the music in 1923 as a concert suite for large orchestra.
He returned to the small orchestra with his Chamber Symphony (1917)
for twenty-three instruments, a work strongly influenced by Schoenberg's Chamber Symphony no. 1. Shreker's *Kleine Suite für Kammerorchester* (1929) is neoclassical in spirit. It was written expressly for broadcast
by Breslau Radio, which made the use of a large orchestra superfluous.

Germans composing in the neoclassical vein between the world wars
also favored small orchestras. Hindemith, in his *Kammermusik* series,
revived a baroque orchestral sound, and he also used small orchestras in
his three compositions entitled *Konzertmusik* (1930–1931), in the ensemble songs *Die junge Magd* (1922) and *Die Serenaden* (1925), and in his
essays in *Gebrauchsmusik* ("music for use"), including the *Spielmusik*, Opus
43, no. 1 (1927), and parts of the *Plöner Musiktag* (1932). The music of
Ernst Toch is related in style to that of Hindemith. Toch's Chamber Symphony of 1906 (unpublished) launched his career as a composer, and his
later essays for small orchestra include his *Tanz-Suite* (1923), Five Pieces
(1924), Concerto for Cello (1925), *Die chinesische Flöte* (1923), and several
chamber operas. Like Hindemith and Toch, Ernst Křenek used the
chamber orchestra repeatedly in his music of the 1920s. In that decade
his works for small orchestras included *Symphonic Music* (1922) for nine
instruments; Concertino (1924) for flute, violin, harpsichord, and strings;
Symphony (1925) for winds and percussion; and Suite (1927) for small
orchestra.

France, Italy, and Spain. The chamber orchestra enjoyed its greatest
popularity among French composers in the decade after World War I. Its
frequent use in France stemmed from a strong reaction against German
music and the growth of the neoclassical idiom, with which small orchestras have a natural alliance. French composers of this time were also influenced by the innovative and economical orchestrations of Stravinsky.
"One of the characteristics of the music of Stravinsky," wrote Erik Satie
in 1922, "is its sonorous transparency. This quality is always found
among pure masters, who never allow residue in their sonorities—residue
which you will always find in the musical substance of impressionist composers and even in that of certain romantic musicians."

After *The Rite of Spring* (1913), Stravinsky made a clean break with
the large romantic orchestra, to which he did not return until the late
1920s. His first orchestral essays employing reduced instrumentation were
three sets of ensemble songs: *Three Japanese Lyrics* (1913), *Pribaoutki*, and
Berceuses du chat. The instrumentation of the first of these—a few wood-

winds, strings, and piano—may have been suggested to Stravinsky by his encounter with Schoenberg's *Pierrot lunaire* in Berlin in 1912. Stravinsky later had great praise for the instrumental and contrapuntal sonority of this work, which he deemed a "brilliant instrumental masterpiece" (1959, 76).

Stravinsky then composed a series of dramatic works utilizing chamber orchestra: *Renard, Les noces, L'Histoire du soldat,* and *Pulcinella.* Among his concert works, *Rag-Time,* the two Suites for small orchestra (1925, 1921), the Octet (1923), *Dumbarton Oaks* Concerto, and the Concerto in D are for reduced media. No two of these call for the very same orchestra, as Stravinsky at this time applied a succession of novel instrumental combinations. Most of them emphasize woodwinds, brass, and percussion. In *Oedipus rex* (1927) and subsequent works, Stravinsky returned to a more conventional style of orchestration in which larger orchestras are deployed and in which the string choir is again central.

All of the orchestral music of Erik Satie was written for an ensemble of modest size, which contributed to the understatement and "sonorous transparency" that he sought in all of his work. Satie's music for the comedy *Le piège de Méduse* (1913) is scored for seven instruments, percussion, and piano. His *musique d'ameublement,* on which he collaborated with Darius Milhaud, was background music heard during intermissions in a concert at the Galérie Barbazanges in 1920. The composer's "musical furniture" was scored for trombone, piano, and three clarinets, the available instruments at the concert.

Maurice Ravel did not compose for chamber orchestra except in his early *Introduction and Allegro* (1907) and in two sets of ensemble songs: *Trois poèmes de Stéphane Mallarmé* (1913) and *Chansons madécasses.* The Mallarmé settings—for soprano, piano, and eight instruments—are closely related to Stravinsky's *Three Japanese Lyrics.* Both were inspired by Stravinsky's enthusiasm for *Pierrot lunaire.*

Among composers of "Les Six," Darius Milhaud made the greatest use of small orchestras. His music for Paul Claudel's translations of the *Oresteia* by Aeschylus achieves striking dramatic effects through the use of percussion ensemble and narrator. Milhaud was drawn to the small orchestra also because it seemed appropriate to his experiments with contrapuntal polytonality. He essayed this idiom in his music to Claudel's *Euménides* (1927). "What I wanted," he wrote in his memoirs, "was to eliminate all nonessential links and to provide each instrument with an independent melodic line or tonality. In this piece polytonality is no longer a matter of chords, but of the encounter of lines." Milhaud refined his conception of polytonality in a series of six *petites symphonies* for seven to ten instruments (1917–1923). "I was attracted by the musical quality of small groups of instruments," he wrote. "I was most eager to hear these experiments in tonal independence." The orchestration of the chamber symphonies is varied: the first three, subtitled *Le printemps, Pastorale,* and *Sérénade,* use woodwinds and four solo strings; the fourth and fifth are for ten strings and ten winds, respectively; and the sixth calls for a vocal quartet, oboe, and cello.

Milhaud's earliest ensemble songs, *Machines agricoles* (1919) and *Catalogue des fleurs* (1920), use an orchestra similar to his chamber symphonies. The ballets *L'Homme et son désir* (1921), *Le boeuf sur le toit* (1920), and *La création du monde* and the cantatas *Le retour de l'enfant prodigue* (1922) and *Pan et Syrinx* use small ensembles. In 1924, at the invitation of the Princess Edmond de Polignac, Milhaud composed *Les malheurs d'Orphée,* his first in a series of chamber operas calling for reduced orchestra. Throughout his lengthy career, Milhaud returned to the small ensemble, as in his film scores (*Actualités* and *La petite Lilie,* both 1929), dramatic music ('*adame Miroir, Les songes*), and numerous concert works, including the Concerto for Percussion and Small Orchestra (1930), two serenades (1921), *Concert champêtre, Sinfonietta,* and *Symphonie concertante.*

Francis Poulenc's early music for small orchestra shares the rambunctious high spirits of Satie and Cocteau. In the third movement of Poulenc's *Rapsodie nègre* (1917), a baritone chants nonsensical pseudo-African doggerel, accompanied by seven instruments. *Cocardes* (1919) allies a dadaist text by Cocteau to a music-hall band of violin, cornet, trombone, and percussion. *Le bestiaire* (1919) and the "secular cantata" *Le bal masqué* (1932) also utilize chamber ensembles. Poulenc returned to the chamber orchestra in a more serious vein in several concert works of the late 1920s through the 1940s, including the "choreographic" piano concerto *Aubade* (1929), *Suite française,* and *Deux marches et un intermède* (1938). Arthur Honegger wrote a few works for chamber orchestra during his brief period of collaboration with Les Six, notably *Pastorale d'été* (1921) for woodwinds, horn, and string quartet, and the dramatic psalm *King David* (1921). He later returned to a more romantic style of orchestration.

The spirit of Les Six was rekindled in the 1930s and 1940s by Jacques Ibert, André Jolivet, and Jean Françaix in a series of works for chamber orchestra. Ibert's music for small ensembles includes the *Capriccio* (1938) for ten instruments, *Divertissement* (1930), *Suite symphonique* (1932), and Symphony no. 1 (*Symphonie marine,* 1931). Stravinsky and the French neoclassicists were guiding lights to the Czech composer Bohuslav Martinů during his period of residence in Paris from 1923 to 1940. After his *Half-time* (1924), Martinů dispensed with the large orchestra and turned instead to chamber music and numerous works for chamber orchestra. His Serenade (1931) experiments with a polytonality derived from Milhaud. Several works imitate popular music and call for jazz band. Among his concert pieces for small orchestra from his years in France are *Divertimento* (1932), Concerto for Harpsichord and Chamber Orchestra, *Concerto grosso* (1941), the ballet *La revue de cuisine* (1927), and the *Sonata da camera* with cello (1940).

Like the expatriate Martinů, the Spanish composer Manuel de Falla was influenced by Stravinsky and by trends among French composers. Falla resided in Paris from 1907 to 1914, during which time he wrote colorful Spanish pieces in a manner derived from the Spanish-flavored works of Debussy. After about 1919 his music took on a more abstract and international quality, following a direction in which Stravinsky was moving at that time. He composed three pieces employing small orchestra: *El retablo de maese Pedro*; Concerto for Harpsichord, Flute, Oboe, Clarinet, Violin, and Cello; and *Psyché* (1924) for soprano and five instruments. Falla was also a cofounder in 1922 of the Orquesta Bética de Cámara (Chamber Orchestra of Andalusia), which toured Spain playing baroque and twentieth-century works.

The Italian composer Alfredo Casello was also much influenced by musical developments in France, where he lived from 1896 until 1915. Casella's music for small orchestra includes the children's ballet *La camera dei disegni* (1940), *Scarlattiana*, *Three Sacred Songs* (1943), and numerous transcriptions of his own works originally in other media, such as the *Serenata*, Opus 46b (1930), *Caricatures*, Opus 27c (1920), and *L'Adieu à la vie*, Opus 26b (1926). *Scarlattiana*, for piano and small orchestra, is based on themes from the keyboard sonatas of Domenico Scarlatti; it owes its conception to Stravinsky's *Pulcinella*.

Ottorino Respighi's training in the Russian school of orchestration under Rimsky-Korsakov is reflected in his picturesque Roman trilogy for large orchestra (*Fountains of Rome*, 1917; *Pines of Rome*, 1924; and *Roman Festival*, 1929), but his discovery of early music in the 1920s led him to a new style of orchestration that emphasized small ensembles. His chamber-orchestra work *Trittico botticelliano* (1927) consists of three musical interpretations of paintings by Botticelli. The suites *Antiche danze ed arie per liuto* and *Gli uccelli* are transcriptions for chamber orchestra of Renaissance and baroque music.

England and the United States. The strength in England of the romantic tradition of orchestral music did not allow as decided a shift away from the large orchestra as occurred in Paris or Vienna. Most orchestral music by the major English symphonists of the early twentieth century—

Edward Elgar, Frederick Delius, and Ralph Vaughan Williams—is scored for a moderately large ensemble. Gustav Holst's *Savitri* (written 1908 but not performed until 1916) is an early example of chamber opera, a genre that enjoyed popularity among later English composers. Holst's concert works for small orchestra include *Brook Green Suite* (1934) and the *Fugal Concerto* (1923) for flute, oboe, and strings.

The flippancy of Les Six is reflected in works of the 1920s for voice and chamber ensemble by William Walton and Arthur Bliss. Walton's *Façade* (1923) combines a recitation of Edith Sitwell's poetry with music for six instruments. Bliss's series of ensemble songs composed after World War I—*Madame Noy* (1918), *Rout*, and *Rhapsody* (1923)—reflects his interest in the music of his Parisian contemporaries. Bliss wrote in *As I Remember*, "I greatly enjoyed being part of the stir that the young hornets Honegger, Poulenc, Auric, as well as Milhaud were causing." Both *Rhapsody* and *Rout* use nonsense words reminiscent of Poulenc's *Cocardes*, *Rout* being a musical portrait of the sounds of a carnival as "overheard at a distance."

Benjamin Britten's Sinfonietta (1932) for ten instruments is modeled upon the counterpoint and motivic style of Schoenberg's Chamber Symphony no. 1. Britten later adopted an orchestra of moderate size as his standard orchestral medium. His chamber operas *The Rape of Lucretia* (1946) and *Albert Herring* (1947) use reduced resources partly because of the limited size of the opera house at Glyndebourne, where these works were first heard.

The large romantic orchestra had become a major cultural institution in the United States by the turn of the century. It was accepted from the 1920s through the 1940s as the standard orchestral ensemble by many American composers, including Aaron Copland, Roy Harris, and Walter Piston. Copland occasionally wrote for reduced forces, as in his *Three Latin American Sketches* (1972), *Music for the Theatre*, and *Music for Movies* (1943), the last of which incorporates excerpts from music for the films *The City*, *Of Mice and Men*, and *Our Town*.

But the gradual emergence in the United States of an important musical avant-garde ultimately led to a substantial literature for small ensembles. Between approximately 1900 and 1917, Charles Ives composed over twenty-five works for chamber orchestra, with and without voices. Many of these also exist as songs for voice and piano or in versions for other forces. Ives usually wrote for chamber orchestra in an attempt to re-create the sound of theater orchestras in which he had played since his adolescence. His *Ragtime Pieces*, *All the Way Around and Back*, *The Gong on the Hook and Ladder*, *Over the Pavements*, *The See'r*, *Luck and Work*, and *Set of*

Pieces for Theatre or Chamber Orchestra call for the distinctive mixture of piano, brass, woodwinds, and percussion derived from the theatre orchestra. Other pieces by Ives for chamber groups such as *Central Park in the Dark, The Unanswered Question, From the Steeples and the Mountains, Incantation, Tone Roads,* and *Washington's Birthday* (from the *Holidays* Symphony) use reduced orchestration to facilitate the composer's experiments in sound. Ives described their purpose in his *Memos:*

> Some of these shorter pieces like these (for a few players, and called chamber music pieces) were in part made to strengthen the ear muscles, the mind muscles and perhaps the Soul muscles too.... Right or wrong, things like these—some hardly more than memos in notes—show how one's mind works. The only value probably of some of these things was that, in working these sound-pictures out (or trying to), it gave the ears plenty of new sound experiences.

Ives's experiments with chamber orchestra were prophetic for the future of American avant-garde composition. Later in the century the chamber orchestra as a vehicle for experimentation with sound and texture would be cultivated by Edgard Varèse, Henry Cowell, John Cage, and their successors.

Although Ives occasionally had his works for small orchestra played privately, they were virtually unknown to a larger public until the 1930s. In 1931, Nicolas Slonimsky led the Boston Chamber Orchestra in performances of *Three Places in New England,* in a version for chamber orchestra that the composer arranged for Slonimsky's use. This work and movements from the *Set of Pieces for Theatre or Chamber Orchestra* were subsequently conducted by Slonimsky in Europe under the aegis of the Pan-American Association of Composers.

The Pan-American Association and its predecessor, the International Composers Guild, were important stimuli to avant-garde American composers to write for chamber groups. Between 1922 and 1927, the Guild presented concerts of modern music in New York, and its policy was to program only works for small ensembles. As a result of this restriction Carl Ruggles, one of the leading composers of the Guild, wrote two works for chamber orchestra. The first, *Men and Mountains,* uses music from his earlier orchestral suite *Men and Angels* (1922). *Men and Mountains* was first heard at a concert of the Guild in 1924. It was followed by *Portals,* which Ruggles originally scored for chamber orchestra and revised for string ensemble; it was premiered at a Guild concert in 1926.

In 1927, Edgard Varèse reorganized the Guild as the Pan-American Association of Composers. The Association was dedicated to bringing to light works by avant-garde composers of the United States and Latin America. In addition to music of Ives and Ruggles, the Association gave the first performances of music for chamber orchestra by Adolph Weiss (Chamber Symphony for ten instruments, 1927; *American Life*) and Wallingford Riegger (*Dichotomy*, Opus 12, 1932; *Scherzo*, Opus 13, 1933).

Music for chamber orchestra by Varèse and Cowell figured prominently on programs of the Guild and the Association. Between 1922 and 1934, Varèse composed six works for mixed ensembles: *Offrandes* for soprano and chamber orchestra; *Hyperprism* for winds and percussion; *Octandre* for winds and string bass, *Intégrales* for winds and percussion; *Ionisation* for percussion ensemble; and *Ecuatorial* for voice, brass, percussion, and keyboard instruments. These small ensembles were the ideal medium for Varèse's sonic and textural experiments.

Cowell's earliest work for chamber orchestra was a version of his string quintet *Ensemble*, which was orchestrated for a performance in 1925 by the International Composers Guild. This work was again revised in 1928 and titled *Sinfonietta* for a performance by Slonimsky's Boston Chamber Orchestra. Cowell returned to the small orchestra in many later works, including some of his twenty symphonies and eighteen *Hymn and Fuguing Tunes*; character pieces such as *Polyphonica* (1930), Suite for small orchestra, *American Melting Pot* (1940), *Ancient Desert Drone* (1940), *Characters* (1959), *Concerto grosso* (1963), and *Heroic Dance* (1931), and in his evocations of oriental orchestras in works such as the *Persian Set* (1957) concertos for koto and orchestra (1962, 1965), and Symphony no. 13 (*Madras*, 1959).

Cowell's students on the West Coast, including John Cage and Lou Harrison, specialized during the 1930s and 1940s in compositions for percussion ensemble. Cage's works for percussion from 1935 to 1942 include a quartet, a trio, the first three *Imaginary Landscapes*, three *Constructions in Metal*, Double Music (with Lou Harrison), and the dance piece *Credo in Us*. Most of these use unconventional percussion instruments—tin cans are prominent—as well as phonograph equipment, radios, and other electronic devices.

Eastern Europe and Scandinavia. Twentieth-century symphonists of eastern Europe in general have preserved in their music a romantic style of orchestration and a predilection for the large orchestra. The only major exceptions are figures such as Stravinsky and Martinů who emigrated to France, where the chamber orchestra enjoyed a much larger popularity. The leading symphonic composers in Russia, including Scriabin, Rachmaninoff, Prokofiev, and Shostakovich, seldom wrote for small orchestra. Shostakovich used reduced instrumentation mainly in incidental music and film scores, such as his music for *Hamlet* (1932). As mentioned previously, Prokofiev employed an orchestra of classical size in his *Sinfonietta* and *Classical* Symphony. His *American* Overture (1927) is scored for seventeen instruments; this work was commissioned by the Pianola Company of New York for the opening there of the Aeolian Concert Hall, and the small size of this auditorium limited the number of players. Prokofiev later revised the overture for full orchestra.

Bartók's three major works for small orchestra—*Music for Strings, Percussion and Celesta*, Divertimento for String Orchestra, and Sonata for Two Pianos and Percussion (1938)—were commissioned by Paul Sacher for the Basel Chamber Orchestra. Except for a few less important works, such as the early Suite no. 2 for small orchestra, and a few transcriptions, all of Bartók's orchestral music is for full orchestra.

Jean Sibelius wrote numerous works for an orchestra of small to moderate size. Most were composed as incidental music to spoken plays given in small theaters, which required the reduced means. The scores for *Belshazzar's Feast* (1906), *Kuolema* (1903), *Pelléas et Mélisande* (1905), and *Svanevit* (1908) are of this type. A few other pieces—including *Autrefois* (1920), *Suite mignonne* (1921), and *Suite champêtre* (1921)—call for an orchestra of moderately small dimensions.

BIBLIOGRAPHY

Alte und neue Musik: Das Basler Kammerorchester (1952). Arthur Bliss, *As I Remember* (1970). Jean Cocteau, "Cock and Harlequin," in *A Call to Order*, Rolo H. Myers, trans. (1974). Michael de Cossart, *The Food of Love: Princesse Edmond de Polignac (1865–1943) and Her Salon* (1978). Theo Hirsbrunner, "La rôle de la musique de chambre dans la première moitié du 20ème siècle," in *Hindemith Jahrbuch*, 11 (1982). Charles E. Ives, *Memos*, John Kirkpatrick, ed. (1972). Alfred Kerr, *Gesammelte Schriften* (1917). Ernst Křenek, *Horizons Circled: Reflections on My Music* (1974).

Darius Milhaud, *Notes Without Music*, Donald Evans, trans. (1953). Hans Moldenhaur, *Anton von Webern* (1979). Gabriel Pierné and Henry Woollett, "Histoire de l'orchestration," in *Encyclopédie de la musique et dictionnaire du conservatoire*, edited by Albert Lavignac and Lionel de la Laurencio, part 2, vol. 4 (1929). Princess Edmond de Polignac, "Memoirs of the Late Princess Edmond de Polignac," *Horizon: A Review of Literature and Art*, 12 (1945). Gardner Read, *Style and Orchestration* (1979).

Cecilia Saltonstall and Henry Saltonstall, *A New Catalog of Music for Small Orchestra*, Music Indexes and Bibliographies no. 14 (1978). Erik Satie, *Écrits*, edited by Ornella Volta (rev. ed., 1981). Arnold Schoenberg, "Composition with Twelve Tones," "Eartraining Through Composing," and "Gustav Mahler," in

Style and Idea, Leonard Stein, ed., Leo Black, trans. (1975); and "Interview with Myself," David Johnson, trans., in pamphlet accompanying Columbia Records M2L 294 (1962). Igor Stravinsky and Robert Craft, *Conversations with Igor Stravinsky* (1959); and *Expositions and Developments* (1962).

Kurt Weill, "Die neue Oper," translated as "New Opera" by Kim Kowalke, in *Kurt Weill in Europe* (1979). Egon Wellesz, *Die neue Instrumentation* (2nd ed., 1928). Rudolf Weys, *Cabaret und Kabarett in Wien* (1970). Hellmuth Christian Wolff, "Die Kammermusik Paul Hindemiths," in *Hindemith Jahrbuch*, 31 (1973).

The Orchestra and Recorded Sound

Lance W. Brunner

Recorded sound probably has been the most significant development in musical life in the West since the development of music writing during the ninth century. The technology of notation brought about a distinction between composer and performer and helped make possible a millennium of stylistic change that embraced increasingly complex and sophisticated harmonic, rhythmic, and textural developments, culminating in nineteenth- and twentieth-century orchestral music. But the written score demands re-creation of notated sound by performers, and its interpretation is subject to change through a variety of factors.

The technologies of recording, from the earliest phonographs to magnetic tape and digital recording, permit storage of the actual sound of a score, which can then be reproduced indefinitely at different times and in different places. This has precipitated profound changes in almost every aspect of musical life. Although recorded sound has long since become basic to musical life and helped transform the substance, repertoire, transmission, reception, and functions of music, it is usually taken for granted and its influences have been relatively little studied. To "know" an orchestral work, for example, means something very different today than it did a hundred years ago.

The present essay examines the relationship between orchestras, their repertoire, and the business of creating sound recordings. The focus is the realm of so-called classical or art music written for concert-hall performance and recorded primarily in Western Europe and the United States. Concertos and works for chamber orchestra are included, but operas and choral works are not.

Tens of thousands of orchestral recordings have been made since the first orchestras played into collecting horns in the early recording studios at the turn of the century. To trace the history of these recordings is to probe into the complex symbiotic relationship between art, technology, and business that has transformed the nature and meaning of cultural life in the modern world. Such a study must consider the inevitable compromises that exist between aesthetic aspirations and the realities of business. It will also reveal how musical life has been influenced by the talent and vision of the people making the records, by those performing on them, and by the tides of economics, politics, and public taste. The principal areas of study here include the expansion of the recorded repertoire, its dissemination, and changes in performance and patterns of listening brought about by recordings. Before considering the relationship of records to the orchestra, it is necessary to recount briefly the development of recording techniques and the history of the recording industry, since technological change and the state of the economy have exerted such a strong influence on the history of orchestral recordings.

THE DEVELOPMENT OF RECORDING TECHNOLOGY

The first successful experiments with sound recording and playback were carried out by Thomas Alva Edison in 1877 with his invention of the phonograph. Edison's primitive instrument consisted of a grooved drum or cylinder covered with tinfoil and rotated by a crankshaft. Sound patterns were inscribed in the foil by a metal stylus, which was connected to a speaking tube. When the metal point retraced the grooves, some semblance of the original sound became audible. With his invention, the principles of sound recording and reproduction were essentially in place. What followed was a long chain of technological advances, still being pushed forward today, that led to vastly improved sound reproduction and more efficient dissemination of music.

The next far-reaching innovation was the gramophone, developed and patented in 1888 by Emile Berliner, a German-born citizen of the United States. The gramophone used flat discs rather than the cylinders of the phonograph. Both gramophone and phonograph were commercially available well into the 1920s, when the disc prevailed in the marketplace. The fierce competition between different companies and differing approaches to recording accelerated the pace of change, and improvements were introduced in every aspect of the technology.

In the period up to 1925, recordings were made by a purely acoustical process. A new era of recording began then with the commerical introduction of electrical recordings. The new process employed microphones and electrical amplifiers, which had been developed for radio broadcasting. Electrical recordings, operating at seventy-eight revolutions per minute, introduced profound advances over the acoustical in both frequency and dynamic range, as well as in the depth and balance attainable in the recorded sound.

The next two milestones in the development of recorded sound appeared after World War II: the long-playing, microgroove record (LP), introduced by Columbia in June 1948, and magnetic tape, which by 1948 was rapidly replacing discs for master recordings made in the studio. The LP had distinct advantages over the 78-rpm disc in increased playing time (about twenty-five minutes of music per side), continuity of longer works, ease of storage, and better value. Tape had the advantages of increased fidelity, flexibility in the studio in both its increased length and ease of editing, the possibility it afforded for the recording of multiple tracks at the same time, and greatly reduced recording costs, which made it possible for hundreds of smaller companies to begin to produce recordings.

The major developments of the next generation involved improved fidelity. Stereophonic or two-channel records, introduced in 1957, created a sense of spaciousness, clarity, and separation of sound that approached the effect of a live performance. By the late 1970s the most promising new technology was digital recording, in which the audio signal is translated into a binary code rather than preserved as an imitation, or analogue, of the original sound wave. In 1983 the digital process was introduced in yet another format: the compact disc (CD), on which digitally encoded signals are read by a laser beam. Each major development in the technology of recorded sound has had significant effects on the recorded repertoire, much of which has been rerecorded with each major breakthrough.

THE GROWTH OF THE RECORD INDUSTRY

Making records has always been a business fraught with risks caused by fluctuations in the economy, new technological advances, fads, and quickly changing musical tastes. As the musical marketplace has changed, so have the corporate strategies of the recording companies. The most comprehensive picture of the record industry has been drawn in 1983 by Pekka Gronow, whose work forms the basis of the summary below.

Before the turn of the century the growth of the record industry was slow and sporadic. By 1900, the industry had solved two of its most important problems—the securing of reliable techniques for the duplication of recordings and the refining of the reproducing equipment—and was ready to begin cultivating an international mass market. The major companies competing at this time, many of which survive today, included, in the United States, Edison's National Phonograph Company (founded in 1896 and closed in 1929), Columbia (founded in 1889, now known as CBS), and the Victor Talking Machine Company (founded in 1901, now known as RCA), and in England, the Gramophone Company (founded in 1898, now known as EMI), in Germany, Deutsche Grammophon (founded in 1898), and in France, Pathé (founded in 1896).

By 1910, the industry had thriving markets around the world. Sales in the United States grew from an estimated 3 million records in 1900 to around 10 million a decade later. Recordings were issued at a dizzying pace. The Gramophone Company alone issued about 200,000 titles from 1898 to 1920.

After World War I, the industry expanded rapidly, shaking off a temporary setback in 1923 and 1924 caused by competition with radio broadcasting. Gronow estimated that in 1929 there were over 10,000 releases in the United States alone, with sales reaching $75 million. The prosperous industry collapsed, however, with the Great Depression. By 1933, record sales in the United States had plummeted 92 percent below their 1929 level. The bleak economy caused a number of bankruptcies and led to mergers, most importantly the creation of the giant EMI (Electric and Musical Industries), embracing the Gramophone Company, Columbia, Parlophone, and other companies in Europe. Starting in the mid-1930s the industry began to expand again, and although the European market was sharply curtailed during World War II, the American market continued to expand through 1947. New technologies, coupled with the rock music explosion of the mid-1950s, led to a dramatic expansion of sales. Today, cassette tapes and inexpensive playback equipment help make music accessible to almost everyone.

THE CONCEPT OF REPERTOIRE

A repertoire is that body of works that a musician or ensemble is prepared to perform. More broadly, it is a list of pieces available for performance. The advent of recording has affected the entire conception of repertoire. Once recorded, a piece joins the catalog of music "prepared for performance," although future performances will be through a reproducing medium that permits anyone at any time to hear the realized musical sound. The difference between recorded and performance repertoires lies in the difference between preserved performances and transitory ones: a recorded performance always adds to the total available stock of documented performances of a given piece; a concert performance not documented through recording is preserved only in the memories of those present and as a statistic, although each performance presumably increases the orchestra's preparedness to repeat the work.

While the repertoire of pieces available for the concert hall and the recording studio remains the same, decisions about this repertoire are affected by the differing market demands on each venue. Orchestras most frequently play the favorite, hallowed classics demanded by conservative concert audiences, and thereby create a concert repertoire that has not expanded significantly in over half a century. Most record companies, on the other hand, can afford to be more venturesome, so that the recorded repertoire grows through the addition of less well known or newer compositions.

The relationship of recordings to concert repertoire is not a simple one. Recordings can serve to familiarize audiences with music outside the standard fare and thus increase their acceptance of less-familiar music. On the other hand, the existence of recordings can encourage orchestras to relinquish their responsibility to broaden their performance repertoire. Recordings make vast amounts of music readily available, but indications are that concert repertoires continue to be rooted firmly in the core of the standard canon. For example, in his thesis on late-romantic piano concertos, Allan Ho lists recorded performances of ninety such concertos, all but a few of which appear infrequently.

Translating perceptions of public taste into finished product is no easy matter, for the forces shaping repertoires are complex and dynamic, both in the concert hall and on disc. At most record companies, a number of contending financial priorities enter into decisions concerning which proposed projects become completed recordings. Sometimes this process is bypassed through the patronage of foundations, universities, or corporations, or the efforts of small record companies that develop specialized markets, or even through large companies that subsidize losses to produce an esoteric repertoire. In general, the business end of the industry has been a decisive factor. As Fred Gaisberg observed, "The recording art never had time to develop at leisure, but was urged on by rapidly expanding trade and the profits that were to be earned" (p. 37).

Until recently the key person at the intersection of recording art and commerce has been the person in charge of the record companies' artists and repertoire (A&R) department. The greatest A&R executives have often combined the talents of making and selling recorded music, and although they generally work behind the scenes, they nevertheless have been most instrumental in deciding what will be recorded and by whom. They have molded recorded repertoire and public taste. Currently A&R duties are often split between the producer and the product marketing director. The products of the record companies are the subject of the following survey, which falls into three distinct periods, each created by a major technological advance: the acoustic period (through 1925), pre-LP electrical recordings (1926–1948), and the LP period (1948 to the present).

THE ACOUSTIC PERIOD

The principal sources for this study are manufacturers' catalogs and monthly supplements. Other information can be gathered from catalogs of collections and libraries (for example, the *Rigler and Deutsch Record Index*) and from periodical literature. An accurate picture of the available repertoire from this period is difficult to piece together.

In the discussion of acoustical recordings of orchestral works I have focused on significant examples of change, in particular the trend to record larger works in unabridged versions. The tables used to summarize the recorded repertoire are arranged, whenever possible, according to record-issue dates, in order to show how and at what pace the repertoire was expanded.

In Milan in March 1902, Fred Gaisberg, chief recordist and talent scout for the Gramophone Company, recorded ten arias by tenor Enrico Caruso. These recordings brought Caruso international stardom. By 1915 he had seventy-nine solo recordings and forty-nine recordings with other singers in ensembles in the Victor Red Seal catalog. Caruso's recordings also helped establish the gramophone as a serious instrument for listening to music and opened up markets for recordings by many other distinguished vocal artists. After Caruso's initial success, and throughout the acoustic period, catalogs of classical music, particularly the "celebrity" series like Victor's Red Seal and HMV's Red Label, were dominated by operatic voices. For example, of the ninety-three musicians listed in the Victor Red Seal catalog of 1915, eighty-three were vocal artists, and the other ten were solo instrumentalists. Opera singers, already the stars of the concert world, found their celebrity enhanced on records by the medium's clear preference for the human voice.

If the process flattered the singing voice, it played havoc with orchestral sound. During the 1900s, recording equipment, with its limited frequency and dynamic range, could not capture anything approaching the complex sound of the orchestra. Furthermore, recording demanded that scores be reorchestrated and that instruments such as tubas and bassoons be substituted for the lower strings (Table 8). Regular violins were often replaced by Stroh violins, having an aluminum body connected to an amplifying horn, invented in 1901 by Charles Stroh expressly for recording. Conditions in the early studios were also inhibitingly cramped and uncomfortable. Under such circumstances major orchestras were reluctant to record.

The orchestral selections that appeared in company monthly supplements before 1910 or 1911 consisted mostly of opera overtures, short light classics, popular dances, and song arrangements, all played by house orchestras or by popular theater and hotel orchestras. A catalog produced by the Gramophone Company in 1899 lists fifty-one orchestral selections played by five orchestras. The few classically oriented pieces include "Selections from Lohengrin" and "Waltz" from Faust.

Arnold has listed a number of historically important orchestral recordings made before 1914. These include dance music recorded in Vienna as early as 1901 with an orchestra conducted by Carl Wilhelm Drescher; two years later Johann Strauss III began his long association with recordings. About 1901, members of the Metropolitan Opera House Orchestra, conducted by Nahan Franko, made nineteen cylinder recordings, several of which contained excerpts from Wagner's music dramas. Walter Damrosch made a series of recordings for Columbia in 1903, although only one excerpt from Carmen was commercially released. European companies had begun to add shorter orchestral selections to their catalogs by 1906, when the La Scala Orchestra entered the Gramophone Company's catalogs. The next year Léon Jehin began conducting for Odeon and Édouard Colonne recorded for Pathé.

During this period classical orchestral pieces were also recorded by military or concert bands. Winds were far better suited to the acoustic medium than the string-dominated standard orchestras, and therefore band recordings far outnumbered those by orchestras. Military bands formed an important part of public concert life in the late nineteenth and early twentieth centuries, reflecting perhaps more than any other kind of music the substantial changes in taste and social and economic conditions. (The articles by Williams review this repertoire in relation to changing social conditions.) The 1913 Victor catalog lists more than six hundred band records. The most prolific of all recording bands, the Pryor Band, made an estimated two thousand records for Victor from 1903 to 1929. From 1900 to 1908 the major portion of its repertoire consisted of arrangements of classical works, especially opera overtures, most of which were substantially cut. The extent to which recording companies would trim and rearrange popular classics is illustrated by the 1911 recording of the first movement of the *Moonlight* Sonata by Vessella's Italian Band.

The need to redress the balance of the recorded repertoire to include major symphonic works in their original form began to be felt strongly by enthusiasts and critics about 1910. The first to respond to that demand were the European record companies, particularly those in England and Germany. This expansion of the recorded orchestral repertoire was due, in part, to economic considerations. American companies had exclusive contracts with the most famous and most marketable singers. These companies left the bulk of the orchestral literature a relatively untapped resource, one that their European counterparts soon began to cultivate. One of the most important voices calling for a serious commitment to orchestral recording was the German composer and critic Max Chop, who wrote a record-review column, "Phonokritik," from 1906 to 1914 for the weekly German trade magazine *Phonographische Zeitschrift*. Chop called attention to the wealth of vocal recordings and the dearth of recordings of serious literature for orchestra. He called for recordings of preludes to Wagner's music dramas and movements from symphonies, with fidelity to the composers' scores:

> The original orchestration should be employed as far as the characteristics of the recording diaphragm and sound box permit. It is true that double basses and cellos must be discarded *a priori* and replaced by the lower woodwinds and brasses. This is but yielding to necessity.... On the other hand, arbitrary replacement of the higher strings (violins) by high-pitched winds (flutes, clarinets, trumpets) is definitely objectionable.... Such policies may perhaps bring an initial profit, but they will surely embarrass their perpetrators in the end, when a gradually awakening public begins to recognize the artistic impossibility of such instrumental manipulations. That serious critics are repelled goes without saying.
>
> (Gelatt, 175)

Chop's comments were prophetic, coming at the beginning of an expansion of the recorded repertoire that in succeeding decades would produce a tremendous legacy of orchestral recordings. This type of critical commentary has served throughout the history of recorded sound to both heighten public awareness and pressure recording companies. Critical writings constitute an important resource for tracing the development of the recorded repertoire.

England, 1909–1918. The foremost early producers of orchestral recordings were English companies; they maintained their supremacy, with some substantial challenges from Germany, until 1939. The period before 1914 was critical in the establishment of strategies and patterns for expansion that continued until the development of the LP. In April 1909, Tchaikovsky's *Nutcracker* Suite, performed by the London Palace Orchestra and conducted by Hermann Finck, was released by the English branch of the German-owned Odeon Company, marking the first recording of a large orchestral work—it occupied four double-sided discs. In October 1910 the same company released, in identical format, Mendelssohn's incidental music to *A Midsummer Night's Dream*.

The most prolific conductor of recorded orchestral music in this early period was Landon Ronald, whose association with the Gramophone Company began in 1900 when he recorded a piano transcription from *Tristan und Isolde*. In 1901 he was engaged as the company's musical adviser and in that capacity had a powerful influence in shaping the Gramophone Company's catalog. (Moore documents Ronald's critical role in a series of Elgar's recordings.) In November 1909 the Gramophone Company issued Ronald's first orchestral recordings: three selections from Grieg's *Peer Gynt* Suite (see Table 1). The company supplement praised the performance by the New Symphony Orchestra, in hyperbole that would become typical of advertising copy, as "by far the finest orchestral recording ever issued" and asserted that the discs "inaugurate a new era of orchestral recording." The recordings did, in fact, open a new era. By December the Gramophone Company issued the first recording of a piano concerto, on two single-sided twelve-inch discs: the abridged first and third movements of the Grieg Piano Concerto, with Wilhelm Backhaus as soloist and Ronald leading the New Symphony Orchestra. In December 1911, Ronald began a series of monthly releases of orchestral music with the New Symphony. Table 1 lists these releases through the outbreak of World War I. The pieces are still relatively short or are abridged, but the systematic expansion and exploration of repertoire would soon lead to complete recordings of large-scale works.

The breakthrough for recording unabridged, larger-scale orchestral works came in Germany in the fall of 1911, when Odeon issued Beethoven's Symphony no. 5 on four double-sided discs, each side being assigned a number. Early in 1913 Odeon followed up with a complete version of the Symphony no. 6 on five double-sided discs. These works, the first complete symphonies on record, were performed by the Odeon-Streichorchester, presumably conducted by Eduard Künneke, and were enthusiastically reviewed by Chop as great artistic achievements. By the end of the year, Odeon had issued three more complete symphonies (see Table 5).

The Gramophone Company soon ventured into the market for complete symphonic recordings with their own landmark, a recording of the Beethoven Fifth Symphony with the Berlin Philharmonic Orchestra led by Arthur Nikisch. This recording, issued in Germany in February 1914 on four double-sided discs, and in England in four installments from January to August of that year (Table 1), was the first orchestral recording by a world-renowned conductor and orchestra.

The Nikisch recording, made in November 1913, was soon followed by another Gramophone Company coup: Landon Ronald's arrangement, early in 1914, for Sir Edward Elgar to record his own music. Elgar's collaboration with His Master's Voice (the company's label) lasted twenty years, until his death in 1934, and yielded music from fifty-seven recording sessions. These recording activites are chronicled in great detail by Jerrold Northrop Moore in his book *Elgar on Record*. Elgar's first recording, *Carissima*, was recorded on 20 or 21 January 1914 and released that April. A substantially cut version of the *Pomp and Circumstance* March no. 1, recorded on 26 June with several other works, was released in October. (For an idea of the problems involved in adapting music for the recording techniques of 1914, see Moore.)

The outbreak of the war in the summer of 1914 generated a wave of nationalistic feeling that soon affected the recorded repertoire in England. Recordings there, and in Italy as well, were used in the war effort as a psychological tool, a means of kindling patriotic fervor and determination. The Gramophone Company's new-records supplement of October 1914 proudly announced *Pomp and Circumstance* as follows: "At a time when patriotism is welling up in the breast of every British born citizen, Elgar's super-patriotic suite is doubly welcome.... Every Britisher should possess this unique record." Nikisch, who in the July supplement was still referred to as "Herr," had become "maestro" by the next month. The patriotic sentiment led to the virtual boycott of orchestral recordings by German composers, with the exception of an occasional recording of a Wagner prelude. Despite the hardships imposed by the war, the repertoire was systematically expanded with works by French, Russian, and especially British composers. In addition to Elgar, the composers Edward German, Ethel Smyth, Frederic Cowen, Alexander Mackenzie, and Charles Villiers Stanford conducted recordings of their own orchestral works.

HMV's principal competitor, English Columbia, had an early popular success in 1911 with an abridged version of Schubert's *Unfinished* Symphony, which actually was recorded in the United States. But not until 1915 did Columbia, under its energetic general manager, Louis Sterling, set about to match its archrival in the orchestral market. Armed with sizable profits from recordings of musical revues, Sterling hastened to expand Columbia's existing repertoire. Although he could not break the Gramophone Company's monopoly on British composers conducting their own works, in that year he signed up two distinguished conductors, Henry J. Wood and Thomas Beecham, to record for his company. By 1918, Wood had produced twenty-eight double-sided discs and Beecham thirteen. A significant early recording of a concerto was Wood's 1916 recording of Elgar's Violin Concerto (in a substantially abridged version) with Albert Sammons as soloist. This recording enticed the Gramophone Company to record the work under the composer's direction.

England, 1919–1925. Despite the landmark recordings of complete symphonies made before 1914, most of the works issued on record throughout the 1910s were relatively short works or arrangements that would fit onto one or two sides of a twelve-inch disc. This all changed in the new, postwar marketplace as more of the orchestral repertoire began to be explored. In Germany both Parlophon and Deutsche Grammophon initiated series of recordings of orchestral excerpts from Wagner's music dramas that were unabridged and faithful to the composer's scores. However, the English companies were the first to embark enthusiastically on recording programs that embraced unabridged performances of large-scale orchestral works, with the German companies soon following suit. By 1924 there was vigorous recording activity on both sides of the English Channel, and the repertoire expanded at a remarkable rate.

In 1922 the Gramophone Company secured the services of conductors Albert Coates and Eugene Goossens, who along with Ronald and Elgar added significantly to the catalog. From 1922 to 1925, the last three years of the acoustic period, the Gramophone Company issued a number of large-scale orchestral works in its Black Label series, the most impressive of which are listed in Table 2. Coates's recording of Beethoven's Ninth—an impressive undertaking for the acoustic period—was issued in May 1924, to commemorate the one-hundredth anniversary of the first performance of the work (the Polydor recording having been issued six months earlier).

There were many other shorter works or excerpts added to the Gramophone Company's orchestral catalog in these years as well. (For a complete listing, see Michael Smith's catalog.) The International Red Label series also produced important records during this period, including

Ronald's recording of Schumann's Piano Concerto, with Alfred Cortot as soloist (issued September 1924) and a recording of Bach's Violin Concerto no. 2 in E Major with Jacques Thibuad as soloist and an unspecified orchestra and conductor (issued September 1925).

English Columbia began to provide competition for the Gramophone Company by the early 1920s. From 1918 to 1925, Wood had added forty-six more discs to the catalog. Columbia's recordings of large-scale orchestral works lagged somewhat behind HMV's, but by the end of the acoustic period, there was stiff competition in this repertoire. Table 3 lists many of the significant orchestral works Columbia issued before the shift to the electrical process. (For a complete listing, see Smith and Cosens' catalog.)

Wood's abridged 1922 recording of Beethoven's *Eroica* Symphony met with sharp criticism, indicating that both critics and the public by that time demanded performances of complete works that were true to the score. A number of conductors were called upon to meet that demand. Columbia added to its conducting roster Felix Weingartner, Hamilton Harty, and Bruno Walter, and also entered into competition with HMV by enlisting the composers Richard Strauss, Gustav Holst, Frank Bridge, and Arthur Bliss to conduct their own music. The repertoire was expanding so rapidly at this time that a February 1924 essay in *Gramophone* magazine bemoaning shortcomings in record catalogs was out of date by the time it was printed and needed an editorial apology.

Other companies in England also began to offer competition to the Gramophone Company and Columbia. From 1923 to 1926, the Aeolian Company issued a number of recordings of orchestral music, as well as vocal and chamber music, on the Vocalion label. The larger orchestral works, generally performed by the Aeolian Orchestra, are listed in Table 4. Contemporary music on Vocalion included two of the rare recordings of Vaughan Williams conducting his own works, as well as McEwen's *Solway* Symphony. Vocalion's prices were also considerably lower than those of the major companies, almost half that of comparable orchestral records on HMV in 1923. Another less expensive label issued in England was Velvet Face, manufactured by Edison-Bell. The recording on this label of Elgar's oratorio *The Dream of Gerontius* won critical praise when it was issued in October 1924. The larger orchestral works on Velvet Face are also listed in Table 4. Anderson Tyrer was the featured pianist in works for piano and orchestra. Recordings by the American firm Brunswick were also issued in England, but most of its orchestral offerings during the acoustic period were of shorter selections.

The founding of *The Gramophone* by Compton Mackenzie in April

1923 was also a significant event in the development of the recorded repertoire. It was operated by record enthusiasts, not by professional musicians or critics, for other enthusiasts. Its role was expressed in the prologue to the first issue: "To encourage the recording companies to build up for generations to come a great library of good music." As an intermediary between companies and consumers, *The Gramophone* offered a new type of market stimulus setting it apart from the trade journals of the day. Its monthly reviews and articles had a powerful influence on the nature of the repertoire, as well as on the quality of recordings and performances. There were constant calls to explore new repertoire throughout the 1920s and, when necessary, admonitions to adhere to the score and the intention of the composers. The omission of the triangle in the Velvet Face recording of Liszt's Piano Concerto no. 1, for example, raised the ire of one reviewer (June 1924).

The Gramophone was also the vehicle for the National Gramophonic Society, founded by Mackenzie in 1924. The Society produced noncommercial recordings in limited editions for its members, who were able to vote for the music they wanted on record. Mackenzie formed the Society in order "to persuade the recording companies that there is an articulate body of potential buyers of records, clamouring for the best and willing to pay for it." Although most of the Society's issues were chamber music, there were some orchestral works issued during the electrical period. The Society was also influential as a model for other societies formed during the 1930s.

Germany, 1910–1918. Several German companies were active in orchestral recording around 1910. The Anker label, for example, issued pioneering recordings of Bruno Weyersberg conducting the Blüthner Orchestra of Berlin, beginning in that year. Weyersberg made first recordings of movements from Beethoven symphonies, uncut for the most part, and was the first to record the complete *Leonore* Overture no. 3 (Anker E 9189–90, issued May 1911). (Arnold has a complete listing of Anker orchestral recordings.) Odeon, as mentioned earlier, issued landmark recordings of the Beethoven Symphonies nos. 5 and 6. Other important orchestral works on the label are listed in Table 5.

The most extensive orchestral catalog before 1914 was that of Deutsche Grammophon, which began to develop its catalog along the lines of its parent company in England. Deutsche Grammophon, in fact, issued a number of Ronald's recordings with the New Symphony Orchestra. His recordings of the *Marriage of Figaro* Overture, the *Peer Gynt* Suite, and Weber's *Oberon* Overture, for example, were issued by Deutsche Grammophon only a few months after their first appearance in England.

In fact, Ronald's recording of Tchaikovsky's *Romeo and Juliet* Fantasy-Overture (DG 040735-6) was issued in Germany but apparently never in England. By 1913 the Deutsche Grammophon catalog seemed even richer than that of its English parent, since it enlisted German conductors and orchestras for recordings that were not issued in England. Bruno Seidler-Winkler recorded a number of shorter works before 1914. In 1913, Alfred Hertz recorded a series of orchestral excerpts from *Parsifal* with the Berlin Philharmonic Orchestra (040772-9).

In Germany, unlike England, World War I brought the record industry to a virtual halt. Relatively few orchestral recordings were made from August 1914 until after the war. Important exceptions were the recordings of Richard Strauss conducting his own music, which were made in the fall of 1917 for Deutsche Grammophon and included *Der Bürger als Edelmann*, *Don Juan*, *Till Eulenspiegel*, and waltzes from *Der Rosenkavalier* (Morse, 11).

Germany, 1919–1926. In the postwar period, Germany resumed a vigorous schedule of recording orchestral music. The two principal labels competing in this area were Polydor, issued by Deutsche Grammophon, and Parlophon, a subsidiary of the Carl Lindström Company.

Before the war, Deutsche Grammophon had relied on matrices from its European and American affiliates to fill out its catalog. The legal separation from its parent company in England demanded that it develop a new catalog relying exclusively on German artists. The company enlisted many of the most prominent conductors of the day, including Richard Strauss, Leo Blech, and Bruno Seidler-Winkler, who had already recorded for Polydor, as well as, among others, Otto Klemperer, Hans Knappertsbusch, Hans Pfitzner, and Bruno Walter. By the end of the acoustic period, Polydor's repertoire of orchestral music was extensive indeed. Table 6 lists some of the most impressive releases. By 1925 the Polydor catalog offered a complete set of the Beethoven symphonies, as well as works otherwise not available on disc. Oskar Fried's performances of complete versions of Bruckner's Seventh Symphony and Mahler's Second were landmarks of their day, the only complete recordings of symphonies by either composer to be made during the acoustic period.

After the war the Lindström Company issued its important orchestral recordings on the Parlophon label, which had hitherto released innocuous popular and operatic records. In 1919, Parlophon launched its series of recordings of Wagner orchestral excerpts conducted by Eduard Mörike. The series was proudly announced as being unabridged and true to the scores. By 1925, Mörike had contributed twenty-three

double-sided discs of Wagner's music to the series. Wagner's son, Siegfried, also made five recordings of his father's music. It was Mörike who
had revived the trend begun before the war of recording unabridged
symphonies, with a recording of Schubert's *Unfinished* Symphony. He also
recorded a number of symphonic poems. However, most of the large-scale
works were conducted by Frieder Weissmann, who recorded all of the
Beethoven symphonies but the Seventh. But Parlophon was the first
company to issue, in March 1925, all the symphonies, on forty-four double-sided twelve-inch discs. This Beethoven cycle was also issued on the
Odeon label, another Lindström affiliate. Two of the last acoustic recordings of orchestral works issued by the company were conducted by
George Szell; curiously, these were issued in England on the Parlophone
label and in Germany only on the Odeon label. Table 7 lists many of the
important orchestral recordings issued by Parlophon after 1914.

Other Western European Countries, 1910–1926. England and Germany were the most prolific sources of orchestral recordings in the acoustic period, but there was activity in other European countries as well,
particularly through the affiliates of the Gramophone Company. Italy's
recording output was predominantly vocal, but the early recordings of
shorter orchestral works by the La Scala Orchestra were among the most
important in the Gramophone Company's catalog. By the end of 1910,
the English catalog listed fourteen ten-inch and thirty-four twelve-inch
records by this orchestra. Apparently a number of these recordings were
never issued in Italy.

In France, the Gramophone Company issued Debussy's *Prélude à
l'après-midi d'un faune* by L'Orchestre Symphonique du Gramophone in
March 1913. Significant postwar orchestral recordings included works
performed by L'Orchestre des Concerts Pasdeloup: Franck's Symphony
in D Minor (December 1924) and interludes from Debussy's *Pelléas et
Mélisande* (April 1925), both conducted by Piero Coppola; Berlioz'
Symphonie fantastique (April 1925), also issued in England, conducted by
Rhené-Baton; and Honegger's *Pacific 231* (October 1925), conducted by
the composer. The Pathé Company was also very active in France, with
François Ruhlmann as its leading conductor. Among his recordings were
complete versions of Beethoven's Symphonies no. 2 and no. 5. Girard
and Arnold provide listings of orchestral and instrumental selections on
cylinders and vertical-cut discs.

In 1917 the Gramophone Company in Spain issued two of the earliest complete concerto recordings: the violin concertos by Mendelssohn
and Beethoven, with the Orquesta Sinfónica de Barcelona, Concordio
Gelabert conducting and Juan Manen as soloist. Manen was also the

soloist with an unspecified orchestra and conductor in the Bruch Violin Concerto no. 1 (October 1922).

The United States, 1911–1925.   During most of the acoustic period, American record catalogs were sparse in classical orchestral repertoire compared to European catalogs. At the end of the period, a critic in The Gramophone (March 1926), commenting on the latest Brunswick records, summed up the situation as follows: "The American orchestras are satisfied to record such trifles. We ought to be thankful for the far better things we get from our British firms." A comparison of American and British catalogs from 1911 on confirms the critic's assessment. Throughout the period, the focus of the American classical record market was vocal music, but there were some important seeds sown in the realm of orchestral music that would flower in the electrical period and that many Europeans would envy and try to emulate.

American Columbia issued a number of orchestral recordings, beginning in 1911 with the Russian Symphony Orchestra of New York, led by Modest Altschuler. Most were lighter pieces, but the series did feature an unabridged recording of Glinka's Kamarinskaya (August 1912). Charles Prince's Symphony Orchestra also recorded for Columbia, serving as its house band. Its drastically abridged recording of Schubert's Unfinished Symphony on a single double-sided twelve-inch disc was issued in April 1911. It was also issued in England that July, where the orchestra was listed as the Court Symphony Orchestra. Many other records with the Court Symphony Orchestra issued in England were actually made by Prince's Orchestra, which during this period served as an experimental ensemble for improving recording technology and led the way for recording sessions by major American orchestras. It may have been Prince's Orchestra that Ernest Ansermet conducted in his Russian-ballet series, which included four double-sided discs recorded in April 1916.

Columbia was the first American firm to record a major American symphony orchestra with its own conductor. The Chicago Symphony, conducted by Frederick Stock, held recording sessions in May 1916. As a result of those sessions two double-sided twelve-inch discs appeared in the 1916 Columbia catalog, one containing Mendelssohn's "Wedding March" and Grieg's "Spring," the other containing "Two Spanish Dances" from Bizet's Carmen and the "Waltz" from Tchaikovsky's Sleeping Beauty. Other releases from those sessions included excerpts from Wagner's music dramas: Lohengrin Prelude, the "Procession of the Knights of the Holy Grail" from Parsifal, and the "Ride of the Valkyries" from Die Walküre. The next year, after the United States had entered the war,

Stock recorded his own arrangements of "The Star Spangled Banner" and "America."

In January 1917, Columbia recorded the Cincinnati Orchestra under Ernst Kunwald and the New York Philharmonic under Josef Stransky. The Cincinnati Orchestra recorded eleven sides in their first two sessions, although only four were issued. Kunwald was a victim of the anti-German sentiment engendered by World War I, which resulted in his arrest in December 1917 as an enemy alien, perhaps explaining why Columbia did not issue more of his recordings. Kunwald was succeeded by the Belgian violinist Eugène Ysaÿe, who, during three sessions in 1919, conducted the only other acoustic recordings made by the Cincinnati Orchestra. The studios used for these recordings apparently could only accommodate about thirty-five musicians. (A description of these early sessions and a complete listing of the recordings made are contained in Fellers and Meyers.) From the New York Philharmonic sessions, Columbia issued six works, including the *Andante* from Beethoven's Symphony no. 5 and the *Largo* from Dvořák's *New World* Symphony. From 1917 to 1921, twenty-four discs by Stransky and the New York Philharmonic were issued.

Victor recorded Victor Herbert and his orchestra from 1911 to 1923. Herbert had previously recorded on Edison cylinders from 1909 to 1911. The recordings of his own music and that of other composers rank among the most successful recordings made in the United States during the acoustic period. Victor also made orchestral recordings in the early 1910s with its house bands: the Victor Concert Orchestra, the Victor Orchestra, and Pryor's Orchestra.

Victor's first recording session with a major American orchestra was in October 1917, with the Boston Symphony Orchestra under the German conductor Karl Muck. Their recordings of the finale to Tchaikovsky's Symphony no. 4 (single-sided records), Wagner's Prelude to *Lohengrin* (ten-inch record), and Tchaikovsky's "Marche Miniature" from his First Orchestral Suite (ten-inch record) were enthusiastically received. But Victor's plans to promote a series of recordings were foiled as Muck, like Kunwald, fell victim to the anti-German feelings. In March 1918, Muck was jailed and then deported. The Boston Symphony did not record again until 1928, under Serge Koussevitzky.

Victor had also recorded the Philadelphia Orchestra under Leopold Stokowski in October 1917, with happier and more far-reaching results. Their first recording was Brahms's Hungarian Dances nos. 1 and 2. The orchestra held six recording sessions in 1917, but none in 1918. Recording engagements became more regular in the early 1920s. The ledger sheets for the first recording sessions show over ninety musicians; this large number produced rather cloudy results and led Stokowski to reduce his forces considerably in later sessions. Most of his acoustic recordings were of short popular classics, but he did record two full-length works in 1924 and 1925: Schubert's *Unfinished* Symphony and Stravinsky's *Firebird* Suite. In 1924, Stokowski also recorded the second and third movements of Rachmaninoff's Piano Concerto no. 2, with the composer as soloist. Stokowski had a profound impact on the history of orchestral recordings, although the full force of that impact was not to be felt until the electrical period. (An assessment of his acoustic recordings appeared in *The Gramophone* of April 1925.)

Other orchestras featured in the 1925 Victor catalog were the New York Philharmonic, under Willem Mengelberg, and the La Scala Orchestra, under Toscanini. Their recordings were primarily of overtures, short pieces, and movements from symphonies. In 1925, Alfred Hertz and the San Francisco Symphony also made several recordings for Victor, mostly Wagner excerpts. Another significant recording in the 1925 catalog was an abridged version of Gershwin's *Rhapsody in Blue* with the composer as soloist and Paul Whiteman conducting his own orchestra.

Brunswick also issued a number of orchestral recordings during the acoustic period. Among them were some fifteen recordings by the Cleveland Orchestra under Nikolai Sokoloff, issued in 1924 and 1925, including Tchaikovsky's *1812* Overture. By the end of the acoustic period Brunswick also offered several recordings by the Minneapolis Symphony and the New York Philharmonic.

The gradual improvement of recording equipment and the urge to expand the existing repertoire produced an impressive cross section of orchestral music on records. The most impressive catalogs were those amassed by the English and German companies; American companies were far less adventurous. Independent labels also contributed marginally to the repertoire.

PRE-LP ELECTRICAL RECORDINGS, 1925–1948

The development of the electrical process—the switch from acoustic collecting horns to microphones—had a profound impact on recording. Although there was some initial skepticism, particularly in *The Gramophone*, the advantages and possibilities were quickly understood and exploited. In *The Gramophone* (December 1928), conductor Stanley Chapple described the remarkably difficult conditions under which orchestras had to perform during acoustic recording sessions, as compared with those using the new electrical process. Under the new process orchestral forces were greatly expanded, as Table 8 indicates.

It was possible to record with a full orchestra in a spatial arrangement similar to the concert hall, and this, combined with the expanded frequency and dynamic range and greater sensitivity of the electrical recording process, yielded more sumptuous and lifelike recordings. The new process enticed many more conductors and orchestras into the studios, although the new technology did not initially produce as happy results as many of the later acoustic recordings. The new electrical recordings shifted the spotlight away from the opera singer to the orchestra conductor, who, as David Hall (1948, 123) remarked, had become "the god among musical performers."

The resulting repertoire of orchestral music on pre-LP electrical recordings is extensive and difficult to summarize. Unlike the situation with acoustic records, there are a number of reference tools that can be used to survey the repertoire and trace its development. The most comprehensive is *The World's Encyclopedia of Recorded Music* (WERM), which attempts to list "every record of permanent music issued since the advent of electrical recording up to April, 1950, throughout the world." This is an indispensable reference tool, but because it is arranged alphabetically by composer, it cannot be used to trace the development of the repertoire and establish the contribution of individual conductors or orchestras. Given the extent of the repertoire and the number of important conductors and orchestras, the following discussion is of necessity highly selective.

The electrical recording process was developed in the United States by the Bell Telephone Laboratories during the early 1920s. By March 1925 both Columbia and Victor had signed contracts with Bell and had begun recording. The first Columbia disc (50013-D) was a spectacular demonstration of the monumental forces the microphone could capture: made at New York's Metropolitan Opera House, it had, on one side, "John Peel" sung by 850 voices and, on the other, "Adeste Fideles" sung by an estimated 4,850 voices. The first orchestral recording using the electrical process was Victor's *Danse macabre* by Saint-Saëns, performed by Stokowski and the Philadelphia Orchestra. It was the European companies, however, that first exploited the potential of the electrical process to record large-scale orchestral works.

Table 9 shows some of the significant orchestral recordings issued from 1925 to 1929. These records have been taken from monthly reviews in *The Gramophone* and from company catalogs. This table shows how vigorously large-scale works were rerecorded to replace the acoustic recordings, many of which were made only a year or two earlier. Shorter orchestral works were just as quickly rerecorded. The standard repertoire was rapidly duplicated with the coming of the new technology—a trend that still operates in the industry.

The electrical process also inspired composers to pursue more active recording schedules as conductors. Strauss began conducting works for recordings from the standard repertoire, as well as his own. Igor Stravinsky began the most extensive series of a major composer's interpretations of his own orchestral music. His recording career lasted over forty years. According to Hamilton, Stravinsky recorded for French Columbia the *Firebird* Suite in Paris in 1927 and the *Rite of Spring* in 1928; both recordings were later issued in England and the United States.

The adoption of the electrical process in England fostered the commemoration of the centennial of Beethoven's death with an international celebration in March 1927. English Columbia sponsored the project and issued more than one hundred discs. Columbia's Beethoven records clearly demonstrated the commitment (further borne out by Table 9) of the major companies to large-scale works from the standard repertoire.

Columbia decided to celebrate the centennial of Schubert's death in 1928 in an entirely different, and more outrageous, way, by sponsoring a contest to finish the *Unfinished* Symphony. An international outcry caused Columbia to change the competition to one for an entirely new symphony, although a prize was given to Frank Merrick for completing the Schubert symphony. The competition drew over five hundred entries from twenty-six countries. The grand prize went to Swedish composer Kurt Atterberg for his Symphony no. 6, which both Beecham and Atterberg recorded. Columbia abandoned the idea of such promotional tactics after the Schubert competition, but during the age of the LP, companies would continue to commemorate anniversaries with a flood of recordings. For example, in 1970, Deutsche Grammophon released a twelve-volume, seventy-five-LP edition of Beethoven's music for the bicentennial of his birth. In 1974, Columbia similarly honored Charles Ives with a special boxed set for the centennial of his birth.

During the final years of the acoustic period, conductors such as Ronald and Coates for HMV; Wood, Harty, and Weingartner for English Columbia; Mörike and Weissmann for Parlophon; and a number of conductors for Polydor (see Table 6) had led the movement to record unabridged large-scale orchestral works. Most of them continued to record throughout the 1920s and into the 1930s. Weingartner's Beethoven recordings with the Vienna Philharmonic during the 1930s were to become classics, and conductors such as Klemperer and Walter would have long and distinguished careers that extended well into the age of the LP. As Table 9 shows, the recording of orchestral music remained vigorous in the early years of electrical recording at HMV, Columbia, and Polydor, but Parlophon's activities dropped off significantly. Weissmann went back to recording shorter orchestral works, and Mörike died in 1929. After 1925, however, a number of other conductors began to record frequently for other companies, and they had an important influence on recorded performance between the wars.

Leopold Stokowski's recordings with the Philadelphia Orchestra had a profound effect in Europe as well as in the United States. His recordings—made in the United States for Victor and issued in England on HMV—set a standard. Furtwängler was said to have been so disappointed with the sound of his own recordings compared to Stokowski's that he changed from Polydor to EMI, but without satisfaction. There was much discussion about how Stokowski managed to produce such excellent recordings. The best explanation was offered by Charles O'Connell, music director of Victor:

> This superiority has been attributed to almost every circumstance except the really causative one.... The truth of the matter is that Stokowski understands the recording of sound and conducts his orchestra accordingly. To begin with, he was always more interested in orchestral tone than any other conductor and knew more about it—how to produce it, how to employ it, how to make it register on a record. Secondly, he decided that...he could accomplish more by manipulation of the orchestra than by revolving a rheostat, and he rightly concluded that having learned the limitations of recording, he could register more convincing music on records by operating in his own way, within those limitations, than by applying to so plastic and sensitive an instrument as the orchestra the artificialities that are possible in any recording system. He accomplished his results, therefore, through conducting technique; leaving entirely to me the adjustment of the electronic-mechanical factors. In his last several seasons with the Philadelphia Orchestra we had become so completely en rapport...that we could go through a recording session from start to finish, from ppp to fff, without the necessity for the recording engineers to touch their instruments. I have never worked with any other musician who could do this.
>
> (pp. 297–298)

As recording equipment became more sophisticated and sensitive, as elaborate mixing boards, multitrack tape recorders, and digital equipment became standard in recording studios, it became easier to manipulate the sound in the control room or through editing. Recordings could be made more "perfect" than a live performance. But in the early days of electrical recording it was the orchestra that had to be adjusted, and Stokowski understood this better than any conductor.

Stokowski's repertoire was as impressive as the sound he produced. Although his boldest exploration of the repertoire on records came after he left the Philadelphia Orchestra in 1938, he did explore a wider repertoire than most other major figures during this period. It should also be noted that the collapse of the record market during the Great Depression limited the range and number of releases. Nevertheless, in 1929, Stokowski recorded Stravinsky's *Rite of Spring;* in 1932 he made first recordings of Schoenberg's *Gurrelieder* and Sibelius' Symphony no. 4; he also recorded Scriabin's *Poem of Ecstasy* and *Prometheus.* In 1939, Stokowski recorded his own orchestration of Mussorgsky's *Pictures at an Exhibition;* he also recorded three Shostakovitch symphonies: no. 1 in 1933, no. 5 in 1939, and no. 6 in 1940. Stokowski's recordings of standard works, particularly his later ones, were often idiosyncratic and controversial, but his interpretations always had to be reckoned with, and many of his recordings are of enduring value.

Serge Koussevitzky's recordings for Victor with the Boston Symphony Orchestra rivaled Stokowski's in both quality of performance and breadth of repertoire. During his tenure in Boston (1924–1949), Koussevitzky was drawn to the Russian and French literature in particular, and his recordings of Stravinsky, Prokofiev, Mussorgsky, Tchaikovsky, Debussy, and Ravel brought international recognition to the orchestra. Koussevitzky also made impressive recordings of works by Sibelius and Richard Strauss. Koussevitzky promoted new music through the Koussevitzky Music Foundation, and his own recordings of American music on Victor included Copland's *El Salón México* in 1939, *Appalachian Spring* in 1946, and *A Lincoln Portrait* in 1947, and Roy Harris' Symphony no. 3 in 1940. (Stokowski also recorded a number of American works after he left Philadelphia.)

The third powerful conductor working at this time in the United States was Arturo Toscanini. From 1928 on, after an active conducting career at La Scala, Toscanini began working principally in the United States. He was the director of the New York Philharmonic from 1930 to 1936. In 1937 the NBC Symphony Orchestra was formed especially for him, and he remained with it until his final concert in 1954. Before 1936, Toscanini made relatively few recordings because of his dissatisfaction with the quality of recorded sound. In 1936, however, when he was sixty-nine, he began to record liberally and left a legacy of about 160 recorded works. He was criticized for his neglect of contemporary music and American composers, but his boundless energy, musical genius, fidelity to the score, and severe demands on both himself and his musicians produced remarkable performances and made Toscanini one of the most powerful cult figures of the period. Unfortunately, many of his recordings did not capture the brilliance of his live performances, a situation Hall referred to as "one of the tragedies of recorded music in our time" (1940, 125). Toscanini, like many other conductors, came to place great importance on documenting performances through recording, and the competition to make the first recording of a work led to bitter conflict between him, Stokowski, and Koussevitzky.

In England the formation of EMI (Electric and Musical Industries) in 1931 brought together many of the most significant European labels and musicians in one company. EMI's only serious competitors were Decca and Telefunken. The number of prominent conductors and orchestras recording with EMI during the 1930s makes only a brief and selective summary possible here. Bennett and Hughes list recordings by 157 conductors and 93 orchestras.

The most prolific British conductors of the 1930s and 1940s were Beecham, Adrian Boult, and John Barbirolli. Beecham's distinguished recording career helped establish the highest standards in Europe. In addition to outstanding recordings of works by Haydn, Mozart, Beethoven, Mendelssohn, Berlioz, and Tchaikovsky, among others, he recorded many of the works of Delius and Sibelius.

Boult made several recordings with different orchestras and labels in the acoustic period, but his most impressive work was his series of recordings with the BBC Symphony Orchestra, which he directed from its inception in 1930 until 1950. Most of these recordings are from the standard repertoire, but he was a champion of English composers and recorded, among others, works by Elgar, Vaughan Williams, Holst, and Bliss.

Barbirolli explored a somewhat broader spectrum of repertoire on records. After conducting a number of works for the National Gramophonic Society from 1925 to 1927, he began a series of recordings for HMV in 1928 with various orchestras, including the London Symphony and London Philharmonic. He succeeded Toscanini in 1936 as director of the New York Philharmonic but returned to England in 1943 to conduct the Hallé Orchestra. In addition to the standard repertoire, Barbirolli recorded a number of baroque works and works by British composers. Later in his career he made influential recordings of Mahler symphonies.

Many other prominent conductors made recordings between 1914 and 1939. Those recording primarily in Europe included Wilhelm Furtwängler, Bruno Walter, Erich Kleiber, Willem Mengelberg, Karl Böhm, and Malcolm Sargent; those whose primary recording activities were in the United States included Pierre Monteux, Dimitri Mitropoulos, Eugene Ormandy, Fritz Reiner, and Eugene Goossens.

In the 1930s , the trend in the industry was to duplicate works in the standard repertoire, rather than to explore new territory. A comparison of the recordings of the twelve prominent conductors listed by Wooldridge reveals considerable overlap. For example, all the conductors, except for Clemens Krauss, recorded Beethoven's Fifth Symphony at least once. Not only did rival companies and conductors duplicate works, but as recording techniques improved or conductors changed orchestras they rerecorded favorite works themselves. Toscanini, for example, made five recordings of the "Scherzo" from Mendelssohn's *Midsummer Night's Dream.*

One response to the duplication of standard works in the record catalogs was the development of societies modeled after the National Gramophonic Society. The impetus for these societies came from Walter Legge, the influential recording manager of the Gramophone Company. Legge founded the Philharmonia Orchestra in 1945 and produced many of the most important recordings in the EMI catalog through the 1970s. Through the formation of subscription societies, Legge wanted to make available recordings of neglected works and underexposed composers. His first venture was to form the Hugo Wolf Society, which produced its first recording (with Elena Gerhardt) in 1932. Its success led to the formation of a number of other societies, including one for the Beethoven piano sonatas (with Arthur Schnabel), the Bach *Goldberg* Variations (with Wanda Landowska, harpsichord), and the Glyndebourne Opera performances of Mozart's operas. In the orchestral repertoire the most important society issues were those for Delius (with Beecham), Sibelius, and Medtner. The Finnish government had already subsidized recordings of Sibelius' Symphonies nos. 1 and 2 for Columbia, but the six Sibelius Society volumes, containing eighty-four sides of his orchestral music, did far more to secure the composer's international reputation.

Another attempt to broaden the repertoire began in 1931 when HMV set up a special *Connoisseur's Catalogue* to ascertain the demand for a still wider range of records. By December 1934, nearly a thousand records were in the catalog. These records were not carried by most dealers; in order to protect retailers against losses from stock that did not sell, they had to be specially ordered. The catalog did provide greater breadth of repertoire, but the orchestral works consisted essentially of works that had already been available.

The first comprehensive encyclopedia of recorded music, R. D. Darrell's *Gramophone Shop Encyclopedia of Recorded Music* (1936), provides a good indication of the achievement of the first ten years of electrical recordings. However, from our perspective fifty years later, we can recognize substantial gaps in the repertoire recorded up to 1936. The 78-rpm disc was still most congenial for shorter works, arias, or excerpts. The longest section in Darrell's *Encyclopedia* is devoted to the music of Wagner: over fifty columns, listing more than eleven hundred discs, not including releases of the same recording on different labels in other countries. Even these listings are not complete, since all duplicates are not listed—many items simply have "etc." at the end. Abridged recordings are listed of *Tannhäuser, Tristan und Isolde,* and *Die Walküre,* on thirty-six, thirty-eight, and twenty-eight sides, respectively. Most of the recordings were excerpts. Duplicate recordings of popular excerpts abound: there are thirty-four recordings listed of various versions of the "Prize Song" from *Die Meistersinger,* including instrumental arrangements, and fifteen of the Prelude to Act 1.

Many of the most popular symphonies, symphonic poems, ballet suites, and concertos were also available in 1936 in multiple performances. In addition, the symphonic works of Elgar, Stravinsky, and Richard Strauss were particularly well represented, owing largely to the composers' own recordings. But there was no orchestral music of Bartók other than an orchestration of five Romanian folk dances, only two recordings of a single complete Bruckner symphony (no. 7), and one of Mahler (no. 2). Eight of Mozart's symphonies had received complete recordings, ten of Haydn's, and two of Dvořák's. Only a few Vivaldi concertos were available, most of which were abridged and arranged for other than the original instruments.

Comparing the orchestral items of the 1942 edition of the *Encyclopedia* with the 1936 edition, trends toward both duplication of standard works and gradual expansion of the repertoire are obvious. For example, in the later catalog there are eighteen new recordings of Brahms symphonies, eight new recordings of Beethoven piano concertos, and five new recordings of Tchaikovsky's Sixth Symphony. Bruckner's Symphonies nos. 4, 5 and 9 were added to the catalog, as were Mahler's Symphonies nos. 1 and 9. The number of Haydn symphonies available jumped from ten to twenty-one, and those of Mozart from eight to thirteen. Six piano concertos of Mozart had been added, bringing the total of those recorded to sixteen. Louis Krasner's recording of the Berg Violin Concerto, with the Cleveland Orchestra under Rodzinski, was a bold addition to the recorded repertoire. The same trends of gradual expansion and substantial duplication continue into the 1980s.

During World War II, recording activity, especially in Europe, was severely curtailed. Shortages of material and manpower also caused many deletions from the catalogs. In the United States there was some activity in 1941 and 1942, but the ban on recordings called by the American Federation of Musicians starting in August 1942 closed the Victor, Decca, and Columbia studios for over two years. One significant event was Columbia's decision in August 1940 to cut the cost of Masterworks records from $2 to $1. Victor quickly followed suit, and the result was to make the record industry "big business," with emphasis on volume sales and low-risk, standard repertoire. By 1948, a number of independent record companies were active, providing competition with the multinationals and enriching the repertoire. Independents would play an increasingly more important role during the age of the LP. Hall estimated that about twenty-five thousand discs were available in 1948. But what seemed remarkable then would be dwarfed by the expansion set in motion by the advent of magnetic tape and the LP.

THE AGE OF THE LP, 1948 AND AFTER

When Columbia Records introduced its new long-playing microgroove record at a press conference in June 1948, it was met with some skepticism. In the past, promises to increase playing time had only raised false hopes. RCA Victor's reaction to Columbia's announcement was to develop the seven-inch 45-rpm record, precipitating the so-called war of the speeds, which was to throw the public into confusion. But the advantages of the LP for classical music were overwhelming, and within two years most companies had tooled for LP production.

The response of the industry to the new technologies was not surprising: improved fidelity and new equipment had already provided impetus to rerecord the standard repertoire en masse, while the saturation of the market with standard works had led to the exploration of previously unrecorded music. The same patterns were to be followed with the introduction of stereophonic sound in 1957, digital recordings in the 1970s, and the compact disc in the 1980s. What was new with the introduction of tape and the LP was the rate of growth of the repertoire—an explosive expansion unimaginable a generation earlier.

Since the classical LP catalog is so enormous, only selective observations are possible, most of which will concern the broadening of the repertoire into new areas. Reference works, however, are readily available that permit more detailed investigation.

The introduction of magnetic tape and the LP had a profound impact and initiated rapid changes. The best summary of the developments of this transitional period is by Hall (1950), who estimated that "of the current serious music repertoire available on American labels, and totaling about 3,500 works by some 400 composers, nearly half is now available on two dozen LP labels.... As of early 1950, new LP releases of art music are being added to the catalogue at the rate of 25 per month" (p. 7). The rate was soon to increase dramatically as RCA Victor entered the LP market. The first *Schwann Long Playing Record Catalog* (October 1949) contained listings on 11 labels. By October 1950, 64 labels were listed, and a year later, 112. The deluge became so great that there was concern that the record companies would run out of music to record.

Hall pointed out that the LP repertoire was growing in a remarkably well balanced fashion, owing mostly to the contribution of independent companies. Domestic companies like Allegro, Bartók, Capitol, Concert Hall, Dial, Haydn Society, Westminster, and Vox were quick to record unexplored repertoire. European companies were also focusing on new repertoire, including a systematic recording of national music, notably of Czech and Swedish music, after World War II.

The large multinational record companies—for whom maximizing profit is the rule—remained fairly conservative in their choice of repertoire. With an internationally esteemed conductor and orchestra, plus the promise of improved fidelity, yet another recording of Berlioz' *Symphonie fantastique* or a Brahms symphony would be a certain moneymaker. Furthermore, most well-known conductors feel compelled to record their interpretations of the popular classics at least once. The most prominent conductors of the LP period, Bernstein, Böhm, Klemperer, Ormandy, Reiner, Solti, Szell, Karajan, and Walter, to name only a few, have built up discographies with a common foundation in the standard repertoire, no matter how adventurous they might otherwise be and no matter what their specialties.

The multinational companies, in particular Columbia, did on occasion venture into more challenging repertoire. Goddard Lieberson, who was with Columbia Records from 1939 until his retirement in 1975 and who was president of the company (1955-1966, 1973-1975), was largely responsible for the adventurous recording policy that embraced the music of Ives, Schoenberg, and Webern. He also initiated the innovative Modern American Composers series. Most of Stravinsky's rich recorded legacy on LP is on Columbia. Columbia's classic recordings from the early 1940s of Schoenberg conducting *Pierrot lunaire* and Krasner performing the Berg Violin Concerto were reissued on LP. Deutsche Grammophon also issued a number of recordings of new music in its Avant Garde series. In general, however, it was the independent companies that were the most adventurous. The LP did help some works join the standard concert repertoire and hence attracted prominent conductors and orchestras. The most notable of these works are the Bruckner and Mahler symphonies, the monumental structures of which were not well suited to the 78.

The early years of the LP saw not only the favorite works of the most popular composers rerecorded but the exploration of their other music. For example, C. G. Burke's survey of Beethoven's music on LP in *High Fidelity* (Spring 1952) considered 230 recorded versions of 119 works, occupying 329 sides. In 1952 nearly four hundred more sides of his music were issued. By 1955 the Haydn Society had recorded thirty-two of Haydn's lesser-known symphonies and the Concert Hall label had issued most of Mozart's early symphonies and piano concertos. In 1956, Westminster began to issue all the Mozart symphonies, conducted by Erich Leinsdorf.

The LP had a considerable impact on recordings of American music. In his foreword to Oja's work in 1982, William Schuman observed,

> As late as the mid-1930s, there were few recordings of contemporary American music. Over the years, however, ... some 13,000 record releases of nearly 8,000 works by 1,300 composers have been issued. Of these releases, 9,000 (8,500 33's and 500 78's) were issued by small commercial firms and by nonprofit organizations, often subsidized by the composers themselves. Of these, some 4,300—approximately 47%—are currently extant. The other 4,000 releases (3,000 33's and 1,000 78's) were recorded by major commercial manufacturers (EMI, CBS/Columbia, RCA/Victor, Philips/Mercury, Deutsche Grammophon Gesellschaft) and their subsidiaries. Unfortunately, only 750 of these 4,000 recordings—approximately 18%—are now available. And this points to one of the most serious problems facing recordings of contemporary American music.

The problem, of course, is that if the sale of records falls below a certain level, they are often deleted from the catalogs of larger companies. Recordings of contemporary music or of repertoire that is off the beaten path often need some type of patronage to survive.

An example of such patronage was the Louisville Orchestra's New Music Project. From 1948 to 1957 the orchestra, with civic funds and substantial help from the Rockefeller Foundation, commissioned new works by prominent composers to be performed and recorded by the orchestra. LP recordings figured in the project from the start and, initially at least, the guidelines gave suggested lengths of works that would fit conveniently on one or two sides of an LP. More than one hundred commissioned works were recorded before the New Music Project had to abandon its regular commissions in 1957. The first recording, William Schuman's *Judith,* was issued in 1951 on Mercury. From 1951 to 1954, commissioned works were issued on Columbia Masterworks and, from then on, the orchestra's own First Editions label. Recordings established the Louisville Orchestra's reputation and helped create a substantial body of new orchestral music.

Another label devoted exclusively to contemporary music is CRI (Composers' Recordings, Inc.). Formed in 1954 through the American Composers' Alliance, its mission was plainly stated as "the discovery, circulation, and preservation of the best music of our time." Since 1977 it has been a nonprofit corporation. Its current catalog contains over five hundred recordings and is growing at a rate of about twenty entries a year. Unlike commercial companies, CRI has a policy of keeping all of its records in print. It was the first to record many orchestral works by American composers that have since taken their place in the concert repertoire, including works by Barber, Copland, Cowell, Harrison, Riegger, and Sessions. The selection process is highly competitive—less than 1 percent of the scores submitted are accepted—and the composers themselves must arrange to meet production costs.

The number of small, independent record companies that market new and more esoteric music is vast. A recent catalog of the New Music Distribution Service—set up for independent companies producing new music, including jazz—lists around 225 labels. Although many of these have only a few issues, and most do not feature orchestral music, their number and diversity testify to the enterprise and venturesomeness of the smaller companies.

The postwar period was also witness to the systematic exploration of early music. A wealth of baroque music was recorded for the first time on LP. Such a popular work as Vivaldi's *Four Seasons,* for example, was not recorded as a set until 1948 on the Concert Hall label. Recordings of early music paralleled the dramatic rise in scholarly interest in that music as the field of musicology grew in the 1950s and 1960s. Musical research has led not only to the editing and recording of tens of thousands of preclassical works but also to the discovery of how that music was actually played. "Authentic" performances demand interpretations that are true to the period and are performed on original or reconstructed instruments. As new sound images began to emerge from the historical instruments, even standard works like Bach's *Brandenburg* Concertos were rerecorded, resulting in multiple performances and a wide range of interpretive possibilities. Recent *Schwann* catalogs list over thirty complete performances, and Myers' *Index* lists sixty-three. Croucher (1981) lists 671 LP recordings of late-baroque orchestral music, principally by Bach, Handel, Telemann, and Vivaldi, available in English catalogs. The quest for greater historical accuracy in performance practice has gradually led to the performance on period instruments of music written well into the nineteenth century.

The most systematic recording program in this field has been Deutsche Grammophon's Archiv series, which began in 1947. From an early focus on the music of Bach, inspired by the bicentennial of his death in 1950, the project has expanded to include music that now ranges from Gregorian chant to Schubert. Other labels that have explored early orchestral music include Argo, Bach Guild, Concert Hall, Erato, Harmonia Mundi, Haydn Society, Musical Heritage Society, Nonesuch, L'Oiseau-Lyre, Telefunken, and Vox. The resulting recorded repertoire now covers the entire spectrum of orchestral literature, from works by the earliest ensembles to the most contemporary groups.

SOME EFFECTS OF RECORDED SOUND

In the present study, I have concentrated on the expansion of the recorded repertoire of orchestral music, particularly the ways in which this repertoire has been shaped through aesthetic, economic, and technological influences. However, an assessment of the ways that this expansion and increasingly more lifelike sound reproduction have affected musical life is a more complex proposition. It will be helpful to briefly outline some of the most important developments.

Recordings have produced not only an astounding quantitative change in the orchestral repertoire but a qualitative one. Casals commented that he thought violinists before Eugène Ysaÿe did not play in tune. Whether or not this surprising assertion is true, there can be little doubt that recordings have drastically raised the general level of performance. With the possibility of indefinitely repeating any given performance for study and criticism, recordings demand the most accurate and accomplished performances possible. In addition, they provide pressure for ensembles to match the level of performance achieved on recordings, in which, through editing and manipulation, performances reach levels of perfection in both accuracy and balance that a live performance cannot realistically match. Nevertheless, initial fears that recordings would keep concert audiences at home and therefore threaten the very survival of orchestras have proved to be unfounded. The number of orchestras and other performance-related organizations has steadily increased in recent years. For example, Parakilas reports that the number of symphonic ensembles in the United States rose from 1,204 in 1972 to 1,572 in 1983.

With the advantages of increased access to music through recordings come disadvantages as well. The huge quantity of records now available to the average listener can breed a passive consumption of music rather than active and engaged listening. Excessively manipulated recordings can give a false impression of the music and of performances. Although works from the standard repertoire are recorded again and again, contemporary works are likely to be recorded only once, if at all. And as Reynolds points out (Hitchcock), "the single representation ... has a tendency to *become* the work, even for the composer. The authority of sound prevails over the abstract prescription in score. The goal (let alone the fact) of multiple realizations fades, and the creative person's aims are inevitably re-directed."

A wealth of technically fine recordings does not necessarily mean better performances. Irving Kolodin felt in 1955 that many of the recordings made during the first six years of LP production fell short of the achievements of earlier recordings: "It is my belief that the total of great performances now on records is substantially smaller than it was in 1941." The flexibility of magnetic tape had distinct advantages, but in Kolodin's opinion "encouraged lax standards and diminution of artistic integrity." Furthermore, recordings tend to set standards, fix expectations, and hence serve to narrow interpretive freedom in performance, creating a more homogeneous repertoire.

Despite these drawbacks, the effects of recorded sound on orchestral music have been predominantly positive, particularly through its democratizing influence and the possibility of intense, prolonged study of the music as sound. There are strong indications that recordings have actually produced more active, sophisticated listeners. Recorded sound has given us access to vast amounts of orchestral repertoire and afforded the possibility to come to know this music intimately and in depth, to an extent unimaginable in earlier generations.

TABLE 1 Gramophone Company New Releases on "His Master's Voice" (HMV) of Orchestral Records, November 1910–August 1914

Date Issued in England (Month/Year)	Catalog No.	Composer, Work	Orchestra*/Conductor
11/09	0594	Grieg, *Peer Gynt*, "Morning"	NSO/Ronald
11/09	0595	Grieg, *Peer Gynt*, "Anitra's Dance" and "In the Hall of the Mountain King"	NSO/Ronald
12/09	05523–4	Grieg, Piano Concerto, mvmts. 1,3	NSO/Ronald (Backhaus)
12/11	0681	Mendelssohn, "Scherzo," *Midsummer Night's Dream*	NSO/Ronald
12/11	0682	Mozart, *Marriage of Figaro Overture*	NSO/Ronald
12/11	0683	Sibelius, *Finlandia*	NSO/Ronald
1/12	0701–3	Beethoven, *Leonore* Overture no. 3	NSO/Ronald
2/12	0717–20	Grieg, *Peer Gynt* (4 movements)	NSO/Ronald
3/12	0725	Mendelssohn, *Ruy Blas* Overture	NSO/Ronald
3/12	0724	Weber, *Oberon* Overture	NSO/Ronald
4/12	0726	Liszt, *Hungarian Rhapsody*	NSO/Ronald
4/12	0739	Mascagni, "Intermezzo," *Cavalleria Rusticana*	NSO/Ronald
4/12	0738	Mendelssohn, "Spring Song" and "Bee's Wedding"	NSO/Ronald
5/12	0734	Beethoven, *Egmont* Overture	NSO/Ronald
6/12	0746	Berlioz, "Marche Hongroise"	NSO/Ronald
6/12	0735	Nicolai, *Merry Wives of Windsor* Overture	NSO/Ronald
9/12	0731–2	Schubert, *Unfinished* Symphony, movement 1	NSO/Ronald
10/12	0733	Schubert, *Unfinished* Symphony, movement 2	NSO/Ronald
10/12	0757	Tchaikovsky, Symphony no. 6, movement 3	NSO/Ronald

11/12	0753-4	Rossini, *William Tell* Overture	NSO/Ronald
12/12	0755	Mendelssohn, "Wedding March"	NSO/Ronald
12/12	0756	Mendelssohn, "Nocturne," *Midsummer Night's Dream*	NSO/Ronald
1/13	0792-4	Tchaikovsky, "Theme and Variations," Suite no. 3	NSO/Ronald
2/13	0799	Grieg, *Lyric Suite*, no. 1, "Shepherd's Boy"	NSO/Ronald
2/13	0800	Grieg, *Lyric Suite*, no. 2, "Norwegian Rustic March"	NSO/Ronald
2/13	0797-8	Coleridge-Taylor, *Petite Suite de Concert*	IPO/Pitt
3/13	0817-8	Wagner, *Die Meistersinger* Overture	NSO/Ronald
4/13	0835	Wagner, "Dance of the Apprentices," *Die Meistersinger*	NSO/Ronald
4/13	0836	Wagner, "Procession of the Meistersingers," *Die Meistersinger*	NSO/Ronald
5/13	0864	Schubert, *Marche Militaire*	NSO/Ronald
6/13	0865-6	Wagner, *Tannhäuser* Overture	NSO/Ronald
7/13	0887	Grieg, *Lyric Suite*, no. 3, "Nocturne"	NSO/Ronald
7/13	0888	Grieg, *Lyric Suite*, no. 4, "March of the Dwarfs"	NSO/Ronald
8/13	0848	Gounod, "Funeral March of the Marionette"	NSO/Ronald
9/13	0839	Meyerbeer, "Krönungsmarsch," *Le Prophète*	NSO/Ronald
9/13	0863	Bizet, Prelude, *Carmen*	NSO/Ronald
10/13	0834	Bizet, *L'Arlésienne* Suite, "Farandole"	NSO/Ronald
10/13	0841	Meyerbeer, "March Indienne," *L'Africaine*	NSO/Ronald
11/13	0828	Bizet, *L'Arlésienne* Suite, "Prelude and Minuet"	NSO/Ronald
11/13	0837	Bizet, *L'Arlésienne* Suite, "Adagietto"	NSO/Ronald
1/14	040786-7	Beethoven, Symphony no. 5, Andante	BPO/ Nikisch
2/14	040772-4	Wagner, Prelude to Act 1, *Parsifal*	BPO/Hertz
3/14	040778-9	Wagner, "Verwandlungsmusik," *Parsifal*, Act 1	BPO/Hertz
3/14	040775	Wagner, "Verwandlungsmusik," *Parsifal*, Act 3	BPO/Hertz
4/14	0967	Elgar, *Carissima*	SO/Elgar
4/14	040776-7	Wagner, "Good Friday Music," *Parsifal*	BPO/Hertz

TABLE 1 (*Continued*)

Date Issued in England (Month/Year)	Catalog No.	Composer, Work	Orchestra*/Conductor
5/14	040784–5	Beethoven, Symphony no. 5, movement 1	BPO/Nikisch
6/14	0845	Delibes, "Cortège de Bacchus," *Sylvia*	NSO/Ronald
6/14	0849	Delibes, "Intermezzo and Valse Lente," *Sylvia*	NSO/Ronald
7/14	040788–9	Beethoven, Symphony no. 5, Finale, parts 1 and 2	BPO/Nikisch
8/14	040790–1	Beethoven, Symphony no. 5, Finale, parts 3 and 4	BPO/Nikisch

*BPO = Berlin Philharmonic Orchestra
IPO = Imperial Philharmonic Orchestra
NSO = New Symphony Orchestra
SO = Symphony Orchestra

TABLE 2   Large-Scale Orchestral Works Issued in the Gramophone Company Black Label Series, 1922–1925

Date Issued (Month/Year)	Catalog No.[1]	Composer, Work	Orchestra[2]/Conductor (Soloist)
4/21–5/22	536–7; 587; 613	Dvořák, Symphony no. 5 [i.e., no. 9]	RAHO/Ronald
11/21–3/22	578 582; 602; 596	Elgar, Enigma Variations	SO/Elgar
4/22	608–9	Strauss, Till Eulenspiegel	SO/Coates
9/22	625–9	Beethoven, Piano Concerto no. 5	RAHO/Goossens (Lamond)
2/23	665–8	Beethoven, Symphony no. 5	RAHO/Ronald
3/23	670–1	Strauss, Don Juan	SO/Coates
4/23	683–4	Bach, Brandenburg Concerto no. 3	RAHO/Goossens
6/23	697–8	Franck, Symphonic Variations	RAHO/Ronald (de Greef)
7/23	708–9	Ravel, Mother Goose Suite	SO/Coates
8/23	713–7	Tchaikovsky, Symphony no. 6	RAHO/Ronald
9/23	732–4	Rimsky-Korsakov, Le coq d'or Suite	SO/Coates
10/23	743–4	Strauss, Death and Transfiguration	SO/Coates
11/23	767–71	Beethoven, Violin Concerto	RAHO/Ronald (Menges)
4/24	853–5	Stravinsky, Petrushka Suite	RAHO/Goossens
6/24	759–54	Tchaikovsky, Symphony no. 5	SO/Coates

TABLE 2 (Continued)

Date Issued (Month/Year)	Catalog No.[1]	Composer, Work	Orchestra[2]/Conductor (Soloist)
6/24	842–9	Beethoven, Symphony no. 9	SO/Coates
9/24	871–4	Brahms, Symphony no. 2	RAHO/Ronald
10/24	890–2	Liszt, Piano Concerto no. 1	RAHO/Ronald (de Greef)
12/24	934–6	Schubert, Symphony no. 8	RAHO/Ronald
1/25	942–5	Mozart, Symphony no. 41	SO/Coates
2/25	951–2	Tchaikovsky, Francesca da Rimini	SO/Coates
4/25	958–9	Stravinsky, Firebird Suite	SO/Coates
4/25	969–71	Mendelssohn, Piano Concerto no. 1	RAHO/Ronald (Moiseiwitsch)
5/25	987–92	Berlioz, Symphonie fantastique	OSCP/Rhené-Bâton
9/25	1012–7	Elgar, Symphony no. 2	RAHO/Elgar

[1]All numbers have the prefix D.

[2]RAHO = Royal Albert Hall Orchestra (before 1916, New Symphony Orchestra)
OSCP = L'Orchestre Symphonique des Concerts Pasdeloup
SO = Symphony Orchestra

TABLE 3 Selective List of Significant Orchestral Recordings Issued by English Columbia (Acoustic Process), 1922–1926

Date Issued (Month/Year)	Catalog No.[1]	Composer, Work	Orchestra[2]/Conductor (Soloist)
4/22	1419–20	Strauss, Don Juan	LSO/Strauss
10/22	1437–8	Handel, Water Music	HO/Harty
11/22	1447–9	Beethoven, Symphony no. 3	NQHO/Wood
2/23	1459	Holst, The Planets, "Jupiter"	LSO/Holst[3]
6/23	1475–6	Bliss, Conversations	SO/Bliss
9/23	1480–4	Beethoven, Symphony no. 7	LSO/Weingartner
10/23	1489–92	Tchaikovsky, Symphony no. 6	NQHO/Wood
11/23	1500–1	Bridge, Sea Suite	LSO/Bridge
2/24	1523–7	Dvořák, Symphony no. 5 [i.e., no. 9]	HO/Harty
4/24	1538–41	Beethoven, Symphony no. 8	LSO/Weingartner
9/24	1563–5	Mozart, Symphony no. 39	LSO/Weingartner
10/24	1569–72	Franck, Symphony in D Minor	NQHO/Wood
11/24	1586–7	Holst, Beni Mora Suite, "Oriental"	LSO/Holst
12/24	1592–5	Mozart, Violin Concerto no. 5	HO/Harty (Catterall)
1/25	1596–1600	Brahms, Symphony no. 1	LSO/Weingartner
3/25	1613–5	Bach, Concerto for 2 Violins in D Minor	HO/Harty (Catterall, Bridge)
3/25	1617–9	Saint-Saëns, Carnival of the Animals	HO/Harty
4/25	1621–3	Strauss, Death and Transfiguration	RPO/Walter
4/25	1624–6	Bach, Clavier Concerto no. 1	SO/Wood (Cohen)
5/25	1629–32	Elgar, Enigma Variations	NQHO/Wood
7/25	1640–3	Beethoven, Symphony no. 5	LSO/Weingartner

TABLE 3 (Continued)

Date Issued (Month/Year)	Catalog No.[1]	Composer, Work	Orchestra[2]/Conductor (Soloist)
10/25	1668–70	Haydn, Symphony no. 94	NQHO/Wood
11/25	1648–9	Holst, St. *Paul's* Suite	StrO/Holst
12/25	1680–2	Bruch, Violin Concerto no. 1	SO/Harty (Sammons)
1/26	1686–9	Beethoven, Piano Concerto no. 3	SO/Harty (Murdoch)
4/26	1717–22	Vaughan Williams, Symphony no. 2	LSO/Godfrey

[1]All catalog numbers listed have the prefix L.

[2]HO = Hallé Orchestra
LSO = London Symphony Orchestra
NQHO = New Queen's Hall Orchestra
RPO = Royal Philharmonic Orchestra
SO = Symphony Orchestra
StrO = String Orchestra

[3]Holst's *The Planets* was released on individual discs periodically through May 1924. The others include: "Venus" (L1499), "Uranus" (L1509), "Mars" (L1528), "Saturn" (L1532), "Neptune" (L1542), and "Mercury" (L1543). All were rerecorded in 1926 using the electrical process and assigned the same number with the suffix R.

TABLE 4 Selected Acoustic Recordings of Large-Scale Orchestral Works on the Vocalion and Velvet Face Labels, 1923–1926

Date Issued (Month/Year)	Catalog No.	Composer, Work	Orchestra*/Conductor (Soloist)
		VOCALION	
6, 8/23	J.04041–3	McEwen, Solway Symphony	AO/Whitemore
9, 10/24	K.05105–6	Mozart, Symphony no. 40	AO/Greenbaum
	K.05112–3		
12/24	K.05125–7	Haydn, Symphony no. 92	AO/Greenbaum
3/25	K.05148–50	Mendelssohn, Symphony no. 4	AO/Chapple
9/25	A.0237–40	Beethoven, Piano Concerto no. 4	AO/Chapple (Bowen)
11/25	A.0242–4	Mozart, Violin Concerto no. 3	AO/Chapple (d'Aranyi)
12/25	A.0247–8	Vaughan Williams, Old King Cole Ballet	AO/Vaughan Williams
1/26	A.0249	Vaughan Williams, The Wasps Overture	AO/Vaughan Williams
5/26	A.0259–62	Tchaikovsky, Piano Concerto no. 1	AO/Chapple (Sapellnikoff)
		VELVET FACE	
5/23	540–2	Schubert, Symphony no. 8	BSO/Boult
7/23	557–8	Liszt, Piano Concerto no. 1	RSO/Boult (Tyrer)
9/24	599–600	Franck, Symphonic Variations	BSO/Boult (Tyrer)
6/25	624–5	Liszt, Piano Concerto no. 2	RSO/Batten (Tyrer)
12/25	655–7	Strauss, Burleske	RSO/Batten (Tyrer)

*AO = Aeolian Orchestra
BSO = British Symphony Orchestra
RSO = Royal Symphony Orchestra

TABLE 5   Significant Orchestral Works Issued in Germany on the Odeon Label, 1911–1914[1]

Year Issued	Catalog No. (by Side)	Composer, Work	Orchestra/Conductor[2]
1911	xx76147-54	Beethoven, Symphony no. 5	OSO/Künneke
1913	xx76292-301	Beethoven, Symphony no. 6	OSO/Künneke
1913	xx76308-11	Tchaikovsky, *Capriccio italien*	OSO/Künneke
1913	xx76312-7	Haydn, Symphony no. 94	OSO/Künneke
1913	xx76325-30	Mozart, Symphony no. 40	OSO/Künneke
1913	xx76331-6	Mozart, Symphony no. 39	OSO/Künneke
1914	xx76434-9	Wagner, Prelude to Act 1 and "Good Friday Music," *Parsifal*	BPO/Hildebrand

[1] I am grateful to Claude Arnold for supplying record numbers, dates, and other information contained in this table.
[2] OSO = Odeon-Streichorchester (Eduard Künneke was presumably the conductor for all of these recordings)
BPO = Berlin Philharmonic Orchestra

TABLE 6   Selected Large-Scale or Significant Orchestral Works Issued by Deutsche Grammophon on the Polydor Label, 1919–1926

Date Issued (Month/Year)[1]	Catalog Nos.[2]	Composer, Work	Orchestra[3]/Conductor (Soloist)
?/19	69543-4/65842-3	Mendelssohn, Overture and "Scherzo," *Midsummer Night's Dream*	BSOO/Blech
?/19	69546-7/65845-6	Smetana, *The Moldau*	BSOO/Blech
?/19	69548-9/65847-8	Schubert, *Rosamunde* Overture	BSOO/Blech
?/19	69550-1/ —	Liszt, *Les préludes*	BSOO/Blech
?/21	69562-3/65876-7	Grieg, *Peer Gynt* (four selections)	BPO/Blech
?/21	69566-7/65906-7	Liszt, Hungarian Rhapsody no. 1	BPO/Nikisch
?/22	69569-70/65879-80	Wagner, *Siegfried Idyll*	BPO/Blech
1/23	69584-6/65871-3	Strauss, *Death and Transfiguration*	BPO/Abendroth
?/23	69597-9/66278-80	Schubert, Symphony no. 8	BPO/Blech
?/23	69603-4/65902-3	Mussorgsky-Rimsky-Korsakov, *A Night on Bald Mountain*	BPO/Kuper
12/23	69607-13/65267-73	Beethoven, Symphony no. 9	NSO/Seidler-Winkler
?/23	69625-7/66282-4	Schumann, Symphony no. 4 [movs. 1,2,4]	BSOO/Pfitzner
12/23	69638-41/66250-3	Beethoven, Symphony no. 5	NSO/Seidler-Winkler
12/23	69642-7/66254-9	Beethoven, Symphony no. 6	NSO/Pfitzner
1/24	— /65782-4	Haydn, Symphony no. 45	TO/Seidler-Winkler
3/24	69655-8/66286-9	Mozart, Symphony no. 41	BSOO/Heidenreich
3/24	69659-62/66260-3	Beethoven, Symphony no. 7	BSOO/Wohllebe

TABLE 6 (Continued)

Date Issued (Month/Year)[1]	Catalog Nos.[2]	Composer, Work	Orchestra[3]/Conductor (Soloist)
8/24	69663–7/66245–9	Beethoven, Symphony no. 4	BSOO/Pfitzner
8/24	69861–91/66290–300	Mahler, Symphony no. 2	BSOO/Fried
8/24	69692–3/65931–2	Tchaikovsky, 1812 Overture	COHO/Blech
8/24	69698–9/ —	Liszt, Les préludes	COHO/Blech
8/24	69701–5/66304–8	Brahms, Symphony no. 1	BSOO/Fried
8/24	69706–11/66239–44	Beethoven, Symphony no. 3	BSOO/Fried
8/24	69723–5/66309–11	Haydn, Symphony no. 94	COHO/Blech
8/24	69726–8/66312–4	Haydn, Symphony no. 88	COHO/Blech
8/24	69742–4/66315–7	Strauss, Also sprach Zarathustra	BSOO/von Schillings
11/24	69753–9/66318–24	Bruckner, Symphony no. 7	BSOO/Fried
12/24	69760–3/66231–4	Beethoven, Symphony no. 1	BSOO/Klemperer
12/24	69764–7/66325–8	Bruckner, Symphony no. 8, Adagio	BSOO/Klemperer
1/25	— /66014–5	Bach, Brandenburg Concerto no. 3	BSOO/Höberg
2/25	69768–70/66329–31	Schrecker, Der Geburtstag der Infantin	BSOO/Schrecker
3/25	69771–5/66332–6	Tchaikovsky, Symphony no. 6	BSOO/Walter
4/25	69776–7/66337–8	Stravinsky, Firebird Suite	BSOO/Fried

5/25	69786-8/66264-6	Beethoven, Symphony no. 8	BSOC/Klemperer
5/25	69789-93/ —	Beethoven, Violin Concerto	BSOC/Thierfelder (Wolfsthal)
9/25	69783-5/66344-6	Haydn, Symphony no. 92	BSOO/Knappertsbusch
9/25	69803-7/66351-5	Strauss, An Alpine Symphony	BSOO/Fried
9/25	69808-11/66356-60	Berlioz, Symphonie fantastique[4]	BSOO/Fried
10/25	69795-8/66347-50	Schumann, Symphony no. 1	BSOO/Pfitzner
10/25	69799-802/66235-8	Beethoven, Symphony no. 2	BSOO/Fried
10/25	69815-8/ —	Beethoven, Piano Concerto no. 1	BSOO/? ? (Kempff)
1/26	— /66067-9	Rimsky-Korsakov, Scheherazade	BSOO/Fock
1/26	— /66117-8	Liszt Mazeppa	BSOO/Fried
2/26	69788-90/66339-41	Schubert, Symphony no. 8	BSOO/Klemperer
?/26	69812-4/66361-3	Liszt, Tasso	BSOO/Hausegger
?/26	69828-32/66366-70	Schumann, Symphony no. 2	BSOO/Pfitzner

[1] I am grateful to Claude Arnold for supplying issue dates and catalog numbers for many of the works listed in this table.

[2] Polydor orchestral records were usually issued in the 69000 Violet Label series and subsequently reissued on the less expensive 65-66000 Black Label series. Records also bore numbers for each side of a disc (Arnold).

[3] BPO = Berlin Philharmonic Orchestra
BSOO = Berlin State Opera Orchestra (Kapelle der Staatsoper, Berlin)
COHO = Charlottenberg Opera House Orchestra (Kapelle des Berliner deutschen Opernhauses, Charlottenberg)
NSO = Neues Symphonie-Orchester, Berlin
TO = Tonkünstler-Orchester, Berlin

[4] Initially issued in the 69000 series without the third movement. The third movement was probably recorded in early 1926, when the complete work was issued in the 66000 Black Label series. See Weber (1983), 56.

TABLE 7   Selected Large-Scale or Significant Orchestral Works Issued by Parlophon in Germany and Parlophone in England, 1921–1926

Date Issued[1] (Month/Year) Germany (England)	Catalog Nos.[2] Germany (England)	Composer, Work	Conductor[3] (Soloist)
?/21 (UK 12/23)	1265–7 (UK 10052–4)	Schubert, Symphony no. 8	Mörike
?/23 (UK 12/24)	1638–42 (UK 10207–12)	Tchaikovsky, Symphony no. 6	Weissmann
?/23 (UK 10/24)	1676[4] ⎱ (UK 19175–8)[4] ⎰ 1719–21	Mendelssohn Violin Concerto { mvmt. 2 / mvmts. 1, 3	Hildebrand (Lorand) / Weissmann (Brown)
?/23 (UK 12/24)	1638–42 (UK 10207–12)	Tchaikovsky, Symphony no. 6	Weissmann
?/24 (UK 2/25)	1730–4 (UK 10227–31)	Rimsky-Korsakov, *Scheherazade*	Mörike
?/24 (UK 1/25)	1781–5 (UK 10222–6)	Beethoven, Symphony no. 7	Mörike
?/24 (UK 4/25)	1786–8 (UK 10256–8)	Beethoven, Symphony no. 8	Weissmann
?/24 (UK 6/25)	1792–5 (UK 10284–7)	Beethoven, Symphony no. 5	Weissmann
1/25 (UK 3/25)	1821–3 (UK 10242–4)	Haydn, Symphony no. 94	Weissmann
1/25 (UK 4/25)	1824–5 (UK 10254–5)	Strauss, *Don Juan*	Mörike
2/25 (UK 7/25)	1826–30 (UK 10318–22)	Beethoven, Symphony no. 6	Weissmann
3/25 (UK 7/25)	1845–51 (UK 10299–305)	Beethoven, Symphony no. 3	Weissmann
3/25 (UK 7/24)	1852–60 (UK 10137–45)	Beethoven, Symphony no. 9	Weissmann, Mörike[5]
3/25 (UK 6/25)	1861–4 (UK 10280–3)	Beethoven, Symphony no. 4	Weissmann
3/25 (UK 5/25)	1865–7 (UK 10270–2)	Strauss, *Death and Transfiguration*	Mörike
3/25 (UK 7/25)	1886–8 (UK 10311–3)	Beethoven, Symphony no. 1	Weissmann

3/25 (UK 7/25)	1889-92 (UK 10314-7)	Beethoven, Symphony no. 2		Weissmann
5/25 (UK 7/25)	1915-9 (UK 10306-10)	Strauss, *Ein Heldenleben*		Mörike
5/25 (UK —)[6]	1934-9 (UK —)	Berlioz, *Symphonie fantastique*		Weissmann
7/25 (UK 10/25)	1952 (UK 10353)	Siegfried Wagner, *Der Bärenhäuter* Overture		S. Wagner
7/25 (UK 7/25)	1953-4 (UK 10323-4)	Wagner, *Siegfried Idyll*		S. Wagner
7/25 (UK 8/25)	1955-5 (UK 10334-5)	Wagner, *The Flying Dutchman* Overture		S. Wagner
9/25 (UK 11/25)	1970-1 (UK 10364-5)	Strauss, *Till Eulenspiegel*		Mörike
9/25 (UK 11/25)	1978-30 (UK 10383-5)	Mozart, Violin Concerto no. 4		Weissman (Queling)
11/25 (UK 4/26)	2022-4 (UK 10423-5)	Strauss, *Macbeth*		Mörike
12/25 (UK —)[6]	2053-3 (UK —)	Strauss, *Aus Italien*		Mörike
4/26 (UK 11/25)	2164-5 (UK 10366-8)	Mozart, Symphony no. 40		Weissmann
11/26 (UK 1/26)	2240-2 (UK 10392-4)	Mozart, Symphony no. 39		Weissmann
— (UK 5/26)[7]	— (UK 1433-6)	Mozart, Symphony no. 41		Weissmann
— (UK 10/25)[8]	— (UK 1487-90)	Brahms, Symphony no. 1		Szell
— (UK 11/25)[9]	— (UK 1498-500)	Haydn, Symphony no. 88		Szell

[1] I am grateful to Claude Arnold for supplying the German catalog numbers and issue dates used in this table.

[2] German catalog numbers all have the prefix P, and English numbers, the prefix E.

[3] All works were performed by the Berlin State Opera Orchestra (Kapelle der Staatsoper, Berlin), except for the Beethoven Symphony no. 9 and the second movement of the Mendelssohn Violin Concerto, both of which are by the Blüthner Orchestra.

[4] Eddy Brown was the soloist for movements 1 and 3, and Edith Lorand, for movement 2 (*Gramophone*, October 1924).

[5] Apparently for the English recordings the entire Ninth Symphony was recorded by Frieder Weissmann and the Blüthner Orchestra. Arnold reports that the finale was recorded as early as 1921, while the other three movements were recorded in 1923. The finale was rerecorded for the German set by Mörike and the Berlin State Opera Orchestra with different soloists. This set was issued in the United States in 1925 as Odeon 5077-85.

[6] Not issued in England.

[7] Apparently not issued in Germany.

[8] Issued in Germany only on the Odeon label (O 8549-52).

[9] Issued in Germany only on the Odeon label (O 8553-5).

TABLE 8 Comparison of Orchestras Used for Recording in the Acoustic
Process (*ca.* 1914) and the Electric Process (1928)[1]

1914	1928
4 1st violins	10 1st violins
2 (Stroh) 2nd violins	8 2nd violins
1 or 2 (Stroh) violas	6 violas
1 clarinet	
1 cello	5 cellos
1 bassoon	
1 contrabassoon	4 basses
1 tuba	
2 flutes	2 flutes
2 oboes	2 oboes
2 clarinets	2 clarinets
2 bassoons	2 bassoons
4 horns	4 horns
2 trumpets	2 trumpets
3 trombones	3 trombones
timpani	timpani
2 or 3 percussion	1 percussion
harp or piano[2]	harp

[1]Adapted from Stanley Chapple, "In the Recording Studio," in *Gramophone*, December 1928.
[2]In addition, 1 or 2 euphoniums, a bass clarinet, and a bassoon were used to fill up the "middle" of a score.

TABLE 9 Selective List of Electrical Recordings of Large-Scale Orchestral Works Issued in England and Germany, December 1925–May 1929

Year Issued	Company[1] and Catalog No.	Composer, Work	Orchestra[2]/Conductor (Soloist)
1925	HMV D.1037–41	Tchaikovsky, Symphony No. 4	RAHO/Ronald
1926	HMV D.1102	Elgar, *Pomp and Circumstance Marches* nos. 1, 2	RAHO/Elgar[3]
	HMV D.1110–11	Elgar, *Cockaigne Overture*	RAHO/Elgar
	HMV D.1121	Saint-Saëns, *Danse macabre*	PO/Stokowski
	HMV D.1130–33	Tchaikovsky, Piano Concerto no. 1	RAHO/Ronald (Hambourg)
	Col L.1708–13	Berlioz, *Symphonie fantastique*	LSO/Weingartner
	Col L.1764–6	Tchaikovsky, *1812 Overture*	NQHO/Wood
	Col L.1775–82	Beethoven, Symphony no. 9	LSO/Weingartner
	Col L.1783–5	Mozart, Symphony no. 35	HO/Harty
	Col L.1791–3	Schubert, Symphony no. 8	NQHO/Wood
	Pol 69833–5	Mozart, Symphony no. 39	BSOO/Strauss[4]
	Pol 69836–9	Beethoven, Symphony no. 7	BSOO/Strauss
	Pol 69840–4	Strauss, *Ein Heldenleben*	BSOO/Strauss
	Pol 69845–8	Mozart, Symphony no. 41	BSOO/Strauss
	Pol 69849–52	Strauss, *Death and Transfiguration*	BSOO/Strauss
1927	HMV D.1150–3	Beethoven, Symphony no. 5	RAHO/Ronald
	HMV D.1154–7	Elgar, *Enigma Variations*	RAHO/Elgar
	HMV D.1158–63	Beethoven, Symphony no. 3	SO/Coates
	HMV D.1164–71	Beethoven Symphony no. 9	SO/Coates
	HMV D.1190–4	Tchaikovsky, Symphony no. 6	SO/Coates
	HMV D.1198–1201	Beethoven, Piano Concerto no. 5	RAHO/Ronald (Backhaus)

TABLE 9 (Continued)

Year Issued	Company[1] and Catalog No.	Composer, Work	Orchestra[2]/Conductor (Soloist)
1927	HMV D.1214–6	Tchaikovsky, Nutcracker Suite	PO/Stokowski
	HMV D.1230–5	Elgar, Symphony no. 2	LSO/Elgar
	HMV D.1237–40	Grieg, Piano Concerto	RAHO/Ronald (de Greef)
	HMV D.1250–4	Dvořák, Symphony no. 5 [i.e., no. 9]	RAHO/Ronald
	HMV D.1265–70	Brahms, Symphony no. 4	LSO/Abendroth
	HMV D.B. 997–1000	Mendelssohn, Violin Concerto	BSSO/Blech (Kreisler)
	Col L.1864–7	Beethoven, Symphony no. 2	LSO/Beecham
	Col L.1868–74	Beethoven, Symphony no. 3	NQHO/Wood
	Col L.1875–9	Beethoven, Symphony no. 4	HO/Harty
	Col L.1880–3	Beethoven, Symphony no. 5	RPO/Weingartner
	Col L.1889–92	Beethoven, Symphony no. 1	RPO/Henschel
	Col L.1893–7	Beethoven, Symphony no. 6	RPO/Weingartner
	Col L.1898–1902	Beethoven, Symphony no. 7	RPO/Weingartner
	Col L.1903–5	Beethoven, Symphony no. 8	RPO/Weingartner
	Col L.1938–41	Mozart, Symphony no. 41	SO/Godfrey
	Par E 10533–6	Beethoven, Piano Concerto no. 4	SO/Weissmann (Szreter)
	Pol 69855–9	Beethoven, Symphony no. 5	BP/Furtwängler
	Pol 69864–6	Mozart, Symphony no. 40	BSOO/Strauss
	Pol 66410–3	Schumann, Symphony no. 4	BSOO/Pfitzner
	Pol 66460–2	Beethoven, Symphony no. 8	BSOO/Klemperer
	Pol 66467–72	Beethoven, Symphony no. 6	BSOO/Pfitzner

Year	Catalogue	Work	Orchestra/Conductor
1928	HMV D.1359-62	Mozart, Symphony no. 41	LSO/Coates
	HMV D.1390-5	Schubert Symphony no. 9	LSO/Blech
	HMV D.1404-8	Franck, Symphony in D Minor	PO/Stokowski
	HMV D.1428	Bach-Stokowski, Toccata and Fugue in D Minor	PO/Stokowski
	HMV D.1454-8	Brahms, Symphony no. 1	LSO/Abenroth
	HMV D.1475-7	Beethoven, Symphony no. 6	VP/Schalk
	HMV D.1481-3	Beethoven, Symphony no. 8	VP/Schalk
	Col L.2079-85	Schubert, Symphony no. 9	HO/Harty
	Col L.2088-91	Haydn, Symphony no. 101	HO/Harty
	Col. L.2145-9	Brahms, Symphony no. 1	RPO/Weingartner
	Col. L.2151-5	Brahms, Symphony no. 2	NYSO/Damrosch
	Col. L.2160-3	Auerberg, Symphony no. 6	RPO/Beecham
	Col. L.2173-5	Stravinsky, Petrushka Suite	SO/Stravinsky
	Pol 95030-2	Tchaikovsky, Nutcracker Suite	BSOO/Fried
	Pol 95052-3	Stravinsky, Firebird Suite	BSOO/Fried
	Pol 95093-5	Beethoven, Symphony no. 1	BP/Pfitzner
	Pol 95096-100	Beethoven, Symphony no. 4	COHO/Pfitzner
	Pol 69869-72	Mozart, Symphony no. 40	BSOO/Strauss
	Pol 66657-63	Beethoven, Symphony no. 9	BSOO/Fried
	Pol 66669-70	Mozart, Eine kleine Nachtmusik	BSOO/Fried
	Pol 66717-9	Schubert, Symphony no. 8	BP/Kleiber
	Pol 66750-2	List, Piano Concerto no. 1	BP/Prüwer (Brailowsky)
	Pol 66753-6	Chopin, Piano Concerto no. 1	BP/Prüwer (Brailowsky)
	Pol 66784-6	Schubert, Symphony no. 8	BP/Prüwer
	Pol 66787-8	List, Mazeppa	BP/Fried
	Par E 10672-4	Schubert, Symphony no. 8	BSOO/von Schillings
1929	HMV D.1499-1503	Brahms, Symphony no. 1	PO/Stokowski
	HMV D.1507-9	Elgar, Cello Concerto	NSO/Elgar (Harrison)

TABLE 9 (Continued)

Year Issued	Company[1] and Catalog No.	Composer, Work	Orchestra[2]/Conductor (Soloist)
1929	HMV D.1511–6	Tchaikovsky, Symphony no. 5	NSO/Ronald
	HMV D.1518–20	Haydn, Cello Concerto	SO/Barbirolli (Suggia)
	HMV D.1521–4	Stravinsky, Petrushka Suite	LSO/Coates
	HMV D.1525–7	Strauss, Death and Transfiguration	LSO/Coates
	HMV C.1608–10	Haydn, Symphony no. 104	BCO/Barbirolli
	Col L.2176–82	Tchaikovsky, Symphony no. 5	CO/Mengelberg
	Col L.2209–12	Schumann, Symphony no. 4	MFO/Walter
	Col L.2215–8	Mozart, Piano Concerto no. 17	BSO/Dohnanyi
	Col L.2220–2	Mozart, Symphony no. 34	RPO/Beecham
	Col L.2265–9	Brahms, Violin Concerto	HO/Harty (Szigeti)
	Col L.2279–2	Stravinsky, Firebird Suite	OSP/Stravinsky
	Col 9616–9	Schumann, Piano Concerto	RPO/Ansermet (Davies)
	Par E 10807–12	Brahms, Symphony no. 1	BSOO/Klemperer
	Par E 10844–6	Haydn, Symphony no. 94	BSOO/Knapertsbusch
	Pol 95193–5	Atterberg, Symphony no. 6	BP/Atterberg
	Pol 95243–7	Beethoven, Violin Concerto	BP/Gurlitt (Wolfsthal)

Pol 66802–8	Bruckner, Symphony no. 7	BP/Horenstein
Pol 66812–3	Liszt, *Les préludes*	BP/Fried
Pol 66814–7	Beethoven, Symphony no. 5	BSOO/Strauss

[1]HMV = "His Master's Voice" (Gramophone Company)
Col = Columbia (English branch)
Par = Parlophone
Pol = Polydor (Deutsche Grammophon)
[2]BCO = Barbirolli Chamber Orchestra
BP = Berlin Philharmonic
BSO = Budapest Symphony Orchestra
BSOO = Berlin State Opera Orchestra
CO = Concertgebouw Orchestra
COHO = Charlottenberg Opera House Orchestra
HO = Hallé Orchestra
LSO = London Symphony Orchestra
MFO = Mozart Festival Orchestra
NQHO = New Queen's Hall Orchestra
NSO = New Symphony Orchestra
NYSO = New York Symphony Orchestra
OSP = Orchestre Symphonique, Paris
PO = Philadelphia Orchestra
RAHO = Royal Albert Hall Orchestra
RPO = Royal Philharmonic Orchestra
SO = Symphony Orchestra
VP = Vienna Philharmonic
[3]For details on Elgar's recordings, see Moore.
[4]For details on Strauss's recordings, see Morse.

BIBLIOGRAPHY

Hollis Alpert, "A&R: These Men Shape Your Listening," in *High Fidelity*, December 1957 and January 1958. Claude Arnold, work in progress. Jeanne Belfy, *The Louisville Orchestra New Music Project: Selected Composers' Letters to the Louisville Orchestra* (1983). John R. Bennett and Eric Hughes, *Voices of the Past*, vol. 4, *The International Red Label Catalogue of "DB" and "DA" His Master's Voice Recordings, 1924–1956, Book I: "DB" (12-inch)* (1961). David Bicknell and Robert Phillip, "Gramophone," in *New Grove Dictionary of Music and Musicians*, Stanley Sadie, ed. (1980). Kurt Blaukopf, *The Phonogram in Cultural Communication* (1982). John Borwick, ed., *The First Fifty Years: Celebrating the Fiftieth Anniversary of the IFPI* (1983).

Jim Cartwright, *Leopold Stokowski Acoustical Recordings* (1977); and "The Recordings of Alfred Hertz," in *Le Grand Baton*, 50 (June 1981). Stanley Chapple, "In the Recording Studio," in *Gramophone*, December 1928. Francis F. Clough and C. J. Cuming, eds., *The World's Encyclopedia of Recorded Music*, 3 vols. (1966). David Edwin Cooper, *International Bibliography of Discographies* (1975). Trevor Croucher, *Early Music Discography from Plainsong to the Sons of Bach* (1981). John Culshaw, *Putting the Record Straight* (1981).

R. D. Darrell, ed., *The Gramophone Shop Encyclopedia of Recorded Music* (1936; 3rd ed., 1948). Christopher Dyment, "Albert Coates Discography," in *Recorded Sound*, nos. 57-58 (January–April 1975), with errata in no. 59 (July 1975); and *Felix Weingartner: Recollections and Recordings* (1976). Ted Fagen and William Moran, *The Encyclopedic Discography of Victor Recordings*, vol. 1 (1983). Frederick P. Fellers and Betty Meyers, *Discographies of Commercial Recordings of the Cleveland Orchestra (1924–1977) and the Cincinnati Symphony Orchestra (1917–1977)* (1978). Peter Ford, "History of Sound Recording," in *Recorded Sound*, 1, no. 7 (Summer 1962), 1, no. 8 (Autumn 1962), 2, nos. 10-11 (April–July 1963), 2, no. 12 (October 1963), 2, no. 13 (January 1964).

Frederick W. Gaisberg, *The Music Goes Round* (1942). Peter Gammond and John Atkinson, "The Role of the Record Producer," in *Hi-Fi News and Record Review*, August 1978. Roland Gelatt, *The Fabulous Phonograph, 1877–1977* (1977); and "The Pangs of Progress," in *High Fidelity*, January 1958. Victor Girard and Harold M. Barnes, *Vertical-cut Cylinders and Discs* (1964). Gary-Gabriel Gisondi, "Sound Recording Periodicals," in *Association for Recorded Sound Collections Journal*, 10, no. 1 (1978). Michael H. Gray, *Beecham: A Centenary Discography* (1979); and "Discography: Its Prospects and Problems," in *Notes*, 35 (1979). Michael H. Gray and Gerald D. Gibson, *Bibliography of Discographies*, vol. 1, *Classical Music, 1925–1975* (1977). Pekka Gronow, "The Record Industry Comes to the Orient," in *Ethnomusicology*, 25 (1981); and "The Record Industry: Growth of a Mass Medium," in *Popular Music*, 3 (1983).

David Hall, *The Record Book* (1940; supplements 1941 and 1943); *Records: 1950 Edition* (1950); and *The Record Book, International Edition* (1948; repr. 1978).

David Hamilton, "Igor Stravinsky: A Discography of the Composer's Performances," in *Perspectives on Schoenberg and Stravinsky*, B. Boretz and E. T. Cone, eds. (1972). Hugh Wiley Hitchcock, *The Phonograph and Our Musical Life: Proceedings of a Centennial Conference 7–10 Dec. 1977*, 14 (1980). Allan Ho, "The Late-Romantic Piano Concerto Finale: A Stylistic and Structural Analysis," Ph.D. diss., University of Kentucky (1985). John L. Holmes, *Conductors on Record* (1982). Edward Johnson, ed., *Stokowski: Essays in Analysis of His Art* (1973). Michael Kennedy, *Barbirolli: Conductor Laureate* (1971). Joseph Kerman, "A Few Canonic Variations," in *Critical Inquiry*, 10 (September 1983). Irving Kolodin, *The Guide to Long-Playing Records: Orchestral Music* (1955).

Erich Leinsdorf, "Will We Run Out of Music to Record?" in *High Fidelity*, January–February 1954. Compton Mackenzie, *My Record of Life* (1955). Antoinette O. Maleady, *Index to Record and Tape Reviews* (1975). Jerrold Northrop Moore, *Elgar on Record: The Composer and the Gramophone* (1974). Peter Morse, "Richard Strauss's Recordings: A Complete Discography," in *Association for Recorded Sound Collections Journal*, 9 (1977). Julian Morton Moses, *Collector's Guide to American Recordings: 1895–1925* (1949; repr. 1977). John H. Mueller, *The American Symphony Orchestra: A Social History of Musical Taste* (1951). Kate Hevner Mueller, *Twenty-Seven Major American Symphony Orchestras: A History and Analysis of Their Repertories, Seasons 1842–43 through 1969–70* (1973). Kurtz Myers, *Index to Record Reviews*, vols. 1–4 (1978) and vol. 5 (1980). Kurtz Myers and Richard S. Hill, eds., *Record Ratings* (1956).

Charles O'Connell, *The Other Side of the Record* (1948). Carol J. Oja, *American Music Recordings: A Discography of 20th Century U.S. Composers* (1982). James Parakilas, "Classical Music as Popular Music," in *Journal of Musicology*, 3, no. 1 (Winter 1984). John F. Potte, "American Symphony Orchestras," in *Gramophone*, April 1925. Oliver Read and Walter L. Welch, *From Tin Foil to Stereo* (2nd ed., 1976).

David Sachs, "CRI at 30: Celebration and Challenge," in *Fanfare*, September–October 1984. Alan Sanders, *Sir Adrian Boult: A Discography* (1980); and *Walter Legge*, Discographies Series, vol. 11 (1984). Harold C. Schonberg, "A Half Century of Orchestral Recording," in *Musical Courier*, 1 December 1945. Elisabeth Schwarzkopf, *On and Off the Record: A Memoir of Walter Legge* (1982). D. E. L. Shorter and John Borwick, "Sound Recording, Transmission and Reproduction," in *New Grove Dictionary*. Michael Smith, *The Catalogue of "D" and "E" His Master's Voice Recordings*, vol. 5 of *Voices of the Past* (1961). Michael Smith and Ian Cosens, *Columbia Graphophone Company Ltd.: English Celebrity Issues*, vol. 8 of *Voices of the Past* (1971). John Swan, "The Anonymous, the Pseudonymous, and the Missing: Conductors on Record Revisited," in *Association for Recorded Sound Collections Journal*, 15 (1983). J. F. Weber, *Bruckner*, Discography Series, vol. 10 (1971); *Mahler*, Discography Series, vol. 9 (2nd ed., 1974); and "Clues to Composer Discography," in *Association for Recorded Sound Collections Journal*, 15 (1983). Frederick P. Williams, "The Times as Reflected in the Victor Black Label

Military Band Recordings from 1900 to 1927," in *Association for Recorded Sound Collections Journal,* 4, nos. 1–3 (1972); 8, no. 1 (1976); 8, no. 3 (1981). David Wooldridge, *Conductor's World* (1970).

I would like to express my gratitude to Michael H. Gray, President of the Association for Recorded Sound Collections, and Claude Arnold for their generous and expert help in preparing this article, as well as to Ruth Edge of the EMI Music Archives in Hayes, England, and to the staffs of the Rodgers and Hammerstein Archives of Recorded Sound of the New York Public Library and the Library of Congress.

The New Amateur Player and Listener

Edward Rothstein

"There are probably few cities where musical amateurism is as general as it is here," wrote a Viennese correspondent of the *Allgemeine musikalische Zeitung* in 1800. "Everybody plays, everybody learns music." Those must have been halcyon days, indeed. The words were written at the dawn of the century that has given us most of our orchestral repertoire, most of our musical customs, many of our best concert halls, and most of our currently performed composers. Haydn was still composing. Beethoven was entering his maturity. Music was beginning to acquire the sort of status with the bourgeoisie that would forever change its style and audience. And everybody seemed to know how to play.

But the correspondent went on to complain of a pretentious, vacuous amateurism: "Music is being looked upon as something easy, as if it were something that could be learned in passing as it were: one thinks one knows everything right away, excuses one's self finally with the word 'amateur,' and regards the whole thing more as a matter of *galanterie* and good form." In upper-class houses "private academies" were common — social gatherings organized around performances of music, punctuated by idle chatter: "This widespread all-too-easy amateurism has spoiled taste and allowed the sense for greater things to fall asleep."

One would think, then, that we are in no similar danger today, for no one could complain of widespread amateurism. In fact, if a correspondent were to assess the musical scene in America's most important musical city, New York, the evaluation would have to be precisely the opposite. There are probably few cities where musical professionalism is as widespread. Music has become, to put it simply, a business. During a single week at the peak of the season, more than 150 concerts are given in the numerous grand and small halls and playing spaces around the city; the players are not young ladies fashionably toying with the latest piano sonata but young yet polished graduates of our finest conservatories. A score of artist-management companies books them around the country, touting their virtues with blurbs from newspaper reviews, supplemented occasionally by the efforts of a public relations firm. Everything is professional, everything is marketable, but very little is worth hearing. It is similar to the situation described by Virgil Thomson in 1939: "Enormous quantities of music are consumed but none of it means much.... The concert world is taken over by incompetent soloists and by overcompetent orchestral conductors who streamline the already predigested classics to a point of suavity where they go through everybody like a dose of castor oil."

Much had changed in the world between these two journalistic accounts of nineteenth-century Vienna and twentieth-century New York, not the least of which was the status of the amateur. Between the dominance of the amateur and that of the professional, the musical culture underwent radical transformations; if "the sense for greater things" seemed asleep in 1800, the scene now, as Thomson said, is at the point of decadence. It is worth repeating the broad outlines of this failure: for all the professionalism of contemporary musical life, contemporary music, itself a refuge of our most brilliant performing professionals, has never succeeded in reaching the mainstream public; for all the economic prosperity, the concert halls play almost exclusively nineteenth-century music; for all the polish of today's orchestral players, there is hardly an orchestra that sounds as forcefully *musical* as it does on recordings made more than two decades ago. For all the dedication to greater things, we repeat, over and over, those great things which we have inherited without embracing those that we are creating; for all the expanding audiences, created and inspired by grants, recordings, promotion, and the increase in the number of concerts, musical illiteracy and lack of contact with the *making* of music have never been more prevalent among nonprofessionals.

THE ORIGINS OF THE AMATEUR

The shift in importance of the amateur during the last century would seem crucial to this decline in the vitality of musical life. But the amateur's role is hard to pinpoint in history; the amateur is necessarily out of the public eye, a person playing for private pleasure whose playing is incidental to his livelihood. In the Europe of the seventeenth and eighteenth centuries, there was almost no room at all for the concept of amateur as we understand it. Musical life centered on either the church or the court; in either place the concept of amateur would be inappropriate. In the church a player was engaged in worship; in the court he was fulfilling a social function and collecting a wage. Some musicians, of course, did not fit either category: Frederick the Great, for example, could be called an amateur flutist, and he was neither the first nor the last monarch to take upon himself the pleasures of music making. Town musicians such as those of the Bach family also sang or played for the pleasures of the village or family.

But the amateur came to maturity with the bourgeoisie when the cultivation of music in the home was modeled on the practice thriving in the court; his prestige was connected to the growing prestige of his class. As early as the sixteenth century, the social benefits of amateurism were clear.

Here, again, the Viennese correspondent who is quoted above is enlightening:

> Every well-bred girl, whether she has talent or not, must learn to play the piano or to sing: first of all, it's fashionable; secondly (here the spirit of speculation comes in), it's the most convenient way for her to put herself forward attractively in society and thereby, if she is lucky, make an advantageous matrimonial alliance, particularly a moneyed one. The sons likewise must learn music: first, also, because it is the thing to do and is fashionable; secondly, because it serves them too as a recommendation in good society; and experience teaches that many a fellow (at least amongst us) has musicked himself to the side of a rich wife, or into a highly lucrative position.... If somebody wants to be a lawyer, he acquires a lot of acquaintances and clients through music by playing everywhere; the same is true of the aspiring physician.

Castiglione's *The Courtier*, for example, recommended musical skill as appropriate polish to a gentleman. In the seventeenth century, the accomplished bourgeois might join an amateur musical society in London, like the one Roger North called a "society of gentlemen of good esteem." In *The Anatomy of Melancholy* (1621), Robert Burton wrote of music as a part of a "gentlewoman's bringing up," as the "way their parents think to get them husbands." But the bourgeoisie at the beginning of the nineteenth century turned these notions into public strategies. Musical training was no longer just a sign of cultivation among the upper classes but a necessity for all who desired entrance into the world of commerce.

The result was astonishing. In London, in 1750, there were no more than 12 music shops; in 1794, about 30; and in 1824, about 150. Music catalogs typically listed no more than several hundred compositions in the 1700s; by 1824, there were 10,000 foreign publications alone listed in the 280 pages of Boosey's catalog. Morsels of amateurish music were published throughout Europe and consumed voraciously. Virtually everything that was available was transcribed for the piano, ranging from the polka currently in vogue to the arias of the latest operatic hit. Arthur Loesser, in his grand social history *Men, Women and Pianos,* makes it clear how that instrument was at the heart of the new amateurism. With the development of industry and the increase in commerce, pianos could be manufactured in quantities that would have been impossible for the handmade clavichords and spinets in earlier years. Between 1802 and 1824, Broadwood produced an average of 1,680 pianos a year. In Paris, by 1834, the Pleyel company was manufacturing 1,000 pianos annually. Erard, in 1855, manufactured 1,500. The piano became an institution in the home as in the concert hall, and the thousands of pianos manufactured by the great European companies served an ever-expanding market of amateurs. The bourgeois instrument par excellence, the piano was a potential introduction into the home of the same sounds that had charmed the aristocracy.

Although many amateurs had a passionate devotion to music in itself, amateurism must still be considered a social phenomenon. The amateur is not just someone who plays an instrument; the amateur is one who *wishes* to play, who wishes to be *known* to play, and who wishes the social benefits from *being known* to play. In Jane Austen's *Pride and Prejudice,* for example, Lady Catherine de Bourgh, though better-born than most, is just as calculating about music: "It is of all subjects my delight. I must have my share of the conversation if you are speaking of music. There are few people in England, I suppose, who have more true enjoyment of music than myself, or a better natural taste." The nature of the amateur was bound up with the aspirations of the bourgeoisie as a class.

What music offered the amateur was not just the emblems of sensitivity and taste. Skill also could be displayed, or at least the appearance of skill; complicated passage-work on the piano could be impressively made to seem simple; simple passage-work could be impressively made to seem complicated. In either case, authentic skill or the image of skill served its purpose. The amateur was coming into his own when music itself was becoming increasingly difficult to play—as if there were a causal relation between the complexity of passages in Chopin, Liszt, and Thalberg, and the intricate social ambitions of those whose drawing rooms were equipped with the requisite pianoforte.

Extraordinary technical demands, such as those made by Liszt and Paganini, were partly an attempt to distance the performer-composer from the amateur, but the effect also suited amateur taste. The challenge of the music—"Can you do this?"—represented precisely the challenge that the world posed to the amateur's social ambitions. The difficulties were suitably called "transcendental." Unlike earlier expert players, such as Bach, the nineteenth-century virtuoso was the image of the amateur triumphantly transcending his origins. He was far from being a professional figure; he was too unpredictable, too much the individualist, rejecting the social world even as he courted it. Paganini and Liszt were acclaimed not for their professionalism but for their frightening mastery and demonic power. The amateur's impulse to display his cultivation and skill is just a moderated version of that of the virtuoso, whose entire musical existence is based upon grand display.

Desires for display thus led to the beginning of a public musical life. The amateur who played at home was ready to play in public. Patronage was always a sign of status, and in the nineteenth century, its venue became the concert hall, which was effectively the court of the bourgeoisie. While amateurism was an attempt to attain public status through private activity, concerts helped to realize private ambitions in public places. They created an arena in which the virtuoso could dramatize these ambitions.

In that arena the orchestra played a distinctive role in the social drama. During the eighteenth century, particularly in England, upper-middle-class aspirants formed their own orchestras, meeting in assembly halls and taverns. Tickets could be sold and professionals occasionally hired for support. Paul Honigsheim, sociologist of music, wrote:

Traveling soloists frequently had difficulty advertising, selling tickets, and even securing a performance hall. The following pattern emerged: After coming to the city, a foreign virtuoso would first play, accompanied by an amateur orchestra, in a program sponsored by the orchestra. The amateur associations would then allow him to perform his own concert rent-free in their hall.

This relationship must have been ideal: the amateur orchestra could display itself through the achievements of the soloist. But the orchestra eventually became a professionalizing force. As the wealthiest amateurs endowed the orchestra and as the municipality became sponsor as well as host, the orchestra became institutional, requiring extensive income to maintain itself in the image to which its sponsors aspired. It required professional management at the very least, professional discipline at best. And as civic support grew, the orchestra became fully professional, closely affiliated with the city and its government. We speak of Berlin, New York, and Chicago and hardly need name the orchestras themselves. As an organization, not an individual, the orchestra required structure, regularity, planning—exactly what the mercurial and temperamental virtuoso soloist appeared to disdain.

The orchestra could even appear a model of the world being built so industriously outside the concert hall, with disparate individuals of varying skills and temperaments professionally bound together for the purpose of production. The concerto form could serve to dramatize tensions between the virtuoso individual and the professional society, between the improvisatory and the structured. The conductor, in turn, was a mediator between virtuoso and society: he was an authority but also a soloist, at once the consummate professional and the tempestuous virtuoso, embodying two of the contradictory impulses that dominated musical life.

These various conflicts were enacted in a quite particular way within the music itself. Indeed, the only way to fully appreciate the transformations wrought in nineteenth-century musical life by the bourgeoisie and the spirit of the amateur is to step back from the century as a whole to notice the central preoccupations of its seemingly varied music. The major transformation in musical style during this period involved a rejection of the static presentation of images and themes in baroque suites and programs. Kuhnau's *Biblical Sonatas* are simple imitations of a single image; Vivaldi's *Four Seasons* is a series of still-lifes in sound; Bach's various suites get their energy not through the dynamic development of

themes and rhythms but through their cascading variety. By the end of
the eighteenth century, this was changing.

Beginning with the sonatas of Haydn and his contemporaries, music
became increasingly concerned with the transformation of themes. In
Haydn such transformation is witty, dealing with sudden conjunctions
and surprising contexts. In Beethoven the rhetoric becomes more expansive. Typically, a theme of a certain character is subjected to various musical events, suffering tensions and oppositions in an almost picaresque
manner, before finally returning to its original form. For the listener, that
return is experienced as a transformation; the theme cannot be heard in
the same way again. The musical emphasis is on evolution rather than
on demonstration. When the theme of the first movement of the *Eroica*
Symphony, for example, returns in the recapitulation, the mysterious C-
sharp of the opening theme does not resolve upward to a D as it did in
the exposition but moves downward to a C: this is an act of reinterpretation and so affects our understanding of the events of the symphony
as a whole. One does not get this sense, for example, from Bach's *Goldberg*
Variations, another work that involves intricate transmutations of a
theme; those variations are not evolutionary or developmental but contemplative and analytical.

The elements of the new musical style can be specified quite clearly,
as Charles Rosen did in his study *The Classical Style*. But they also represent a more pervasive mode of thought. The style of sonata form beginning in the classical period is a form of romantic archetype, a recurrent
pattern in nineteenth-century writing and philosophy that M. H.
Abrams, distinguished literary critic, has called "the circuitous journey."
Here is his description:

> The mind of man, whether generic or individual, is represented as discip-
> lined by the suffering which it experiences as it develops through successive
> stages of division, conflict, and reconciliation, toward the culminating stage
> at which . . . it will achieve a full and triumphant awareness of its identity,
> of the significance of its past, and of its accomplished destiny.

In the novels of the period, the journey involved a character's departure
from home, his succeeding education through a series of encounters, and
his final return home, transformed by his passage through experience.
Their musical counterpart was sonata form.

As the century progressed, the sonata form became part of a more
general style. Abrams' description is quite germane: this was a music of

experience. It increasingly assumed a narrative function, often with reference to specific literary works, as in the *Faust* Symphony of Liszt; programmatic music also dramatically invoked journeys of introspection and conflict, as in Berlioz' *Symphonie fantastique*. What the listener—the amateur listener—heard in the music of this century, ranging from the symphonies of Beethoven to the symphonies of Mahler, were musical tales, with quite similar preoccupations. The symphonies of Beethoven, the nocturnes of Chopin, the operas of Verdi—all, in various ways, suggest expression of the self. The melody in a work—its theme and germinating idea—can seem like the voice of an individual, encountering in musical surroundings the sorts of trials and struggles faced by characters like Pip in *Great Expectations* and Dorothea in *Middlemarch*; the novel, after all, was the literary form that came to maturity with the bourgeoisie, telling of the course of individual life in a newly forming society. For the listener in the concert hall, as for the reader of the novel, that was no abstract tale. The music's melody could be experienced as a personal voice; the music became an autobiography. This is the repertoire of "identification."

Similar themes could be heard in the opera house, where the narrative became quite concrete. The plots of romantic opera, beginning with those of late Mozart, inevitably involve the struggles of the individual, within a world bounded by the state, the army, the society, the family. These are themes far different from those of baroque opera and opera seria. The works of Verdi, for example, from *Nabucco* to *La Traviata* and *Aida,* for all their variety of setting and costume, can be interpreted as explorations of the intricate relations of citizens to the social order and the results of violations of that order. Stable social hierarchies are threatened by the hero's yearning, as Germont's family is by his son's affair or as the Egyptian royal family is by Radames' love. There may be royalty and priests involved, but Verdi was writing about what he knew at first hand: the struggles between the unpredictable, irrational, or passionate individual and the demands of the society and family. In Bizet's *Carmen* as well, this causes the downfall of Don José, tempted away from his mother's deathbed and his love for his fiancée by an outsider to such bourgeois manners—by a gypsy, a figure who reappears again and again in nineteenth-century cultural life.

The melodic line, elevated to the center of attention, issuing from the belly and chest of the singer, links the music directly to the listener, and the listener to the tale. Melody, in a highly metaphorical sense, may even be considered a musical expression of the interior life of the individual in society. When a long melodic line gracefully descends to its final tone, when it soars suddenly and flirts with a distant key, when it surprises the ear with a sudden turn—wherever it moves—it is experienced as the listener's own voice, his own feelings and dreams. Because it is the listener's own, that voice may be linked to the amateur; the music belongs to the untrained as well as the trained; it is of private as well as public importance. The professional, as professional, executes the music; but this is not a music addressed to the professional (as some music is today); it is a music specifically addressed to the amateur. The amateur is not concerned with the technical aspects of the music. He is attracted to the psychological or social situations embodied in the music; given the social nature of the themes, the concert hall and the opera house, with their gatherings of citizens, adds resonance: it is where the playing amateur finds fulfillment as a listener.

Amateurism in the nineteenth century, then, should be looked at as a complement to concert life. In the concert hall the amateur saw the transcendental amateur on display, the virtuoso, possessed by the music and possessing the audience's attention, rising out of bourgeois origins yet clearly in contact with forces outside the social order. The amateur could also see that order demonstrated in the organization of the orchestra, with passions and dangers controlled and overcome on a professional scale. The professional musician was the orchestra player who submerged his individual ambitions and desires for the sake of the ensemble, just as the amateur had to outside of music, in the ensemble activities of his daily life.

Ultimately, much of the music of the later nineteenth century—from Wagner to Mahler, from Lizst to Brahms—was beyond the personal reach of the amateur except in simplified transcriptions. But there was recompense. If the amateur yearned to transcend his origins—to be more than bourgeois—and to do so through display, virtuosity, and manners, the music expressed a yearning no less clear. This is a way we can understand the constant "state of desire" heard in this repertoire, its yearning for resolution in the face of the ever more intricate tensions of tonality. The music, of course, ultimately succeeded in its latent ambitions. It transcended its audience, becoming too difficult for the amateur player. But it still spoke to him; more and more the amateur player became, in the late nineteenth century, the amateur listener.

Meanwhile, the music world itself became more and more professional, in image as well as substance. Quite early this was seen as a potential danger. In "The Amateur Orchestra" (1893) George Bernard Shaw wrote:

> To me the amateur orchestra is all-important; for out of every ten people who support music in England, at least nine and three-quarters must have acquired their knowledge of it as amateurs and from amateurs. The musician of professional antecedents is an incorrigible deadhead: whether he performs or listens, music has to support him, instead of being supported by him.

Shaw, himself a self-taught amateur, had already reached a verdict on the professional. Although he mocks the amateur elsewhere in his writings, Shaw knew that something was being sacrificed by the removal of music from the amateur's hands.

THE END OF THE AMATEUR

The amateur during the nineteenth century derived pleasure not only from playing music but also from being seen playing it. By the dawn of this century, the pleasure in playing was replaced by the pleasure in listening and in being seen listening. The European middle class had become firmly established as the new patron and audience for serious music; the concert hall had supplanted the home as the focus of musical life. The repertoire had also solidified to comprise almost exclusively the music of the same century that gave birth to the public concert on a grand scale.

Certainly the increasing technical difficulty and complexity of music helped this process along, changing the relationship of the amateur to the art. But there were also technological reasons for the decline in the amateur's status: he had become unnecessary. By the 1920s, for example, the player piano had achieved such sophistication that the major pianists of the day were under contract to produce piano rolls for sale to the public. The same works that an amateur might have learned or played in simple versions could now be had by wealthier aspirants in their original form. "Perfection without practice" was one advertising claim in 1905. By 1919, player pianos constituted more than half of the pianos manufactured in America. The best were quite expensive and became signs of cultivation and social position.

But the increasing popularity of recordings made even that sort of contact with an instrument superfluous. It became possible to hear music divorced from its players and the circumstances of its performance. With the growth of urban society, the home, moreover, came to have less and less social and public importance. The amateur soiree could not be as great a social occasion as opening night at the city's most prestigious concert hall or opera house. Shaw, at the age of ninety, hailed radio for making symphonic music available to anyone at any time, noting that "my own familiarity with the orchestral classics was gained by playing arrangements of them as piano duets with my sister." The sheer pleasure of playing had to bow to the pleasure of listening without practice.

The orchestra, in the meantime, had become thoroughly professional. The philharmonic societies had become civic institutions that themselves conferred prestige, as if the individual yearnings of the last century were being elevated to a municipal or even federal scale. That prestige could be conferred without labor, merely by the purchase of a ticket; this prestige gradually displaced pride in playing. Concert sponsorship and attendance grew, resulting in a nearly geometric growth in the number of concerts given each season.

But most important, the cultural ambition that defined the amateur had become deflected. For a small number of people, it successfully blended into professional ambition—hence, the increased enrollment and expansion of conservatories for training professional musicians. The rise of academic musical studies had much the same effect; the theory of music was something to be taught apart from the playing of music. The professionalization of musical studies grew extravagantly. While Harvard gave the first American doctoral degree in music only in 1905, by 1952 there were 231 dissertations on musical subjects being written in the United States; 1,917 dissertations were in progress by 1970.

The cultural ambitions that supported amateurism in the nineteenth century have also diffused in a more idiosyncratic way. Part of the amateur's initial urge to play was a desire to share the signs of cultivation established by the upper class; once that goal had become historically remote, the desire was simply to share in the rewards of success that other members of the bourgeoisie had established. The pleasures of culture were partly the pleasures of belonging, of success, of "making it." In recent decades, playing an instrument became a sign of very little; the culture in question was not contemporary; proficiency in playing did not lead to proficiency in social life. Instead, to a great extent, these pleasures were claimed by the embrace of a new form of culture granted the name *popular*.

The new popular culture was vastly different from the culture that caused Verdi to be carried on the shoulders of crowds following an operatic success or that made London readers eagerly await a new installment of Dickens' latest novel. It was on a scale that dwarfed earlier notions of "popular" in economic size as well as in following. Moreover, it did not make the demands of literacy that had existed earlier. The pop culture of television and movies is, by definition, specifically intended to be popular, to provide for the widest number the greatest sense of pleasure in belonging. It requires no training for understanding or participation; all are eligible. Hence, all are automatically amateurs, lovers of sensation, whose ambitions become simple because so easily sated. The amateur becomes the consumer.

Many of the compositions written during this century appealed not to the amateur listener but to a figure who might be called the professional listener, the listener who had a trained ear and had taken music on as a discipline and who, moreover, chose to discard the bourgeois aesthetic that had shaped the tradition. The professional listener is the critic, the academic, the historian, the composer—anyone who depends on the development and nature of the art for his living. And while not every professional listener had a taste for the new, few enough others did. It is primarily the professional listener who turns his attention to Elliott Carter or Pierre Boulez; the amateur listener in the concert hall remains moored in the music of the past. This is the most problematic aspect of the contemporary musical scene. Its remedy is not to be found simply in exposing the amateur listener to new music because the purpose of his listening is intrinsically different. There were changes in the music as well. The new amateur listener is the direct heir of the nineteenth-century amateur player and is listening for exactly the same thing: identification with the music. The same narrative tales that appealed to the amateur player appeal to the amateur listener. He repeats, again and again, the great works of the last century, which have come to define for him what music should be.

This repetition goes far beyond the desire simply to gain appreciation of the great works of the past; it demands very little variation, encouraging the professionalization of musical performance, turning it into mere recitation. Sigmund Freud identified the demand for repetition with the child's desire to hear the same tale again and again. In *Beyond the Pleasure Principle* (1920), he wrote, "If a child has been told a nice story, he will insist on hearing it over and over again rather than a new one: and he will remorselessly stipulate that the repetition shall be an identical one and will correct any alterations of which the narrator may be guilty." In the musical world the results are the same. The works that grew out of the bourgeois dreams of the nineteenth century can never be repeated often enough on the concert stage. Such compulsive repetitions could be, Freud suggested, an attempt "to restore an earlier state of things," to gain control over the conflicts and tensions expressed within a story. In concert life this means attempting to master the narratives of bourgeois musical culture, the tales of social order and threatening desire that fill the concert halls.

This music is also mythological in its import. Claude Lévi-Strauss has suggested in *Myth and Meaning* (1979) that as mythical thought passed to the background in Western thought, music began to take its place, beginning in the seventeenth century but culminating in the nineteenth. This is quite literally the case. If myth shows how a culture develops out of nature, this music dramatizes how modern society is connected to the threatening natural world around it and how forces of nature are barely tamed within its citizens. Many of Verdi's operas are set in periods when the nation-state was just coming into existence. Most of the explicit themes of the programmatic music of the period are concerned with the boundaries of the social world and with the forces of nature and the irrational that impinge upon it—hence, this music's concern with the demonic (Mephisto, Faust, Robert le Diable), with the figure of the gypsy (Carmen), with the carnival (*Carnaval, Faschingsschwank aus Wien*), with the dream (*Symphonie fantastique*). This music enacted mythic reconciliations between the rational and the irrational, between order and desire, between society and the individual. While for the nineteenth-century amateur musical works were revelatory tales, for the new amateur they are restorative reminders of his past. So the new amateur listener hears the music of the standard repertoire differently: partly as a dissent from the compositions currently being written and partly as a nostalgic re-creation of the past. Something of its original power is lost.

When playing a piano sonata, for example, even the most superficial of amateur performers needs to attend to a vast amount of detail—the harmonic progressions, the articulation of multiple voices, the shifts in dynamics. When listening to that sonata, the new amateur need not attend to very much at all, because the function of his listening may be mostly mythic rather than artistic. The music can do its work passively. The only element that is given attention is melody.

Indeed, it may be that never before has melody become so important at the expense of harmony or the other elements of music. In the Western tradition, melody and harmony serve nearly opposite functions, with rhythm providing physical energy. Melody is feeling, harmony is law; melody provides expanse, harmony defines limits; melody can be considered an image of the self, harmony an image of society; melody is desire, harmony is order. For the mainstream audience—that is, for the class of new amateur listeners—melody eclipses all other factors. How does that go? has become the fundamental question. Melody is the focus of music-appreciation courses and provides the means by which we recognize and remember music.

The melodies in question are also quite peculiar: when we think of melody we think not of Gregorian chant, Renaissance madrigals, or modal folk songs or tone rows but rather of the themes of Schubert and Verdi, Mahler and Mendelssohn, Wagner and Chopin. The melody focused on is felt as "my" individual voice. The new "melodies" of this century's serious music—in Stravinsky, Bartok, Schoenberg, and more recent figures—have qualities different from the old that make them better suited for the professional musical class: they are cut off from the faith in social institutions and law that traditional harmony seemed to represent, leaving shaky ground for the individual's melodic voice and little context for the grand public dramas nurtured in the last century. So for the large public, traditional melody has become an object of longing. And during the last fifty years or so, such melody has become stylized and self-conscious.

This has been most clear in the development of the popular-music industry, which has attempted to speak directly to the middle class. In the pop industry, nineteenth-century melody became transmuted and transformed for this new public. We can hear the stylized remnants of Chopin, Schubert, and Brahms in the love ballads crooned by Frank Sinatra or Tony Bennett.

Another result of this new popular culture is that melodies become commodities on a scale unimagined in the past. A melody can be called "catchy"—possessing a quality that so captivates a listener that it could not be dismissed. Such a melody is well crafted, tapping a popular sentiment or invoking comforting gestures, eagerly replayed. There were such popular melodies in the past, tunes used and reused in medieval music for example; and Verdi even schemed to keep the theme of "La donna è mobile" top-secret so that it would not become a hit before its time. But with the commercialization of popular culture and the focus upon melody within music, the catchy tune has become a part of commerce. The commercial "jingle," for example, is a melody so catchy yet so unassuming and undemanding that it can easily be linked to a product rather than a person.

Jingles, popular tunes, and show tunes often tap the spirit of nineteenth-century melody, which still hovers somewhere in the background of modern consciousness—melodies that tell of our social origins and speak of our passions. Out of the second movement of Beethoven's *Emperor* Concerto, for example, come the melodic gestures of "There's a Place for Us" in Leonard Bernstein's *West Side Story*; out of Rachmaninoff comes "Full Moon and Empty Arms." But such "popular" creations remain ghosts of their parents. Nearly every hit song and jingle has a limited life; its strength comes from associations that accrue during the heyday of its marketability, not from the profound connections with the listener's own voice that melody had in the past.

Of course, the audiences for popular culture and concert life are now radically separated, but the spirit of melody evident in popular culture also suffuses concert life. Along with the obsessively repeated repertoire of the nineteenth century, its great melodies have taken on a commercial value; they help book concert halls and sell subscription series and recordings. The decline in musical interpretation since 1950 is partly the result of the increase in the commerce of melody. Performers began to lose the context for the singing line, treating music as a product rather than a process. The classical melody in the modern marketplace often seems curiously barren, as if the longing in its line had become dutiful and routine.

Some contemporary composers have responded to contemporary culture and are writing directly for the new amateur listener; their style is sometimes called neoromanticism, but it is more "neo" than "romantic." Melodies often bear a strong resemblance to nineteenth-century melodies or deliberately evoke them. John Corigliano, George Rochberg, and John Adams all pay homage to nineteenth-century gestures; the works of several lesser-known younger composers are still more eclectic, and even a Soviet composer such as Alfred Schnittke has chosen this route to expressive invention.

The overall goals of such composers are complex, but the result, as far as melody is concerned, is a curious stylization. Melody seems to be posing artificially, drawing attention to itself. David del Tredici's enchanting "Alice" theme from his works based upon the Lewis Carroll character (notably *Final Alice*), for example, often seems passed through a looking glass, exaggerated, interrupted, and then indulgently caressed. This ironic treatment of classical melody is similar to the sort of appropriation and exaggeration that take place in punk music or styles of clothing.

We would seem, then, to be living in the twilight of the age of melody, in which the strengths of earlier melodies are invoked to give body to those of today, which in turn exist only to comment on those now past. Like the bulk of contemporary musical life, what exists is a distant image of the last century; and what is promised is never fulfilled. The cause of this situation is not simple, nor is blame to be facilely assigned to the composer, performer, listener, or manager; it represents nothing less than a wholesale transformation of cultural life.

Indeed, the new amateur listener is not at all distressed by this. He can even be quite serious and educated: he becomes a record collector, opera fan, or subscriber to a major municipal music organization. He listens to the twenty-four-hour classical radio stations, surveys the musical feature stories in the newspapers, tunes in to "Live from Lincoln Center," and assiduously tapes broadcasts from the Met. He becomes a highly educated listener, able to discern performances and styles, argue with friends over virtues and failings of this rendition or that of one of the warhorses. He becomes the model listener for "serious" music making. His passion is voracious; music becomes paramount. This has much to do with the powers of music itself, but this passion is also directed toward an accumulation of experience of music and toward the status conferred by such accumulation.

But rarely does even this most serious amateur listener become a player. So his experience of music always lacks the internal knowledge that performance brings, the ways in which physical gestures are reproduced in sound and attentive hearing leads to finely wrought playing. The new amateur remains a listener and thus an ardent consumer in a contemporary musical scene already flooded with commodities.

Meanwhile, the music world continues on the road to ever greater financial successes, building its audiences out of amateur listeners at best, while professional players parade across the stages, endlessly repeating the great music of the past. The concert scene of the last century had more vitality; ours has more professional polish. The concert scene then was the home of virtuosos and showmen and urgent music making; it was the dream of the amateur writ large. The current scene not even an amateur could wish for.

BIBLIOGRAPHY

M. H. Abrams, *Natural Supernaturalism* (1971). Paul Honigsheim, *Music and Society*, K. Peter Etzkorn, ed. (1973). Arthur Loesser, *Men, Women and Pianos* (1954). Charles Rosen, *The Classical Style* (1971). Edward Rothstein, "Why We Live in the Musical Past," in *New York Times*, 11 April 1982; and "Dr. Shaw's Music Lessons," in *New York Review of Books*, 1 April 1982; and "Liberace: The King of Kitsch," in *New Republic*, July 1984. George Bernard Shaw, *Shaw's Music*, Dan H. Laurence, ed., 3 vols. (1981). Virgil Thomson, *The State of Music* (1939), partially reprinted in *A Virgil Thomson Reader* (1981).

The Star Conductor and Musical Virtuosity

Rufus Hallmark

Star: A person of brilliant qualities, who stands out pre-eminently among his fellows.—*Webster's New Collegiate Dictionary*, Merriam-Webster, 1956

An actor, singer, etc., of exceptional celebrity, or one whose name is prominently advertised as a special attraction to the public.—*Oxford English Dictionary*

The history of music is filled with the names of great conductors, but certain figures stand out larger than life. They achieved a prominence among their peers and with succeeding generations that has invested them with a star quality. In every case, the star conductors have been possessed of superior musical talent and artistic insight, but nonmusical factors have also played a role in establishing their stardom. Sometimes an early career opportunity has catapulted them into the public's eye, or the historical moment—musical and otherwise—has proved ideally suited to their particular talents, vision, and ambitions. Occasionally conductors' personalities, avocational interests, and offstage lives have drawn the attention of the media. And it cannot be denied that the bearing and movements of conductors on the podium—whether pertinent to how the musicians play or not—has been a factor in determining their popularity with audiences. In all instances, star conductors have an intense commitment to sharing their musical vision with others, combined with a supreme confidence in their ability to realize that vision. This essay is a survey of the careers and achievements of only a representative sample of star conductors; it makes no attempt at a general history of conducting (for which readers should consult items in the bibliography).

The engagingly different definitions of "star" given above, though not framed by their authors with conductors in mind, draw one into a consideration of the nature of the famous person on the podium. Which better describes the star conductor, Webster's idealistic version or the slightly cynical entry in the O.E.D.? Just what does the conductor do to merit stardom? "He seems to receive a larger share than his orchestra of the audience's applause, though he has not normally played a note. And ... he also receives the largest fees in an age which his kind has replaced all but the most extraordinary sopranos as principal object of public respect and adulation" (Jacobson, 11).

The word *star* for an actor or entertainer first came into use in the late eighteenth century; its application to the musical world soon followed because of the rise of public concerts and of virtuoso instrumental performers and singers. The identification of conductors as stars came later, for conducting as a formally recognized and professional activity arose gradually during the nineteenth century.

The history of conducting is inextricably bound to the evolution of musical institutions, the sociology of music, and the history of musical composition. Before the nineteenth century, the size of an average orchestra, which played for the most part in the large public rooms of royal and aristocratic households or on the floor in front of the stage in small opera theaters, ranged from one dozen to three dozen players. The person in charge of the performance, the *Kapellmeister*, was more often than not a composer and frequently the composer of the music being played. He rehearsed and led the playing from a keyboard instrument placed in the center of the group. In the seventeenth and much of the eighteenth century, the keyboard part, or *continuo*, was an integral part of the music. The use of *continuo* disappeared in the late eighteenth century, and although the composer still sometimes rehearsed from a keyboard, the performance was more and more held together by the first-chair player of the first violins, the concertmaster. The nineteenth-century composer, no longer considered a servant employed to direct a private musical establishment, began to lose intimate touch with the execution of his music for large ensembles. Partly for this reason, composers began to annotate their scores more heavily with performance directions and expression markings so that their wishes would be understood by musicians not under their direct control. To a certain extent, composers worked more abstractly and were no longer conceiving music for players whose strengths in talent and number they knew, but for an ideal orchestra. And the increase of performances in concert halls for paying public audiences created new opportunities, demands, and constraints on the composer. The result of these conditions—and others—was that new orchestral scores frequently called for larger forces in new acoustical circumstances, and the greater difficulty of the new music required more rehearsal. In the absence of the composer, such scores needed an understanding and authoritative musical mind to direct.

This rather mechanistic explanation is only part of the story. Important aesthetic and stylistic changes also set the stage for the conductor's entrance. Whereas the role of *Kapellmeister* had been musically important, his task had been relatively straightforward. He oversaw the performance of music that was almost exclusively of his own day, composed in one of a few clearly defined national styles, and frequently of his own composition. The broad brushstroke and relatively restricted color palette of baroque affectations gave way to the new classical style, with its dynamic (as opposed to static) expressiveness. This meant changes of tempo, more modulation of volume, harmonic complexity, greater variety of melodic and rhythmic gesture—in short, drama. With nineteenth-century romanticism, nationalism, and individualism, these tendencies toward variety, drama, and complexity increased, and musical styles proliferated. Though many orchestras in the early nineteenth century performed with the concertmaster starting the music and occasionally directing with his bow (some, like François Antoine Habeneck's orchestra in Paris, truly excelled), it began to be apparent that this situation was inadequate.

Some composers were hired or self-appointed to assume directorial responsibility. A number of composers in the first half of the nineteenth century established firm reputations as conductors. Among them were Weber, Spontini, and later Wagner, who were known primarily for their opera direction, and Mendelssohn and Berlioz, who achieved reputations as leaders of orchestral concerts. It seems also to have been with these composer-conductors that the baton became a standard accoutrement. Berlioz wrote the first tract on conducting, *L'Art du chef d'orchestre* (1856), as an appendix to his treatise on orchestration. Mendelssohn's case illustrates the rise of the civic orchestra, which is the nature of almost all major symphony orchestras today. He established his reputation as conductor of the already famous Leipzig Gewandhaus Orchestra, which served as a model of artistic standards for many others. As Ewen noted, because of Mendelssohn's work with the Gewandhaus, conductors began to personalize their performances, making them reflect their individual temperament and genius (Ewen, 1936, 79).

Ironically, music criticism, the bane of many a conductor's existence, must be given some credit for describing musical problems that the professional conductor would eventually be in a position to correct. Late-eighteenth- and early-nineteenth-century observers have left testimony to the standards of musical performance of the time (instrumental proficiency, intonation, ensemble playing). Travelers, like Dr. Charles Burney, made comparisons and offered certain ensembles, such as the Mannheim orchestra, as exemplars of fine orchestral playing. Composers who heard the better orchestras knew what was ideally possible, in the same way that they knew what kind of solo music they themselves or virtuosi could play.

Between concertmasters and composer-conductors, on the one hand, and the first professional conductors, on the other, there is no clear distinction in musical education or inherent ability but only in the external circumstances that the newer conductor was generally neither a performing member of the ensemble nor a composer of the music that it played. What perhaps set the conductor apart from the average *Kapellmeister* or concertmaster was his strong sense of conviction about performance standards and repertoire and his directorial authority over programming. What distinguished him from the composer-conductor was his zeal for correct interpretation and flawless performance without the motivation of vested interest in his own music or vicariously vested interest in the music of other composers. There emerges, in fact, an interesting new alignment of loyalty. The *Kapellmeister* had been the servant of his employer; in a figurative sense, the new conductor became the servant of the composer and his music. He was hired not to give music lessons or to compose at his employer's command but to conduct and direct the musical organization.

The professional conductor also became an important means of getting works accepted by the performing musicians and by the public. Orchestral musicians and middle-class audiences, on the whole, have always been notoriously conservative. The conductor inspired and disciplined the orchestra for the performance of new works; in some cases he lectured the audiences about them. Unlike their aristocratic predecessors, the new bourgeois concertgoers were little trained in music, and except for the acquisition of a modest ability on the piano or flute by young ladies, they were not amateur performers. For musical entertainment they heard others perform rather than making music themselves, beyond the simplest or most trivial. They were enthralled by virtuoso soloists like Paganini and the young Liszt, and doted on their orchestral counterpart, the conductor.

Hans von Bülow is considered the first musician to have achieved eminence primarily in the role of conductor. Although von Bülow did compose (Wagner recognized him as a composer), he was neither prolific nor publicly acclaimed for his music; and when he toured Europe and America as a solo piano recitalist in the 1870s, he had already established his reputation as a conductor, specifically of Wagner's opera, in Munich.

In his teens, von Bülow had begun to form his own strong opinions about how music should be played (and conducted) and had, over his mother's objections, set a career in music as his goal. He sought out Liszt and Wagner as teachers. Having gained practical experience in St. Gall and elsewhere, von Bülow was named director of the Bavarian State Opera in Munich, a post he held from 1864 to 1869. There he conducted the premieres of *Tristan und Isolde* and *Die Meistersinger.* These were very difficult works for their day, and the successful performances under von Bülow's direction were regarded as distinct achievements. (His ability to inspire, lead, and discipline the orchestra and singers for the premiere of *Tristan* has been compared with conductor Erich Kleiber's feat of bringing about the first performance of Berg's *Wozzeck* some eighty years later.) From 1880 to 1885, von Bülow conducted the orchestra of the duke of Meiningen, which became the most famous orchestra in Europe under his direction.

What qualities and practices made von Bülow a star conductor? There was first his own discipline. He rehearsed and conducted performances from memory. He said to Richard Strauss, "You must have the score in your head and not your head in the score." He studied music intensely and tirelessly. Imbued with didactic zeal, he explained to his players how each of them fit into the whole and lectured to audiences about the music they were about to hear. He expected his musicians, too, to memorize their music. Autocratic and sharp-tongued, he was not satisfied with a rehearsal until the tiniest detail was correct.

He espoused the music of Wagner and later of Brahms and Richard Strauss, while deriding Verdi and all Italian composers. Von Bülow developed a distinctly personal style of interpretation. An exponent but not a slavish imitator of Wagner, he believed in the expressive use of tempo modification, a flexibility not prescribed in composers' markings but meant to be inferred by the sensitive musician. He also retouched scorings in classical works, as Wagner had done, and became known for his virtuosic baton technique. These practices made him controversial, and observers heard, described, and reacted to him in different ways. Felix

Weingartner, whose essay on conducting was partly a response to von Bülow's style, deplored his tempo modifications, accusing him of starting a fashion for musical sensationalism. Eduard Hanslick charged that his music making lacked sensuousness, and Ferdinand Hiller found it "dull, dry, unimaginative, and unfeeling." On the other hand, others heard in von Bülow's conducting a subtle, spiritual quality of tone reminiscent of Liszt. Bruno Walter, an ardent and eloquent advocate, spoke of von Bülow's "sublime artistic purity." Walter's desire to conduct originated at a concert of the Berlin Philharmonic under von Bülow:

> I saw in Bülow's face the glow of inspiration and the concentration of energy. I felt the compelling force of his gestures, noticed the attention and devotion of the players, and was conscious of the expressiveness and precision of their playing. It became at once clear to me that it was that one man who was producing the music, that he had transformed those hundred performers into his instrument, and that he was playing it as a pianist plays the piano.
>
> (Brook, 209)

The Meiningen Orchestra took unprecedented tours under von Bülow's direction (1880–1885), and in addition to his regular posts, he was frequently called as guest conductor of other orchestras. His fiftieth appearance as guest conductor of the Berlin Philharmonic in the 1891–1892 season received worldwide press coverage.

In summary, von Bülow was ambitious and single-minded in his pursuit of a conducting career. He had some lucky and not altogether accidental breaks (such as the Wagner connection and the *Tristan* premiere) that thrust him into the public's awareness. He had a sense of mission about what he did, from which stemmed his own stern discipline and that which he demanded of others. He fervently desired that his musicians and audiences understand the music. He cultivated idiosyncratic interpretations and an impressive manner on the podium (with baton and without score). He devoted himself to a particular repertoire. He was held in either high or low regard, the former approaching wonder and worship. He placed himself and his orchestras frequently and widely before the public.

Many of von Bülow's traits are characteristic of subsequent star conductors, and quality of interpretation is one of the chief factors distinguishing eminent conductors: "Conducting had grown [by the late nineteenth century] far beyond the confines of mere technical skill and had developed what might well be called a virtuosity of its own. At this stage, the personality of a conductor, the individuality of his readings, and his own interpretation of the music he directed, began to count for more than technical correctness" (Seltzer, 97). Weingartner's criticism of von Bülow's tempo modifications calls attention to an interpretive distinction among conductors that has been made ever since. Although not always apt or helpful—or easily made—the distinction nevertheless identifies issues about musical interpretation pertinent to an investigation of star conductors: it is that between strict and free (or between objective and subjective) interpretation. The strict or "purist" conductor has the orchestra play the music exactly as written; the subjective conductor takes liberties and can become the object of adoration (or scorn) for what is regarded as his individual conception of the music. The former can similarly be applauded (or derided) for what is considered fidelity to the composer's intentions.

Ever since Wagner first addressed the matter in "On Conducting" (1869), a major issue for conductors has been the nature of tempo. Wagner devoted a large section of his treatise to the question of finding the correct tempo for a movement and its parts. He deplored what he considered insensitively fast performances and in this regard was critical of Mendelssohn, to name only the best-known object of his criticism. In addition, Wagner argued for an elasticity of the beat within the movement, slowing an *allegro* movement, for example, for the entrance of a *cantabile* theme. Such *tempo rubato* was not unknown in solo literature, but it was unheard of in orchestral music, where the musical ensemble depended on the regularity of the established beat and on occasional motions of the concertmaster. Begging the aesthetic question, the use of tempo modification enhances the conductor's apparent role, for it gives him a palpable control over the music that is conceived and realized by him alone. It invests him with one of the powers of the virtuoso soloist and provides one of the most apparent bases for the metaphor so beloved by the conductor—that the orchestra is an instrument on which he plays.

It is important to recognize that Wagner stressed subtlety; the changes of tempo that he recommended were to be made almost imperceptibly. Later adherents often tended to broaden this effect and turn it into a mannerism; this is apparently what von Bülow did on occasion. Early opponents, accustomed to the unaltered tempos of an earlier style, understandably decried tempo modification as a distortion. Again putting purely musical judgment aside, the steady tempo of tradition was for conductors wishing to make their mark an open invitation to introduce variation. When the orchestral *tempo rubato* had become widely accepted, it in turn provided the opportunity for younger conductors, such as Toscanini, to "purify" practice by eliminating it. We can trace the lineage of the heavy-handed interpreters, such as Wagner, Nikisch, Richter, and Furtwängler, and of the light-handed interpreters, such as Mendelssohn, Weingartner, Toscanini, and Szell. The question of tempo, as only one representative issue, remains controversial; and while each conductor will claim that he reaches his decisions on purely musical grounds, it is undeniable that controversy leads to notoriety, a step on the road to stardom.

The public image of the conductor came almost inevitably to play a major role in his career. His appearance, dress, and bearing could be a crowd-pleasing factor. Von Bülow did not cut a fine figure, but photographs and contemporary accounts show Artur Nikisch as a strikingly handsome man, always carefully coiffed and elegantly attired. He is said to have practically mesmerized his orchestra and audience with his eyes and gestures. His movements were not in the least flamboyant but, on the contrary, quiet and restrained. Tchaikovsky once described him as a "wonderful master" and commented that his manner was "sparing of superfluous movements, and yet so extraordinarily commanding, powerful, full of self-control" (Schonberg, 212). Though Wagner, under whom young Nikisch had played, may have originated the subtler guidance of the baton with wrist and fingers, instead of using only arm motion, it was Nikisch who popularized the technique. Adrian Boult said that Nikisch "made his stick say more than any other conductor" (Schonberg, 212). He also pioneered the use of the left hand for cueing entrances, indicating dynamics, and giving expressive directions.

Nikisch excelled in the romantic repertoire, especially Bruckner, Wagner, and Tchaikovsky, although he did not promote contemporary music. His persistent use of tempo fluctuation and melodic sentimentality were perhaps out of place in the classic repertoire. (One can hear the very perceptible slackening of tempo at the entrance of the second theme in the Nikisch recording of Beethoven's Fifth Symphony.) Nikisch directly influenced Furtwängler, who succeeded him in Leipzig and Berlin, and Boult, who was inspired by Nikisch's example to take up conducting. Both Stokowski and Koussevitzky were also deeply impressed by Nikisch.

Choice of repertoire, in addition to innate ability, training, personal magnetism, and interpretive skill, defines a conductor. Many nineteenth-century conductors—Wagner prominent among them—made their interpretive points (in their writings as well as their performances) with Beethoven's symphonies. Beginning with Habeneck's concerts in Paris and Otto Nicolai's in Vienna, these nine symphonies became the staples of the orchestral repertoire and the touchstones of a conductor's ability. The retention of true masterworks in performance would in itself be laudable, had not the tendency to plan retrospective orchestral concerts grown disproportionately.

Concert programs in the early nineteenth century comprised mainly contemporary works; special concerts were set apart for the creations of a bygone era, such as Mendelssohn's famous revival in 1829 of Bach's *St. Matthew Passion*. By midcentury, while there was still a preponderance of new and recent works, older pieces continued to be played and were taking a larger place on the program. By the turn of the century, the notion of a "standard repertoire" of "classics" was being formed, partly defined in contradistinction to the newer, more difficult music that was failing to find a place regularly in orchestral concerts. After their premieres, few modern works received repeated performances. Today it is new works that are rare. Programs of most orchestras consist almost entirely of works from the standard repertoire plus a handful of early-twentieth-century works that have found acceptance.

Today's orchestras are museums of musical art; conductors are the curators. Audiences seem eager to hear different conductors' interpretations of the same standard repertoire and are generally reluctant to listen to new music. Orchestral boards, mindful of budgetary concerns and ticket sales, adjust to this situation and encourage, if not require, artistic directors to cater to audiences' tastes. Recording companies delight in one new boxed set of Beethoven symphonies after another, confident that the star conductors' interpretations of the standard works, graced with the latest technical improvements in recording technique, will sell their products. The modern conductor who conducts the same Beethoven symphony in his regular season, on tour, in guest appearances with other orchestras, and in summer festivals has an easier time of it than the conductor who programs different works for each such engagement. One of the marks of many great conductors—though it may detract from their stardom—is a consistent commitment to the performance of new music.

The Germanic tradition in conducting has on balance produced the greatest international stars, but stars of other countries have achieved international recognition. After Berlioz, Édouard Colonne and Charles Lamoureux were the most outstanding French conductors. Both founded concert series and achieved notable results with their orchestras, which they handled in an autocratic manner. Colonne championed the new music of Massenet, Lalo, Franck, and Saint-Saëns, and also programmed Berlioz; Lamoureux was better known for his conducting of Wagner and for his performances of the *St. Matthew Passion* and Handel's *Judas Maccabaeus* and *Messiah*. Saint-Saëns considered Lamoureux "more precise; he is colder. Colonne is more elastic, more inspired" (Schonberg, 200).

Of the next generation of French conductors, Pierre Monteux

achieved the greatest international stature. Indicative of the affection and fascination he inspired the public curiosity as to whether his coal-black hair, as contrasted with his white mustache, was dyed. (Good-natured Monteux invited anyone to test his hair color.) Monteux directed the orchestra for Diaghilev's Ballet Russe, including the premieres of Stravinsky's *Petrouchka* and *Rossignol*, Ravel's *Daphnis et Chloë*, and Debussy's *Jeux*. From 1920 to 1924 he was music director of the Boston Symphony, where he introduced new works by Stravinsky, Honegger, Respighi, and Vaughan Williams. He conducted the San Francisco Symphony Orchestra (1936–1952). He subsequently made guest appearances (including many with the Boston Symphony) and was principal conductor of the London Symphony Orchestra from 1961 until his death in 1964. Musicians enjoyed Monteux; he was easygoing and made no enemies. His beat was precise, and he stood almost motionless on the podium. Stravinsky once remarked that of all the conductors he knew, Monteux was "the least interested in calisthenic exhibition for the entertainment of the audience" (Schonberg, 329). He never created the excitement and public interest of Toscanini or Stokowski.

Other notable conductors in the French tradition on the international scene have been the Alsatian Charles Munch and the Swiss Ernest Ansermet. Munch studied under Furtwängler at the Leipzig Gewandhaus and later served as concertmaster there. He conducted the Paris Conservatoire Orchestra and followed Koussevitzky as director of the Boston Symphony (1949–1962). Ansermet, a longtime friend and associate of Stravinsky and conductor of many premieres of his works, was relatively unknown internationally until after World War II. Much of his fame rests on his recorded interpretations of Stravinsky and modern French composers, and much of his notoriety on his outspoken criticism of twelve-tone music.

In England, the nineteenth-century conducting scene was dominated by foreigners. Michael Costa, an Italian singer who went to England in 1829, became keyboard player at the King's Theatre in London in 1830 and assumed orchestral direction there in 1833. He instilled the musicians with strict discipline and turned the orchestra into a professional group. He subsequently conducted the Philharmonic Society Concerts and the Birmingham Festival. He won the respect of Mendelssohn and Rossini, and George Bernard Shaw considered him the only conductor in England before Hans Richter. He was known to conduct rather metronomically, fast, and pedantically, and to retouch scores egregiously; for example, he added ophicleide, piccolo, bass drum, and cymbals to *Don Giovanni*.

Exceeding Costa in outrageous practices and a prototype of extreme showmanship was Louis Antoine Jullien. Born and trained in France, Jullien made his career in England, where he was active from 1840 to 1859. While Jullien does not rank among the great conductors as a musician, he merits a place in the development of conductors' stardom. It is said that Jullien in England, Johann Strauss in Vienna, and Philippe Musard in Paris were the first conductors who drew audiences to see them, regardless of the music. As conductor of the Promenade Concerts, Jullien attracted a

> huge, devoted audience; ... won by a fine orchestra and choir, skilled programme building and, above all, by his combination of brilliant showmanship, blatant sensationalism and genuine musicianship. ... Elegantly eccentric, with splendid moustaches and luxuriant black hair, he had a gilt armchair behind him on the podium, and into this he would sink exhausted after acknowledging the applause. At the climax of any work he would seize a violin, or perhaps a piccolo, and play with the orchestra.
>
> (Raynor, 103)

Jullien gradually introduced more serious works into the repertoire, beginning with short excerpted movements and opera arias and later moving to whole symphonies. Even then he could not resist a touch of the sensational, such as rattling a tin box of dried peas to imitate hailstones during the storm section of Beethoven's *Pastoral* Symphony or reverently using a jeweled baton when conducting any of that composer's works. Jullien also delighted in using oversized and unique instruments, such as the colossal fifteen-foot octobass. His escapades were far removed from the world of serious conducting, but his showmanship, if excessive, was not so distinct in kind from that of other notable conductors such as Stokowski.

Though German-born Charles Hallé and his namesake orchestra in Manchester came to rival the London Philharmonic, it was the latter under Hallé's compatriot Hans Richter that outshone other English orchestras of the time. Richter had achieved his reputation in association with Wagner. (Many turn-of-the-century conductors were quite accomplished, but none made the same international impact as those who had worked with Wagner, including Hermann Levi, Felix Mottl, and Anton Seidl.) Though musically and technically deficient—Wagner admitted as much—Richter nevertheless could stir an audience. After he conducted the first Bayreuth Festival in 1876, he was catapulted to fame and was in demand in Vienna and London: "Hans Richter became in London something of a legendary figure, and his name inspired myth and adulation. The conductor-idol was now an institution in {English} musical life" (Ewen, 1936, 121).

Undoubtedly the best-known native-born star among English con-ductors was Sir Thomas Beecham. Born into a wealthy family (makers of Beecham's Pills), he was able to hire his own orchestras and halls. He was witty and urbane, and many anecdotes relate his comical and sometimes scathing remarks in rehearsals. He founded the Beecham Symphony Orchestra in 1909 and programmed Berlioz and Vaughan Williams on the first concert. He continued to conduct these composers and new Brit-ish, French, and Russian music. Beecham was a universal musician, with catholicity of taste in repertoire (with the exception of expressionism and atonality). He conducted the Prom Concerts during World War I (and excluded German music) and insisted on native English singers in his opera productions. During the 1920s he was a guest conductor. In 1932 he was instrumental in forming the London Philharmonic Orchestra. He was by then a leading conductor, and his peppery comments on a wide variety of subjects frequently found their way into the press. During World War II he conducted in the United States. In 1946 he created the Royal Philharmonic, with which he toured abroad and made numerous recordings.

Beecham had no conventional baton technique or poise on the podium. His gyrations included crouching, standing with one knee crooked, and leaning over worryingly near the edge of the podium. Yet he got amazing results and created the first topnotch, well-disciplined English orchestras. Beecham was heavily influenced by the German atti-tude toward flexibility of interpretation, but it was combined with his innate sense of proportion and decorum, precluding excess. He was a romantic who believed that Richard Strauss and Delius were the last great composers. He was totally unsympathetic to musicological authenticity in the performance of baroque music: "No conductor in English history came near the fame, prestige, popularity and controversial quality of Sir Thomas Beecham. His was virtually a household name all over the world" (Schonberg, 290). No other British conductors of the first half of the twentieth century, including John Barbirolli, Adrian Boult, and Malcolm Sargent, equaled his star status.

In America, which lacked Europe's cultural traditions and aristocracy, appealing conductors and programs of popular music were the drawing card. It is no surprise that when Jullien toured America his eccentricities assured his success. The conductor in America had to attract an audience and win it to the music he wanted to conduct. (A latter-day incarnation of Jullien-type concerts is the Boston Pops, strongly identified with Arthur Fiedler, who conducted it for fifty years and became a star in his own right.)

As a shaping force in the history of music in America, Theodore Thomas deserves admission to a gallery of star conductors. Born in Germany, he moved to New York City with his family when he was ten. Convinced that music is a necessity, not a luxury, he set out with evangelistic zeal to cultivate good musical habits among American audiences. He began conducting in 1859 and founded his own orchestra in 1864. In addition to his regular concerts, Thomas also offered popular concerts in Central Park Gardens. Like Jullien, he insinuated more serious music into basically trivial programs—at first an occasional overture, by 1870 complete symphonies, and in 1872 an all-Wagner program. Thomas and his orchestra made famous tours of the United States and Canada. Thomas was director of the New York Philharmonic from 1877 until 1891; he then founded the Chicago Symphony, which he conducted until his death. In both cities Thomas created professional orchestras that compared favorably with the best in Europe. Fierce and autocratic, and an unswerving programmer of good music, he endured hostile audiences and critics. On balance, it may fairly be said that Thomas had elevated American musical taste and made the public receptive to symphony concerts.

American orchestras have been dominated by foreign-born conductors mainly in the Austro-German tradition since their beginnings, with conductors like Leopold Damrosch, Mahler, and Mengelberg (New York Philharmonic); Gericke, Max Fiedler, Karl Muck, Nikisch, Leinsdorf, and Steinberg (Boston Symphony); Frederick Stock and Fritz Reiner (Chicago Symphony); Scheel and Ormandy (Philadelphia Symphony). But other cultures have also been represented: the Frenchmen Monteux and Munch (Boston), the Greek Mitropoulos (New York), the Russian Koussevitzky (Boston), the Italian Toscanini (New York). For conductors, as for other European immigrants, America was a land of opportunity. Political concerns such as Nazism, as well as the positive lures of better orchestras and more authority, drew many conductors to its shores. As Henry Raynor wrote:

American orchestras have been unmistakably American since the end of the first World War, with a brilliance that is strictly national and a virtuoso quality that European orchestras have rarely tried to achieve. This style is in part the gift of conductors, for until after the second World War any major American orchestra looked for a conductor who, having won a great European, preferably German, reputation, was given a degree of authority uncurbed, as conductorial tyranny is normally curbed in Europe, by a variety of imponderables of custom and orchestral tradition; nowhere else had a conductor had so free a hand to make what he wished of an orchestra, so long as he was supported by the committee which manages the orchestra's business affairs, and the adherence of the orchestra, as he had in the United States.

(pp. 180–181)

Three European-American conductors stand out as stars in the first half of the twentieth century: Arturo Toscanini, Leopold Stokowski, and Serge Koussevitzky. Harold Schonberg calls them "the conducting heroes of the American musical scene in the decades from the mid-twenties to the late forties" (p. 309). By virtue of their personality, authority, musicianship, popularity, and influence, these men stood apart from other conductors. Each in his own way set standards for conducting and established himself as a star. Toscanini was the musical purist; Koussevitzky, the most irascible; and Stokowski, the greatest showman. All were worshiped by the public, which they, aided by modern technology and media, greatly increased: "The intensely competitive organisation of American music, especially of its orchestras, insisted always on the finest performers directed by the most spectacular conductors.... In America a conductor had to be flamboyant, romantic, eloquent, extravagant in one way or another; he had to dominate not only an orchestra but also its audience" (Raynor, 174).

Many Americans who never entered a concert hall came to know Arturo Toscanini from his radio broadcasts with the NBC Symphony and from recordings of those broadcasts issued later by RCA. Toscanini retired in 1954 (at the age of eighty-seven) as conductor of the NBC Symphony, which he had led since 1937. Prior to that he had conducted the Metropolitan Opera (1908–1915), the La Scala Opera (1898–1929), and the New York Philharmonic (1926–1936). His conducting career began at age nineteen in Brazil, in a dramatic way. He was a cellist in a touring Italian opera troupe. On the day of a performance of *Aida,* the conductor resigned. Toscanini's fellow players knew how absorbed the young cellist was in the music of Verdi, and they proposed him as an impromptu substitute. Toscanini knew the score from memory and mounted the podium without music, confidently leading an impressive performance. Success and notoriety followed him ever after.

Toscanini was one of the very few Italian conductors until recently to have gained an international reputation. Many Italian conductors seemed to have limited their vision to their native opera repertoire, but as conductor of the La Scala Opera Orchestra concerts (1896), Toscanini programmed much German and Russian music. He was the first non-German conductor to conduct Wagner at Bayreuth (1930). Regardless of varying appraisals, Toscanini's versatility with a variety of music and styles is undeniable.

Opinions differ with regard to Toscanini's involvement with contemporary music. In 1936, David Ewen described him as "volcanic" in his conducting of modern music; a decade or so later, the composer and critic Virgil Thomson disparaged Toscanini's lack of commitment to contemporary music. The truth lies somewhere in the middle; Toscanini gradually conducted less new music, though he had earlier been a firm supporter of the then new Puccini and Debussy.

Toscanini was revolutionary in his musical objectivity. He insisted that a score be stripped of its overlay of romantic performance practices (such as *tempo rubato* and string glissandos). He demanded clear textures, unretouched orchestration, and consistent tempos (generally faster than those of romantic conductors). George Szell said that Toscanini "wiped out the arbitrariness of the postromantic interpreters. He did away with the meretricious tricks and the thick encrustation of the interpretive nuances that had been piling up for decades" (Schonberg, 252). Toscanini's related impatience with programmatic interpretations of music is exemplified in his well-known remark about Beethoven's *Eroica* Symphony: "Some say this is Napoleon, some Hitler, some Mussolini. For me it is simply *allegro con brio*" (Schonberg, 254). Detractors say that Toscanini's performances were metronomical, denying any spontaneity and expression on the part of the players with his rigidity. If Toscanini's purism was an extreme, it served to temper the excesses of a previous age and to establish a healthy model for a generation of younger conductors.

Gifted with a prodigious memory, Toscanini knew not only hundreds of scores by heart but also detailed expression markings of different editions. He possessed an extremely keen ear: when balancing an orchestra to bring out what he considered the important notes from the texture, he instantly knew when a player or section was not playing as he wished. Although capable of displaying his temper, he withheld his severest criticism for himself; he could not enjoy the applause if he considered the performance less than perfect.

In rehearsal Toscanini went through the entire score meticulously. Spot-checking problem points was not enough, for he believed "in every performance a work must be reborn" (Ewen, 1936, 193). He would drill particular passages until they were played exactly as he wanted them. He was capable in rehearsal of verbal and physical histrionics to coax what he wanted from his players. In performances, his gestures were more restrained, and it is claimed that "a peculiar characteristic of his genius" was "his profound unawareness of the audience" (Brook, 163). Stokowski said that Toscanini's beat was amazingly clear and that he created perfect ensemble with the orchestra. Musicians felt privileged to play under him; it is said that for Toscanini musicians took their parts home and practiced. The New York Philharmonic developed a heretofore unknown discipline under Toscanini's direction.

Leopold Stokowski is probably best known for his participation in the Walt Disney film *Fantasia,* for which he conducted an array of orchestral music (including his arrangement of Bach's Toccata and Fugue in D Minor) and in which his silhouetted figure shakes hands with Mickey Mouse. A showman who was perfectly comfortable with such an unprecedented collaboration, Stokowski was also an outstanding musician. As conductor of the Philadelphia Orchestra from 1912 to 1936, he whipped it into "one of the most brilliant groups that had ever existed, a marvel for its color, precision, power and virtuosity" (Schonberg, 314). Stokowski was also a champion of modern music.

Stokowski was born in England to an Irish mother and Polish father whose name had been anglicized to "Stokes." He was deeply impressed by the elegant and romantic figure of Artur Nikisch and decided to invest himself with glamour by affecting a Polish accent. Thus his showmanship began. He had a sound musical education at the Royal College of Music, went to the United States in 1905, and became organist at Saint Bartholomew's Episcopal Church in New York City. He made his conducting debuts in Paris (1908) and London (1909). He impressed a representative of the recently founded Cincinnati Symphony Orchestra and was invited to become its conductor. After three seasons (1909–1912), he was called to the Philadelphia Orchestra, where he remained until 1936. He then conducted a succession of orchestras, including the All-American Youth Orchestra, the New York Symphony Orchestra, the Hollywood Bowl Symphony Orchestra, the Houston Symphony, and the American Symphony Orchestra, the first and last of which he founded. Stokowski brought a "new kind of glamour" to the Cincinnati Orchestra and at the same time "a new set of instrumental standards" (Schonberg, 309). He raised the Philadelphia Orchestra from provincial status to an orchestra of international consequence.

In addition to other musical values and issues, Stokowski was perhaps most interested in the sheer sound of the orchestra. With the Philadelphia Orchestra, Stokowski developed what came to be known as the

"Philadelphia sound," a sonority based on a rich string section and on exaggerated dynamics and tempos, and affected by some "retouching" of scores. In the latter regard, Stokowski was the opposite of Toscanini and took great liberties with orchestrations. Early in his career he was known for "Stokowski-izing" composers he conducted and reputedly said, "You must realize that Beethoven and Brahms did not understand instruments" (Schonberg, 313). Stokowski also experimented with different seating arrangements of the orchestra in order to achieve what he considered the optimal balance and projection of sound to the audience.

His interest in sound also led him early in his career to investigate recording. From 1917, when he conducted a recording with the Philadelphia Orchestra, he was deeply interested in, and committed to, the improvement of recorded sound. He even authorized Bell Laboratories to set up a lab underneath the stage in order to study orchestral sound and recording techniques.

One of Stokowski's most praiseworthy accomplishments is his consistent support of new music. It is estimated that by 1971 he had conducted two thousand premieres. His modern repertoire in Philadelphia included Stravinsky, Schoenberg, Berg, Shostakovich, Bartók, Vaughan Williams, Hindemith, and Varèse. He held regular Wednesday-morning readings of new works. Because of his insistence on the inclusion of modern music, the Philadelphia orchestra suffered financial difficulties in his early years there and survived only through the generosity of an anonymous benefactor. Throughout his career Stokowski conducted numerous first performances, the most illustrious of which were the American premieres of Wozzeck, The Rite of Spring, and Mahler's Eighth Symphony, and—in 1965 with the American Symphony Orchestra—the world premiere of Charles Ives's Fourth Symphony. For the last, Stokowski is especially praised for his thorough understanding and excellent musical performance, which "served to give universal sanction to the work of Charles Ives" (Wooldridge, 136).

In what did Stokowski's special glamour consist? As a musician inspired by Nikisch, he gave "romantically passionate readings" (Ewen, 1936, 198). He re-created Bach keyboard works in his own orchestral image. He subscribed to many nineteenth-century practices such as exaggerated dynamics and fluctuating tempos. He impressed his listeners with the beautiful sonority of his orchestra. David Ewen recognized Stokowski's musical genius, but gave this characterization of Stokowski in the 1930s: "To become an almost legendary figure, ... to be spoken of everywhere with awe and reverence, to inspire obedience and terror in [others], to be literally worshipped by an audience, ... to be always a fresh topic for discussion, controversy and conversation, to be front-page news ... for this it is infinitely more essential to be an impressive personality than an outstanding musician" (Ewen, 1936, 201–202).

How did Stokowski create this impression? Among other things, through his striking appearance, with his trim figure, mane of hair, distinctive profile topped by a prominent brow, and delicately expressive hands. Stokowski was the first American conductor (he was naturalized in 1915) to conduct without a baton or score. He was not above enhancing his appearance by having the lights dimmed and his head and hands spotlighted. The slightly rotund Pierre Monteux bitterly resented Stokowski's greater popularity, deriding Americans' desire for a "tailor-model" as a conductor (Ewen, 1936, 199). Stokowski lectured to his audiences on the music they were about to hear and would occasionally chastise them for their rudeness. He experimented with the clavilux, a device that displayed colors on the walls of the concert hall while the orchestra performed. Besides *Fantasia*, Stokowski appeared in other films, occasionally speaking as well as conducting. He tried to suppress his birth date and enjoyed the controversy surrounding his real name. It is indicative of the public interest in such extraneous matters that the *New York Times* dispatched a reporter to investigate and write an article about his age, parentage, and name.

Musicians, intellectuals, and scholars have generally scorned Stokowski for his falsification of fact, platitudinous remarks about music, and manhandling of musical scores (such as making huge cuts in Beethoven symphonies). His emphasis on details sometimes resulted in his failure to make a dramatic whole of a work. Though these weaknesses may deny Stokowski a place among the truly great conductors, they contributed to his stardom. With his showmanship and musical verve, Stokowski helped to build a broad, modern audience for the orchestral repertoire, including twentieth-century music. And his recordings constitute one of our largest legacies of recorded sound.

Serge Koussevitzky may not have been the virtuosic conductor that Toscanini or Stokowski was, but he made important contributions on many fronts besides that of conductor: as a music publisher, a commissioner of new compositions, and the founder of Tanglewood, one of America's most important summer music centers. And in his own way, he was a star, idolized by his audiences.

Koussevitzky was born and trained in Russia, where he became a virtuoso player on the double bass. At his conducting debut with the Berlin Philharmonic in 1908 he was hailed by the press as "the Russian Nikisch," a conductor he intensely admired. He married into a wealthy family, and his father-in-law and wife financed his early career. He founded the publishing house Éditions Russes de Musique, which published Stravinsky, Prokofiev, Rachmaninov, and Scriabin. He created his own orchestra, toured, and commissioned works. It was for Koussevitzky that Ravel orchestrated Mussorgsky's *Pictures at an Exhibition.* In 1924, Koussevitzky went to the United States as conductor of the Boston Symphony Orchestra, a post he held until 1949, the longest tenure of any conductor of that orchestra. He had a lifelong interest in modern American music and conducted the works of Copland, Barber, Hanson, Harris, Piston, and William Schuman. For the fiftieth anniversary of the Boston Symphony (1931) he commissioned a number of works, including Stravinsky's *Symphony of Psalms,* Hindemith's *Konzertmusik* for brass and strings, Ravel's Piano Concerto in G, and works by Copland, Gershwin, Prokofiev, and Roussel. He established the Berkshire Music Center and the Tanglewood Concerts in 1940; there he counted among his conducting students Leonard Bernstein. After the death of his wife, he set up the Koussevitzky Foundation in her memory to commission new works; the foundation's first operatic commission was Britten's *Peter Grimes.*

Flamboyant and egocentric, Koussevitzky wore a cape, which he removed with a flourish when he arrived at rehearsals. He used his body as well as his arms and hands to conduct. In addition to late-romantic and modern music, he conducted the standard orchestral repertoire but treated the classics in an unorthodox way; he "illuminated familiar works in an unfamiliar manner" (Brook, 105). He never lost his heavy Russian accent, and his English was spiced with malapropisms. He was famous for his rages and feuds (and tender reconciliations); a Boston Symphony member described Koussevitzky as "the best-hated conductor we ever had to play under" (Wooldridge, 147).

The case of Koussevitzky raises the question whether a great conductor brings fame to an orchestra or vice versa. There is disagreement over how important Koussevitzky was in his capacity as conductor of the Boston Symphony, in comparison with his other institutional involvements with commissions, programming of American works, and Tanglewood. Many believe that Koussevitzky would not have amounted to much as a conductor had his predecessor, Monteux, not prepared the orchestra for him. At first, its members did not like Koussevitzky. They thought he was a bluffer, and indeed, he did make mistakes. He was a poor score reader and required someone (often the composer) to play through a new score at the piano repeatedly until Koussevitzky learned it. Some think that the superior esprit and ensemble of the Boston Symphony was due to the musicians' need to achieve cohesiveness by themselves in the years before Koussevitzky gained firm control. Gradually he won the orchestra over and molded it to his ideals. He was jealous of other conductors who directed his orchestra, wanting it to play only his way; the Boston Symphony seldom had guests during his regime. In the opinion of some, the Boston Symphony became the greatest orchestra in the world under Koussevitzky.

At the same time in Europe, an entire generation of conductors was active, including many who, like Toscanini and Koussevitzky, eventually brought the eminence they had achieved in Europe to head major orchestras or guest-conduct in America. Among those in the Austro-German tradition were Karl Böhm, Fritz Busch, Otto Klemperer, Erich Kleiber, Clemens Krauss, Erich Leinsdorf, Willem Mengelberg, Eugene Ormandy, Fritz Reiner, Artur Rodzinski, Georg Solti, George Szell, Bruno Walter, and Felix Weingartner. None of these names, however, is as electrifying as that of Wilhelm Furtwängler. Both a throwback and a visionary, Furtwängler was a controversial but almost universally admired musician, and often vilified on account of his much-debated position in Nazi Germany.

After a conventional apprenticeship at four opera theaters, Furtwängler was director of the Lübeck Opera (1911–1915), of the Mannheim Opera (1915–1920), and then of the Berlin State Opera symphony concerts (1920–1922). He emerged as the leading young German conductor and succeeded Nikisch as director of both the Berlin Philharmonic and the Leipzig Gewandhaus orchestras in 1922. He remained with the Berlin Philharmonic until his death in 1954. He toured annually with the Berlin orchestra and made guest appearances abroad, including concerts in the mid-1920s with the New York Philharmonic and the Royal Philharmonic in London. He also was conductor of the Vienna Philharmonic in 1927–1930 and returned regularly thereafter.

With the advent of Nazism, Furtwängler continued at his posts, never expecting conditions would become as bad as they did. In 1933, witnessing the repressive measures of the Third Reich, he wrote an open letter to Goebbels arguing for the neutrality of art and of the artist in political considerations. The letter was tolerated by the Nazis, and Furtwängler succeeded in delaying the removal of many Jewish musicians from the Berlin Philharmonic. He protested in other ways, too, refusing to give the Nazi salute or to conduct in occupied countries. But in 1934 there was a showdown. Furtwängler was preparing a production of Hindemith's opera *Mathis der Maler* when Hitler banned Hindemith's music. It is not clear whether Furtwängler resigned in protest or was dismissed. Further-

more, one is not sure whether the authorities had asked him to recon-
sider his resignation or whether he was allowed to return four months
later by becoming somehow reconciled to the Nazi regime (as the government claimed). Furtwängler could have left Germany, as many non-
Jewish as well as Jewish musicians did, but he chose to stay. Many urged
him to remain (including Schoenberg) in order to be a symbol of German musical culture. In any case, even after he was cleared of any Nazi
offenses in 1946, his equivocal position hounded him. Successful vilifi-
cation campaigns in America prevented him from becoming conductor
of the New York Philharmonic in 1936 and of the Chicago Symphony
in 1949, and Furtwängler never again conducted in the United States.

Furtwängler had a remarkable and effective, but neither conventional
nor pleasing, conducting manner. He was tall and gangly (one German
critic likened him to a stalk of asparagus), and his gestures were inimitable and, to those unfamiliar with them, indecipherable: "Furtwängler's
beat was a phenomenon unduplicated before or since: a horror, a nightmare, to musicians.... He would gesticulate, shout, sing, make faces, spit,
stamp. Or he would close his eyes and make vague motions. Until orchestras worked with him and got used to that curious, quivering, trembling
baton they could be in a complete mess" (Schonberg, 272). According to
Donald Brook, "During brisk crescendoes he staggers ecstatically from
back to front of the rostrum with a tremor of hands.... The stick waves
so frantically that...it is not seen any more" (p. 74). But there was
method to Furtwängler's madness, and the impression that he was
untrained in technique is erroneous. Furtwängler intentionally avoided
standardized conducting patterns, which he felt led to precision but
nothing else. He deliberately cultivated an imprecise beat because he
wanted to avoid sounding the beat and the bar lines, seeking instead to
bring out the larger units of phrase and section. He wrote that the preparation of the beat was more important than the beat itself, that professional musicians did not need to rely on a conductor to beat time. He
was aware that onlookers were puzzled by his conducting, but he also
knew that musicians could come to understand him and in fact play with
great precision and ensemble.

In his aesthetic, Furtwängler continued the Wagnerian tradition of
looking for the long line, or *melos*, of the music. He studied for many
years with the theorist Heinrich Schenker and, like his mentor, was interested in discovering the inner plan of a composition. To articulate that
structure, Furtwängler, like others of the Wagnerian school, used tempo
modification and even unwritten pauses. But the music he conducted
never sounded disjointed. Fritz Sedlak, who played under him in the

Vienna Philharmonic, said that Furtwängler was "a master of transitions" and that he "worked ... to unite tempo changes within a movement with the smoothness that prevented the dissolution of the movement's structure" (Schonberg, 271).

Like Nikisch, Furtwängler mesmerized his orchestras and his audiences. He seemed to radiate a mystical comprehension of, and communion with, the music. He excelled in and conducted principally the German classics, especially Beethoven and Wagner, but he also performed non-German music (Tchaikovsky, Berlioz, Debussy, Sibelius) and modern repertoire (Schoenberg, Stravinsky, Bartók). Furtwängler demanded the utmost concentration from musicians. He wrung tremendous tone and color from the orchestra, in part by improving the playing in the cello and double bass sections and introducing continuous vibrato into sectional string playing. In the final analysis, Furtwängler's interpretations of preromantic music were anachronistic, and the modern aesthetic of objectivism, associated with Toscanini, held sway. Yet Furtwängler will remain beside Toscanini as one of the greatest conductors of his era.

There can be little debate that two conductors rival each other today as superstars: Herbert von Karajan and Leonard Bernstein. Each has a commanding podium presence, a multifaceted intellect, a romantically handsome figure, and a glamorous personality. Both received attention as conductors at an early age, have been covered doggedly by the media, and have taken great advantage of modern audio and video technology for the realization of their conductorial and musical visions.

The Austrian-born (1908) Herbert von Karajan has been called the "Generalmusikdirektor der Welt" because of his "empire" of musical enterprises. He has the unique status of holding a lifetime contract with a world-class orchestra, the Berlin Philharmonic. Possessed with a compulsion for perfection and a voracious appetite for overseeing every detail of his musical projects, Karajan has exercised more influence on conducting than anyone since Toscanini.

Karajan's career can be divided into two parts, separated by the end of World War II. He began conducting professionally in 1929 in Ulm, where he apprenticed for five years as director of the opera orchestra. He was fired from that position, his superior later claiming that he recognized the young conductor's great talent and did not want him to get stuck in Ulm. Karajan's next appointment began a period of political favoritism and ostracism and professional jealousy and rivalry. In 1934, he found a position as assistant conductor in Aachen. He learned that in order to be hired he would have to join the Nazi party. In consequence, he unwittingly became a pawn in a power struggle between Goering, who favored Karajan, and Goebbels, who favored Furtwängler. Throughout the Nazi period, Karajan suffered the disdain and antagonism of Furtwängler and occasionally of Hitler. When Furtwängler fell into disfavor with the Nazis for his support of Jewish musicians and Karajan was released from the military draft through Goering's influence, the older conductor's resentment increased. Despite these problems, Karajan continued to build a strong reputation for himself. During his seven years at Aachen good fortune smiled three times. To prevent his being lured away by tempting offers in Karlsruhe, the Aachen opera administration promoted him, at the age of twenty-seven, to become Germany's youngest general music director. Invited by Bruno Walter to conduct *Tristan* at the Vienna State Opera in 1937, he was told he would have three rehearsals but ended up with none; in spite of this, the performance was a triumph. And after a guest appearance with the Berlin Philharmonic, he was hailed by the press as "das Wunder Karajan" (which only increased Furtwängler's enmity toward him). After Aachen dismissed him for too frequent absences, he did little conducting from 1942 to 1947, partly because Furtwängler used his influence to deny Karajan a number of posts. At the end of the war, the Russians banned him from conducting in Vienna for two years, where he had gone to do guest appearances.

After being denazified, Karajan began his rise to international fame. He was appointed director of Vienna's Singverein der Gesellschaft der Musikfreunde and transformed the amateurish Singverein into a great choral organization. In 1948 he was named director of the German season at La Scala. In 1951 and 1952, he conducted at Bayreuth. When his old rival Furtwängler (whose conducting he greatly admired) died in 1954, the Berlin Philharmonic called on Karajan as his replacement. In the 1950s, Karajan was also artistic director of the Vienna State Opera and the Salzberg Festival. He has made many tours with the Berlin Philharmonic and many appearances at home and abroad as guest conductor. His ubiquitous presence has given rise to many jokes: Asked by a cab driver, "Where to, buddy?" he replies, "It doesn't matter; they want me everywhere." In addition to his concert career, Karajan has equally impressive achievements in recordings, film, and television. The Herbert von Karajan Foundation sponsors a competition for young conductors and a festival of youth orchestras. The academy he established teams young musicians with members of the Berlin Philharmonic for training and performance.

Because Karajan conducts with his eyes closed and ahead of the beat, he often seems disconnected from the music. But this is not so. Behind his eyelids he is focusing intensely on his conception of the music; he knows the score by memory and prefers to "see" the music, not the notation, in his mind. He says of the conductor's preparation that he must not only know what comes next but also have a picture of the whole in his mind. Though the musicians joke about paying no attention to him at all, they have in fact adjusted to his manner and follow him closely, playing with precision. Karajan claims to rehearse every detail of a score and always begins to study his programmed works months ahead, even if he has conducted the music countless times before. When invited to conduct in Berlin in 1938, he demanded sectional rehearsals. The orchestra balked at the idea but submitted and came to respect him for his methodical preparation of the music. Once he has sufficiently rehearsed, he gives the orchestra a certain freedom in performance. He speaks not of carrying the orchestra with him but of being carried by the orchestra, and of the orchstra, himself, and the music becoming one in the performance. When he conducts operas, he demands full artistic control over every element, and he has even staged a number of his own productions. His demeanor on the podium, with restrained but electrifying gestures and his head of silvery hair thrown back, has made a matinee idol of him.

Deutsche Grammophon must regard Karajan as one of its most precious commodities, for most of his more than eight hundred recordings were made for that label. His 1977 boxed set of Beethoven symphonies sold 8 million copies. Even his recordings of Schoenberg, Berg, and Webern (for which Karajan had waived his normal fee) surpassed his and the company's expectations. In addition to recordings, Karajan has filmed *Otello, Madame Butterfly, La Bohème, Carmen, Der Rosenkavalier,* and *Das Rheingold,* and has made numerous video cassettes of concerts.

Karajan claims Toscanini as his idol, but it is clear that he also combines Furtwängler's fantasy, vision, and elasticity with Toscanini's clarity and precision. He has brought the Berlin Philharmonic to a peak of professionalism and discipline. "Lionized wherever he goes, selling more records than any other conductor, endlessly written up and photographed at the controls of his private jet, the wheel of his fast cars, the helm of his racing yacht" (Matheopoulos, 212) and still the musical wonder he was half a century ago, Karajan defines the modern superstar conductor.

Karajan's American counterpart is Leonard Bernstein. Known to millions through his Broadway musical *West Side Story,* televised lectures and concerts, and books, Bernstein, like some other star conductors, works in many areas in addition to conducting. Talented, articulate, versatile, handsome, he is said to be "the most important conductor—by far—that the United States has produced.... He has captured the imagination of the public to a degree unprecedented in history" (Schonberg, 352).

"Today there is hardly an orchestra board ... that does not hope to find ... its local version of Leonard Bernstein" (Hart, 1973, 461).

Born in 1918, Bernstein studied at Harvard and the Curtis Institute of Music but received his training as a conductor under Fritz Reiner and at Tanglewood, where he was Koussevitzky's best pupil. After serving as Koussevitzky's assistant there, he became assistant conductor of the New York Philharmonic under Rodzinski. On 14 November 1943, when the scheduled guest conductor, Bruno Walter, fell ill, Bernstein stood in for him, and his performance was front-page news. He conducted the New York City Symphony in the late 1940s, taught at Brandeis University during the early 1950s, and conducted at Tanglewood throughout the better part of his career. He became co-conductor of the New York Philharmonic with Dimitri Mitropoulos in 1957 and succeeded him as music director the following year. He held that post until 1969. Since then, Bernstein has guest-conducted around the world, made many television appearances, and continued to lecture and write.

By the time he came to the New York Philharmonic, Bernstein had already established himself as a considerable composer of both serious and light music. The public knew him best for his shows On the Town, Wonderful Town, Candide, and West Side Story. In fact, there was some resentment when this "show-business type" was appointed to head the New York Philharmonic. Bernstein definitely brought a new style to the post. A native American with an urban background, a Harvard education, and a keen interest in jazz, he was not the model of Old World gravity and aloofness that had characterized so many immigrant conductors. But Bernstein overcame the initial resistance of the musicians. For one thing, he acted in their interests by getting the orchestral season extended until the players had yearlong contracts. His concerts sold out completely. The number of recordings and television appearances increased the orchestra's revenues: "Bernstein has not only become a conductor of international stature ... but has set the example for a new and distinctly American conception of conductor's charisma, breaking down the remoteness often inherent in the earlier foreign style of leadership, and opening up the symphonic institution to wider public interest" (Hart, 1973, 461).

Bernstein generated much of this interest by doing on television and before audiences of young people what von Bülow and Stokowski had done. He talked about the meaning and performance of music, promoting it by using his own idiosyncratic appeal. His television lectures and other essays were published as The Joy of Music (1959) and The Infinite Variety of Music (1966).

Bernstein has doubtless mesmerized his audiences (as well as drawn the scorn of some musicians) with his podium manner: "Bernstein is the most choreographic of all contemporary conductors ... a specialist in the clenched fist, the hip swivel, the pelvic thrust, the levitation effect, ... the uppercut, the haymaker" (Schonberg, 357). His critics deplore his gyrations, imputing them to showmanship and ego gratification. Bernstein himself claims that his movements are unpremeditated, that he tries to elicit from the orchestra what he wants in the only way he knows how, and that he regrets that some find his actions distracting. Many people enjoy the distraction; in fact, a generation of less critical concertgoers has probably grown up believing that a conductor less agile or extroverted than Bernstein is his inferior.

For the most part, Bernstein has conducted the standard repertoire; that is to say, he has not ventured far into avant-garde or early music. He has been responsible in large part for revived interest in Gustav Mahler, with whose music Bernstein strongly identifies. Some deplore as a tragically lost opportunity that he did not bring the same enthusiasm to new music. In dealing with the standard repertoire, Bernstein has been in many respects commendable. His is the only recorded performance of the Schumann symphonies, for example, that does not tamper with the composer's orchestration.

"Bernstein," wrote Harold Schonberg, "became famous overnight and has remained famous—a controversial figure, a showman, a romantic, a glamour boy not fully accepted by his peers, disliked by many critics in America and Europe throughout much of his career, yet ... the only native-born conductor to be musical director of a major American orchestra" (p. 352). Bernstein became director of the New York Philharmonic during the Eisenhower era, just a year after *Sputnik*, when America was looking for native achievements to celebrate. His tenure lasted into and beyond the Kennedy years, during which serious music—for the first time since Thomas Jefferson's presidency—was recognized, honored, and actively promoted by the White House. Bernstein was one of the first "jetset" conductors, who, like Karajan, can hold positions and honor guest engagements not only in their own countries but all over the world.

Jet-setting, some have argued, has diminished the individuality of orchestras. Few major conductors spend most of their time with one orchestra, and conversely, few orchestras now are molded to the ideal of a single musical mind. All major orchestras are much more technically proficient than in the past and play well under any good conductor, but most of them lack the stamp of a strong personality. Since one ingredient of stardom has usually been the development by a conductor of the reputation and style of his orchestra, the present system works against the starworthy achievements of bygone eras.

Today's ministars, it might be argued, are those who have identified a special sector of the repertoire and formed their own ensembles to perform it. These are the conductors of "early music" and of new music. In the former category, Nikolaus Harnoncourt, Neville Marriner, Raymond Leppard, and Christopher Hogwood come to mind. Harnoncourt, with his Vienna Concentus Musicus, and Leppard have specialized in seventeenth- and early-eighteenth-century music; Marriner, with his Academy of St. Martin-in-the-Fields Orchestra, and Hogwood, with the Academy of Ancient Music, pay more attention to music of the late eighteenth century. All of these conductors share a strong interest in the well-known and the neglected music of these periods as well as in the use of period instruments and/or performing forces. Within this group we can perceive a philosophical division analogous to the subjective-objective distinction between conductors of the standard repertoire. On the one hand, a conductor like Harnoncourt is insistent on purging Monteverdi and Bach of romantic performance traditions, on using only authentic instrumentation, and on adhering as far as ascertainable to the performance style of the earlier period. This school of thought has strong supporters as well as detractors. On the other hand, Leppard, although he records Monteverdi madrigals with solo singers instead of large choirs, still chooses to use rich voices and full vibrato rather than the purer tones presumably more apposite for this music. In both cases, these conductors have become stars in their own right by promoting music that few conventional conductors had programmed and by approaching it with strong personal points of view. Their achievements—whether Leppard's lush readings of Cavalli operas or Harnoncourt's drier performances of Bach cantatas—are major contributions. (In the even more remote realm of medieval and Renaissance music, Thomas Binkley's Early Music Quartet, Konrad Ruhland's Capella Antiqua, and the late David Munrow's Early Music Consort of London deserve mention for their verve, musicality, recorded legacy, and influence.)

In the area of new music, a number of composer-conductors have formed chamber ensembles that specialize in their own and their contemporaries' music. Among them are Charles Wuorinen and his Group for Contemporary Music, Ralph Shapey and the Contemporary Chamber Players, Peter Maxwell Davies and the Fires of London, and Karlheinz Stockhausen and Philip Glass and their own performing ensembles. These musicians have ventured into a repertoire with a following even more sparse than that of early music and pursue it—perhaps for that reason—with even more dogged conviction.

In both the early- and new-music ensembles, it is also the virtuosity cultivated by the individual players that contributes to the star quality.

In the case of new music, the virtuosity extends to conventional instruments and electronic devices. In many of the new-music groups, conducting has again become the domain of composers. And their repertoire, like that of the early nineteenth century, is again the music of the recent past. And yet for all this historical precedent, it is unlikely that the Philip Glasses of this world will ever enjoy the mass adulation of the older star conductors.

A number of younger conductors of the standard orchestral and operatic repertoire have become prominent. Their international reputation is, in some cases, attested by their holding important permanent or guest positions outside their native countries; all of them travel widely as guests. Some of them may still become stars.

Colin Davis (born 1927), successor to Georg Solti in 1971 as music director of the Royal Opera at Covent Garden, was called the "best since Beecham" when he replaced the ailing Otto Klemperer in a performance of *Don Giovanni* in 1959. Davis has led the late-twentieth-century revival of interest in the music of Berlioz (including the stage works) with his performances and recordings. Indeed, Davis' work was probably a contributing factor in the British-led *New Berlioz Edition* of the complete works; he has also been associated with Michael Tippett, many of whose works he has premiered. Davis was formerly director of the BBC Symphony Orchestra and principal guest conductor of the Boston Symphony Orchestra.

One of Germany's leading young conductors of the postwar period is Christoph von Dohnányi (born 1929), music director of the Cleveland Symphony Orchestra since 1984. Dohnányi distinguished himself primarily in opera, having assisted Solti in Frankfurt and then held the chief posts in the opera houses of Lübeck, Kassel, Frankfurt (1968–1977), and Hamburg (1977–1984). He has conducted premieres of Henze's operas and has been generally praised for his promotion and direction of the modern repertoire (such as his production of Schoenberg's *Moses und Aron* in Frankfurt).

Claudio Abbado (born 1933) and Zubin Mehta (born 1936) attended the Vienna Academy of Music and Tanglewood together. Abbado, in addition to his post as music director of La Scala, is a principal conductor of the London Symphony Orchestra and of the Chicago Symphony. He has raised La Scala's playing to high symphonic standards. Zubin Mehta's arrival in Los Angeles in 1962 as music director of its orchestra coincided with plans for a new civic arts center, and the city made him the star of its fund-raising drive. He turned the Los Angeles Symphony into a fine orchestra and in 1978 succeeded Pierre Boulez as music director of the

New York Philharmonic, where one of his decisions has been to feature a particular composer each season (Schubert in 1978–1979, Stravinsky in 1980–1981, Bartók in 1981–1982, Schoenberg in 1982–1983, Copland in 1985–1986).

Born in 1935 into a poor Japanese family, Seiji Ozawa rose in his profession by virtue of determination and sacrifice. He earned, saved, and borrowed enough money to get to Paris, where Charles Munch (then conductor of the Boston Symphony) heard him in a competition and invited him to Tanglewood. He studied with Leonard Bernstein there and with Karajan in Berlin and was appointed assistant conductor of the New York Philharmonic in 1961. Ozawa subsequently conducted the Toronto and San Francisco symphonies. As music director of the Boston Symphony since 1973, he has made two European tours, a triumphant tour of Japan (1978), and a historic tour of China (1979).

Riccardo Muti (born 1941), music director of the Philadelphia Orchestra since 1980, has proved that a principal conductor can still make an orchestra in his own image. The Philadelphia Orchestra under his direction has turned from the lush Ormandy sound and standard nineteenth-century repertoire to a leaner timbre and a range of music from Haydn to Penderecki.

By virtue of the direction of James Levine (born 1943) the orchestra of the Metropolitan Opera deserves attention. Levine was a child prodigy, making his debut as solo pianist with the Cincinnati Symphony when he was ten. By the age of twenty-three he was assisting George Szell at the Cleveland Orchestra (1964–1970). After an engagement as a guest conductor with the Metropolitan Opera in 1971, he was appointed principal conductor in 1973, a title created for him under music director Rafael Kubelík, whom he succeeded in 1976. Levine joined the Met when it was in difficult artistic, administrative, and financial straits. The new management solved the practical problems, and Levine raised the musical standards. He also eliminated a bit of the reputation of the Metropolitan Opera for stodginess, by setting out to include neglected repertoire (including Berg's Lulu, Weill's Mahagonny, Gershwin's Porgy and Bess, and Britten's Billy Budd) and to revive works not heard there for many seasons (Smetana's Bartered Bride and Janáček's Jenufa).

The kind of stardom typified by Toscanini, Furtwängler, or even Bernstein does not seem to be in evidence among this younger generation—at least not yet. This may be in large part because of the way these conductors think of themselves. There is apparently more recognition than before that a musical work belongs to the composer—not to the interpreter. After a performance of the Verdi Requiem conducted by

Carlo Maria Giulini, a fan praised him for "his" *Requiem,* whereupon the conductor chided, "It is Verdi's, not mine" (Matheopoulos, 167). Many modern conductors are modest, without exaggerated ideas of their own importance. Davis is described as "modestly free of any 'star conductor' consciousness" (Jacobson, 103); Muti dislikes the "cult of the conductor." Egalitarian principles have gradually infiltrated orchestras, too, and the age of autocratic or dictatorial conductors is over. Abbado "hates being called 'Maestro'" and greatly values the fact that he was elected by the members of the orchestra he directs (Matheopoulos, 76). Muti says that a conductor today can transmit—but not impose—his idea of a work to an orchestra. These are reflections of a changed age, of a different aesthetic climate. Both music and the conductor have been relieved of their nineteenth-century aura of mystery and divinity. We have all become perhaps a bit jaded by, and suspicious of, the promotional efforts of orchestral boards and public relations managers. And finally, for the conductors themselves, it is better to make a clean break than to try to live up to the real and legendary achievements of the past.

In the final analysis, it is impossible to be precise about what characteristics and abilities define the star conductor. Some outstanding conductors have had impeccably clear baton techniques, others have appeared awkward or careless, and at least one deliberately cultivated ambiguity. Some have been tyrants with their orchestral players, while others have asserted their authority in more congenial ways. Some stars have emoted in extreme movements on the podium; others have maintained the utmost poise and grace. Some have championed new music or revived old music; some have seldom strayed from the standard repertoire. Some stars have liberally doctored scores with their own reorchestrations, cuts, and performance nuances, while others have conducted the music with absolute fidelity to the composer's written intentions. Some have been richly cultured and articulate spokesmen; others have shown little verbal acumen and practically no interest in anything beyond music. Some were instrumentalists with established performance careers; some were composers; some cultivated no musical activities besides conducting. Some exhibited prodigious memories and conducted without benefit of scores, while others have consistently worked with the printed music before them. Some have had the advantages of being born to wealth or being endowed with a handsome appearance; others have not enjoyed these privileges. Some stars have had an undeniable penchant for showmanship, while others have eschewed self-promotion. It is clear that no single set of "star" characteristics can be formulated.

Of course certain traits have been more important at given times and places. The actual emergence of conducting as a professional career could have been predicted, and authoritarianism was probably a necessary device for instilling discipline and high standards in nineteenth-century orchestras or in any orchestra founded where no orchestral tradition had preceded it. Baton technique was bound to have been more straightforward in the early era of conducting because the conventions were being established. Only after the turn of the twentieth century could a conductor be characterized as adhering to the "standard repertoire," which was only then taking shape. Score memorization is always remarkable when dauntingly large and complex compositions are at issue. In the first three quarters of the nineteenth century, conducting a Beethoven symphony from memory was a feat, whereas it is no longer considered so. Being an articulate speaker has never been a requisite for the conductor dealing directly with his musicians, but such an ability definitely enhances one's public image in our era of interviews in the mass media and in books devoted to conductors. The change in emphasis from heavy-handed interpretations in the late nineteenth century to more objective renditions in the twentieth followed a general aesthetic turn away from romanticism and a greater awareness of historical styles.

In considering the relatively short history of conducting one is tempted to regard most of the changes in the conductor's role, status, and characteristics, as well as the individual differences between conductors, as superficial or inessential to the accomplishment of the musical ends. Yet there seems to be one factor that has been basically and perhaps irretrievably altered—the relationship of the conductor to the living composer. This issue has already been touched on in this essay, but seems nevertheless a fitting thought on which to conclude. The major conductor originally championed new music, but now he does not. Thus, there is a greater distance than ever before between the conductor and the audience. Whether the star conductor has played a critical role in creating this predicament by failing to program more modern music, has merely gone along with the trend, or has become a victim himself, being prohibited from exercising his artistic will by the demands of the box office, is beyond the scope of this discussion. But one is tempted to speculate that the institution of conductor and the nature and quality of those who pursue this profession are bound to suffer the longer the conductor is prevented from being the creative link between the living composer and the performance of new orchestral and operatic music.

BIBLIOGRAPHY

Warren A. Bebbington, "The Orchestral Conducting Practice of Richard Wagner," Ph.D. diss., City University of New York, 1984. Donald Brook, *Inter-*

national Gallery of Conductors (1951). Robert Chesterman, ed., *Conversations with Conductors* (1976). Will Crutchfield, "Orchestras in the Age of Jet-Set Sound," in *New York Times*, 6 January 1985. David Ewen, *The Man with the Baton* (1936); and *Dictators of the Baton* (1943). Peter Paul Fuchs, *The Psychology of Conducting* (1969). Philip Hart, *Orpheus in the New World: The Symphony Orchestra as an American Cultural Institution* (1973); and *Conductors: A New Generation* (rev. ed., 1983). Bernard Jacobson, *Conductors on Conducting* (1979). Helena Matheopoulos, *Maestro: Encounters with Conductors of Today* (1983). John H. Mueller, *The American Symphony Orchestra: A Social History of Musical Taste* (1951). Henry Raynor, *Music and Society Since 1815* (1976). Harold C. Schonberg, *The Great Conductors* (1967). George Seltzer, *The Professional Symphony Orchestra in the United States* (1975). Bernard Shore, *The Orchestra Speaks* (1938). David Wooldridge, *Conductor's World* (1970).

The Extended Orchestra

Tod Machover

During the twentieth century, the symphony orchestra has undergone many transformations, some involving new uses of traditional instrumental forces and some the addition of new elements into the ensemble. Many of these transformations have been reponses to the increasing complexity and changing emphasis of the composer's demands, but some have been by-products of the development of technology, which has fundamentally changed our concept of the very word *instrument*.

This essay will trace certain of the more significant contributions of new technology to the orchestra. In so doing, it will combine reflections based on recent and current compositional activity with a certain amount of reasoned speculation necessitated by the fact that until now, very little music has actually been written for the combined forces of the orchestra and sophisticated electronics. Why this is so will be treated later on. Also this essay will extrapolate from the results of musical research, the evolution of electronic-music technology, the disappearance of electronic music as an independent genre, and numerous musical works that combine electronics and modest instrumental resources. This evidence suggests a movement toward a union of electronic and instrumental forces, one in which distinctions between, and juxtapositions of, them will be scarcely useful or interesting and in which what might be truly termed the "extended orchestra" will exist.

Since the beginning of the twentieth century, composers have attempted to extend the sonic capabilities of the symphony orchestra, to accommodate the changing needs for expression and the conditions of contemporary musical language. As often stated, the epoch preceding World War I represented the end of a long period of continuous historical and cultural development in Europe and the United States. Music reflected these changes at least as much as the other arts.

The traditional configuration of the nineteenth-century symphony orchestra reflects the priorities of Western musical discourse. Orchestral groupings favor the massed and unified deployment of each orchestral family, which best conveyed the melodic and harmonic movement of such music. Rhythmic structure is of secondary importance, and major phrase units are conveyed with percussion support. The supportive role of percussion is even more apparent in the realm of color, or timbre. Until the early part of the twentieth century, nonpercussive instruments were used primarily for their single-line, melodic ability, for which purpose they were, in fact, originally designed. Timbre was never considered to be an independent musical element, in the same way that musical "noise" was not, and both served only to add extra emphasis to the fundamental pitch orientation of the music.

The development of art in all ages inevitably involves the artist's search for intensification of impact and expression, because of a natural maturing process of artistic materials and a need to avoid what have become clichéd and hackneyed techniques, devoid of freshness. Such development continues until the new expressive language becomes so saturated and hypercharged that necessary contrast and objective distance are completely lost. Then a period of creative equilibrium becomes inevitable. Such a saturation point was experienced in Western music at the beginning of the twentieth century. Since music had so long depended primarily on pitch relationships to convey its meaning, pitch was stretched and intensified before the other aspects of music. (In this, Western music is quite different from such musics as those of Africa and Japan, cultures that favor rhythm and timbre, respectively, as the fundamental building blocks of expression.) By the time that Wagner had composed his music dramas, the implications of harmonic extension through modulation had been so expanded that the original tension between a tonic key and its closely related harmonic regions was all but lost. In any case, many composers found it useless to attempt to invest music with a new intensity by using harmonic means, and many original and personal solutions were proposed. Schoenberg attempted to reorganize pitch relationships completely. But a more radical approach was to search for tools of expression that favored those elements of Western music so long neglected: rhythm and timbre. This placed new demands on the orchestra and led to the development of electronic means to enlarge the capabilities of instruments designed for more limited purposes.

Many twentieth-century composers became concerned with exploring new rhythmic and timbral possibilities of the orchestra. Stravinsky has long been associated with the use of pulsating, often irregular primitive rhythms in an orchestral context. Varèse was clearly influenced by the power of such rhythms and constructed entire pieces on the blaring and insistent repetition of rather static tonal units. In his symphonic and chamber music he used enormous percussion sections, often introducing either non-Western instruments or materials originally designed for unmusical purposes, such as sirens. Since then, the use of percussion has achieved a new prominence in orchestral music, notably in such diverse works as John Cage's various *Constructions in Metal* of the 1940s, Steve Reich's pulsating ensembles based on rhythms and sonorities he heard in Africa and Bali, and Hugues Dufourt's impressive *Saturne* (1979) for chamber orchestra, in which the constantly changing sound masses are created by an enormous and inventive use of percussion.

This novel use of percussion in so many twentieth-century scores simply emphasizes a fundamental fact: to compensate for the breakdown of the diatonic harmonic system ("common practice" tonality), composers liberated noise and color, and sound itself, as a major element—perhaps *the* major element—of musical discourse. In Debussy and in Schoenberg's famous "Farben" movement from the *Five Pieces for Orchestra* (1912) the delicate transformation of orchestral color was used to convey expressive content. The same timbral richness can be found in many composers since World War II, most notably Pierre Boulez, György Ligeti, and George Crumb. Most important is the fact that such changes have been motivated by profound musical needs and concepts. Whereas the carefully linear construction of traditional tonal music, based on the association and development of discrete and easily recognizable melodic and harmonic elements, was best adapted to the formal and dramatic unravelings of sonata-form prosody, the holistic and massive movements of noise and color suggest a contemplative, rather static, listening experience.

Many composers have felt that the sonic and expressive resources offered by the traditional symphony orchestra are not adequate to convey the powerful and subtle music that the liberation of timbre has made possible. This conviction prepared the way for the acceptance of electronics. The electronic domain—starting with the introduction of the tape recorder, then the analogue synthesizer, and more recently the digital computer—allows aspects of music to be controlled with a precision and suppleness that are not possible with traditional instruments. At least this seemed to be the case during the first, naive period of electronic experimentation.

During this period—roughly from the end of the 1940s until the middle of the 1970s—a general feeling of intense optimism surrounded the new medium. This same euphoria greeted each subsequent technological improvement and contributed to a climate in which the greatest developments of electronic music tended to occur independently of the world of traditional instruments. In many ways, electronic music was treated as a separate genre with a small, characteristic public and mode of presentation and distribution (staring at rectangular loudspeakers in a concert hall or listening to the radio or records). At that time composers were more interested in exploring the specificity of the electronic medium than in attempting to combine it with the orchestra, for several reasons.

First was the genuine feeling that all possible sounds could be created with electronics and that the traditional orchestra would soon become obsolete. Second, a more historicist point of view held that electronics must, by definition, entertain a complete break with the past and thus be disassociated from the culture-laden references of any orchestral instrument. Most important, the original separation of electronic and instrumental resources resulted from the terrible crudeness of early electronic-music materials. The two classic approaches to electronic music can be illustrated by observing the Cologne Radio Studio and the Paris Radio research group in the 1950s and early 1960s (with both approaches observable at the Columbia-Princeton Studio in New York). These studios adopted opposite approaches to the development of electronic music. The Cologne group based its research (and many of its compositions, as witnessed by the work of Karlheinz Stockhausen) on the construction of purely synthetic, electronic sounds from what were considered to be elemental acoustical particles. The Paris group (following the inspiration of Pierre Schaeffer and his *objets sonores*) treated only prerecorded natural, nonmusical sounds, which were held to be already complex and in need only of slight, delicate manipulations and placement in a compositional context. In New York the development of "pure" electronic synthesis (although often combined in musical discourse with traditional instruments) was pursued by Milton Babbitt and Mario Davidovsky, while the manipulation of prerecorded sounds was explored by

Vladimir Ussachevsky and Otto Luening. These two approaches—constructing complex sound worlds from simple electronic elements and organizing and transforming already complex and meaningful materials—are still the aesthetic and technical poles of electronic music. And both were plagued for at least thirty years with severe technical limitations.

"Additive synthesis" is the electronic technique suggested by the early experiments of the Cologne, Columbia-Princeton, and similar studios. This technique is based on Fourier's theorem, which states that any sound is made up of a relatively large number of independent frequencies, or "harmonics," which all vary a great deal in amplitude and slightly in frequency over the course of a sound or musical note. The presence of certain harmonics and not others and the way that these vary over time give each sound its individual timbre. To define and control such sounds in a musically interesting way is far more difficult than was originally imagined in the early days of electronics. Any sound of even moderate richness contains many partials, often numbering in the hundreds (as in a single low piano note). If a high-quality synthesis is to be achieved, each of these partials, as well as its microscopic movement, must be very precisely reproduced. And an enormous amount of research is needed in order to ascertain exactly which partials are present in a single sound and how each of these partials varies. Even to acquire sufficient data to allow a single note performed by a professional violinist on a good instrument to be synthesized is a considerable task. All of the above procedures were considerably beyond the reach of equipment available until recently.

The situation involved with the appropriation and transformation of prerecorded sounds (often noninstrumental), or *musique concrete*, already rich in musical information, is quite analogous to the one described. Here the difficulties enter for the opposite reason: to provide interesting and musical results, it is necessary to decompose and separate the components of a recorded sound. If this is not done, the sound keeps too much of its own identity and is not neutral enough to be treated in a musical discourse, always retaining an independent identity. We are all familiar with the banal and cloying sound of a recording of a human voice sped up to the point where it resembles a hyperactive chipmunk or slowed down to sound like a lobotomized elephant. To achieve the opposite effect—to have a very treble but intelligible and "human" speaking voice, for instance—requires the ability to disassociate, and therefore treat independently, different physical aspects, or parameters, of a given sound. This in turn requires quite complex and powerful mathematical and acoustical analyses of a sound. The techniques that make this possible have become available only recently and still need a great deal of improvement.

With all of these problems and limitations, it is understandable that until recently composers often treated electronic music as an independent genre, feeling that what they could produce with electronics was in some way not worthy of being combined or contrasted with the subtlety of the orchestra. However, since the mid-1970s, many developments in electronic music and the general musical culture have begun to bridge the gap between electronics and the orchestra. With the introduction of digital computers, the sonorities of traditional instruments could be simulated with ever greater accuracy, and what is probably even more important, an understanding of producing and controlling rich, interesting abstract sound structures is being acquired. Composers are now in a position to explore the many different ways in which electronics and traditional instruments might be combined, unified, and juxtaposed. To carry out this work efficiently and fruitfully, three major classes of developments are called for: first, further improvement of electronic-music systems and the musical concepts that underlie their use; second, an expansion and renewal of traditional instrumental techniques and the incorporation of these techniques into an orchestral setting; and third, the establishment of situations involving the unification of orchestras with electronics—a sort of extended-orchestra laboratory, in which musical experiments could be made and much indispensable experience gained.

In the late 1960s and early 1970s, pioneering work was done in the use of digital computers to achieve greater control over the production of new sonorities, first at the Bell Telephone Research Laboratories (Mathews and Risset) and later at Stanford University (Chowning and Grey). Initial research was conducted into discovering which aspects of sounds created the distinction between a "lively, natural" sound and a "dull, dead" one. To do this, comparisons had to be made between existing sounds and computer versions of these same sounds, which had been reconstructed after careful spectral analysis. Thus, additive synthesis forced researchers to select musically rich models on which to base their tests. Traditional instruments and the human voice were chosen as the materials best suited for close observation. This research necessity is one of the main reasons composers have often stayed close to these instrumental models and to combinations with orchestralike ensembles in musical contexts. By 1980, most musical research centers around the world contained computerized libraries that allowed for the reconstruction of orchestral sounds in most ranges of each instrument. Of course, these data remain quite limited, since such elements as performance nuance and subtle color change are often quite difficult to calculate and incorporate in such models. Still, powerful instrumental synthesis systems do exist, and although they are often housed in large, expensive, mainframe computer installations such as Stanford and Paris' Institut de Recherche et de Coordination Acoustique/Musique (IRCAM), the data are widely available.

Computers can produce "any sound in the universe" and are not limited to imitating existing instruments. Much work has been done to apply synthesis models originally developed for known sounds to the creation of completely new structures. Two such models, frequency modulation, or FM (developed by John Chowning at Stanford), and formant synthesis, or CHANT (developed by Xavier Rodet at IRCAM), demonstrate this point. Both of these methods were first developed to reproduce instrumental sounds, FM for percussion and CHANT for the singing voice. Both evolved into general systems from which an enormous variety of sounds could be generated. FM can be easily used to synthesize enormously complex harmonic or inharmonic spectra, and CHANT can do the same with a greater ease of transformation from one spectral state to another. Of equal importance is the fact that both have been conceived to permit the greatest ease of use by composers, who are easily overawed by the enormous wealth of nonmusical data needed to synthesize even the simplest sonorities. FM reduces this data to one simple formula that the composer can master as he would a musical instrument. CHANT is perhaps even more intuitively accessible, allowing a musician to conceive of an imaginary resonating object that functions as the vocal tract would, although it may be assigned any bizarre and wonderful physical characteristics that one wishes, even if they do not exist in nature.

This principle of abstraction from physical objects is at the heart of much computer-music research. Composers have not, of course, been content to rely on exact models of existing sounds (a process that is in any case aesthetically dubious). One of the most exciting frontiers has, in fact, been the musical exploration of inharmonic sounds—that is, those based on complex spectra unlike those of most existing instruments. The science of musical psychoacoustics (David Wessel and Stephen McAdams are the major proponents) has helped to chart this unknown region, extrapolating from existing sound structures and using the physical limits and psychological functioning of the ear as guides.

Since computer synthesis involves the construction of complex sounds, composers have recognized the power and musical interest of modeling the "interior particles" of individual sounds and performing transformations from one sound group to another. The idea of leading a listener to follow musical developments not of notes or phrases but of individual partials is a major musical contribution of our time. The difference between this attitude and traditional compositional practice is that instruments are no longer thought to be rigidly fixed, confined within the physical limits of their construction. Any instrument can modify and take on the musical characteristics of any other; it is, in fact, the trajectory of this timbral change that conveys musical sense and beauty. The examples of this practice are many, but a particularly clear and elegant composition is Jonathan Harvey's *Mortuos Plango, Vivos Voco* (1980), in which a child's voice, a large church bell, and wide-ranging inharmonic sound complexes are all woven and merged together to produce a contemplative yet ever-changing sound world. This domain of "artificial timbre as continuum" is one of the areas in which electronics can most fruitfully complement and add to the world of the traditional orchestra.

With such tools and concepts, composers have developed the ability to synthesize and reproduce a very wide variety of sounds. This has led to new curiosity and daring in combining these sounds with traditional instruments. Activity in this domain has been especially rich since 1980, and diverse combinations have been tried. Through the works that have been composed, a new sense of orchestration has begun to be developed.

One of the fundamental impulses on the part of composers has been to increase the volume of the orchestra. For the generation that has matured listening to a great deal of music diffused over high-fidelity systems rather than in concert halls, a live performance—even of a symphony orchestra—can seem slightly lacking in presence. Our ears have also become accustomed to the sound of rock music, which has pushed decibels to new levels of human pain. The point is not that recorded or rock music is either good or bad as a musical or social phenomenon; it is simply important to note that the standard of absolute loudness (and therefore expressive power) changes with each generation, in somewhat the form of a large crescendo.

Therefore it is not strange to find that many composers have been motivated to apply amplification to orchestral instruments. Even traditional instrumentalists have done this, notably the Kronos String Quartet of San Francisco, which has given amplified performances of Beethoven quartets in what they consider to be oversized concert halls, such as the Bay Area's Cow Palace. In Pierre Boulez' *Répons* (1981/in progress) such amplification is used both to increase the sound level at climaxes and to highlight a group of soloists against a chamber-orchestral *tutti*. Another aspect of amplification also becomes clear when one listens to *Répons* in a live performance (since the phenomenon is not clearly conveyed on record): amplification changes the timbre of instruments as well as their loudness. Depending on the microphone used, the treble or bass components of an instrument are exaggerated, and the simple fact of being heard through a loudspeaker rather than from a physical sounding box "neutralizes" and changes a sound. Some composers have made conscious and dramatic use of timbral changes caused by amplification. Lorenzo Ferrero, in his opera *Marilyn* (1978), uses a different amplification technique to individualize each character, as well as to highlight different moments in Marilyn Monroe's career.

Once an instrument is amplified, it emanates from, and is therefore perceived through, a loudspeaker, not its acoustic sounding box. It follows that the instrument can therefore be heard through any loudspeaker, thus introducing the concept of "spatialization." This procedure, although technically simple, can be invested with extreme musical subtlety, for by making it appear as if the sound of an instrument is detached from its own body and can even dance through a concert space, the composer can use electronics to tread the fine line between reality and imagination. In this simple case it is possible to observe a phenomenon that underlies all successful interaction of orchestral instruments and electronics: mixing is most successful when both forces can meet on common ground, when they can resemble each other, and then split off to their own specificities. By exploiting these similarities, the musician avoids the risk of having the two worlds exist in never-meeting parallel planes.

Of course, amplification and spatialization are only the simplest techniques that help instruments move a step closer to the electronic world. Many methods of instrumental transformation have been developed. The first category of these transformations takes the entire signal of the instrument, processes it with an electronic circuit, and diffuses the sonic result from a loudspeaker. Most of these techniques were developed before the utilization of digital equipment, and computers have contributed only by adding greater precision and cleaner sonic results. The most common of these techniques are ring modulation, frequency shifting, harmonizing, and filtering. The first three add spectral complexity to the sound, either by combining that spectrum with a new source or by transposing the entire spectrum so that the partial relationships remain arithmetically correct but proportionately wrong, since they are not expanded or contracted to correspond to the new frequency region. For instance, a harmonic spectrum transposed up an octave would be expanded, finding its respective partials farther apart than those of a "natural" harmonic spectrum based on the same new fundamental. Filtering subtracts from, rather than adds to, the spectrum of the transformed instrument, much as stone is reduced and modeled by the sculptor's chisel. If controlled carefully, these procedures create new sonorities while keeping certain identifying characteristics (envelope, or constant change in amplitude for the duration of a sound; phrasing; spectral shape, or the distribution of frequency energy that determines the timbre of a given sound; and the like) of the original instrument, thus satisfying the condition of "common ground" mentioned above.

However, these techniques, because they operate on the entire instrumental signal, are quite limited. Except for filtering, the electronic algorithms, or processes, are quite rigid and do not vary over the course of a note or phrase. Each modulation technique produces a characteristic sound, one that is spectrally quite rich and easily identified. In ring modulation, for instance, it is almost impossible to control the degree of spectral richness or density of the modulated signal. Any modulation is so dense that an increase runs the risk of producing aggressive and noisy saturation. Also, these modulations affect the incoming instrumental signal in the same way, regardless of what note is played. Normal instruments change in timbre as they change in pitch; a trumpet played at the top of its range is spectrally richer, or brighter, than when played at the bottom of its range. Such transformations and modulations do not take the subtle variety of instrumental tones into account and tend to produce the timbral equivalent of parallel fifths—noisy, undifferentiated timbral blocks moving relentlessly throughout the frequency range. But the ear soon tires of such sounds and fails to detect important musical distinctions.

Current research is directed toward the use of computers to perform "intelligent transformations" on orchestral instruments, with the goal of controlling independently many different aspects of instrumental sound, much as multiple sound parameters are controlled in the synthesis techniques described above. To achieve this, the computer must be aware of what the instrument is playing, how it is playing, and in certain instances (involving structural transformations) even why it is playing certain music at a specific time. Therefore, the computer employs various techniques, some mathematically based on the analysis of the spectrum at a given moment, some based on physical monitoring of a player's movement (such as using optical sensors to detect what fingering a flutist is employing in order to determine what pitch is being played), or some on artificial-intelligence techniques (such as a program that can make musical deductions from a phrase that a particular instrumentalist has just performed). The goal of these and other such techniques is the same—to permit the computer to shape its electronic reaction with the greatest subtlety and to follow truly the gesture and intent of the performer.

Much research has been done in the area of intelligent transformations. But because vast and complicated calculations are often necessary to allow the computer to accumulate such information, most of the more sophisticated of these processes (for example, stretching a sound in time from four seconds to four minutes without affecting its timbre) are now possible only on the largest computers. They are usually performed in the studio and rarely on the concert stage. But this also is changing, and it is not impossible to imagine in the near future the existence of hybrid instruments that will combine certain aspects of a traditional, acoustical instrument and playing technique with built-in high-speed computer interaction. An instrument based on the violin might have sensors that would aid a microcomputer to analyze the minutest spectral transformations of the normal violin sound. In turn, another microcomputer might contain a collection of preprogrammed modifications of spectral information that could delicately reconstruct violin sounds in many ways. The bridge of the same instrument might be fitted with a highly sensitive mechanism to measure the most delicate fluctuations in bow pressure and speed. The signals measured at the bridge could be directly connected to the microcomputer to control the spectral transformations contained in memory. Such an interactive hybrid instrument would couple established playing techniques with very sophisticated technology to allow the performer to control his own electronic modifications with a finesse and musicality unheard of at present. Such instruments (which, by adding new levels of automated response and interaction, would change the very concept of "instrument") would provide a necessary link between the orchestra and the new technology.

So far, direct transformation and the hybridization of traditional instruments have been suggested as powerful methods for assuring a meaningful and convincing marriage between electronics and the traditional orchestra. It is essential that electronic materials develop sufficient sophistication to participate in a live musical situation. During the initial stages of analogue and computer electronic music, the fundamental medium for diffusing a finished product was magnetic tape. Until the end of the 1970s computer music was especially plagued by this problem because enormous calculations were necessary for the machine to produce even the simplest sounds. General-purpose computers (those not specially designed for musical purposes) were simply not rapid enough to calculate sound samples in real time. In other words, when using such systems, the composer always experienced considerable delay from the moment he specified a particular musical idea to the machine to the moment when he could hear and evaluate the sonic result. This separated musical gesture and intuition from the creative process and was highly undesirable to most composers and performers.

To overcome this problem, much research was conducted at the end of the 1970s to design technology specifically adapted to musical needs. Numerous types of such real-time digital synthesizers have become available since 1980. Basically they can be divided into two large categories: first, highly powerful (and very expensive) machines that have few limitations in terms of musical performance but are usually operable only by very skilled musicians or, more often, technicians; second, commercially manufactured inexpensive machines that offer limited possibilities but are easy to use and to transport. In a sense, the first are basically research machines or are usable for the final stages of a major creative production (somewhat like a performance with a major symphony orchestra), while the second are daily tools for study, tests, experiments, and easy performing.

In fact, there is a reciprocal relationship between the two. First, because large, powerful systems are "transparent" and can be easily modified (through programming changes) to perform a multitude of operations, they can provide a laboratory for developing musical materials that can later be standardized and miniaturized for commercial production. Such was the experience of John Chowning, who worked on Stanford University's powerful digital synthesizer, the Samson Box. He developed the algorithm for frequency modulation described above and subsequently sold the patent for this algorithm to the Japanese instrument manufacturer Yamaha. It is now the basis of Yamaha's revolutionary series of DX digital synthesizers. (The process has been reciprocal, since royalties from Yamaha helped to fund further musical research at Stanford.)

Second, and perhaps more important, it is possible to imagine that these small and large computer music systems will evolve into a similar relationship that now exists, for instance, between the individual composer and his working tools (pencil, paper, nonconcert piano, and the like), on the one hand, and an orchestral performance, on the other. No individuals and not many institutions are likely to be able to afford the most powerful computer systems that are available; these are likely to remain the property of a relatively few important music centers such as Stanford, Massachusetts Institute of Technology, IRCAM, and the University of California at San Diego. However, inexpensive systems will be developed to allow the composer or researcher to do preparatory and creative work at home, away from the institution, and to contact the performance center for information, advice, and its final production and performance of a new piece. For this system to work (and this appears to be the only way that computer music will survive into the twenty-first century as a vital medium), a technology must be conceived that offers complete compatibility between the work that the composer does at home with his private machine and the contact that he needs to have with the electronic orchestra.

Some progress is being made in this field. LucasFilm in San Rafael, California, has developed, under the direction of J. A. Moorer, what is at present probably the world's most sophisticated sound-editing system, the ASP. This expensive machine allows a composer to manipulate delicately, and reconfigure, any recorded sound with the greatest ease. A similar but less powerful (and much less expensive) system has been developed by the Compusonics Corporation in Cambridge, Massachusetts. It is not impossible to imagine that such a machine, which uses a small microcomputer, could be owned and manipulated by an individual composer but connected by phone line to an institution possessing an ASP. The same is true with the 4X digital computer, developed by Giuseppe di Giugno at IRCAM in Paris. This machine allows the composer great freedom with synthesis and transformation of live instruments but is far beyond any composer's budget. Research has begun at various centers to develop a true composer's work station that could be in communication with such a machine as the 4X. Such a work station would use a microcomputer and commercially available synthesis and transformation hardware (like that manufactured by Yamaha) to permit the composer to try many different timbral combinations, structural changes, phrasing nuances, and the like and to hear the results immediately. Entire compositions could be worked on in this way: notation—in the form of either programs or abstract gestural notation—could be generated automatically by the machine and sent to one of two performance sources, the powerful studio machines or a live symphony orchestra.

Musical use has already been made of such digital synthesizers. Popular performers like Stevie Wonder and Herbie Hancock are enormously proficient, especially on keyboard-oriented machines. I have done experiments with powerful digital synthesizers used in a concert situation, especially in *Fusione Fugace* (1982), composed for IRCAM's 4X machine. The goal of this composition was to create a work of chamber music for three performers and a live computer. Chowning, on commission from

Yamaha, is working on a real-time composition that will incorporate the many, diverse, and sophisticated transformations of complex inharmonic sounds into music for preprogrammed and inexpensive digital synthesizers.

With all of these tools, some composers have approached the question of combining computer electronics with the orchestra. Although the number of important pieces in this domain is limited, progress and trends have already become clear. Tristan Murail, as part of the French Ensemble Itinéraire, is interested in the use of complex sonorities (harmonic and inharmonic spectra) as a basis for musical composition. He considers each orchestral instrument as an integral part of a larger ensemble sonority or timbre and has long felt the necessity to incorporate electronic materials into his instrumental works to fill out and complement their dense sound complexes. The best example of this tendency is his work *Désintégrations* (1983) for chamber orchestra and computer tape. The computer part adds or reinforces spectral material that is not present in orchestral instruments and functions as a sort of timbral glue that holds together the work's large, complex sonorities. The form of the piece is defined by large-scale transformation of these spectra, which over the course of the piece move from harmonic to inharmonic and from fused to nonfused episodes.

Another approach is that of the German York Höller. In a series of pieces for orchestra and computer sounds, notably *Arcus* (1979) and *Resonance* (1983), he strives to relate them as absolutely equal participants. The musical material performed by both groups is identical, using the same melodic and harmonic procedures. Höller often bases his computer sounds on actual instrumental recordings or on close synthetic reproductions of these sounds. He also strives to create combination or hybrid timbres that function paradoxically in the gray area between instrumental families with the computer or between "real/physical" sound and "abstract/electronic" sound. The result is a sort of *concerto grosso* form, in which a dramatic but closely connected interplay takes place between matched partners.

Roger Reynolds has recently employed technical concepts similar to Höller's but has achieved strikingly different musical results. In *Archipelago* (1983) an ensemble of thirty players is subdivided into many smaller groups (duos, trios, quartets, and so on), and each of these groups has its own computer-transformed shadow. These many separate elements are meant not to combine or to clash but rather to function as equal parts of an intricate puzzle. The computer allows greater control over musical detail and clarity of the sonic result than would be possible with traditional instruments alone.

As stated above, one of the most powerful aspects of computer-generated music is the ability to control the finest, most microscopic details of individual sounds. Such an approach has been extended to the electronic-instrumental domain by Peter Eötvös in his *Intervalles intérieures* (1984). Here an instrumental ensemble performs material closely based on arpeggiations and melodic derivations of the natural harmonic series. Eötvös uses electronics to draw the ear further into the reductive process; one listens to complex and ever-changing spectral components freely derived from "real" spectra based on each of the performing instruments.

An even stronger connection between the orchestra and electronics can be made by creating a direct, live concert link between the forces. Morton Subotnick, in such works as *Ascent into Air* (1981), enables instrumentalists to control directly an electronic result by performance gesture. Two cellists are wired to a real-time digital synthesizer. By changing amplitude, phrasing, and pitches, they determine how preprogrammed events are triggered or started in the machine and in what ways musical aspects of these electronics (spectral density) are shaped during performance. A more complicated approach is taken by George Lewis in his *Rainbow Family* (1984). In this work, scored for any number of improvising musicians and live computer system, the performers are not directly wired to the machine; rather, the machine is programmed to be intelligent enough to listen to the music being played (through microphones), to make certain musical assumptions based on this music, and to generate immediately its own musical response. Possibly a new form of concerto might evolve from this practice—the individual, skilled, articulate soloist opposed to the mass of the orchestra, with the electronics acting as mediator in the dispute.

In *Déplacements* (1979) and *Light* (1979), I explore a different path. Rather than being concerned with destroying distinctions between instruments and electronics, these works establish dramatic tension by the exaggeration of differences and the juxtaposition of these forces. Musical form is created by the attempt to find underlying principles of unity beneath what appears to be endless division on the sonic surface. In *Spectres Parisiens* (1984) for chamber orchestra and computer electronics, I use large-scale electronic spectral transitions to determine the overall form of the work, to provide an inevitability and directionality to its development much as tonal harmony provided in past music. Therefore, electronic spectra become not independent material but the very material from which the entire musical discourse is woven. The orchestral instruments give, in a sense, specific instances or examples of each timbral state. The *tutti* orchestra mediates between solo instruments and electronics, constantly altering between fused ensemble textures (approaching the dense spectra of the computer) and intricate individual polyphony (mirroring or answering the soloists). *Spectres Parisiens* employs time-variant spectra to provide a context within which instrumentalists can assert their individuality and freedom.

In such experiences with the combination of electronics and the orchestra, much has been learned and many seemingly obvious phenomena contradicted. For instance, it has often been a shock for composers to realize that a rather bad electronic sonority that tries to copy a live instrument tends to mix too well with the real instrument, to be covered and masked, in fact, rather than to protrude in an ugly fashion. Composers have had to learn, among other things, which electronic sonorities fuse or mix better than others, what exaggerations are necessary to make independent sonic layers audible, and how instruments must be slightly amplified to compete in presence with electronic sounds that emanate from loudspeakers. It is obvious that a totally new concept of orchestration is being developed, one that will link advanced electronics to ever-changing orchestral textures.

In this process, one thing is painfully evident; theoretical precepts can never replace practical, empirical auditory experience and judgment. Just as the harmonic series provided a metaphor and conceptual model for the tonal system, so psychoacoustic laws and spectral analysis of instruments can point to interesting directions in which composers might look. It is indispensable to make musical experiments combining orchestral and electronic forces, to make changes based on sonic results, to formalize and generalize the acquired knowledge, and to thereby improve compositional, instrumental, and computer skills.

We are at the beginning of such profound exploration and must seriously ask, Where are the forums that permit and facilitate the frequent encounter and collaboration of symphony orchestras and advanced technology? For the moment such forums do not exist. Today's symphony orchestras, because of social and economic reasons, are hard-pressed to keep up with the twentieth-century repertoire and risk becoming museums of past music. But we cannot resort to making recriminations or to resigning ourselves to such a seemingly impossible situation. If one believes that we are in need of mixed orchestral and electronic forces to express truly the musical ideas of our time, then a solution can surely be found.

Part of the problem resides in the camp of the electronic-music world and in the glaring lack of standardization one finds from studio to studio, machine to machine, and even program to program. It was such standardization of orchestral forces (number and type of instruments, social environment of the concert hall, and so on) that made it possible for so many great composers in the eighteenth and nineteenth centuries to develop their symphonic genius. Today, technology changes so rapidly that before a composer has learned to be fluent on a particular computer music system, it is already outdated and ready for retirement.

But one need not despair, for many researchers and manufacturers are moving in the direction of standardization. A decision has been made to unify the way that information is sent from a computer to a synthesizer or from one synthesizer to another (the MIDI interface). And manufacturers are increasingly working directly with independent or university research groups to design subsequent generations of music technology. Those designs and concepts formulated by composers and musical researchers that are selected for incorporation into the future machines of the big manufacturers are those that will become standard. The field of electronic music has become such big business that it is no longer realistic for an individual inventor to purvey his splendid machine in isolation. In fact, the true task of independent research groups will be to lobby intensively to the large manufacturers in order to assure that the computer instruments of the future incorporate the highest musical sophistication and flexibility rather than just the lowest common standards of the marketplace.

If this is the current goal of computer-music research groups, what of those who systematically attempt to combine instruments and electronics? We can hope for two different situations at present: first, the formation of small, intensive work groups to test computer-instrument interaction in a sustained way, and, second, an increasing number of flexible forums wherein research centers and orchestral laboratories can collaborate on musical projects.

In the first instance, the goal is to achieve a sophisticated balance between the most advanced technology and individual performers and eventually to create a family of such hybrid instruments as described above. Such a musical research group would contain a small number of composer-performers and a team of computer scientists and instrument builders. Experiments would constantly be tested in the concert hall by encouraging music to be composed for such a specialized ensemble. The various musical research institutes that already exist would provide the ideal context for the residency of such ensembles.

To extend the discoveries that would be made in this way to a wider forum, research centers must establish strong and long-lasting relationships with already existing symphonic organizations. It is not enough for an orchestra to perform a piece with electronics from time to time; rather, a forum is necessary wherein ideas from the laboratory can be tested in a rehearsal situation, modified, presented in concert, and modified again until composer and performers are satisfied.

What will the extended orchestra of the future look like? Today, it is not uncommon for classically trained composers to be knowledgeable about technological concepts. As computers become a more natural part of our culture and education, concepts of computer music will be integrated into the conservatory and university music curriculum. This trend should apply to instrumentalists, whether those destined for solo or orchestral careers. So we can imagine a future when amplification, digital synthesizers, and hybrid instruments will be fully integrated into the symphony orchestra and will represent the sound-image that composers hold up as their ideal. It is, of course, also possible that with increasingly powerful machines and faced with orchestral conservatism and inflexibility, orchestras of electronic instruments will be forced to establish themselves independently of traditional instruments.

But in my view, the modernist mode of purely electronic sounds is quickly passing. We are moving toward a time when the entire range of electronic instruments will simply become part of the orchestral resources available to the composer. Whereas compositional ideas at present still emphasize the distinctness of each world, soon there will be no difference between them.

BIBLIOGRAPHY

Milton Babbitt, "Twelve-Tone Rhythmic Structure and the Electronic Medium," *Perspectives of New Music*, 1 (1962). John Chowning, "The Synthesis of Complex Audio Spectra by Means of Frequency Modulation," *Journal of the Audio Engineering Society*, 21 (1973); and "John Chowning on Composition," in Roads, *Composers*. A. Gerzso, "Reflections on *Répons*," *Contemporary Music Review*, 1, pt. 1 (1984). P. Griffiths, "Three Works by Jonathan Harvey: The Electronic Mirror," *ibid*. Y. Höller, "*Resonance*: Composition Today," *ibid*. D. Jameux, "Boulez and the Machine," *ibid*. G. Lewis, "Improvisation," in Roads, *Composers*. S. McAdams, "Spectral Fusion and the Creation of Auditory Images," in M. Clynes, ed., *Music, Mind, and Brain* (1982). Tod Machover, "Computer Music With and Without Instruments," in *Contemporary Music Review*, 1, pt. 1 (1984); and "Some Thoughts About Computer Music," in Roads, *Composers*. M. V. Mathews, *The Technology of Computer Music* (1969).

Tristan Murail, "Spectra and Pixies," in *Contemporary Music Review*, 1, pt. 1 (1984). J. C. Risset, *An Introductory Catalog of Computer-Synthesized Sounds* (1969). Curtis Roads, ed., *Composers and the Computer* (1985). D. Wessel, "Timbre Space as Musical Control Structure," *Computer Music Journal*, 3, no. 2 (1979).

Glossary

ABSOLUTE MUSIC   Music that is absolutely free of literary or pictorial references.

A CAPPELLA   Term originally applied only to sacred choral music, indicating that it was sung without instrumental accompaniment, but now used for unaccompanied vocal music in general.

ACCIDENTAL   Signs (sharp, flat, double sharp, double flat, and natural) used in musical notation to alter, or cancel alteration, of the pitch of a note.

ADAGIO   Tempo indication meaning "very slow," from Italian word for "at ease" or "leisurely"; often—but not always—used to indicate tempo slower than *andante* but not as slow as *largo.*

ALLEGRO   A general term indicating quick tempo, also implying bright or cheerful mood.

ALLEMANDE   A dance of possibly German origin, in moderate tempo, often followed by a quicker dance in triple meter (*tripla,* or later the *courante*). Frequently used as the first movement (or first after prelude) of a baroque suite.

ALTO   The vocal part above the tenor, from Italian for "high." In the sixteenth through eighteenth centuries, alto parts in sacred music were sung by men, while in secular music they were sung by women. Now commonly applied to low-registered female voices (also "contralto") in the standard, four-part choral grouping.

AMPLITUDE   The maximum amount of deviation from equilibrium in a vibration or wave.

ANALOGUE SYNTHESIZER   Synthesizer that produces sound through electronic means (as opposed to computers that produce sound digitally).

ANDANTE   A tempo designation indicating a relaxed, "walking" tempo, often between that of *allegretto* and *adagio.* Also used as title of movement or work performed at such a tempo.

ARCO   Italian for "bow." Used in score to indicate the end of a pizzicato passage. Also written *coll'arco*.

ARIA   Italian for "air." A self-contained solo vocal piece in an opera, oratorio, or cantata. Also written as independent work (concert aria) for orchestra and voice from seventeenth century to the present. See also DA CAPO.

ARIETTA   A solo vocal piece shorter and less elaborate than an aria and usually in binary form. Often adopted for instrumental pieces of similar character.

ARPEGGIO   The playing of the notes of a chord in succession rather than simultaneously.

ATONALITY   The absence of any key center or mode.

AUTOGRAPH   Manuscript written in the composer's hand.

BASSE DANSE   Main court dance of the late Middle Ages and Renaissance, disappearing after the middle of the sixteenth century. Several early instrumental techniques evolved from the musical practice surrounding it.

BASSO CONTINUO   Term (usually shortened to *continuo*) for the part played by the keyboard instrument in concerted music of the seventeenth and eighteenth centuries. This part consisted of a bass line with figures underneath the notes (called the *figured bass*), which indicated how the player was to "realize," or fill in, the harmonies.

BINARY FORM   Musical structure consisting of two complementary parts, either or both of which may be repeated.

BOLERO   Spanish song or dance in moderate tempo and triple meter, popular in the late eighteenth and nineteenth centuries. Ravel's piece in this form is particularly famous.

BORE   Interior of the tube of a wind or brass instrument, which determines the pitch of the lowest note obtainable.

BOW   A flexible wooden stick with horsehair or nylon stretched across it, drawn across a string instrument to produce sound.

BOWING   The method or style of applying the bow to strings; *down-bow* is movement of the arm away from the instrument, and *up-bow,* toward instrument. The term is also used as a marking in a score to indicate in which direction the bow is to move.

CADENCE   A melodic or harmonic pattern or progression that concludes a phrase, a section of a composition, or a composition itself.

CANON   A strict method of contrapuntal imitation, in which a melody is echoed note for note by another voice or voices. "Three Blind Mice" is an example of an unaccompanied "perpetual canon."

CANTABILE   In a "singing" style.

CANTILENA   A smoothly lyrical instrumental passage or vocal melody, as opposed to one that is dramatic or virtuosic. In choral music, the part carrying the main melodic line.

CANTOR   In the Lutheran church, the person in charge of the music, often a performer himself (as with Bach in Leipzig). In synagogues, the cantor is the solo singer.

CANTUS FIRMUS   Latin for "fixed melody". In the Middle Ages and Renaissance, a preexisting melody, generally taken from church liturgy, that was used as the basis for a polyphonic composition. It was usually stated in notes of long duration against which other voices were set in counterpoint. In the sixteenth century, the term was also used to identify the highest vocal line in a choral work.

CANZONA   A polyphonic instrumental piece of the sixteenth and seventeenth centuries, developed from the Netherlands chanson. In the eighteenth and nineteenth centuries the term signified a lyrical or poetically expressive instrumental or vocal composition.

CAPRICCIO   Originally applied to madrigals and, in the seventeenth century, to keyboard pieces, the term was later used for any musical work of a sprightly, imaginative, or capricious nature.

CASSATION   A term used in the late eighteenth century for a composition or movement of a light nature and often written to be performed outdoors; stylistically similar to the divertimento and the serenade.

CAVATINA   In eighteenth-century opera, a brief, songlike aria without *da capo*, performed on its own or inserted in a recitative. Also used for songlike instrumental pieces. In nineteenth-century Italian opera the term described an elaborate and often virtuosic aria.

CHACONNE   A musical form, very similar to the passacaglia, usually in triple meter, moderately slow, and with a ground bass over which continuous variations are essayed.

CHAMBER MUSIC   Music intended to be played in a room rather than in a concert hall. As presently used, the term refers to music for small groups of players (excluding solo players or duos) in which the various parts are treated on equal terms.

CHANT   Declamatory, nonmetrical vocal music of the Western Christian church. The major type is Gregorian chant, which is the final evolutionary form of plainsong, the style of chant developed in the earliest centuries of Christianity. Plainsong and Gregorian chant are strictly monophonic, with all voices singing in unison.

CHORALE   The congregational hymn of the German Protestant (Lutheran) church, with vernacular texts and simple melodies sung in unison. Bach's chorale harmonizations, still in wide use, are models for the writing of four-part harmony.

CHORD   Simultaneous combination of three or more pitches.

CHROMATIC   Based on the division of the octave into twelve semitones, as opposed to diatonic.

CIRCLE OF FIFTHS   The arrangement of the twelve major or minor keys by ascending or descending perfect fifths; used by theorists as a measure of relative harmonic remoteness of two keys.

CODA   Italian for "tail." The concluding section of a movement or work that is an addition to that piece's design or formal scheme. It may contain new development of themes or even present new thematic material.

COLLA PARTE   Italian for "with the part." Indication to follow or play in tempo with another part.

COLL'ARCO   See ARCO.

COLLEGIUM MUSICUM   Latin for "musical guild." A society of musical amateurs that originated in German-speaking countries in the sixteenth century and was the germ from which concert societies developed.

CONCERTANTE   The solo group in a *concerto grosso*, as distinct from the instruments of the orchestra (the *tutti* or *ripieno*); the term *concertino* is also used for this solo group. *Concertante* is also used by composers to denote the use of soloist(s) in a way similar to a concerto, as in a *sinfonia concertante*.

CONCERTINO   A short concerto for soloist and orchestra. See also CONCERTANTE.

CONCERTMASTER   The first-chair player of the first-violin section of an orchestra.

CONCERTO   A work for soloist and orchestra, usually in three movements, in which a solo instrument or small group is contrasted and blended with the orchestra. See also CONCERTO DA CAMERA, CONCERTO DA CHIESA, CONCERTO GROSSO.

CONCERTO DA CAMERA   Type of *concerto grosso*, structured similarly to the *sonata da camera* (chamber or court sonata), consisting of an introduction followed by three or four dance movements.

CONCERTO DA CHIESA   Type of *concerto grosso*, structured similarly to *sonata da chiesa* (church sonata); standard form is four movements with a slow-fast-slow-fast ordering.

CONCERTO GROSSO   Early form of multimovement baroque concerto, in which a small group of instrumentalists (*concertino, concertato,* or *concertante*) alternates with a larger body of instruments (*ripieno*). Some twentieth-century composers have used the term for works that highlight more than one soloist.

CONSORT   Old spelling of *concert,* a small instrumental ensemble or the music played by such a group.

CONTREDANSE   Dance popular in eighteenth-century France, developed from an English country dance; Mozart and Beethoven, among others, wrote *Kontretänze*.

CORRENTE   Italian version of the French courante, a popular dance of the seventeenth and early eighteenth centuries, often used as a movement of a suite.

COUNTERPOINT   The ordered combination of two or more melodic lines according to a system or set of rules. See also CANON, CANTUS FIRMUS, IMITATION, SPECIES.

CRESCENDO   An increase in loudness.

CROOK   Detachable tubing applied to the mouthpiece of brass instruments to alter the length of the tube and thus the fundamental pitch of the instrument. Also used for bent metal tubing that connects mouthpiece to body of some wind instruments.

CYCLICAL FORM   The reintroduction of thematic or motivic material, in order to establish cohesion in a movement or an entire work. The foundations of cyclical principles, laid by Beethoven, Schubert, and Berlioz, assumed even greater importance in the late romantic era.

CZARDAS   Hungarian dance popular in the mid-nineteenth century and used by Liszt as the basis for many compositions.

DA CAPO   Italian for "from the beginning, " usually abbreviated D.C., an instruction to repeat all or part of the first section of a work after the second (or later) section.

DESCANT   Also *discant.* Originally a technique for improvising polyphony, now denotes the uppermost part of a polyphonic composition; the highest-pitched member of an instrumental family, such as the descant viol; or the freely written or improvised part that soars above a hymn tune.

DESSUS   The highest part or voice in an ensemble; also used in the seventeenth and eighteenth centuries to mean violin (from *dessus de violin*).

DEVELOPMENT   The reshaping, elaboration, or transformation of a motive or theme through various means. In a sonata-form movement, the development section follows the exposition, in which the main thematic material is presented.

DIATONIC   Term describing the major and minor scales, as well as melodies, intervals, and chords and harmonies made up of notes of these scales.

DIMINISHED SEVENTH CHORD   A harmonically ambivalent and unstable chord and the most common chromatic sonority of tonal music.

DIMINUENDO   A gradual decrease in loudness. Opposite of *crescendo.*

DISSONANCE   Any musical sound that creates a feeling of instability or discord, according to the context of a given harmonic system.

DIVERTIMENTO   A musical form originating in the eighteenth century, consisting of a series of movements arranged in suitelike form, often containing dance movements. Written primarily to provide background entertainment at large gatherings. Also name given to a group of dances inserted into an opera. See also CASSATION, SERENADE.

DIVISI   Term used in orchestral scores to indicate the division of an instrumental group (such as first violins) into two or more subgroups, each playing a separate line.

DODECAPHONIC   Music written in the twelve-tone system. See also ATONALITY, SERIALISM.

DOMINANT   The fifth note of the diatonic scale or a chord built upon that note; of fundamental importance in tonal music.

DOTTED RHYTHM   Rhythmic figures consisting of alternating notes of long and short value. Named for the dot used in notation to indicate the prolongation of the first note, usually by half its value.

DOUBLE-STOPPING   In string-instrument playing, the simultaneous depression of two strings; but the term is often used loosely to mean the playing of two strings simultaneously, even if one of the strings is "open" (that is, not depressed).

DRONE   Any long, sustained sound. See also MUSETTE.

DYNAMICS   The gradation and variation of the volume of sound in musical performance. First notated in scores in the early sixteenth century, dynamic instructions came into currency in Italy in the seventeenth century. See also CRESCENDO, DIMINUENDO.

EIGHTH NOTE   Note with one-eighth the value of a whole note; it is written by adding one flag to the stem of a quarter note.

EMBOUCHURE   The coupling of the player's air supply and the mouthpiece of a wind or brass instrument; also French term for the mouthpiece.

EMPFINDSAMKEIT   German for "sensibility" or "sentimentality." An aesthetic propounded by eighteenth-century North German composers, most notably C. P. E. Bach, that aimed at attaining intimacy and sensitivity in musical expression, with little use of ornamentation or embellishment.

ENTR'ACTE   Orchestral music played between acts of a play or opera.

ENVELOPE   A graph depicting variations in the amplitude of a musical wave over time, including its beginning (attack) and end (decay).

EXPOSITION   The initial statement of the main theme or themes in an extended movement or work. In a fugue, the exposition is the opening section in which the subject is stated by each voice in turn. In a sonata-form movement, it is the opening section (sometimes preceded by an introduction), which usually begins in the tonic key.

EXPRESSIONISM   Term taken from the movement in literature and the visual arts (ca. 1905–1930) that implies a subjective, symbolic, distorted, and exaggerated mode of expression. Among the composers associated with expressionism are Schoenberg, Berg, and Webern.

FANFARE   A short, lively passage for trumpets (sometimes with other brass and percussion), usually employed on festive or ceremonial occasions.

FELDMUSIK   Term originally used in the seventeenth century (along with Feldstücke) for fanfares and other pieces to be played outdoors by brass and wind instruments, particularly at military events. In the eighteenth century, Feldmusik became popular with amateur musicians.

FERMATA   A musical symbol, also known as *hold* or *pause,* indicating the prolongation of a note, rest, or end of a phrase.

FIFTH   The interval between two notes of the diatonic scale that are separated by four notes—for example, D to A.

FIGURE   A short melodic or rhythmic idea, with a particular identity, often used with other figures to create a larger melodic idea or theme.

FORTE   Loud (abbreviated *f*).

FORTISSIMO   Very loud (abbreviated *ff*).

FOURTH   The interval between two notes of the diatonic scale that are separated by three notes—for example, D to G.

FREQUENCY   The number of complete cycles per second of a vibrating medium, such as a violin string or column of air.

FRET   A strip of material placed at appropriate intervals across the fingerboard of certain string instruments, against which the player presses a finger to shorten the vibrating length of the string and produce specific pitches.

FROG   The device at the bottom of the bow used for string instruments that secures the hairs and, in modern bows, regulates their tension by means of a screw mechanism.

FUGAL   Term applied to compositional procedures associated with the fugue.

FUGATO   An imitative passage, in fugal style, within a primarily noncontrapuntal composition.

FUGUE   A composition or technique using imitative counterpoint involving one main theme as the primary or most characteristic means of formal elaboration.

GAGLIARDA   Also *galliard.* A court dance of the sixteenth and early seventeenth centuries, often paired with the slower pavane.

GALANT   Term used in the mid-eighteenth century for a graceful style of instrumental writing (*style galant*) that featured simple harmonies and minimal counterpoint, in contrast to strict (church) style.

GAVOTTE   A French court dance and instrumental form popular at the court of Louis XIV and remaining in vogue until the French Revolution. It became an optional movement of the baroque suite.

GIGA   An Italian dance and instrumental form related to the French gigue but faster and written in 12/8 time, with regular phrases and a more homophonic texture.

GIOCOSO   Italian for "jocular." A performance instruction usually coupled with a tempo indication (for example, *allegro giocoso*).

GLISSANDO   An instrumental effect obtained by sliding up or down between two pitches without articulating individual notes, although each of them is audible.

GROUND BASS   In a composition, a melody or figure in the bass that is repeated over and over and upon which variations are built in the other voices. Used prevalently in the seventeenth century. See also CHACONNE, OSTINATO.

HARMONICS   Individual pure sounds (overtones) that result from the vibration of a string or column of air in sections, as well as in its entirety, and that blend with the fundamental pitch to sound as a single note.

HARMONY   The element of music dealing with the nature and consequences of simultaneously sounding tones and with the principles governing such combinations.

HETEROPHONY   Simultaneous variations of the same melody; term has frequent application in ethnomusicology.

HOFMUSIK   Music of the court.

HOMOPHONY   Applied to music in which one melodic voice is accompanied in simple chordal style; it is also used to describe music in which all voices move together rather than exhibiting the independent characteristics found in polyphony.

IDÉE FIXE   French for "obsession" or "fixation." Term originated by Berlioz to describe a musical idea recurring obsessively, as does the principal theme of the *Symphonie fantastique*, which symbolizes the artist's obsession with his beloved.

IMITATION   The exact or approximate repetition of a phrase or motive appearing in another voice, often at a different pitch and overlapping the original phrase. Exact and extensive imitation forms a *canon* with the original; a *fugue* features imitation of one (and sometimes more than one) subject throughout its length.

IMPRESSIONISM   Term borrowed from late nineteenth-century movement in painting. In music, applied most often to Debussy, along with Ravel, Griffes, Delius, and others, whose works are perceived as attempting to convey a musical impression through the use of minute detail, orchestral color, ambiguous tonality, exotic scales, and extreme chromaticism.

INCIDENTAL MUSIC   Music composed for, or interpolated into, a nonmusical stage work.

INTERLUDE   Any smaller or less important piece played between larger sections of a musical work, play, or opera.

INTERMEDIO   In the fifteenth and sixteenth centuries, a sequence of music and dance inserted between the acts of a play or musical work, primarily to provide lighthearted contrast and to allow performers to relax. During the seventeenth century, the intermedio became absorbed into opera, which did, however, sometimes have its own intermedios, called *intermezzi*.

KAPELLMEISTER   Originally the music director of a German court chapel, the *Kapellmeister* was later in charge of all music at the court, including orchestral concerts and opera. In the nineteenth century the term was applied to the director of any musical ensemble.

KEY   The tonal center toward which a musical passage or composition is perceived as gravitating; a piece is described as "being in" a certain key. The term is also used for devices depressed by fingers on wind and keyboard instruments.

LEGATO   Italian for "linked" or "connected." Smoothly connected, with no discernible interruption of sound. See also STACCATO.

LEITMOTIV   An easily identifiable theme or other musical idea connected with a particular character, incident, place, emotion, or any other element of a dramatic work. Recurring throughout the work, it is often combined, extended, altered, or otherwise developed, in referential conjunction with the drama. Developed by Weber, the leitmotiv was a paramount musical and structural device in Wagner's music dramas and in those of several twentieth-century composers.

MADRIGAL   Term originally applied to lyrical poetry of fourteenth-century Italy but revived in the sixteenth century to cover many types of secular polyphonic works.

MADRIGAL COMEDY   Type of work produced in Italy in the late sixteenth century; it comprises a series of secular vocal works, unified by a plot or story, in which the music describes the action, situation, or characters.

MANNHEIM SCHOOL   A group of German composers at the court of Mannheim (1740–1780) known mainly for exploiting dynamic effects in their orchestral music, either through abrupt changes or long crescendos. Other characteristics include the melodic importance given to the violins and the frequent use of solo winds.

MARTELLATO   A detached, "hammered" bow stroke; on the piano, a hammered staccato.

MASQUE   An entertainment for the court and nobility originating in sixteenth-century England, based on allegorical or mythological subjects, incorporating poetry and music, and featuring elaborate costumes, scenery, and machinery.

MASS   The ritual service of the Eucharist in the Roman Catholic liturgy, the music of which became a seminal form of Western music. Many composers have also set the mass for nonliturgical use.

MAZURKA   A class of Polish country dances in triple time, extended and refined by Chopin in his group of about sixty mazurkas.

MEAN-TONE TEMPERAMENT   A system of tuning the scale; widely used from the sixteenth through eighteenth centuries (and superseded by equal temperament). Mean-tone temperament left remote keys virtually unusable.

MEASURE   Metrical unit between two bar lines.

METER   The basic pulse of rhythmic impulses or beats, as distinguished from rhythm, which is the deployment of notes over the underlying pulse or meter.

MEZZO-   Prefix meaning "half," as in *mezzo-soprano* (half-soprano, midway between soprano and alto) and *mezzo-forte* (half loud, or moderately loud).

MINUET   A seventeenth-century French court dance. Incorporated into the baroque suite, it later became a standard movement of late eighteenth-century forms such as the sonata and the symphony. Beethoven and later composers replaced the minuet with the scherzo.

MODE   The arrangement of tones into a scale used as the basic tonal foundation of a piece of music. The two modern modes are the major and minor. *Modal* normally refers to the eight so-called ecclesiastical or church modes, which dominated European music from about 400 to 1500 and remained influential into the seventeenth century.

MODERATO   A tempo designation indicating a moderate speed; also used to modify another term, such as *allegro moderato*.

MODULATION   The transition from one key or tonal center, to another, through various harmonic devices. By contrasting various keys, modulation sustains harmonic interest by articulating their relationship in large-scale compositions.

MONOCHORD   Ancient device with single string stretched over a resonating board, and a movable bridge to alter the pitch. It was used as a teaching device up to the nineteenth century.

MONOTHEMATIC   A description of any movement or work that is based on a single theme.

MOTET   One of the major forms of polyphonic composition (1200–1750), particularly during the Middle Ages and Renaissance. Although its characteristics varied, it was generally an unaccompanied choral composition based on a sacred Latin text and preexisting melody (*cantus firmus*) to which other melodies and texts were added in counterpoint. After Bach, the term was used rather loosely, sometimes for accompanied choral works or even solo works with accompaniment.

MOTIVE   A brief harmonic, melodic, or rhythmic idea with a recognizable identity. The four-note opening of Beethoven's Fifth Symphony is a well-known rhythmic motive.

MUSETTE   A pastoral, dancelike piece incorporating a long drone.

MUTE   A device used to muffle the tone or change the timbre of an instrument.

NEOCLASSICAL   Refers to a twentieth-century musical movement, particularly widespread between the two world wars, in which certain formal and stylistic features of the seventeenth and eighteenth centuries were adopted in reaction to the excesses of romanticism, including a more objective, detached style; a revival of classical forms; reduction of orchestral forces; and increased emphasis on counterpoint. Stravinsky was perhaps its foremost exponent.

OBBLIGATO   Italian for "indispensable." Refers to an instrumental part in concerted music that, ranked in importance second only to the principal melody, must not be omitted. Term has come to be used for a solo passage that provides a supplementary or counter theme of a decorative nature, despite implication of term's literal definition.

ODE   In classical antiquity, a poem in free meter and verse structure, written in honor of a special occasion or as part of a play, and usually sung or recited to music. Odes were set to music by Renaissance composers, and in the baroque period the ode became a cantatalike ceremonial work.

OPERA   A drama set to music for soloists, orchestra, and often chorus. It arose around 1600 from the attempts of a group of Florentine composers (among them, Peri and Caccini) called the Camerata to re-create the drama of classical antiquity, which had employed music, chant, and dance.

OPERA BUFFA   Italian comic opera, evolving in the early eighteenth century from the intermezzo. By the end of the century it had incorporated elements of serious or sentimental drama. Unlike other forms of comic opera, it always used recitative rather than spoken dialogue. See also INTERMEDIO.

OPÉRA COMIQUE   In the eighteenth century, the term applied to light French comic opera with spoken dialogue. In the next century it came to mean any opera with spoken dialogue.

OPERA SERIA   Serious Italian opera; the chief operatic genre of the seventeenth and eighteenth centuries, usually on a heroic, mythological, or tragic subject.

ORATORIO   An unstaged dramatic work, usually an extended musical setting of a religious text, and commonly employing orchestra, chorus, and soloists. Extremely popular in the seventeenth and eighteenth centuries, oratorios usually incorporated operatic forms and styles of the period. Notable examples include Bach's *Christmas Oratorio* and Handel's *Messiah*.

ORGANOLOGY   The study and analysis of musical instruments.

ORNAMENTATION   The embellishment of a melody by a performer, employing trills, roulades, and the like.

OSTINATO   A pattern or figure repeated persistently throughout all or part of a composition. In the seventeenth and eighteenth centuries the basso ostinato, or ground bass, was a common feature of the ground, chaconne, and passacaglia.

OVERTONES   See HARMONICS.

OVERTURE   A composition intended to introduce another, larger work, such as an opera, ballet, or oratorio. Also written as an independent work (concert overture).

PARALLEL MOTION   The movement of two or more voices or parts in the same direction, with the interval between the two remaining constant.

PART   One line of a composition, to be performed by one instrument or voice, or group of instruments or voices. Also, music from which that line is read.

PARTIALS   The constituent vibrations of a musical note. The fundamental is the first partial; the overtones are the upper partials. See also HARMONICS.

PART-SONG   A usually unaccompanied secular composition for more than one voice in a single movement, frequently with a homophonic texture.

PEDAL POINT   A sustained or repeated note (usually in the bass) above which the harmonies change. In an inner part rather than in the bass, it is called an inverted pedal.

PHRASE   A unit of varying musical length, generally bearing a melodic connotation. The aspect of performance concerned with the articulation of a work's phrase structure is called *phrasing*.

PIANISSIMO   Very soft (abbreviated *pp*).

PIANO   Soft (abbreviated *p*).

PIZZICATO   Direction to players of bowed string instruments to pluck a string with the finger rather than bowing it (abbreviated *pizz.*).

PLECTRUM   Small piece of horn, wood, or ivory used to pluck the strings of an instrument such as the mandolin. Also, the part of the keyboard action that plucks a harpsichord string.

POLYPHONY   The combination of two or more musical lines or voices, each of which maintains some degree of melodic independence and individuality. See also COUNTERPOINT.

POLYTONALITY   The simultaneous use of more than two keys, or tonalities (two is called bitonality).

POSITIONS   The various points on the fingerboard to which the left hand slides when playing a string instrument; also, the various degrees of extension of the trombone slide.

POSTLUDE   A piece played at the end of a composition; also used for an organ piece (sometimes improvised) played as the congregation exits at the end of a church service; opposite of *prelude*.

PRELUDE   A piece intended to introduce a larger work (such as a suite or opera). In the nineteenth century the term was used by composers for a nonspecific category of character piece, particularly for piano, with no intended prefatory function.

PROGRAM MUSIC   Narrative or descriptive instrumental music written with specific references to extramusical material, literary or otherwise. Introduced by Liszt, the term denotes the antithesis of *absolute music*. See also SYMPHONIC POEM.

QUINTUPLET   A group of five notes of equal length, to be played in the time taken to play four notes of the same kind indicated by the time-signature.

REAL-TIME SYNTHESIZER   Electronic instrument capable of producing music in live, "real time" concert situations.

RECAPITULATION   The third (and usually last) section of a movement in sonata form, following the exposition and development and re-presenting material of the exposition.

RECITATIVE   Declamatory vocal music in opera, oratorio, and cantata, used for dialogue or declamatory passages, and following the natural rhythms and accents of speech.

REGISTER   A portion of the total range encompassed by an instrument or voice. Register may be based on the distinctiveness of a tonal quality (such as the chalumeau register of the clarinet) or a particular compass (such as high and low registers of instruments). Also, used for a set of organ pipes controlled by one stop, which may include several ranks.

RELATIVE KEY   A key with the same key signature as another key; D minor is the relative minor key of F major.

RESOLUTION   The conclusion of a musical idea; in counterpoint, the progression from a dissonance to a consonance.

RETROGRADE   The backward reading of a melodic line (last note to first). Used as a canonic device as early as the fourteenth century, it is important today as one of three main operations performed on a tone row in the twelve-tone system, others being transposition and inversion.

RICERCAR   Italian for "to seek out." Applied in the sixteenth and seventeenth centuries to various types of contrapuntal instrumental music, including the imitative ricercar for ensembles, keyboard, or lute, and to works more improvisatory in style. In the seventeenth century the ricercar became a particularly sophisticated and complex form of keyboard composition.

RING MODULATOR   A device used in electronic music to modify the frequency component of a given sound in relation to a second signal input. Used to create new and complex sound mixtures.

RIPIENO   The full instrumental body in the baroque concerto, as distinguished from the solo instruments. See also CONCERTANTE.

RITORNELLO   Italian for "little return." Applied in seventeenth and eighteenth centuries to the orchestral material that acts as a recurring refrain, in addition to appearing at opening and closing, in arias and concertos, especially the *concerto grosso*.

ROLL   A rapid succession of drumbeats, producing an almost continuous sound.

RONDO   A musical form comprising recurrent material that alternates with contrasting material. Often used for the final movement of symphonies and concertos.

RUBATO   Italian for "robbed." A distortion of strict rhythm for expressive purposes, by prolonging one note and "robbing" the time from another. The analogous distortion of strict tempo is called *tempo rubato*.

SALTARELLO   A sprightly Italian dance first mentioned in the fourteenth century. In the sixteenth century it was virtually indistinguishable musically from the French galliard, both dances commonly being coupled with the pavane.

SARABANDE   A stately dance of Spanish origin, regularly included in baroque suites.

SCHERZO   Italian for "joke." A type of movement, established by Beethoven as successor to the minuet and trio in the symphony. Typically light and playful in mood, it often contains a slower contrasting section, inherited from the minuet-and-trio format. Also used as independent character piece by composers such as Brahms and Chopin.

SEQUENCE   The repetition, at a different pitch, of a melody or harmonic sequence.

SEMITONE   The smallest interval of the traditional Western tonal system, equal to a minor second in the diatonic system.

SERENADE   Originally a form of musical greeting from lover to beloved, performed outdoors and in the evening. The term was used for eighteenth-century multimovement instrumental compositions written to be performed outdoors; closely related to cassation, divertimento, and notturno. In the nineteenth century the term was applied to multimovement works written for traditional concert purposes.

SERENATA   A cantatalike work of the seventeenth and eighteenth centuries, performed to commemorate an event, featuring costumes and minimal staging. Also applied occasionally to the instrumental serenade.

SERIALISM   A twentieth-century compositional technique in which all the elements of a composition (dynamics, timbre, rhythm, and so on) are subjected to the methods of the twelve-tone system. See also TWELVE-TONE SYSTEM.

SEXTUPLET   A group of six notes of equal length, to be played in the time taken to play the number of notes of the same kind indicated by the time-signature; thus, in a passage marked 4/4, it would be played in the time needed to play four notes.

SFORZANDO   Italian for "forcing." Strongly accented; abbreviated *sf* or *sfz*.

SICILIANA   A dance of the seventeenth and eighteenth centuries, originating in Sicily, and a popular instrumental movement. Its flowing accompanimental figures and lyrical melodies were used by many composers of the time.

SINFONIA   An orchestral piece of the baroque period used as the introduction to an opera (or to an individual scene), suite, or cantata. Operatic sinfonias became standardized in the late seventeenth century as the Italian overture.

SINFONIA CONCERTANTE   Multimovement work of the late eighteenth and early nineteenth centuries, for two or more soloists (as many as nine) and orchestra. Though the name implies symphonic form, such a work is closer in structure to the concerto.

SINFONIETTA   An orchestral work similar to the symphony but smaller and more modest; the term is sometimes used for a small orchestra.

SIXTEENTH NOTE   A note with one-sixteenth the value of a whole note, written by adding two flags to the stem of a quarter note.

SONATA   A solo instrumental work, commonly in three or four movements, that shares features of other types of multimovement instrumental music such as the symphony and string quartet. The term originated in the sixteenth century for any piece intended to be played rather than sung.

SONATA FORM   Construction normally used in first movements of symphonies, sonatas, concertos, and other multimovement works, and sometimes in other movements, as well. It is generally in three sections: the exposition, with a first theme (or group of themes) in the tonic key, a second theme (or group) in the dominant or other closely related key; the development, often beginning in the dominant and traveling through other key areas leading back to the tonic; and the recapitulation, with both themes in the tonic. The movement may begin with an introduction (usually slow) and/or conclude with a coda. Also known as *sonata-allegro form*, *compound binary form*, or *first-movement form*.

SPECIES   As enumerated by Johann Joseph Fux in *Gradus ad Parnassum* (1725), the five basic techniques for adding a contrapuntal line to a given *cantus firmus*. These have since been the basis for much instruction in strict counterpoint.

SPECTRUM   A term used in electronic music for the number and relative strength of harmonics present in a given signal.

STACCATO   Italian for "detached." The playing of a note in such a way that it is given less than its written value and is thereby detached from the notes flanking it. Indicated in score by a dot over or under note.

STAFF   The set of five horizontal lines on and between which notes are written to indicate their pitch.

STILE ANTICO   A term given to church music written after 1600 utilizing the strict contrapuntal procedures of Palestrina.

STOP   The mechanism that allows the player to use or shut off the various registers of an organ or harpsichord.

STRETTO   Italian for "narrow" or "tight." The introduction of two or more subject entries in contrapuntal writing, in substantially closer succession than in their exposition, producing an intensifying effect. Also used for any faster tempo at the conclusion of a section or piece.

STURM UND DRANG   German for "storm and stress." A movement in late eighteenth-century German literature, and reflected in other arts, that emphasized emotionalism, terror, and an antirational, subjective approach to art.

SUITE   A multimovement instrumental work originally based on dance forms and styles; the term was later used for any group of pieces extracted from a larger work, such as an opera or ballet.

SUSPENSION   A note sustained from a chord in which it is consonant into a chord in which it is dissonant.

SYMPHONIC POEM   A term invented by Liszt to describe a large orchestral work, usually in one movement, based on literary or other extramusical ideas.

SYMPHONY   An extended, usually multimovement orchestral work created in the eighteenth century, and since then, the major genre of orchestral music.

SYNCOPATION   The shifting of a beat ahead of or behind its previous position in a metric pattern.

SYNTHESIZER   Electronic apparatus invented by Robert Moog in 1965, to synthesize sounds, permitting control of various parameters such as frequency, duration, intensity, envelope, and wave form. Some synthesizers are controlled with a piano-type keyboard. See also REAL-TIME SYNTHESIZER.

TACTUS   A beat or pulse in medieval and Renaissance music.

TAILLE   A middle voice, usually tenor, or an instrument of similar register.

TEMPERAMENT   An adjustment to the tuning of fixed-pitch instruments (such as the piano, organ, and harpsichord), in which intervals are made to deviate from the "pure" intervals of the harmonic series, making it easy to play in any key. The standard method today is equal temperament, in which the octave is divided into twelve equal semitones. See also MEAN-TONE TEMPERAMENT.

TERNARY   A musical structure comprising two independent sections followed by an exact (or nearly exact) repetition of the first. Normally referred to as an ABA structure.

TEXTURE   A combination of acoustic characteristics, including tone color, the number of parts, spacing of chords, and thickness of sonority. The major distinctions are between homophonic and polyphonic textures.

THIRTY-SECOND NOTE   A note with one thirty-second the value of a whole note; written by adding three flags to the stem of a quarter note.

THOROUGHBASS   The English term for *basso continuo* or figured bass.

TIE   A curved line written between two notes of the same pitch, used to sustain a note over a bar line or to indicate a single note of combined time values.

TIMBRE   The quality of tone that distinguishes one instrument (or voice) from another.

TONAL   Pertaining to principles of tonality, as opposed to atonality.

TONALITY   A system of relationships between pitches that have a common or central pitch (tonic) as their organizing harmonic element. This tonic defines the key.

TONE ROW   See TWELVE-TONE SYSTEM.

TONIC   The first note, or key note, of a diatonic scale; the chord built on that note is the tonic chord.

TOURTE BOW   A bow made by developer of the modern bow, François Tourte (1747–1835).

TRANSCRIPTION   An arrangement of a composition for an instrument or medium other than that for which it was written or for the same medium but in a different style.

TRANSPOSITION   The performance or notation of music from one pitch (or key) to another. Instruments that sound tones different from the pitch of those notated are called transposing instruments (for example, the B-flat clarinet, which sounds a B-flat when C is written).

TREBLE   A high vocal or instrumental part, generally superseded by the term *soprano* in the eighteenth century but still applied to certain older instruments.

TREMOLO   Italian for "quivering" or "trembling." A rapid, arrhythmic repetition of a single note or the back-and-forth repetition of two notes.

TRIAD   A three-note chord traditionally comprising one pitch, called the root, and those a third and fifth above it. Depending upon the exact size of those intervals, the triad may be major, minor, augmented, or diminished.

TRILL   A rapid alteration of a note with the one below or above it.

TRIO   The second of two alternating dances or dance movements, as in minuet and trio; later applied to an instrumental piece for obbligato parts. Also, any group of three performers or a work written for such a group.

TRIO SONATA   The central form of baroque chamber music, for two upper parts and continuo. Despite its name, it was usually performed on four instruments, including a low string instrument playing the figured bass line along with the harpsichord.

TRITONE   An interval of three whole tones (that is, an augmented fourth or diminished fifth), long considered the "devil in music," to be avoided for its harmonic instability and tonal ambiguity. Since the Renaissance, composers have taken advantage of its ambivalence, used it to depict evil, or deployed it to suspend or extend the limits of tonality.

TUNING SLIDE   The U-shaped tube on brass instruments or the tenon-and-socket joint on wind instruments, used to adjust pitch. Also, the device attached to the end of an organ pipe, used to adjust its length and thus its pitch.

TUTTI   Italian for "all." Used to indicate a passage for orchestra, especially as contrasted with those for soloist(s), in a concerto. In an orchestral work the term indicates a passage for the entire orchestral body.

TWELVE-TONE SYSTEM   A twentieth-century technique of composition, most commonly attributed to Arnold Schoenberg, in which all twelve chromatic tones within the octave are ordered into a "tone row" as a unifying basis for a composition. Permutations and combinations of this row are used throughout: the row may be transposed to begin on any of the twelve pitches and may be altered in any of several prescribed ways. See also SERIALISM.

UNISON   The sounding of the same note by more than one instrument or voice. Also, the interval formed by two notes of identical pitch. Two or more musicians performing the same part are said to "play in unison."

VALVE   On brass instruments, a mechanism, invented around 1815, that increases or decreases the length of the tube in which air vibrates, thus altering the fundamental pitch and making all notes of the chromatic scale attainable.

VARIATION   A musical form in which thematic material is modified or transformed through a variety of techniques and re-presented in altered settings retaining one or more features of the original. Theme and variations has been a popular form since the sixteenth century, when they were called "divisions on a ground".

VIBRATO   A slight, rapid fluctuation of pitch used by singers and instrumentalists for expressive purposes.

VOICE   A single line of music, whether or not intended for the voice or for more than one performer. Synonymous with *part*.

VOICE-LEADING   The aspect of composition relating to the motion and progression of individual lines of music.

WHOLE NOTE   A note with time value equal to four quarter notes. The sign for it is an open circle with no stem.

WHOLE TONE   The interval of a major second, or one whole step on the diatonic scale.

ZARZUELA   Spanish opera interspersed with spoken dialogue, on either comic or tragic subjects. Named for the royal country palace of La Zarzuela, where it was first performed in the early seventeenth century, it reached the height of its popularity in the nineteenth century, gaining the status of the Spanish national operatic genre.

Index
